BUCKS
COUNTY
PENN

MISCELLANE
1755-1857

THOMAS G. MYERS

WILLOW BEND BOOKS
2004

WILLOW BEND BOOKS
AN IMPRINT OF HERITAGE BOOKS, INC.

Books, CDs, and more – Worldwide

For our listing of thousands of titles see our website
at
www.HeritageBooks.com

Published 2004 by
HERITAGE BOOKS, INC.
Publishing Division
65 East Main Street
Westminster, Maryland 21157-5026

Other Books by the Author:
Bucks County, Pennsylvania Orphans' Court Records 1685-1852
Bucks County, Pennsylvania, Orphans' Court Records: 1852-1900
1930 Census Index: Bucks County, Pennsylvania
Bucks County, Pennsylvania, Will Abstracts, 1825-1870
Bucks County, Pennsylvania, Will Abstracts, 1870 - 1900

International Standard Book Number: **1-58549-935-8**

BUCKS COUNTY MISCELLANEOUS DEED DOCKETS 1785-1857

The Bucks County Recorder of Deeds began the Miscellaneous Docket series in 1785 to record various transactions other than standard transfers of real estate. The transactions included in the Miscellaneous Dockets include powers of attorney, releases of executors and administrators, releases of guardians, dower releases, assignments of property, bills of sale and freeing (manumission) of slaves. Since many of these transactions are related to estate settlements, they contain a wealth of valuable genealogical information.

This work contains abstracts of transactions recorded in Miscellaneous Docket Volumes 1-12, recorded during the period 1785-1857. Each entry contains a summary of the transaction, the volume and page where recorded and the date of the transaction (which may differ from the date the transaction was recorded). Not all transactions were abstracted—the emphasis was on transactions containing information of genealogical interest.

Among the more interesting finds in these dockets are 63 transactions related to the freeing (manumission) of slaves. On March 1, 1780, the Pennsylvania state legislature passed "An Act for the Gradual Abolition of Slavery". This Act provided that all persons born in Pennsylvania after that date could not be deemed slaves, although children born to slaves after that date could be bound to serve their masters until age 28. In addition, slave owners were required to register all of their slaves by November 1, 1780. Any person not registered could not be held in slavery. And slaves who were brought from other states could only be held in slavery for a period of seven years or until age 28 whichever was later.

Many slave owners voluntarily agreed to free their slaves prior to the date required by the Act or to free slaves at age 28 who were born prior to the passage of the Act. In other cases, slaves were purchased for the specific purpose of setting them free. In order to provide an official record of these manumissions, they were recorded by the Recorder of Deeds in the Miscellaneous Dockets.

One of the common transactions found in the Miscellaneous Dockets are dower releases. Through the mid-19th century, a widow was generally entitled to one-third of her husband's property upon his death. In the case of real estate, it was common practice upon the sale of the decedent's land for the widow to retain a dower lien for her one-third of the value of the land, rather than taking that value in cash. The purchaser of the land would be required to pay the widow annual interest on the dower principal during her life which provided her with a source of ongoing income. Upon the widow's death, the decedent's heirs would be entitled to receive the dower principal from the current owner of the property. Until extinguished, the dower served as a lien on the property through any subsequent sales. As a way of proving clear title on property, owners frequently required the heirs to sign a release upon payment of the dower principal with the release recorded by the Recorder of Deeds in the Miscellaneous Dockets. In cases where dower releases were not recorded, subsequent property owners sometimes needed to petition the Bucks County court in order to eliminate the lien and provide a clear title.

Similarly, executors, administrators and guardians frequently required heirs to sign releases upon payment of their shares of a decedent's estate in order to prove extinguishment of their liability to their heirs. To provide a permanent record of these releases, the executors, administrators or guardians sometimes had the releases recorded by the Recorder of Deeds in the Miscellaneous Dockets.

Jacob Bishop of Lower Milford Twp, innkeeper, and Samuel Foulke of Richland Twp, yeoman, executors of the will of Michael Bishop, late of Lower Milford Twp, acknowledge payment of bequest to Michael's daughter Anna Barbara (wife of George Kline Jr.).   Bk 1/pg 1   Dec 20, 1785

Joseph Hart of Warminster Twp, Esq., sets free his Negro slave ____ and his wife Jane.   Bk 1/pg 2   Dec 24, 1785

Leonard Heaninger of Rockhill Twp. agrees to support his father John Heaninger of Rockhill Twp.   Bk 1/pg 3   Jan 25, 1786

George Brown of Falls Twp, yeoman, sells land in Falls Twp to his son Samuel Brown of Falls Twp, yeoman.   Bk 1/pg 6   Mar 26, 1726

Elizabeth Crout, widow of Henry Crout, late of Bedminster Twp, yeoman, releases Henry's sons Henry Jr. and Jacob and Henry's son-in-law Philip Crots, administrators of Henry's estate, and all the other heirs of her right to dower.   Bk 1/pg 8   Jun 13, 1781

Henry and Jacob Oberholtzer and Jacob Wisler, all of Bedminster Twp, testify that they saw Agness Geil, daughter of Henry Kraut, late of Bedminster Twp, and her husband Jacob Geil sell their share of Henry's land and grist mill to Jacob Kraut.   Bk 1/pg 9   Feb 11, 1786

John Bland of London, goldsmith, and wife Prisilla and John Mann of London, merchant, and wife Mary, through their attorneys, sold land in Bucks County to Robert Mearns in 1729. Robert bequeathed half this land to his wife Jane and at her death or marriage to children Hugh, Agnes, Gennet, Mary and a child his wife was then bearing. Gennet and her husband William Smith of Middleton Twp, Cumberland Co, yeoman, sell their share to her brother Hugh Mearns of Warwick Twp, miller. Bk 1/pg 10   Jun 26, 1785

Samuel Jones, late of Horsham Twp, Montgomery Co, died intestate leaving estate to his daughter Dorothy (widow of Isaac Marple, late of Horsham Twp) who has since married Isaac Van Horn of Salsbury Twp, Bucks Co [sic], joyner. Isaac agrees to pay part of the estate to Dorothy's son Jonas and David Marple when they are 21 years old (Jonas to be paid on Feb 25, 1800 and David to be paid on Mar 1, 1802).   Bk 1/pg 13   May 15, 1786

James and John Gregg of Middletown Twp, yeomen, sons of Patrick Gregg, late of Middletown, agree to the division of their father's real estate.
                                        Bk 1/pg 15   Jun 21, 1785

Conrad Klein of Nockamixon Twp, yeoman, agrees to give his livestock, utensils and household goods to sons George and John (when he is 21) in consideration of the services they did for him.　Bk 1/pg 22　Apr 22, 1785

William Wallace of Warwick Twp, yeoman, Margaret Wallace of Warwick, spinster, Robert Wallace of Warwick, yeoman and Issable Wallace of Warwick, spinster, children of James Wallace, late of Warwick, yeoman, (who also left a widow Issable) sell to daughter Jane Carr and her husband John a part of their father's real estate.　Bk 1/pg 34　Oct 30, 1786

Stephen Williams, late of Philadelphia, merchant, left land and mill at PennyPack in Bucks Co. to Rev. Stephen Roe who died leaving only daughter Maria Olivia Barnes, heretofore of Parish of St. James's Clerkenwells in Middlesex Co. but now of Parish of John Hackney in Middlesex Co. and their son Richard Stephen Barnes of Parish of Christ Church, Newgate Street, London, gentleman, acknowledge sale of this land by attorney Rev. Dr. William Smith of Philadelphia.　Bk 1/pg 37　Feb 19, 1771

Thomas Whilson of Sadsbury Twp, Lanhester[?] Co. due to being stricken in years and weak in body gives power of attorney to son Thomas Whilson of the same county to recover money due him.　Bk 1/pg 44　Dec 26, 1786

John Vanosdol, late of Northampton Twp, yeoman, died intestate leaving widow, two sons (Simon—eldest son and Garret) and three daughters. Simon of Reading Town, Hunterdon Co, NJ, clerk, due two shares as eldest son, sells one-fourth of his share to his brother Garret so that Garret will be equally situated. Their sister Elizabeth (wife of John Cornel) died leaving two sons, John and Wilhellmus, who died in their minority so that Elizabeth's share's descended to Simon. Simon also sells half of this share to Garret.
Bk 1/pg 46　May 24, 1785

John Zelly of Northampton, Burlington Co, NJ, farmer, and wife Hannah, daughter of Elizabeth Collins, deceased, who was a legatee of James Tunnicliff/Tunecliff, sell their share in James' estate to Peter Vansant of Lower Makefield Twp.　Bk 1/pg 56　Dec 18, 1786

Henry Reikert and wife Catharine, late widow of Jacob Kintzing, acknowledge payment of dower by John Kintzing.
Bk 1/pg 65　Jun 25, 1769

2

James and Mary Hunter of Philadelphia give power of attorney to friend Hannah Harris of Newtown to recover money due Mary by will of William Stewart, late of Kentucky.　　　Bk 1/pg 66　May 7, 1786

Thomas and Margaret Hamilton of Abbeville Co, SC give power of attorney to friend William Hutton of Abbeville Co. to recover money from James and Sarah Bussen of Springfield Twp. due by will of Stephen Twining, late of Wrightstown Twp.　　　Bk 1/pg 67　Apr 2, 1787

Hezekiah Rogers of Hampshire Co, VA, yeoman, administrator of late Hezekiah Rogers, gives power of attorney to friends James Hanna, Esq. of Newtown and William Doyle of Plumstead Twp, yeoman, to recover money due the estate.　　　Bk 1/pg 70　Apr 10, 1786

Gabriel Vansant of Lower Makefield Twp, due to sundry misfortunes, sells the estate he received by will of father Isaiah Vansant to brother Peter Vansant of Lower Makefield.　　　Bk 1/pg 72　Apr 14, 1787

Joseph Martindale of Upper Makefield Twp, yeoman, agrees to pay back all or part of the money received by his orphan daughter from the estate of Isaac Buckman, late of Upper Makefield to his administrators Isaac and Abraham Buckman, if the estate suffers additional debts.　Bk 1/pg 76　Apr 13, 1787

Abraham Buckman of Upper Makefield Twp, yeoman, agrees to pay back all or part of the money he received from the estate of Isaac Buckman, late of Upper Makefield, to administrator Isaac Buckman if the estate proves to have additional debts.　　　Bk 1/pg 77　Apr 13, 1787

Isaac Buckman, late of Upper Makefield, died intestate leaving widow and two sons and a granddaughter Rachel Martindale, daughter of late Hannah Martindale). Joseph Martindale, father and guardian of Rachel, and Abraham Buckman acknowledge payment of estate by eldest son Isaac Buckman who inherited the real estate.　　　Bk 1/pg 78　Apr 13, 1787

Joseph Youst of Tinicum Twp. and wife Mary sell to Conrad Youst of Bedminster Twp. his share in estate of father Michael Youst.
　　　Bk 1/pg 83　Sep 10, 1787

Joseph Hart, partly of Warminster Twp. and partly of Warwick Twp, sets free all his Negro slaves when they reach the age of 28 (Isaac on Oct 15, 1803, Amos on Oct 20, 1805, David on Nov 12, 1807 and George on Jul 18, 1809). He also had two other Negro slaves who were born after the Act of Abolition

3

took place who by law are entitled to freedom at the age of 28 (Moses born Jan 29, 1783 and Jane born Nov 20, 1784).   Bk 1/pg 84   Jan 9, 1788

Thomas Miller of Philadelphia, clerk, gives power of attorney to brother Robert Miller of Northampton Twp, carpenter, to sell land in Mount Bethel Twp, Northampton Co.   Bk 1/pg 86   Feb 15, 1788

John Durn[?], late of Lower Makefield Twp. bequeathed money to daughter Eleanor (wife of Joseph Clark) along with his Negro chef Sarah. Joseph and Eleanor acknowledge receipt of their legacy from John's son and executor John Durn.   Bk 1/pg 88   Jun 14, 1786

Jacob and Sarah Houseman of Washington Twp, Fayette Co, heir to John Johnson, give power of attorney to Archibald M. Latton[?] to recover estate from John Chapman of Bucks Co.   Bk 1/pg 95   Mar 4, 1788

Margaret Dunn, widow of George Dunn, releases her share of real estate to John Pilner.   Bk 1/pg 96   Apr 2, 1788

Thomas and Hannah Lee are entitled to one-tenth of one-third of the dower on real estate of Reubin Pownal, deceased, which was adjudged to eldest son Reubin. They sell their share to Jonas Ingham.   Bk 1/pg 101   Mar 26 1788

Thomas Thomas of Maryland, farmer, gives power of attorney to brother David Thomas of Bucks Co. to recover estate from Owen Thomas, executor of his father Joseph Thomas.   Bk 1/pg 105   Mar 12, 1788

Jacob and Catharine Hertzel, Abraham and Christina Cobe, Adam and Margaret Cobe, John and Sophia Althouse, Henry and Elizabeth Bleyler, Henry and Hannah Drumbore and Peter and Susanna Scholl, daughters of Henry Hertzel, late of Rockhill Twp, yeoman, acknowledge payment of estate by executors Paul and Henry Hertzel and Abraham Stout.
                              Bk 1/pg 107   Aug 16, 1788

Paul Hertzel, Henry Hertzel, Jacob and Catharine Hertzel, Abraham and Christina Cobe, Adam and Margaret Cobe, John and Sophia Althouse, Abraham and Magdalena Stout, Henry and Elizabeth Bleyler, Henry and Hannah Drumbore and Peter and Susanna Scholl, children of Henry Hertzel, late of Rockhill Twp, yeoman, and brothers of Michael Hertzel who died intestate soon after his father, acknowledge payment of estate by Michael's widow Catharine and Jacob Reed and Abraham Stout, administrators to the estate.   Bk 1/pg 109   Aug 16, 1788

4

John Ashburn of Newtown sold land received by will of his father Wm Ashburn to his daughter Agness and her husband Asa Carey of Newtown Twp. in return for supporting his during his natural life.

Bk 1/pg 112   Nov 29, 1784

John Kemmerly and wife Catharine (late wife of Christian Hegeman) sell land to Arion Hegeman.   Bk 1/pg 116   Nov 26, 1788

Charles Shoemaker of PetersBerg, VA and Margaret Merrick of Bristol Borough were married in Bucks Co. on Jan 7, 1789.

Bk 1/pg 120   Jan 7, 1789

Mary Herwick and Ulrich, Joseph and John Drissel release Mary's right to dower from her husband John Herwick.   Bk 1/pg 122   Dec 27, 1788

John Clinker, late of Nockamixon Twp, yeoman, died leaving children including eldest son John who since died intestate, over age 21. John Sr.'s heirs Christian Klinker of Nockamixon Twp, yeoman, and Michael and Magdalena Strebey of Nockamixon Twp, earthen potter, and Jacob and Catharine Stout of Nockamixon Twp. agree to partition of John Sr's real estate.   Bk 1/pg 125   Mar 7, 1789

Phillip Walter of Richland Twp, acknowledges payment of estate by executor Peter Walter from his father Peter Walter, late of Rockhill Twp, due upon death of his mother Catharine and agrees to indemnify Peter if the estate has additional debts.   Bk 1/pg 128   Dec 8, 1788

William Stackhouse of Lower Makefield Twp, administrator of John Stackhouse, late of Nova Scotia, gives power of attorney to friend William Green of Annapolis, Nova Scotia to recover money due estate.

Bk 1/pg 133   Apr 20, 1789

Adam and Dorothy Sheffer give power of attorney to friend Andrew Trapp of Springfield Twp. to recover legacy due by will of Philip Trapp.

Bk 1/pg 134   Oct 24, 1788

Ann Seller, widow of John Seller, late of Hilltown Twp, blacksmith, releases to her son Samuel Seller all right to dower.   Bk 1/pg 136   May 25, 1789

Abraham Seller and Philip and Elizabeth Sheetz, children of John Seller, late of Hilltown Twp, blacksmith, acknowledge payment of estate by John's son Samuel Seller who inherited John's real estate.   Bk 1/pg 136   May 26, 1789

Elias Beitleman of Lower Milford Twp, house carpenter, Isaac Rothrock of Lower Saucon Twp, yeoman, and wife Gertraut, and Elizabeth Beitleman of Lower Milford, spinster, children of Leonard Beitleman, late of Lower Milford, acknowledge payment of estate by Leonard's son Jacob who inherited the real estate.   Bk 1/pg 137 Feb 2, 1789

Daniel Dologhan, late of Dublin, Ireland, but now of Northampton Co, heir of Michael Down, gives power of attorney to James Hanna of Newtown Twp, to recover estate from John Lynn of Philadelphia, wheelwright.
                                        Bk 1/pg 141   Aug 19, 1789

Michael Dowd of Lower Dublin Twp, Philadelphia Co, yeoman, bequeathed estate to Daniel Dologhan of County Down, Ireland. Daniel acknowledges payment by executors Hugh Tomb, Joseph Fenton and James Howe.
                                        Bk 1/pg 142 Aug 18, 1789

Joshua Glass, late of Bucks Co, bequeathed estate to nephew James Kerr, now of Banbridge, Ireland, son of his sister Hannah (wife of John Kerr). James Kerr gives power of attorney to uncle Isaac Glass to receive estate from executors Matthew Greer and Robert Glass. Bk 1/pg 143 May 14, 1789

Joshua Glass, formerly of Parish of Sea Patrick in County Down, Ireland, who moved to America and died in Bucks Co, bequeathed estate to brother Daniel Glass in Ireland who is since deceased leaving two daughters, Jane Glass— wife of James Stenson and Hannah Glass. They give power of attorney to Isaac Glass to received estate from executors Matthew Greer and Robert Glass.   Bk 1/pg 143   May 12, 1789

Joshua Glass, late of Hilltown Twp, bequeathed estate to brother Samuel Glass of Parish of Seapatrick in County Down, Ireland who since died intestate and his estate descended to eldest son James Glass. James Glass gives power of attorney to his uncle Isaac Glass of Southampton Twp. to recover estate from administrator George Kelso. Bk 1/pg 144 Aug 25, 1789

Dame Elizabeth Baxter, widow of Coll. William Baxter, late of Warwick Twp, upon payment by guardian William Scott, releases dower right to her children Jane, Robert, Sarah, Mary, Daniel, William and John Baxter.
                                        Bk 1/pg 151 Jan 17, 1787

Philip and Margaret Barron of Springfield Twp, yeoman, old and infirm, convey land to son Jacob Barron on condition that he care for them.
                                        Bk 1/pg 161 Dec 28, 1780

Samuel Yardley of Newtown Twp, yeoman, places his Negro boy James as servant to Mark Hapeny of Newtown Twp, yeoman, until James reaches age 21 on Feb 6, 1792 and then he is to be set free. Bk 1/pg 164   Apr 8, 1790

William White of Kent Co, DE owned a Negro slave named Isaac who was taken up in Pennsylvania and confined as a runaway in the public jail in Bucks Co. and sold at his order for a period of years by Josias Ferguson, keeper of the jail. William gives power of attorney to Josias Ferguson to set Isaac free at the expiration of his term.   Bk 1/pg 164   Jan 23, 1790

Abraham Larew of Bensalem Twp. bequeathed estate to wife Alice, son Abraham and daughters Elizabeth (wife of Garret Vansant), Eleanor (wife of Joseph Sackett) and Ann Larew. Heirs agree to abide by terms of will.
Bk 1/pg 165   Apr 5, 1790

Jonathan Davis of Hennery Co, VA gives power of attorney to brother-in-law Thomas Jones of New Britain Twp. to recover money due him.
Bk 1/pg 167   Oct 15, 1784

Joseph Vandegrift, John Vandegrift, Jonathan Vandegrift and Ann Vandegrift, heirs of John Vandegrift, late of Bensalem Twp, acknowledge payment of their shares by brother Joshua Vandegrift.
Bk 1/pg 168   Nov 10, 1789

Samuel and Jane Hanin and Judith or Judea Fenton, daughters of Josiah Fenton, late of Buckingham Twp, acknowledge payment of estate by executors and brothers.   Bk 1/pg 169   Jul 29, 1789

Thomas Lewis, formerly of Hilltown Twp. but now of Queens Co, New Brunswick Province, Nova Scotia, son of John Lewis, late of Hilltown Twp, yeoman, assigns his share of estate to Jeremiah Thomas of Hilltown Twp.
Bk 1/pg 172   Jun 7, 1790

Jacob Kulp of Bedminster Twp. and Henry and Elizabeth Rosenbury of New Britain Twp, children of Tilman Kulp, late of Bedminster Twp, acknowledge payment of estate by their brother Henry Kulp of Bedminster Twp.
Bk 1/pg 173   Nov 14, 1789

Conrad Bohn of Secheim, Hessen Darmstadt, Germany, yeoman, and wife Maria Margaretha, daughter of John Desh, late of Secheim, yeoman, who was eldest brother of John George Desh, late of Haycock Twp, yeoman, and Adam Fieberling of Secheim, yeoman, and wife Eve, daughter of Jacob Schaf and wife Maria Elizabeth, deceased, who was also a daughter of John Desh, give power of attorney to John Deter Weigand of Baltimore, MD to sell the estate on their behalf and behalf of Maria Elizabeth's minor children Catharine Margaret and Eve Elizabeth.   Bk 1/pg 176   Apr 28, 1790

John Young of Lower Milford Twp. acknowledges payment by his guardian Christian Clymer of money due from his father's estate.
Bk 1/pg 177   Oct 24, 1790

James Flack of Buckingham Twp, guardian of grandson James Anderson, gives power of attorney to friend John Hough the younger, saddler, of Warwick Twp. to recover estate from executors of Joseph Anderson, late of Baltimore, MD, merchant.   Bk 1/pg 180   Dec 9, 1790

Francis Baird, executor of John Baird, late of Warwick Twp. gives power of attorney to William Mains of Louden Co, VA to recover money that Robert Jamison of VA owes to his father's estate.   Bk 1/pg 183   May 21, 1791

William McKinstry of Green Bryar Co, VA gives power of attorney to Robert McKinstry of Buckingham Twp. to estate of father Nathan McKinstry, late of Buckingham Twp.   Bk 1/pg 183   Apr 9, 1791

Abraham Reasor, Abraham and Anna Funk and Abraham and Susanna Sliver, heirs of Abraham Reasor, agree to valuation of their father's real estate.
Bk 1/pg 184   Jun 7, 1791

Mary McNair of Philadelphia, spinster, daughter of Andrew McNair, late of Philadelphia, gives power of attorney to William Linton of Bucks Co. to enter satisfaction of a mortgage.   Bk 1/pg 188   Jul 18, 1791

Margaret Grier of Hilltown Twp. gives power of attorney to cousin Joseph Grier (with whom she lives) to recover money from estate of her father George Grier, late of Philadelphia.   Bk 1/pg 189   Feb 7, 1791

John Booze of Bristol Twp. and Mary Atkinson of Bristol Twp. have entered into a marriage contract and agree to keep their estates separate.
Bk 1/pg 192   Dec 2, 1791

Andrew Beyer, only son and heir of Jacob Beyer, late of Rockhill Twp, innholder, gives power of attorney to Philip Zeigler Sr. and Philip Zeigler Jr. of Upper Salford Twp, Montgomery Co. to sell his father's land and to pay

the proceeds to his sons Jacob and Andrew and daughter Mary Elizabeth
(wife of Andrew Zeigler). Bk 1/pg 192 Dec 30, 1791

Samuel Wright of Bristol Borough sets free his Negro woman Maria, now
about 20 years old), formerly the property of Ann Wright, deceased, since
residing with Aaron Schuyler, deceased, and late residing with Archibald
McElroy. Bk 1/pg 195 Feb 4, 1792

John Johnson of Plumstead Twp. acknowledges that he previously set free his
mulatto girl Tamar. Bk 1/pg 195 Feb 12, 1792

Nicholas Houpt of Nockamixon Twp. gives power of attorney to son George
Houpt of Nockamixon to sell his land. Bk 1/pg 195 Oct 10, 1791

Negroes Jack and Ned of New Britain Twp. have by their free will
apprenticed themselves to Thomas Stewart of New Britain Twp, yeoman to be
taught husbandry. Bk 1/pg 199 Apr 7, 1792

William Pettit of Solebury Twp, yeoman, sets free six Negroes: Nell (about 26
years old), Jim (about 21 years old), Cate (about 17 years old), Cate's
daughter Hager[?] (about 2 years old), Omme[?] and Tile (about 10 years
old). Bk 1/pg 201 Apr 15, 1790

John Barton acknowledges payment by Joseph Barton of estate from father
Thomas Barton, late of New Britain Twp. Bk 1/pg 204 Oct 2, 1792

Margaret Wentz of Upper Salford Twp, Montgomery Co, widow and
daughter of Mary Elizabeth Miller, late of Upper Salford, widow, gives power
of attorney to son-in-law John Derr of Upper Salford, yeoman, to recover
estate from her mother's administrator, Jacob Nunnemaker, Jr.
Bk 1/pg 205 Sep 7, 1785

Gilliam Cornell of Northampton Twp, yeoman, sets free his Negro slave Will
(about 29 years old). Bk 1/pg 207 Apr 10, 1792

Robert Shirley of Bartley Co, VA who married Rachel Gilbert, daughter of
Nathan Gilbert, late of Bartley Co, who will be due estate upon death of his
grandmother Elizabeth Gilbert which is in the hands of Joseph Hart in Bucks
Co, acknowledges payment of estate by Rachel's guardian Andrew Long,
Esq. who was appointed by Bucks Co. Orphans Court.
Bk 1/pg 221 Dec 24, 1792

James Ruckman of Plumstead Twp, yeoman, sets free his Negro slave Cate, about 23 years old. Bk 1/pg 221 May 9, 1793

John Dunlap of Plumstead Twp, yeoman, and wife Jane, late widow of William McFaddon of Allen Twp, Northampton Co. and on behalf of heirs of John McFadden, deceased, agree that William Heslet of Northumberland Co. and wife Margreth, daughter of William McFaddon, should receive a certain portion of the estate. Bk 1/pg 225 Aug 11, 1790

Barthelemy Cowasier of Bensalem Twp. sets free his Negro slaves Modist, now 17 years of age, and Crispin, now 10 years of age.
Bk 1/pg 226 Jul 13, 1793

Mary Ramsey of Tinicum Twp, widow, gives power of attorney to friend Frances Willson of Tinicum Twp. to sell land now occupied by son Robert Ramsey. Bk 1/pg 228 Jul 11, 1793

Lydia Thomas, widow of Leonard Thomas, late of Lower Milford Twp, yeoman, agrees that daughter Elizabeth Smith should receive an equal portion of estate with the other children. Bk 1/pg 230 Sep 12, 1793

William M. Henry [McHenry?] of Bedminster Twp, yeoman, sets free his Negro woman Nancy, now under 27 years of age, and his Negro man Jack, now under 28 years of age. Bk 1/pg 230 Aug 20, 1793

John D. Coxe of Philadelphia, attorney at law, purchased from Richard Rue of Bensalem Twp. a certain Negro slave named Cuffee, about 25 years old. John now sets him free. Bk 1/pg 231 Nov 9, 1793

Margaret Clark, widow of John Clark, sets free her mulatto female slave named Flora, aged between 25 and 26 together with her son Jim, about 2 years old. Also the Negro slaves named Ceasar (which she bound to William Hewsen/Hixsen of Bristol Twp) and Peter (which she bound to Charles Shoemaker of Bristol Twp) are to be set free at the end of their indenture.
Bk 1/pg 231 Nov 11, 1793

Henry Wynkoop of Northampton Twp, Esq., sets free his Negro slave Phebe and his Negro slave Tony, both over 28 years old, and his Negro slave Tom, under age 28. Bk 1/pg 232 Dec 16, 1793

John Meredith, late of New Britain Twp, but now of Annapolis Co, Nova Scotia bequeaths money due from British Parliament to reimburse his losses to friend Abraham Chapman of Annapolis and his wife Mary and son John. He also appoints brother Simon Meredith to recover money due from father's estate which money is to go to Charles and Elizabeth Meredith, children of his brother Hugh.   Bk 1/pg 234   Jun 27, 1787

Is. Hicks acknowledges payment of mortgage by John Leedom, acting executor of William Carter by virtue of marriage to William's widow Mary.
                                                         Bk 1/pg 235   Dec 21, 1793

Joseph Thornton of Northampton Twp. sets free his Negro slave Pompey, now about 25 years old.   Bk 1/pg 245   Feb 28, 1794

Bartholomy Cowasier of Bensalem Twp. sets free his Negro slave Benjamin, about 11 years old.   Bk 1/pg 248   Apr 5, 1794

Frederick Murray of Lancaster Co. and wife Elizabeth (late Hanes) and Mary Haines (for whom Frederick is guardian) give power of attorney to John Stokes to recover money due from estate of Valentine Rhore.
                                                         Bk 1/pg 252   Feb 27, 1794

Elizabeth Salliday, widow of Frederick Salliday Jun., late of Bedminster Twp, acknowledges payment of estate by administrator Michael Weisel Jun.
                                                         Bk 1/pg 258   Apr 14, 1786

Frederick Salliday, late of Bedminster Twp, died intestate leaving four children: Immanuel, John, Catherine and Frederick, all minors, for whom Michael Wisell of Bedminster Twp. was appointed guardian. Immanuel Salliday, eldest son, now 21, acknowledges payment of estate by his guardian.
                                                         Bk 1/pg 258   Feb 22, 1794

George Rogers, son and administrator of Elizabeth Rogers who was a daughter of John Sebring, late of Solebury Twp, acknowledges payment of estate by John's administrator Smith Price of Plumstead Twp, shopkeeper.
                                                         Bk 1/pg 259   Jul 22, 1794

James Ryan sells his Negro boy Aaron to George Meade.
                                                         Bk 1/pg 260   Feb 17, 1794

Robert Meade, son of George, sells Negro boy Aaron to James Hanna.
                                                         Bk 1/pg 260   Jul 15, 1794

11

Aaron Linton of Northampton Twp, blacksmith, gives power of attorney to brother John Linton of Northampton to recover money due him.

Bk 1/pg 262   Apr 4, 1793

John Carr of Warwick Twp, yeoman sets free his Negro slave Job, age 27.

Bk 1/pg 266   Nov 3, 1794

Margaret Gilbert of Moreland Manor, Montgomery Co. gives power of attorney to cousin Jonathan Gilbert of Moreland, yeoman, to sell land in Warminster Twp.

Bk 1/pg 267   Nov 30, 1794

John Longstreth of Warminster Twp. sets free his Negro slave Abraham, age 23 the 16th of this month.

Bk 1/pg 269   Jan 23, 1795

Nathaniel Burrows of Middletown Twp, miller, sets free his Negro woman Jane, age 19.

Bk 1/pg 269   Dec 20, 1794

Benjamin and Richard Corson, executors of their father Benjamin Corson, late of Northampton Twp, pursuant to agreement of all the heirs, set free two female slaves named Dinah and Sarah, both under the age of 28.

Bk 1/pg 270   Feb 11, 1795

Bernard Taylor, late of Newtown Twp, gave bonds to Peter Taylor of Newtown Twp. who bequeathed them to his granddaughter Mary Taylor, now wife of Benjamin Price and who is now deceased. Benjamin Price acknowledges payment of the bonds by Benjamin Taylor, executor of Bernard Taylor.

Bk 1/pg 271   Aug 20, 1794

Rebecca Biles of Falls Twp, administratrix of Hannah Biles, late of Falls Twp, gives power of attorney to her sister Sarah Pennington of Philadelphia to recover money due her.

Bk 1/pg 271   Mar 10, 1795

Jacob and Cornelia Vandegrift, Simon Vanartsdalen, Joshua and Jane Praul, Abraham and Margaret Lefferts, Derick Vanartsdalen, Jacob Vanartsdalen, John Vanartsdalen, Elizabeth and Mary Vanartsdalen, heirs of Simon Vanartsdalen, late of Southampton Twp, agree to settlement of estate.

Bk 1/pg 275   Mar 30, 1795

Joseph Thornton of Northampton Twp. sets free his Negro girl Violletta, now over 21.

Bk 1/pg 279   May 6, 1794

Richard Gibbs of Bensalem Twp, Esq. gives power of attorney to daughter Hannah Gibbs and son-in-law Doctor John Ruan to sell his land in Baltimore Co, MD.   Bk 1/pg 280   May 15, 1795

Peter Blaker of Loudown Co, VA gives power of attorney to his son John Blaker to recover money due him.   Bk 1/pg 282   Nov 21, 1794

Jesse Keil, Mary Keil and Conrad Keil [heirs of Conrad Keil?] release Henry Rosenberger and James Thomas from a bond due to John Keil and Susanna Keil for their administration of the estate of Conrad Keil, late of New Britain Twp.   Bk 1/pg 285   Apr 23, 1794

John Bennet of Northampton Twp. sets free his Negro slave Anthony Limehouse, age 37 years.   Bk 1/pg 287   Nov 5, 1795

John Bennet of Northampton Twp. sets free his Negro slave Joseph Limehouse, age 33.   Bk 1/pg 287   Nov 5, 1795

Samuel Gibbs, Mary Cary, Sarah Rodman, Elizabeth Ruan (late Gibbs), Hannah Gibbs, Euphemia Gibbs, Gilbert Rodman and John Ruan, legatees of Richard Gibbs, late of Bensalem Twp, Esq. agree to acknowledge the strikeouts and erasures present in Richard's will. Bk 1/pg 288   Oct 20, 1795

Henry Wynkoop of Northampton Twp. sets free his Negro slave Peter, age 27 years and 11 months.   Bk 1/pg 290   Dec 11, 1795

John Rhoar, late of New Britain Twp, yeoman, died intestate leaving only heirs Catharine (wife of John Frick of Hatfield Twp, Montgomery Co, taylor) and Elizabeth Frick of New Britain Twp, spinster, full sisters. They give power of attorney to their uncle Christian Wireman of Union Town, Fayette Co, storekeeper, to pay off the patent on John's land.
                                          Bk 1/pg 290   Nov 30, 1795

Ann Mason, widow of Benjamin Mason, late of Loudoun Co, VA, gives power of attorney to son-in-law Levi Hole of Loudoun Co. to recover legacies due under wills of Elizabeth Warder of Lower Makefield Twp and Ellen Mead of Loudon Co.   Bk 1/pg 291   Nov 12, 1795

Andrew Schlichter acknowledges payment by Andrew Ruth, executor of Christian Ruth, late of New Britain Twp, yeoman, of share of John Ruth in dower of Christian's widow (now deceased) which share John assigned to Andrew.   Bk 1/pg 293   Nov 26, 1795

Phillip Jacob Overpeck, late of Springfield Twp, bequeathed his estate to children Andrew, George, Phillip, Henry, John, Elizabeth and Mary. Peter Keysor of Hambleton Twp, Northampton Co, Mary's newly appointed guardian by her choice, acknowledges payment of estate by Phillip Harple of Bedminster Twp, who had been appointed Mary's guardian when she was under age 14. Bk 1/pg 294   Jan 22, 1796

John Moyer of Plumstead Twp. sets free his Negro slave Peter (Tom's son), now age 40. Bk 1/pg 297   Apr 8, 1796

John Leedom of Northampton Twp, miller, releases to his wife Mary, all the goods she received by will of her late husband William Carter.
Bk 1/pg 298   Apr 4, 1796

Rebeckah Biles, Charlott Biles and Ann Biles, heirs to Hannah Biles, late of Falls Twp, with agreement from the other heirs, set free Natt Johnson, a black man who belonged to Hannah. Bk 1/pg 298   Mar 31, 1796

Peter Vansant of Lower Makefield Twp, yeoman, sets free his Negro slave Richard Gibbs. Bk 1/pg 300   May 31, 1796

Joseph Brown of Bristol Twp, yeoman, died intestate on Apr 17, 1796 leaving widow Sarah and only son William and only daughter Sarah (wife of Benjamin Larzalere). Benjamin and Sarah agree to allow William two-thirds share of the estate per the wishes of their father. Bk 1/pg 301   May 18, 1796

Sarah Brown, widow of Joseph Brown, late of Bristol Twp, yeoman, releases son William Brown and daughter Sarah (wife of Benjamin Larzalere) from dower right. Bk 1/pg 302   May 18, 1796

Abraham DuBois, Esq. of Northampton Twp. sets free his Negro slave Esther, age 31 years. Bk 1/pg 303   Aug 1, 1796

Rachel Mearns, widow of Hugh Mearns, late of Warwick Twp, accepts her husband's bequests in lieu of dower. Bk 1/pg 303   Sep 27, 1796

Joseph Thomas of Annapolis, Nova Scotia, farmer, gives power of attorney to brother David Thomas of Bucks Co. to recover money from Owen Thomas, executor of his father Joseph Thomas. Bk 1/pg 304   Aug 20, 1788

Samuel Gibbs, Mary Cary, Sarah Rodman, Elizabeth Ruan, Hannah Gibbs, Gilbert Rodman and John Ruan, children and legatees of Richard Gibbs, Esq., acknowledge additional bequests that Richard made to: his sister Mary (wife of John Rodman of Bensalem Twp), Mary Johnson (widow of Lawrence Johnson in whose house he was married), James Miller (now of Philadelphia, weaver), neighbor Isaac Jackson, children of late sister-in-law Hannah Cornwall (late Palmer), Rachel Titus (who now lives with him), negro woman Sick.   Bk 1/pg 308   Feb 22, 1796

John Kroesen of Northampton Twp. sets free his Negro slave Harry, age 26 years sometime next month.   Bk 1/pg 314   Sep 13, 1796

Conrad Seager and wife Mary of Shannandoah Co, VA give power of attorney to friend Abraham Snyder of Bucks Co, farmer, to recover money due from estate of Catharina Young, late of Bucks Co.
                                          Bk 1/pg 314   Feb 6, 1797

William Bennett, administrator of Isaac Bennett, late of Northampton Twp, yeoman, sells to Sam Malony of Northampton Twp, a free Negro man, a Negro slave named Syll, age 28, and her Negro child named Sall or Sarah, now above 18 months.   Bk 1/pg 317   Jun 10, 1797

William Bennett, eldest son and administrator of Isaac Bennett, late of Northampton Twp, yeoman, sets free Isaac's Negro slave Sam Malony, now 28 years old, upon payment by Derrick Kroeson for the purpose of setting Sam free.   Bk 1/pg 317   Jun 9, 1797

Abraham Larrue of Bensalem Twp, practitioner in physic, sets free his Negro slave Tobias Butler, age 26 years and one month.   Bk 1/pg 318   Jun 17, 1796

Hannah Harris, late of Woodford, KY but now of Bucks Co. and Mary Hunter of Bucks Co, widow, sisters of William Stewart, late of Kentucky, give power of attorney to Thomas Allen of Mercer Co, KY and Thomas Todd of Franklin Co, KY to partition William's real estate.   Bk 1/pg 322   Jun 30, 1797

Hannah Harris, widow of John Harris, late of Newtown, Esq., who is about to set out for the state of KY where she is entitled to one-half part of John's yet unsold lands by deed of the eldest and only son, John, and who is also entitled with her sister Mary Hunter to land from their father Charles Stewart, late of Upper Makefield, gives power of attorney to Daniel Martin and John D. Murray, both of Bucks Co. to represent her interests in Bucks Co.
                                          Bk 1/pg 325   Jul 25, 1797

Thomas Stewart of New Britain Twp, yeoman, had agreed to free his two Negro slaves Ned (age 27 years, 3 months) and Jack (age 25 years, 6 months) upon their turning 28 but there being some doubt about their freedom, he gives up all right and claim to these two Negroes. Bk 1/pg 326   Aug 7, 1797

Kitty Youngkin declares that her son Henry Youngken was not 21 years old when he sold land in Bedminster Twp. to his brother Rudolph Youngkin as the agreement was made in Sept, 1794 and Henry was not 21 until Oct 9, 1794.   Bk 1/pg 327   Jun 7, 1797

Derick Krewson of Northampton Twp. sets free his Negro slaves Timothy (age 19, to be free at age 28) and Hannah (age 22, to be free now).
                                        Bk 1/pg 329   Sep 28, 1797

George Waggoner of Rockhill Twp, hatchet maker, gives power of attorney to son Emanuel Waggoner of Rockhill Twp, yeoman, to recover money due from Jacob Waggoner and Jacob Sox.   Bk 1/pg 330   Sep 21, 1797

Lucy Dobel, widow and administratrix of William John Benger Dobel, late of Philadelphia, now about to move to New England, gives power of attorney to William Waln of Philadelphia to recover money due her.
                                        Bk 1/pg 330   Oct 31, 1797

Joseph Thornton sets free his mulatto woman Rose, age 26, on Aug 13, 1797.
                                        Bk 1/pg 332   Mar 23, 1797

Andreas Everandus VanBeam Houckgust of Chinas Retreat, Bristol Twp. and Johanna Egberta Constantia VanSchulen of Chinas Retreat are about to be married and agrees that Johanna shall keep any money she has or shall inherit.
                                        Bk 1/pg 336   Feb 2, 1798

Samuel Huff, late of Maryland, left estate which descended to his brother Richard Huff and sisters Mary, Ruth, Elizabeth and Rachel of whom Richard Stockton is trustee or attorney. Albert Douglas and wife Elizabeth and Joseph Colter and wife Rachel give power of attorney to Matthias Hutchinson of Bucks Co, Esq. to recover their shares from Richard Stockton.
                                        Bk 1/pg 338   Mar 7, 1798

William Waln of Philadelphia, attorney for Lucy Dobel, administratrix of Benger Dobel, MD, late of Philadelphia, and Peter Dobel, Samuel and Ruth (Dobel) Bennet and Sarah Dobel, acknowledge payment of a mortgage due to Benger, Peter, Ruth and Sarah.   Bk 1/pg 340   Mar 16, 1798

Richard Leedom of Northampton Twp. sells to James D. Lancie his black man Peter D. Lancie whom he purchased from John Fenton, deceased.

Bk 1/pg 342   Apr 14, 1798

James Delancie of Northampton Twp. sets free Peter D. Lancie whom he purchased from Richard Leedom.

Bk 1/pg 342   Apr 14, 1798

Jonathan Willett, late of Southampton Twp, yeoman, sets free his Negro woman Jude who will be 25 years old next Sept. 10.

Bk 1/pg 343   Apr 23, 1798

Jacob Dean, son of John Dean, late of Philadelphia Co, yeoman, sells to his uncle John Duer of Lower Makefield Twp. his share in his father's estate.

Bk 1/pg 349   Feb 9, 1798

Thomas Hutchinson of Northampton Twp, son-in-law of David Twining, deceased, husband of David's daughter Sarah, abates the interest which might have accrued on a mortgage due by will of David.   Bk 1/pg 350   Mar 29,1798

John Praul of Middletown Twp. sets free his Negro wench [sic] Jude, aged 23 years and 9 months.   Bk 1/pg 351   Jun 5, 1798

John Praul of Middletown Twp, yeoman, sets free his Negro wench [sic] Suk, age 18.   Bk 1/pg 352   Jun 5, 1798

Joseph Bloomfield and wife Mary (late McIlvain) acknowledge payment of a mortgage by John Burges.   Bk 1/pg 352   May 16,1798

David Forst of Solebury Twp. and wife Sarah have agreed to separate due to unhappy differences between them.   Bk 1/pg 357   Feb 4, 1796

Paul Cramer, son of John Cramer, late of Hilltown Twp, sells his share of his father's estate to his mother Christina.   Bk 1/pg 363   May 21, 1798

John Longstreth of Warminster Twp, Esq. sets free his Negro slave Cesar when he arrives at the age of 28 on the 12th of next month.

Bk 1/pg 364   Oct 20, 1798

Adam Bootzman of Limerick Twp, Montgomery Co. agrees with Catarina Trumboar of Milford Twp. that he will not demand or be an heir to the legacy Catarina may receive from the estate of her father Henry Huber.

Bk 1/pg 366   Apr 21, 1788

17

Robert Miller of Upper Makefield Twp, blacksmith, is due a certain part of the estate of his father Robert Miller and sells that right to Charles Carter of Buckingham Twp, mason.   Bk 1/pg 368   Sep 22, 1787

Daniel Dean, eldest son of John Dean, late of Philadelphia Co, yeoman, sells his share of estate to his uncle John Duer of Lower Makefield Twp.
Bk 1/pg 369   Jan 15, 1799

Augustin Willett of Southampton Twp, son of Samuel Willett, late of Bucks Co, yeoman, acknowledges payment of estate by Joseph Thornton and his wife Elizabeth (his mother, late Elizabeth Willett).   Bk 1/pg 370   Dec 27,1783

Joseph Thornton sets free his Negro wench [sic] Viollet, age 20.
Bk 1/pg 372   May 10, 1794

Elias Dungan of Northampton Twp. sets free his Negro slave Patty.
Bk 1/pg 372   Feb 6, 1799

Charles Stuart Sen. of Plumstead Twp. agreed in 1780 to sell his plantation to George Stuart and Charles Stuart Jun. subject to a lifetime annuity for himself and maintenance for his daughter Rachel Stuart (an infirm person).   Charles Stuart Jun. now sells his right to George Stuart.   Bk 1/pg 376   Oct 6, 1781

Samuel Benezet of Bensalem Twp, administrator of James Benezet, late of Bensalem, with consent of his mother and sisters, sets free a Negro slave named Abraham Cummings, under age 28, belonging to his father's estate.
Bk 1/pg 381   Jan 24, 1799

Mary Backhouse, James Backhouse, John Barclay and William Bryan, all of Bucks Co, guardians, heirs and representatives of Richard Backhouse, Esq., late of Bucks Co, give power of attorney to friend Col. John Smith of Springfield Twp. to sell land in Westmoreland Co.
Bk 1/pg 383   Apr 2, 1799

Johann Georg Desch, late of Haycock Twp, died intestate without issue so his estate descended to his eldest brother Johannes Desch who subsequently died intestate leaving children Maria Margaretha (wife of Conrad Bohn) and Maria Elizabetha (wife of Jacob Scharf).   Maria Elizabeth Scharf died intestate leaving three daughters: Eva (wife of John Adam Fieberling), Catharina Margaretha (wife of Joh. Conrad Schaemer, yeoman) and Eva Elizabetha (wife of G. Paul Pfeifer).   On April 28, 1790, Maria Margaretha Bohn and Eva Fieberling gave power of attorney to Johann Peter Weygand of

Baltimore, innkeeper, but the other two heirs were not of age at that time. Catharina Margaretha and Eva Elizabetha, both of Secheim, Hessen Darmstadt, Germany, give power of attorney to Peter Uhbrich of Philadelphia, merchant, to recover their shares of the estate.   Bk 1/pg 392   Apr 13, 1798

John McNair of Southampton Twp. sets free his Negro woman Dina, age 25.
Bk 1/pg 399   Sep 17, 1799

Rebecca McNeely, widow of Robert McNeely, late of Bedminster Twp, acknowledges payment by executors William McNeely of dower.
Bk 1/pg 400   Jun 13, 1799

John and Sarah Bye of Nelson Co, KY give power of attorney to friends Hezekiah Dean of Frederick Co, MD and Joseph Dean of Bucks Co. to recover their share of dower of Martha Dean, deceased.
Bk 1/pg 403   Jun 8, 1799

John Simpson of Solebury Twp, miller, died intestate in 1747 leaving widow Hannah and sons John and James and other children. Hannah later married Robert Thompson of Solebury Twp. John Simpson of Solebury and James Simpson of Warminster Twp. give power of attorney to Robert Smith of Buckingham Twp. to recover their share of estate from Robert Thompson.
Bk 1/pg 404   Nov 13, 1799

Jane Hilborn, widow of Robert Hilborn of Newtown Twp, yeoman, releases her son Amos Hilborn from her dower right.   Bk 1/pg 405   Apr 1, 1799

Hannah Livezey, daughter of Enoch Ingby/Drigby[?] of Pelham Twp, Lincoln Co, Upper Canada, now about 18 years, chooses her husband Richard Livezey of Pelham Twp. as guardian of her estate.   Bk 1/pg 406   Oct 25, 1799

Henry Opdyck of Sussex Co, NJ, administrator of Nicholas Depue and Abraham Depue, son of Jno. Depue and his wife Sarah who married Nicholas Lazeler, deceased, give power of attorney to friend William Aspy of Lower Makefield Twp. to recover the share agreeable to an article between my [Abraham's?] mother and Nicholas Lazelere.   Bk 1/pg 408   Jan 15, 1800

Samuel Jones of Warrington Twp. gives power of attorney to John Brinton of Ross Co, North Western Territory of the U.S.A., one of the executors of John Thomas, late of Bucks Co, to sell land in Hilltown Twp. bequeathed to Samuel by John Thomas.   Bk 1/pg 409   Nov 28, 1797

John Duer of Lower Makefield Twp. sets free his Negro slave Harry who has faithfully served him for 25 years.   Bk 1/pg 410   Jan 30, 1800

Christian Gross of Springfield Twp, yeoman, gives power of attorney to friend Christopher Kessler of Springfield Twp, yeoman, to recover estate from Christopher Wagner and Charles Rentzhimer, executors of Christian Gross, late of Lower Saucon Twp, Northampton Co.
                                              Bk 1/pg 411   Dec, 1797

Garret Vanartsdalen of Northampton Twp. sets free his Negro slave Tom who has served him faithfully for nearly 25 years.   Bk 1/pg 412   Feb 5, 1800

John Simpson of Solebury Twp, miller, died intestate about the year 1747 leaving widow Hannah who subsequently married Robert Thompson of Solebury Twp. who then became responsible for settling John's estate. As Robert is now old and infirm, he gives power of attorney to John Beaumont of Upper Makefield Twp. to carry out the administration.
                                              Bk 1/pg 412   Feb 3, 1800

Walter Hill of Washington Co. gives power of attorney to friend Joseph Trager of Washington Co. to recover all moneys due his wife Elizabeth by bequest of Lawrence Brown, which money is in the hands of Jacob Trager of Bucks Co.   Bk 1/pg 413   Feb 10, 1798

Mary Warner, Amos Warner and wife Susanna, and John Warner, children of Croasdale Warner, deceased, give power of attorney to Isaac Warner of Montgomery Co. to sell Croasdale's land.   Bk 1/pg 414   Mar 10, 1800

Thomas Hutchinson of Northampton Twp. purchased a Negro woman named Euphemia, now about 24 years old, from Edward Duffield for the purpose of setting her free. Euphemia had been registered by Hugh Tomb and sold by him to Edward Duffield in 1791. Upon receipt of payment by David Story who wished to help pay for this act, Thomas now sets Euphemia free.
                                              Bk 1/pg 414   Apr 8, 1800

Hugh Tomb of Byberry Twp, Philadelphia Co. sells to Edward Duffield his Negro girl Euphemia, age 15 years, she having been registered with the Clerk of Quarter Sessions of Bucks Co.   Bk 1/pg 415   Aug 5, 1791

Thomas Wright of Luzerne Co. gives power of attorney to Joseph Erwin, Esq. of Bucks Co. to recover money due him from estate of Thomas Dyer, Esq., late of Bucks Co. now in the hands of John Dyer Jun. and Jesse Dyer, executors of Jane Dyer who was executrix of Thomas.

Bk 1/pg 418   Apr 11, 1800

John Wilson, Esq. of Buckingham Twp. and George Piper of Bedminster Twp. set free Rachel Irwin, daughter of Katherine Lewis, age about 24 years, who was born and recorded as a slave agreeable to law.

Bk 1/pg 421   May 7, 1800

Mary Paxson of Solebury Twp, only daughter and representative of James Paxson, deceased, who was a son of Thomas Paxson of Middletown Twp, deceased, who died intestate leaving estate now administered by Mary's well-respected uncles Thomas and William Paxson, acknowledges payment of estate by Simon Gillam, administrators of her late uncle William and Benjamin Buckman, guardian of Ann and Mary Paxson.

Bk 1/pg 424   Aug 9, 1799

Charles Kirk of Lower Mount Bethel Twp, Northampton Co, laborer, and wife Sara, sister to Samuel and Thomas Bond and heir to John Bond, ratify sale to Christian Shimmel of Springfield Twp. of a tract of land in Springfield which was sold by Sara's brothers, subject to trust for Sara.

Bk 1/pg 425   Apr 17, 1800

Samuel Bond of Pikeland Twp, Chester Co, weaver, and Thomas Bond of Springfield Twp, cordwainer, sell land in Springfield Twp. to Christian Shimmel of Upper Saucon Twp, weaver, subject to one-third of purchase price being held in trust for benefit of their sister Sarah Keith.

Bk 1/pg 426   Feb 6, 1800

Christian Wilour of Lower Milford Twp, son of late Adam Wilour of Lower Milford, and Abraham Shelly of Lower Milford, yeoman, gave a bond to Peter Wilour of Lower Milford, another son of Adam, for payment of part of estate now and part after the death of the widow Mary. Peter gives power of attorney to Henry Freed of Norriton Twp, Montgomery Co. to recover payment from Christian and Abraham.   Bk 1/pg 430   May 13, 1800

Joseph Carver and wife Elizabeth acknowledge receipt from Jesse Pickering, John Sheldon[?], Henry Paxson and Joseph Paxson, executors of Anthony Kimble, of a portion of proceeds from the sale of Anthony's land.

Bk 1/pg 434   Apr 1, 1800

21

Harman Vansant of Warminster Twp, yeoman, sets free his Negro man John when he arrives at the age of 27 years, 11 months and 20 days.

Bk 1/pg 437   Sep 15, 1800

Jacob Hockman, late of Bedminster Twp, bequeathed land to his son Jacob upon turning 20, subject to Jacob and the executors (Ulry Hockman and Jacob Leatherman) choosing men to appraise its value. They now choose men to make an appraisement per the provisions of the will.

Bk 1/pg 438   Jan 9, 1790

William Margrove and wife Mary, who is widow and sole administratrix of Erasmus Kelly, clerk, who was grandson of John Kelly, late of Bucks, sell their right to land bequeathed by Erasmus grandmother Eleanor Kelly.

Bk 1/pg 440   May 31, 1800

Amos White, Joseph White, Ann White, John White and Abraham Clark and wife Mary, heirs of Daniel White, late of Buckingham Twp, acknowledge payment of the dower due the widow Mary but Samuel Gilbert, grandson of Thomas Gilbert, late of Buckingham Twp, who purchased Daniel's land.

Bk 1/pg 442   Nov 24, 1800

Ann Sagers of Lower Milford Twp, daughter and heir of William Sagers who was a legatee of Peter Sagers, late of Richland Twp, acknowledges payment of estate by executor John Stover.   Bk 1/pg 447   Dec 4, 1800

Martha Brown, Robert Kennedy, Amos Bradshaw, Rachel Brown, David Gilbert, David Bradshaw and James Bradshaw, heirs of James Bradshaw, late of Buckingham Twp, acknowledge payment of estate by executors John and William Bradshaw.   Bk 1/pg 448   Apr 7, 1785

Jacob Letherman and Anne Letherman, children of Michael Letherman, late of Bedminster Twp, yeoman, acknowledge that their brother Henry has paid the one-third dower due to their mother Anne, now wife of John Loux.

Bk 1/pg 450   Feb 3, 1801

John Loux of Plumstead Twp, yeoman, and wife Anne, widow of Michael Letherman, late of Bedminster Twp, acknowledge payment of the dower by Michael's son Henry Letherman of Bedminster Twp.

Bk 1/pg 450   Feb 3, 1801

Gabriel Sagers and Conarad Sagers of Shanadore Co, VA, Christian and Elizabeth Young of Northampton Co. and Elizabeth Daymote[?] and Jonas

Furry and wife Barbara, heirs of William Sagers, late of Springfield Twp, and John Harwick, guardian of Mary Bedler, late Sagers, heirs of Peter Sager, late of Richland Twp, acknowledge payment of estate by executor John Stover.

Bk 1/pg 451   Nov 14, 1795

Barbara Moyer (late Sager), legatee of Peter Sager, late of Richland Twp, acknowledges payment of estate by executors John Stover.

Bk 1/pg 452   Nov 17, 1795

Edith Hough of Warminster Twp, widow, gives power of attorney to son Oliver Hough of Upper Makefield Twp. to recover money due her.

Bk 1/pg 453   Oct 24, 1800

Margaret Colvin of Baltimore, widow of Patrick Colvin of Baltimore, acknowledges payment of dower by Patrick's son Samuel.

Bk 1/pg 454   Aug 23, 1800

James Lefferts of Southampton Twp. sets free his Negro slave Anthony Brown, now about 27 years old.   Bk 1/pg 455   Oct 1, 1800

Gilliam Cornell of Southampton Twp, yeoman, sets free his Negro woman Jude/Judeth Derry, now about 35 years old, as well as her mulatto son named Moses Derry, aged about 12 months.   Bk 1/pg 458   Apr 14, 1801

Joseph Galloway of Walford Parish, Kerts Co, Great Britain, Esq., gives power of attorney to friends Joseph Richardson Jenks and Thomas Story of Pennsylvania to recover money due from estate of Lawrence Groudon, late of Bucks Co, Esq.   Bk 1/pg 460   Mar 4, 1800

David Landis of Middletown Twp. sets free his Negro woman Flourow, about 43 years old, whom he purchased of James Boyd of Newtown.

Bk 1/pg 461   Feb 23, 1801

Jacob Godshalk, guardian of Samuel, Ann and Gabriel Atherholt, children of Frederick Atherholt, late of Bedminster Twp, acknowledges payment of estate by Frederick's son Frederick.   Bk 1/pg 462   Feb 25, 1801

Joshua Vanhorn sold to Abdon Buckman land in Newtown Twp. which his father Henry Vanhorn owned at his death and which Joshua inherited as eldest son, subject to dower for his mother of which he is entitled to two-ninths upon his mother's death.   Bk 1/pg 465   May 4, 1801

David Kulp, late of Bedminster Twp, bequeathed his land to his three sons Jacob, Abraham and David. David Kulp the younger died after his father intestate and without issue. David and John Yoder of Bedminster Twp. sell to Abraham Kulp of Bedminster Twp, yeoman, their one-fifth share of the estate of David Kulp the younger.   Bk 1/pg 466   Feb 28, 1801

Henry Landis of East Nantmill Twp, Chester Co, yeoman, sells to Abraham Kulp of Bedminster Twp, yeoman, his one-fifth share of the estate of David Kulp the younger, who was an heir of David Kulp Sr.
    Bk 1/pg 467   Feb 28, 1801

David Kulp, Anne Kulp and Elizabeth Kulp of Bedminster Twp. sell to Abraham Kulp of Bedminster Twp, yeoman, their three-fifths part of one-fifth share of the estate of David Kulp the younger, who was an heir of David Kulp Sr.   Bk 1/pg 469   Feb 28, 1801

George Cramer and wife of Hilltown Twp. sell to Christiana Cramer of Hilltown his share in a plantation left to him by his late father John Cramer.
    Bk 1/pg 470   Jan 26, 1801

Thomas and Ann Hutchison of Buckingham Twp, yeoman, and Samuel and Margaret Cary of Buckingham Twp, yeoman agree to redraw the line between land they all received under the will of William Person.
    Bk 1/pg 482   Jun 8, 1801

Mary Hunter of Upper Makefield Twp. gives power of attorney to her son William Stewart Hunter of Newtown Twp. to recover all moneys due her.
    Bk 1/pg 487   Jun 10, 1801

Elizabeth Beans of Buckingham Twp. gives power of attorney to friend Samuel Johnson of Buckingham and son Joseph Rice of Solebury Twp. to recover dower from her son John Rice due on the estate of her former husband Edward Rice.   Bk 1/pg 488   Aug 1, 1801

Griffith Miles of Northampton Twp. sets free his Negro woman Isabel, now 28 years old, whom he purchased from Henry Debois for the purpose of freeing her.   Bk 1/pg 491   Aug 6, 1801

Jane Burley, widow of John Burley, late of Upper Makefield Twp, and her four daughters Sarah Burley, Jane Burley, Phebe Burley and Mary Burley, release Joshua Burley of the widow's dower which would otherwise be due upon Joshua's purchase of John's real estate. Bk 1/pg 498   May 12, 1801

24

James Dixey, late of Georgia, bequeathed estate to the children of his brother William, namely William, James, Thomas, Isaiah, Elenor and Hannah (James having also specifically received two Negroes). Isaiah Dixey gives power of attorney to Frederick Mooze[?] of Lincoln Co, NC to recover estate from his brother James who is now deceased.   Bk 1/pg 501   Sep 23, 1801

Mary Booze, widow of Peter Booze, late of Bristol, yeoman, swears that she heard her husband say that he sold land to his brother John Booze which he received by will of his father.   Bk 1/pg 504   Oct 16, 1801

Joseph Carver acknowledges payment by Jesse Pickering, John Shelton, Henry Paxson and Joseph Paxson, executors of Anthony Kimble, of one-fifth portion of the proceeds of the sale of Anthony's real estate which was due to his wife Elizabeth as daughter of Anthony.   Bk 1/pg 505   Mar 30, 1801

Samuel Richardson of Falls Twp. sets free a Negro woman named Hager Johnson, age 29 years.   Bk 1/pg 508   Sep 12, 1801

John Ramsey of Warwick Twp, yeoman, sets free his Negro slave Peter, age 27 years.   Bk 1/pg 509   Nov 6, 1801

Samuel Y. Thornton of Middletown Twp, innkeeper, sets free a Negro boy named Amos Freeman, age 8 years and being a slave until age 28, born the property of John Krusen of Northampton Twp. who transferred him to Christopher Snyder who sold him to Samuel.   Bk 1/pg 509   Oct 25, 1800

Joseph Pool, William Pool and wife Martha, John Pool and Joseph and Martha Mettlen, children of Edward Pool, late of Warwick Twp, weaver, agree to partition of part of Edward's real estate to their brother James.
Bk 1/pg 510   Mar 9, 1801

Gilbert Rodman and William Rodman, executors of William Rodman, late of Bensalem Twp, set free two Negro slaves named Plymouth and Ceasar when they are 28 years old (Plymouth on Sep 26, 1802 and Ceasar on Dec 6, 1807) as provided in William's will.   Bk 1/pg 518   Nov 22, 1801

Abraham Larew, late of Bensalem Twp, yeoman, left land to his three daughters (Ellenor—wife of Joseph Sacett, Ann—wife of John Larselere and Elizabeth Vansant) upon the death of his wife Alice, excluding a portion given to his son Abraham. Alice is now deceased and the three daughters agree to partition of the real estate.   Bk 1/pg 521   Nov 30, 1801

Ephraim Addis of Warwick Twp. sets free his Negro slave Ben, age 24 years, on condition that he immediately bind himself to John Hulme for three years and six months who has paid for such service. Bk 1/pg 542   Oct 9, 1801

John Hill and Cathrine Hill (formerly Cathrine James), being Baron and Feme, give power of attorney to friend Asa Thomas of Bucks Co. to collect a legacy devised by William James of Bucks Co. now in the hands of executors David Evans and Rebecca Smith.   Bk 1/pg 543   Aug 22, 1797

Maria Mallam Brooks, wife of David Brooks of Runebeck, Dutchess Co, NY, acknowledges payment of dower by James Carrel Jun. of Tinicum Twp. on land he purchased from Joseph Brooks, Benjamin Brooks and her husband David Brooks as heirs of James Brooks, late of Tinicum Twp.
                                        Bk 1/pg 546   Jun 6, 1800

David Brooks of Rynebeck, Dutchess Co, NY gives power of attorney to brother Joseph Brooks of Tinicum Twp. to sell his share of the farm of his father James Brooks, late of Tinicum Twp.   Bk 1/pg 547   Mar 7, 1796

Joseph Winner of Bristol Twp. gives power of attorney to friend Thomas Barton of Bristol Twp. to recover money due from administrators of Peter Brown, late of Bristol Twp.   Bk 1/pg 548   Sep 11, 1801

Abraham and Mary Geil, Christian Crotz, Catharine Crotz (late Geil), John Geil, Samuel Godshalk (in right of late wife Mary Geil), Samuel and Barbury Swarts, all of Bucks Co, give power of attorney to friend Christian Funk of Rockingham Co, VA, cooper, to sell land in Rockingham Co. (the shares of Jacob Geil, Christian Funk and Jacob Beury in this land already being sold).
                                        Bk 1/pg 551   Feb 1, 1802

David Willson Sen. of Nockamixon Twp. gives power of attorney to Francis Willson of Tinicum Twp. to recover money from Robert Stewart Jun. and Maria Willson, executors of Samuel Wilson, late of Nockamixon Twp.
                                        Bk 1/pg 552   Sep 26, 1798

William Silvius Jun. and Jacob Silvius, both of Rockingham Co, VA, acknowledge payment by their father William Silvius of Rockhill Twp. of the shares they would receive at their father's death. Bk 2/pg 10   Mar 19, 1802

John Roth, eldest son of Jacob Roth, late of Rockhill Twp, yeoman, acknowledges payment of estate by his brother Jacob who inherited their father's real estate.   Bk 2/pg 13   May 31, 1792

Andrew Heller and wife Elizabeth, daughter of Jacob Roth, late of Rockhill Twp, acknowledge payment of estate by her brother Jacob.

Bk 2/pg 15   May 27, 1796

Samuel Foreman of Beaver Dam Twp, Northumberland Co. and wife Katern, daughter of Jacob Rode, late of Rockhill Twp, acknowledge payment of estate by executors Jacob and Henry Rode.   Bk 2/pg 16   Mar 29, 1798

Henry Roth, son of Jacob Roth, late of Rockhill Twp, yeoman, acknowledges payment of estate by brother Jacob Roth.   Bk 2/pg 17   May 29, 1797

Henry Miller and wife Charlotte, daughter of Jacob Roth, late of Rockhill Twp, acknowledge payment of estate by brother Jacob Roth.

Bk 2/pg 18   Aug 30, 1794

Peter Roth, son of Jacob Roth, late of Rockhill Twp, acknowledges payment of estate by Jacob Roth.   Bk 2/pg 19   May 27, 1796

Roderick Connor of Solebury Twp, farmer, gives power of attorney to John Worthington of Solebury Twp, farmer, to recover money due out of estate of his father-in-law Peter Vickers due his wife Susanna.

Bk 2/pg 26   Sep 6, 1802

Robert Stockdale of Lewistown, Mifflin Co. gives power of attorney to brother George Stockdale of Moorland Twp, Montgomery Co. to recover estate of late father Robert Stockdale now in hands of guardian Thomas Wilson of Southampton Twp.   Bk 2/pg 29   Sep 14, 1802

Peter Plais[?] of Philadelphia Co, yeoman, and wife Barbara, daughter of John Shearer, late of Bucks Co, give power of attorney to Joseph Hart of Northern Liberties Twp, Philadelphia Co. to recover estate due her.

Bk 2/pg 32   May 4, 1801

Mathias Cowell of Solebury Twp. gives power of attorney to son Joseph and son-in-law Thomas Hambleton, both of Solebury, to sell real estate in Rye Twp, Cumberland Co.   Bk 2/pg 36   Oct 27, 1802

Henry and Ann (Harris) Innes, Thomas and Elizabeth (Harris) Todd, John Harris, Sarah (Harris) Smith, Rachel Harris and Hannah Harris, children of John Harris, late of Newtown, authorize the widow Hannah to sell her dower right in John's real estate.   Bk 2/pg 45   Oct 1, 1802

John Klinker of Northampton Co. gives power of attorney to Philip Jacoby of Hilltown Twp. to recover rent from Abraham Otherholt of Haycock Twp. who lives on the plantation where Arnt Klinker lived at the time of his decease.   Bk 2/pg 47   Dec 11, 1802

John Praul of Middletown Twp, who owns a slave named Samuel Derry by will of his late father John Praul, sets his slave free.   Bk 2/pg 48   Feb 5, 1803

Ruth Merrick of Newtown Twp, widow, gives power of attorney to Jonathan Heston of Buckingham Twp. to recover dower from Robert Merrick.
                                    Bk 2/pg 51   Jan 12, 1801

John Waldman of Upper Saucon Twp, Northampton Co, grandson of Henry Wenig, late of Lower Milford Twp, and heir to his mother's sister as well, sells his share of estate to Daniel Cooper, of Upper Saucon Twp, innkeeper.
                                    Bk 2/pg 53   Feb 2, 1803

Edward Roberts of Cumberland Twp, Green Co, yeoman, son and heir (with Everard Roberts, Rebecca Foulk and Rachel Carr) of Everard Roberts, late of Richland Twp, sells to Susanna and Ann Roberts of Richland Twp, single women, his share of estate due upon death of his mother Ann.
                                    Bk 2/pg 57   Jan 10, 1803

Andrew Ellicott of Baltimore Co, MD gives power of attorney to son Thomas Ellicott of Baltimore Co. to recover money from Whiston Canby of Bucks Co.   Bk 2/pg 60   Jan, 1803

Abraham Pevikiser of Bedminster Twp, yeoman, sells to his son Daniel and Daniel's wife Agness all his household goods and stock.
                                    Bk 2/pg 62   Jan 24, 1803

Henry Riegel acknowledges payment by his father George Reigle of Nockamixon Twp. of Henry's share of George's estate.
                                    Bk 2/pg 66   May 1, 1798

Amey Clark acknowledges payment by William Crawford of dower due on real estate previously belonging to her late husband John Clark.
                                    Bk 2/pg 79   May 5, 1803

Dr. William Delaney on Feb 7, 1801 executed an agreement to pay his wife Lydia Delany for the education of their daughter Eliza but that agreement did

not specify the amount of payment. Dr. Delaney now agrees to a specific
amount of payment.   Bk 2/pg 83   Mar 5, 1803

Joseph Swift of Bensalem Twp. sells to Charles Swift of Philadelphia,
Esquire, in consideration for a bond from Charles' brother John White Swift,
Joseph's share in the estate of his late father John Swift, Esq. of Bensalem
Twp.   Bk 2/pg 85   Apr 2, 1803

Jacob Kesler and wife Elizabeth, daughter of Amos Strickland, deceased,
acknowledge payment of ground rent by Amos' widow Margaret Gordon of
Newtown.   Bk 2/pg 89   Jul 26, 1803

Able and Margaret Thomas of Rockbridge Co, VA give power of attorney to
brother Asa Thomas of Hilltown Twp. to recover all moneys due them.
                                            Bk 2/pg 92   Nov 1, 1793

Samuel Canby of Mason Co, KY gives power of attorney to John Stapler of
Bucks Co. to recover estate from Thomas Yardley and Thomas Yardley,
executors of his uncle Thomas Yardley, late of Trenton, NJ.
                                            Bk 2/pg 93   Jul 25, 1803

John Gittilman, eldest son of Henry Gettelman of Rockhill Twp, yeoman,
acknowledges payment by his father of John's share in three tracts of land in
Rockhill Twp.   Bk 2/pg 94   Apr 2, 1802

Frederick Meyer, married to Christiana Riter, widow of George Reiter, late of
Milford Twp, give power of attorney to David Spinner to recover dower due
to Christiana.   Bk 2/pg 99   Oct 8, 1803

Obed Aaron of Hilltown Twp. sets free his two slaves: Negroe Jenny (age 21)
and Negroe Lidia (age 19).   Bk 2/pg 103   Jul 11, 1798

Jonathan and Charity Tomlinson of Munsy Twp, Lycoming Co. give power of
attorney to his brother Henry Tomlinson of Bucks Co. to sell two tracts of
land in Attleborough in Middletown Twp.   Bk 2/pg 105   Mar 17, 1803

Joseph Fulmer of Haycock Twp, yeoman, sells his real estate to his son
Joseph Fulmer Jun.   Bk 2/pg 111   Jul 25, 1794

Joshua Paul and Hannah Paul of Warrington Twp. and Seneca Lukens of
Horsham Twp, Montgomery Co. (guardian of Yeamans Paul), children of

Hannah Paul, late of Warrington Twp, acknowledge payment by Joseph Longstreth of a mortgage given to Hannah Paul.   Bk 2/pg 123   Apr 9, 1804

Aaron Linton of Northampton Twp, blacksmith, gives power of attorney to uncle Aaron Winder of Lower Makefield Twp. to recover moneys due him.
Bk 2/pg 124   Apr 11, 1795

Joseph Long of Solebury Twp, son of Ludwick Long, late of Tinicum Twp, gives power of attorney to Elias Shull Jun. of Tinicum Twp, joiner, to recover his one-eighth share of estate from his mother Elizabeth and brother Peter, executors of Ludwick.   Bk 2/pg 127   Feb 13, 1804

Philip Shitz Jun. of Limerick Twp, Montgomery Co, guardian to his children, the grandchildren of Peter Hedrick, late of Richland Twp, acknowledges payment of estate by executors John Benner and John Hedrick due previous to the deceased of widow Catharine.   Bk 2/pg 131   Feb 20, 1802

Samuel Coats of Philadelphia, executors of his sister Alice Longsale[?] who was executrix of their mother Mary Coats, acknowledges payment by Jacob Walton and Timothy Taylor of mortgages held by his mother.
Bk 2/pg 132   Feb 16, 1804

Elizabeth Buckman of Buckingham Twp, widow of Thomas Buckman, late of Newtown Twp, gives power of attorney to friend John Carver of Buckingham Twp. to recover dower.   Bk 2/pg 140   May 12, 1804

Nicholas Hoft of Easton, son of Deiter Hoft, late of Richland Twp, gives power of attorney to friend John C. Sams of Haycock Twp. to recover estate from administrator Peter Long, late of Rockhill Twp.
Bk 2/pg 141   Sep 12, 1803

Madalana Wanech of Milford Twp, widow of Henry Wanech, late of Milford, gives power of attorney to son-in-law John Freck[?] of Upper Milford Twp, Northampton Co. to recover estate from administrators John Young and Thomas Boyer.   Bk 2/pg 147   Aug 2, 1804

Sarah Twining, widow of John Twining, late of Warwick Twp, gives power of attorney to William Hill of Warwick Twp. to acknowledge payment of a mortgage from Joseph Twining.   Bk 2/pg 150   Aug 15, 1804

30

Charles Bessonett of Bristol Twp, executor of father John Bessonett, gives power of attorney to friend Abraham Chapman, Esq. of Newtown to record satisfaction of a mortgage.   Bk 2/pg 153   Oct 17, 1804

James Dungan of Northampton Twp. frees the slave Jacob, 25 years of age, which his father Elias Dungan recorded as a slave.   Bk 2/pg 154   Oct 24, 1804

Henry and Margaret Bissey, Andrew and Catherine Steer, George and Barbara Lida, Henry and Susanna Hertzel and Michael and Eve Eckart, daughters of Jacob Ahlum, late of Haycock Twp, acknowledge payment of estate by Jacob Ahlum and Philip Tatisman.   Bk 2/pg 159   Nov 19, 1804

Michael Ahlum, Philip Ahlum, George Ahlum, John Ahlum and David Ahlum, all of Bucks Co, sons of Jacob Ahlum, late of Haycock Twp, acknowledge payment of estate by administrators Jacob Ahlum and Philip Tatesman.   Bk 2/pg 160   Nov 19, 1804

William Scott of Turbot Twp, Northumberland Co, yeoman, gives power of attorney to his uncle Alexander Meckleroy of Nockamixon Twp, yeoman, to take possession of one-fifth part of land in Nockamixon due by will of grandmother Jean Meckleroy.   Bk 2/pg 163   Dec 13, 1802

Frederick Moyer who married Christiane, widow of George Reiter, late of Milford Twp, assign their dower right to John Huber of Milford Twp.
                  Bk 2/pg 164   Sep 24, 1804

Jonathan Vastine and wife Elizabeth of Shemokin Twp, Northumberland Co. give power of attorney to son John Vastine of Northumberland to recover from Thomas Campbell of Hilltown Twp. a legacy due them.
                  Bk 2/pg 167   Feb 4, 1805

Abraham and Elizabeth Johnson, Sarah Johnson, William and Mary Parker, Robert and Jane Cunningham, Joseph and Rebecca Jenkins, siblings of Joseph Johnson, late of Bucks Co, give power of attorney to John Johnson of Bucks Co. to sell Joseph's land.   Bk 2/pg 171   Jan 10, 1805

George Aston of Philadelphia, guardian of Ann Mayburry, gives power of attorney to Abraham Gerhart of Rockhill Twp. to enter satisfaction of a mortgage from George Snyder to Rebecca Mayburry, John Warden and James Vaux, administrators of Thomas Mayburry.   Bk 2/pg 174   Dec 30, 1803

Priscilla Merrick, widow of Robert Merrick, late of Bristol Borough, gives power of attorney to friend William Hulme of Middletown Twp. to recover rents or dower from Jason and Robert Merrick. Bk 2/pg 181   Jun 2, 1803

Rebecca Ashton, widow of Abraham Roberts, late of Bucks Co, yeoman, gives power of attorney to her father Thomas Ashton of Lower Dublin Twp, Philadelphia Co. to recover estate due her.   Bk 2/pg 182   Apr 30, 1805

Robert Shirley of Jefferson Co, VA who married Rachel Gilbert, daughter of late Nathan Gilbert who was due money upon the death of his mother Esther Gilbert, now in the hands of Reading Howell of Philadelphia, acknowledges receipt of estate from Andrew Long, Esq. who was appointed Rachel's guardian in 1789 by the Bucks Co. Orphans Court.

Bk 2/pg 186   Feb 12, 1805

John A. Flack of Mercer Co, KY gives power of attorney to brother-in-law Absolom Calleson of Garrard Co, KY to recover estate from executors of James Flack.   Bk 2/pg 192   May 18, 1805

William Brewis, administrator of Robert Irvan Jun, late of Chansford Twp, York Co. and grandson of John Boyle, late of Plumstead Twp, gives power of attorney to brother Robert Brewis of Chansford Twp. to recover estate from John Boyle, son of late John Boyle.   Bk 2/pg 211   Oct 22, 1804

George Waggoner of Hempfield Twp, Westmoreland Co, yeoman, gives power of attorney to friend Henry Daub of Montgomery Co. to recover estate due from father George Martin Waggoner of Lower Milford Twp, now in hands of Emanuel Waggoner.   Bk 2/pg 213   May 14, 1805

Giles Craven of Northampton Twp. sets free his slave Tone, aged about 27 years.   Bk 2/pg 216   Oct 8, 1805

Jacob Detweiler, George and Barbara Roth and Samuel Detweiler, children of Jacob Detweiler, late of Upper Hanover Twp, Montgomery Co, give power of attorney to Michael Gaugler to recover money from administrator John Detweiler.   Bk 2/pg 220   Dec 2, 1805

Melcher Hevener of Bedminster Twp, yeoman, gives power of attorney to son Jacob of Bedminster, yeoman, to recover money due him.

Bk 2/pg 229   Mar 6, 1806

John Kirk of Manarcuningham, County Donegall, Ireland, gentleman, and wife Jane, only surviving sister of Andrew Kennedy, late of Langhorn Park, gentleman, give power of attorney to her brother John Kennedy of Baltimore to recover her share of estate.   Bk 2/pg 237   Jun 9, 1803

Joseph Long of Plumstead Twp, innkeeper, due one-eighth part of estate of Ludwig Long, revokes the power of attorney he previously gave to Elias Shull Jr. of Tinicum Twp, joiner.   Bk 2/pg 240   May 3, 1806

George Frantz, Paul Frantz, Jacob and Tobias Frantz (and on behalf of brother Michael Frantz), Philip Frants (and on behalf of sister Sarah Starky), Nancy Frantz and Elizabeth Hocksworth, all late of Hilltown Twp and now in PA and heirs of their father Paul Frantz, late of Hilltown Twp, acknowledge payment of estate by administrators Nicholas Frantz and George Shull.
Bk 2/pg 245   May 5, 1804

John A. Flack of Mercer Co, KY, sadler, son of late Benjamin Flack who was a son of James Flack, late of Buckingham Twp, gives power of attorney to Nathaniel Irwin, clerk, and John Hough, miller, to acknowledge payment of estate by Joseph Flack of Buckingham Twp (eldest son of James).
Bk 2/pg 248   Sep 5, 1805

Maria Catharine Felicity Francis Dupont, widow of James Peter Brissot de Warville, practitioner of Law, residing at Versailles, France, heiress of her brother Francis Clery Dupont who died in America near Philadelphia, and on behalf of her sisters Maria Theresa Dupont (of age) and Anne Dupont, widow of Citizen Aublay, merchant, (their other sister Henrietta Felicity Augustina Dupont being dead), gives power of attorney to Miers Fisher, Jacob Shoemaker and Joshua Gilpin, all of Philadelphia, merchants, to sell the land of her brother, signed on the 18th day of Germinal, 10th year of the Republic.
Bk 2/pg 253

Marie Catharine Felicite Francosa Dupont Brissol of Versailles, France, widow, Marie Therese Dupont of Birmingham, England, gentlewoman, and Ann Dupont Aubly of Birmingham, widow, only sisters of Francis Clery Dupont, formerly of Philadelphia, who died intestate without issues leaving these three sisters and a fourth sister Henrietta Julie Augustine Dupont who is since deceased, give power of attorney to Miers Fisher of Philadelphia, Esq., John Warder of Philadelphia, merchant, Jacob Shoemaker of Philadelphia, merchant and Joshua Gilpin of Philadelphia, merchant, to sell the property of their brother.   Bk 2/pg 256   Feb 6, 1802

John Mitchener and wife Martha, daughter of Daniel Longstreth, late of Warminster Twp, about to move to Ohio, acknowledge payment of estate by executors John and Joseph Longstreth.   Bk 2/pg 274   Sep, 1805

Henry S. and Hannah Drinker, late of Falls Twp. but now of Philadelphia, give power of attorney to brother William Drinker of Philadelphia and friend Thomas Porter of Newtown Twp. to recover money due them.
          Bk 2/pg 276   Nov 12, 1806

Frederick and Peter Sailer, executors of father Peter Sailer, late of Williams Twp, Northampton Co, acknowledge payment of a judgment against Jacob Seigle.   Bk 2/pg 280   Nov 17, 1806

Martin Althouse of Bedminster Twp, yeoman, gives power of attorney to brother Daniel, now of Bedminster but about to leave for Upper Canada, to sell a half interest in land in Creamsby Twp, Clinton Co, Upper Canada.
          Bk 2/pg 302   May 30, 1807

John Stevens of Blount Co, PA and wife Grizzal, daughter of James Cummings, late of Bucks Co, give power of attorney to Nathaniel Irwin to recover estate due her.   Bk 2/pg 309   Nov 10, 1806

Samuel Dean of Springfield Twp, yeoman, gives power of attorney to son William to liquidate and settle his business with the Sheriff of Bucks Co.
          Bk 2/pg 315   Aug 12, 1807

Philip Rapp of Alexandria Twp, Hunterdon Co, NJ and George Maust of Tinicum Twp, yeoman, heirs of Peter Stones, late of Nockamixon Twp, give power of attorney to Henry Calf of Tinicum Twp. to enter satisfaction of bonds from Henry Calf, George Wykers, Philip Rapp and Frederick Stone related to the settlement of the estate.   Bk 2/pg 319   Nov 16, 1807

James James of Roan Co, Buans Settlement, NC, farmer, gives power of attorney to friend Joseph Mathews of New Britain Twp. to recover estate from father John James, late of New Britain.   Bk 2/pg 322   Nov 30, 1792

Zillah Thomas of Hilltown Twp, administratrix of the part of estate of Manasseh Thomas, late of Hilltown, which were not administered by executor Eber Thomas (who is lately died intestate), gives power of attorney to William H. Rowland and George Leidigh, both of Hilltown Twp, to handle these affairs.   Bk 2/pg 324   Dec 29, 1807

Peter Snyder, Henry Snyder, William Snyder, George Snyder, Barnard and Barbara Hellepot, heirs of Peter Snyder, late of Tinicum Twp, yeoman, give power of attorney to friend Michael Heaney of Tinicum Twp, yeoman, to sell Peter's land.   Bk 2/pg 329   Dec 19, 1807

Elizabeth Hibbs of Bristol Twp. gives power of attorney to son Jacob Hibbs to recover moneys due her.   Bk 2/pg 338   May 2, 1808

George Heinline of Easton, yeoman, sells to Jacob Abel Jun. of Easton and David Stem of Durham Twp, yeoman, a part of the one-thirteenth portion of the estate of his father George Heineline, late of Durham Twp, yeoman, due from executors Sarah Heineline, William Heineline and William Long.
                                   Bk 2/pg 340-3   Nov 25, 1806

Agness Sample, now of Ohio Twp, Allegheny Co, widow of John Sample, late of Buckingham Twp, give power of attorney to Robert Smith of Buckingham, to recover money due her.   Bk 2/pg 347   Oct 13, 1806

Robert and Elizabeth Blackledge Jun. of Columbiana Co, OH owns land in Buckingham Twp. now or previously in possession of his father Robert and gives power of attorney to Samuel Johnson of Buckingham Twp, Esq., to sell this land.   Bk 2/pg 348   Jun 3, 1807

Alice Vanartsdalen, widow of Simon Vanartsdalen, late of Northampton Twp, gives power of attorney to son-in-law Thomas Fenton of Southampton Twp, yeoman, to recover moneys due her.   Bk 2/pg 353   Jan 13, 1806

Absalom Calleson of Garrard Co, KY, yeoman, and wife Anne, daughter of late Benjamin Flack who was son and heir of James Flack, late of Buckingham Twp, give power of attorney to Nathaniel Irwin, clerk, John Hough, miller and Samuel Gillingham, miller, all of Bucks Co, to recover their share of estate from eldest son Joseph Flack of Buckingham.
                                   Bk 2/pg 354   Aug 30, 1808

Daniel Craig of Pittsburgh, heir of his uncle Henry Miller of Bucks Co, gives power of attorney to friend David Knox of Norristown to recover his share of estate.   Bk 2/pg 357   Jun 21, 1808

Elizabeth Hartly of Solebury Twp. give power of attorney to son Joseph Hartly of Maryland to enter satisfaction of a mortgage.
                                   Bk 2/pg 359   Apr 5, 1809

Thomas Evans of Bensalem Twp, one of the children of John Evans, late of Bensalem, gives power of attorney to Daniel Knight to sell John's real estate.
Bk 2/pg 359   Apr 8, 1809

Joseph Parker Jun. of Hanover Twp, Burlington Co, NJ having married Mary Meredith, daughter of late Richard Meredith, a brother of William Meredith, late of Bucks Co (who died intestate without issue but brothers Thomas and Jonathan and late brother Richard), gives power of attorney to friend Hugh Ross of Newtown to recover estate due his wife.   Bk 2/pg 360   Mar 8, 1809

Mary Erwin, widow of Arthur Erwin, late of Tinicum Twp, gives power of attorney to Thomas Ross and Abraham Chapman, attorneys, to record satisfaction of a bond from Joseph Erwin.   Bk 3/pg 3   Apr 1, 1809

Nicholas Hammerstone, Philip Hammerstone, Ann Margaret Roofner, Christina Ecc, Jacob and Mary Ruple and Simon and Barbara Raesner, heirs of Andrew Hammerstone, late of Nockamixon Twp, agree to selection of men to partition Andrew's real estate.   Bk 3/pg 5   Jun 23, 1809

Susanna Stokesberry of Culpeper Co, VA gives power of attorney to William and David Stokesberry of Culpeper Co. to recover money due from estate of John Thomas of Bucks Co.   Bk 3/pg 6   Dec 21, 1807

Jacob Ranner of Penn Twp, Northampton Co. gives power of attorney to John Roth of Rockhill Twp. to recover from executors Michael Crowman and Adam Dimigh, both of Richland Twp, a legacy due by will of Michael Crowman, late of Richland Twp.   Bk 3/pg 8   Jul 4, 1809

Samuel Houp of Mindon Twp, Montgomery Co, NY, son of Henry Houpt, late of Durham Twp, gives power of attorney to friends Henry Funk and Jacob Funk, both of Springfield Twp, to take any part of his father's real estate that they may think proper.   Bk 3/pg 8   Jul 18, 1809

Adam Stewart of Crawford Co, PA and wife Jane, daughter of David Feaster, late of Northampton Two, give power of attorney to friend David Taggert of Northampton Twp. to recover estate now in hands of Jane's brother Aaron Feaster of Northampton Twp.   Bk 3/pg 10   Oct 11, 1809

Jacob Weisel of Washington Co, MD, shoemaker, gives power of attorney to Daniel Weisel of Washington Co, tanner, to recover money from George Weisel, administrator of Jacob Weisel, late of Bucks Co.
Bk 3/pg 12   Apr 6, 1809

David Climer of Milford Twp. gives power of attorney to Abraham Olwine of Milford to recover money due from estate of his father Christian Clymer.
Bk 3/pg 13   Oct 10, 1809

Abraham Freed of Machodunco Twp, Northumberland Co, son of Jacob Freed, late of Richland Twp, gives power of attorney to Israel Foulke of Richland to record payment of his share of estate by brother Henry Freed.
Bk 3/pg 14   Oct 6, 1809

Susanna Towman of Tyrone Twp, Fayette Co, daughter of Casper Crose, late of Richland Twp, gives power of attorney to son Jacob Toman of Tyrone Twp. to recover estate due by father's will.   Bk 3/pg 21   Nov 14, 1807

Jacob Toman of Tyrone Twp, Fayette Co, attorney for mother Susanna Toman, acknowledges payment of estate due from Casper Grose, late of Richland Twp, by executors Adam Bartholomew and Rudolph Shough.
Bk 3/pg 22   Dec 7, 1807

William Crawford of Fayette Co, son of John Crawford, late of Warwick Twp, Esq., sells his share of estate to John Barclay Esq. of Philadelphia.
Bk 3/pg 24   Apr 23, 1808

John Vandegrift of Turbot Twp, Northumberland Co. gives power of attorney to brother Jacob Vandegrift of Lamberton, NJ to sell land in Bensalem Twp.
Bk 3/pg 27   Apr 26, 1808

Jona. Meredith authorizes Hannah Wallas (wife of Joseph Wallas, formerly Hannah Meredith) to receive her share of estate of her uncle William Meredith.   Bk 3/pg 30   May 4, 1810

John Crawford of Eaten Twp, Worrand Co, OH, son of Mary Crawford who was a daughter of late John Crawford, gives power of attorney to James McKee, merchant, of Millersburgh, Burbon Co, KY to recover estate from Samuel Mann of Horsham Twp, Montgomery Co, executor to John's estate.
Bk 3/pg 32   Oct 20, 1808

Mary Crawford (widow of Samuel Crawford) and Mary Heddleson, Samuel Crawford, William Crawford and Issabella Crawford, children of the said Mary and Samuel Crawford, of Nicholas Co, KY, give power of attorney to James McKee, merchant, of Millersburg, Bourbon Co, KY, to recover estate from Samuel Mann of Horsham Twp, Montgomery Co, executor of late John Crawford.   Bk 3/pg 33   Jul 5, 1808

Grace LeRay deChaumont, wife of James Donatianus LeRay deChaumont of Leraysville, Jefferson Co, NY, gives power of attorney to Nicholas Arnous of Philadelphia, to sell her dower interest in land in Middletown Twp, formerly owned by John Strickland.   Bk 3/pg 40   May 4, 1810

George Child and wife Ann and Jonathan and Elizabeth (late Iden) Evans acknowledge payment by Thomas Iden of Richland Twp. of dower due them upon death of their mother.   Bk 3/pg 41   Jan 2, 1810

Job Strawhen of Franklin Twp, Fayette Co, son of Jacob Strawhen, late of Haycock Twp, acknowledges payment of bonds due from Abel and Daniel Strawhen of Haycock Twp.   Bk 3/pg 42   May 25, 1810

Abraham Bussey of Rockhill Twp, yeoman, and wife Margaret, daughter of Jacob Rule, late of Hilltown Twp, yeoman, give power of attorney to Jacob Bussey of Tinicum Twp, yeoman, to recover dower due upon death of widow Appolonia now in hands of Jacob and Tobias Rule and John Fluck and Frederick Koder.   Bk 3/pg 43   Apr 13, 1810

Harriet Harvey, executrix of John Harvey, late of Bordentown, Burlington Co, NJ, gives power of attorney to Azariah Hunt of Lamberton, Burlington Co, merchant, to recover money due her.   Bk 3/pg 52   Jan 22, 1810

Thomas Edwards and wife Hannah, who is entitled to one-ninth part of estate of Nathan Roberts, late of Richland Twp, give power of attorney to Everard Edwards of Muncy Creek Twp, Lycoming Co, to recover her share from executors Everard Foulke and James Chapman, both of Richland.
                Bk 3/pg 55   Jun 6, 1808

Joseph Church of Muskingum Co, OH gives power of attorney to Dr. John Wilson of Bucks Co. to recover money from Thomas Betts, executor of Zachariah Betts who was Joseph's guardian. Bk 3/pg 56   May 8, 1809

John Booz of Bristol Twp, yeoman, gives power of attorney to friend Amos Gregg of Bristol Borough, physician, to recover all moneys due his including that due from Mary Jolly (late Booz).   Bk 3/pg 58   Jan 11, 1811

Isaac Worthington of Chester Co. gives power of attorney to his father David Worthington to New Britain Twp. to recover money due him.
                Bk 3/pg 61   Feb 9, 1811

Hannah Wallas, entitled to some estate from uncle William Meredith, late of Plumstead Twp, but her husband has now eloped after establishing Jonathan Meredith of Philadelphia as her trustee, who has since released the trust, she now gives power of attorney to her brother Thomas Meredith of Philadelphia to recover her share from administrator David Meredith.

Bk 3/pg 64   May 7, 1810

William Beans gives power of attorney to his son Joshua Beans to enter satisfaction of a mortgage.   Bk 3/pg 64   Apr 13, 1811

Daniel Lawrence and wife Phebe, William Lawrence and wife Hannah, Benjamin Lawrence and wife Rebecca and Mahlon Lawrence (son of Charity West), children and heirs of late Mary Lawrence who was a daughter of Catherine Severns, give power of attorney to brother Samuel Lawrence to sell their share of Catharine Severns real estate.   Bk 3/pg 65   Mar 23, 1811

Lydia McCall, widow of George McCall, late of Philadelphia, gives power of attorney to Joseph Erwin of Bucks Co. to record satisfaction of a mortgage.

Bk 3/pg 66   Feb 3, 1793

Samuel Willslayer of Allegheny Co, son of John Willslayer, late of Bucks Co, give power of attorney to Henry Stover of Bucks Co. to recover money from administrators of his late guardian Isaac Burson.   Bk 3/pg 76   Jan 15, 1812

Henry Walter Livingston, Esq. of Columbia Co, NY and wife Mary Martin Livingston give power of attorney to William Tilghman of Philadelphia, Esq. to record deed for sale of land Mary inherited from her grandfather William Allen.   Bk 3/pg 79   Apr 7, 1804

William Crawford of Franklin Co, IN gives power of attorney to James Crawford of Bottetout[?] Co, VA to recover money due from estate of late William Bailey.   Bk 3/pg 80   Nov 19, 1811

James Crawford of Sullivan Co, TN, son of late Thomas Crawford, gives power of attorney to Hugh Crawford of Sullivan Co. to recover money due from estate of late William Bailey.   Bk 3/pg 80   Mar 24, 1812

Samuel Crawford and James Simpson, heirs of Eleanor Simpson (formerly Crawford) and heirs of late Mary Crawford, give power of attorney to brother Hugh Crawford to recover money due from estate of their mother's brother William Bailey.   Bk 3/pg 81   Feb 19, 1812

James Crawford of Bottetout[?] Co, VA gives power of attorney to Hugh Crawford of Sullivan Co, TN to recover money from estate of deceased uncle William Bailey.   Bk 3/pg 81   Apr 4, 1812

Hugh Crawford of Sullivan Co, TN (but currently of Bristol Borough) makes known that Mary Crawford (late Bailey), wife of Samuel Crawford but now deceased, now of Bottotout[?] Co, VA who left issue Eleanor (wife of James Simpson of Knox Co, TN), Samuel Crawford Jr. of Knox Co, William Crawford of Franklin Co, IN, Hugh Crawford, Thomas Crawford (now deceased leaving only child James Crawford Jr. of Sullivan Co, TN) and James Crawford of Bottetout Co, VA. Mary (Bailey) Crawford was a sister of William Bailey, late of Bucks Co. Hugh Crawford gives power of attorney to kinsman William Crawford and friend Dr. Amos Gregg, both of Bristol Borough, to recover Mary's share of estate. Bk 3/pg 82   May 4, 1812

Jacob Bechtel acknowledges payment by Benjamin Rosenberger, executor of Julius Rosenberger, of legacy due his wife. Bk 3/pg 85   May 1, 1810

Jesse McKinstry of Willistown Twp, Chester Co. gives power of attorney to friend Andrew McMickin of Buckingham Twp. to sell land he received from late Samuel McKinstry.   Bk 3/pg 86   Sep 3, 1812

Jacob Baker of Rockhill Twp, tobacconist, grandson of late Mary Doyling of New York City, gives power of attorney to brother Charles Baker of New Britain Twp. to recover legacy due him.   Bk 3/pg 89   Feb 26, 1813

Michael Stoneback and wife Magdalene of Haycock Twp. assign to John Stokes of Haycock the legacy due from her father Michael Ditterly now in hands of Michael Ditterly and Philip Wemer. Bk 3/pg 89   Jan 7, 1813

John Giveans of Vernon, NY and Isaac Smith of Warwick, Orange Co, NY give power of attorney to Israel Wood of Warwick, NY to recover money from Silas Twining, administrator of James H. Benjamin, late of Bucks Co. due to them by right of their wives who were sisters of James.
                                   Bk 3/pg 90   Mar 16, 1813

Charles McMickin Jun. of Felinana[?] Parish, LA gives power of attorney to friend Dr. John Wilson of Buckingham Twp. to recover money due him from estate of deceased uncle Andrew McMicken, late of Warwick Twp.
                                   Bk 3/pg 96   Apr 1, 1813

Jacob Keller, Michael Keller, John Ott and John Ott acknowledge payment by
Henry Keller of their shares of estate of John Keller, late of Haycock Twp.
Bk 3/pg 97   Jun 11, 1813

Jacob Baker of Bedminster Twp, tobacconist, son of Dr. Jacob Baker, late of
Augusta Twp, Northumberland Co, gives power of attorney to brothers
Charles Baker of New Britain Twp. and Dr. Ephraim Baker of Maxatawny
Twp, Berks Co. to recover estate from widow Elizabeth Baker.
Bk 3/pg 97   Jul 12, 1813

Clement Richardson gives power of attorney to his son Joseph Richardson to
settle his business.   Bk 3/pg 98   Apr 24, 1813

William Magill and wife Jane of Solebury Twp, Sarah Paxton of Solebury,
Rachel Paxton, Deborah Paxton, Betsy Paxton, Mary Paxton, Letitia Paxton,
Hester Paxton and Jonathan Paxton, all of Newtown Twp, give power of
attorney to friend Jacob Magill of Solebury Twp. to settle their concerns in
relation to the estate of their uncle Isaiah Paxton, late of Solebury Twp.
Bk 3/pg 100   May 29, 1813

James C. Morris, now of Philadelphia but about to move to Ohio or
somewhere near there, due a legacy from David Caldwell of New Castle, DE
upon death of widow Mary, gives power of attorney to friend Enos Morris of
Newtown, attorney at law, to recover his legacy.   Bk 3/pg 102   Nov 12, 1805

Mary Reed of Adams Co, daughter of Thomas Craig Esq., late of Bucks Co,
gives power of attorney to son Thomas Craig Reed of Millertown, Adams Co.
to recover estate from Thomas' executrix.   Bk 3/pg 103   Nov 26, 1813

William Miller of Millerstown, Adams Co. and wife Margaret, daughter of
Thomas Craig Esq., late of Bucks Co, give power of attorney to son Thomas
Craig Miller of Millerstown to recover estate due them.
Bk 3/pg 104   Nov 29, 1813

Isaiah Paxson, late of Solebury Twp, died intestate leaving no issue but
siblings including Joseph Paxson, late of Sadsbury Twp, Chester Co, who
died before Isaiah leaving several children including Benjamin, Jacob, Aron
and Jonathan Paxton, all of Sadsbury Twp, James and Mary Cooper of
Sadsbury Twp, Rachel Paxton of Sadsbury, John Truman Jun. of Sadsbury
and wife Amelia, Calvin and Sarah Cooper of Columbia, Hempfield Twp,
Lancaster Co, John and Abigail Vickers of East Caln Twp, Chester Co, and
widow Mary Paxton of Sadsbury, guardian of daughter Esther Paxton, and

Ann Paxton of Sadsbury, another daughter, all give power of attorney to Joseph Paxton of Sadsbury (eldest son of late Joseph) to recover estate due them.   Bk 3/pg 106   Sep 4, 1813

Job M. Carty of Muncy Creek Twp, Lycoming Co. and wife Jane give power of attorney to friend Hugh Ely of Solebury Twp. to attend to business involving estate of Isaiah Paxson.   Bk 3/pg 108   Apr 7, 1813

John Trittenbach of Easton, shoemaker, and wife Catharine, only daughter of George Barron, late of Bucks Co, give power of attorney to Valentine Weaver of Easton, tanner, to recover estate from George Barron who took the land of the late George Barron.   Bk 3/pg 110   Dec 31, 1813

Abraham Bennet of Alexandria Twp, Hunterdon Co, NJ, son of Richard Bennet and legatee of Abraham Bennet, late of Solebury Twp, assigns his legacy to Isaac Bennet of Plainfield Twp, Northampton Co.
                                         Bk 3/pg 112   Jan 24, 1814

George Ink, Charles Ink, Able Miller and Phila Cool of Upper Mount Bethel Twp and Mary Crowell, all of Northampton Co, legatees of Joseph Wilkinson, give power of attorney to Joseph Ink of Upper Mount Bethel to settle with Oliver and Aaron Paxson of Bucks Co, guardians of the children of Peter Ink.   Bk 3/pg 113   Jan 8, 1814

Robert McNeely of Cumberland Twp, Green Co. and wife Elizabeth, daughter of William Roberts, late of Bucks Co, give power of attorney to friend Paul Dowlan of Cumberland Twp. to recover legacy due her.
                                         Bk 3/pg 115   Mar 25, 1814

Magdalena P. Swift gives power of attorney to friend John Hulme Esq. of Hulmeville to sell land bequeathed to her by her grandfather Thomas Riche Esq. in Penns Manor.   Bk 3/pg 116   Jul 5, 1810

Mary Cline, daughter of Ludwick Craven, late of Milford Twp, gives power of attorney to Andrew Reed Esq. to acknowledge payment of bond from Andrew and Jacob Craven, Jacob Kremer and Adam Levy, all of Milford Twp. which became due upon her mother's death.   Bk 3/pg 118   Jan 8, 1814

Mary Snyder of Tinicum Twp, widow and administrator of Peter Snyder, on account of her age and ill health gives power of attorney to Henry Ridge of Bucks Co. to administer the estate in her stead.   Bk 3/pg 120   Jun 22, 1814

Abigail Wood of Loudoun Co, VA gives power of attorney to son Joseph Wood to recover estate from her father Charles Poulton and mother Ruth Poulton.   Bk 3/pg 121   Jul 30, 1814

Martha Poulton (widow of John), Ruth Poulton, Reed Poulton and James and Tamor Tribby, heirs of John Poulton, give power of attorney to Thomas Poulton of Loudoun Co, VA to recover estate from grandfather Charles Poulton.   Bk 3/pg 121   Aug 3, 1814

Jacob Hollowbush of Northern Liberties, Philadelphia Co. assigns to William Groves of Northern Liberties the right his wife Mary may have in estate of Philip Hinkle, late of Bucks Co.   Bk 3/pg 124   Jun 13, 1814

Ruth Rich of Philadelphia[?], widow, daughter of Charles Poulton, late of Bucks Co, gives power of attorney to Benjamin Combs of Buckingham Twp, wheelwright, to recover estate from her father and her deceased brother Thomas Poulton who was executor of her father's will.
                                    Bk 3/pg 125   Nov 23, 1812

Morgan N. Thomas of New Britain Twp, about to enter the service of his country, gives power of attorney to brother Maron James of New Britain to handle his affairs.   Bk 3/pg 127   Sep 16, 1814

Samuel Thomas of Richland Twp, yeoman, and wife Elizabeth, Sarah Foulke (wife of Judah) of Richland, daughters of Thomas McCarty, late of Muncy Creek Twp, Lycoming Co, and Samuel Foulke of Richland, saddlemaker, grandson of Thomas, give power of attorney to friend Judah Foulke of Richland, cooper, to recover estate in hands of executors John and William McCarty.   Bk 3/pg 128   Oct 13, 1814

Joshua C. Canby, Joseph Hulme, William Lownes, Henry B. Slack, Robert Smith Jr. and Hanameul[?] Canby, children of late Thomas Canby, acknowledge payment of estate by their guardian William Lownes.
                                    Bk 3/pg 129   [not dated]

Nathan Huddleston of Hampshire Co, VA gives power of attorney to John Ray of Chester Co, SC in his name as executor of his father Henry Huddleston, late of Plumstead Twp, to sell Henry's land.
                                    Bk 3/pg 129   Jul 9, 1814

Joseph Funk acknowledges payment by his guardian Abraham Rieser of estate due from his father Abraham Funk.   Bk 3/pg 130   Oct 29, 1812

Elizabeth Hartley of Solebury Twp. gives power of attorney to friend Joseph Rice and son Samuel Hartley, both of Solebury, to recover money due her.
Bk 3/pg 132   Oct 31, 1814

Abel Mathias, son of Thomas Mathias, merchant, of Hilltown Twp, acknowledges payment of estate by guardian Joseph Mathias.
Bk 3/pg 133   Nov 1, 1814

Susanna Drissel, wife of John Drissel of Tinicum Twp, is due one-fourth part of estate of her father Jacob Stover, late of Haycock Twp. John and Susanna acknowledge payment of estate by executors Henry Stover Jun. of Haycock Twp. and John Fretz of Nockamixon Twp.   Bk 3/pg 133   Oct 6, 1814

John Knowles of Upper Makefield Twp, far advanced in life, gives power of attorney to son-in-law Joseph Taylor of Lower Makefield Twp. to take care of his affairs.   Bk 3/pg 134   Oct 15, 1814

William Newbold, John Watson, Jacob Paxson, Jacob Magill, Oliver Paxson, Benjamin Paxson, Hugh Ely (attorney for Job McCarthy and wife), John Paxson and Mary Paxson, heirs of Isaiah Paxson, acknowledge payment of their shares by administrator Aron Paxson by agreement with widow Mary.
Bk 3/pg 135   Oct 14, 1814

Henry Stout, Jacob and Anna Hartman, Tobias and Margaret Rool, Hannah Worman and John and Magdalena Gerhart, children of Abraham Stout, late of Rockhill Twp, yeoman, acknowledge payment of estate by executors Jacob and Abraham Stout.   Bk 3/pg 136   Jun 13, 1814

Sarah Vastine, only daughter of Evan Mathias, late of Hilltown Twp, died intestate leaving real estate which descended to the heirs of her only brother Benjamin Mathias: John, Elizabeth (wife of Daniel Gerhart), Thomas, Nathaniel, Mary (wife of Thomas Thomas), Abel and Jonah D. These heirs acknowledge payment of estate by John Mathias.   Bk 3/pg 138   [blank], 1798

Catharine Mathias, widow of the above named Nathan Mathias, acknowledges that her husband before his death received his share from John Mathias.   Bk 3/pg 139   Apr 4, 1800

Lewis Alloway of Northern Liberties, Philadelphia, cooper, and wife Eleanor, who was widow of Peter Deroche, assign to their son Peter Deroche, her dower right in land in Nockamixon Twp.   Bk 3/pg 141   Mar 28, 1807

Mary Hinkle, widow of Philip Hinkle, and children Joseph, Casper, Elizabeth, Anthony, Nancy, Samuel Beake, Charles, Catharine [blank], Wm and Barbara Groves, Wm Groves as assignee of Jacob Holobush, and Catherine Richards, agree to the sale of Philip's land.   Bk 3/pg 142   Oct 20, 1814

Barbara Yerger, widow of Peter Yerger, late of New Hanover Twp, Montgomery Co, releases her dower interest in plantation bequeathed to son Samuel.   Bk 3/pg 145   Mar 28, 1815

Barbara Delp, widow of George Delp, late of Warwick Twp, agrees on settlement of estate with sons and administrators George and John Delp on behalf of herself and other children.   Bk 3/p 145   Apr 8, 1815

John and Catharine Searl, Robert and Mary Jolly, Thomas and Rebecca Barton, Samuel and Charity Wright, Joseph Cooper, Joseph and Ann Vandegrift, John and Letitia Vansant, children of Elizabeth Cooper (late Elizabeth Severns) who was a daughter of Catherine Severns, give power of attorney to John Vansant to sell their share of Catherine's real estate.
          Bk 3/pg 148   Feb 14, 1811

Abraham Myers, son of Gerge Wendle Myers, late of Lower Milford Twp, assigns his share of estate to George Mumbaur of Lower Milford Twp.
          Bk 3/pg 150   Jun 12, 1815

Samuel, Joseph and Silas Carey own two farms in Newtown Twp. in common by bequest of their father Sampson Carey. The brothers agreed on the division of these farms.   Bk 3/pg 151   Feb 19, 1807

John Frederick and Elizabeth Kern of Charlestown, SC are entitled to land in PA by will of John Daniel Kern, late of Bucks Co. They give power of attorney to Adolph Ehringhaus and John Geyer, executors of John Daniel, to sell this land.   Bk 3/pg 154   Jan 18, 1815

Godshalk Godshalk of Towamensing Twp, Montgomery Co. and wife Mary, daughter of Hubert Cassel, late of Hilltown Twp, acknowledge payment of estate by Hubert's son Isaac Cassel.   Bk 3/pg 156   Jun 11, 1810

Griffith Owen acknowledges payment by John and Elizabeth Pugh, two heirs of Owen Owens, late of Hilltown Twp, of which Griffith is administrator and to whom he sold some of Owen's land.   Bk 3/pg 158   Mar 4, 1814

Michael Althouse, son of Daniel Althouse, late of Bedminster Twp, now 21, acknowledges payment of estate by guardian Jacob Godshalk.

Bk 3/pg 158   Mar 19, 1814

Thomas Shaw and wife Rachel, daughter of Charles Poulton, late of Bucks Co, give power of attorney to Martin Andrews of Steubenville, Jefferson Co, OH to recover estate from administrators John Moon and Ambrose Poulton.

Bk 3/pg 160   Oct 21, 1814

James Carrels acknowledges payment of estate by Joseph Vandick, executor of Lambert Vandick.   Bk 3/pg 160   Apr 8, 1813

Jonathan Vandyke acknowledges payment of estate by Joseph Vandyke, executor of his father Lambert Vandyke, late of Warminster Twp.

Bk 3/pg 161   Jun 19, 1815

John Kessler of Northern Liberties, baker, gives power of attorney to wife Mary to recover money she is due from estate of her father George Meyers.

Bk 3/pg 161   Nov 23, 1814

Joseph Booz of Bristol, windsor chair maker, gives power of attorney to brother-in-law Stephen Hibbs of Bristol, farmer and innkeeper, to recover money due him.   Bk 3/pg 164   Jul 22, 1815

William Bailey formerly of Kilwaughter, County Antrim, Ireland but late of the United States, had two brothers and one sister: Robert and James Bailey of Kilwaughter, now deceased, and Mary (deceased, wife of Samuel Crawford, formerly of Kilwaughter but late of the United States). Robert Bailey left two sons and two daughters: Hugh and James, both of Kilwaughter, Harman and Jane Agnew, now deceased, and Janet (wife of James Bell) of Camory, County Antrim. James Bailey is long since deceased unmarried and without issue. Mary Crawford left children in America.

Bk 3/pg 167   Jul 13, 1815

Margaret (wife of John Ludwig of Shepherdstown, VA), daughter of John Adam Scheetz of Nockamixon Twp, gives power of attorney to son Conrad Alshouse to receive her share of her father's estate upon his death.

Bk 3/pg 170   Sep 11, 1815

Elias Carter of Cumberland Co, eldest son of Charles Carter, late of Bucks Co, gives power of attorney to Amos Carter of Bucks Co. to refuse to accept Charles' real estate.   Bk 3/pg 172   Nov 15, 1815

William Williams of Nockamixon Twp, yeoman, gives power of attorney to son Charles Williams of Nockamixon to recover money due him.
Bk 3/pg 174   Jan 12, 1815

John P. Cosbey and wife Mary of Chester District, SC give power of attorney to friend and relation Henry Montgomery of Hanaway Co, VA to recover money from estate of grandfather Henry Huddleson of Bucks Co.
Bk 3/pg 174   Sep, 1815

Frederick and Elizabeth Hanley of New York state give power of attorney to Adam Bartholomew of Richland Twp. to recover estate from Philip Mumbower, executor of her father George W. Meyer, late of Lower Milford Twp.   Bk 3/pg 176   Aug 8, 1815

Samuel Woolaslager of Aleghany Co. acknowledges payment by his attorney Henry Stouffer of Bucks Co. of money Henry received from Samuel's former guardian Isaac Burson, due from the estate of Samuel's father John Wolslager.   Bk 3/pg 179   May 8, 1816

John Ray Jun, Sally Ray, Alexander and Patsey (Ray) Dorsey, Aaron and Betsey (Ray) McONeelly and John P. Cosby and wife Mary (late Montgomery), all of Chester District, SC, give power of attorney to John Ray Sen. of Chester District to collect money due by will of Henry Huddleson, late of Plumstead Twp. willed to Huldah Montgomery (late Huldah Ray).
Bk 3/pg 179   Sep 20, 1814

Thomas Gibson of New Britain Twp, administrator to Eleanor Gibson (alias Eleanor Verity), acknowledges payment of estate by Nicholas Youngken, administrator of Jesse Verity, late of Springfield Twp, of dowry due Eleanor from estate of Jacob Verity.   Bk 3/pg 180   Jan 26, 1815

Morgan Morgan Jun. of Montgomery Twp, Montgomery Co, blacksmith and wife Ann and Mary Custard of Richland Twp, daughters of Joseph Custard, late of Richland, acknowledge payment of estate by brother George Custard.
Bk 3/pg 181   Apr 18, 1814

Barbara Swarts acknowledges payment of estate by Jacob Rhoar, executor of her grandfather Christian Rhoar, late of New Britain Twp.
Bk 3/pg 182   Feb 24, 1816

Frederick and Catharine Rook, Jacob Sellers, Henry and Elizabeth Fresher, all of Bedford Co, all over age 21, three of the five children of John Sellers and wife Anna Maria, deceased, who was a daughter of Benjamin Summer, late of Bucks Co, give power of attorney to Jacob Schell of Shellesburg, Bedford Co, merchant, to recover estate due them.　　　Bk 3/pg 182　Jan 23, 1816

Benjamin Summers, late of Tinicum Twp, yeoman, bequeathed estate to daughter Ann Maria, wife of John Sellers of Bedford Co. She died previous to her father leaving five children. Jacob Schell, attorney for the three children of age, acknowledges payment of estate by executor Lewis Summers.
　　　Bk 3/pg 183　Mar 12, 1816

Amos Wilson, Rachel Wilson, Asa and Ann Comfort, Mary Wilson, Elizabeth Wilson, Jane Wilson and Wm B. Wilson, children of Hampton Wilson of Bucks Co. and legatees of William Briggs, late of Sadsbury Twp, Chester Co, give power of attorney to their father Hampton to recover estate due them.
　　　Bk 3/pg 184　Dec 4, 1815

Amos Briggs (for himself and David Briggs), Thomas Briggs, Isaac Ashton (for Elizabeth Ashton—late Briggs), Ann Briggs, James Briggs, Benjamin Smith (for Mary Smith—late Briggs) and Joshua Smith (for Rachel Smith— late Briggs), David Heston Jun, Tacy Smedly (late Heston) and Rachel Sills (late Heston), all of Bucks Co, give power of attorney to friend and relation Edmund Smith of Upper Makefield Twp, yeoman, to recover estate from James Cooper and John Williams, executors of their uncle William Briggs, late of Sadsbury Twp, Chester Co, they being children of James Briggs and Rachel Heston, deceased.　　　Bk 3/pg 186　Mar 23, 1816

Margaret James of New Britain Twp, widow of Morgan James, late of New Britain, gives power of attorney to friend Levi James of New Britain, yeoman, to help administer the estate.　　　Bk 3/pg 187　[blank] 7, 1816

John Fritz of Loyalsock Twp, Lycoming Co. gives power of attorney to friend Henry Hinkle of Lower Milford Twp. to recover money due by will of Valentine Kreamer of Hilltown Twp.　　　Bk 3/pg 190　Dec 7, 1812

Mary Erwin of Easton, widow of Arthur Erwin, late of Bucks Co. gives power of attorney to son John Erwin of Easton, practitioner of physic, to recover estate from administrator William Erwin of Bucks Co.
　　　Bk 3/pg 190　May 16, 1816

Rowland Mathias, now 21, acknowledges payment by guardians John and Joseph Mathias (appointed after petition by his mother Margaret) of estate due

from his father Thomas Mathias, late of Hilltown Twp. and grandfather John
Mathias.   Bk 3/pg 191   May 6, 1816

John Thompson Carothers of Alexandria Twp, Hunterdon Co, NJ, legatee of
John Thompson, late of Tinicum Twp, acknowledges payment of legacy by
executor William Long.   Bk 3/pg 192   Aug 18, 1815

Paul Cramer and Nicholas Frantz and wife Christiana, children of John
Cramer, late of Hilltown Twp, yeoman, acknowledge payment of estate by
executors Samuel Moyer and Henry Egle for themselves and on behalf of
Andrew, Henry and Daniel Cramer.   Bk 3/pg 192   Apr 4, 1816

John Carver purchased land in Plumstead Twp. 1812 from heirs of Samuel
Shaw subject to payment of interest to Sarah Chapman during her life and
then to the heirs of Samuel Shaw. Sarah died May 3, 1815. Anna Shaw, heir
of Samuel Shaw, acknowledges payment of her one-eighteenth share of estate
by John Carver.   Bk 3/pg 193   May 29, 1816

Sarah Thomas, widow of Joseph Thomas, late of Hilltown Twp,
acknowledges receipt from her son Ephraim (who is now deceased) of dower
due her by will of her husband for land that Ephraim received along with his
brothers Nathan and Abner.   Bk 3/pg 194   Jun 27, 1816

Sarah Thomas, daughter of Joseph Thomas, late of Hilltown Twp,
acknowledges payment of estate by her brothers Ephraim and Abner which
was due by will of her father for land that they received along with their
brother Nathan.   Bk 3/pg 195   Jun 27, 1816

Henry Fisher of Haycock Twp, weaver, and wife Elizabeth, daughter of Jacob
Cressman, Late of Durham Twp, assign to John McCarty of Haycock Twp. a
bond from Christian Cressman, Michael Snider and Peter Long to secure
payment of estate to Henry and Elizabeth Fisher upon the death of Jacob's
widow Mary M.   Bk 3/pg 196   Jun 27, 1816

John Wilson of Notingham Twp, Washington Co. gives power of attorney to
brother Samuel Wilson of Nockamixon Twp. to recover moneys due him.
                                            Bk 3/pg 196   Oct 10, 1810

Jean Ramsey, Mary Ramsey, John Ramsey and Betsey Ramsey of Prince
Georges County, MD give power of attorney to Samuel M. Ramsey of Prince
Georges Co. to sell land of William Ramsey, late of Bucks Co. one-third

share of which was bequeathed after death of his nephew William to the aforesaid children of Robt. Ramsey.   Bk 3/pg 199   Feb 27, 1816

Adam Shreyer of Rockhill Twp, heir to estate of J. Philip Shreyer of Haycock Twp. acknowledges payment of estate by administrator Philip H. Shreyer.
Bk 3/pg 208   Apr 3, 1809

George Nickolas of Springfield Twp, John Haring of Chillisquaky Twp. and Abraham Shreyer of Turbut Twp, both of Northumberland Co, all heirs to estate of John Philip Shreyer of Haycock Twp, acknowledge payment of estate by administrator Philip H. Shreyer.   Bk 3/pg 208   Aug 20, 1816

John Michael of Plainfield Twp, Northampton Co. and wife Susannah, daughter of Jacob Yearling, late of Bucks Co, now 21, acknowledge payment of estate by guardian Lewis Allgard.   Bk 3/pg 209   Jun 3, 1816

Johann Lorentz Kern of the free Hanseatic City of Hamburgh, merchant, and his wife Johann Louisa Prale, give power of attorney to Theodore Francis Lavezzari of Paris, now in the U.S., merchant, to recover estate from John Geyer and Adolph Ehringhauss of Philadelphia, executors of his brother John Daniel Kern, late of Bucks Co.   Bk 3/pg 210   Sep 5, 1815

Dorothea Maria Catherina Kern, widow of Philip John Joseph Lagan, residing at Paris, gives power of attorney to Theodore Francis Lavezzari of Paris, now in the U.S., to recover estate from John Geyer and Adolph Ehringhauss of Philadelphia, executors of her brother John Daniel Kern, late of Bucks Co.
Bk 3/pg 212   Sep 14, 1815

John and Elizabeth Miller and Henry and Sophia Black, daughters of Anthony Height, acknowledge payment of estate by Nicholas Swartz, executor of Michael Swartz who was Anthony's administrator. Bk 3/pg 214   Jun 10,1816

Phineas Willett of Southampton Twp. gives power of attorney to Robert Manson of Moorland Twp Philadelphia Co. to recover estate due from his mother Martha Willett.   Bk 3/pg 215   Sep 21, 1816

Phineas Willett of Southampton Twp, heir under will of Martha Willett, late of Southampton, assigns his legacy to Robert Manson.
Bk 3/pg 216   Sep 25, 1816

Elizabeth Markley, widow of George Markley, late of Warrington Twp, gives power of attorney to Jacob Cassel of Montgomery Twp, Montgomery Co, yeoman, to help her administer her husband's estate.

Bk 3/pg 217   Oct 22, 1816

Joseph Hinkle, Charles Hinkle, Philip Hinkle, Catharine Richards, Jacob and Mary Hollobush, William and Barbara Groves, Elizabeth Hinkle, Samuel and Margaret Beaks and Ann Hinkle, children of Philip Hinkle, late of Plumstead Twp, acknowledge payment of estate by administrators George Burgess and Casper Hinkle.   Bk 3/pg 218   Apr 1, 1816

Ann Grace Roberts of Gloucester Place, Portman Square, Saint Marylebone Parish, Middlesex Co, England, spinster, only child of Elizabeth Roberts, late of York Street, Saint Marylebone, gives power of attorney to Joseph Richardson Jenks of Philadelphia, merchant, and William Rawle the elder and William Rawle the younger of Philadelphia, to sell all lands belonging to Elizabeth Roberts.   Bk 3/pg 220   Apr, 1816

John Singley, Joseph Singley, John Hill and Joseph Rees, heirs of Andrew Singley, late of Bensalem Twp, agree to pay an annuity to Andrew's widow Agness.   Bk 3/pg 223   Dec 6, 1814

Charles Dennis and Nathan Heacock and wife Dinah (late Dennis) of Greenwood Twp, Columbia Co, children of Amos Dennis, late of Richland Twp, give power of attorney to friend Everard Foulke, Esq. of Richland Twp. to sell Amos' real estate.   Bk 3/pg 225   May 22, 1816

William Allen, son of late Mary Allen who was a daughter of Wm Bidgood (the elder), deceased, gives power of attorney to John Hellings of Bristol Twp. to sell his one-third share of a house in Bristol Twp.

Bk 3/pg 225   May 28, 1816

Henry Myer, Abraham Meyer and Christian Meyer, sons of John Meyer, late of Plumstead Twp, agree to selection of men to value the land bequeathed to youngest son Christian.   Bk 3/pg 227   Nov 1, 1816

Andrew Swartz and Jacob and Susanna Shane, all of Muncy Twp, Lycoming Co, children of Michael Swartz, late of Plumstead Twp, acknowledge payment of estate by executor Nicholas Swartz.   Bk 3/pg 230   Nov 18, 1816

Elizabeth Long, Michael Swartz and Thomas Swartz, devisees under will of Michael Swartz, acknowledge payment of legacy by executor Nicholas Swartz.   Bk 3/pg 230   Oct 11, 1816

Elias Jones, Samuel Jones and Nathan Jones of Frederick Co, VA give power of attorney to William Jones of Frederick Co. to recover money from John Pew, executor for their grandfather John Thomas.   Bk 3/pg 231   Nov 8, 1804

William Jones on his own behalf and as attorney for Elias, Samuel and Nathan Jones, acknowledges payment by John Pugh, executor of John Thomas, of estate bequeathed to John's daughter Leah Jones which since her death is now due to her children.   Bk 3/pg 231   Feb 1, 1805

Thomas Thomas bequeathed estate to Sarah Jones, daughter of Samuel Jones, when she came of age. Sarah Jones, now of full age, gives power of attorney to Benjamin Jones of Mercer Co. to recover legacy from John Pew and John Briton.   Bk 3/pg 232   Nov 11, 1807

Benjamin Jones acknowledges payment by John Pugh, executor of Rev. John Thomas, late of Bucks Co. of legacy to sister Sarah Jones of Washington Co, daughter of Leah Jones.   Bk 3/pg 233   Nov 23, 1807

Rev. John Thomas, late of Hilltown Twp. bequeathed estate to daughter Leah (wife of Samuel Jones) and after her death to her children. Benjamin Jones of Mercer Co. acknowledges payment of his share by executor John Pugh.
                                    Bk 3/pg 233   Nov 23, 1807

Daniel Jones acknowledges payment by John Pugh, executor of Rev. John Thomas of his share of bequest to his mother Leah Jones.
                                    Bk 3/pg 233   Apr 12, 1808

Thomas Jones of Washington town, Washington Co. gives power of attorney to friend George Nixon of Washington Co. to recover money from John Pew, Esq. of Hilltown Twp, executor of Leah Jones, wife of Samuel Jones, late of Hilltown, bequeathed by his grandfather John Thomas.
                                    Bk 3/pg 234   May 21, 1805

George Nixon acknowledges payment of Thomas Jones' share by executor John Pugh.   Bk 3/pg 235   Jun 4, 1805

Erasmus Jones of Ross Co, OH gives power of attorney to Thomas Worthington, Esq. of Ross Co. to recover estate due from Rev. John Thomas from executor John Pugh.   Bk 3/pg 235   Jan 1, 1806

T. Worthington acknowledges payment of Erasmus Jones' share by executor John Pugh.   Bk 3/pg 235   Feb 23, 1806

Isaiah Jones of Mercer Co. acknowledges payment by John Pugh, executor of Rev. John Thomas, of his share of legacy left of John's daughter Leah Jones who was Isaiah's mother.   Bk 3/pg 235   Jan 13, 1803

Peter Jacoby of Durham Twp, yeoman, and wife Catharine, daughter of Christian Trauger, late of Nockamixon Twp, yeoman, acknowledge payment of estate by executor Frederick Trauger.   Bk 3/pg 237   Jan 23, 1816

Catharine Long (formerly Catharine Laudenstone), wife of George Long of Muncy Twp, Lycoming Co, daughter of Elizabeth Loudenstone and granddaughter of Christian Trauger, late of Nockamixon Twp, gives power of attorney to husband George Long to recover estate due her.
                Bk 3/pg 237   Jan 1, 1816

Christian Drauger, late of Nockamixon Twp, bequeathed estate to daughter Barbara, wife of Peter Loudenstone of Tinicum Twp, who died before him and her one-sixth share descended to her children. George Long acknowledges payment of Catharine (Loudenstone) Long's share by executor Frederick Trauger.   Bk 3/pg 238   Jan 20, 1816

George Fenner and wife Magdalena, daughter of Barbara Loudenstone who was a daughter of Christian Trauger, acknowledge payment of estate by executor Frederick Trauger.   Bk 3/pg 238   Mar 30, 1816

Christopher and Christian Drauger of Nockamixon Twp, yeoman, sons of Christian Drauger, late of Nockamixon, yeoman, acknowledge payment of estate by executor Frederick Drauger.   Bk 3/pg 239   Dec 10, 1814

John Loudenstone, Abraham Loudenstone, Isaac Loudenstone and Susanna Loudenstone of Tinicum Twp and Adam and Elizabeth Clemens of Haycock Twp, children of Barbara Loudenstone who was a daughter of Christian Drauger, late of Nockamixon Twp, acknowledge payment of estate by executor Frederick Drauger.   Bk 3/pg 239   Jan 9, 1815

Christian Loudenstone of Nockamixon Twp, son of Barbara Loudenstone who was a daughter of Christian Drauger, late of Nockamixon, acknowledges payment of estate by executors Christopher and Frederick Drauger.

Bk 3/pg 240   Dec 5, 1814

William Harrold, on behalf of wife Elizabeth, gives power of attorney to John Ely Jun. of Buckingham Twp. to recover estate due Elizabeth from Samuel Gillingham, Samuel Ely and Thomas Ely, executors of Amon Austin Hughs, late of Buckingham Twp.   Bk 3/pg 241   Oct 20, 1815

Magdalena Wireman, widow of Martin Wireman, now of New Britain Twp, gives power of attorney to son-in-law John Delph to handle her affairs.

Bk 3/pg 242   Mar 25, 1817

Samuel Harris, Edith Reinbrough and M. Duke Reinbrough, legatees of Isaac Harris, late of NC, give power of attorney to Robert Shannon Jr. of Hilltown Twp. to recover money due from John Harris of Bucks Co. and Thomas Wilson of Montgomery Co, executors of John Harris, late of Montgomery Co.

Bk 3/pg 242   Oct 23, 1813

Robert Ramsay Sen., Jean Ramsay, Mary Ramsay, John Ramsay and Betsey Ramsay and Samuel M. Ramsey and James B. Ramsey, all of Prince George Co, MD give power of attorney to Stephen Beans of Bucks Co. to recover money from Robert Ramsey and William R. Blair, executors of William Ramsey.   Bk 3/pg 244   Feb 27, 1816

Brice Purcil of Warren Co, OH gives power of attorney to Joseph Kitchen of Warren Co, OH to recover money from George Wyker and John Williams, executors of John Purcil, late of Bucks Co.   Bk 3/pg 245   Feb 15, 1817

The church wardens of the Evangelical Reformed and Lutheran Congregation of Nockamixon Twp. with the consent of the members of the congregation unite and resolved to build a house of publick worship. Signed by Revs. Saml Staehr and Jno. N. Mensch and Elders and Wardens Michael Kol, Abraham Fulmer, Jacob Weidemoyer, John Hager, John Neiss, Solomon Wolfinger, Philip Hager, Jacob Shick, Nicholas Gruker, Lawr. Frankenfield, Jacob Trauger, Fredk. Trauger, Peter Long, and Church Officers Geo. Adams, Henry Leidigh, Abraham Fulmer, Fredk. Trauger, Peter Long, Nicholas Gruker, Treasurer Philip Leidigh and Secretary Henry Miller.

Bk 3/pg 246   [blank], 1814

John Dannehower, late of Hilltown Twp, willed that his real estate be sold when youngest child attains her age. Widow Elizabeth and children John, Abraham, Jacob, Philip, Elizabeth (wife of Jacob Fluck), Mary (wife of Peter Sheive) and Hannah (youngest daughter), acknowledge payment of estate by executor John Pugh.   Bk 3/pg 247   Apr 1, 1816

Frederick Diehl of Richland Twp. died intestate leaving widow Susanna (now also deceased) and twelve children. Jacob Wyker and wife Mary, daughter of Frederick, acknowledge payment of their share by Frederick's son Abraham Diehl.   Bk 3/pg 248   Oct 26, 1815

Christiana Bleyler, administratrix of husband David Bleyler, late of Bukerson Twp, Cumberland Co, gives power of attorney to John Bleyler of Philadelphia to recover money due her husband from the executors of his father Henry Bleyler, late of Bucks Co.   Bk 3/pg 250   Jun 13, 1817

Sarah Thomas, widow of Joseph Thomas, late of Hilltown Twp, releases son Abner of dower obligation in land he received (along with brothers Ephraim and Nathan) from his father.   Bk 3/pg 251   Aug 21, 1814

John Troxell of Hilltown Twp. acknowledges payment by guardian John Pugh of Doylestown to estate due him.   Bk 3/pg 251   Jun 28, 1817

Robert Stockdale of Baltimore, MD gives power of attorney to Joseph Skelton of Bucks Co. to recover estate from Isaac Chapman and David Warner, executors of his father David Stockdale, late of Bucks Co.
                    Bk 3/pg 252   Feb 1, 1817

John Stockdale of Muskingum Co, OH gives power of attorney to Joseph Skelton Jun. of Solebury Twp. to recover estate from Isaac Chapman and David Warner, executors of his father David Stockdale, late of Buckingham Twp.   Bk 3/pg 253   Mar 30, 1817

Samuel Mettler and wife Letitia, daughter of Robert Eastburn, late of Bucks Co, assign their share to William Mettler to pay a debt.
                    Bk 3/pg 254   Jul 2, 1817

Isaac Wynkoop, late of Bucks Co. but now of Franklin Co, IN and wife Ann, daughter of James Winder, late of Bucks Co, give power of attorney to Dr. Phineas Jenks of Newtown to refuse to accept her father's real estate.
                    Bk 3/pg 255   Jun 24, 1817

Henry Haldeman of Schibach[?] Twp, Montgomery Co, father-in-law of Henry Rosenberger, late of Hilltown Twp, miller, acknowledges payment of estate by administrator Benjamin Rosenberger. Bk 3/pg 257   Apr 8, 1817

John Keil of Sugarloaf Twp, Columbia Co. is due a legacy by will of his father Conrad Keil, late of New Britain Twp, due upon the decease of his mother (which has since taken place). John gives power of attorney to brother Conrad Keil of Union Twp, Erie[?] Co, PA to recover estate from Casper Hinkle of Plumstead Twp.   Bk 3/pg 260   Oct 8, 1817

Geo. Johnson of Northern Liberties, Philadelphia, cordwainer, is due money by Benjamin Johnson upon the death of George's mother Hannah, widow of Henry Johnson, late of Richland Twp. George assigns his right to Lydia Johnson of Easton, tutoress.   Bk 3/pg 261   Sep 23, 1817

Daniel Nicholas of Bedminster Twp. gives power of attorney to Christopher Keller and John Ott, both of Haycock Twp. to recover dower of Susanna Nicholas, widow of his father Christian Nicholas, late of Haycock which will become due at Susanna's decease and now held by John Nicholas.
Bk 3/pg 262   May 27, 1817

Samuel Nichola of Haycock Twp. assigns to John Nichola of Haycock a legacy due him after the decease of his mother Susana, widow of Christian Nichola, late of Haycock Twp.   Bk 3/pg 265   Oct 11, 1817

William Reeder (husband and guardian of Mary Gourley), John Wilkinson (guardian and husband of Elizabeth Gourley and administrator of Joseph Gourley, late of VA) and Joseph Gourley (administrator of Samuel Gourley, late of Montgomery Co), heirs of John Gourley, late of Bucks Co, to a dower due now that the widow is deceased, acknowledge payment of dower by John Smith of Wrightstown who now holds the lands subject to dower.
Bk 3/pg 266   Dec 22, 1817

Christian Draysbach of Tischelbach, Wittgenstein County, son of Bernhard Draysbach who died in Bucks Co. in 1815 gives power of attorney to the proper authority of his country, the grand Duke of Hesse, Court/Count of Wittgenstein's Office of Justice at Laasphe to recover estate.
Bk 3/pg 268   Nov 12, 1816

Christina, the legitimate daughter of Bernhard Draysbach and wife Ann Christina, was born Jul 21, 1771 according to record of births of Parish Tischelbach.   Bk 3/pg 268   Nov 7, 1816

Joseph Puff of Warminster Twp, son of Henry and Mary Puff who were legatees of Joseph Miller, late of Warminster, gives power of attorney to Francis G. Lukens of Warminster to recover estate due from Joseph Miller.
Bk 3/pg 270   Dec 31, 1817

Abraham Fox, George Fox, Barnet Fox, John Fox and Daniel Fox of Tinicum Twp. give power of attorney to brother Jacob Fox Sr. of Tinicum to recover estate from grandfather Jacob Fox, late of Bedminster Twp.
Bk 3/pg 271   Feb 2, 1818

Mary Booz, now wife of Peter W. Appleton, daughter of Peter Booz, late of Bristol Twp, acknowledges payment of estate by guardian Joseph Brown, Esq.
Bk 3/pg 272   Dec 17, 1817

John Frederick and Elizabeth Kern of Lawrence District, SC give power of attorney to Adolph Ehringhaus, merchant, and John Geyer, Esq. of Philadelphia to sell land inherited from brother John Daniel Kern, late of Bucks Co.
Bk 3/pg 272   Aug 17, 1816

Abraham Hundsberger of Clinton Twp, Lincoln Co, Upper Canada, quilldriver, legatee of Christian Hunsberger, late of Milford Twp, acknowledges payment of estate by executors Jacob Clymer and Peter Strunk.
Bk 3/pg 275   Nov 15, 1817

Christiana Dreisbach, only daughter of Bernhard Dreisbach of Lower Makefield Twp. who died in 1815, previously gave power of attorney to Judge Abreish but now revokes that power and give power instead to J.C. Benfer of Philadelphia as recommended by the Orphans Court of Bucks Co.
Bk 3/pg 279   Dec 23, 1817

John Vandyke, late of Warrington, bequeathed estate to daughter Elizabeth McGooken and after her deceased to her children, including William Walker of Warrington. Administrator William Garges has paid this legacy to Elizabeth's husband Hugh McGooken. William Walker assigns his share to William Garges.
Bk 3/pg 281   Apr 1, 1818

Nathaniel and Cynthia Shewell and Jane Titus, daughters of Margaret Fell who was a daughter of John Gourley, late of Wrightstown Twp, acknowledge payment of dower by John Smith of Wrightstown.
Bk 3/pg 281   Apr 27, 1818

Daniel Kerr of Derry Twp, Columbia Co. and wife Sarah (late Cooper) and John Cooper of Point Twp, Northumberland Co, give power of attorney to Rudolph Sechler of Danville, Columbia Co. to recover estate from Sarah's grandfather John Hoppaugh, late of Hunterdon Co, NJ from administrator John Hoppaugh Jr.   Bk 3/pg 282   May 5, 1818

Mary Hoppoch, widow of John Hoppoch Sr., late of Amwell Twp, Hunterdon Co, NJ acknowledges payment of estate by administrators Jacob Hoppoch and Daniel Boileau.   Bk 3/pg 283   Apr 7, 1818

John Iliff Jr. of Alexandra Twp, Hunterdon Co, NJ, hatter, now 21, acknowledges payment by guardian and uncle John Iliff of estate due from grandfather John Iliff and some of his other uncles.
                        Bk 3/pg 283   Apr 22, 1816

Valentine Iliff of Shamokin Twp, Northumberland Co, yeoman, now 21, acknowledges payment by guardian and uncle John Iliff of estate from grandfather John Iliff and some of his other uncles.
                        Bk 3/pg 284   Apr 4, 1818

Mary Moore, wife of Jacob Moore of Augusta Twp, Northumberland Co, yeoman, gives power of attorney to husband Jacob to recover estate from late father John Hoppock of Amwell Twp, Hunterdon Co, NJ.
                        Bk 3/pg 284   May 19, 1818

Rebecca McKeen, daughter of Arthur Erwin, Esq., gives power of attorney to Josiah Shaw, Esq. to record satisfaction of a mortgage.
                        Bk 3/pg 285   May 13, 1818

Catherine Vansant acknowledges payment of estate by Daniel Hogeland, executor of Derrick Hogeland.   Bk 3/pg 287   Jul 4, 1813

Jacob and Margaret Kulp, Jacob and Mary Kendich, Sarah Moyer, Modelena Moyer (by guardian Henry Freed) and Samuel Moyer (by guardian Jacob Moyers), children of Christian Moyers, late of Richland Twp, acknowledge payment of estate by administrators Henry Young and John Smith.
                        Bk 3/pg 287   Apr 3, 1818

Abel Knight, eldest son of Isaac Knight, late of Bucks Co, and Isaac Knight (2nd son), presently at Baltimore, MD, give power of attorney to Jonathan Thomas to take possession of land in Bensalem Twp.
                        Bk 3/pg 288   Dec 8, 1817

Elizabeth Cooper of Augusta Twp, Northumberland Co, daughter of John Hoppock, late of Amwell Twp, NJ, gives power of attorney to friend Samuel Bloom of Augusta Twp. to recover estate due her.
Bk 3/pg 291   May 8, 1818

Jacob Ruth of Elizabethtown, Lancaster Co. gives power of attorney to Abraham Landes of Lancaster Co. to recover money from Abraham Wismer of Bucks Co, executor of Henry Wismer, late of Hilltown Twp.
Bk 3/pg 292   Jul 6, 1818

Theodore F. Lavazzari (on behalf of wife who is sister of John F. Kern) of Paris, France, John Loretz Kern of Hamburg and Dorothea Maria Catherine Logan of Paris (by attorney Theodore F. Lavazzari) acknowledge payment of estate by Adolph Ehringhaus, executor of John F. Kern, late of Bucks Co.
Bk 3/pg 293   Jun 11, 1818

Elizabeth Detwiler, Barbara and Henry Swartley, Magdalena and Joseph Fretz, Catherine and John Swartley, Susannah and John Loux, John Loux (administrator of Isaac Delp) and Abraham Delp, heirs of George Delp, late of Bucks Co, acknowledge payment of estate by administrators John and George Delp.
Bk 3/pg 294   Apr 11, 1818

George Delp, Elizabeth Detwiler, Barbara and Henry Swartley, Magdalena and Joseph Fretz, Catherine and John Swartley, Susannah and John Loux, John Loux (administrator of Isaac Delp) and Abraham Delp, heirs of Henry Delp, late of Hilltown Twp, acknowledge payment of estate by administrator John Delp.
Bk 3/pg 294   Apr 11, 1818

Adam and Agness Bryan and George and Barbara Geddes of Plumstead Twp, and Joseph, Abraham and William Nash of Plumstead Twp, children of Abraham Nash, late of Plumstead Twp, acknowledge payment of estate by administrator Joseph Nash of Tinicum Twp.   Bk 3/pg 295   Apr 1, 1818

Theodore Frances Lavazzari and wife Jane Amelia Philipina Logen, both of Paris but now of Geneve, give power of attorney to Charles Chauncey, Esq., attorney at law, of Philadelphia and Charles Nicholas Buck, Esq. of Philadelphia, merchant, to recover estate from John Geyer and Adolph Ehringhaus of Philadelphia, executors of John Daniel Kern, late of Bucks Co. who was uncle to Jane Amelia.   Bk 3/pg 300   Mar 18, 1817

James Shaw of Alexandria, VA and wife Elizabeth, daughter of John Watson, late of Bucks Co, give power of attorney to brother Charles Shaw of Bucks Co. to petition Orphans Court for partition of John Watson's real estate.

Bk 3/pg 301 Jun 22, 1818

Joseph Coon of Upper Saucon Twp, Lehigh Co. and Samuel Coon of Springfield Twp. give power of attorney to brother John Coon of Springfield to sell land owned by Henry Coon, late of Springfield.

Bk 3/pg 302   Apr 2, 1818

Thomas Wood of Mount Heacock Twp, Jefferson Co, OH gives power of attorney to friend Robert Wood of Buckingham Twp. to petition Orphans Court for partition of land devised to his father Uriah Wood, late of Plumstead Twp. by his father Thomas Wood.   Bk 3/pg 302   Jul 18, 1818

Hugh and Edith (formerly Hepburn) Erwin of Erwinna, Bucks Co. agree to separate due to unhappy differences between them. They executed a marriage contract on Feb 3, 1817 recorded in Northumberland Co.

Bk 3/pg 303   Sep 8, 1818

Martha Kerr, widow of John Kerr, agrees with James Kerr on behalf of himself and other legatees to increase the annuity due to Martha.

Bk 3/pg 304   Aug 13, 1817

Susanna Troxell (widow and administratrix of Jacob Troxell the younger who was eldest son), Elizabeth (wife of George Kern), Mary Troxell, Margaret (wife of Benjamin Vanluvanee), John Troxell and Sarah Troxell (by guardian John Pugh, Esq.), children of Jacob Troxell, late of Hilltown Twp, acknowledge payment of estate by widow and administratrix Elizabeth Troxell.   Bk 3/pg 305   [blank], 1818

John Cooper of Northampton Co. in right of wife Mary, daughter of Arthur Erwin, late of Bucks Co, gives power of attorney to Josiah Y. Shaw, Esq. of Bucks Co. to record satisfaction of a mortgage. Bk 3/pg 306   Jul 30, 1818

Thomas Leonard of Bristol, harnessmaker and coach trimmer, gives power of attorney to brother Charles Leonard of Philadelphia, house carpenter, to recover money due him.   Bk 3/pg 308   Nov 3, 1818

Abraham G. Vandegrift, only son of Abraham Vandegrift, late of Bensalem Twp, gives power of attorney to Jacob Larue of Bensalem to sell his father's estate.   Bk 3/pg 309   Oct 17, 1818

Ann Shafer and Margaret Shaver, both of Tinicum Twp. give power of attorney to Michael Haney of Tinicum to recover money due from estate of their father William Shafer/Shaver and other moneys due them.
Bk 3/pg 309   Nov 23, 1818

William Williams of Springfield Twp, physician, gives power of attorney to brother-in-law Jehu Morris of Hilltown Twp. to collect all moneys due him.
Bk 3/pg 311   May 13, 1818

Peter Ulmer, late of Nockamixon Twp, died intestate leaving widow Barbara and seven children: Mary Rapp, John, Henry, Peter, Jacob, Catharine and Samuel. Heirs give power of attorney to George Rapp of Nockamixon Twp. (husband of Mary) to sell Peter's real estate.   Bk 3/pg 312   Jan 23, 1819

Ann Grace Roberts of Gloucester Place, Portman Square, Middlesex Co, England, spinster, only child of Elizabeth Roberts, late of York St, Portman Square (formerly Elizabeth Galloway), who was only child of Joseph and Grace (formerly Growdon) Galloway, late of Philadelphia, entitled through her grandmother Grace to land in Durham Twp. previously belonging to Durham Company as well as land in Bensalem Twp. Ann Grace gives power of attorney to Joseph Jenks of Philadelphia, merchant and William Rawle the elder and William Rawle the youngest of Philadelphia, Esquires, to sell this land.   Bk 3/pg 314   Mar 4, 1817

Andrew Reed, Esq. of Rockhill Twp, guardian for minor children of George Moyer and David Moyer, sons of George Wendle Moyer, late of Milford Twp, acknowledges payment of estate by executor Phillip Mumbower.
Bk 3/pg 319   Feb 16, 1819

Peter Stouffer of East Huntington Twp, Westmoreland Co. gives power of attorney to Henry Stouffer of East Huntington Twp. to recover money from Samuel Stouffer of Northampton Co. due from estate of his father John Stouffer, late of Bucks Co.   Bk 3/pg 322   Sep 12, 1818

Henry Stouffer, for himself and as attorney for Peter and John Stouffer, sons of John Stouffer, late of Milford Twp, acknowledges payment of estate by executor Samuel Stouffer.   Bk 3/pg 323   Dec 14, 1818

John Stofer of Tyrone Twp, Fayette Co. gives power of attorney to brother Henry Stofer of Westmoreland Co. to recover money from brother Samuel Stofer of Lower Milford Twp. due from father John Stofer.
Bk 3/pg 324   Oct 13, 1818

John Stoufer, Henry Stoufer, Abrm Stoufer (by guardian George Peter Driesback), Mary Stoufer (by guardian David Acreman), Jacob and Sarah Stoufer (by guardian Jacob Acreman), all of Northampton Co, children of late Jacob Stoufer who was a son of John Stoufer, late of Milford Twp, acknowledge payment of estate by executor Samuel Stoufer.

Bk 3/pg 324   Nov 21, 1818

Deborah Titus of Buckingham Twp. gives power of attorney to William Vandegrift of Bensalem Twp. to recover money due under will of John Gallahan, late of Bensalem or as heir to his widow Rebecca and legacies due under will of Lawrence Vandegrift, late of NJ.   Bk 3/pg 326   Dec 21, 1818

Isaac Bennet, son of George Bennet, late of Tinicum Twp, assigns to William Tomlinson his share of estate due upon death of widow Charity.

Bk 3/pg 327   Mar 3, 1819

Michael Deihl of Richland Twp. bequeathed estate to his son Michael in trust due to Michael's incapacity with son-in-law Jacob Moyer, Jacob's father Abraham Moyer and Michael's nephew David Deihl as trustees. Son Michael, now of Upper Milford Twp, Lehigh Co. has now so far settled himself in marriage, industry and sobriety that his trustees Abraham Moyer of Springfield Twp. and David Deihl of Richland Twp. (Jacob Moyer being deceased) agree to give him his full legacy. Agreement also obtained by Michael's other children and representatives: William Moyer, William Moyer, Henry Messmer, Jacob Deihl, Susanna Moyer.

Bk 3/pg 329   Feb 19, 1819

Teenah Cooper of Augusta Twp, Northumberland Co. gives power of attorney to friend John Malich of Augusta Twp. to recover estate due from grandfather John Hoppaugh, late of Huntingdon Co, NJ.

Bk 3/pg 334   Aug 23, 1817

John Cooper of Point Twp, Northumberland Co. assigns to John Mellick of Augusta Twp, Northumberland Co. his share to estate of grandfather John Hoppock, late of Hunterdon Co, NJ.   Bk 3/pg 335   Oct 26, 1818

Elizabeth Mehlick (late Cooper) of Augusta Twp, Northumberland Co, daughter of Daniel Cooper and wife Malue[?] who was daughter of John Hoppock, late of Hunterdon Co, NJ, gives power of attorney to husband John Mehlick to recover money due from grandfather's estate.

Bk 3/pg 335   Mar 27, 1819

Michael Moyer, late of Hilltown Twp, died intestate leaving widow Magdalena and five children: John, Catherine (wife of Abel Bitting), Elizabeth (wife of David Cope), Hannah (wife of Henry Fuhrman) and Mary Moyers. Heirs acknowledge payment of estate by administrator Wm H. Rowland.   Bk 3/pg 337   Mar 31, 1819

Senica Fell, son of late Seneca Fell, acknowledges payment of legacy by his brother Stacey Fell.   Bk 3/pg 339   Apr 12, 1819

Anna, widow of David Herr, late of Rockhill Twp, acknowledges payment of estate by administrators Jacob Beihn and David Herr.
                                 Bk 3/pg 340   Mar 25, 1819

John Herr and Christina Herr, siblings of Jacob Herr and Henry Cope and John Detweiler, guardians to the minor children of David Herr, another brother of Jacob, acknowledge payment of estate by Jacob Beihn and David Herr, administrators of Jacob Herr.   Bk 3/pg 340   Mar 21, 1819

George Herr, Samuel and Margaret Herr, Elizabeth Herr and Magdalena Herr, children of John Herr and legatees of Catharine Herr, late of Rockhill Twp, acknowledge payment of estate by executor David Herr.
                                 Bk 3/pg 341   Mar 19,1819

Jacob and Mary Stauffer and David and Barbara Stauffer, daughters of Henry High of Butler Co. give power of attorney to brother Henry Stouffer of Montgomery Co, yeoman, to sell land of late father Christian Stouffer in Montgomery Co. in agreement with stepmother Catharine Stouffer.
                                 Bk 3/pg 342   Oct 13, 1823

Ann Beal of Warwick Twp. gives power of attorney to friend Eleazer T. McDowell, Esq. of Doylestown Twp. to recover estate on which her brother Joseph Beal now lives.   Bk 3/pg 344   May 1, 1824

Jacob Hempt of Springfield Twp. gives power of attorney to brother Adam Hempt of Eastpenns Borough, Cumberland Co. to recover money due him.
                                 Bk 3/pg 345   Jun 4, 1824

Mathias Case of Plumstead Twp. and wife Mary, daughter of Joseph Howell, late of Amwell Twp, Hunterdon Co, NJ, give power of attorney to Jacob Hansel of Amwell Twp. to recover estate due them.
                                 Bk 3/pg 346   Apr 28, 1824

Elias Rosenberger of Hilltown Twp, administrator for his late wife Barbara who was a daughter of Joseph Fretz, late of Haycock Twp, acknowledges receipt of estate from executors Henry and Martin Fretz.
Bk 4/pg 3   May 13, 1819

Elias Rosenberger of Hilltown Twp. and his father Benjamin give bond to Henry and Martin Fretz, executors of Joseph Fretz, to repay part of legacy if needed to pay Joseph's debt.   Bk 4/pg 3   May 13, 1819

William Bailie of Bristol died intestate without issue. Patrick Agnew of Ballygowan, Ballow Parish, Antrim Co, Ireland, farmer, and Jane Agnew, spinster, are entitled to one-fourth share of half of William's property as children of the late Jane Agnew, daughter of Robert Bailie who was William's brother. Patrick and Jane give power of attorney to William Crawford of Bristol to receive their shares.   Bk 4/pg 5   Aug 9, 1815

Michael Landis of Coventry Twp, Chester Co. and wife Ann, daughter of Peter Hunsperger and heir of Christian Hunsperger, late of Bucks Co, give power of attorney to friend Samuel Hunsperger of Coventry Twp. to recover estate.   Bk 4/pg 7   May 7, 1819

Henry and Catharine Trumbour Jun. of Richland Twp, shoemaker, and John and Hannah Shull of Upper Salford Twp, Montgomery Co, yeoman, daughters of Henry Blyler, late of Milford Twp, acknowledge payment of estate by Henry's son Peter.   Bk 4/pg 8   Nov 14, 1812

Conrad Poth acknowledges payment of estate by Philip Mumbower, executor of George Windle Myer of Lower Milford Twp. who was father to Conrad's lately beloved wife Catherine.   Bk 4/pg 9   Feb 9, 1819

Hannah White and Mary Ditterlin/Ditloh, daughters of George Windle Moyer, late of Lower Milford Twp, acknowledge payment of estate by executor Philip Mumbower.   Bk 4/pg 9   Apr 9, 1819

Geo. Willet of Warrington Twp, house carpenter, son of late Gilbert Willet and grandson of Martha Willet, late of Southampton Twp, acknowledges payment of estate by his guardian Samuel Arnwine of Bensalem Twp.
Bk 4/pg 10   Jun 3, 1819

Samuel Preston of Stockford, Wayne Co, son of late Paul Preston of Plumstead Twp, acknowledges payment of estate by brother Silas Preston of Plumstead.   Bk 4/pg 10   Jun 3, 1819

Frederick Hartman of Franklin Co, IN gives power of attorney to Michael Hartman of Montgomery Co, to recover moneys due him.

Bk 4/pg 10   Apr 21, 1819

Eli Thomas of Hilltown Twp. acknowledges payment by Zillah Thomas, administrator of Eber Thomas, of legacy from grandfather Monasa Thomas which was left to Eber Thomas.   Bk 4/pg 12   Dec 18, 1817

Henry Cope of Hilltown Twp. guardian of Lidia, Anna, Enos and Sarah Thomas, heirs of Eber Thomas, acknowledges payment of estate due them under will of their grandfather Monasa Thomas, late of Hilltown Twp.

Bk 4/pg 12   Jun 14, 1816

John Applebach of Lehigh Twp, Northampton Co. acknowledges payment by Henry Applebach of his share of valuation (including widow's dower) of real estate of late Henry Applebach of Springfield Twp.

Bk 4/pg 13   May 14, 1819

Lewis Lewis of Richland Twp, yeoman, and wife Abigail, daughter of Abraham Roberts, late of Milford Twp, assign her one-eighth share of estate (payable upon death of widow Peninnah) to William Green of Richland Twp, merchant.   Bk 4/pg 14   [blank], 1819

John Vandyke, late of Warminster Twp, willed that after death of his sister-in-law Rebecca Evans, late of Trenton, NJ, a lot that John got through his late wife Margaret should be sold and proceeds paid to Elizabeth McGooken and heirs of his son Abraham Vandyke and Mary Bartly, widow of Hugh Bartley of Ballston. Mary's share to be put out at interest and residue paid after her death to her four children: Rebecca (wife of Jacob Dunn of Hartford, Susquehanna Co), Betsey Warner, John E. (of Saratoga) and Maria Bartley (of Ballston, Saratoga Co, NY). Betsey, John and Maria have assigned their shares to their mother Mary who acknowledges through her attorney (Rev. Reuben Smith of Ballston) payment of estate by John Vandyke's executor William Garges of Newville, Bucks Co.   Bk 4/pg 16   Apr 26, 1819

Mary Vandyke of Hamilton Twp, Franklin Co. gives power of attorney to Josiah Wood of Upper Dublin Twp, Montgomery Co. to recover estate from William Garges, executor of John Vandyke, late of Bucks Co.

Bk 4/pg 17   Mar 31, 1819

Maria Horn of Richland Twp, widow of Stephen Horn, gives power of attorney to sons Benjamin and Daniel Bartholomew of Haycock Twp. to recover money due her. Bk 4/pg 19 Mar 22, 1819

Peter Traugh of Durham Twp, yeoman and wife Ann Maria, daughter of Christian Draugher, late of Nockamixon Twp, acknowledge payment of estate by executor Frederick Draugher, this being a duplicate release and Frederick lost the original release. Bk 4/pg 20 Apr 29, 1819

Esther Jameson, wife of James L. Jameson, and her child are being supported by the County. The Directors of the poor of Bucks County obtained a warrant against James L. Jameson who was arrested and indicated that he could not support his wife and child but offered with his brother John Jameson to pay the county $200 if the county will not in future prosecute him for support of his wife and child. Bk 4/pg 21 Oct 20, 1817

James L. Jameson and wife Esther agree to separate due to unhappy circumstances. Bk 4/pg 21 Oct 20, 1817

James Ewing, guardian of Elizabeth Ewing by will of her father, said Elizabeth being an heir of Margaret Tate, late of Trenton, NJ, gives power of attorney to Abraham Chapman of Doylestown to refuse to accept Margaret's real estate. Bk 4/pg 26 Aug 7, 1819

Hugh McNair of Canandaigua, Ontario Co, NY and wife Elizabeth (formerly Elizabeth T. Boyd) who is an heir of Margaret Tate, late of Trenton, NJ, give power of attorney to Abram Chapman of Doylestown to refuse to accept Margaret's real estate. Bk 4/pg 27 Aug 4, 1819

Samuel Keith, guardian of Caroline Matilda Tate who is an heir of Margaret Tate, late of Trenton, NJ, gives power of attorney to Abraham Chapman, Esq. to refuse to accept Margaret's real estate. Bk 4/pg 28 Aug 24, 1819

Margaret and Sarah Boyd, heirs of Margaret Tate, late of Trenton, NJ, give power of attorney to Abraham Chapman, Esq. of Doylestown to refuse to accept Margaret's real estate. Bk 4/pg 28 Aug 24, 1819

Mercy Pursel, wife of John Pursel, late of Nockamixon Twp, and John's children Margaret, Brice, Else and Jane (wife of Joseph Kitchen), all of Butler Co, OH, give power of attorney to Benjamin Pursel of Butler Co, OH (another of John's children), who is about to depart for PA, to recover estate from

John's executors John Williams and George Wyker of Bucks Co.
Bk 4/pg 29   Mar 2, 1819

Benjamin Renner of Lower Milford Twp, yeoman, Jacob Renner of Shamokin Twp, Northumberland Co, weaver, and Adam Renner of Hilltown Twp, blacksmith, sons of Jacob Renner, late of Milford Twp, acknowledge payment of estate by executors Jacob Smith and Philip Singmaster.
Bk 4/pg 30   Jun 1, 1819

Samuel Stover, son of Abraham Stover of Rockhill Twp. and Mary Schoch, daughter of Rudolph Shoch of Richland Twp, consummated marriage on Apr 10, 1819 since which an unhappy difference has taken place and they have agreed to separate and agree that neither will call upon the other for expenses with respect to a certain male child of Mary's for which Samuel is the reputed father.
Bk 4/pg 31   Aug 31, 1819

Samuel Hall of Doylestown Twp, husband of Ann Delp, daughter of George Delp, late of Warwick Twp, assigns his share of estate to Abraham Delp of Hilltown Twp.
Bk 4/pg 32   Sep 3, 1819

John Widner of Lower Milford Twp, yeoman, gives power of attorney to brothers Daniel and Jacob of Lower Milford to recover his share of estate of Daniel Widner due upon death of his mother Edith.
Bk 4/pg 32   Aug 5, 1819

Abraham Low of Reading Twp, Hunterdon Co, NJ died intestate leaving widow Phebe and four children: John, Esther (wife of Daniel P. Schamp), Peter B. and Catharine (minor). Heirs give power of attorney to Cornelius Wykoff of Amwell Twp, Hunterdon Co. to sell Abraham land in New Hope.
Bk 4/pg 33   Aug 17, 1819

Susanna Overholt, wife of Stouts Overholt of Clinton Twp, Lincoln Co, Niagara District, Upper Canada, gives power of attorney to friend Jacob Myer of Clinton Twp. to recover estate from Peter Strunk and Jacob Clymer, executors of Christopher Hunsberger, late of Lower Milford Twp.
Bk 4/pg 35   Sep 7, 1809[19?]

Moses and Susanna Fretz of South Twp, Niagara District, Upper Canada give power of attorney to Jacob Myer of Clinton Twp, Niagara District to recover estate from executors of Christian Hunsperger of Bucks Co.
Bk 4/pg 36   Sep 4, 1819

Christian Hunsberger, late of Milford Twp, bequeathed money to sister Susanna Overholt and remainder among children of his brothers and sisters which include Susanna, wife of Moses Fretz. They, through their attorney Jacob Myer, acknowledge payment of estate by executor Jacob Clymer.
Bk 4/pg 36   Sep 29, 1819

Jacob Bachtel of Springfield Twp. and wife Helena had given power of attorney to John Hoot of Rockhill Twp. to recover legacies from Benjamin Rosenberger, executor of Julius Rosenberger. They now revoke the power of attorney as John Hoot has abused his privilege.   Bk 4/pg 37   Oct 15, 1819

George and John Kramer, sons of John Kramer, late of Hilltown Twp, acknowledge payment of estate by executors Henry Eckle and Samuel Moyer.
Bk 4/pg 37   Apr 8, 1819

Sarah Freeman of Warwick Twp, widow and administratrix of Caesar Freeman, late of Warwick, gives power of attorney to friends John Crawford Sen. and Jonathan Roberts of Warwick to transact business on her behalf.
Bk 4/pg 39   Oct 17, 1819

Henry Ulmer of Nockamixon Twp. acknowledges payment of estate by his mother Barbara Ulmer and George Rapp, administrators of late Peter Ulmer.
Bk 4/pg 39   Mar 11, 1819

James and Eleanor McDougal of Chillicothe, Ross Co, OH, John and Sarah Roads of Ross Co, John and Ann Timmons of OH, Nathan Britten, Evans Britten and John Britten of OH, heirs of Elijah Britten, late of PA, give power of attorney to John Britten of Champaign Co, OH and John Pugh of Doylestown to sell Elijah's real estate.   Bk 4/pg 40   Sep 20, 1819

Catherine Moyer of Bedminster Twp. acknowledges payment of legacy by Isaac and Samuel Moyer, executors of Samuel Moyer, late of Hilltown Twp.
Bk 4/pg 41   Oct 11, 1819

Christian Moyer of Bedminster Twp. and Jacob Moyer of Clinton Twp, Lincoln Co, Upper Canada and Abraham and Henry Moyer, both of Hilltown Twp, sons of Samuel Moyer, late of Hilltown Twp, acknowledge payment of estate by executors Isaac and Samuel Moyer. Bk 4/pg 41   Oct 11, 1819

Giles Craven on May 27, 1794 recorded birth of negro child Jacob to his slave Polly which said Jacob was bound by laws of PA to serve Giles until age 28.

Giles sold Jacob to Lambert Vandyke, late of Northampton Twp. who willed the slave to his son Joseph Vandyke. Joseph now sets Jacob free.
                                              Bk 4/pg 42   Nov 1, 1819

Joseph Longbing of Nockamixon Twp, yeoman, son of Stophel Longbing, late of Nockamixon who died intestate with issue, sells his share of estate to Michael Heany of Tinicum Twp, storekeeper.   Bk 4/pg 43   Oct 30, 1819

Peter Rodrock of IN, husband of Margaret Hevender, daughter of Melchior Hevender, late of Bedminster Twp, acknowledges payment of estate by executors Abraham Hevender and Jacob Kulp.   Bk 4/pg 43   May 28, 1819

Jacob Beidler of Bedminster Twp, guardian for William Moyers, minor son of Jacob Moyers, late of Springfield Twp, acknowledges payment of estate by administrator Jacob Clymer.   Bk 4/pg 44   Nov 11, 1819

Adam Leghner of Rockhill Twp, yeoman, assigns his share in estate of father Adam Leghner, late of Northampton (now Lehigh) Co, due upon death of his mother Susanna, to Abraham Stull of Rockhill Twp, shoemaker.
                                              Bk 4/pg 44   Oct 11, 1819

John McMullen of Bensalem Twp. gives power of attorney to son Abraham McMullen of Bensalem to recover money due him. Bk 4/pg 45   Jun 20, 1818

Samuel Humphreys of Haverford Twp, Delaware Co. gives power of attorney to Eleazer B. Shaw to recover money due him from estate of Mathew Hunges, late of Plumstead Twp.   Bk 4/pg 46   Aug 30, 1819

Benjamin and Isaac Scott, both of Bensalem Twp. give power of attorney to Rebert Manson of Moreland Twp, Philadelphia Co. to recover money due from estate of their father Samuel Scott which will be due on death of their mother Mary and at death of aunt Abigail Scott.   Bk 4/pg 46   Nov 29, 1813

Abel Knight, Isaac Knight, Hester Knight, George Knight, Nathan Knight and Abigail Knight, children of Israel Knight, late of Bensalem Twp, give power of attorney to John Townsend of Bensalem to refuse to accept Israel's real estate.   Bk 4/pg 47   Aug 3, 1819

Emanuel Roudenbush of Augusta Co, VA, heir of George Roudenbush, late of Bucks Co, gives power of attorney to friend Conrad Harble of Bucks Co. to recover estate from brothers Abraham and Nicholas Roudenbush.
                                              Bk 4/pg 49   Sep 24, 1819

Isaac and Susanna Ziegler of Dublin Twp, Bedford Co. give power of attorney to daughter Nancy Zigler of Bedford Co. to recover legacy from Christian Hunsberger.   Bk 4/pg 52   Oct 13, 1819

Daniel Appelbach of Haycock Twp. assigns share in estate of his father Henry Applebach due at death of widow to Abraham Myers of Springfield Twp.
                                        Bk 4/pg 54   Jan 1, 1820

John Kinsey of Rockhill Twp, yeoman, gives power of attorney to son [sons?] Jacob Kinsey and Abraham Kinsey, one of Montgomery Co. and one of Bucks Co, yeoman, to recover money due him.   Bk 4/56   Jan 11, 1820

Jacob and Helena Bechtel of Springfield Twp. give power of attorney to Benjamin Bechtel of Springfield to recover money from Benjamin Rosenberger of Rockhill Twp. due under will of Yelles Rosenberger.
                                        Bk 4/pg 57   Jan 15, 1820

Richard Groom and wife Sarah, daughter of Samuel Scott, late of Bensalem Twp, give power of attorney to friend Robert Manson of Moreland Twp, Philadelphia Co. to recover estate due at death of mother Mary and aunt Abigail Scott.   Bk 4/pg 59   Dec 8, 1819

Henry Blank, John and Catharine Trumbore, Mottelena Blank, Abraham and Mary Gerhart and Amos Richardson (guardian of Elizabeth Blank), children of Michael Blank, late of Rockhill Twp, acknowledge payment of estate by executors John Blank and Benjamin Foulke, due at death of their mother Elizabeth.   Bk 4/pg 60   Jan 8, 1820

James Buckman of Falls Twp, executor of Martha Scott, late of Bucks Co. (formerly of Philadelphia), gives power of attorney to Jonah Briggs of NJ on his behalf and on behalf of heirs Jonah Briggs, John Briggs, Abbot Chapman and Martha Briggs to sell stock in Bank of Philadelphia.
                                        Bk 4/pg 63   Feb 22, 1820

Rebecca Griffin of Philadelphia gives power of attorney to Benjamin Atkinson of Bensalem Twp. to recover money due her and settle with Adam Vandegrift of Bucks Co, laborer, the father of her child.
                                        Bk 4/pg 64   Feb 12, 1820

Daniel Nicholas of Bedminster Twp. assigns to Christopher Keller of Haycock Twp. his dower right from Elizabeth Kover, widow of his father-in-law George Adam Kover, late of Rockhill Twp.   Bk 4/pg 65   Sep 6, 1819

Barbara Kramer, widow of Henry Kramer, late of Hilltown Twp, acknowledges payment of estate by administrators John Cramer and Michael Snider. Bk 4/pg 66   Jan 22, 1820

Barbara Cramer (widow), Jacob Doub (husband of Elizabeth—late Cramer), George Cramer, Henry Cramer and Conrad Snider (guardian of Mary Artman—late Cramer and Michael Cramer), all of PA, widow and children of Henry Cramer, late of Hilltown Twp who died intestate, give bond to administrators John Cramer and Michael Snider to repay their shares if needed to pay Henry's debts. Bk 4/pg 66   Jan 22, 1820

Jacob Bachtel and wife Helena revoke power of attorney given to Benjamin Bachtel. Bk 4/pg 67   Feb 26, 1820

John Cowden of Philadelphia, stonemason, and wife Catharine, eldest daughter of Michael Broutler, late of Bucks Co, Elizabeth Broutler (2nd daughter) and Mary Broutler (3rd daughter) give power of attorney to Francis B. Shaw, Esq. to refuse to accept Michael's real estate. Bk 4/pg 67   Dec 23, 1819

Abraham Obrist [Christ?] of Milford Twp, yeoman, and wife Hannah, daughter of Felix and Hannah Bruner, late of Milford Twp. agree that her mother Hannah's administrator Caleb Foulke should pay Hannah's debts and give them the overplus to cover debts that were due them from Hannah. Bk 4/pg 67   Feb 18, 1820

Felix Brunner, late of Milford Twp, has been weak for several years and was attended by his daughter Hannah, wife of Abraham Obrist [Christ?]. They acknowledge payment of estate plus extra to cover services rendered by administrators Jacob Brunner and Philip Singmaster. Bk 4/pg 68   May 17, 1819

Amos and Lucretia Bennet, children of Isaac Bennet of Buckingham Twp, acknowledge payment by guardian Samuel Gilbert of legacy due them from Amos A. Hughs. Bk 4/pg 69   Nov 30, 1819

Henry Slack and wife Margaret, sister and heir to William Geddes, late of Plumstead Twp, give power of attorney to Mahlon Smith of Tinicum Twp. to recover their share of estate. Bk 4/pg 69   Nov 4, 1819

David Simpson and John Lacey (for their wives) and Sarah Wiggins acknowledge payment by Benjamin Wiggins of estate due them under will of Benjamin Wiggins, late of Upper Makefield Twp. Bk 4/pg 69 Feb 22, 1816

Jacob Seiple of Forks Twp, Northampton Co, miller, and wife Elizabeth, daughter of Martin Sheive, late of Haycock Twp, yeoman, who died intestate, assign their share of estate to Peter Shive of Haycock Twp.
Bk 4/pg 70 Mar 7, 1820

Samuel Seiple of Hilltown Twp, yeoman, and wife Magdalena, daughter of Martin Sheive, late of Haycock Twp, yeoman, assign their share of estate to Pete Sheive of Haycock Twp, yeoman. Bk 4/pg 71 Mar 11, 1820

John Bailey, late of Tinicum Twp, owned land which was adjudged to eldest son John, 2nd son and to son Samuel S. Bailey subject to payment to eldest daughter Elizabeth Bailey upon decease of widow Isabella. Elizabeth acknowledges payment by her three brothers. Bk 4/pg 72 Mar 12, 1817

George Kern, late of New Britain Twp, bequeathed estate to wife Deborah and after her death, to his children, including Susana, wife of Elias Lewis of Doylestown Twp. Elias and Susan assign their share to John Brunner of Doylestown Twp. to pay a debt. Bk 4/pg 75 Feb 26, 1820

Henry Ulmer of Nockamixon Twp, son of Peter Ulmer, late of Nockamixon, assigns his share due upon death of his mother Barbara to Isaac Weaver.
Bk 4/77 Mar 30, 1820

Levi Hott, late of Bucks Co. but now of Hallifax Twp, Dauphin Co. gives power of attorney to Edward Millon of Hallifax Twp. to recover money from Samuel Gardner of New Britain Twp. due by death of his mother Mary Reece. Bk 4/pg 78 Dec 25, 1819

George Kressler is due one-eleventh share of estate of his father George Kressler, late of Bucks Co. and gives power of attorney to Joseph Afflerbach of Springfield Twp. to recover same from executors Henry Kressler and William Long. Bk 4/pg 79 Apr 5, 1820

Henry and Catharine Nase, Jacob and Barbara Smith and Adam Wenhold, children of Jacob and Susanna Wenholt, late of Rockhill Twp, yeoman, acknowledge payment of estate by administrator Abraham Wenholt.
Bk 4/pg 81 Feb 14, 1812

Jacob Vanhold, John Vanhold, Adam Vanhold, Henry Vanhold, Adam and Elizabeth Wagner, David and Margaret Wambold, Mary Vanhold and Adam and Susanna Wetzel, children of Jacob and Susanna Vanhold, late of Rockhill Twp, both deceased, acknowledge payment of estate by administrator Abraham Vanhold.   Bk 4/pg 82   Dec 28, 1810

James Carver of Solebury Twp. gives power of attorney to brother David Carver of Solebury to money due him.   Bk 4/pg 85   Apr 7, 1820

Joseph Narregang of Bushkill Twp, Northampton Co, administrator of wife Anna, daughter of Julius Rosenberger, late of Rockhill Twp, acknowledges payment of estate by executor Benjamin Rosenberger.
                                      Bk 4/pg 86   May 10, 1816

Jacob Bechtle of Springfield Twp. and wife Helena, daughter of Julius Rosenberger, late of Rockhill Twp, acknowledge payment of estate by executor Benjamin Rosenberger.   Bk 4/pg 86   Mar 10, 1820

Jacob Krout of Westnantmill Twp, Chester Co, son of Henry Krout, late of Bedminster Twp, acknowledges payment of estate by executors Joseph and Henry Kinsey.   Bk 4/pg 88   Apr 4, 1818

Philip and Abraham Krout of Plumstead Twp, Henry and Catharine Krout of Bedminster Twp. and Daniel Krout of Rockhill Twp, children of Henry Krout, late of Bedminster Twp. acknowledge payment of estate by executors Joseph Krout and Henry Kinsey.   Bk 4/pg 88   Apr 3, 1820

Jacob and Elizabeth Doub of Salford Twp, Montgomery Co, George Cramer, Henry Cramer and Conrad Snyder (guardian for Mary Artman—late Cramer and Michael Cramer), children of Henry Cramer, late of Hilltown Twp, acknowledge payment of estate by administrators John Cramer and Michael Snyder.   Bk 4/pg 90   Jan 22, 1820

Joseph Artman of Hilltown Twp. and wife Mary, daughter of Henry Cramer of Hilltown Twp, acknowledge payment of estate by her guardian Conrad Snyder of Hilltown Twp.   Bk 4/pg 90   May 5, 1820

Jacob Hevender, son of Melchior Hevender, late of Bedminster Twp, acknowledges payment of estate by executors Abraham Hevender and Jacob Kulp.   Bk 4/pg 96   Dec 15, 1819

John Smith and wife Sarah, daughter of John Sellers, late of Franklin Co. who was a son of Leonard Sellers, late of Hilltown Twp, yeoman, acknowledge payment of estate by Leonard's son Abraham Sellers of Hilltown.

Bk 4/pg 96   Dec 8, 1809

Mary Dungan of Bedford Co, daughter of Leonard Sellers, late of Bucks Co, acknowledges payment of widow's dower by Leonard's son Abraham Sellers.

Bk 4/pg 96   Aug 25, 1814

Maria Kinsey (widow) of Bedford Co, daughter of late John Sellers and granddaughter of Leonard Sellers, late of Bucks Co. by her attorney Jacob Schell of Schellsburg, Bedford Co, merchant, acknowledges payment of estate by Abraham Sellers.   Bk 4/pg 97   Jun 15, 1819

John Beale of Warwick Twp, grandson of John Beal of Buckingham Twp, is entitled to one-sixth share of estate upon death of John's widow (along with Joseph Beal, Elizabeth Davis, Jane Breece, Rebecca Ann Beal and Oram [Beal?]). John and his wife Lucinda assign his share to John Pugh of Doylestown to pay for land bought from John and his wife Elizabeth.

Bk 4/pg 99   May 29, 1820

Merab Cooper gives power of attorney to friend Joseph Wilkinson Jun. to recover annuity by will of her father John Ely, late of Solebury Twp, from her brother Asher Ely who was John's executor. Bk 4/pg 103   Aug 14, 1819

Christian Fluck Jr. of Hilltown Twp, hatter, now 21, acknowledge payment by guardian George Siple of estate due from father Christian Fluck.

Bk 4/pg 103   Sep 10, 1817

John Sheive of Bedminster Twp. and wife Magdalena, acknowledge payment by her guardian George Siple of estate due from her father Christian Flook, late of Hilltown Twp.   Bk 4/pg 104   Mar 14, 1815

Sarah Fluck of Richland Twp, spinster, now 21, acknowledges payment by guardian Jacob Ruhl of estate from her father Philip Fluck.

Bk 4/pg 106   Jun 20, 1820

Christian and Samuel Hunsberger, John Hunsberger Jr., Samuel and Catherine Fretz, John and Susanna Hane and Barbara Hunsberger, children of John Hunsberger Sen. of South Twp, Lincoln Co, Niagara District, Upper Canada, yeoman, give power of attorney to friend Samuel Moyer of Clinton Twp,

Lincoln Co. to recover estate from Jacob Clymer, executor of Christian
Hunsberger.   Bk 4/pg 108   Aug 12, 1820

Isaac and Christopher Overholt, Susanna Singer, Elizabeth Fisher and Mary
Ruth, children of Stats Overholt, and Joseph and Samuel Hunsberger, Lany
King, Mary Wolker and Barbary Farefield, children of Abraham Hunsberger,
all of Clinton Twp, Lincoln Co, Niagara District, Upper Canada, give power
of attorney to friend Samuel Myers of Clinton Twp. to recover estate from
Peter Struck or Jacob Clymer, executors of Christian Hunsberger, late of
Lower Milford Twp.   Bk 4/pg 109   Aug 5, 1820

Mary Jones of Port Tolbot, Upper Canada give power of attorney to father
John Hunsberger of South Twp, Lincoln Co, Upper Canada to recover money
from Jacob Clemmer of Bucks Co. due from estate of Christle Hunsberry.
                               Bk 4/pg 109   Feb 15, 1820

Samuel Moyer, attorney for children of John Hunsberger, Susanna Overholt
and Abraham Hunsberger, siblings of Christian Hunsberger, acknowledge
payment of estate by Christian's executors Jacob Clymer and Peter Strunk.
                               Bk 4/pg 110   Sep 18, 1820

Ludwick Richard of Rockhill Twp, yeoman, and wife Elizabeth, daughter of
Felix Brunner, late of Milford Twp, yeoman, assign their share in estate to
Philip Singmaster.   Bk 4/pg 110   Aug 21, 1820

David Yeakel of Milford Twp. died intestate and eldest son Jacob took the
real estate. Second son George Yeakel gives power of attorney to Abraham
Shelly of Milford, practitioner of physic, to recover his share of estate.
                               Bk 4/pg 115   Oct 9, 1820

Mary Ann Pursell (formerly Iliff) and husband Wm of Alexander Twp,
Hunterdon Co, NJ, now 21, acknowledges payment by guardian John Iliff of
estate from grandfather John Iliff Sr.   Bk 4/pg 120   Jul 28, 1820

John Brunner of Rockhill Twp, shoemaker, gives power of attorney to Jacob
Hartzel of Lehigh Co. to recover money from brother Jacob Brunner and
Phillip Singmaster, administrators of late father Felix Brunner of Lower
Milford Twp.   Bk 4/pg 120   Sep 16, 1820

Elizabeth Hockman, late of Bedminster Twp. bequeathed part of estate to
daughter Elizabeth, wife of Rudolph Youngkin of Perry Co, OH. Elizabeth
Youngkin gave power of attorney to son John of Perry Co. to recover her

share. John acknowledges payment of estate by Henry Stover and Jacob Stover, executors of Ulrick Stover who was executor to Elizabeth Hockman.
Bk 4/pg 121   Dec 1, 1820

Elizabeth Youngkin of Perry Co, OH gives power of attorney to son John of Perry Co. to recover estate due from mother Elizabeth Hockman, late of Bucks Co.   Bk 4/pg 122   Nov 2, 1820

Henry and Samuel Youngkin of Perry Co, OH give power of attorney to John Youngkin of Perry Co. to recover estate due by will of Elizabeth Hockman, late of Bucks Co.   Bk 4/pg 122   Nov 2, 1840

Henry Cope and John Detweiler, guardians of minor children of David Herr, late of Rockhill Twp, acknowledge payment of estate by administrators Anna Herr, Jacob Biehn and David Herr.   Bk 4/pg 123   Apr 1, 1809

David Stover of Williams Twp, Northampton Co, son of David Stover, late of Nockamixon Twp, now 21, acknowledges payment of estate by guardian Henry Miller.   Bk 4/pg 123   Apr 25, 1818

Abraham Christ of Milford Twp, wheelwright, and wife Hannah, daughter of Hannah Brunner, late of Milford Twp, acknowledge payment of estate by administrator Caleb Foulke.   Bk 4/pg 124   Jan 11, 1821

Abraham Wismer of Bedminster Twp. acknowledges payment of wife's share of estate of Samuel Meyer, late of Hilltown Twp. by executors Isaac and Samuel Meyer.   Bk 4/pg 125   [blank], 1820

Thomas Edwards of Germantown Twp, Philadelphia Co, weaver, previously gave power of attorney to Michael Baum of Whitemarsh Twp, Montgomery Co, innkeeper to recover estate from father William Edwards, late of Richland Twp. Thomas now revokes this power of attorney.
Bk 4/pg 128   Dec 11, 1820

Henry Drumbor of Philadelphia assigns to brother Elias Drumbor of Philadelphia, coachpainter, his share in estate of brother John Drumbor, late of Bucks Co.   Bk 4/pg 129   Mar 1, 1821

John Brunner of Rockhill Twp, son of Felix Brunner of Lower Milford Twp. gives power of attorney to Robert Smith of Rockhill to recover his share of estate.   Bk 4/pg 132   Mar 12, 1821

Mary Barkley of Battstown, Saratoga Co, NY gives power of attorney to Jacob P. Dunn of Hartford Twp, Susquehanna Co. to recover money from William Garges of Warminster Twp, executor of William Whittingham, being part of legacy from John Vandyke, late of Warminster.

Bk 4/pg 133   Aug 19, 1820

Thomas Wier of New Britain Twp, storekeeper and wife Mary, daughter of James Bradshaw of Warrington Twp, assign her share of estate to Hamilton Roney of Montgomery Twp, Montgomery Co, weaver.

Bk 4/pg 140   [blank], 1821

Hannah Stelle, widow of Samuel Steele, late of Northampton Twp, releases to executor Thomas B. Montanye her dower right.   Bk 4/pg 151   Apr 2, 1821

Jane Edams of Northampton Twp, widow, releases James and Gayne Edams of Northampton Twp. of dower obligation due under will of Gayn Edams, deceased.   Bk 4/pg 160   Mar 5, 1821

John Vandyke, Samuel Vandyke, Isaac Vandyke, Rebekah Hubart, Margeret Martin, Mary Vandyke, Nancy Vandyke and Rachel Vandyke, heirs of Abraham and Mary Vandyke of Franklin Co. who were entitled to one-third share of property in Philadelphia under will of John Vandyke of Warrington Twp, assign their rights in John's estate to their mother Mary.

Bk 4/pg 160   Aug 1, 1820

Mary Vandyke of Franklin Co, widow of Abraham Vandyke, gives power of attorney to Josiah Wood of Upper Dublin Twp, Montgomery Co. to recover estate from William Garges of Warrington Twp, acting executor of John Vandyke, late of Bucks Co.   Bk 4/pg 161   Aug 1, 1820

Moses Murdock of Warwick Twp, singleman, gives power of attorney to brother William Murdock of Warminster Twp, shoemaker, to recover moneys due him.   Bk 4/ pg 165   Apr 14, 1821

Frederick Hartman of Brookville Twp, Franklin Co, IN, yeoman, gives power of attorney to brother Michael Hartman of Montgomery Twp, Montgomery Co. to recover moneys due him.   Bk 4/pg 169   Apr 27, 1820

Michael Funk of Clinton Twp, Lincoln Co, Niagara District, Upper Canada, weaver, gives power of attorney to brother John W. Funk of Plumstead Twp, clockmaker, to recover estate from Abraham Wismer of Bedminster Twp, administrator of John Funk, late of Hilltown Twp.   Bk 4/pg 172 Jul 12, 1820

John Miller of Easton, blacksmith, assigns to daughter Catharine of Easton, single woman, his share in estate of his grandfather Thomas Thomas, late of Bucks Co, in trust for herself, his wife Pheobe and his other children.
Bk 4/pg 180   Dec 27, 1820

Joseph Rodman of Bensalem Twp. gives power of attorney to brother Samuel Rodman of Doylestown Twp. to recover moneys due him.
Bk 4/pg 182   May 21, 1821

Jacob Nease of Milford Twp, joyner and George William Reichart of Upper Milford Twp, yeoman, and wife Christina, children of Nicholas Nease, late of Rockhill Twp, yeoman, acknowledge payment of estate by administrator Henry Nease of Rockhill, yeoman.   Bk 4/pg 183   May 24, 1821

Leonard Sellers of Hilltown Twp. died intestate leaving a widow and several children with eldest son Abraham as administrator. Abraham assigns his share of dower to his sureties John Beringer and John Frantz.
Bk 4/pg 187   Apr 20, 1821

Anthony Rue died intestate leaving land in Middletown Twp. and eight children: George W. Rue, Mary Rue, Benjamin Rue, Anthony Rue, Joseph Rue, John and Edith Watt, Sarah Rue and Samuel Rue. They appoint men to value the estate.   Bk 4/pg 187   Sep 30, 1820

Daniel McCalmont of Bath, Steuben Co, NY, late of Bucks Co. gives power of attorney to brother Samuel of Montgomery Co. to recover money from guardian Jacob Trichler of Bucks Co.   Bk 4/pg 188   Apr 5, 1821

Rebbeca Strawn of Saucon Twp, Northampton Co, spinster, daughter of William Strawn, late of Haycock Twp, gives power of attorney to friend Caleb Foulke of Richland Twp. to enter satisfaction of bond given her by brother William.   Bk 4/pg 189   Aug 20, 1821

Jean Price of Alexander Twp, Hunterdon Co, NJ, widow, acknowledges payment by brother Samuel Wilson of Nockamixon Twp. of a mortgage.
Bk 4/pg 189   Jun 2, 1821

Phebe Cooper of Highland Co, OH gives power of attorney to brother John Cooper of Highland Co. to recover money from estate of late father Jonathan Cooper of Bucks Co.   Bk 4/pg 189   May 19, 1821

Francis Booz, now wife of Cheri Borie/Boize[?] and daughter of Peter Booz, late of Bristol Twp. acknowledges payment of estate by her guardian Joseph Brown, Esq.						Bk 4/pg 190 Sep 10, 1821

David Carr of West Chester, Chester Co. and wife Abi (late Carlile) give power of attorney to her mother Abi Carlile to recover estate from Daniel and Benjamin Carlile, executors of her grandfather John Carlile, late of Plumstead Twp.						Bk 4/pg 190 Sep 21, 1821

Isaac Klein of Upper Milford Twp, Lehigh Co. (creditor of Jacob Stahr) gives power of attorney to Abraham Shelly of Milford Twp. to obtain legal partition of land willed to Jacob and Samuel Stahr by their mother Susanna Stahr.
						Bk 4/pg 192 Jun 15, 1821

Edward and Sarah Otto acknowledge payment by guardian Joshua Knight.
						Bk 4/pg 198 Dec 5, 1820

Seth and Martha Chapman of Newtown and Robert and Ruth Croasdale of Middletown Twp. agree to a partition of land jointly willed to Martha and Ruth by their father Joshua Richardson, late of Middletown.
						Bk 4/pg 198 Sep 30, 1811

Elizabeth Sease of Rockhill Twp, widow of Jacob Sease, late of Rockhill, yeoman, renounces her right to administer husband's estate and asks son Michael and sons-in-law Christopher Socks and William Getman to handle.
						Bk 4/pg 200 Feb 19, 1816

Peter Ott of Upper Mount Bethel Twp, Northampton Co. and wife Mary, daughter of Melchoir Heavener, late of Bedminster Twp, acknowledge payment of estate by executors Abraham Heavener and Jacob Kulp.
						Bk 4/pg 200 Jun 19, 1821

Ann Hertzel, widow of Jacob Hertzel, late of Richland Twp, and John Hertzel and Jacob Smith of Milford Twp. (guardian of Jacob and Solema Hartzel), children of Jacob, acknowledge payment of estate by administrators Everard Foulke and Abraham Hertzel.		Bk 4/pg 201 Jun 8, 1821

Henry Trumbower, George Trumbower, Samuel Trumbower, Joseph Trumbower, Philip Trumbower, Michael Trumbower, John and Elizabeth Friese, Samuel and Mary Moyer, children of Henry Trumbower, late of Richland Twp, yeoman, acknowledge payment of estate by executors John and Jacob Trumbower.		Bk 4/pg 202 Apr 12, 1819

George Schwenk of Lower Milford Twp, yeoman, acknowledges payment by son Daniel Schwenk for certain goods.   Bk 4/pg 202   Jun 15, 1821

Isabella Bailey of Tinicum Twp, widow of John Bailey, late of Tinicum, acknowledges payment of dower by her son Samuel S. Bailey of Tinicum.
Bk 4/pg 203   Aug 25, 1821

Nathan Shelmire, Abraham and Daniel Shelmire of Montgomery Co, Benjamin Shelmire of Philadelphia Co, Edward and Maria Yerkes of Bucks, children of John Shelmire, late of Warminster Twp, for themselves and on behalf of children of Jesse Shelmire, late of Hindeston[?], IL, George Shelmire of Redding Twp, NY and George, Jesse, Thomas M., Elizabeth and Jacob Rutherford, children of Elizabeth Rutherford, other children of John Shelmire, and John Shelmire, minor son of late John Shelmire who was eldest son of John, authorize executors Thomas B. Montanye and John Vanartzdalen to take back real estate previously sold to John Edwards.
Bk 4/pg 204   Aug 20, 1821

Samuel Wismer of South Twp, Lincoln Co, Niagara District, Upper Canada, yeoman, gives power of attorney to Joseph Fretz of South Twp. to recover estate from Abraham Wismer of Bedminster Twp, executor of Henry Wismer, late of Hilltown Twp.   Bk 4/pg 207   Aug 20, 1821

Jacob Overholt, son of Staats Overholt, and Elizabeth Mills, daughter of Abraham Hunsberger, both of Baam Twp, Middlefort Co, London District, Upper Canada give power of attorney to Joseph Fretz of South Twp, Upper Canada to recover estate from Peter Strunk and Jacob Clymer, executors of Christopher Hunsberger, late of Lower Milford Twp.
Bk 4/pg 207   Mar 9, 1821

Rachel Mathew, widow of Benjamin Mathew, late of New Britain Twp, releases dower right to sons Benjamin and Joseph Mathew.
Bk 4/pg 209   Oct 19, 1821

William Larkin of Bethel Twp, Delaware Co. and wife Sarah, daughter of Jonathan Carlile and granddaughter of John Carlile, late of Plumstead Twp, give power of attorney to friend Joseph Carr of Plumstead, farmer, to recover estate from executor Benjamin Carlile.   Bk 4/pg 212   Nov 9, 1821

Margaret Ray, minor daughter of Nathaniel Ray, late of Chester District, SC, is entitled to goods in state of PA and requests that her grandfather John Ray of Chester District be appointed her guardian. Bk 4/pg 214 Oct 21, 1816

Thomas Fell of Buckingham Twp, having become aged and infirm, gives power of attorney to sons Benjamin Fell of East Caln Twp, Chester Co. and Jesse Fell of Little Britain Twp, Lancaster Co. and friend Jonathan Fell of Buckingham to handle his affairs. Bk 4/pg 218 Dec 3, 1821

Peter Trolinger of Tinicum Twp, son of Peter Trolinger, late of Franconia Twp, Montgomery Co. gives power of attorney to John Snyder of Tinicum Twp. to recover estate from Andrew Trolinger, administrator of mother Sophia, late of Franconia. Bk 4/pg 223 Mar 30, 1821

John Swift, Esq, late of Bucks Co. willed property to son Charles and wife Mary subject to disposition to Charles' children as he should will. Charles bequeathed to the children by his last marriage: Robert, Henry and Lewis. Samuel Swift, executor of John assigns property to Robert, Henry and Lewis.
Bk 4/pg 224 Mar 14, 1822

Elizabeth Balderston of Solebury Twp. gives power of attorney to Robert Smith of Buckingham Twp. to recover estate from late husband John Balderston. Bk 4/pg 225 Jun 5, 1821

Veronica Meyer (widow), Henry and Anna Meyer, John and Anna Gingrich, Joseph and Elizabeth Gingrich, Joseph and Mary Light, John and Veronica Ober and John Gingrich as guardian for John and Sarah Meyer, widow and children of Henry Meyer, late of Annville Twp, Lebanon Co, give power of attorney to George F. McCawly of Annville Twp. to execute titles for certain land in Bucks and Montgomery Co. Bk 4/pg 226 Feb 14, 1822

Abraham Clemens acknowledges payment by Abiah James Jr. of New Britain Twp. for one-eighth part of William Callender's share of plantation of his father John Callender now in possession of Abraham.
Bk 4/pg 227 May 5, 1818

Jonathan Huntsman died intestate possessing certain tracts of land and leaving children Jonathan Jr., David, William, Elizabeth Morris, Mary Bowers, Susan, Sarah, Margaret Case and Priscilla. Son William and wife Mary give power of attorney to brother David to sell his share. Bk 4/pg 228 Jul 29, 1820

Mathias Meyer, husband of Hannah (late Winhold) of Easton holds by right of wife a judgment against George Hinkle, late of Richland Twp. Mathias acknowledges payment by Peter Zeginfoos, assignee of George.

Bk 4/pg 228   Apr 4, 1822

Margaret Toman of South Huntingdon Twp, Westmoreland Co. and Ezekiel Sample of South Huntingdon Twp, guardian of Elizabeth Toman, children of Andrew Toman and wife Susanna (late Gross), late of Fayette Co, who was a daughter of Casper Gross, late of Richland Twp, gives power of attorney to Henry Stouffer of East Huntington Twp, Westmoreland Co. to recover estate.

Bk 4/pg 230-2 Dec 27, 1820

George Toman of South Huntingdon Twp, Westmoreland Co. gives power of attorney to brother Jacob Toman of South Huntingdon to recover estate from Adam Bartholomy and Rudolph Shough of Richland Twp, executors of Casper Gross, late of Richland Twp.   Bk 4/pg 233   Oct 6, 1811

Henry Stouffer of East Huntingdon Twp, Westmoreland Co, yeoman, attorney for Margaret and Andrew Toman and guardian of Joseph Toman, children of Andrew Toman and grandchildren of Casper Gross, late of Richland Twp, acknowledges payment of estate by executor Adam Bartholomew.

Bk 4/pg 233-5   Apr 17, 1815

George Sterner of Richland Twp, yeoman and wife Margaret, daughter of Casper Gross, late of Richland Twp, acknowledge payment of estate by executors Adam Bartholomew and Rudolph Shough.

Bk 4/pg 235   Oct 18, 1817

Jacob Toman of South Huntingden Twp, Westmoreland Co, eldest son of Susanna Toman and legatee of Casper Gross, late of Richland Twp, acknowledges payment of estate by executors Adam Bartholomew and Rudolph Shough.   Bk 4/pg 236   Sep 17, 1810

Mark Balderston, Merab Balderston, John and Hannah Mitchell and Anna Balderston, children of John Balderston, late of Solebury Twp (died May 16, 1821), acknowledge their father's bequest of land to brother John.

Bk 4/pg 237   Jun 11, 1821

Hannah Custard, Jane Foulke and Rachel Foulke (by guardian Evan Penrose), daughters of Benjamin Foulke, late of Richland Twp, give power of attorney to friend George Custard of Richland Twp. to decline their father's real estate.

Bk 4/pg 238   Mar 4, 1822

Mary Penrose, widow of David Penrose, late of Richland Twp, and Joseph and Samuel Penrose, sons of David, acknowledge payment by Charles Foulke and George Custard, administrators of Benjamin Foulke, late of Richland Twp, which was due to Mary from the estate of her father Jacob Hartzel.
Bk 4/pg 239   Dec 22, 1821

Abraham Derstine, Henry Derstine, Samuel Derstine, Henry and Catharine Felman, Christian and Hannah Detwiler, Jacob and Magdalin Halderman, children of Isaac Derstine, late of Rockhill Twp, acknowledge payment of estate by executors George and Isaac Derstine.   Bk 4/pg 240   Oct 13, 1821

Thomas Warner bequeathed estate in seven shares to children of brother John, brother Joseph, nephew James Wildman, children of brother Croasdale, brother Isaac with the other two shares undisposed. Heirs believe it was his intent to bequeath other two shares to children of sister Sarah Wiggins and children of brother Abraham. Signed by heirs Mercy Green, John and Hannah Townsend, Seneca Warner, Anthony and Martha Paxson, Aaron Warner, Agness C. Warner, James Wildman, Amos Warner Jr., Rachel Weaver, Rachel Flood, John and Rachel Heston, Banner and Elizabeth Taylor, Mary Warner, Amos Warner, John Warner, Isaac Warner, David Warner, Isaiah Warner, Jonathan Warner, Sarah Flood, Joseph Warner, Silas Warner, Cuthbert Warner, Hannah Ely, Crosdale Warner, Asa Warner, Simeon Warner and Jonathan Warner.   Bk 4/pg 240   Mar 3, 1821

Elias Klinker of Lancaster Co, singleman, son of John Klinker, late of Northampton Co, died about two years ago intestate leaving siblings but no other heirs. Sister Sarah and husband Jacob Cope of Hilltown Twp. assign their share to Abraham Jacoby of Hilltown in order to pay debt.
Bk 4/pg 242   Mar 9, 1822

Sarah Johnson of Warwick Twp, widow, gives power of attorney to Silas Roney of Mooreland Twp, Montgomery Co. and Daniel Roberts of Warwick to recover share in estate of late Joseph Ball in hands of administrators in Philadelphia.   Bk 4/pg 247   Apr 16, 1822

Jacob and Magdalena Fretz, children of William Fretz, now 21, acknowledge payment of estate by guardian Joseph Fretz Jun.   Bk 4/pg 248   Mar 22, 1822

Samuel Strawn, minor son of William Strawn, late of Haycock Twp, gives power of attorney to Caleb Foulke of Richland Twp. to record payment of bond due from William Strawn and others received prior to the death of Samuel's mother.   Bk 4/pg 248   May 11, 1822

83

Solomon Nunemaker of Milford Twp, yeoman and wife Ann, granddaughter of Baltzer Wynberry, late of Milford Twp, acknowledge payment by executors Henry Landes and Abraham Geisinger of one-fourth part of the share of her mother Barbara Landes.   Bk 4/pg 249   Mar 9, 1822

Samuel Wynberger of Forks Twp, Northampton Co. acknowledges payment by Henry Landes and Abraham Geisinger, executors of John Landis who held a bequest due to Samuel from his father Baltzer Wynberger, late of Milford Twp.   Bk 4/pg 249   Mar 5, 1822

Baltzer Winberry and Samuel Landes of Milford Twp, yeoman, and wife Francia, children of Baltzer Wynberry, late of Milford Twp, yeoman, acknowledge payment by Henry Landes and Abraham Geisinger, executors of John Landis, late of Milford Twp, yeoman, of money bequeathed to them upon the death of John Landis and his wife Elizabeth who was a daughter of Baltzer Wynberry.   Bk 4/pg 250   Mar 9, 1822

Benjamin Wynberger, son of John Wynberger, late of Bedminster Twp and grandson of Baltzer Wynberger, late of Lower Milford Twp, acknowledges payment of one-fourth share of bequest due his father from Henry Landes and Abraham Geisinger, executors of John Landis.   Bk 4/pg 251   Mar 18, 1822

William Wilson of Rockhill Twp. and wife Sarah, daughter of Jonah Thompson, late of Plumstead Twp and John Thompson of Haycock Twp. give power of attorney to friend Eliaser Shaw of Plumstead Twp. to recover money due from father's estate.   Bk 4/pg 253   Jun 4, 1822

Anna Leatherman, widow, Jacob and Susanna Beidler, Christian and Elizabeth Rosenberger, Isaac and Mary Kulp and Hester Crout, children of Jacob Crout, late of Bedminster Twp, acknowledge payment of estate by executor Henry Crout.   Bk 4/pg 254   Apr 3, 1820

Jane Wright, widow of John Wright, late of Falls Twp, accepts mortgage from sons Samuel and Benjamin in lieu of dower right due from sons Samuel, Benjamin, Stephen and Amos.   Bk 4/pg 255   Mar 11, 1822

Elizabeth Lunn, widow of Thomas Lunn, late of Montgomery Twp, Montgomery Co, releases administrator Joseph Lunn from dower right.
                Bk 4/pg 257   Jun 20, 1819

John and Catharine Frick and Charles and Elizabeth Selnor, daughters of
Jacob Rhoar, late of New Britain Twp, wheelmaker, acknowledge payment of
estate by executrix Anna Rhoar.　　　　Bk 4/pg 258　Jun 13, 1796

Walter Evans of Montgomery Twp, Montgomery Co. gives power of attorney
to son Walter S. Evans of Nottingham Twp, Burlington Co, NJ to recover
mortgage due from Henry Moyer of Bucks Co.　Bk 4/pg 259　Apr 8, 1822

Conrad Shellenberger of Hilltown Twp, guardian of Hannah, Abraham,
Barbara and Susanna Fluke, minor children of Christian Fluke, deceased,
acknowledges payment of estate by executors Philip Fluke and Daniel
Housekeeper.　　　　Bk 4/pg 262　Apr 20, 1822

David and Susanna Shelly of Rockhill Twp, yeoman, grant to John Clemmer
(farmer), Jacob Clemmer (yeoman), John Roth (in right of wife Elizabeth,
deceased), all of Rockhill, Henry and Catharine Geisinger of Saucon Twp,
Lehigh Co, and Martin and Barbara Overholtzer of Berks Co, yeoman, heirs
of Jacob Clemmer, late of Rockhill Twp. and equal right to the property of
Jacob sold to David and Susanna by administrators Isaac Clemmer, John
Clemmer and John Roth.　　　　Bk 4/pg 267　Apr 12, 1822

Peter Knight of Durham Twp. died intestate and his land was sold subject to
dower right by widow Catharine who is also now deceased. Daniel Scaman
of Sandiston Twp, Sussex Co, NJ who married Peter's daughter Susanna,
assigns his dower share to Micha Scaman of Sandiston Twp.
　　　　　　　　　　　Bk 4/pg 268　Apr 29, 1822

Jacob Fox of Pottsgrove Twp, Montgomery Co. and his brother-in-law John
Ditlow of Lower Milford Twp. give power of attorney to friend Jacob Fox,
Sen. of Tinicum Twp. to recover estate from grandfather Jacob Fox, late of
Bedminster Twp.　　　　Bk 4/pg 269　Jul 29, 1822

John Stapler of Hunterdon Co, NJ and Susanna Betts of Upper Makefield
Twp. intend to be married and agree to maintain Susanna's property
separately.　　　　Bk 4/pg 270　Apr 13, 1822

Adam Reidenauer of Upper Saucon Twp, Lehigh Co. gives power of attorney
to David Koons of Lower Milford Twp. to recover estate from John
Reidenauer, executor of Christopher Reidenauer, late of Lower Milford.
　　　　　　　　　　　Bk 4/pg 271　Jul 29, 1822

Daniel Carr and wife Sarah, daughter of Else Hoppack, daughter of John Hoppack, late of NJ who married Daniel Coopper, Jacob and Christiana Waggoner, Daniel and Frany Waggoner, Daniel Coopper as guardian for Catharine, George, Mary and Rudolph Coopper (minor children of Daniel Cooper of Derry Twp, Columbia Co.), give power of attorney to Rudolph Sichler of Mahoning Twp, Columbia Co. to recover Else Coopper's share in estate of John Hoppack in hands of Henry Allen, John G. Trimmer and Jacob R. Fisher.   Bk 4/pg 272   May 26, 1820

John and Magdalena Fretz of Loyalsock Twp, Lycoming Co. give power of attorney to Jacob Kreamer Sen. of Bedminster Twp. to recover money from estate of mother Mary Kreamer, late of Haycock Twp.
                                                Bk 4/pg 275   Aug 29, 1822

Henry Hinkle and wife Mary (formerly Fretz) of Washington Twp, Lycoming Co, granddaughter of Maria Kreamer of Haycock Twp. give power of attorney to John Fritz of Loyalsock Twp, Lycoming Co. to recover money due from Maria's estate.   Bk 4/pg 276   Aug 9, 1822

Asa Beck of Fayette Co, IN and wife Ann, daughter of John Percil, late of Bucks Co, give power of attorney to John Iliff of Huntingdon Co, NJ to recover money from Ann's guardian Brice Purcel of Bucks Co.
                                                Bk 4/pg 276   Jul 30, 1822

Jacob and Elizabeth Daub of Upper Salford Twp, Montgomery Co, George Cramer, Henry Cramer, Joseph and Mary Artman, and Conrad Snider, guardian of Michael Cramer, children of Henry Cramer of Hilltown Twp, acknowledge payment of estate by administrator John Cramer.
                                                Bk 4/pg 280   Apr 26, 1822

William and Elizabeth (late Smith) Scott and Samuel and Catharine (late Smith) Fretz, granddaughters of Barnet Keplar, late of Plumstead Twp, now 21, acknowledge payment of estate by guardian Nicholas Swartz.
                                                Bk 4/pg 282   May 6, 1822

John Solliday and wife Elizabeth, daughter of George Geddes, late of Plumstead Twp and heir of Henry Geddes, late of Plumstead Twp, acknowledge payment of estate by guardian Nicholas Swartz.
                                                Bk 4/pg 282   Dec 25, 1821

Jacob Reed, late of New Britain Twp, bequeathed land to son Philip or to sons Jacob or Andrew in his stead. Philip died before his father. Jacob Reed of

Sugarcreek Twp, Stark Co, OH, yeoman, and Andrew Reed of Hilltown Twp, yeoman, acknowledge payment of estate by executor Jacob Conver.
Bk 4/pg 283   Apr 1, 1822

Sarah Stever (wife of Henry Allum of Bedminster Twp), now 21, acknowledges payment by guardian Baltzer Stever of estate from father Philip Stever.
Bk 4/pg 284   Mar 30, 1822

Rebecca Peirce of Plymouth Twp, Montgomery Co. gives power of attorney to brother John Eastburn of Upper Makefield Twp. to recover moneys due her.
Bk 4/pg 284   May 10, 1822

Susana Letherman, daughter of Christian Letherman, now 21 and married to Abraham Fretz of Bedminster Twp, acknowledges payment of estate by guardian Conrad Harpel.
Bk 4/pg 285   Mar 1, 1822

John Wismer of Yearmouth Twp, Middlesex Co, London District, Upper Canada, yeoman, gives power of attorney to John Moyers of Clinton Twp, Lincoln Co, Niagara District, Upper Canada, yeoman, to recover from Abraham Wismer of Bedminster Twp, yeoman, a legacy due from father Henry Wismer, deceased.
Bk 4/pg 286   Sep 7, 1822

Samuel Landes of Rockhill Twp, son of John Landes, late of Rockhill, now 21, acknowledges payment of estate by guardian Caleb Foulke.
Bk 4/pg 288   Apr 3, 1822

John Groff of Rockhill Twp, yeoman, and wife Christina, daughter of John Fulmer, late of Rockhill, acknowledge payment of estate by administrators Henry Cope and Caleb Foulke.
Bk 4/pg 288   Oct 1, 1821

Michael Yost of Hanover Twp, Northampton Co, yeoman, Abraham and Catharine Zeigenfus of Bedminster Twp, Benjamin Jacoby of Haycock Twp. (guardian of Samuel Yost), children of Catharine Yost who was a daughter of John Fulmer, late of Rockhill Twp, acknowledge payment of estate by administrators Henry Cope and Caleb Foulke.
Bk 4/pg 289   Nov 24, 1821

John Groff of Rockhill Twp, yeoman, administrator of Barbara Fulmer, late widow of John Fulmer, late of Rockhill Twp, acknowledges payment of estate by administrators Henry Cope and Caleb Foulke.
Bk 4/pg 290   Oct 1, 1821

Henry Groff and John Karn, both of Rockhill, guardians of Catharine, Anna and John Fulmer, minor children of John Fulmer the younger, late of

Springfield Twp, grandchildren of John Fulmer, late of Rockhill Twp, acknowledge payment of estate by administrators Henry Cope and Caleb Foulke.   Bk 4/pg 290   Oct 1, 1821

John Baldwin assigns to Walter Baldwin of Bristol his right to an annuity under will of his sister Sarah R. Baldwin, late of Bucks Co.
                                      Bk 4/pg 291   May 1, 1822

Margretha Nease, widow of Abraham Nease, late of Rockhill Twp, and Abraham Nease of Rockhill Twp, and Abraham Heany of Upper Salford Twp, Montgomery Co. (guardian of Jacob Nese), children of Abraham, acknowledge payment of estate by administrators George and John Nease.
                                      Bk 4/pg 291   Aug 1, 1822

George Burges, administrator of Isaac Michener, late of Plumstead Twp, acknowledges payment by John Townsend of dower due upon death of widow Martha who is now deceased.   Bk 4/pg 293   Jan 17, 1822

Jacob G. Server, son of John Server, late of Warrington Twp, acknowledges payment of estate by Samuel Garner, surety for widow Elizabeth who was administratrix.   Bk 4/pg 293   Jul 2, 1821

In 1800, Thomas Mathias, Isaac and Elizabeth Morris, Abel and Sarah Mathias and John and Elenor Mathias (since deceased without issue), heirs of Thomas Mathias the elder of Hilltown Twp. sold to brother Joseph Mathias land in Hilltown subject to dower right by widow Elizabeth who is now deceased. Heirs Abel Mathias of Hilltown Twp, Isaac Morris of Hatfield Twp, Montgomery Co. and Mathias Morris of Doylestown (only heirs of late Elizabeth Morris), Ashbel Mathias of Hilltown and Abel Mathias of Philadelphia (only heirs of Thomas Mathias the younger, late of Hilltown), acknowledge payment of dower by Joseph Mathias.
                                      Bk 4/pg 294   Feb 20, 1822

George Wertzner, husband of Esther Server and Jacob Markley, husband of Rachel Server, heirs of John Server, late of Warrington Twp, acknowledge payment of estate by Samuel Garner, surety for widow Elizabeth who was administratrix.   Bk 4/pg 296   Nov 27, 1821

Jacob Gerhart of Upper Salford Twp, innkeeper, gives power of attorney to mother-in-law Barbara Sallady of Upper Salford to recover money due him from estate of father-in-law, late of Milford Twp. Bk 4/pg 297 Apr 17, 1822

Deborah Preston, Samuel Preston, Ann Preston, Naioma Price, Uphemia Preston, Paul Preston and Silas Preston, children of Hannah Preston, late of Plumstead Twp, give power of attorney to James Price of Buckingham Twp. to collect their mother's estate.　　　　Bk 4/pg 298　[not dated]

Jesse Johnson, late of Bristol Twp, bequeathed land to wife Catharine and after her death to nephew Jesse Johnson. The nephew Jesse and his wife Catharine of Middletown Twp. sell this land to Anthony Taylor of Bristol Twp.　　　　　　　　　　　　Bk 4/pg 298　Apr 13, 1822

Frederic Hartman Sen. of Franklin Co, IN gives power of attorney to son Frederick Hartman Jun. of Bucks Co. to recover moneys due him.
　　　　　　　　　　　　　　Bk 4/pg 300　Aug 26, 1822

Jacob Gerhart and wife Anna (late Salady), both of Upper Salford Twp, Montgomery Co. assign their share of estate of Anna's father Jacob Salady, late of Milford Twp, to her mother Barbara.　Bk 4/pg 300　Jun 1, 1822

David Carver of Solebury Twp, grandson of Samuel Harrold, deceased, for himself and as attorney for brother James, acknowledges payment of estate by executor David Harrold.　　　　　　Bk 4/pg 302　Sep 13, 1820

Isaac Michener, late of Plumstead Twp, gave bond to Charles and Elizabeth Plumly in 1803 to secure payment of Elizabeth's share in estate of her father William Michener with final payment due upon death of widow Martha. Charles Plumly acknowledges payment of bond by Isaac's administrator George Burges.　　　　　　　　Bk 4/pg 302　Jun 11, 1822

Abraham and William Griffith of Richland Twp. and Thomas and Jane Jackson and Nathaniel and Hannah Kinsey, all of Millcreek hundred, New Castle Co, DE, children of John Griffith, Esq., late of Richland, give power of attorney to brother John G. Griffith of Richland to refuse to accept their father's real estate.　　　　　　　Bk 4/pg 303　Mar 2, 1822

Owen Owen of Greenhood Twp, Perry Co. and Zelophehad Owen of Perry Twp, Union Co, administrators of Abel Owen, late of Perry Twp, give power of attorney to friend Capt. Wm Magill of Doylestown to enter satisfaction of a bond from Griffith Owen, administrator of estate of Owen Owen.
　　　　　　　　　　　　　　Bk 4/pg 305　Jun 15, 1822

Abel Owen and Peter and Margaret Castner, heirs of Owen Owen, late of Hilltown Twp, acknowledge payment of estate by heir and administrator Griffith Owen who took their father's real estate.   Bk 4/pg 305   Apr 5, 1811

Mary Magdalena Benner of Bedminster Twp. gives power of attorney to Jacob Kramer of Buckingham Twp. and Adam Benner of Haycock Twp. to recover dower due under will of husband John Benner, late of Hilltown Twp. of which Adam and John Benner are executors.   Bk 4/pg 305   Dec 10, 1822

Henry Shelly, late of Lower Milford Twp. died intestate leaving widow and six children: Henry, Susanna (wife of John Landes Jr.), Molly (wife of David Shelly), John, William and Daniel, last two minors. John Landis and David Shelly acknowledge payment of their shares by Henry Shelly who took his father's real estate.   Bk 4/pg 307   Oct 4, 1821

Samuel Fellman of Rockhill Twp, yeoman and wife Elizabeth, late widow of Jacob Fluke of Richland Twp, acknowledge payment of estate by administrators John Heany and Everard Foulke.   Bk 4/pg 308   Jun 8, 1822

Samuel Fluke and Hannah Fluke, children of Jacob Fluke, late of Hilltown Twp, acknowledge payment of estate by administrators John Heany and Everard Foulke, which was due when Hannah turned 21.
                                              Bk 4/pg 308   Jun 8, 1822

Barbara Fretz, Mary Fretz, Ann Fretz, Joseph Fretz and Sarah Fretz, heirs of Henry Fretz, late of Bedminster Twp, give power of attorney to Henry Moyers to refuse to accept the real estate.   Bk 4/pg 309   Nov 20, 1821

Christian and Hannah Ruhl have made agreements to resolve differences between them and agree that Hannah is to receive certain moneys, including legacy left by her father and in return releases Christian from any obligation to support her.   Bk 4/pg 310   Sep 10, 1822

Jonathan Fell and wife Mary, daughter of Joseph Townsend, late of Bedminster Twp, acknowledge payment of estate by executor John Townsend.   Bk 4/pg 311   Apr 19, 1822

Abraham Delp of Hilltown Twp. assigns to brother John Delp of New Britain Twp. his claim against Samuel Hall.   Bk 4/pg 312   Apr 3, 1820

Jacob Leidy Jr. of Franconia Twp, Montgomery Co, shopkeeper and wife Hannah, Thomas Sellers and Francis Sellers, children of Samuel Sellers, Esq.,

late of Rockhill Twp, acknowledge payment of estate by administrator
Everard Foulke. Bk 4/pg 314 Oct 12, 1822

Henry Raquet, Mary H. Wirtz, Silas Vansant, James Raquet and Reading
Beatty acknowledge payment by executor Jona. Wynkoop of moneys due
them under will of Henry Wynkoop, Esq. Bk 4/pg 315 Mar 16, 1822

George Merrick and Christianna Lundy, both of Bristol Borough, are about to
be married and agree to disposition of property. Bk 4/pg 316 Mar 6, 1793

John Crossley, son of James Crossley who married Susanna Brunner
(deceased), daughter of Felix Brunner, late of Milford Twp, acknowledge
payment of estate by administrator Jacob Brunner. Bk 4/pg 317 Oct 28, 1822

Catharine Weidner of Butler Co, OH, daughter of Felix Brunner, late of
Bucks Co, gives power of attorney to husband Jacob Weidner to recover
estate from executors Jacob Brunner and Philip Zingmaster.
Bk 4/pg 317 Sep 13, 1822

John Paxson acknowledges payment by guardian Joshua Knight of estate due
to him. Bk 4/pg 319 Sep 3, 1822

Samuel Young of Number Six, Frederick Co, MD and wife Elizabeth,
daughter of Nicholas Neace, late of Rockhill Twp, acknowledge payment of
estate by administrator Henry Neace of Rockhill. Bk 4/pg 319 Nov 14, 1822

John and Catharine Hedrick of Springfield Twp, weaver, and Jacob and
Elizabeth Cramer of Hilltown Twp, blacksmith, daughters of John Benner,
late of Hilltown Twp, acknowledge payment of estate by executors John and
Adam Benner. Bk 4/pg 323 Aug 27, 1814

Henry Benner of Wayne Twp, Columbiana Co, OH, yeoman, son of John
Benner, late of Hilltown Twp, acknowledges payment of estate by executors
John and Adam Benner. Bk 4/pg 323 Sep 2, 1815

Mary Magdalena Benner of Rockhill Twp, widow of John Benner,
acknowledges payment of estate by sons John and Adam Benner.
Bk 4/pg 324 Aug 27, 1814

Jacob Ettleman of Stark Co, OH and wife Cleary acknowledge payment by
administrators John and Adam Benner of estate from John Benner, late of
Bucks Co. Bk 4/pg 324 Apr 14, 1815

Everard Foulke of Richland Twp, yeoman, gives power of attorney to son Samuel Foulke of Richland, yeoman, to receive funds due from saving fund society in Philadelphia.   Bk 4/pg 325   Mar 19, 1823

John Price, Esq. of Plumstead Twp, guardian of Jonas Brooks, minor child of Joseph Brooks, late of Plumstead, acknowledges payment of estate by executors Daniel Boileau, Esq. and Anthony Fretz.
                                            Bk 4/pg 328   Jan 8, 1823

Phillip Parry of Buckingham Twp. is indebted to brother Samuel and to the house for the employment and relief of the Poor in York County. He assigns to them his share of estate of father Phillip Parry, late of Buckingham Twp.
                                            Bk 4/pg 332   Jan 20,1823

Isaac Chapman was appointed trustee under will of Henry Cooper, late of Northampton Twp. to Henry's daughter Sarah, now married to Amos Scarborough. Isaac transfers this trust to Amos of Wrightstown Twp.
                                            Bk 4/pg 332   Jan 23, 1822

Abraham Biehn and Michael Headman of Rockhill Twp, guardians of Abraham, Enos, John and Catharine Zeigenfus, minor children of John Zeigenfus, late of Rockhill Twp, acknowledge payment of estate by Henry Cope and Caleb Foulk, administrators of former guardian Jacob Stout, late of Rockhill Twp, including portion due to widow Catharine Zeigenfuss.
                                            Bk 4/pg 336   Aug 17, 1822

John S. Hough, Tho. Humphrey (guardian of John Lunn), Silas Lunn, Oliver Lunn, Joseph Lunn Jr. and Elizabeth Lunn, heirs of Thomas Lunn, late of Montgomery Twp, Montgomery Co, acknowledge payment of estate by administrator Joseph Lunn.   Bk 4/pg 337   Apr 5, 1822

Henry and Maria (late Senn) Schlichter of Rockhill Twp, yeoman, and James and Anna (late Senn) Casseda of Newtown Twp, Sussex Co, NJ, now 21, acknowledge payment of estate by Henry Cope and Caleb Foulk, administrators of former guardian Jacob Stout, late of Rockhill Twp.
                                            Bk 4/pg 338   Mar 5, 1822

Abraham Fluke of Haycock Twp, wheelwright, son of Christian Fluke, late of Hilltown Twp, now 21, acknowledges payment of estate by Henry Cope and Caleb Foulk, administrators of former guardian Jacob Stout, late of Rockhill Twp.   Bk 4/pg 338   Apr 22, 1822

John Ruth of Springfield Twp, weaver, son of Barbara Ruth who was a daughter of Henry Landis, late of NJ, acknowledges payment of estate by Henry Cope and Caleb Foulk, administrators of former guardian Jacob Stout, late of Rockhill Twp.   Bk 4/pg 339   Sep 15, 1821

Philip Deiley of Springfield Twp, tailor, son of Christian Deiley, deceased, acknowledges payment of estate by executors Joseph and Christian Deiley.
                                                Bk 4/pg 339   Apr 15, 1822

Jacob Diley of Williams Twp, Northampton Co, joiner, assigns share in father's estate to brothers Joseph and Phillip Diley.   Bk 4/pg 340   Jul 26, 1820

Michael Creamer of Hilltown Twp, acknowledges payment by guardian Conrad Snyder of Hilltown of estate from father Henry Creamer, late of Hilltown.   Bk 4/pg 340   Mar 22, 1823

John and Catharine Trumbore of Rockhill Twp, mason, daughter of Michael Blank, late of Rockhill Twp, acknowledge payment of estate by Michael's son John.   Bk 4/pg 341   Mar 24, 1816

Henry and Motilina Miller of Milford Twp, yeoman, Abraham and Mary Gerhart of Milford Twp, blacksmith, Henry and Elizabeth Mumbower of Milford Twp, wheelwright, daughters of Michael Blank, late of Rockhill Twp, acknowledge payment of estate by John and Henry Blank.
                                                Bk 4/pg 341   Mar 22, 1822

Ulrich Beeler of Milford Twp, Christian Rood of Richland Twp. and Jacob Beeler of Milford Twp. give power of attorney to Joseph Himmelwright Jr. of Milford Twp, sawmiller, to record satisfaction of bond from Ullerick Hockman as payment of their shares of estate of Ullerick Hockman, late of Bedminster Twp.   Bk 4/pg 342   Apr 8, 1823

John Pickering of Solebury Twp. gives power of attorney to sons Yeamans Pickering of Buckingham Twp. and Stacy Pickering of Solebury to manage his estate.   Bk 4/pg 345   Apr 14, 1823

Jacob Kohl Sen. of Nockamixon Twp, yeoman, sells land to Nicholas Kohl of Nockamixon, yeoman, subject to Nicholas caring for widow Elizabeth.
                                                Bk 4/pg 346   Aug 14, 1819

David Fox of Chatham Co, NC and Jacob and John Fox, administrators of Nicholas Fox, late of Chatham Co, NJ, give power of attorney to friend Jacob Fox of Tinicum Twp. to recover estate of father Jacob Fox, late of Bucks Co.
Bk 4/pg 347   Mar 24, 1823

Joseph and Mary Heany, Diannah Kelly (late wife of Samuel Cooper), Isaac Weaver and Henry Weaver, heirs of Jacob Weaver, late of Tinicum Twp, agree that executors John, Moses and William Weaver should sell Jacob's real estate.
Bk 4/pg 351   Dec 30, 1822

Martha Blankenhorn of Doylestown Twp, seamstress, legatee of John Blankenhorn, late of Doylestown Twp, gives power of attorney to friend Robert McDowell, farmer, to recover estate due her.
Bk 4/pg 352   Dec 25, 1822

Mary Geiger of New York City gives power of attorney to John Jacob Gatteker of NYC to recover estate from grandfather Michael Stoneback, late of PA.
Bk 4/pg 355   Apr 12, 1823

Jane Wright of Falls Twp. gives power of attorney to son Benjamin Wright to recover moneys due her.
Bk 4/pg 355   Mar 11, 1822

John Wasser, late of Hilltown Twp, bequeathed one-fourth of estate to David Roderock of New Britain Twp. and wife Catharine to be paid by executors Jacob Wasser of Hatfield Twp. and Henry Cop of Hilltown Twp. after death of widow Mary.   David and Catharine assign their share to Jacob Clinker Jr. of New Britain Twp. in order to pay their debt to him.
Bk 4/pg 356   Apr 22, 1823

Mary Watson of Middletown Twp. gives power of attorney to son Nathan Watson of Middletown to recover moneys due her.
Bk 4/pg 356   Apr 22, 1823

Elenor Blood of Northern Liberties, Philadelphia Co, widow, gives power of attorney to son Rowland Blood of Northern Liberties, cordwainer, to recover moneys due her.
Bk 4/pg 361   May 15, 1823

Eve George, widow of Jacob George, late of Tinicum Twp, releases George Hillpot Jr. of dower obligation, upon assurance by Jacob George's heirs (George Wyker, Jacob Fulmer, Frederick Sollada and George Hillpot Jr.) that they will pay her an annuity.
Bk 4/pg 361   May 10, 1823

William Vansant of Bristol Twp. contracted marriage with Sarah Brelsford in 1794. Sarah is now deceased and Williams acknowledges payment of estate by executors John Brelsford and William Sisom.   Bk 4/pg 363   Mar 18, 1822

William Vansant of Bristol Twp, schoolmaster, contracts marriage with Sarah Brelsford of Middletown Twp, widow.   Bk 4/pg 363   Feb 8, 1794

John and Mary Bechtle of Springfield Twp, yeoman, and Samuel Bryan of Mercy Creek Twp, Lycoming Co, children of William Bryan, late of Springfield Twp, acknowledge payment of estate by executors James and Joseph Bryan.   Bk 4/pg 364   May 26, 1823

Michael Snyder, late of Hilltown Twp, gave land to brother Conrad Snyder of Hilltown, subject to dower right by widow Margaret who is now married to Abraham Moyers Jr. of Hilltown. Abraham and Margaret Moyers acknowledge payment of dower by Conrad Snyder. Bk 4/pg 365 Apr 7, 1823

Thomas Morris of Doylestown Twp. was guardian of Ephraim Fenton. John Jones, administrator of Ephraim and Tench C. Kintzing of Montgomery Twp, Montgomery Co. and wife Mary, sister to Ephraim, release Thomas Morris of his guardianship.   Bk 4/pg 368   Jun 26, 1823

Michael Moyer, late of New Britain Twp, bequeathed land to son Michael subject to payment to other heirs (John, Abraham, Joseph, Samuel and Elizabeth) after decease of widow. Abraham Myers of Doylestown Twp. assigns his share to Abraham Geil of Doylestown Twp. in order to pay debt.
Bk 4/pg 369   Jul 3, 1823

Lewis C. Vanuxem of Morrisville gives power of attorney to brother James Jr. of Morrisville, storekeeper, to recover money due him on his own behalf or as part of late firm of L.C. & J. Vanuxem Jr. of Morrisville, millers.
Bk 4/pg 371   Dec 23,1822

Mercy Purcel of Butler Co, OH, widow of John Purcel, late of Bucks Co, Brice Purcel of Butler Co. and Aaron and Else (late Purcel) Beek of Fayette Co, IN, give power of attorney to Joseph Kitchen of Butler Co. to recover money due as heirs of John Purcel.   Bk 4/pg 372   May 13, 1823

Bolder and Catharine Isly of Guilford Co, NC give power of attorney to friend Jacob Fox of Bucks Co. to recover money due from grandfather's estate.   Bk 4/pg 372   May 24, 1823

Anthony and Catharine Gale of Washington, DC agree to separate due to unhappy differences.　　　　　　　　　　Bk 4/pg 373　Aug 15, 1820

Thomas Longshore and wife Jane, daughter of Thomas Gaine, late of Wrightstown Twp, acknowledge payment of estate by Thomas' son and administrator James Gaine.　　　　　　　　Bk 4/pg 376　Apr 1, 1822

Henry and Elizabeth Vanhorn acknowledge payment by administrator James Gawn of their share of estate of Thomas Gawn, late of Wrightstown Twp.
　　　　　　　　　　　　　　　　Bk 4/pg 377　Mar 16, 1822

James Houge of Solebury Twp. gives power of attorney to grandson George Lewis of Solebury, shoemaker, recover money due him.
　　　　　　　　　　　　　　　　Bk 4/pg 377　Sep 8, 1823

David A. Huntsman (attorney of Wm and Mary Huntsman), John and Mary Bowers, Susanna Huntsman, Sarah Ann Huntsman, William and Margaret Case, David A. Hunstman, Priscilla Huntsman and Jonathan Huntsman, heirs of Jonathan Huntsman, acknowledge payment by administrator Elias Morris of debts to Margaret Lewis and Andrew Shattinger.
　　　　　　　　　　　　　　　　Bk 4/pg 378　May 13, 1823

Jacob Loh of Milford Twp, Lehigh Co, executor (with George Wonsidler) of estate of John Loh, late of Rockhill Twp. gives power of attorney to friend William H. Long, Esq. of Milford Twp, Lehigh Co. to perform in Jacob's stead.　　　　　　　　　　　　Bk 4/pg 379　May 16, 1823

John Ulmer of Nockamixon Twp. acknowledges payment by Wilson Housel of Alexandria Twp, Hunterdon Co, NJ of money due from estate of his father Peter Ulmer by administrators Barbara Ulmer and George Rapp.
　　　　　　　　　　　　　　　　Bk 4/pg 380　Sep 22, 1823

Isabel Owen (widow), Chloe Davis, Agness Davis and Salome Davis, daughters of Joanna Davis, late of New Britain Twp, acknowledge payment of estate by administrator Griffith Owen.　　　Bk 4/pg 384　Oct 20, 1823

Robert and Solomon Ramsey of Lincoln Co, NC testify that they were acquainted with Mary Ramsey, late wife of David Ramsey, deceased, who was Mary Anderson before marriage and understood to have had a brother Israel Anderson in Bucks Co. Mary died some years ago leaving six children: James, Anne (wife of John Eaton), Thomas, Mary (wife of Joshua Hooper who left her 12 or 13 years ago), Samuel (moved to western country and reported to be dead) and William (moved to Spartenburgh Dist, SC where he died leaving widow and several children). Robert and Solomon were also acquainted with Mary's sister Sarah Vandike, wife of Richard Vandike, deceased, who has been dead a number of years past leaving children Letitia (wife of Peter Beft and since deceased leaving family of children), Joseph (died many years ago leaving a son Joseph), Sally Vandike, Joshua (died some years ago leaving children Lewis and Salley—wife of Christian Earney), Anderson, Ester Vandike, Peter, John and Jonathan Vandike. Robert and Solomon have also known Mary's sister Elizabeth Robinson for 45 years and she is now a widow living in Lincoln Co. Mary Anderson was the wife of their uncle David Ramsey and they were acquainted with her from their infancy and they were acquainted with Sarah Anderson (wife of Richard Vandike) for 30 years before her death. Robert Ramsey is about 62 years old and Solomon about 52 years old.   Bk 4/pg 384   Mar 31, 1823

James Spencer testifies in Spartanburg District, SC that he was acquainted with Richard and Salley Vandike for 30 years and believes that both are dead leaving children Tisha (wife of Peter Biss), Joseph (died 17-18 years ago), Jonathan, Joshua (believed to be dead), Sally, Anderson, James, Hester (wife of Isaac White) and John.   Bk 4/pg 385   Apr 9, 1823

Isaac White and wife Easter, daughter of Richard and Sally Vandike, both deceased, Sally being sister of Israel Anderson, give power of attorney to friend John Vandike of Spartenburg Dist, SC to recover money from estate of Israel Anderson, late of Bucks Co.   Bk 4/pg 385   [not dated]

John Vandike for himself and as attorney for Isaac and Easter White, acknowledges payment of estate by John Watson, executor of Israel Anderson, late of Bucks Co.   Bk 4/pg 386   May 12, 1823

Mary Anderson (alias Ramsey) of Spartanburgh Dist, SC gives power of attorney to John Vandike of Spartanburgh to recover money from estate of Israel Anderson.   Bk 4/pg 386   Mar 15, 1823

Joseph Vandike, son of late Joseph Vandike who was son of late Salley Vandike, wife of late Richard Vandike and sister of Israel Anderson, deceased, and Thomas Ramsey, son of late Mary Ramsey, wife of late David Ramsey and sister of Israel Anderson, and Peter Bess, husband of late Letitia Vandike, daughter of late Sally Vandike (as father and guardian of Peter, Joshua, John, Delilah, Visa, Joseph and Adeline Bess), all of Lincoln Co, NC, give power of attorney to John Vandike of Spartenburgh Dist, SC to recover money from estate of Israel Anderson.   Bk 4/pg 387   Mar 27, 1823

Anderson Vandike and Salley Vandike, children of late Salley Vandike, and John Eaton who married Anne Ramsey, daughter of late Mary Ramsey, both sisters of Israel Anderson, all of Pendleton Dist, SC, give power of attorney to John Vandyke of Spartanburgh Dist, SC, to recover money from estate of Israel Anderson.   Bk 4/pg 388   Apr 7, 1823

Elizabeth Robinson, sister of Israel Anderson, and James Ramsey, son of late Mary Ramsey, also a sister of Israel Anderson, all of Lincoln Co, NC, give power of attorney to John Vandike to recover money from estate of Israel Anderson.   Bk 4/pg 389   Mar 26, 1823

Mary Hooper, daughter of late Mary Ramsey, and James Vandike, son of late Salley Vandike, and Christopher Earney and wife Sally, daughter of late Joshua Vandike who was son of late Sally and Richard Vandike, all of Lincoln Co, NC, give power of attorney to John Vandike of Spartenburgh Dist, SC to recover money from estate of Israel Anderson.
                    Bk 4/pg 390   Mar 28, 1823

John Mason and Robert McClure, guardians of Hannah and Eliza Brooks, minor children of John Brooks, late of Lycoming Twp, Lycoming Co. give power of attorney to Nicholas Funstan of Lycoming Twp. to recover money from John Watson, executor of Israel Anderson, due to Hannah and Eliza as heirs of John Brooks.   Bk 4/pg 391   Oct 18, 1823

John Mason and Robert McClure, by attorney Nicholas Funstan, acknowledge payment by executor John Watson of estate bequeathed by Israel Anderson to Hannah Brooks, grandmother of Hannah and Eliza Brooks, children of late John Brooks.   Bk 4/pg 392   Oct 25, 1823

Jared and Mary Welsh of Dunstable Twp, Lycoming Co. and Sarah Gwynn (widow of Daniel) of Bald Eagle Twp, Lycoming Co. give power of attorney to Nicholas Funston of Newbury Twp, Lycoming Co. to recover estate from John Watson, executor of Israel Anderson, late of Buckingham Twp. bequeathed to their mother Hannah Brooks. Bk 4/pg 392   Oct 14, 1823

John Jacoby, guardian for Samuel and Susannah Jacoby, children of Peter Jacoby, late of Durham Twp, acknowledges payment of estate by administrators Benjamin Jacoby and Frederick Laubough.
                    Bk 4/pg 398   Apr 5, 1817

Henry Cope of Hilltown Twp, guardian of Elizabeth Senn, daughter of Jacob Senn, late of Rockhill Twp, acknowledges payment of estate by Caleb Foulke, administrator of former guardian Jacob Stout, late of Rockhill Twp.
Bk 4/pg 400   Apr 25, 1823

Henry Schwenk of Philadelphia, innkeeper, husband of late Elizabeth Trumbauer and guardian of Catharine, Anna, Hester, Rueben, Harriet and Ezra Schwenk, releases Henry Trumbauer from any obligations.
Bk 4/pg 401   Dec 8, 1823

John Smith acknowledges payment by Abraham Smith of money due under will of his father Robert Smith, late of Wrightstown Twp.
Bk 4/pg 402   Jan 15, 1800

Samuel Smith, late of Philadelphia, flour merchant, bequeathed in 1814 shares of stock to nephew Samuel Smith of Wrightstown Twp, subject to payment to Samuel Smith, son of Thomas Smith. The latter bequest was paid by Benjamin Smith of Buckingham Twp and Samuel Smith of Wrightstown gives Benjamin power of attorney to sell some of the stock to reimburse said payment.
Bk 4/pg 402   Nov 24, 1823

Samuel Smith received payment from Benjamin Smith of legacy from Samuel Smith, late of Philadelphia, flour merchant.   Bk 4/pg 403   Nov 24, 1823

Charles Gilbert of Buckingham Twp. assigns portion of estate from father Samuel Gilbert, late of Buckingham Twp. to Benjamin Walton of Solebury Twp. to pay debt.
Bk 4/pg 403   Dec 27, 1823

George Grubham of Falls Twp. is due considerable estate from his father George Grubham, late of Falls Twp, yeoman, but is subject to convulsion fits which frequently deprive him of memory and understanding, chooses David Heston of Falls Twp, yeoman, and John Kirkbride of Falls Twp, yeoman, to serve as his trustees.
Bk 4/pg 407   Jan 2, 1824

Eve Piper, widow of Col. George Piper, late of Bedminster Twp. acknowledges payment of estate by executors Joseph Piper and Jacob Kichline.
Bk 4/pg 408   Jan 6, 1824

Joel and Maria Carver of Northampton Twp, yeoman, inherited land from will of Joel Carver, deceased, but assigns this to Abraham Smith and John Chapman of Wrightstown Twp. in order to pay debts.
Bk 4/pg 410   Dec 30, 1823

Andrew Snider of Richland Twp, joiner, son of Andrew Snider, late of Richland Twp, acknowledges payment of estate by administrators Henry and George Snider.   Bk 4/pg 412   Apr 5, 1820

Phillip Stoneback of Nockamixon Twp, laborer, gives power of attorney to Jacob Deemer of Williams Twp, Northampton Co, merchant, to recover estate from George Afflebach, executor of Balser Stoneback, late of Haycock Twp, wheelwright.   Bk 4/pg 413   Jan 24, 1824

Peter Zigler of Hains Twp, Centre Co. gives power of attorney to brother Jacob Zigler of Limestone Twp, Columbia Co. to recover estate from late father, now in hands of his executors.   Bk 4/pg 423   Mar 23, 1824

Isaac and Mary Overholt of Plumstead Twp. agree with his brother Abraham on the division of the real estate bequeathed to them by their father Abraham Overholt, late of Plumstead Twp.   Bk 4/pg 424   May 1, 1814

Strickland Foster Jr. of Washington Twp, Burlington Co, NJ gives power of attorney to father Strickland Foster of Bristol Borough, M.D., to recover estate from grand-parents Mathew and Sarah Banes, late of Southampton Twp.   Bk 4/pg 428   Mar 27, 1824

Martha Blankenhorn of Bucks Co, sister of John Blankenhorn, late of Doylestown Twp, acknowledges payment of estate by executor Jonathan Large.   Bk 4/pg 433   Jan 28, 1824

Elizabeth Sees of Rockhill Twp, widow, previously gave power of attorney to John Benner of Rockhill Twp. to recover estate of late husband Jacob Sees. She now revokes that power of attorney.   Bk 4/pg 434   Apr 21, 1824

David Jackson of Bensalem Twp. gives power of attorney to Joseph Vandegrift of Bensalem to recover legacy from William T. Vandegrift, administrator of Philip Sipler, late of Bensalem. Bk 4/pg 434   Jan 3, 1824

John Johnson of Montgomery Co. and wife Mary, sister of John Blankenhorn, late of Doylestown Twp, acknowledge payment of estate by executor Jonathan Large.   Bk 4/pg 435   [blank], 1823

Jacob Clymer, Christian Clymer, Mary Clymer of Rockhill Twp, and George Landis of Haycock Twp (guardian of Elizabeth Leidy, late Clymer), heirs of Samuel Clymer, late of Rockhill Twp, acknowledge payment of estate by administrator John Clymer.   Bk 4/pg 435   Apr 8, 1823

Jacob and Samuel Filman and George and Ann Ziegenfus, children of John Fillman, late of Rockhill Twp, acknowledge payment of estate by executors John and Henry Filman.   Bk 4/pg 436   Feb 23, 1824

Rev. Samuel Stahr of Nockamixon Twp. and wife Catharine Anne sell to Isaac Kline of Milford Twp. land that Samuel was willed (along with brother Jacob) by his mother Susanna, widow of John Stahr, late of Milford Twp.
                                                    Bk 4/pg 437   Dec 28, 1821

Charles Leidy of Rockhill Twp. and wife Sarah (late Stout), Tobias Ruhl of Rockhill (guardian of Anna and Magdalena Stout), Frederic Althouse of Rockhill (guardian of Isaac, Abraham and Elizabeth Stout) and John Gerhart of Franconia Twp, Montgomery Co. (guardian of Jacob and Samuel Stout), children of Jacob Stout, late of Rockhill Twp, acknowledge payment of estate by administrators Henry Cope and Caleb Foulke.   Bk 4/pg 439   Apr 3, 1823

Godfrey Fishler of Springfield Twp. and wife Maria (late Younken), assign to Jacob Shank of Springfield their fourth part of a share of land in Springfield Twp. being part of property of Jessy Varity, late of Springfield.
                                                    Bk 4/pg 440   Jan 31, 1824

Andrew Long, Mary Vanhorn and Harman and Margret Yerks, children of Andrew Long, late of Warrington Twp. and Andrew Long Jr., George Harigan (married to Mary West), Sarah Long, Alexander R. Long, Jane Miller, Hugh S. Long, Ann Long and John Long (last two by guardian Andrew Long), children of late John Long who was a son of Andrew Long, William Hart, Samuel and Jane Craven, Solomon Hart, Andrew Hart and John and Elizabeth Craven, children of late Isabella Hart who was a daughter of Andrew Long acknowledge payment by Andrew's son William Long of dower due now that the widow Mary is deceased.   Bk 4/pg 444   Apr 1, 1822

Andrew Overpeck of Springfield Twp, yeoman, now 21, acknowledges payment by guardian Jacob Barron of estate due from father Andrew Overpeck.   Bk 4/pg 450   Sep 5, 1823

George Swinker of Haycock Twp. died intestate leaving widow Catharine and children George and Catharine. Son George received part of estate subject to dower right by widow Catharine (now Barnet). Son George of Haycock Twp, yeoman releases Martin Wack of Haycock, yeoman, and William Stokes of Haycock, yeoman for dower obligation.   Bk 4/pg 451   Feb 25, 1824

Jacob Kepley of Richland Twp, yeoman, gives power of attorney to son-in-law John Kichline of Richland, yeoman, to recover mortgage from Christian Smith.   Bk 4/pg 452   Mar 6, 1824

William Kealer Sen. of Bedminster Twp. gives power of attorney to son Jacob Kealer of same place to enter satisfaction of mortgage held against Henry Swartz of same place.   Bk 5/pg 1   Feb 23, 1824

Samuel Palmer and wife Anna of Falls Twp. sell right in land to Joseph Howell and Harvey Gillingham in order to settle debt of about $1550, the amount of store and Tavern licenses due from Samuel as late Treasurer of Bucks County to the state of Pennsylvania, as well as other of Samuel's debts.
                                          Bk 5/pg 2   Feb 28, 1824

Mary Kern, widow of Adam Kern, late of Hilltown Twp, and daughter of Henry Huber, late of Huntington Co, PA gives power of attorney to John Riel and Jacob Huber (both of Montgomery Co.) to settle estate of father.
                                          Bk 5/pg 4   Aug 24, 1824

Catherine Slutter of Salem Twp, Columbiana Co, OH, late of Bucks Co, widow of Christian Slutter of Bucks gives power of attorney to John Slutter of Bucks to sell land in New Britain that was part of estate of father John Wisler, deceased.   Bk 5/pg 5   Feb 9, 1824

Magdalena Myers gives power of attorney to Abraham Delp of Buckingham Twp. to file settlement of mortgage she held against Henry Grove and David Grove Jr.   Bk 5/pg 6   Apr 2, 1824

Robert McNeely and wife Martha of N. Liberties, Philadelphia Co, weaver sell land in Plumstead Twp. to James Davidson of Plumstead Twp, yeoman in order to settle debts. This land was inherited from Martha's parents Thomas and Margaret Henry.   Bk 5/pg 7   Apr 2, 1824

Charles and Ann Krusen, James and Elenor Krusen, Garret N. and Elizabeth Carver, Thomas and Charity Hart, John M. and Jane V. Craven, children and legatees in will of Derrick Krusen of Northampton Twp. appoint appraisers to divide the estate into five equal shares.   Bk 5/pg 8   Jan 22, 1824

Charles Krusen and wife Ann, James Krusen and wife Elinor, Garret N. Carver and wife Elizabeth (formerly Krusen), Thomas Hart and wife Charity (formerly Krusen) file release to John M. Craven and wife Jane (formerly Krusen) for Jane's share of father's estate.   Bk 5/pg 10   Mar 26, 1824

Stephen Woolston of Falls Twp. releases Joshua Woolston of same place from a judgment bond.   Bk 5/pg 11   Apr 5, 1824

Micha Seamen of Sandyston Twp, Sussex Co, NJ gives power of attorney to son Daniel Seamen of same place to sue Jacob Ruth and John Searfos, administrators of late Peter Knight. Daniel's wife Susannah was a daughter of Peter.   Bk 5/pg 13   Nov 1, 1823

Samuel Ashton of Bucks and David Davis and wife Sarah (late Ashton), children of late Peter Ashton of Springfield Twp, release Everard Roberts and Robert Ashton, Peter's administrators for receipt of their share of estate.
                     Bk 5/pp 13-14   Apr 8, 1824

George Seiple of Hilltown Twp and Conrad Harpel of Bedminster Twp, trustees of Lutheran Congregation formerly called Kichline's Church in Bedminster Twp release Conrad Snyder and Jacob High, executors of late Michael Snyder of Hilltown for receipt of legacy.   Bk 5/pg 14   Mar 22, 1824

Samuel Moyer, George Beringer, John Cramer and Daniel Housekeeper, trustees of Beringer's and Fretz's schoolhouse in Hilltown Twp. release Conrad Snider and Jacob High, executors of Michael Snider for receipt of legacy.   Bk 5/pg 15   Apr 21, 1824

John Martin, Michael Martin, Jacob Ruhl and wife Mary, and Catharine Martin, all of Richland Twp. children and legatees of Michael Martin, late of Richland Twp. release executors Peter Martin and Abraham Beihn for receipt of their legacies.   Bk 5/pg 15   Apr 3, 1824

John Brunner of Doylestown Twp sells right to mother's dower in father's estate to Thomas Stephens of same place in order to settle a debt.
                     Bk 5/pg 16   Apr 13, 1824

Johanna Corson, widow of Richard Corson the Elder, late of Solebury Twp releases dower right to John Bye and wife Hannah, only daughter of Richard and stepdaughter of Johanna. Only son Dr. Richard Corson previously released his right to his sister Hannah.   Bk 5/pg 16   Apr 14, 1824

Susanna Green, widow of Joseph Green, late of Bedminster Twp. releases executors Wm Neely and Andrew Wilson for receipt of legacy.
                     Bk 5/pg 17   Aug 2, 1823

103

Esther Richardson, Elizabeth Millard, Mary Doan and Aaron Doan, all of
Upper Canada and heirs of Esther Doan give power of attorney to their
brother Joseph Doan of Wallpole, Norfolk Co, London District, Upper
Canada to recover money from executors of Bridget Smith of whom Esther
was an heir.   Bk 5/pg 18   Jun 1, 1823

John Huber of Milford Twp. and wife Margaret, a daughter and legatee of late
Abraham Ditlow of Milford give power of attorney to Christian Huber of
Milford to sue executor David Ditlow for legacy that was due upon the death
of widow Hannah.   Bk 5/pg 23   Jan 1, 1824

Joshua Yardley, son of Hanna Yardley a daughter of late Edward
Baily/Bayley is due one-fourth part of a legacy upon his mother's death. He
sells right to this legacy to Jacob Janney to settle debts.
                                                Bk 5/pg 24   Apr 29, 1819

Henry Ruhl, surviving administrator of will of Michael Hillegas, Esq., late of
Philadelphia gives power of attorney to Benjamin Wright and Stephen
Woolston to file settlement of mortgage from Charles Patterson to George
Stockham.   Bk 5/pg 26   Apr 2, 1824

Mary Paxson, Mercy Paxson and Amy Worthington, all of Solebury Twp,
give power of attorney to nephew Joseph Wilkinson of Solebury to recover
money from James Hambleton of Dunmore Twp, Lancaster Co.
                                                Bk 5/pg 26   Sep 8, 1824

William Cooper of Clerk Co, IL gives power of attorney to Cadwallader
Cooper of same place but currently of Montgomery Co, PA to settle estate of
Mary Cooper, late of Montgomery Co.   Bk 5/pg 27   Jun 17, 1824

Henry Johnson holds bond from brother Benjamin Johnson for payment upon
death of Hannah Johnson, widow of Henry Johnson, late of Richland Twp.
He assigns interest to George W. Coulston of Philadelphia to settle debt.
                                                Bk 5/pg 28   Jul 10, 1824

George Swinker, late of Haycock Twp died intestate leaving widow Catherine
(now Barnet) and two children: George and Catherine. George Jr. of
Haycock, yeoman is due part of dower upon death of his mother. George Jr.
files release to John Matts of Richland Twp. for payment of part of dower.
                                                Bk 5/pg 29   Feb 25, 1824

William Wharton, David Palmer and wife Mary, Phineas Wharton, Ann Wharton and Phebe Wharton, all of Lower Makefield Twp. Their father William Wharton Sr., late of same place devised land to son Johnson Wharton but without title. Other heirs file to perfect title. Bk 5/pg 30 Apr 13, 1824

Charles Krusen and wife Ann, James Krusen and wife Eleanor, John M. Craven and wife Jane, and Thomas Hart and wife Charity acknowledge right of Garret V. Carver and his wife Elizabeth (formerly Krusen) to her share in their father's estate.   Bk 5/pg 33 Mar 26, 1824

William Wharton and wife Elizabeth, David Palmer and wife Mary, Phineas Wharton, Ann Wharton and Johnson Wharton, all of Lower Makefield file to perfect title in land bequeathed by father William Wharton Sr. to their sister Phebe Wharton.   Bk 5/pg 35 Apr 13, 1824

Joseph Hicks, Gilbert Hicks, Isaiah Hicks, William Hicks, Jacob Woolsey and wife Elizabeth, Elias Slack and wife Mary, children of Joseph (deceased) and Margaret Hicks of Upper Makefield Twp. They and their brother Charles Hicks and Joshua Knight (guardian for children of their sister Margaret Corlile) are due money upon the death of their mother Margaret.
                                   Bk 5/pg 36 Apr 22, 1822

Henry Eckel of Lower Saucon Twp, Northampton Co. gives power of attorney to John Eckel of Bedminster Twp to sue for money due from Andrew Loux of Bedminster.   Bk 5/pg 39 May 10, 1824

Moses Rich of Buckingham Twp. gives right to mother Mary Rich of the same place to live in the building where they now live until the time of her death.   Bk 5/pg 40 May 7, 1824

Samuel Yost, minor son of late Michael Yost, is now 21 and releases his guardian Benjamin Jacoby for payment of Samuel's share in the estate of his grandparents John and Barbara Fulmer as well as share in his father's estate.
                                   Bk 5/pg 41 Apr 13, 1824

Enos Randal and wife Mary, Jacob Randal and wife Susan, George Rampson and wife Ann, Jonathan Randal, Jesse Randal, Eliza Randal and Mary Randal, heirs of late Jacob Randal of Middletown Twp who died intestate. Widow Elizabeth since married to Jonathan Ring, late of same place, but is now deceased. Heirs release George Harrison for payment of dower.
                                   Bk 5/pg 41 Dec 10, 1823

Trustees of New Britain Baptist Church file release to Rev. Thomas B. Montayne and Rev. Joseph Mathias, executors of Dr. Silas Hough for payment of money held in trust by Dr. Hough from the estate of John N. Thomas, M.D., upon agreement with Silas' widow Elizabeth.

Bk 5/pg 44   Apr 10, 1824

Sarah Powers of Philadelphia, Jonathan Livezey of Warwick Twp. and wife Euphamia (late Powers), Maria Powers of Northampton Twp, and Ann Powers of Warwick Twp. (single woman) give power of attorney to friend Col. John Davis of Southampton Twp. to obtain their shares in estate of father William Powers, late of Southampton Twp. from executors of Harman Vansant, Esq. who was their guardian.

Bk 5/pg 46-49   Jun 19, 1824, Apr 14, 1824, May 1, 1824, Jun 10, 1824

George Cole and Jacob Cole, both of Plumstead Twp, yeoman, two of the sons of George Cole, late of same place, yeoman promise to widow Catharine Cole and John and Nicholas Cole, two other sons, and Elizabeth Cole, Catharine Gordon and Mary Cole, three daughters to accept their father's estate and pay for same to the other heirs.   Bk 5/pg 50   Feb 3, 1810

Ann Showaker of Germantown, Philadelphia, widow of Jacob Shewaker, late of Bedminster Twp. who died intestate and without issue. Ann releases Barnet Heller for payment for real estate intended to be purchased during life of Jacob.   Bk 5/pg 51   Apr 20, 1819

William McNeely and Andrew Wilson, executors of late Joseph Greer of Bedminster Twp appoint appraisers for Joseph's real estate as his widow Susanna is now also deceased.   Bk 5/pg 58   Dec 30, 1823

John Mann, guardian of James G. Wilson, one of the grandsons of Joseph Greer, agrees to take the real estate of Joseph at the valuation declared by the appraisers.   Bk 5/pg 59   Dec 30, 1823

Harman Vansant, Esq. was named guardian to Ann, Maria, Euphemia, Sarah, Elizabeth and Rachel Powers. The first four have given power of attorney to Col. John Davis who releases Alice Vansant and James Vansant, executors of Harman, for payment of the money due to the Powers heirs.

Bk 5/pg 60   Jun 24, 1824

Heirs of John Landis, late of Rockhill Twp. (Elizabeth Landis—widow[?], Henry and Susanna Derstein, Abraham Landis, Samuel Landis, John and Ladavina[?] Stauffer, and Samuel Gahman—administrator of Jacob Landis) agree to adjust value of lands bequeathed by John to sons Abraham, Jacob and Samuel.   Bk 5/pg 60   Oct 20, 1823

Peter Heft, William Heft, George Heft, Daniel Heft, Margaret Heft and Henry Heft, children and legatees of Peter Heft, late of Haycock Twp release executors Henry Heft and George Sheive for payment of their shares of estate.
                                        Bk 5/pg 61-62   Jul 19, 1806

Thomas R. Swift and wife Ann P. of Norfolk Co, VA give power of attorney to Aquilla A. Brown of Philadelphia to sell land in Pennsbury Manor, Falls Twp.   Bk 5/pg 64   Mar 5, 1824

A.E. Large of New Brunswick, Middlesex Co, NJ gives power of attorney to Samuel Large of Bucks to settle share in estate of mother Rachel Large who died about Oct 1, 1823.   Bk 5/pg 65   Aug 17, 1824

Huldah Anderson, widow of Daniel Anderson of Lower Makefield Twp. releases dower right to Andrew Smith and his wife Rachel.
                                        Bk 5/pg 67   [blank], 1824

Jacob Gross of East Huntington Twp, Westmoreland Co, PA sells to Andrew Shadinger of Plumstead Twp all right to estate of late father Daniel Gross of Plumstead.   Bk 5/pg 70   Sep 15, 1824

John George Long of Marlborough Twp, Montgomery Co. died intestate leaving widow and three children: Jacob, Margarade Long, George. Son George of Trumbauersville gives power of attorney to John Mumbauer to pursue his share of the dower upon the death of widow Anna Mary.
                                        Bk 5/pg 72   Jun 5, 1824

Martin Fretz, surviving executor of late Joseph Fretz of Haycock releases Conrad Harpel, administrator of late Abraham Slutter of Haycock for payment for land and fulling mill.   Bk 5/pg 73   Apr 3, 1823

Henrietta, widow of Leopold Nottnagle, has dower right payable by John Newbold of Bristol Twp to Louis Leopold Nottnagle, William Godfried Nottnagle, Lisetti Julie Nottnagle and Bernard Wykoff Nottnagle upon Henrietta's death. Henrietta (now Disborough) sells part of dower right to Jacob L. Walton of Bristol Twp.   Bk 5/pg 75   Nov 6, 1824

John Dice of Rockhill Twp, stonemason, and wife Elizabeth, one of the daughters of George Cressman, late of Franconia Twp, Montgomery Co. sell

her share to Philip Dise of Rockhill, said share now in hands of executors
George Cressman and Michael Snyder.   Bk 5/pg 76   Apr 10, 1821

William Young of Northampton County, farmer, legatee of Michael Young,
late of Philadelphia Co. gives power of attorney to Samuel Ziegler of
Philadelphia, innkeeper.   Bk 5/pg 76   Oct 30, 1824

David Vansant (son of Gabriel) and sister Letitia (wife of William
Alexander), both of Liberty Twp, Columbia Co, PA are legatees of late Isaiah
Vansant of Lower Makefield Twp. who bequeathed estate to son Gabriel who
lately died leaving five daughters and two sons. David and Letitia sell their
shares to brother Amos Vansant (eldest son of Gabriel) of Lower Makefield.
     Bk 5/pg 77   Nov 25, 1824

Christopher Bloom of Bedminster Twp, saddler, and wife Catharine (late Ott),
daughter and legatee of late Peter Ott of Bedminster Twp, sell her share to
Samuel A. Smith of Rockhill Twp.   Bk 5/pg 78   May 21, 1824

Henry Kramer of Salsburg Twp, Lehigh Co. gives power of attorney to
Michael Kulp of Bedminster Twp. to recover money from John Wearts,
administrator of [blank] Anderson.   Bk 5/pg 82   Jan 31, 1824

Ann, wife of Frederick Hartman of Franklin Co, IN gives power of attorney to
friend John Williams of Tinicum Twp. to sign deeds that her husband may
have made regarding land in Nockamixon Twp. Bk 5/pg 83   Dec 8, 1823

Charles Krusen and wife Ann, James Krusen and wife Eliner, Garret V.
Carver and wife Elizabeth and John M. Craven and wife Jane acknowledge
share of sister Charity (wife of Thomas Hart) in estate of father Derrick
Krusen, late of Northampton Twp.   Bk 5/pg 84   Mar 26, 1824

John Lay of Haycock Twp. and wife Elizabeth, daughter of Henry Nase, late
of Rockhill Twp, give power of attorney to friend Morgan Custard of
Haycock Twp. to recover share of estate in hands of her brother Frederick
Nase.   Bk 5/pg 86   Dec 20, 1824

Christian Young, executor of late Michael Young of Philadelphia gives power
of attorney to Jacob Stover and George Mast to sell land of Michael Young in
Bedminster and Haycock Twp.   Bk 5/pg 92   Jan 11, 1825

Charles Krusen and wife Ann, Garret P. Carver and wife Elizabeth, Thomas
Hart and wife Charity, and John M. Craven and wife Jane acknowledge share

of brother James Krusen and wife Eleanor in estate of father Derrick Krusen, late of Northampton Twp.   Bk 5/pg 93   Mar 26, 1824

Catharine Kuter of Milford Twp. gives power of attorney to friend David Spinner, Esq. of Milford to recover dower in the estate of late husband Peter Kuter, now in hands of George Bruch or George Mumbower.
                                                Bk 5/pg 94   Jan 22, 1825

Philip Leatherman, Henry Leatherman and Jacob Leatherman of Bedminster Twp. and John Leatherman of Plumstead Twp. agree to divide the real estate left them by the will of Abraham Leatherman, late of Bedminster.
                                                Bk 5/pg 96   May 3, 1824

Elizabeth Buttemore, widow of Jacob Buttemore of Connellsville Twp, Fayette Co. gives power of attorney to Andrew Stillwaggon of same place to recover money from estate of her father Andrew Zagefuse which had been in hands of executors Michael and Peter Sagefuse, both of whom are now deceased.   Bk 5/pg 97   Nov 25, 1824

Anthony Schlotter of Bedminster died intestate leaving two children: Magdalene (wife of Henry Kilmer) and Anthony. Henry and Magdalena of Tinicum Twp. release Anthony for payment of her share of estate.
                                                Bk 5/pg 102   Jul 24, 1816

Solomon Leibgabp of Nockamixon Twp. gives power of attorney to son John of Durham Twp. to collect moneys due yearly from William Schaeffer of Saucon Twp, Northampton Co.   Bk 5/pg 104   Nov 27, 1824

Benjamin Jones of Warminster Twp and Samuel Daniels of Southampton Twp. give power of attorney to friend Henry Miller, Esq. of Nockamixon Twp. to sell land formerly belonging to Alexander McElroy in Nockamixon Twp.   Bk 5/pg 105   Jan 14, 1825

Richard Mather of Warren Co, OH assigns to his brother Joseph T. Mather of Philadelphia (but now in Cincinatti, OH) his share of father Benjamin Mather's (late of Montgomery Co.) estate which is due from brother Jonathan Mather.   Bk 5/pg 105   Jan 22, 1823

Robert Hanna Jr., Henry Hartman and Ann Hartman, administrators of Frederick Hartman (late of Franklin Co, IN) give power of attorney to John Williams of Bucks Co. to collect money due from Mordecai Roberts and John Houseworth.   Bk 5/pg 106   Jan 14, 1825

Joseph Ratzel of Hilltown Twp. and wife Mary assign property to Abraham Jacoby and Isaac Godshalk in order to pay debts.   Bk 5/pg 108   Feb 5, 1825

Cassandra Anderson acknowledges receipt of her legacy from will of her father Joshua Anderson (late of Buckingham Twp) from executor Joseph Anderson.   Bk 5/pg 109   Dec 8, 1824

James Kirk of Buckingham Twp. and wife Letitia (late Anderson) acknowledge receipt of legacy from will of her father Joshua Anderson paid by executor Joseph Anderson.   Bk 5/pg 110   Apr 1, 1824

Mary Oliver, executrix of John Oliver (late of Bordentown, NJ) gives power of attorney to Thomas Cooper of Falls to file settlement of a mortgage paid by William Moore.   Bk 5/pg 110   Feb 9, 1825

Mary Black of Springfield Twp. acknowledges receipt of payment by Jacob Kooker, Esq., administrator of John Black, late of Springfield Twp.   Bk 5/pg 111   Jan 1, 1825

Benjamin J. Houghton assigns to Thomas Montayne of Southampton Twp. money which is due from estate of his late father-in-law Joseph Harvey.   Bk 5/pg 111   Jan 1, 1825

Pierson Mitchell gives power of attorney to son J. Allen Mitchell of Middletown Twp. to file settlement of a mortgage from John Reed.   Bk 5/pg 112   Feb 28, 1825

Henry Pearson of Springfield Twp. and wife Sarah (late Overpeck), daughter and legatee of Andrew Overpeck (late of Springfield Twp) acknowledge payment of legacy by executor Jacob Overpeck.   Bk 5/pg 112   Mar 27, 1822

Mary Swartslander of Doylestown Twp, daughter of Andrew Overpeck receives payment from executor Jacob Overpeck.   Bk 5/pg 113   Mar 5, 1825

John Claxton of Philadelphia, merchant, and William Bethell of Philadelphia, merchant, executors of Robert Bethell, late of Falls Twp. give power of attorney to Robert Bethell of Doylestown (William's son) to recover any moneys due them.   Bk 5/pg 113   Mar 10, 1825

John Gillingham Jr. of Buckingham Twp. assigns to John Jones, administrator of Ann Gillingham, all right to share of his mother Ann's estate.   Bk 5/pg 114   Mar 14, 1825

Amy Worthington of Solebury Twp, widow, gives power of attorney to Jacob Balderson of Morgan Co, OH to buy land there for son Mahlon Worthington.
Bk 5/pg 115   Mar 19, 1825

Harrison Erwin Weaver, minor son of late Christian Weaver of Tinicum Twp, now age 21, releases his guardian Isaac Weaver.
Bk 5/pg 115   Mar 21, 1825

Henry Moll of Upper Salford Twp, Montgomery Co, taylor, and wife Elizabeth assign property to Joseph Miller of Lower Milford Twp, Bucks Co, yeoman, for payment of debts.   Bk 5/pg 116   Apr 13, 1825

Phineas Kelly of Buckingham Twp. assigns share of dower in estate of George Kelly due from James Simpson upon death of Phineas' mother to William Cathers, Isaac Scarborough and John Pearson for payment of debts.
Bk 5/pg 119   Apr 29, 1820

Joseph Wolf of Rockhill Twp. and wife Elizabeth assign property to Christian Neas and Abraham Heaney, Esq., both of Salford Twp, Montgomery Co. for payment of debts.   Bk 5/pg 119   May 9, 1825

Samuel Moon and Joseph Burges, both of Falls Twp, yeoman, assign real estate to trustees of Falls Monthly Meeting.   Bk 5/pg 121   Mar 7, 1825

Amy Worthington of Solebury Twp, widow, gives power of attorney to friend Jesse John, Esq. of Blue Rock, Meshkingum Co, OH to purchase land for son Mahlon Worthington.   Bk 5/pg 126   Jun 24, 1825

Hannah Austen of Philadelphia, daughter of late John Smith of Bucks Co. gives power of attorney to brother Daniel Smith of Bucks to recover money due from brother James Smith.   Bk 5/pg 129   Apr 6, 1825

William Swope of Plumstead Twp, guardian of Elizabeth Wildonger, minor child of Leonard Wildonger of Plumstead Twp, releases former guardian George Fox of Bedminster Twp.   Bk 5/pg 130   Feb 25, 1825

William Swope of Plumstead twp, guardian of Samuel, Mary, Catharine and Elizabeth, minor children of late Leonard Wildonger, acknowledges receipt of legacy from Abraham Wyker, executor of Mary Trauger.
Bk 5/pg 131   Feb 25, 1825

Martha Carver of Solebury Twp, daughter and legatee of Elizabeth Addis, late of Northampton Twp. acknowledges receipt of legacy from executor Richard Duffield. Bk 5/pg 131 Feb 23, 1825

Peter Hardy and wife Hannah (widow of Christopher Weaver of Tinicum Twp) and Harrison E. Weaver, only son of Christopher, acknowledge receipt of dower from John, Moses and William Weaver, executors of late Jacob Weaver who was administrator for Christopher. Bk 5/pg 132 Apr 5, 1825

Walter Thomas of Union Twp, Clearmount Co, OH and George Leidy, administrator of Elizabeth Thomas, acknowledge receipt from John Miller for payment of dower of Elizabeth who was Walter's mother. Bk 5/pg 133 Jul 20, 1822

John Reasner of Nockamixon Twp, husband of Catharine (widow of Abraham Nicholas of Tinicum Twp) releases Michael Shitz of Nockamixon Twp. for payment of Catharine's dower. Bk 5/pg 133 Apr 23, 1825

Jacob Frank of Upper Salford Twp, Montgomery Co, weaver, and wife Polly, daughter of Frederick Dill of Rockhill Twp. who died intestate leaving widow and children, give power of attorney to John Donahour of Marlboro Twp, Montgomery Co, yeoman, to recover Polly's share from brother Jacob Dill. Bk 5/pg 135 Apr 13, 1825

William Cope of Rockhill Twp. and wife Mary assign right to one-ninth of dower of late Henry Hartzel upon death of widow Susanna (Mary's mother) to Thomas Cope of Hilltown for payment of debts. Bk 5/pg 137 Apr 23, 1825

Margaretta Lombeart of Morrisville Borough gives various items to John W. Wynkoop of Newtown in trust for Margaretta's daughter Mary Ann (wife of Peter Gwinner). Bk 5/pg 137 Jan 12, 1825

Henry Stover of Springfield Twp, guardian for minor children of Jacob Stover (late of Haycock Twp) acknowledge payment from Christian Fretz, administrator of John Fretz who was also testamentary guardian for Jacob Stover's children. Bk 5/pg 138 Apr 16, 1825

Barbara Kolb, widow of Dillman Kolb of Toamensen Twp, Montgomery Co, daughter and legatee of Hubert Cassel of Hilltown Twp. acknowledges payment from brother Isaac Cassel. Bk 5/pg 139 Apr 9, 1825

Abraham Heany of Upper Salford Twp, Montgomery Co, administrator of George Loh, formerly of Marlborough Twp, Montgomery Co but late of Kingsington, Philadelphia Co. who died intestate and George's widow Christina acknowledge receipt of payment by William Edwards and Caleb Foulke, both of Richland Twp, for the balance of money they obtained to pay the debts of George and Christina Loh.   Bk 5/pg 141   Dec 17, 1824

John Bewighouse of Bedminster Twp, lately married to Esther Leatherman, minor daughter of Christian Leatherman (late of Bedminster Twp) releases Esther's guardian Joseph Landis of Bedminster Twp.
                                        Bk 5/pg 142   Apr 4, 1825

Christopher Bloom and wife Catharine, daughter of Catharine Ott who was a daughter of John Heany Sr. of Rockhill Twp. acknowledge payment by John Heaney Jr. (eldest son of John Sr.) for Catharine's share of estate.
                                        Bk 5/pg 143   Sep 15, 1808

Adam Loux of Haycock Twp. and wife Elizabeth, heir of John Heany of Rockhill Twp. acknowledge payment by administrator John Heany of Rockhill Twp, miller.   Bk 5/pg 143   Aug 13, 1810

Henry Loux of Winsor Twp, York Co, PA acknowledges payment by John Heany of Rockhill Twp. (eldest son of late John Heany who died intestate) of share of late wife Barbara, daughter of John Heany Sr.
                                        Bk 5/pg 144   Feb 10, 1800

Jacob Sallade Jr. of Bedminster Twp and wife Esther, daughter of late John Heany of Rockhill Twp. acknowledge payment by John Heany, her surviving guardian.   Bk 5/pg 144   Apr 24, 1802

John Krouthamel of Bedminster Twp. and wife Catharine, daughter of Elizabeth Saleday late of Rockhill Twp. release Catharine's guardian John Heany.   Bk 5/pg 145   Apr 1, 1801

Jacob Heany of Rockhill Twp, son of late John Heany of Rockhill, acknowledges payment by brother John.   Bk 5/pg 145   Apr 30, 1825

Emanuel Saleday of Bedminster Twp. and wife Magdalena, daughter of late John Heany of Rockhill Twp. acknowledge payment by brother John Heany.
                                        Bk 5/pg 146   Aug 9, 1814

Philip Stine and wife Susanna, daughter of late John Heany of Rockhill Twp, and John Beaver (Susanna's son by former husband), all of Rockland Twp, Berks Co, acknowledge payment by John Heany, Jr.

Bk 5/pg 147   Jun 4, 1792

Henry Pearson of Springfield Twp. and wife Sarah, daughter and legatee of Andrew Overpeck (late of Springfield Twp) acknowledge payment by Andrew Overpeck Jr.   Bk 5/pg 148   Mar 26, 1825

Mary Swartslander of Doylestown Twp, daughter and legate of Andrew Overpeck (late of Springfield Twp) acknowledges payment by Andrew Overpeck Jr.   Bk 5/pg 149   May 30, 1825

Michael Yost of Upper Hanover Twp, Northampton Co, son of Catharine Yost (late Fulmer), daughter of Barbara Fulmer (late of Rockhill Twp), Abraham Zeigenfuss of Haycock Twp and wife Catharine (daughter of late Catharine Yost), and Benjamin Jacoby of Haycock Twp, guardian of Samuel Yost (son of late Catharine Yost) acknowledge payment by John Groff, administrator of Barbara Fulmer.   Bk 5/pg 149   Nov 24, 1821

Henry Groff and John Kern, guardians of minor children of John Fulmer (late of Springfield Twp), son of Barbara Fulmer, late of Rockhill Twp. acknowledge payment by John Groff, Barbara's administrator.

Bk 5/pg 150   Nov 24, 1821

Esther and Susannah Gross acknowledge payment by Samuel Wismer, executor of Sarah Gross, late of Plumstead Twp.   Bk 5/pg 151   Apr 8, 1825

Margaret Shaffer of Haycock Twp, widow of John Shaffer and daughter and legatee of Michael Young of Northern Liberties Twp, Philadelphia Co, gentleman, gives power of attorney to friend George Smith of Haycock Twp, yeoman, to recover money from executor Christian Young.

Bk 5/pg 152   Apr 1, 1825

Jesse C. Barnes, son of Elizabeth Mosser who was a daughter of late William Barnes of Warminster Twp. acknowledges payment by William's executors Samuel Hart and Robert Ramsey.   Bk 5/pg 153   Jun 2, 1825

Mary Bye, Martha Bye and Sarah Bye of Buckingham Twp pledge their property to each other upon death.   Bk 5/pg 153   May 1, 1810

Thomas Bye, father of late Martha Bye, releases Martha's estate to daughters Mary and Sarah Bye.   Bk 5/pg 153   Feb 28, 1820

Mary Hillpot, widow of John Hillpot (late of Tinicum Twp) and Margaret Tice, daughter and legatee of John agree with John D. Hillpot, son of John to pay part of Margaret's legacy to widow Mary.   Bk 5/pg 154   Jun 17, 1825

Samuel Berger of Springfield Twp. and wife Mary, Jacob Treichler of Richland Twp, John Beidler of Milford Twp. and wife Ann, Samuel Treichler of Richland Twp, Henry Trumbower of Richland Twp and wife Sarah, and Samuel Ritter of Springfield Twp and wife Elizabeth, children of John Treichler (late of Richland Twp) acknowledge payment by brother John Treichler of Richland Twp.   Bk 5/pg 156   Jun 18, 1825

Enoch Edwards, late of Richland Twp but now of Munery[?] Twp, Lycoming Co, PA, yeoman, releases Caleb Foulke and John G. Griffith and on behalf of late Abel Penrose, for payment of balance of money available after they had paid Enoch's debts.   Bk 5/pg 158   May 26, 1825

Henry Koons and wife Mary of Berks Co. release Henry Trumbower for any claims they may have against him.   Bk 5/pg 159   May 9, 1825

Daniel Nicholas and wife Christiana of Bedminster Twp. give power of attorney to Peter Shive of Bedminster Twp. to recover money from Abraham Cover, administrator of Elizabeth Cover of Rockhill Twp.
                    Bk 5/pg 161   Jun 20, 1825

Abraham Grose of Wayne Co, OH gives power of attorney to David Funk of East Huntingdon Twp, Westmoreland Co, PA to receive money from Isaac Grose and Henry Wismer, administrators of father Daniel Grose.
                    Bk 5/pg 162   May 6, 1825

George Shitz of Rockhill Twp, yeoman, and wife Machdalena (late Carl) release her guardian George Nese for payment of her share of estate of grandfather John Carl of Bedminster Twp.   Bk 5/pg 163   Sep 10, 1825

William Wharton and wife Elizabeth, David Palmer and wife Mary, Phineas Wharton, Johnson Wharton and Phebe Wharton, all of Lower Makefield Twp, children of William Wharton Sen., late of Lower Makefield release to sister Ann Wharton the property devised to her in father's will.
                    Bk 5/pg 163   Apr 13, 1824

Samuel Humphreys, grandson of Mathew Hughes (late of Plumstead Twp) assigns to Isaac Closson of Tinicum Twp one-third part of one-fourth part of land in Plumstead Twp willed to Mathew's daughter Jane Hughes.

Bk 5/pg 166   Sep 19, 1825

Stephen Simmons, guardian of Benjamin Cooper's children, gives power of attorney to Enos Morris, Esq. to record satisfaction of a mortgage paid by John Hulme which was held by James Cooper (Benjamin's father).

Bk 5/pg 166   Jul 14, 1825

Anna Bergstrasser of Tinicum Twp, widow, gives power of attorney to son Philip of Alexandria Twp, Hunterdon Co, NJ, yeoman, except power already given to son Frederic to collect a legacy from her father's estate.

Bk 5/pg 167   May 21, 1825

John Kirkbride and wife Ann Eliza (late Gregg) of Philadelphia agree to sell to Nathaniel Walton of Bucks County land in Bristol Borough due Ann Eliza from her father's estate.   Bk 5/pg 169   Nov 7, 1825

Joseph Michener, Londongrove Twp, Chester Co, son of William and Martha Michener, late of Plumstead Twp. gives power of attorney to friend Francis Good of New London Twp, Chester Co. to recover his share of dower.

Bk 5/pg 170   Nov 30, 1825

Elleanor Field and Peninnah Hayhurst of Cattawissa Twp, Columbia Co, PA and Phebe Gearhart of Bloom Twp, Columbia Co, daughters of late Robert Field and late wife Priscilla (formerly Roberts), who was a daughter of Abraham Roberts, give power of attorney to Bezaleel Hayhurst of Cattawissa.

Bk 5/pg 172   Jul 26, 1824

Henry Cope of Hilltown Twp, guardian of David Ertman (now compas mentis), son of late Yost Ertman of Hilltown Twp, acknowledge payment by George Leidy and Conrad Snyder, executors of Yost Ertman.

Bk 5/pg 174   Oct 29, 1825

Isaac Mill and wife Mary, daughter of late Daniel Aflebough of Haycock (who died intestate), sell Mary's share to Elizabeth Afleboch.

Bk 5/pg 175   Dec 21, 1825

George Shelmire Sen. of Moreland Twp, Montgomery Co. gives power of attorney to son George A. Shelmire to recover money due from Peter

Bartleson of Bucks, farmer, and to settle any matters with Thomas and John Longstreth, administrators of Thomas Longstreth of Moreland Twp.
Bk 5/pg 176   Dec 26, 1825

Mary Mathias of Hilltown Twp. releases her guardians John and Joseph Mathias for payment of estate from father Thomas Mathias and grandfather John Mathias.   Bk 5/pg 177   Dec 22, 1825

Hannah Rhoads of Philadelphia, widow, gives power of attorney to Thomas Rhoads of Philadelphia.   Bk 5/pg 178   Dec 20, 1823

Lester Rich of Hilltown Twp, cabinet maker, gives power of attorney to sister Levina Hickscock of Westhaven Twp, Rutland Co, VT to sell land in Bristol Twp, Hartford Co, CT.   Bk 5/pg 178   Jan 27, 1826

Christian Snyder, Jacob Hoche and wife Catharine and Frederick Shull and wife Hannah acknowledge payment from Conrad Snyder, executor of Michael Snyder, late of Hilltown Twp. Children of late Jacob Snyder: George, Michael, John L. Shellenberger and wife Catharine, William Swenk (guardian of Enos and Elizabeth Snyder) and Abraham Jacoby (guardian of Elias and Christian Snyder) provide similar release.   Bk 5/pg 180   Apr 23, 1825

Henry Garber of Rockhill Twp, yeoman and wife Christina, daughter and legatee of Henry Neas of Rockhill, acknowledge payment by administrator Fredrick Neas.   Bk 5/pg 180   Jan 28, 1826

Mary Walmsley of Brandywine Hundred, New Castle Co, DE gives power of attorney to Josiah D. Banes of Byberry Twp, Philadelphia Co. to sell land in Southampton Twp.   Bk 5/pg 181   Jan 30, 1826

Barbara Fisher, spinster, and William Ott and wife Catharine (late Fisher), daughters of John Fisher, late of Rockhill Twp, release guardian George Nase.
Bk 5/pg 182   Feb 7, 1826

John Keen of Bensalem Twp. gives power of attorney to son Samuel of Bensalem.   Bk 5/pg 183   Dec 14, 1825

Sebasten Horn, Barbara Horn (wife of Sebasten Brong), Seble Horn (wife of Michael Crowman) and Mary Horn, children and legatees of Sebastin Horn, late of Richland Twp. acknowledge payment by executor Daniel Horn.
Bk 5/pg 184   Apr 12, 1816

Jacob L. Walton and wife Lisette Julia (late Nottnagle) assign to Samuel Badger, Esq. of Philadelphia the right to dower of mother Henrietta, widow of Leopold Nottnagle.   Bk 5/pg 184   Jul 27, 1822

Isaac Black, minor son of late Abraham Black of Bedminster Twp, having arrived at age 21 releases his guardian Henry Rosenberger of Hilltown Twp.
Bk 5/pg 186   May 22, 1820

Abraham Landes, son and legatee of John Landes of Rockhill Twp, acknowledges payment by executrix Elizabeth Landes and payment by Samuel Landes and Samuel Gehman, administrators of Jacob Landes, late of Rockhill, the said Samuel and Jacob being two other sons of John Landes.
Bk 5/pg 186   May 15, 1824

Samuel Landes of Rockhill Twp, son and legatee of John Landes of Rockhill Twp, acknowledges payment by executrix Elizabeth Landes and by Abraham Landes and Samuel Gehman, administrators of Jacob Landes, late of Rockhill, the said Abraham and Jacob being two other sons of John Landes.
Bk 5/pg 187   May 15, 1824

Samuel Gehman and Mary (late Landes, now the wife of Jacob Schwink), administrators of Jacob Landes, late of Rockhill Twp who died intestate acknowledge receipt from Elizabeth Landes, executrix of John Landes of Rockhill Twp, and from Abraham and Samuel Landes, two sons of John.
Bk 5/pg 188   May 15, 1824

Joseph Cary of Rochester, NY but late of Buckingham Twp. assigns to Isaiah Jones of Buckingham Twp. a note received from his father Thomas Cary in order to pay debts.   Bk 5/pg 188   Feb 7, 1826

John Neimond of Greenwood Twp, Mifflin Co, PA gives power of attorney to friend John Moyers of Haycock Twp. to recover from Henry Amey and [blank] Jones, Esq., executors of John's mother.   Bk 5/pg 189   May 22, 1823

Peter Smith of Springfield Twp, cordwainer and wife Elizabeth, daughter of late Stephen Horne of Richland Twp, yeoman, acknowledge payment by James Bryan of Springfield Twp, yeoman, for dower of widow Mary.
Bk 5/pg 190   Apr 8, 1825

Abraham Stover, surviving executor of Ralph Stover, late of Bedminster Twp, releases William Stover of Bedminster for any debts that might be due.
Bk 5/pg 191   [blank] 1826

Elizabeth Moss (alias Barnes) of Warminster Twp, daughter of legatee of William Barnes, late of Warminster gives power of attorney to John H. Hill of Moreland Twp, Montgomery Co. to recover estate from executors Samuel Hart and Robert Ramsey.   Bk 5/pg 192   Jan 25, 1826

Mahlon Atkinson, late of Byberry, Philadelphia Co. but now of Lancaster Co. gives power of attorney to brother-in-law Francis Mahan of Newtown to collect any moneys due.   Bk 5/pg 197   Jan 27, 1821

Jonathan Leedom, eldest son of late Benjamin Leedom, and Rebecca Leedom, Anna Leedom and Sarah Leedom, daughters of Benjamin, all heirs of Richard Leedom, late of Bucks Co, give power of attorney to Jacob Sommer of Moreland Twp, Philadelphia Co. to accept Richard's land.
                    Bk 5/pg 197   Mar 14, 1826

John Klein of Upper Milford Twp, Lehigh Co, yeoman, gives power of attorney to William Dillinger of Upper Milford, yeoman, to recover money due from estate of mother Barbara (wife of George Klein) who was daughter and legatee of Michael Bishop of Lower Milford Twp, Bucks Co.
                    Bk 5/pg 200   Apr 10, 1826

Solomon Nese of Nockamixon Twp and wife Lydia (late Fisher) acknowledge payment by her guardian Henry Nese for estate from father John Fisher, late of Rockhill Twp.   Bk 5/pg 204   Apr 6, 1826

Henry Funk of Springfield Twp, now 21, releases guardian Jacob Funk for payment of estate from late father Henry Funk.   Bk 5/pg 204   Oct 5, 1825

John W. Gooken of Warrington Twp, laborer, son of late Henry W. Gooken and his wife Elizabeth (daughter and legatee of John Vandike) releases to William Walker (who is another son of Elizabeth) and claim to land devised to Elizabeth.   Bk 5/pg 205   Apr 14, 1826

Jacob Nese of Rockhill Twp. acknowledges payment by guardian Abraham Heany for estate from late father Abraham of Rockhill Twp.
                    Bk 5/pg 207   Feb 9, 1826

Solomon Seider of Upper Saucon Twp, Lehigh Co, yeoman, and wife Mary (late Weidner), minor child of Daniel Weidner, late of Milford Twp, now 21, release guardian Peter Gruber.   Bk 5/pg 207   May 19, 1823

Joseph Weidner of Milford Twp, guardian of Leanna Weidner, minor daughter of late Daniel Weidner of Milford acknowledges payment by former guardian Peter Gruber of Springfield Twp.   Bk 5/pg 208   Apr 12, 1826

Septimus Hough of East Penn Twp, Northampton Co. is indebted to Rebecca Hough (wife of John Meredith of Buckingham Twp). He assigns share in estate of late Joseph Hough of Warwick Twp to pay debt.
Bk 5/pg 208   Apr 20, 1826

Jacob and Abraham Yost, sons of Jacob Yost, late of Bedminster Twp. and George and Sarah Fullmer, daughter of Jacob Yost, acknowledge payment by administrators Conrad Harpel and Henry Ott.   Bk 5/pg 209   Apr 6, 1826

Philip and Samuel Yost, both of Bedminster Twp, sons of Jacob Yost, late of Bedminster Twp, acknowledge payment by administrators Conrad Harpel and Henry Ott.   Bk 5/pg 210   Jan 26, 1826

Martin and Elizabeth Yost, children of late Daniel Yost and grandchildren of late Jacob Yost of Bedminster Twp, and George Seiple, guardian of Isaac, Catharine and Hannah Yost, other children of Daniel, acknowledge payment by administrators Conrad Harpel and Henry Ott.   Bk 5/pg 210   Apr 6, 1826

Henry Ruhl, surviving administrator of Michael Hillegas, late of Philadelphia, gives power of attorney to John Miller Jr. of Lower Makefield Twp. to file settlement of mortgage paid by George Stockham of Falls Twp, yeoman.
Bk 5/pg 211   Mar 29, 1826

Mary Coon of Springfield Twp, widow of Henry Coon acknowledges payment of dower by John Musselman of Springfield.
Bk 5/pg 213   Apr 27, 1826

Samuel Coon of Springfield Twp, heir of Henry Coon, late of Springfield, gives power of attorney to John Musselman to collect dower from John and Joseph Coon.   Bk 5/pg 214   Apr 27, 1826

Elijah W. Iliff of Greenwich Twp, Warren Co, NJ, now 21, acknowledges payment by guardian John Williams of estate from grandfather John Iliff of Nockamixon Twp.   Bk 5/pg 215   May 10, 1826

Christian Isely of Campbell Co, TN gives power of attorney to friend Jacob Fox of Bucks Co. to recover money due to wife Mary (formerly Fox), daughter of late John Fox.   Bk 5/pg 215   May 15, 1826

John Ruan of Philadelphia entitled to estate by right of wife Susan (daughter of William Rodman, late of Bensalem Twp). He assigns estate to William McIlvaine, Esq. of Philadelphia in trust for use of wife Susan.

Bk 5/pg 216   Apr 13, 1826

Mathew and Mary Humphreys of Muskingam Co, OH give power of attorney to Isaac Closson of Tinicum Twp. to sell land in Plumstead Twp. late in possession of Jane Hughes.   Bk 5/pg 219   Jan 26, 1826

John Michael, administrator of Susana Michael (late Yearling), late of Plainfield Twp, Northampton Co. acknowledges payment by Phillip Groover, executor of Jacob Yearling, late of Tinicum Twp, which represents one-third of dower which was due upon death of widow Magdeline.

Bk 5/pg 220   Apr 24, 1826

James Wigton of Doylestown Twp. assigns to Enoch Harvey his share of estate of William Wigton (late of New Britain Twp) in order to pay debts.

Bk 5/pg 228   Jun 6, 1826

David Gamble of Groveland, Livingston Co, NY and wife Rebecca, daughter and legatee of Barnard Carrol of Warminster Twp. give power of attorney to Hiram McNeill, Esq. of Moorland Twp, Montgomery Co. to collect estate now payable due to decease of widow Lucretia and brother Elias (who died without issue).   Bk 5/pg 231   Nov 22, 1825

Rahel Carrel, James Carrell and Hannah (wife of Robert Service), children of late Barnard Carrel, acknowledge payment by Isaac Carrel of dower due by death of widow Lucretia.   Bk 5/pg 233   Apr 1, 1826

Mary Hooper of Lincoln Co, NC gives power of attorney to Robert H. Burton of Lincoln Co. to recover estate from uncle Israel Anderson in PA.

Bk 5/pg 236   Apr 30, 1825

John Shupe of Milford Twp, taylor, assigns to Jacob Shade of Limerick Twp, Montgomery Co, his right in dower of Magdalena Shupe, widow of Jacob Shupe, late of Milford.   Bk 5/pg 238   Jul 22, 1826

John Stephens of Cape Creertein[?] Co, MO, administrator of Samuel Ramsey of the same place gives power of attorney to Robert Burton, Esq. of Lincoln Co, NC to recover legacy due by right of late mother in Lincoln Co, NC from her uncle Israel Anderson of near Philadelphia.   Bk 5/pg 239   Apr 29, 1824

Mary Crossley, granddaughter of Felix Bruner, late of Milford Twp, now 21, releases her guardian Everard Foulke for payment of estate from grandfather, mother Susanna Crossley and late brother Charles. Bk 5/pg 247 May 1, 1826

Abraham and Henry Shons of Milford Twp. give power of attorney to Abraham Heatrick, Adam Huber, Michael Brish and Eve Neas, all of Milford and Henry Sterner of Maxtany Twp, Berks Co. to recover any money due from father Abraham's administrators and from mother Margrate Shons' estate after her decease.   Bk 5/pg 247   Apr 7, 1826

Samuel Wildonger of Solebury Twp. releases guardian William Swope of Plumstead Twp.   Bk 5/pg 249   Jun 17, 1826

Jacob Schelly and Elizabeth Demute (alias Seacher), both of Westmoreland Co. give power of attorney to Peter Schelly of Lower Milford Twp. to recover money due from estate of John Harwick.   Bk 5/pg 249   Jun 2, 1826

Jesse Leedom of Newtown Twp, yeoman, gives power of attorney to Chapman Buckman of Newtown Twp, yeoman, to recover money due from estate of late father Richard Leedom.   Bk 5/pg 255   Jul 31, 1826

Nicholas Brown of Bensalem Twp assigns to John Paxson of Bensalem all right to estate of late father John Brown of Middletown Twp in order to pay debts.   Bk 5/pg 256   Aug 25, 1826

Mary Wiggins, widow of Bezaleel Wiggins of Upper Makefield Twp (who died intestate leaving five minor children: Jesse, Margery, Joseph, Martha and Margaret) who was a son of Joseph Wiggins releases Crispin Blackfan who is guardian to the minor children.   Bk 5/pg 257   Sep 2, 1826

Robert Murray of Point Twp, North[?] Co, PA acknowledges payment by Amos Vansant in right of wife Nancy (late Vansant) under will of her father Isaiah Vansant.   Bk 5/pg 258   Feb 9, 1825

John Caldwell of Union Twp, Licking Co, OH acknowledges payment by Amos Vansant in right of wife Rachel Vansant, daughter of Gabriel Vansant who was a legatee of late Isaiah Vansant of Lower Makefield Twp.
                     Bk 5/pg 258   Jul 11, 1826

Eveline Burson of Tinicum Twp, daughter of late John W. Burson of Springfield Twp, now 21, releases her guardian Caleb Foulke of Richland

Twp. for payment of estate from grandfather David Burson, late of
Springfield.   Bk 5/pg 259 Sep 6, 1826

Edward Ely and wife Sarah Ann release to sister Elizabeth Ely his share of
estate of father William Ely of Buckingham Twp. Bk 5/pg 260 Jul 29, 1826

John Wismer of Yearmouth Twp, Middlesex Co, London District, Upper
Canada, yeoman gives power of attorney to Jacob Gross of Clinton Twp,
Niagra District to recover money from Abraham Wismer of Bedminster Twp,
administrator of Henry Wismer.   Bk 5/pg 262 Sep 12, 1826

Samuel Autherhold of Brookfield Twp, Trumbull Co, OH, legatee of
Frederick Autherhold acknowledges payment by William Fretz of Bedminster
Twp for share of dower.   Bk 5/pg 264 Oct 3, 1826

Nathan Heacock of Columbiana Co, OH, surviving executor of Martha
Heacock of Bucks Co. and guardian of late Edith H. Jenkins of Bucks Co.
gives power of to Joseph Fisher of Columbiana Co. to recover any moneys
due.   Bk 5/pg 264 Sep 30, 1826

Abraham Letherman of Bullshin[?] Twp, Fayette Co, PA gives power of
attorney to Andrew Shadinger of Plumstead Twp. to settle real estate of father
Henry Letherman, late of Bedminster Twp. Bk 5/pg 268 Oct 5, 1826

Barbara Beitler of Richland Twp, daughter of late Henry Beitler of Richland
Twp gives power of attorney to brother-in-law Joseph Schlifer of Richland
Twp. to refuse to take father's land.   Bk 5/pg 274 Dec 9, 1826

Mary Weaver of Richland Twp, Henry Frankenfield and wife Catharine (late
Weaver) and John Root and wife Hannah (late Mann, daughter of Jacob &
Elizabeth Mann, late Weaver), heirs of Joseph/Yost Weaver, late of Richland
gives power of attorney to brother Joseph Weaver of Richland Twp,
quilldriver[?], to refuse to take father's land. Bk 5/pg 275 Dec 9, 1826

James Watson of Northern Liberties, Philadelphia, storekeeper, assigns to
Lewis David Beck of Kensington, Philadelphia, baker, his right to legacy
from late David Jarrett of Warminster Twp, yeoman.
                                       Bk 5/pg 277 Jun 24, 1826

Mahlon Atkinson of Drumore Twp, Lancaster Co, pump maker, and wife
Martha acknowledge payment by Ezekiel Atkinson of Drumore, farmer, to
land in Southampton Twp which was part of estate of Daniel Walmsley who

died intestate leaving a widow and six children (including Martha), one of whom died a minor. Bk 5/pg 278   Nov 16, 1822

Sara Renner, now 21, daughter of late Adam Renner of Hilltown Twp, releases her guardian Christian Nese of Upper Salford Twp, Montgomery Co. Bk 5/pg 280   Nov 11, 1826

Joseph Weaver, executor of John Bower, late of Richland Twp. and his wife Elizabeth who was a daughter of John acknowledge payment by Christopher Bower, another of John's executors. Bk 5/pg 280   May 31, 1814

Nathan Heacock of Columbiana Co, OH, executor of Martha Heacock, late of Richland Twp. acknowledge (by attorney Joseph Fisher) payment by Caleb Foulke, administrator of Abel Penrose, late of Richland Twp. who was appointed guardian for Edith H. Jenkins, late of Richland Twp.
Bk 5/pg 281   Nov 23, 1826

William Bryan of Hilltown Twp and wife Sarah, daughter of late Issacher Heacock of Bedminster Twp. and legatee of late Martha Heacock of Richland Twp. acknowledge payment from guardian Nathan Heacock.
Bk 5/pg 282   Jan 22, 1824

Charles Reinhart and wife Mary (late Heacock) of Hilltown Twp. acknowledge payment from Nathan Heacock and Abel Penrose, guardians of Edith, daughter of Martha Heacock, whose will indicated that upon the death of Edith in her minority, the estate was to be paid to the three daughters of Issacher Heacock (including Mary). Bk 5/pg 283   Jan 20, 1824

Jane Cooper, widow of Thomas, late of Falls Twp. releases John Rowlett Jr. from payment of dower. Bk 5/pg 287   Dec 18, 1826

Sarah Pritchard of Southampton Twp. gives power of attorney to Jonathan Potts of Moreland Twp, Montgomery Co. and William Delany of Southampton to sell three-fourths of one-eighth of land in Bristol.
Bk 5/pg 288   Jan 26, 1826

John M. Kinsley of Philadelphia, attorney for heirs of Robert McConway of Solebury Twp (brothers and sisters John, Alexander, William, Mary Gamble, Jane McIntire, Catharine Stevenson, Margaret Marshall, Hannah Entniten[?], all in Ireland) acknowledges payment by executors Joseph D. Murray and Merrick Reeder. Bk 5/pg 288   Apr 19, 1826

Sarah Burson of Wrightstown Twp, widow of James, late of Springfield Twp. and former widow of Stephen Twining, late of Wrightstown releases to Jacob Treichler of Springfield Twp all right to dower. Bk 5/pg 289 Dec 11, 1826

Jacob Weaver of Easton and wife Elizabeth (formerly Geiger), granddaughter of Michael Stoneback, late of Hilltown Twp. acknowledge payment by executor Andrew Steer. Bk 5/pg 290 Jul 29, 1826

Mary Geiger of New York City, granddaughter of Michael Stoneback of Hilltown Twp. acknowledges payment by executors Henry Keller and Andrew Steer. Bk 5/pg 292 Mar 6, 1824

Thomas Dannehour of Gwynedd Twp, Montgomery Co, and wife Mary, daughter of Christopher Stoneback, acknowledge payment by Andrew Steer of estate from grandfather Michael Stoneback. Bk 5/pg 292 Aug 2, 1823

Henry King of Montgomery Twp, Montgomery Co. and wife Catharine, daughter of Christopher Stoneback, acknowledge payment by Andrew Steer of estate from grandfather Michael Stoneback. Bk 5/pg 293 Nov 15, 1822

John Geiger of Forks Twp, Northampton Co. and Samuel Stoneback of Norriton Twp, Montgomery Co. acknowledge payment from Andrew Steer of estate from grandfather Michael Stoneback. Bk 5/pg 294 Nov 15, 1822

John Elias Geiger acknowledges payment by Henry Keller of estate from grandfather Michael Stoneback. Bk 5/pg 302 Nov 22, 1822

Grace Fell, minor daughter of Seneca Fell, late of Buckingham Twp, now married to Benjamin J. Buckman of Harrison Co, OH gives power of attorney to Eli Fell of Buckingham Twp. to recover money from guardian Seneca Fell. Bk 5/pg 306 Jan 12, 1827

Charles Wilson and Jonathan Wilson, sons of late Joseph Wilson of Bristol Twp. give power of attorney to John Goslin to refuse to accept father's land. Bk 5/pg 310 Feb 13, 1827

Christian Young of Bethlehem, yeoman gives power of attorney to Henry Jarrett, Esq. of Lehigh Co. to call on Jacob Stoufer and George Most of Bucks sureties for Christian who is administrator of Michael Young, late of Northern Liberties, Philadelphia County to recover money due to Maria (wife of Jacob Shleiffer of Haycock Twp) who was a daughter of Michael. Bk 5/pg 310 Feb 8, 1827

Abraham Zeigenfoos of Rockhill Twp, now 21, son of John Ziegenfoos, late of Rockhill, acknowledges payment by guardian Michael Headman.
Bk 5/pg 314   Mar 28, 1825

Abigail Penrose, widow of Abel Penrose of Richland Twp. acknowledges payment from administrators Caleb Foulke and William Penrose.
Bk 5/pg 314   Jan 4, 1827

Samuel Penrose of Warminster Twp, father and heir of Abel Penrose, late of Richland, acknowledges payment from administrators Caleb Foulke and William Penrose.
Bk 5/pg 315   Jan 2, 1827

John Stouffer of Rockhill Twp, yeoman and wife Catharine, daughter and legatee of John Landes of Rockhill, acknowledge payment by executor Elizabeth Landes and of Abraham Landes, Samuel Landes and Samuel Gehman, administrator of Jacob Landes of Rockhill, sons of John.
Bk 5/pg 316   May 15, 1824

Israel Penrose, Joseph Penrose, James Penrose and Amos Richardson (guardian of minor children of Jane Pugh, deceased), heirs of Joseph Penrose, late of Richland Twp. nominate William Green and Evan Penrose to appraise the estate.
Bk 5/pg 317   Sep 10, 1824

Joseph Keyser is due a legacy from Leonard Keyser, late of Wrightstown Twp, upon the death of this mother Margaret. He assigns this legacy to John S. Grier of Warwick Twp.
Bk 5/pg 319   Mar 9, 1827

Conrad Myers, Esq. of Nockamixon Twp. and Margaret Rodrock (daughter and heir of John Rodrock, late of Plumstead) are about to be married. Margaret assigns her share to John Moore of Plumstead Twp in trust for her use and not the benefit of her intended husband.   Bk 5/pg 322   Apr 4, 1827

John E. Vanhorn, Isaac Vanhorn and William L. Vanhorn and Benjamin Lazalere and wife Mary, children of Barnard Vanhorn, late of Upper Makefield Twp. acknowledge payment by executors Mary Vanhorn, Andrew Vanhorn and William Long.
Bk 5/pg 324   Apr 5, 1827

James Carr of Plumstead Twp, now 21, releases guardians Everard Foulke and Everard Roberts.
Bk 5/pg 324   Dec 3, 1817

Ann Carr of Richland Twp, spinster, now 21, releases guardians Everard Foulke and Everard Roberts.
Bk 5/pg 235   Apr 4, 1827

Jacob Ott, late of Bucks Co. but now of Montgomery Co. assigns his share in estate of late father Jacob Ott to Elias Y. Marple of Norristown.
Bk 5/pg 236   Apr 3, 1827

Benjamin Snodgrass Mann, Anthony Rich and wife Mary, Christian Fretzinger and wife Eliza, and Joseph James and wife Martha, children of John Mann and grand-children of Benjamin Snodgrass, late of Warwick Twp. acknowledge payment by Rev. James Snodgrass of West Hanover Twp, Dauphin Co, including share of late brother James Snodgrass Mann who died without issue.
Bk 5/pg 327   Nov 18, 1823

Mahlon Paxson of Lower Makefield Twp, farmer, gives power of attorney to son-in-law Charles Biles of Lower Makefield to recover any monies due him.
Bk 5/pg 329   Mar 8, 1827

Jacob Kern of Hilltown, yeoman, and wife Susanna, granddaughter and legatee of David Evans of Doylestown Twp, yeoman, assign legacy to Philip Brunner of Warrington Twp, blacksmith.   Bk 5/pg 330   Apr 2, 1827

Susanna Jacoby, minor daughter of late Peter Jacoby of Durham, yeoman, now 21 and married to Jacob Sleifer Jr. of Springfield Twp. releases guardian Christian Trauger of Nockamixon Twp.   Bk 5/pg 332   Jan 1, 1827

Nancy Anderson of Bristol Twp, single woman, gives power of attorney to George White of Bristol Twp, farmer to recover a legacy from father Joshua Anderson in possession of Thomas Cunningham in Lower Makefield Twp.
Bk 5/pg 332   Aug 7, 1826

Elizabeth Shaw of Plumstead Twp. acknowledges payment by William Smith of legacy due from John Smith of Plumstead Twp.
Bk 5/pg 335   Apr 7, 1827

Caleb Ivins of Falls Twp and wife Elizabeth (late Anderson) daughter of late Daniel Anderson of Lower Makefield Twp. acknowledge payment by George White of legacy from Daniel.   Bk 5/pg 338   Apr 27, 1827

John Keller of Rockhill Twp, Henry Keller of Haycock Twp, Michael Keller of Haycock, Samuel Keller of Haycock, Joseph Keller of Haycock, Daniel Keller of Haycock and Catharine Steely of Durham Twp, children of Christopher Keller, late of Haycock agree to division of estate.
Bk 5/pg 339   Apr 1, 1824

Daniel Keller of Durham Twp. and Jacob and Catharine Stealey (late Keller) release John, Henry and Michael Keller, executors of Christopher Keller.

Bk 5/pg 340   Jul 23, 1824

Samuel and Joseph Keller, both of Haycock Twp, release John, Henry and Michael Keller, executors of Christopher Keller.   Bk 5/pg 340   May 5, 1827

Joseph Stoneback, late of Bucks Co. but now a soldier in the 7th Regiment, U.S. Infantry gives power of attorney to John Sheneberger, Esq. of Whitpain Twp, Montgomery Co. to recover money from guardians Henry Keller and Andrew Steer due from will of grandfather Michael Stoneback.

Bk 5/pg 341   Nov 2, 1826

James and Ann Carr, minor children of John Carr, late of Plumstead Twp, and widow Rachel release guardian Everard Foulke.   Bk 5/pg 341   Apr 4, 1827

Lewis Ott of Springfield Twp, husband and administrator of Lovie (late Gerhart, deceased), acknowledges payment by her guardian Christian Nese of her share in grandfather Abraham Gerhart's estate.

Bk 5/pg 342   May 25, 1827

Rebecca Baldwin and Benjamin Swain, administrators of Pamela Baldwin and John McElroy (guardian to Joseph Howard and Eleanor Kirkbride—late Baldwin, heirs of Joseph Baldwin, deceased) give power of attorney to Elijah Cheston of Philadelphia, coachmaker, to record settlement of certain bonds.

Bk 5/pg 343   Apr 23, 1827

Samuel Strawn of Tompkins Co, NY, farmer, gives power of attorney to Daniel Strawn of Haycock Twp. to recover dower from Henry Siple of Springfield Twp.   Bk 5/pg 346   Oct 30, 1826

Jacob Wilhelm of Haycock Twp. and wife Rebecca (late Strawn), daughter of late William Strawn of Haycock give power of attorney to Daniel Strawn of Haycock to recover dower from Henry Seiple of Springfield Twp.

Bk 5/pg 346   Nov 8, 1826

Thomas Z. Smith and William Garges of Fairfax Co, VA give power of attorney to Abraham F. Stover, Esq. of Bedminster Twp. to recover money from Christian Fretz of Warwick Twp, executor of John Fretz of Warwick.

Bk 5/pg 349   Dec 18, 1826

Ely Gorham and wife Latitia of Whitemarsh Twp, York Co, Haine[?] District, Upper Canada give power of attorney to William Herald of same place, yeoman, to recover money from Jonathan Pearson or other executors of estate of her father Joseph Hambleton of Solebury Twp.
Bk 5/pg 350   May 21, 1827

Sarah Walker of Bristol Twp, relict of Thomas Paxson, late of Middletown Twp, sells dower right to Henry Atherton and John Booz, trustees for her son Joshua Paxson.   Bk 5/pg 351   Jun 1, 1827

Samuel Parks of Warminster Twp and wife Julian B., a daughter of James Anderson of Warminster, give power of attorney to Thomas Mifflin Anderson of Warminster to recover share of estate of Sarah McMullin of Northampton Co. who was mother of James Anderson.   Bk 5/pg 354   Aug 18, 1827

Michael Hofford, John Hofford, Joseph Hofford, Jessee Hofford, Mary Loux, Hannah Kidney, Elizabeth Benner, Catharine Rush and Peter Shive (guardian for Rachel Hofford), children of late Mary Hofford release administrator Daniel Hofford for payment of estate.   Bk 5/pg 357   Apr 17, 1827

Rebecca, Anna and Sarah Leedom of Moreland, Philadelphia Co. give power of attorney to James Paul of Montgomery Co, farmer, to recover estate from grandfather Richard Leedom of Bucks Co.   Bk 5/pg 359   Sep 1, 1827

Michael Funk of Clinton Twp, Lincoln Co, Niagara District, Upper Canada province, yeoman, gives power of attorney to brother John Funk of Plumstead Twp. to recover estate from Ralf Funk, executor of Abraham Funk, late of Springfield Twp.   Bk 5/pg 361   Sep 3, 1827

Jesse Edwards, Isaac Edwards and George Edwards of Northampton Twp. acknowledge payment by their father Isaac Edwards of Northampton.
Bk 5/pg 363   Apr 3, 1815

William Harrold, husband of Elizabeth who was widow of Amos A. Hughes, late of Buckingham Twp, gives power of attorney to Hugh B. Ely of Buckingham, yeoman, to recover estate from executors of Amos.
Bk 5/pg 364   Jun 20, 1827

Abraham Dilgart of Springfield Twp. and wife Mary, daughter and legatee of Henry Funk, late of Springfield Twp, acknowledge payment of estate by Henry Funk Jr. of Springfield.   Bk 5/pg 365   Apr 5, 1827

Sarah Parker, daughter of John Parker, late of Wrightstown Twp, gives power of attorney to Timothy Smith of Doylestown to recover her one-sixth share of estate. Bk 5/pg 366 Oct 18, 1827

Samuel Detweiler of Hilltown Twp. and wife Anna have separated themselves by their own free will. Samuel will maintain the children at his own expenses and Anna has the right to come and see her children and be treated in a decent manner. Anna's father Jacob Heistand will see that she follows this agreement. Bk 5/pg 368 May 17, 1826

James Carrell of Tinicum Twp. and wife Jane, daughter and legatee of Hester Abernathy, late of Tinicum Twp, acknowledge payment of estate by Robert Horner and William Long, administrators of late Samuel Abernathy. Bk 5/pg 370 Apr 7, 1824

Samuel Satterthwaite of Falls Twp. acknowledges payment by brother Joseph of legacy from father William Satterthwaite. Bk 5/pg 372 Mar 31, 1827

Joseph Frantz of Philadelphia, now age 21, acknowledges payment by his guardian Paul Frantz of Hilltown Twp. of his share of estate of late father Paul Frantz. Bk 5/pg 373 Dec 17, 1827

Evan Roberts of Richland Twp. and wife Abigal, sister and legatee of Margaret Penrose, late of Richland, acknowledge payment by executor Caleb Foulke. Bk 5/pg 373 Sep 21, 1827

Caleb Edwards of Richland Twp. and wife Sarah, sister and legatee of Margaret Penrose, late of Richland, acknowledge payment by executor Caleb Foulke. Bk 5/pg 374 Apr 21, 1827

Mary Penrose of Richland Twp, widow, mother and legatee of Margaret Penrose, late of Richland, acknowledges payment by executor Caleb Foulke. Bk 5/pg 376 Apr 21, 1827

Amos Richardson, guardian of Hannah and Thomas Pugh, minor children of Samuel Pugh, late of Richland Twp. and his late wife Jane who was daughter and legatee of Joseph Penrose, late of Richland Twp. acknowledges payment by executor Joseph Penrose. Bk 5/pg 377 Oct 6, 1827

James Penrose of Richland Twp, son of Jane Pugh (late Penrose) who was a legatee of Joseph Penrose, late of Richland Twp, acknowledges payment by executor Joseph Penrose. Bk 5/pg 378 Oct 6, 1827

Jacob Herwick of Richland Twp, son and heir of Samuel Herwick, late of Milford Twp. gives power of attorney to Samuel A. Smith, Esq. of Doylestown to refuse to take father's real estate at Orphan's Court hearing.
Bk 5/pg 379   Dec 13, 1827

Jacob Roads of Byberry Twp, Philadelphia Co. died intestate leaving widow Margaret and seven children: John (and wife Elsie), Jacob (and wife Emly), Jonathan (and wife Jane), Silas, Casper, Ann (wife of Michael Stevens), Phebe (wife of Joseph L. Sacket). Heirs release Silas for payment of estate.
Bk 5/pg 380   Mar 19, 1827

William Arthurs and wife Elizabeth (late Vanzant), John Arthurs and wife Rebecca (late Vanzant) and Mary Ann Vanzant, all of Cincinnati, OH, daughters of Jacob Vanzant, late of Bristol, give power of attorney to William Disney of Cincinnati to recover money from estates of Garret H. Vanzant of Bensalem Twp and Harman Vanzant.   Bk 5/pg 384   Oct 17, 1827

Abigail Penrose, widow of Abel Penrose late of Richland Twp, daughter and heir of Everard Foulke, Esq., late of Richland gives power of attorney Peter Lester of Haycock Twp. to refuse to take father's real estate.
Bk 5/pg 384   Feb 11, 1828

Thomas D. Foulke and wife Ann M. of Hamilton Co, OH give power of attorney to David Johnson of Bucks Co. to refuse to take real estate of ancestor Everard Foulke, late of Richland Twp.   Bk 5/pg 385   Jan 14, 1828

Jacob Boyer and John Graber, guardians of minor children of George Heist, late of Milford Twp. who died intestate, acknowledge payment from administrators George Heist and David Kuhns.   Bk 5/pg 386   Dec 15, 1827

Jonathan Woolston Sr. of Middletown Twp, yeoman, gives power of attorney to son Jonathan of Middletown to recover any moneys due him.
Bk 5/pg 387   Dec 15, 1827

Mary Amey (wife of Samuel Amey) of Northern Liberties Twp, Philadelphia Co, daughter of Manus Yost, late of Bucks, gives power of attorney to Henry Ott of Haycock Twp, yeoman, to recover estate from executor John Allum.
Bk 5/pg 387   Feb 7, 1828

John Bergstresser of Wallpack Twp, Sussex Co, NJ, legatee of Dr. Samuel Bergstresser, late of Nockamixon Twp, assigns legacy to Philip Bergstresser of Alexandria Twp, Hunterdon Co, NJ.   Bk 5/pg 388   Jan 5, 1828

Dr. Philip Hinkle of Reading, Berks Co. is indebted to Casper Hinkle of Plumstead Twp, storekeeper, and assigns to him any estate due upon death of his mother, Mary Hinkle, widow of late Philip of Plumstead Twp.

Bk 5/pg 390   Apr 4, 1815

Joseph Hinkle of Plumstead Twp. is indebted to Casper Hinkle of Plumstead and assigns to him any estate due upon death of his mother.

Bk 5/pg 392   Apr 25, 1821

John Keith of Fleming Co, KY gives power of attorney to Isaac Mann of Montgomery Co. to recover money due will of John Keith.

Bk 5/pg 392   Dec 3,1827

Alexander Foresman of Pickaway Co, OH and wife Sarah, heir of John Keith, Esq., late of Bucks give power of attorney to Isaac Mann of Montgomery Co. to recover estate.   Bk 5/pg 393   Dec 1, 1827

Catharine Richards of Philadelphia, widow, is indebted to Casper Hinkle of Plumstead Twp, storekeeper, and assigns to him any estate due upon death of mother Mary Hinkle, widow of late Philip of Plumstead Twp.

Bk 5/pg 396   Apr 4, 1815

Jacob Hollowbush of Northern Liberties Twp, Philadelphia Co. in 1814 assigned to Williams Groves of Northern Liberties his wife Mary's right to estate of Philip Hinkle, late of Bucks. William Groves assigns that right to Casper Hinkle of Bucks, farmer.   Bk 5/pg 397   Dec 25, 1827

Margaret Gillingham acknowledges payment by Israel Lancaster, one of the trustees of her husband Sam'l Gillingham.   Bk 5/pg 399   Apr 15, 1824

Samuel Kauffman of Lower Saucon Twp, Northampton Co. acknowledges payment by Henry Schliffer, executor of Jacob Schliffer, late of Springfield Twp, of share of estate due his wife Elizabeth.   Bk 5/pg 400   Aug 27, 1825

Abraham Sliffer of Springfield Twp. acknowledges payment of his share of estate of Jacob Sliffer, late of Springfield, by executor Henry Sliffer.

Bk 5/pg 400   Feb 12, 1827

Susannah Kramer, executor of Lawrence Kramer, late of Haycock Twp. gives power of attorney to George Hager and Jesse Armstrong, both of Bedminster Twp. to recover any moneys due her.   Bk 5/pg 401   Mar 22, 1828

Benjamin Taylor of Newtown Twp. sells land to son Benjamin Taylor Jr. of Newtown.   Bk 5/pg 403   Apr 1, 1826

Jacob Rufe, eldest son of late George Rufe of Nockamixon Twp, gives power of attorney to Jacob Kintner, Esq. of Nockamixon Twp. to recover estate from executors Frederick and John Rufe.   Bk 5/pg 405   Apr 3, 1828

John and Elizabeth Pennington of Plumstead Twp, son of late John Pennington of New Britain Twp. assign interest in dower due upon death of widow Margaret to Elizabeth and Susan Rich.   Bk 5/pg 406   Apr 10, 1828

Heirs of John Shaw, Esq.: Agnes (widow), Josiah Y., John, Francis B., Mary Shaw, Martha (wife of John Jamison) acknowledge payment of dower by the other heir, William Shaw, who purchased his father's estate.
                                               Bk 5/pg 409   Apr 1, 1828

Joseph Johnson of Orange Co, IN gives power of attorney to wife Sarah to recover money due from estate of her father William Bradshaw, late of Bucks Co.   Bk 5/pg 414   Mar 28, 1828

Adam Lechner of Rockhill Twp, yeoman, acknowledges payment by Enos Schlister, Henry Schlishter and Frederick Althouse, executors of Andrew Schleichter of Rockhill.   Bk 5/pg 414   Apr 29, 1828

John Wambold of Rockhill Twp. assigns to Abraham Wambold of Rockhill all right to share of dower in estate of late John Wambold due upon death of widow.   Bk 5/pg 417   Jun 7, 1828

Christiana, widow of late Andrew Triewig of New Britain Twp (who died intestate) acknowledges payment of estate by administrator Jacob Triewig. Rev. John K. Weiand (husband of Catharine—formerly Triewig) and Abraham Zigafoos (husband of Maria—formerly Triewig) acknowledge payment of their shares by administrators Jacob Triewig.
                                               Bk 5/pg 420   Apr 19, 1828

David D. Marple (who married Mary, daughter of Charles Hinkle), John Gibson (who married Maryann, daughter of Anthony Hinkle), William Campbell (who married Caroline, daughter of Anthony Hinkle), Elizabeth Hinkle, Chas. Hinkle (son of Charles, deceased), John Hinkle (son of Charles, deceased), John Meyers (who married Margaret, daughter of Anthony Hinkle), Charles Morris (who married Ann Mariah, daughter of Chas Hinkle), Wm Groves (who married Barbara, daughter of Philip Hinkle), Ann Hinkle,

Catharine Richards, Mary Hollowbush, Margaret Beck, Thomas Stewart, Esq. (guardian of Elizabeth, Alexander, Philip and Anthony, minor children of Anthony Hinkle), heirs of Philip Hinkle, acknowledge payment of dower (due upon death of widow Mary) by Casper Hinkle.   Bk 5/pg 421   Mar 3, 1828

John Erdman of Milford Twp, Bucks Co, Daniel Eberhart of Milford Twp, Lehigh Co. and wife Mary, David Huber of Milford Twp, Bucks Co. and wife Susanna, John Rudolph of Milford Twp, Lehigh Co. and wife Sarah, children of George Erdman, late of Milford Twp, Bucks Co. acknowledge payment by administrator Jacob Erdman.   Bk 5/pg 423   Apr 7, 1828

John Cosner Jr. of Plumstead Twp. and wife Mary have agreed to separate and live apart for the remainder of their lives. Mary to have management and control of under-age children: Harriet, Elias, Greer and Rebecca.
                                        Bk 5/pg 425   Jun 17, 1828

John Beaumont of Upper Makefield Twp. and Elizabeth Skillman of Upper Makefield intend to be married.   Bk 5/pg 426   Jul 9, 1828

John Strouse assigns legacy due from estate of George Strouse, late of Tinicum Twp, to William Swope of Plumstead Twp.
                                        Bk 5/pg 429   Aug 21, 1828

Frederick Fulmer and wife Elizabeth, daughter of late John Ditterly of Bedminster Twp, give power of attorney to John Ditterly to refuse to accept her father's real estate.   Bk 5/pg 430   Sep 6, 1828

Margaret Haas of Haycock Twp, widow, daughter and legatee of Leonard Hinkle, late of Richland Twp, acknowledges payment of estate by Peter Zigenfoos and Samuel A. Smith, Esq., assignees of executor George Hinkle.
                                        Bk 5/pg 430   Aug 16, 1828

Jacob Althouse, George Heist (husband of Mary) and Joseph Drake (husband of Elizabeth), children of Henry Althouse and grandchildren of John Althouse, late of Franconia Twp, Montgomery Co. give power of attorney to John Freedley of Norristown to refuse to take John's real estate.
                                        Bk 5/pg 431   Feb 18, 1828

Ann Summers, widow of George Summers of Warrington Twp. releases executor Jacob Cassel from all suits that have been initiated by designing and evil disposed persons.   Bk 5/pg 432   Sep 24, 1828

John Yothers of Bedminster Twp. gives power of attorney to trusty friend David Culp of Bedminster to attend inquisition of real estate of late Jacob Yothers.   Bk 5/pg 434   Aug 29, 1828

Henry Yothers of Mount Pleasant Twp, Westmoreland Co, yeoman, gives power of attorney to trusty friend Christian Clemens of Doylestown Twp. to attend inquisition of real estate of late Jacob Yothers.
                                          Bk 5/pg 435   Aug 23, 1828

Nancy and Julia Ann Calbraith, children of George Calbraith by his second wife Hannah, give power of attorney to Hannah, widow of George to recover estate due by will of Hector Calbraith, late of Falls Twp.
                                          Bk 5/pg 436   Oct 28, 1828

Benjamin Williams of Chester Co, yeoman, and wife Eleanor, George Elliot of Mettle Twp, Franklin Co, yeoman, and wife Elizabeth, Daniel Riale of Doylestown Twp, yeoman, and wife Rodah, Huldah James of New Britain Twp. acknowledge payment by Evan James and John E. James, both of New Britain Twp, money due from estate of Josiah James Sr.
                                          Bk 5/pg 439   Feb 10, 1827

Mahlon Higgs of Tredyffin Twp, Chester Co, husband of Mary (late Byerly) acknowledges payment by her guardian Jesse Wharton of the legacy due her from estate of John Blankinhorn.   Bk 5/pg 440   Dec 8, 1828

Abraham Swartz, third son of late Jacob Swartz of Warwick Twp. gives power of attorney to William Randall to refuse to take father's real estate.
                                          Bk 5/pg 443   Sep 10, 1828

Horace, Lewis P. and Mary Ann Smith, children of Jonathan and Elizabeth Smith, both deceased, the latter a daughter of John Parker, late of Wrightstown Twp, give power of attorney to Timothy Smith of Doylestown to refuse to accept John's real estate.   Bk 5/pg 444-5   Nov 6, 1828

Mary Parker, daughter of late John of Wrightstown Twp, gives power of attorney to Timothy Smith of Doylestown to refuse to accept father's real estate.   Bk 5/pg 444   Nov 29, 1828

Michael Musselman of Milford Twp. and wife Sarah, Jacob Moyer of Springfield Twp. and wife Mary, Abraham Geissinger of Richland Twp. and wife Barbara, Jacob Yoder of Saucon Twp, Lehigh Co. and wife Elizabeth, Magdalena and Esther Moyer, both of Springfield Twp, children and heirs of

Christian and Barbara Moyer of Springfield Twp, agree to sell parent's land to brothers Henry and Joseph Moyer. Bk 5/pg 447   Feb 7, 1828

John Myers of Doylestown Twp, Joseph Myers of New Britain Twp, John and Elizabeth Benner of Montgomery Twp, Montgomery Co, and Abraham Geil (assignee of Abraham Myers, late of Doylestown Twp), legatees of Michael Moyer (alias Myers), late of New Britain Twp, acknowledge payment of estate by Michael Myers.   Bk 5/pg 449   Apr 1, 1824

William Smith of Franconia Twp, Montgomery Co, shoemaker, and wife Susana and John Franck of Upper Salford Twp, Montgomery Co, weaver, and wife Mary acknowledge payment by Jacob Dill, Esq. of their share in estate of father Frederick Dill, late of Rockhill Twp, excepting the dower due upon the death of widow Catharine.   Bk 5/pg 451   Jan 24, 1829

Stedman Penrose of Richland Twp, blacksmith, now age 21, acknowledges payment from guardian David Johnson of Richland.
                                        Bk 5/pg 453   Feb 6, 1829

Henry Seagenfoose of Walpack Twp, Sussex Co, NJ and wife Susan, daughter and heir of Michael Kohl Sen., late of Nockamixon Twp, acknowledge payment of estate by administrators Conrad Kohl and Jacob Dech.   Bk 5/pg 453   Jan 22, 1829

Jacob Kohl and Samuel and Magdalena Kraut, all of Upper Mount Bethel Twp, Northampton Co, children of late Michael Kohl of Nockamixon Twp, acknowledge payment by administrators Conrad Kohl and Jacob Dech.
                                        Bk 5/pg 454   Jan 24, 1829

Michael Kohl, John Kohl, George Kohl, Sara Kohl, Hanah Kohl and Elizabeth Trauger (widow of Jacob Trauger), all of Nockamixon Twp, children and heirs of late Michael Kohl of Nockamixon, acknowledge payment of estate by administrators Conrad Kohl and Jacob Dech.
                                        Bk 5/pg 455   Jan 26, 1829

Adam Bartholomew of Richland Twp, guardian of Daniel Horn (minor child of Valentine Horn, late of Richland), acknowledges payment of estate by Jacob Trichler and Joseph Applebach, Daniel's previous guardians.
                                        Bk 5/pg 456   Apr 1, 1822

John Kintner of Nockamixon Twp. and wife Elizabeth (late Horn) acknowledge payment from her guardians Joseph Afflerbach and Jacob Treichler of Springfield Twp.   Bk 5/pg 457   Jan 31, 1829

Michael, Elizabeth, Samuel and Abraham Eckert, all of Rockhill Twp, children of Leonard Eckert, late of Rockhill, and Michael and Abraham Kramer, sons-in-law, acknowledge payment by executors John and Christian Eckert.   Bk 5/pg 458   May 10 1822

John Weaver of Woodbury Twp, Huntingdon Co, Henry Weaver of Allen Twp, Northampton Co, Samuel Weaver of Upper Mount Bethel Twp, Northampton Co, Frederick and Jacob Weaver of Lower Mount Bethel Twp, Northampton Co, and minors Joseph, Jesse and Peter Weaver of Lower Mount Bethel Twp. (by their guardian Frederick Weaver the elder) acknowledge payment of estate by Henry Leicy of Hilltown Twp, executor of John Huntzberger of Hilltown Twp.   Bk 5/pg 461   May 12, 1828

Abraham Ditlow of Milford Twp, blacksmith, gives power of attorney to Abraham Shelly of Milford, physician, to recover money from brother David Ditlow of Lehigh Co, executor of father Abraham Ditlow.
Bk 5/pg 462   Mar 26, 1829

Jesse Fell of Lancaster Co. gives power of attorney to son Joshua Fell of Delaware Co. to recover money from estate of father Thomas Fell now in hands of William Watson, surviving administrator.
Bk 5/pg 466   Mar 18, 1829

George Delp of Franconia Twp, Montgomery Co, Jacob Delp of Franconia, Abraham Delp of Warrington Twp, John Delp of Franconia, Isaac Delp of Franconia, Samuel Delp of Hatfield Twp, Montgomery Co and Henry Delp of Plumstead Twp, children of late John Delp of Warrington Twp, agree to equally divide their father's estate.   Bk 5/pg 466   Nov 20, 1827

Isaac, Abraham, Jacob, Levi Daniel, George and Henry Markley, Jonathan and Catharine Megargee, John and Sarah Garner, John and Elizabeth Weber and John Haldeman (guardian of Joseph Markley), all heirs of late George Markley, and John Markley acknowledge payment of estate by John Delp.
Bk 5/pg 468   Sep 15, 1823

David Walton of Fayette, Seneca Co, NY and John and Levina Roberts (late Walton) and Ann Walton, all of Fairfield Twp, Lycoming Co. assign to their mother Elizabeth Walton all right in estate of grandfather George Rogers, late of Plumstead Twp.   Bk 5/pg 471-2   Jul 3, 1827/Jun 14, 1828

George Walton and wife Martha, Benjn. Warner and wife Mary, Thomas F. Johnston and wife Martha and Jane Walton, children and legatees of David Walton (deceased) and wife Elizabeth who was daughter of George Rogers, late of Plumstead Twp, give power of attorney to Elizabeth Walton of Muncy Twp, Lycoming Co.   Bk 5/pg 472   May 9, 1827

Mary Jenks, widow of William Jenks of Middletown Twp. gives power of attorney to son Michael H. Jenks of Middletown to recover any money due.
                    Bk 5/pg 474   Feb 2, 1828

Isaac S. Keith and Margaret Vansant (late Keith) of Fleming Co, KY give power of attorney to Isaac Mann of Montgomery Co. to collect money from Samuel McNair and Abraham Slack, executors of John Keith, late of Bucks Co as well as money due from estate of Samuel Keith which may come to them as heirs of Isaiah Keith.   Bk 5/pg 474   Aug 2, 1828

Daniel, George, Charles, Jacob and Henry Ditterly, sons and heirs of late Henry Ditterly of Bedminster, acknowledge payment by administrator Charles Zellnor.   Bk 5/pg 475   Apr 4, 1829

Ann Geddes, late of Bucks County, acting as one of the executors of the estate of John Geddes gives power of attorney to Moses Geddes of Bucks County to sell John's real estate.   Bk 5/pg 476   Feb 28, 1829

Leonard, Samuel and Abraham Eckert, yeomen, of Rockhill Twp. gives power of attorney to Michael Kramer, yeoman, of Rockhill to receive from Christian and John Eckert, executors of Leonard Eckert, the 1/9 part of the dower due upon the death of their mother Mary.   Bk 5/pg 477   Mar 14, 1829

John Dietz and wife Magdalena, John Nase and wife Elizabeth, Jacob Hoover and wife Catharine (from Jackson Co, GA) and Philip Ziegler and wife Mary (from Middletown Twp, Cumberland Co, PA), daughters of Lawrence Kreamer, yeoman, late of Rockhill Twp. acknowledge receipt of their share of estate from administrator Michael Kreamer and also the share in mother Catharine's estate.   Bk 5/pg 479-81   Oct 24, 1807

John Nase and wife Elizabeth, Abraham Kramer (farmer of Hilltown Twp), Christian Eckert and wife Susanna, children of Catharine Kramer, late of

Rockhill Twp. acknowledge receipts of their shares of estate from
administrator Michael Kramer.   Bk 5/pg 482   Nov 24, 1806

Elijah Lewis, guardian of Eliza and Reuben Lewis who are minor children of
the late Joseph Lewis, gives power of attorney to Charles DuBois, clerk of the
Orphans Court, to acknowledge bonds received from Caleb Lewis.
                                       Bk 5/pg 484   Mar 31,1829

John P. Lewis, James J. Lewis and Joseph Lewis of Newtown Twp, Delaware
County give power of attorney to Charles DuBois, clerk of the Orphans Court
to record satisfaction of a bond from Caleb Lewis.
                                       Bk 5/pg 484   Mar 31, 1829

John Ditlow of Milford Twp, son of Abraham Ditlow, late of Milford, gives
power of attorney to Daniel H. Klein of Milford to recover estate from David
Ditlow, remaining executor of the estate.   Bk 5/pg 485   Feb 24, 1829

Leonhard Eckert, yeoman, of Rockhill Twp, son of Leonhard Eckerd, late of
Rockhill, acknowledges payment by executors John and Christian Eckert.
                                       Bk 5/pg 486   Sep 20, 1823

Mary B. Baker of Upper Makefield Twp, widow of Henry Baker, gives power
of attorney to Edward Harris of Moorstown, NJ to accept the real estate of
Joseph Baker, late of Upper Makefield.   Bk 5/pg 487   Apr 28, 1828

John Marcellious of Seneca Falls, Seneca Co, NY gives power of attorney to
Albert Smith, Esq. of Doylestown to accept the real estate of his sister Sarah
Marcellious, late of Upper Makefield Twp.   Bk 5/pg 488   Apr 10, 1829

Henry Bibighouse of Philadelphia, executor of John Bibighouse, late of
Bedminster Twp, releases Michael Kulp Senr. of Bedminster for sums he
received from Henry as guardian of Magdalina and Martin Bibighouse,
children of John.   Bk 5/pg 489   Apr 25, 1828

Aaron Wambold, taylor, and David Wambold, weaver, both of Rockhill Twp,
now age 21, acknowledge payment by their guardian Andrew Drumbor of
estate due from their late father David Wambold of Rockhill Twp.
                                       Bk 5/pg 490   Apr 6, 1829

Joseph Collins of Buckingham Twp. assigns right in a certain plantation to
son Enoch of Wrightstown Twp.   Bk 5/pg 491   Apr 18, 1829

Daniel Applebach and wife Catharine of Haycock Twp, daughter of Paul Apple, late of Springfield Twp, acknowledge payment of estate by executor Andrew Apple.   Bk 5/pg 492   Nov 27, 1828

Daniel Dolbey/Dalbey and wife Catharine of Richland Twp. and Benjamin Shroyer and wife Ann of Richland Twp, daughters of late John Fulmer and granddaughters of John and Barbara Fulmer, late of Rockhill Twp, acknowledge payment of estate from guardians Henry Groff and John Karn, both of Rockhill Twp.   Bk 5/pg 493   Apr 11, 1829

Hector Calbraith, late of Penns Manor, bequeathed estate to children of his brother John Calbraith of Drunkendult, Antrim Co, Ireland who is dead leaving children Sarah (wife of William McNaul of Drunkendult, farmer), Nancy (wife of Major Scott of Carncullagh, farmer), Elizabeth (wife of Robert Taylor of Unchenagh, farmer) and Jane (wife of George Washington Thompson, Greensheills, farmer), all of County Antrim. John's heirs give power of attorney to Major Scott, George Washington Thompson and James Thompson (of Penns Manor).   Bk 5/pg 495   Sep 23, 1828

John Stirling of Greenshiels, Antrim Co, Ireland, nephew of Hector Calbraith who died Nov 4, 1827, gives power of attorney to brother-in-law James Thompson of Penns Manor to recover estate from executors Stephen Wilson and Hector Thompson.   Bk 5/pg 503   Aug 16, 1828

Ephraim Addis of Warwick Twp. and Ann Marshall, widow of Warwick, intend to be married soon and intend to keep their respective estates separate.
                    Bk 5/pg 509   May 14, 1829

David and Joseph Atherhold, John Adams and wife Ester, and Solomon Bachman and wife Nancy, children of Frederick Atherhold, late of Bedminster Twp, and Michael and David Wireman, Abraham Rickert and wife Mary and Enos Leidy and wife Rachel, grandchildren of Frederick, acknowledge payment of share of estate by William Fretz of Bedminster, due upon estate of widow Esther.   Bk 5/pg 511   May 8, 1829

Mary Garner of Pikeland Twp, Chester Co, widow of John Garner, late of Warrington Twp, Jacob Garner of Uwchlan Twp, Chester Co (eldest son), John Garner of Pikeland Twp and James Wells and wife Anna of Uwchlan Twp acknowledge payment by Mary and John Garner, widow and son of late Samuel Garner who was administrator to late John Garner of Warrington Twp.   Bk 5/pg 514   Apr 11, 1829

Margaret and Christiana Steer, daughters of late Sabastian Steer of Rockhill Twp. acknowledge payment of estate by executors Andrew and Nicholas Steer.   Bk 5/pg 515   Dec 2, 1796

Andrew Steer of Rockhill Twp, son of late Sabastian Steer of Rockhill acknowledges payment by executor Nicholas Steer.
                                    Bk 5/pg 517   Jun 6, 1829

Samuel Landis of Milford Twp. and wife Elizabeth have recently agreed to separate. John Moyer to act as Elizabeth's trustee.
                                    Bk 5/pg 519   Jul 22, 1829

Mary Nash of Clinton Twp, Lincoln Co, Niagara District, Upper Canada, widow, gives power of attorney to Christian Moyer of Tinicum Twp. to recover estate of her late husband Abraham Nash of Plumstead Twp. now held by Jacob Ledermann of Plumstead Twp.   Bk 5/pg 521   Aug 4, 1828

William Bunting of Middletown Twp. assigned legacy from father William Bunting due upon death of mother Margary to his creditors.
                                    Bk 5/pg 522   Sep 2, 1829

George Wack (dumb man), Martin Wack, Abraham Yost and wife Eve, Duncan McLroy and wife Mary and Catharine Wack, children of Frederick and Elizabeth Wack who was a daughter of Martin Shive, late of Haycock Twp, yeoman, acknowledge payment by Martin's administrator William Stokes.   Bk 5/pg 524   Aug 15, 1829

William Ott and wife Catharine, Barbara Fisher, Sara Fisher and Solomon Nace of Nockamixon Twp, tobacconist, and wife Lydia, heirs of John Fisher, late of Rockhill Twp, acknowledge payment of dower by Henry Fisher, which was due upon the death of widow Barbara. Bk 5/pg 526   Apr 13, 1829

Henry Young of Saucon Twp, Lehigh Co, guardian of Joseph Crosby who is a minor child of James and Susanna (deceased) who was a daughter of Felix Brunner, late of Milford Twp, acknowledges payment by Caleb Foulke, administrator of Everard Foulke, Esq., late of Richland Twp, who was formerly the guardian of Joseph.   Bk 5/pg 528   Jun 16, 1828

Mathias Nase of Rockhill Twp, guardian of Francis Richard, minor son of late Jacob Richard, acknowledges payment by Caleb Foulke, administrator of Everard Foulke, Esq., late of Richland Twp, who was previously Francis' guardian.   Bk 5/pg 528   Jan 5, 1828

Moses Lancaster, late of Richland Twp but now of Milford Twp, gives power of attorney to son Moses of Northern Liberties Twp, Philadelphia Co. to sell land in Richland Twp.　　　　　Bk 5/pg 529　Sep 24, 1829

George Reiter, late of Lower Milford Twp, died intestate leaving widow Christina and seven children, of whom six are now living: Eve (wife of John Hildebeitel), Elizabeth (wife of Daniel Hildebeitel), Barbara, Frederick, Catharine (wife of Jacob Hill) and Michael (the seventh died without issue), acknowledge payment of dower by John Kerwer, present owner of George Reiter's real estate.　　　　　Bk 5/pg 531　Apr 20, 1829

Jacob Funk of Springfield Twp, guardian of Sarah Hess (late Funk), heir of Henry Funk, late of Springfield, acknowledges payment from Henry Funk, another of the heirs.　　　　　Bk 5/pg 535　Mar 29, 1828

Benjamin Riegel and wife Elizabeth of Lower Saucon Twp, Northampton Co, daughter of late Henry Funk of Springfield Twp, acknowledge payment of estate by Henry Funk Jr. of Springfield.　　　Bk 5/pg 535　Feb 19, 1829

Lydia Miles of Southampton Twp. gives power of attorney to brother Samuel Miles and friend Christopher Search, both of Southampton, to recover any money due her.　　　　　Bk 5/pg 535　Oct 24, 1829

Isaac Overrholtzer and wife Elizabeth of Hatfield Twp, Montgomery Co. give power of attorney to John Hunsberger to refuse to accept real estate of late Christian Hunsberger.　　　　　Bk 5/pg 536　Dec 16, 1829

Jacob Adams of Durham Twp. gives power of attorney to Michael Fackenthall Jr. of Durham to recover money due from estates of father John Adams of Durham and father-in-law Jacob Uhler of Durham.
　　　　　Bk 5/pg 538　May 8, 1828

Henry Snyder of Milford Twp, Daniel Snyder of Antrim Twp, Franklin Co. and George Sellers and wife Mary, children of Jacob Snyder, late of Hilltown Twp, give power of attorney to John Snyder of Hilltown Twp. to refuse to accept Jacob's real estate.　　　　　Bk 5/pg 538　Dec 12, 1829

A.V. Banes of Hopewell Twp, Licking Co, OH, physician, and wife Sarah give power of attorney to brother Lemen Banes, Esq. to sell real estate in Southampton Twp.　　　　　Bk 6/pg 5　Nov 7, 1829

Elizabeth Troxel, Charles and Margaret (Troxel) Roeder, Frederick and Catharine (Troxel) Schwartz, Sarah and David Troxel (by guardian Philip Reed, Esq.), Maria and Ann Troxel (by guardian Peter Miller) give power of attorney to Samuel Troxel to refuse to accept real estate of Henry Troxel, late of Upper Hanover Twp, Montgomery Co.   Bk 6/pg 5   Oct 28, 1829

James Bethel of Upper Makefield Twp. assigns his right in legacy under will of John Bethel, late of Wrightstown Twp. (due when the youngest daughter Sarah attains the age of 21) to Rebecca Bethel of Wrightstown Twp.
Bk 6/pg 6   Apr 6, 1829

Ruth Bowen of Schuylkill Twp, Chester Co, widow, gives power of attorney to son Ezekiel of same place, laborer, to recover legacy due from her uncle Joseph Watkins of Bucks Co. as an heir of Thomas and Deborah Pennington.
Bk 6/pg 8   Dec 22, 1829

John Stewart of Montgomery Co, OH and wife Rebecca give power of attorney to William M. White of Bucks Co. to sell real estate in Schuylkill Co.
Bk 6/pg 9   Jul 29, 1828

John Beaumont and Elizabeth Skillman, both of Upper Makefield Twp, were married Jul 19, 1828 by Merrick Reeder, a justice of the peace, but there being some doubt as to the legality of that proceeding, they document the fact that they were married.   Bk 6/pg 10   Jan 2, 1830

Casper Fabian died about 1820 leaving widow Mary and issue George, Catharine (wife of Jacob Shupe) and children of Casper Jr. (deceased). Widow Mary and Jacob and Catharine Shupe of Bucks Co. assign their share to George Fabian.   Bk 6/pg 11   Jan 2, 1830

Josiah Brown and wife Amy of Plumstead Twp. sold land to Charles Price subject to dower of Deborah Brown, widow of late Josiah Brown. They now release Charles from the dower.   Bk 6/pg 12   Jan 17, 1830

John Beaumont of Upper Makefield Twp. annuls the marriage settlement with Elizabeth Skillman that was filed in Misc. Book 5, pg 426 and instead allows her the usual dower right.   Bk 6/pg 13   Jan 21, 1830

Barbara Kramer of Upper Milford Twp, Lehigh Co, widow of Henry Kramer of Hilltown Twp, gives power of attorney to brother-in-law Leonard Detwiler of Hilltown to recover money from husband's estate.
Bk 6/pg 14   Jan 27, 1830

Jacob Yost of Bedminster Twp. and wife Mary (late Ott) who was daughter of Peter Ott, late of Bedminster, acknowledge payment of estate by George Ott (son of Peter).   Bk 6/pg 14   Nov 17, 1826

George Delp of Bedminster Twp. died Dec 28, 1829 having contracted to sell land to Thomas Trower of Bedminster but the transaction was not completed. Court confirms contract.   Bk 6/pg 15   Feb 9, 1830

David Rosenberger, late of Hatfield Twp, Montgomery Co, bequeathed land to daughter Franey (wife of Abraham Rosenberger of Hilltown, yeoman) subject to payment to other heirs. Heir Henry Rosenberger acknowledge payment of his share.   Bk 6/pg 19   Jan 15, 1828

Catharine Dotterer of Frederick Twp, Montgomery Co, widow of Conrad Dotterer and daughter of John Youngken, late of Nockamixon Twp, gives power of attorney to Nicholas Youngken of Nockamixon.
                                        Bk 6/pg 21   Feb 2, 1830

Abraham Younkin of Upper Mount Bethel Twp, Northampton Co, third son of John Younkin, late of Nockamixon Twp, gives power of attorney to Nicholas Younkin of Nockamixon Twp.   Bk 6/pg 22   Feb 11, 1830

John Bergstreser of Walpack Twp, Sussex Co, NJ, yeoman, is entitled to share of estate of father John Bergstresser, late of Tinicum Twp, yeoman, after decease of widow Anna (who is still living). John assigns his share to Philip Bergstreser of Alexandria Twp, Hunterdon Co, NJ.
                                        Bk 6/pg 22   Jan 5, 1828

George Cope, late of Hilltown Twp, died leaving widow Lydia and five children: Thomas, Hester, Christina, Abraham and Carolina. They release Thomas Cope for payment for some of George's land.
                                        Bk 6/pg 23   Feb 24, 1830

Morgan Long of Durham Twp, and wife Mary, daughter of James Wilson, late of Tinicum Twp, acknowledge payment of estate by James Wilson Jr. and Robert Wilson, executors of James. Bk 6/pg 25   Aug 20, 1825

Henry Derstine of Rockhill Twp, miller, and wife Susanna, daughter of John Landes, late of Rockhill Twp, acknowledge payment of estate by surviving executor Elizabeth Landes and from Abraham Landes, Samuel Gayman (administrator to Jacob Landes) and Samuel Landes, the sons of John.
                                        Bk 6/pg 25   Jan 18, 1830

Robert Horner of Allen Twp, Northampton Co. and wife Jane, daughter of James Wilson, late of Tinicum Twp, acknowledge payment of estate by James Jr. and Robert Wilson, executors to James. Bk 6/pg 26   Feb 23, 1827

Samuel Carrel of Tinicum Twp. and wife Ann, daughter of James Wilson, late of Tinicum Twp, acknowledge payment of estate by James Jr. and Robert Wilson, executors of James.   Bk 6/pg 27   Apr 3, 1826

Samuel Abernethy, eldest son of Samuel Abernethy Esq., late of Tinicum Twp, now 21, acknowledges payment of estate by guardian James Wilson Jr.
                                Bk 6/pg 27   Nov 14, 1827

Jacob Casselberry and wife Mary, daughter of John and Sarah Cleaver (alias Watkins) of Lycoming Co, PA, give power of attorney to brother David Cleaver of Columbia Co, PA to recover money from estate of Joseph Watkins in Bucks Co.   Bk 6/pg 28   Jan 20, 1830

Esther Anderson of Wrightstown Twp. gives power of attorney to son-in-law Joseph Reeder of Wrightstown to recover money due her.
                                Bk 6/pg 30   May 4, 1829

Israel Stoneback of Haycock Twp, shoemaker, now age 21, releases Samuel Ruth, administrator of his late guardian Jacob Ruth of Springfield Twp.
                                Bk 6/pg 30   Jan 23, 1830

Christopher Flanagan and wife Mary, daughter of Thomas Buckman, late of Newtown, yeoman, sell land to Thomas Ross, Esq.
                                Bk 6/pg 31   Mar 29, 1810

John Stover of Upper Saucon Twp, Lehigh Co, eldest son of Jacob Stover, late of Haycock Twp, acknowledges payment of estate from late grandfather David Stover of Nockamixon Twp. by executors Abraham and Joseph Stover of Nockamixon. Also for one-half of share of late sister Lydia.
                                Bk 6/pg 37   Mar 16, 1825

Solomon Freas of Hilltown Twp. and wife Anna agree that Solomon will have no share in estate due Anna from her father and now deceased mother (executor Jacob Wasser).   Bk 6/pg 38   Dec 17, 1829

Joseph Subers died about three years ago. Widow Martha died about Oct 6, 1829. Heir George Suber of Warren Co, OH gives power of attorney to Michael H. Jenks of Bucks Co. to recover dower. Bk 6/pg 43   Feb 11, 1830

James Huston and wife Mary Magdalane, Jacob Miller and wife Elizabeth, John Spidle and wife Ann, Edward Sweany and wife Catherine, Philip Etleman, Jacob Etleman Jr. and Henry Etleman, all of Stark Co, OH, heirs of Clorian (deceased, wife of Jacob Etleman of Stark Co) who was a daughter of John and Magdalena Benner of Bucks Co. They give power of attorney to Jacob Etleman to recover estate.   Bk 6/pg 44   Dec 10, 1829

Jacob Bissey of Tinicum Twp, guardian for Lewis Solliday, and Daniel Solliday of Tinicum Twp, guardian of Samuel Solliday, minor sons of Joseph Solliday, late of Plumstead Twp, acknowledge payment of estate by executors John N. and Samuel Solliday.   Bk 6/pg 45   Mar 29, 1830

Samuel Scholl who married Sarah [should be Susanna] Fluck, minor daughter of Christian Fluck, acknowledges payment of estate by Conrad Shellenberger who was Sarah's guardian.   Bk 6/pg 47   Dec 11, 1827

John Johnston of Roxborough Twp, Philadelphia Co. gives power of attorney to Isaac Marpole of same place to recover money from estate of father in Northampton Twp.   Bk 6/pg 47   Apr 1, 1830

Naomi Brodnax, widow of Robert, late of Bristol Twp. releases dower right.
    Bk 6/pg 48   Apr 6 1830

Samuel Bryan of Cecil Co, MD gives power of attorney to Valentine Switzer of Bucks Co. to lease land in Bedminster Twp. which was part of farm of late Samuel Armstrong.   Bk 6/pg 51   Nov 5, 1828

Margret Cope of Hilltown Twp, widow of Henry Cope, late of Hilltown, gives power of attorney to Michael Cope of Marlborough Twp, Montgomery Co to recover moneys due her.   Bk 6/pg 52   May 19, 1829

John Wireman, grandson of Frederick Atherhold, late of Bedminster Twp, acknowledges payment of estate by William Fretz of Bedminster.
    Bk 6/pg 53   Oct 22, 1829

Henry Landis, only son of David Landis of Middletown Twp who left four children: Henry, Anna, Sarah and Eliza. Henry releases share to his three sisters.   Bk 6/pg 56   Mar 1, 1822

John Drissel and wife Margaret of Milford Twp, yeoman, sell real estate to son Ulrich of same place, yeoman.   Bk 6/pg 58   Jan 20, 1757

Jacob Benner and wife Mary, daughter of Abraham Ditlow, late of Milford Twp, give power of attorney to John Alderfer of Rockhill Twp.

Bk 6/pg 61   Mar 23, 1830

Susana Dreisbach of Rockhill Twp. and George Adam Cover of Rockhill, executors of John Nase, yeoman, late of Rockhill, acknowledge payment by John's son Henry for real estate bequeathed to him subject to payment to other heirs.

Bk 6/pg 62   Jan 23, 1828

Daniel Cameron and wife Mary (late Nicely), William Beans and wife Sarah (late Nicely), Benjamin Martin and wife Eliza (late Nicely) and George Nicely, all of Jefferson Co, VA, give power of attorney to Henry Nicely of same place to recover money from estate of John Nicely, late of PA.

Bk 6/pg 63   Mar 22, 1830

William Meyers of Bedminster Twp. and wife Barbara, Tobias Landis of Richland Twp. and wife Verona, Maria Schimmel of Springfield Twp. and Nancy Schimmel (by guardian Jacob M. Meyer) of Springfield, children of late John Schimmel of Springfield, acknowledge payment of their shares by John and Susanna Schimmel, two of the other heirs.

Bk 6/pg 65   Apr 26, 1830

Catharine Gale of Lincoln Co, KY, but formerly of Doylestown Twp. gives power of attorney to George M. Justice and George B. Justice to recover money from Christian Fretz of Warwick Twp.   Bk 6/pg 66   Apr 7, 1830

Samuel Kauffman of Lower Saucon Twp, Northampton Co. acknowledges payment by executor Jacob Schliffer Jr. of legacy due his wife Elizabeth (late Schliffer) from her father Jacob Schliffer of Springfield Twp.

Bk 6/pg 68   Dec 24, 1827

Jacob Schliffer and Jacob Funk of Springfield Twp, administrators of Abraham Schliffer, late of Springfield, acknowledge payment by executor Jacob Schliffer Jr. of Springfield for legacy due from Abraham's father Jacob, late of Springfield.   Bk 6/pg 68   Aug 4, 1828

Christian Swartz, late of New Britain Twp. but now of Upper Canada, son of Jacob Swartz, late of New Britain, assigns his share of estate to brother Peter Swartz of New Britain which is due upon the death of their mother Margaret.

Bk 6/pg 69   Jun 2, 1830

Mary Green of Muncey Creek, Lycoming Co. and Jamima Smith of Springfield Twp, daughters of Garret Vanhorne, late of Springfield Twp, acknowledge payment of estate by administrators James Bryan and William Stokes.   Bk 6/pg 70   Jun 6, 1826

Sophia Walker, widow of Benjamin Walker of Loudon Co, VA, daughter of Garret Vanhorne of Springfield Twp, Thomas and Garret Vanhorne (sons of Barnet Vanhorne, deceased and administrators of William Vanhorne—deceased—who was another son of Barnet), James Swartz (son of Yannaky Swartz, daughter of Garret Vanhorne), all by their attorney Garret Walker of Loudon Co, acknowledge payment of estate by William Stokes.
                                    Bk 6/pg 70   Jul 15, 1826

Henry Siple of Springfield Twp and wife Mary, daughter of Ann Strawn (deceased), who was a daughter of Garret Vanhorn, late of Springfield Twp, acknowledge payment of estate by William Stokes.
                                    Bk 6/pg 72   Jun 6, 1826

Charity Loyd of Withannet[?] Twp, Upper Canada, widow of Thomas Loyd and daughter of Garret Vanhorn, late of Springfield Twp, acknowledges payment of estate by James Bryan and William Stokes.
                                    Bk 6/pg 72   Oct 14, 1826

Jacob Siple of Forks Twp, Northampton Co, miller, and wife Elizabeth, and Samuel Siple of Hilltown Twp, miller, and wife Modlena, daughters of Martin Shive, late of Haycock Twp, gave power of attorney to brother Peter Shive and he acknowledges payment of estate by administrators Daniel Shive and William Stokes.   Bk 6/pg 73   Aug 10, 1824

George Shive of Moore Twp, Northampton Co, shoemaker, son of Martin Shive, late of Haycock Twp, acknowledges payment of estate by Daniel Shive and William Stokes.   Bk 6/pg 74   Nov 21, 1823

Samuel Shive, late of Rockhill Twp but now of East Penn Twp, Northampton Co, son of Martin Shive, late of Haycock Twp, acknowledges payment of estate by Daniel Shive and William Stokes.   Bk 6/pg 74   Jul 24, 1823

Jacob Shive of Haycock Twp, John Shive of Haycock, yeoman, Martin Shive of Haycock, yeoman, Peter Shive of Rockhill Twp, miller, Jacob Smith and Catharine of Richland Twp, weaver, heirs of Martin Shive, late of Haycock, acknowledge payment of estate by Daniel Shive and William Stokes.
                                    Bk 6/pg 75   Aug 10, 1824

Michael Fackenthall of Durham Twp. and Mary Mill of Nockamixon Twp. are shortly to be married. Their respective estates are to remain separate.

Bk 6/pg 75   May 28, 1830

Joseph Myers of New Britain Twp. left estate to be divided between widow Mary and six children. Daughter Rachel and husband Levi Cooper of Amwell Twp, Hunterdon Co, NJ transfer her share in estate to Amos Wilson of Amwell Twp.   Bk 6/pg 78   Mar 3, 1830

Lawrence Moyer of Haycock Twp. died leaving a widow Catharine and nine children: Peter (eldest son), John (2nd son), Jacob, Margaret (wife of John Hofman), Mary (wife of Adam Dimick), Elizabeth (wife of Joseph Muflin), Catharine (wife of Philip Gumbert), Susana (wife of Samuel Harwick), Barbara (wife of John Bergerstreser). John Moyer of Haycock acknowledges payment of dower by William Stokes, administrator of George Fulmer.

Bk 6/pg 79   Mar 19, 1830

Samuel Mofley, Peter Gruver and wife Catharine, Elizabeth Mofley, Sarah Mofley, John Shisler and wife Susanna, Jacob Ritter and wife Lidy, Joseph Ritter and wife Barbara, all heirs of Joseph and Elizabeth Mofley who was a daughter of Lawrence and Catharine Moyer, late of Haycock Twp, acknowledge payment of widow's dower by William Stokes.

Bk 6/pg 80   Mar 19, 1830

Daniel Walton, Ezekiel Walton, Conrad and Margaret Frederic, Mary Walton, Jane Walton and Alice Walton, heirs of Rachel Walton, daughter of Garret Vanhorn, late of Springfield Twp, by their attorney William Walton of Muncey Creek Twp, Lycoming Co, PA, acknowledge payment of estate by James Bryan and William Stokes.   Bk 6/pg 82   Jun 6, 1826

John Whitacre of Loudon Co, VA, guardian of orphan children of Garret Vanhorn, deceased, only heir of John Vanhorn, deceased, who was heir of Garret Vanhorn of Bucks Co, acknowledges payment of estate by James Bryan and William Stokes.   Bk 6/pg 83   Jul 15, 1826

Thomas and Sarah Griffith, Benjamin Vanhorn, Octavia Vanhorn and William Vanhorn, children of John Vanhorn, deceased, all of full age and all of Loudon Co, VA and heirs of Garret Vanhorn of Springfield Twp, acknowledge payment of estate by James Bryan and William Stokes.

Bk 6/pg 83   Jun 24, 1829

Frederick Atherhold of Kingston Twp, Luzerne Co, PA, son of Frederick Atherhold, late of Bedminster Twp, acknowledges payment of estate by William Fretz of Bedminster.   Bk 6/pg 84   May 29, 1830

Heirs of William Watkins, late of Montgomery Co, OH: Joseph Watkins of Lewis Co, KY, David Watkins of Montgomery Co, OH, Joshua Watkins of Warren Co, OH, James and Hannah Mayor of Montgomery Co, OH, George Watkins of Montgomery Co, OH, William and Anna Heath of Mercer Co, OH, William and Rachel Mayor of Mercer Co, OH, Daniel Watkins of Montgomery Co, OH; also Levi and Rachel Hatfield of Brush Co, IN, Jeremiah Allen Watkins, Joseph Watkins and Elizabeth and Martha Watkins, all of Montgomery Co, OH, and Isaac and Mary Moore of Deerburn Co, IN, the latter being heirs of late Jonathan Watkins (3rd son of William); and Elisha and Calinda Jones of Montgomery Co, OH, daughter of late Caleb Watkins of Mason Co, KY (6th son of William). All give power of attorney to William Watkins (4th son of William) to recover estate due from Joseph Watkins of Bucks Co.   Bk 6/pg 84   Apr 17, 1830

Judith Fretz of Tinicum Twp, widow, gives power of attorney to friend Henry Wagner of Tinicum to recover any moneys due her.
                                          Bk 6/pg 87   Mar 6, 1830

Christian Atherhold, son of late Frederick, acknowledges payment by William Fretz of Bedminster Twp. of all estate due from late father and mother.
                                          Bk 6/pg 88   Jun 14, 1830

John A. Gross of Durham Twp, tanner, now 21, acknowledges payment by guardian Jacob K. Riegle of Durham of estate from late father Frederick Gross of Lower Saucon Twp, Northampton Co. Bk 6/pg 90   Apr 1, 1830

Margaret Lombaert, daughter of late Henry Wynkoop, and her children Charles, Marian (wife of Peter Gwinner), Susan (wife of James Vanuxem Jr.) acknowledge payment of estate by Jonathan Wynkoop and Redding Beatty.
                                          Bk 6/pg 91   Nov 20, 1820

Jonathan Leedom of Moreland Twp, Philadelphia Co. gives power of attorney to brother Richard Leedom to recover estate due from late grandfather Richard Leedom of Bucks.   Bk 6/pg 93   Feb 26, 1829

William Watkins of Lewis Co, KY, son of William, late of Montgomery Co, OH and heir of uncle Joseph Watkins, late of Plumstead Twp and attorney for

other heirs of William, acknowledges payment of estate by John W.
Balderston.   Bk 6/pg 93   Jun 19, 1830

Thomas Parker of Schuylkill Twp, Chester Co, administrator for mother
Hannah Foote, formerly Pennington, who was a niece of Joseph Watkins, late
of Plumstead Twp, acknowledges payment of estate by John W. Balderston.
                                               Bk 6/pg 96   Jul 13, 1830

John and Elizabeth Kniceley of Plain Twp, Wayne Co, OH give power of
attorney to Samuel Kniceley of Beaver Co, PA to recover money from estate
of John Kniceley of Quakertown.   Bk 6/pg 97   Apr 26, 1830

John and Mary Pitts, Sarah Nisely and Catharine Rouch (consort of Henry
Rouch of Plain Twp, Wayne Co, OH), daughters of Jacob Nisely of Beaver
Co, PA, give power of attorney to Samuel Nisely of Beaver Co to recover
money from estate of John Nisely of Bucks Co. Bk 6/pg 97   Apr 22, 1830

Jacob Nisely of Beaver Co, PA, guardian for his minor children Jacob,
Stephen, Elizabeth and Peter, gives power of attorney to friend Samuel Nisely
of Beaver Co. to recover legacy due from estate of John Nisely of Bucks.
                                               Bk 6/pg 98   Apr 22, 1830

Mathias Zeiginfus of Haycock Twp, Joseph Zeigenfus of Richland Twp,
Aaron and Sarah Leister of Franconia Twp, Montgomery Co, Jacob and
Hannah Heller of Milford Twp, children of Peter and Catharine Zeigenfus
(late Knizley), sister of John Knizeley of Richland Twp, acknowledge
payment of estate by Caleb Foulke, administrator of Everard Foulke of
Richland Twp. who was John's executor.   Bk 6/pg 100   Apr 12, 1830

Henry Neisley, Daniel and Mary Cameron, William and Sarah Beans,
Benjamin and Eliza Martin and George Neisley, all of Jefferson Co, VA and
minors William, Robert, Drusilla and John M. Neisley by their guardian
Henry Neisley, all heirs of Henry Neisley who was a legatee of John
Neisley/Kniseley of Richland Twp, acknowledge payment of estate by Caleb
Foulke, administrator of Everard Foulke who was John's executor.
                                               Bk 6/pg 101   Apr 6, 1830

John Neicely and Henry and Catharine Rouch, all of Wayne Co, OH, children
of Jacob Neicely who was a brother of John Nicely/Knizely of Richland Twp,
acknowledge through their attorney Samuel Neicly the payment of estate by
Caleb Foulke, administrator of Everard Foulke.
                                               Bk 6/pg 103   May 24, 1830

John Sames of Haycock Twp, guardian of Alexander and Catharine Sames, minor children of Jacob Sames, late of Haycock, who was a son of Elizabeth Sames (deceased), who was a legatee of John Knizely, late of Richland Twp, received payment of estate from Caleb Foulke. Bk 6/pg 104 May 31, 1830

John Sames, Henry Sames, William Sames, Samuel Sames and Gabriel Sames, all of Haycock Twp, heirs of John C. and Elizabeth Sames who was a sister of John Knizely, late of Richland Twp, acknowledge payment of estate by Caleb Foulke. Bk 6/pg 105 Apr 12, 1830

John D. Fenner of Tuscarawas Co, OH gives power of attorney to Owen Rice of Bethlehem to recover estate from Abraham Huber, executor to will of Salome Huber of Bethlehem and from Samuel H. Trauger, administrator of late father Felix Fenner of Springfield Twp. Bk 6/pg 108 Jan 30, 1830

Daniel Fenner of Hanover Twp, Lehigh Co, son of Felix Fenner, late of Nockamixon Twp, farmer, gives power of attorney to Owen Rice of Bethlehem to recover estate from father. Bk 6/pg 109 Apr 5, 1830

John Kephart of Upper Dublin Twp, Montgomery Co, assigns share in estate of father John Kephart, late of New Britain Twp, to Jacob Kephart and John Shutt. Bk 6/pg 110 Aug 20, 1830

Hannah Stelle of Woodbridge Twp, Middlesex Co, NJ gives power of attorney to Edward Stelle of Piscataway Twp, Middlesex Co, NJ to receive annuity from executors of Thomas B. Montanye, late of Bucks. Bk 6/pg 112 Jul 15, 1830

Peter and Mary O'Conner, daughter of Nicholas Buck, late of Nockamixon Twp, give power of attorney to Nicholas Buck to refuse to accept father's real estate. Bk 6/pg 117 Sep 14, 1830

Joseph and Elizabeth Keichline of Newport Twp, Luzerne Co, PA, only daughter and heir of Frederic Premour, late of Richland Twp, acknowledge payment of estate by Samuel Diehl. Bk 6/pg 118 Sep 3, 1830

Barbara Swartz, Samuel Moyer, Abraham Moyer, Jacob Moyer, Anna Wismer, Catharine Moyer and Maria Koch, all of Clinton Twp, Lincoln Co, Niagara District, Upper Canada give power of attorney to friend Andrew Swartz of Clinton Twp. to recover estate from Samuel Moyer of Hilltown Twp, who is executor of Samuel Moyer, late of Hilltown. Bk 6/pg 119 Jul 21, 1830

Frederick and Catharine Deamer, Henry Derr and Magdalena Derr, all of Nockamixon Twp, heirs of John Derr, late of Nockamixon, acknowledge payment of estate by administrator Michael Dech.

Bk 6/pg 121   Sep 28, 1830

John W. Vandegrift of Boston, MA, a soldier in the U.S. Army, gives power of attorney to William Carr of Doylestown to recover estate due under will of his father.   Bk 6/pg 122   May 14, 1830

Samuel H. Dungan of Warwick Twp. due money under will of grandfather Samuel Harrold from his son David Harrold which has now been paid.

Bk 6/pg 123   Oct 26, 1830

Elizabeth Harrold acknowledges payment by David Harrold of legacy from her grandfather Samuel Harrold.   Bk 6/pg 124   Jul 1, 1813

Mary Margerum, widow of Enos, requests that John Miller Jr. administer her husband's estate.   Bk 6/pg 124   Oct 25, 1830

George Young of Plainfield Twp, Northampton Co. and wife Catharine, one of the daughters of Jacob Sterner, late of Bucks Co, give power of attorney to friend James Searle Survior of Forks Twp, Northampton Co.

Bk 6/pg 124   Nov 2, 1830

Widow Magdalena Trauger and Emanuel Trauger, William Trauger and Michael Dech Jr. and wife Hannah (late Trauger), heirs of Frederick Trauger, late of Nockamixon Twp, acknowledge payment of estate by administrators Samuel H. Trauger and Henry Kruger.   Bk 6/pg 125   Oct 29, 1830

Henry G. Stover, son of Jacob Stover, late of Haycock Twp, now age 21, acknowledges payment of estate by guardian Henry Stover and also payment of estate from sister Leadea[sic] Stover.   Bk 6/pg 126   Jul 31, 1830

Michael G. Wisal of Ulysses, Tompkins Co, NY gives power of attorney to friend William McIntire of Tinicum Twp. to recover estate due from father Michael Wisel, late of Tinicum Twp. which had been held by his wife Mary, now deceased.   Bk 6/pg 127   Oct 15, 1830

John Leh of Haycock Twp and wife Elizabeth, late widow of John Keil and daughter of Henry Nase, deceased, assign their share of Henry's estate to Abraham Haney, Esq. of Upper Salford Twp, Montgomery Co. which is due from administrator Frederick Nase.   Bk 6/pg 127   Aug 14, 1830

Conrad Harpel, guardian of Lydia Trauger, daughter of Frederick Trauger, late of Nockamixon Twp, acknowledges payment of estate by administrators Samuel H. Trauger and Henry Groover.   Bk 6/pg 129   Apr 2, 1829

John D. Fenner of Tuscarawas Co, OH (by attorney Owen Rice), Jacob Fenner of Northampton Co, Joseph R. Hess of Lehigh Co. (administrator of George Fenner, late of Lehigh Co. who died intestate), Daniel Fenner of Northampton Co. (by attorney Owen Rice), Valentine Rau of Lehigh Co. and wife Elizabeth and Salome Ott of Northampton Co, children and heirs of Felix Fenner, late of Bucks Co, yeoman, acknowledge payment of estate by administrator Samuel H. Trauger, except the portion reserved for the widow Martha.   Bk 6/pg 129   Oct 23, 1830

Abraham Swartz, minor son of Abraham Swartz, late of Bedminster Twp, now 21, acknowledges payment of estate by guardian Henry Stover.
                                      Bk 6/pg 130   Dec 26, 1829

Sarah S. Spencer, widow, of Penn Twp, Philadelphia Co, sole executrix of will of late husband Joseph Spencer of same place, gives power of attorney to William M. Spencer of Philadelphia to record satisfaction of a mortgage given to James S. Spencer on property in Rockhill Twp. Bk 6/pg 131   Dec 13, 1828

Joseph Johnson of Paoli, Orange Co, IN gives power of attorney to Richard Price of Philadelphia, merchant, to demand legacy from executors of William Bradshaw, late of Plumstead Twp, due to Joseph's wife Sarah who was a daughter of William.   Bk 6/pg 132   Sep 15, 1830

William McIntyre of Tinicum Twp, attorney for Michael G. Weisel, son of Michael Weisel, late of Tinicum Twp, acknowledges payment of estate by executors Jacob Bissey and Nicholas Swartz. Bk 6/pg 132   Nov 19, 1830

Joseph Nicely of Turbut Twp, Northumberland Co, PA, son of Stephen Nicely who was a brother of John Nicely, late of Richland Twp, George and Elizabeth Oyester, Daniel and Sarah Oyster, Anna Nicely and Margaret Nicely, daughters of Stephen and nieces of John, and Joseph as guardian for Stephen's minor children John and Mary, and Joseph as guardian for Samuel and Mary Arnet, minor children of late Susan Arnet who was a daughter of Stephen Nicely, and Elizabeth Schreyer (widow) of Milton, Northumberland Co, daughter of late Elizabeth Sames, another legatee of John Nicely, all acknowledge payment of estate by Caleb Foulke, administrator of Everard Foulke, Esq., late of Richland, who was executor to John.
                                      Bk 6/pg 135   Dec 3, 1830

Samuel Fulmer, minor child of Daniel Fulmer, late of Bedminster Twp, now 21, acknowledges payment of estate (except the widow's dower) by guardian Peter Salladay.   Bk 6/pg 139   Nov 2, 1830

Thomas Krouse of Bucks Co, now 21, acknowledges payment of share of estate of his father Jacob Krouse by his guardian Isaac Stem.
                                                Bk 6/pg 139   Nov 21, 1829

Sally Heist of Milford Twp, now 21, acknowledges payment by guardian Jacob Boyer of her share of estate of late father George Heist, including bond given by brother George Heist.   Bk 6/pg 140   Dec 7, 1830

Henry Nase of Bucks Co. left a will giving estate to his three children Frederick, John and Elizabeth Keil and son-in-law Henry Gerber/Garber. John Keil died shortly before Henry leaving widow Elizabeth (now Ley) who is still alive.   Bk 6/pg 140   Nov 5, 1825

Benjamin E. McCorkle of NJ but formerly of Warwick Twp, now 21, acknowledges payment by guardian Amos Subers of estate from his late father Samuel McCorkle.   Bk 6/pg 141   Jan 3, 1831

Jacob Roathrock and wife Mary, daughter of John Wambolt of Rockhill Twp, deceased, assign her share of father's estate to John Wambolt Jr. of Rockhill Twp. which will be due upon the death of the widow.
                                                Bk 6/pg 142   Jan 8, 1810

George Wambolt, son of late John Wambolt of Rockhill Twp. assigns his share of father's estate to John Wambolt of Rockhill, yeoman, which will be due upon the death of the widow.   Bk 6/pg 143   Oct 7, 1815

George Frantz the elder on Apr 20 1825 executed deeds of conveyance to his three children: Paul, George the younger, Elizabeth Frantz (single woman).
                                                Bk 6/pg 144   Oct 16, 1830

Caroline C. Piper and Sarah Louisa Piper of Chester Borough, Delaware Co, PA give power of attorney to George R. Grantham, Esq. of Doylestown to estate of George Piper from executor Jacob Kechline.
                                                Bk 6/pg 145   Dec 18, 1830

Michael and Mary Stanley, Jesse and Lydia Stanley and John Gourley, all of Guilford Co, NC and heirs of late John and Lydia Gourley, give power of attorney to Jesse Stanley of Philadelphia Co. to recover money from Abraham and David Smith, administrators of John Smith, and Joseph and Thomas Stradling, executors of Moses Smith, all of Bucks Co.

Bk 6/pg 145 [blank] 1830

Abraham and Daniel Fox of Tinicum Twp, sons of late George Fox of Tinicum, acknowledges receipt of estate from executors Jacob and John Fox.

Bk 6/pg 148-150 Apr 3, 1829

Abraham Fox of Tinicum Twp, son of late Elizabeth Fox of Tinicum Twp, acknowledges receipt of estate from executor John Fox.

Bk 6/pg 148 May 15, 1826

Wm and Susannah Spear of Tinicum Twp acknowledge payment by executor John Fox of estate from late Elizabeth Fox of Tinicum.

Bk 6/pg 149 May 1, 1826

Peter and Charles Fox of Lebanon, Hunterdon Co, NJ, executors of Bernet Fox, late of Lebanon, acknowledge payment of estate from Jacob and John Fox, executors of late George Fox of Tinicum Twp.

Bk 6/pg 150 Apr 3, 1826

Wm and Susannah Spear of Tinicum Twp, daughter of late George Fox of Tinicum, acknowledge payment of estate by executors Jacob and John Fox.

Bk 6/pg 151 Mar 30, 1827

Jacob Fox of Tinicum Twp, executors of late George Fox, acknowledges payment of estate by John Fox, the other executor. Bk 6/pg 151 Apr 3, 1829

George Fox of Bedminster Twp and Jacob Fox of Tinicum Twp, sons of late Elizabeth Fox of Tinicum Twp, acknowledge payment of estate by executor John Fox.   Bk 6/pg 152 May 1, 1826

Peter and Charles Fox, executors of late Barnet Fox of Lebanon, Hunterdon Co, NJ, acknowledge payment by John Fox, executor of late Elizabeth Fox of Tinicum Twp.   Bk 6/pg 153 Apr 3, 1826

John and Mary Messer of Nockamixon Twp, daughter of late George Fox of Tinicum Twp, acknowledge payment by executors Jacob and John Fox.

Bk 6/pg 154 May 1, 1826

Daniel Fox of Tinicum Twp and John and Mary Messer of Nockamixon Twp, children of late Elizabeth Fox of Tinicum, acknowledge payment of estate by executor John Fox.   Bk 6/pg 154   May 1, 1826

George Fox of Bedminster Twp, son of late George Fox of Tinicum Twp, acknowledges payment of estate by executors Jacob and John Fox.
Bk 6/pg 156   Apr 3, 1829

Michael Messer of Nockamixon Twp, son of late Lawrence Messer of Nockamixon, acknowledges payment of estate by administrator John Fox.
Bk 6/pg 155   Sep 4, 1819

Michael Lampon of Doylestown Twp gives power of attorney to George Shut of Doylestown Twp. to recover any money due him, including mortgage on property in Nockamixon Twp.   Bk 6/pg 158   Nov 26, 1830

Abraham Overholts of Wilksberry, Lusanna[sic] Co, PA owns woodland in Springfield Twp. He gives power of attorney to Joseph Smith of Nockamixon Twp, cordwainer to sell this lot.   Bk 6/pg 149   Jun 11, 1828

John Eck, late of Montgomery Co, bequeathed legacy to Theodoius Eck of Frederick Co, MD and Joseph Storm (late of Adams Co, PA) in right of his wife Margaret (late Eck) who is now represented by executor Adam Long. Both give power of attorney to friend John Adam of Montgomery Co to recover legacy.   Bk 6/pg 160   Nov 2, 1819

Ann Miller of Donegale Twp, Westmoreland Co, PA, widow of Martin Miller gives power of attorney to son Martin Miller of Donegale Twp to recover money from estate of her father John Eck, late of Montgomery Co.
Bk 6/pg 161   Dec 19, 1812

Martin Miller of Donegale Twp, Westmoreland Co, PA, yeoman, acknowledges payment of estate from John Eck by executor Nicholas Buck.
Bk 6/pg 162   May 5, 1823

Tany Eck, daughter of John Eck, late of Montgomery Co, acknowledges payment of estate by executor Nicholas Buck. Bk 6/pg 163   Aug 19, 1818

Mark Zeigler and wife Sebina, daughter of John Eck, late of Montgomery Co, acknowledge payment of estate by executor Nicholas Buck.
Bk 6/pg 163   May 20, 1817

Margaret Storm, widow of Joseph, late of Canawago Twp, Adams Co, PA, and daughter of John Eck, late of Montgomery Co, acknowledges payment of estate by executor Nicholas Buck.   Bk 6/pg 164   Sep 7, 1816

Conrad Egg of Nockamixon Twp, cordwainer, son of John Egg, late of Upper Salford Twp, Montgomery Co, acknowledges payment of estate by executor Nicholas Buck.   Bk 6/pg 164   Jun 18, 1816

Catharine Adam of Upper Hanover Twp, Montgomery Co, daughter of John Eck, late of Upper Salford Twp, Montgomery Co, acknowledges payment of estate by executors Theodore Eck and Nicholas Buck.
                                    Bk 6/pg 165   Aug 22, 1816

Henry Carver, son of Thomas Carver of Bucks Co, is due a legacy from his grandfather Samuel Harrold, late of Bucks Co. He acknowledges payment by Samuel's son David Harrold.   Bk 6/pg 167   Dec 2, 1830

Nehemiah and Tamer Smith of Guernsey Co, OH give power of attorney to Joseph Smith of Guernsey Co. to recover money from William Large and John Baldison, executors of late Joseph Watkins of Bucks Co, Tamer being a daughter of the late James Watkins who was a brother of Joseph.
                                    Bk 6/pg 168   Jul 13, 1829

Joseph Watkins of Guerney Co, OH gives power of attorney to Stove[?] Hutchinson of Harrison Co, OH to recover estate from William Large and John K. Balderston, executors of Joseph Watkins who was brother to Joseph's late father James Watkins.   Bk 6/pg 170   Mar 5, 1831

William Huntsman of Springfield Twp, Hamilton Co, OH gives power of attorney to brother David Huntsman of Bucks Co. to recover money from John Funk due out of the estate of late Sarah Huntsman.
                                    Bk 6/pg 171   Jan 11, 1831

Belinda Fell, Sarah Fell and Elizabeth Fell, all of Buckingham Twp acknowledge payment of estate from late father David Fell by William Watson and Moses Rich.   Bk 6/pg 172   Apr 1, 1831

Sarah Fell, widow of David Fell, releases William Watson and Moses Rich from the privileges due her under David's will. Bk 6/pg 172   Apr 1, 1831

Martha Rich of Buckingham Twp. gives power of attorney to brother Moses Rich of Buckingham to record satisfaction of a mortgage given to Cyrus Betts.   Bk 6/pg 173   Apr 5, 1830

Margaret McCarty of Haycock Twp, spinster, gives power of attorney to brother-in-law Thomas McCarty of Haycock, yeoman, to recover estate of late father Nicholas McCarty from brother John G. McCarty of Haycock, yeoman.   Bk 6/pg 176   Apr 23, 1829

Samuel Scatton of Philadelphia assigns right in a mortgage to his father William Scatton of Philadelphia.   Bk 6/pg 176   Jan 21,1 830

Joseph and Margaret Fisher of Columbiana Co, OH give power of attorney to Amos Richardson of Bucks Co. to sell land in Richland Twp.
                                                 Bk 6/pg 179   Nov 11, 1829

Hannah Johnson of Easton releases the executors of her late husband Henry Johnson of Bucks Co. from payment of the share of her dower related to her son Henry Johnson.   Bk 6/pg 180   Sep 13, 1824

John Wildman acknowledges payment by Joshua Knight of his share of estate of late father Thomas Wildman.   Bk 6/pg 182   Apr 1, 1831

Jacob Bartels of Rockhill Twp, yeoman and wife Elizabeth, daughter of David Wambold, late of Rockhill, acknowledge payment of estate by Elizabeth's guardian Andrew Drumbor.   Bk 6/pg 182   Apr 2, 1831

Daniel Adams of Durham Twp, now 21, acknowledges payment by guardian John Fackenthall of estate from father John Adams.
                                                 Bk 6/pg 183   Mar 31, 1831

John A. Gross and Hannah of Durham Twp. acknowledge payment by Hannah's guardian John Fackenthall of estate from her father Philip Leidigh, late of Durham.   Bk 6/pg 183   Nov 23, 1830

Israel Shaw of Whitepain Twp, Montgomery Co, now 21, acknowledges payment by guardians George Custerd and Samuel Shaw of estate from father Joseph Shaw of Richland Twp.   Bk 6/pg 184   May 24, 1830

Hezekiah Hughs of Colerain Twp, Belmont Co, OH gives power of attorney to Ephraim Shaw of Plumstead Twp, yeoman, to recover any moneys due him.   Bk 6/pg 184   Oct 5, 1829

Solomon and Margaret Litzenberger of Haycock Twp. assign legacy due Margaret from the will of her father Michael Young, late of Philadelphia Co. to Jacob Mast Jr. of Tinicum Twp.   Bk 6/pg 185   Apr 23, 1831

Thomas Craven of Warminster Twp, yeoman, and wife Margaret have agreed to separate due to uneasiness between them.   Bk 6/pg 187   Apr 23, 1831

Magdalena Hoch of Clinton Twp, Lincoln Co, Niagara District, Upper Canada, widow, gives power of attorney to friend Andrew Swartz of Clinton Twp. to recover money from Philip Lederman of Bedminster Twp, executor of estate of late Catharine Lederman of Bedminster.
                                        Bk 6/pg 187   Jul 21, 1830

Martha Rose of Upper Makefield Twp. acknowledges payment by William Howard for Thomas Briton, both of Kingwood Twp, NJ of widow's right in property formerly belonging to Amos Rose.   Bk 6/pg 189   Apr 23, 1831

Olinda Tomlinson, widow of Joseph, late of Bristol Borough releases dower right upon payment by Thomas Tomlinson.   Bk 6/pg 189   Mar 22, 1831

Amelia Snyder, daughter of Jacob Snyder, late of Hilltown Twp, now married to Levi Sellers, acknowledge payment of estate by her former guardian Conrad Snyder.   Bk 6/pg 190   Mar 4, 1831

Jacob and Lidia Savicool, daughter of Jacob Snyder, late of Hilltown Twp, acknowledge payment of estate by her former guardian Conrad Snyder.
                                        Bk 6/pg 191   May 31, 1828

Henry Benner of Wayne Twp, Columbiana Co, OH, son of Magdalena Benner, late of Haycock Twp, acknowledges payment of estate by executor Andrew Heller.   Bk 6/pg 198   May 28, 1831

David Wambold of Rockhill Twp and wife Martha, daughter of Jacob Senn, late of Rockhill, acknowledge payment of estate by former guardian George Roudenbush of Rockhill.   Bk 6/pg 198   Apr 13, 1830

Henry Schlichter of Rockhill Twp, yeoman, and wife Maria, James Cassady of Sussex Co, NJ, yeoman and wife Ann, George Price of Montgomery Co, tobacconist and wife Elizabeth, sisters and heirs of Matilda Senn, a minor daughter of Jacob Senn, acknowledge payment of estate by Matilda's former guardian George Roudenbush.   Bk 6/pg 199   Jun 14, 1825

Elizabeth Mast of Nockamixon Twp, Susanna Fulmer of Tinicum Twp, Michael and Catharine Worman of Tinicum and Samuel Rufe of Bedminster Twp, heirs of late George Rufe of Nockamixon acknowledge receipt of payment by executors Frederick Rufe and John Rufe.

Bk 6/pg 200   May 28, 1831

Conrad Benner of Knox Twp, Columbiana Co, OH, son of Mary Magdalena Benner, late of Haycock Twp, acknowledges payment of estate by executor Andrew Heller.   Bk 6/pg 204   Jun 20, 1831

Michael Dech, administrator of Jacob Rufe, late of Nockamixon Twp, who was an heir of George Rufe, late of Nockamixon, acknowledges payment of estate by executors Frederick and John Rufe.   Bk 6/ pg 205   Jul 18, 1831

Reuben Miller of Marlborough Twp, Chester Co. and Amos Miller of West _all_owfield[?] Twp, Chester Co, heirs of John Mitchell, give power of attorney to John Allen Mitchell of Middletown Twp to sell land of John Mitchell.   Bk 6/pg 206   Jul 3, 1830

John and Maria Barton (late Miller) and John Miller, all of Mill Creek Hundred, New Castle Co, DE give power of attorney to John Allen Mitchell of Middletown Twp, administrator of John Mitchell, deceased, to recover all moneys due them.   Bk 6/pg 207   Aug 13, 1830

George and Mary White of Nockamixon Twp, daughter of Melchor Weydemeyer, late of Tinicum Twp, acknowledge payment of estate by executors David White and Jacob Weydemeyer.   Bk 6/pg 209   Jul 26, 1831

Catharine Dotterer of Frederick Twp, Montgomery Co, daughter of John Youngken of Nockamixon Twp, deceased, acknowledge payment of estate by brother Nicholas Youngken.   Bk 6/pg 209   Jul 25, 1831

William C. Jamison of Warwick Twp, yeoman, now 21, acknowledges payment by guardian Robert Jamison of estate from late uncle Henry Jamison.

Bk 6/pg 210   Aug 16, 1831

Jacob Snyder of Hilltown Twp. died intestate leaving nine children: John, Michael, Jacob, Henry, Daniel, William, Catharine (wife of John Souder), Mary Magdalena (wife of George Sellers), Sophia (wife of Elias Koch). Jacob, Henry, William, Daniel, John and Catharine Souder, Elias and Sophia Koch and George and Magdalena Sellers acknowledge payment of estate by administrators Michael and John Snyder.   Bk 6/pg 210   Mar 14, 1831

Samuel Doan of Upper Makefield Twp. gives power of attorney to son James Doan of Upper Makefield to recover any moneys due him.

Bk 6/pg 215   Aug 29, 1831

John Wentz, John and Mary Bunker, John and Catharine Hammel, Samuel and Lydia Brand, Jonathan Wentz and Nathan Wentz (by guardian Henry Jacoby), all of Butler Co, OH, children of John and Barbara Wentz and grandchildren of George Erdman, late of Milford Twp, acknowledge payment of estate by administrator Jacob Erdman.   Bk 6/pg 219   May 23, 1831

Anna Brown (widow), John and Elizabeth Schofield, Josiah and Sarah P. Shaw, and Thomas and Lydia Hallowell, daughters of late Thomas Bye of Bucks Co, acknowledge payment of estate by John Bye.

Bk 6/pg 220   Apr 29, 1831

Richard Neeld acknowledges payment by guardian William Palmer.

Bk 6/pg 223   Dec 22, 1830

Joseph Thackary acknowledges payment by guardian William Palmer.

Bk 6/pg 223   Apr 11, 1828

Benj. P. and Samuel Y. Tomlinson acknowledge payment by guardian William Palmer.   Bk 6/pg 224   Oct 18, 1828

Magdalena Trauger, widow of Frederick, Emanuel Trauger, William Trauger, Henry and Mary Kruger, Michael and Hannah Dech Jr., heirs of Lydia Trauger, late of Nockamixon Twp, acknowledge payment of estate by administrator Samuel H. Trauger.   Bk 6/pg 225   Jul 30, 1831

Sarah Cox and Ann Polhemus acknowledge receipt of payment by Garret H. Vanzant, executor of their father Harman Vanzant.

Bk 6/pg 226   Jun 18, 1829

Rebecca Vanzant acknowledges as administrator of her late husband Joseph Vanzant that her husband had received the legacy due from his father Harman Vanzant during his lifetime.   Bk 6/pg 227   May 1, 1830

Joseph Hayes acknowledges receipt from John Paxon, administrator of Garret H. Vanzant of one-fifth of a legacy left by Harman Vanzant to his grandson Harman Vanzant, son of Jacob Vanzant, deceased.

Bk 6/pg 227   Jun 9, 1829

Mary Wilson of Nockamixon Twp, widow of Samuel Wilson of Nockamixon, assigns her dower right to her three daughters Rebecca Wilson, Mary Ann Wilson and Mary Powers.   Bk 6/pg 228   May 15, 1828

Elizabeth Vandegrift of Bensalem Twp. gives power of attorney to Levi D. Vandegrift of Bensalem to sell some land situate in Bensalem.
                                               Bk 6/pg 229   Nov 16, 1831

John Townsend Sr. of Ladsburgh Twp. and wife Mary, daughter of late Robert Walker, give power of attorney to John Walker of Buckingham Twp. to refuse to accept her father's real estate.   Bk 6/pg 232   Nov 29, 1831

Anna Leatherman of Bedminster Twp, now 21, acknowledges payment by guardian William Fretz of estate from late father Christian Leatherman.
                                               Bk 6/pg 233   Mar 7, 1831

John Swartz, son of Abraham Swartz, late of Bedminster Twp, now 21, acknowledges payment of estate by guardian William Fretz.
                                               Bk 6/pg 234   Dec 19, 1831

Frederick Wireman, grandson of Frederick Atherhold, late of Bedminster Twp, acknowledges payment by guardian William Fretz of his share of the dower due upon the death of the widow Ester.   Bk 6/pg 234   Oct 21, 1831

John C. Lester, son of John Lester, late of Richland Twp, and Moses Wilson and Richard Moore, guardians of John's daughter Jane, agree to choose men to value John's real estate.   Bk 6/pg 235   Aug 22, 1831

Leanna Klein (late Heist) of Milford Twp, now 21, acknowledges payment by her guardian John Graber of estate from late father George Heist.
                                               Bk 6/pg 238   Dec 8, 1831

Andrew Allgart died intestate many years ago. His real estate was adjudged to eldest son Lewis Allgart subject to lien during life of widow Magdalena. Heir Jacob Allgart of Nockamixon acknowledges to George Ackerman, administrator of Lewis Allgart, that he received his share of the dower from Lewis.   Bk 6/pg 239   Dec 29, 1831

Christian Trauger Jr. of Nockamixon Twp. and wife Elizabeth (late Elizabeth Mast, widow of Jacob Mast) acknowledge payment from Frederick Rufe, administrator to Jacob Mast, last of Nockamixon. Bk 6/pg 241   Feb 2, 1832

Joseph Fretz, guardian of Margaret and Franey Delp, minor children of George Delp, late of Bedminster Twp, acknowledges payment by George's executors Jacob Delp and Conrad Harpel.   Bk 6/pg 244   Apr 4, 1831

Rebecca and Maryann Wilson of Nockamixon Twp. acknowledge payment by John W. Stover, administrator of Samuel Wilson, late of Nockamixon.
Bk 6/pg 244   Feb 11, 1832

Jesse Ruth of Springfield Twp, now 21, acknowledges payment by guardian Joseph Frey of Springfield for estate of late father Jacob Ruth of Springfield.
Bk 6/pg 246   Mar 19, 1831

Henry G. Stover of Tinicum Twp, son of Jacob Stover, late of Haycock Twp, acknowledges payment by Abraham and Joseph Stover of Nockamixon, executors for his grandfather David Stover of Nockamixon. Henry is also entitled to one-half share of his late sister Lydia's share.
Bk 6/pg 247   Jul 17, 1830

Abby Addis of Northampton Twp, spinster, gives power of attorney to James Cummings of Warwick Twp, yeoman, to recover money from Amos Addis, executor of Nancy Sommers.   Bk 6/pg 249   Jan 16, 1832

Henry Swartz of Tinicum Twp. acknowledges payment by Samuel Funk of New Britain Twp. of legacy from Christian Rohr, late of New Britain Twp.
Bk 6/pg 250   Jan 15, 1827

John and Abraham Heckler of Lower Salford Twp, Montgomery Co, administrators of Christian Roar, acknowledge payment by Samuel Funk who purchased the real estate of Christian Roar the elder.
Bk 6/pg 250   Mar 8, 1824

John Groff of Warrington Twp and wife Anna, Jacob Rohr of New Britain Twp, Jacob Beidler of Tredyffrin Twp, Chester Co, and wife Freany, children of Christian Rohr, late of New Britain Twp, acknowledge payment by Samuel Funk of New Britain Twp. of the dower due upon the death of the widow Barbara.   Bk 6/pg 251   Apr 7, 1830

Jacob Swarts of Warrington Twp, Christian S. Loux of Bedminster Twp (administrator of late Abraham Swartz) and Elizabeth Swartz of Bedminster Twp. acknowledge payment by Samuel Funk of New Britain Twp. of a legacy due from Christian Rohr, late of New Britain.   Bk 6/pg 253   Oct 2, 1826

Susannah Fulmer of Nockamixon Twp, widow of Philip Fulmer, late of Nockamixon, acknowledges payment by Jacob N. Fulmer and Magdalena Fulmer for Philip's real estate.   Bk 6/pg 255   Mar 29, 1831

Philip Brunner of Warrington Twp. acknowledges payment by Richard Riale of Doylestown Twp. of a legacy from estate of David Evans, late of Doylestown which Jacob and Susanna Kern assigned to Philip.
Bk 6/pg 256   Mar 1, 1832

George Wyker of Tinicum Twp. gives power of attorney to son Samuel Wyker to enter satisfaction of a judgment against Jacob Kooker of Nockamixon Twp.   Bk 6/pg 257   Mar 1, 1832

Joseph Williams, guardian of Tyson Jones, gives power of attorney to Benjamin Jones to refuse to accept real estate of Peter Tyson.
Bk 6/pg 258   Nov 29, 1831

Joseph Paul, late of Warrington Twp, died intestate leaving a widow Hannah and four children: Joshua, Yeomans, Sarah and Hannah. Yeomans Paul, Abel and Sarah Thomas and Evan and Hannah Jones acknowledge payment of their shares by Joshua Paul.   Bk 6/pg 260   Dec 3, 1831

Christian Trauger of Nockamixon Twp, yeoman, and wife Elizabeth, legatee in the will of George Rufe, late of Nockamixon Twp, acknowledge payment by executors Frederick and John Rufe.   Bk 6/pg 272   Apr 2, 1832

Barbara Blank, widow of John Blank and daughter of George Kline, late of Milford Twp, acknowledges payment of legacy by George Kline, son of George.   Bk 6/pg 272   Apr 5, 1832

Elizabeth Stover, widow of Henry, late of Bedminster Twp, Samuel and Barbara Detweiler, and Daniel and Elizabeth Rosenberger, heirs of Henry, acknowledge payment of estate by administrators Abraham and Henry Stover.
Bk 6/pg 273   Feb 25, 1832

Ann Leedom, widow of Richard Leedom, late of Northampton Twp, and Enos Morris, Esq. of Newtown are about to be married. Both are to keep their property separate.   Bk 6/pg 275   Mar 15, 1826

Hugh Meredith of Doylestown, heir of Dr. Charles Meredith, gives power of attorney to Charles E. DuBois to refuse to accept Dr. Meredith's real estate.
Bk 6/pg 276   Apr 7, 1832

Joseph Weisel and wife Susanna (widow of Philip Fulmer) acknowledge payment by Jacob N. Fulmer and Conrad Harpel, Philip's administrators.
Bk 6/pg 277   Dec 26, 1831

Catharine Stover of Bedminster Twp, spinster, now 21, acknowledges payment by guardian Abraham F. Stover of estate due from grandfather Ulrick Stover.
Bk 6/pg 277   Mar 14, 1832

Staples Thompson of Butler Co, OH gives power of attorney to David Thompson of Bucks Co. to sell his share of estate of late father Staples Thompson.
Bk 6/pg 278   Sep 29, 1831

Jesse R. Lovett acknowledges payment by executor Samuel L. Booz of estate from late father Samuel Lovett.
Bk 6/pg 280   Nov 1, 1830

Joshua L. Hart and Kinsey Bonham, children and heirs of late Joseph Bonham, acknowledge payment by executors Samuel Kinsey and Jonathan K. Bonham, who also paid what was due to the widow Letitia.
Bk 6/pg 280   Apr 19, 1832

John Landes of Saucon Twp, Northampton Co, cooper and wife Susanna, daughter of Henry Shelly, late of Milford Twp, acknowledge payment by Henry Shelly (son of Henry) for estate due upon the death of the widow Mary.
Bk 6/pg 282   Jan 11, 1827

John Stover of Haycock Twp, now 21, acknowledges payment by guardian William Fretz of estate due from great-grandfather and grandfather.
Bk 6/pg 283   Apr 10, 1832

Jacob Weidemeier Jr. and wife Catharine of Plumstead Twp, grandson of Melchior Weidemeier, late of Tinicum Twp, agree with Jacob Sr. and the other children of Jacob Sr. to retain only his one-eleventh share of the estate of his grandfather. Jacob Jr.'s siblings are John, Samuel, Elizabeth, Catharine, Sarah, Isaac, Susan, Lavina, Mary and Jonas.
Bk 6/pg 285   Apr 21, 1832

Derrick Krewson, late of Northampton Twp, bequeathed his estate to his children Charles, James, Elizabeth (wife of Garret Carver), Charity (wife of Thomas Hart) and Jane (wife of John M. Craven) and to his grandchildren, children of daughter Mary Cornell, deceased (Elizabeth and Jane Matilda Cornell). Elizabeth Cornell married Thomas Purdy of Southampton Twp, but

now of Doylestown Twp. Thomas Purdy acknowledges payment by
Elizabeth's guardian Thomas B. Craven.   Bk 6/pg 287   May 9, 1832

Joseph Hart, Esq., late of Warminster Twp, bequeathed estate to his three sons
(including Lewis F.) and two daughters: Eliza Ann and Clarissa Maria.
Clarissa Maria married Joseph Carver of Solebury Twp. and died after
reaching age 21. Joseph Carver acknowledges payment of Clarissa's share by
Lewis F. Hart.   Bk 6/pg 288   Apr 4, 1832

Henry Meyers, guardian for Henry and Catharine Strouse, minor children of
Henry Strouse Jr., late of Nockamixon Twp, acknowledges payment of estate
by Conard Harpel, administrator for Henry Jr.   Bk 6/pg 290   May 26, 1832

Peter Smith and wife Elizabeth, daughter of Steven Horn, late of Richland
Twp, acknowledge payment by Benjamin Bartholomew of legacy due at
death of Steven's widow.   Bk 6/pg 290   Mar 31, 1827

Abraham W. Overholt of Fairfield Twp, Columbianna Co, OH, innkeeper,
and Martin Overholt, Joseph Overholt, Mary Overholt and Jacob and
Margaret Leatherman, all of Wadsworth Twp, Medina Co, OH, children of
late Joseph Overholt and grandchildren of late Martin Overholt,
acknowledges payment of estate by Jacob Overholt, surviving executor of
Martin.   Bk 6/pg 292   Apr 26, 1832

Peter and Mary Ann Gwinner of Newtown have decided to separate due to
some unhappy differences which have lately arisen between them.
Bk 6/pg 294   Apr 10, 1830

Joseph Hart, Esq., late of Warminster Twp, bequeathed estate to his three sons
(including Lewis F.) and two daughters: Eliza Ann and Clarissa Maria. Eliza
Ann married David Marple of Philadelphia who acknowledges payment of
Eliza Ann's share by Lewis F. Hart.   Bk 6/pg 297   Jun 28, 1832

John Miller of Milford Twp. acknowledges payment by John Eberhard and
Charles Deckenshit, executors for his late wife Maria who was a daughter of
George Kline the elder.   Bk 6/pg 299   Apr 6, 1831

Susana Kline "said to be intermarried with Abraham Olewine" and daughter
of George Kline, late of Milford Twp and John Kline (by attorney William
Dillinger of Upper Milford Twp, Lehigh Co) acknowledge payment of estate
by John Miller.   Bk 6/pg 300   Apr 3, 1830

167

Beulah Carey of Newtown and Thomas Carey of Solebury Twp. are about to be married and wish to keep their property separate.

Bk 6/pg 301   May 10, 1832

John Kinsey, Abraham Kinsey, Daniel and Susanna Stauffer and Henry and Barbara Bechtel of Waterloo Twp. and Jacob Kinsey of Dumfries, Halton Co, Gove District, Upper Canada, give power of attorney to George Probst of South Whitehall Twp, Lehigh Co. to recover money from Abraham Kinsey of Rockhill Twp, executor of late John Kinsey of Rockhill.

Bk 6/pg 303   Feb 15, 1832

George Probst, attorney, acknowledges payment by Abraham Kinsey, executor of John Kinsey, late of Rockhill Twp.   Bk 6/pg 305   Jun 22, 1832

Jacob Krouse of Alexandria Twp, Hunterdon Co, NJ, now 21, acknowledges payment by guardian Isaac Stem of estate of late father Jacob Krouse.

Bk 6/pg 306   Apr 23, 1832

Elias Wildman of Lower Makefield Twp, now 21, acknowledges payment by guardian John Miller Jr. of estate from late father William Wildman.

Bk 6/pg 306   Jul 9, 1832

Samuel Rothrock of Lower Saucon Twp, Northampton Co and Susanna Staufer, widow of Henry Strycker of Milford Twp, both guardians of the children of Henry Strycker (John, Samuel, Margaret—since 21, and Hannah), acknowledge payment from David Deahl and Henry Trumbauer, executors of John Strycker, late of Milford Twp.   Bk 6/pg 309   Mar 24, 1832

Charles Green, Hannah Green, Livy Green, all of Richland Twp, and David and Matilda Yonken of Springfield Twp, acknowledge payment from brother John Green of estate from grandfather Dr. Felix Linn.

Bk 6/pg 310   Oct 16, 1827

Joseph Menchinger/Mininger, Jacob Menchinger, John Menchinger, John and Mary Musselman, John and Elizabeth Young, Henry and Sarah Frick and Susanna Menchinger, children of Joseph Menchinger, late of Richland Twp, choose men to value Joseph's real estate.   Bk 6/pg 311   Nov 12, 1831

Jane Grier of Warwick Twp, widow of John Grier, releases her son John S. Grier from his remaining obligations under John's will.

Bk 6/pg 314   May 12, 1826

James Hogge of Bucks Co, a pensioner of the United States, gives power of attorney to William Carson to collect his pension.   Bk 6/pg 316   Sep 4, 1832

John H. Steiner, administrator for his wife Nancy, late of Frederick Twp, Montgomery Co, acknowledges payment by Nancy's former guardian John Yost of the estate due from her late father Daniel Fulmer of Bedminster Twp.
Bk 6/pg 320   Sep 1, 1832

Joel Doan of Upper Makefield Twp, carpenter, gives power of attorney to son John Doan of Northampton Twp. to recover any money due him.
Bk 6/pg 321   Mar 24, 1832

Mahlon Doan of Muncy Twp, Lycoming Co, PA gives power of attorney to James Johnson of Upper Makefield Twp. to recover money due from estate of his late father Mahlon Doan of Upper Makefield.   Bk 6/pg 323   Dec 19, 1831

Jesse Doan of Upper Makefield Twp, administrator of Eli Doan, late of Solebury Twp, gives power of attorney to friend Thomas Betts of Upper Makefield to sell Eli's real estate.   Bk 6/pg 323   Sep 11, 1832

Jacob Kratz of Hilltown Twp, now 21, acknowledges payment by his guardian Isaac Hunsicker of estate from late father Jacob Kratz.
Bk 6/pg 326   Aug 11, 1832

Mary Rufe, now 21, acknowledges payment by Michael Dech of estate from her late father Jacob Rufe of Nockamixon Twp.   Bk 6/pg 326   Sep 1, 1832

Sarah Vanzant, daughter of Gabriel Vansant of Northumberland Co, PA married John Reed and moved to Armitage Co and died leaving issue Peter, William (since deceased, widow Sarah), James, Nancy, Amos, John and Rebecca, last three still minors. Sarah's heirs give power of attorney to Amos Vansant of Lower Makefield Twp. to receive money due from estate of Gabriel Vansant.   Bk 6/pg 330   Jun 5, 1832

Abraham Person and Elizabeth, wife of Jesse Algert (late Person), give power of attorney to Michael Dech, Esq. of Doylestown to enter satisfaction for bonds given them by Lawrence Person.   Bk 6/pg 331   Oct 5, 1832

Jane Cornell, widow of Gilliam Cornell, late of Southampton Twp and only child Lydia (wife of John M. Neal) sell Gilliam's real estate.
Bk 6/pg 331   Oct 9, 1832

Catharine Dotterer of Frederick Twp, Montgomery Co, widow, daughter of John Youngken, late of Nockamixon Twp, gives power of attorney to David Seip of Nockamixon Twp. to enter satisfaction of a bond from Nicholas Youngken. Bk 6/pg 339 Oct 15, 1832

Felix Fenner Jr. of Lansing Twp, Tompkins Co, NY and wife Elizabeth (late Trauger), heir of Frederick Trauger, late of Nockamixon Twp, yeoman, and of Lydia Trauger, late of Nockamixon, acknowledge payment of estate by administrators Samuel H. Trauger and Henry Kruger.
Bk 6/pg 339 May 1, 1832

Felix Fenner Jr. of Lansing Twp, Tompkins Co, NY, heir of Felix Fenner Sr., late of Nockamixon Twp, yeoman, acknowledges payment of estate by administrator Samuel H. Trauger. Bk 6/pg 341 May 1, 1832

James Vanuxem of Cincinnati, OH is indebted to Mary Wurtz of Philadelphia but is entitled through his wife to one-third share of estate of her late grandfather Henry Wynkoop which is to be paid at the decease of her mother Margaretta Lumbart. James assigns this legacy to John Wurtz of Philadelphia. Bk 6/pg 342 Mar 30, 1827

Henry, Michael and Simon Frankenfield, executors of Adam Frankenfield, late of Springfield Twp, choose men to value Adam's real estate.
Bk 6/pg 346 Oct 17, 1832

John H. Oberteuffer of Philadelphia, administrator of Harman Oberteuffer, late of Springfield Twp, gives power of attorney to Samuel H. Trauger of Nockamixon Twp. to recover moneys due the estate.
Bk 6/pg 350 Nov 30, 1832

Reuben S. Weaver of Dauphin Co, PA, son of Joseph Weaver, late of Philadelphia, gives power of attorney to Catherine S. Weaver of Philadelphia, widow, to recover all moneys due him. Bk 6/pg 350 Nov 29, 1832

Mary Leidy of Hatfield Twp, Montgomery Co, widow, daughter of Abraham Wambold, late of Franconia Twp, Montgomery Co, gives power of attorney to brother Samuel Wambold of Franconia to invest her share of estate.
Bk 6/pg 352 Dec 3, 1832

Alexander Derbyshire acknowledges payment by guardian William Palmer
Bk 6/pg 353 Feb 29, 1832

Samuel Silvester, mariner, late of Baltimore but now residing in Jeremie in the Republic of Haiti, gives power of attorney to wife Eliza Silvester of Baltimore to collect any moneys due him.   Bk 6/pg 353   Oct 12, 1832

James Thornton Bidgood, now of Mobile, AL, youngest son of William Bidgood, late of Bucks Co, gives power of attorney to Charles E. DuBois, attorney at law, to recover money due from dower of late mother Elizabeth Bidgood or late brothers William Bidgood who died in Savanah, GA in 1813, Samuel Bidgood who died in Jackson, AL in 1819 and Joseph Bidgood who died in Albany, NY in 1805.   Bk 6/pg 355   Jun 16, 1832

William Moyer of Milford Twp, Lehigh Co, son of Jacob Moyer, late of Springfield Twp, now 21, acknowledges payment by guardian Jacob Beidler of estate from late father and late grandfather Abraham Moyer of Springfield Twp.   Bk 6/pg 358   Feb 6, 1832

Jane Lester of Richland Twp, now 21, acknowledges payment by guardians Moses Wilson and Richard Moore of estate from late father John Lester.
    Bk 6/pg 358   Dec 27, 1832

John and Mary Coon of Henry Co, IN give power of attorney to Jacob Sider of Sacken [i.e. Saucon] Twp, Leihath [i.e. Lehigh] Co. to sell real estate in Bucks County to Maria Coon of Springfield Twp.   Bk 6/pg 361   Nov 6, 1832

Tobias Weber of Lower Saucon Twp, Northampton Co, heir of Martin Weber, late of Lower Saucon Twp, yeoman, gives power of attorney to John Leith of Lower Saucon Twp. to recover estate from administrators Joseph Ehard [Ehrhard] and Daniel Geissinger.   Bk 6/pg 362   Dec 29, 1832

George Kressler, late of Northumberland Co. but now of Springfield Twp, revokes a previous power of attorney given to Joseph Afflebach of Springfield Twp. to receive legacy from his late father George Kressler's estate.   Bk 6/pg 363   Feb 4, 1833

Jacob and Susanna Krouse of Nockamixon Twp. have decided to separate due to unhappy differences which subsist between them.
    Bk 6/pg 366   Jan 18, 1833

Elizabeth Luger of Plumstead Twp. gives power of attorney to son Christopher Luger of Plumstead to sell real estate where Christopher now resides.   Bk 6/pg 368   Jan 24, 1833

Henry and Elizabeth Afflerbach of Philadelphia acknowledge receipt of payment from Abraham Trauger and John Hager, the surplus of Henry's estate after paying off his debts.   Bk 6/pg 369   Jan 15, 1833

Samuel and Barbara Detweiler, daughter of Henry Stover, late of Bedminster Twp, acknowledge payment by brother Abraham Stover of part of estate.
                                                Bk 6/pg 373   Feb 4, 1833

Hezekiah and Elizabeth Hughs of Belmont Co, OH give power of attorney to fiend James Hampton of Bucks Co. to sell real estate in Bucks Co.
                                                Bk 6/pg 376   Sep 6, 1832

Joseph Fries of Tuscaroras Co, OH, son of Jacob Fries, late of Doylestown Twp, gives power of attorney to Jacob Fries of Doylestown Twp. to recover money from Thomas Stephens of Doylestown Twp. who purchased his father's real estate.   Bk 6/pg 377   Feb 15, 1833

Sarah White of Middletown Twp, widow, gives power of attorney to friend Samuel Everett of Middletown to recover moneys due her.
                                                Bk 6/pg 382   Mar 4, 1833

John, James and Rachel Parry acknowledge payment by Hugh B. Ely, administrator of Thomas Ely, for estate due from their grandfather John Ely of Buckingham Twp.   Bk 6/pg 384   Apr 7, 1832

Elizabeth Rich of Buckingham Twp. gives power of attorney to brother Moses Rich of Buckingham to recover money due her.
                                                Bk 6/pg 387   Mar 27, 1833

Jonathan Bachman of Upper Saucon Twp, Lehigh Co. is firmly bound unto his father Jacob Bachman of Upper Saucon to provide him a room.
                                                Bk 6/pg 388   Apr 8, 1826

Jacob Luger, late of Philadelphia, appointed his wife Elizabeth his sole executor. At Elizabeth's deceased, estate to be divided between John Luger of Plumstead Twp. and Christopher Luger. John sells his right to Christopher.
                                                Bk 6/pg 389   Apr 1, 1833

Martin Loux of Tinicum Twp, guardian of George Smith, minor son of late George Smith, acknowledges payment by Henry Means of Plumstead Twp, George's previous guardian.   Bk 6/pg 395   Apr 6, 1833

Rachel Burges, daughter of late Cornelius Shepherd, acknowledges payment by Moses L. Shepherd of estate from father.   Bk 6/pg 395   Apr 2, 1833

Frederick Jordon of Upper Saucon Twp, Esq., in right of his late wife Catharine, daughter of Michael Hartzel, late of Bucks Co, yeoman, gives power of attorney to Jacob Hartzel of Lehigh CO, to recover money from Michael's estate as a result of the death of Michael's widow Catharine.
Bk 6/pg 396   Apr 4, 1833

Aaron Smith of Plumstead Twp. gives power of attorney to two sons Samuel and Charles Smith to transact all his business.   Bk 6/pg 397   Apr 6, 1833

Catharine Crouthamel, mother of Henry Crouthamel, late of Bedminster Twp, releases sons Andrew, John, George, Abraham, Jacob and Samuel and daughter Elizabeth (wife of Michael Rush), and heirs of deceased daughter Catharine (wife of Jacob Nace) of any right in her son Henry's estate.
Bk 6/pg 399   Mar 21, 1833

Elizabeth Nicholas, daughter of Abraham Nicholas, late of Tinicum Twp, now 21, acknowledges payment by guardian Michael Sheetz of estate from father.
Bk 6/pg 402   Apr 11, 1833

William Chapman of Philadelphia, teacher, and Lucretia Winslow of Philadelphia, instructress, intend shortly to be married.
Bk 6/pg 403   Aug 5, 1818

Daniel Rosenberger and wife Elizabeth, daughter of Henry Stover, late of Bedminster Twp, acknowledge payment of estate by brother Abraham Stover.
Bk 6/pg 406   Feb 25, 1832

Susanna Clemens, daughter of Adam Clemens and grandchild of Peter Laubenstone, late of Tinicum Twp, now 21, acknowledges payment of estate by guardian Jacob Bissey.   Bk 6/pg 410   Jun 3, 1831

Conrad Shitz of Nockamixon Twp, single man, now 21, acknowledges payment by guardian Conrad Overpeck of estate from father and mother.
Bk 6/pg 410   Mar 13, 1833

Robert Walker, late of Buckingham Twp, bequeathed estate to two brothers Phineas and Benjamin Walker subject to payment to administrators of Samuel Shaw, late of Plumstead Twp. Administrators Josiah and Eleazer B. Shaw received payment from Phineas and Benjamin. Bk 6/pg 411   Apr 15, 1833

Euphemia Senn of Sussex Co, NJ, daughter of Jacob Senn, late of Rockhill Twp, now 21, acknowledges payment of estate by guardian George Roudenbush of Rockhill Twp.   Bk 6/pg 412   Apr 30, 1832

Barbara Blank, widow of John Blank and daughter of George Kline, late of Milford Twp, acknowledges payment of estate by George Kline.
                                        Bk 6/pg 413   Apr 15, 1833

Philip Gerhart of Franconia Twp, Montgomery Co, now 21, acknowledges payment by guardian Christian Nease of estate due from father Jacob Gerhart, late of Rockhill Twp.   Bk 6/pg 414   Apr 1, 1833

David Carver, Dinah[?] Walker, Benjamin Walker, John Townsend, Amos Walker, Stacy Walker and Elisabeth Walker, heirs of Robert Walker, late of Solebury Twp, now 21, acknowledge payment of estate by John Walker.
                                        Bk 6/pg 416   Apr 3, 1833

Maria Praul (late Rue), daughter of Elizabeth Vancour, late of Bensalem Twp, acknowledges payment of estate by executor George J. Dungan.
                                        Bk 6/pg 417   Apr 23, 1833

Rachael Bayley of Lower Makefield Twp. gives power of attorney to Samuel H. Bayley of Lower Makefield to recover money due her.
                                        Bk 6/pg 419   Aug 29, 1832

Stephen Yerkes, late of Warminster Twp. gave two bonds to Benjamin Gilbert, John Gilbert, Samuel Gilbert and Hannah (wife of David Wood) payable upon the death of their mother Rebecca Gilbert. They assign their right in the bonds to Harman Yerkes.   Bk 6/pg 419   May 9, 1831

Sarah Shaddinger, widow of Abraham Shaddinger, late of Plumstead Twp, shortly intends to move to Ohio. She gives power of attorney to son Abraham to settle a bond with John Fretz.   Bk 6/pg 421   Sep 26, 1827

John Pope, late of Springfield Twp, bequeathed one-third of his estate to daughter Mary who is now the widow of Andrew Bucher and has four children: Andrew, Catharine (wife of Frederick Kealer), Mary (wife of Frederick Selner), Susanna (wife of Samuel Sterner). They acknowledge payment by administrators Benjamin Jacoby and Andrew Bucher.
                                        Bk 6/pg 424   May 16, 1833

Elizabeth Diehl, widow of Abraham Diehl and daughter of John Pope, late of Springfield Twp, acknowledges payment by administrators Benjamin Jacoby and Andrew Bucher.　　　　　　　　　Bk 6/pg 425　May 16, 1833

Mary Bright, widow of John Bright, late of Springfield Twp, yeoman, acknowledges payment by Samuel Bright, administrator of Elias Bright, late of Springfield Twp, carpenter.　　　　Bk 6/pg 426　May 11, 1833

Cyrus Pearson of Philadelphia assigns his right in estate of his late father Jonathan Pearson of Solebury Twp. to Charles Wood of New York City.
　　　　　　　　　　　　　　Bk 6/pg 427　Jun 3, 1833

Catharine Selser of Montgomery Twp, Montgomery Co. assigns right to son Isaac Selser of Warwick Twp. to real estate in Warwick.
　　　　　　　　　　　　　　Bk 6/pg 430　Apr 7, 1824

Clarissa Pursel, heir of John Pursel, late of Bucks Co. and John Dollahaus, guardian of John Pursel Jr. give power of attorney to friend Samuel Tomlinson of Pinscanes, Knox Co, IN to recover money from estate of John Pursel.　　　　　　　　　　　Bk 6/pg 433　Feb 8, 1833

Clarissa Pursel and John Pursel Jr. through their attorney acknowledge payment by John M. Pursel, one of the administrators of Brice Pursel.
　　　　　　　　　　　　　　Bk 6/pg 434　Aug 3, 1833

John Jacoby of Lower Saucon Twp, Northampton Co, heir of John Wildonger, late of Springfield Twp, acknowledges payment by Samuel H. Trauger, administrator of estate of George Wildonger, late of Springfield Twp.　　　　　　　　　　　　Bk 6/pg 435　Apr 1, 1833

William and Anna Maria Seip and John R. and Catharine Kressler by indenture of release dated Jun 15, 1832 granted to Joseph K. Raub the title to a tract of land subject to the payment of a yearly dower to his mother Maria Raub. Joseph K. provides certain privileges to his mother.
　　　　　　　　　　　　　　Bk 6/pg 436　Jun 15, 1833

Jacob Gayman of Clinton Twp, Lincoln Co, Upper Canada gives power of attorney to Joseph Landis of Bedminster Twp. to petition Orphans Court to divide land of his brother Joseph Gayman.　Bk 7/pg 5　Aug 13, 1833

Henry Hartman of Franklin Co, IN gives power of attorney to John Williams of Bucks Co. to receive estate from executors of Michael Hartman, late of Montgomery Co. Bk 7/pg 6 Apr 13, 1833

George Seas of Milford Twp, innkeeper, heir of Jacob Seas, yeoman, gives power of attorney to friend Peter Cooper of Upper Saucon Twp, Lehigh Co, Esq. to recover estate from executor Frederick Singmaster. Bk 7/pg 7 Aug 16, 1833

Abraham Leatherman of Plumstead Twp, weaver, gives power of attorney to Abm. Overholtzer of Plumstead, farmer, to recover moneys due him. Bk 7/pg 14 Sep 28, 1833

John Nunemaker (husband of Elizabeth), Jacob Henge (husband of Catharine), George Hertzel (husband of Susanna), daughter of Abraham Miller, late of Hilltown Twp, acknowledge receipt of estate from executors John and Henry Miller, excluding the widow's dower. Bk 7/pg 17 Oct 26, 1833

Nathan McCorkle, Charles McCorkle and Samuel McCorkle and his wife Eliza of New York City give power of attorney to Margaret McCorkle of Newtown to dispose of any property due them. Bk 7/pg 23 Oct 25, 1833

Julianna Stewart of Philadelphia, seamstress, now 21 acknowledges payment by guardian Christian Myers of estate from grandfather Peter Stewart. Bk 7/pg 24 Sep 28, 1833

Elizabeth Swift of Lower Dublin Twp, Philadelphia Co. gives power of attorney to son Samuel Swift of Bensalem Twp. to enter satisfaction of a mortgage. Bk 7/pg 25 Dec 4, 1833

William Shaw of Richland Twp, Deborah Wood (late Shaw) and Sarah Dalby (late Shaw), children of Moses Shaw, late of Richland Twp, choose men to value Moses' estate. Bk 7/pg 25 Jun 21, 1833

Rachel Nield (late Johnson) of Philadelphia gives power of attorney to brother John L. Johnson to enter satisfaction for a deed. Bk 7/pg 28 Nov 19, 1833

John W. Yerkes of Mooreland Twp, Montgomery Co, now 21, acknowledges payment by guardian Harman Yerkes of estate from late father Stephen Yerkes of Warminster Twp, except for the widow's dower. Bk 7/pg 28 Apr 3, 1833

Sarah Lovett of Middletown Twp. gives power of attorney to James G. Hibbs of Middletown to recover moneys due her.   Bk 7/pg 30   Nov 19, 1831

John Trichler of Richland Twp. died intestate leaving widow Eva and eight children: John, Jacob, Samuel, Mary (wife of Samuel Bager), Anna, Sarah, Elizabeth and Nancy.   Frederick Wolf and wife Anna (late Trichler) acknowledge payment of estate by John Trichler (Jr.).
Bk 7/pg 31   Apr 13, 1833

John Bartholomew of Haycock Twp. gives power of attorney to father Benjamin Bartholomew of Haycock to recover moneys due him.
Bk 7/pg 32   Dec 6, 1833

John Buckman of Newtown Twp. is 84 years of age and incapable of managing his worldly affairs.   Children Margaret (wife of Benjamin Wiggins), Susanna (wife of Amos Warner), Chapman, John, Jacob, Ann and Ezra appoint Chapman and John Buckman to be trustees.
Bk 7/pg 33   Feb 27, 1832

William Ridge of Bensalem Twp died intestate leaving eleven children and widow Martha.   Martha gives power of attorney to James Ridge of Bensalem to recover estate from administrators.   Bk 7/pg 35   Nov 27, 1833

John Wilson of Warwick Twp and wife Jane, heir of Richard Dale of Warwick, acknowledge payment of estate by executors Benjamin Hough and John Radcliff.   Bk 7/pg 36   Jan 4, 1834

Elizabeth Spencer, late of Warminster Twp, bequeathed estate in six shares to children Martha Hallowell, Elizabeth, Edith Markle, John Marple, Thomas Marple (deceased, children Elizabeth—wife of Cyrus Horner, Kirk, John, Thomas and North), Mary Lukens (deceased, children Ruth—wife of William Toman, Elijah, James and Abner—minor).   Daughter Ruth Towman was removed from estate as she has not been heard from.   Heirs acknowledge payment by executors William Lukens and Isaac Parry.
Bk 7/pg 37   Apr 6, 1832

Solomon Hess of Springfield Twp. and wife Catharina (late Leidy) acknowledge payment by Catharina's guardian Peter Fackenthall of Durham Twp. of estate from father Philip Leidy, late of Durham Twp.
Bk 7/pg 38   Apr 16, 1832

Rebecca Burton of Falls Twp, now 21, acknowledges payment by guardian Anthony Burton Jr. of estate due from father John Burton.

Bk 7/pg 39   Nov 30, 1833

Ely Thomas of Hilltown Twp, tobacconist, now 21, acknowledges payment by guardian John Crator.   Bk 7/pg 42   Jan 5, 1834

Elias Fols of Springfield Twp, heir of John Fols, yeoman, gives power of attorney to Mary Koon of Springfield, widow, to recover estate from executors John Hillagas and John Muselman.   Bk 7/pg 42   Feb 8, 1834

Ann Gaddis, widow of John Gaddis, late of Bucks Co, gives power of attorney to Hesekiah Gaddis of Jefferson Co, OH, to recover estate due her.

Bk 7/pg 44   Sep 19, 1833

Jonas Swartz of Northern Liberties, Philadelphia County gives power of attorney to friend Christian Benner of Doylestown Twp. to recover money from John Burgy of Bucks Co, farmer, due by death of sister Mary Swartz (he being one of her two heirs).   Bk 7/pg 45   Jan 7, 1834

Gaun Opdyke of Warwick Twp, blacksmith, assigns right in estate of John McGrandy, late of Warwick, to William Opdyke of Northampton Twp, cordwainer.   Bk 7/pg 46   Oct 18, 1833

Jesse Messer of Belmont Co, OH and wife Jane, daughter of John C. and Elizabeth Clawson, both of whom died in Bucks Co, said Elizabeth being a daughter of John Praul of Bucks Co, give power of attorney to Jane's brother Isaac Clawson, to recover 1/9 share of Elizabeth's estate from administrator Daniel Belue.   Bk 7/pg 48   Mar 24, 1834

Henry Heft of Bedminster Twp and wife Mary, daughter of John Heacock, deceased, acknowledge payment of estate by George Maugle, executor of Mary's late guardian Henry Ott.   Bk 7/pg 49   Dec 25, 1833

George Rufe, now 21, son of Jacob Rufe, late of Nockamixon Twp, acknowledges payment of estate by administrator Michael Dech.

Bk 7/pg 49   Mar 29, 1834

Elizabeth Hillpot, widow of George Hillpot, late of Tinicum Twp, acknowledges payment of estate by administrators George and Frederick G. Hillpot.   Bk 7/pg 50   Jul 27, 1833

Aaron Vanhorn of Solebury Twp. gives power of attorney to James P. Moore of Solebury to recover money due him.   Bk 7/pg 51   Mar 8, 1834

Samuel Kulp, heir of Michael Kulp, refuses to accept Michael's land. Heir Michael Kulp accepts the land.   Bk 7/pg 53   Apr 1, 1834

Late John Ely bequeathed estate to grandson Seneca Parry to be paid by son Thomas Ely who is now deceased. Seneca's father David of Lancaster Co. gives power of attorney to his son, Dr. Eli Parry, to recover estate from Thomas' administrators.   Bk 7/pg 54   Mar 29, 1834

John Danehower, Abraham Danehower, Philip Danehower, Jacob Fluck and wife Elizabeth, Peter Shive and wife Mary, children of Elizabeth Danehower, late of Rockhill Twp, acknowledge payment of estate by executors Henry Baringer and Adam Fluck.   Bk 7/pg 54   Oct 5, 1833

Joshua Vanhorn of Middletown Twp. assigns right to one-fourth share of estate due upon death of his mother Phebe Vanhorn, widow of John Vanhorn, to Jesse Hellings of Middletown.   Bk 7/pg 55   Mar, 1834

Daniel Stilwell of Madison Twp, Muskingum Co, OH, son of Richard Stilwell who was married to Mary LaRue, sister of Daniel LaRue, late of Middletown Twp, gives power of attorney to Jesse Hellings of Middletown Twp to refuse to accept real estate.   Bk 7/pg 56   Mar 6, 1834

David Yothers of New Britain Twp, yeoman, attorney for John Yothers of Bedminster Twp, acknowledges payment of estate of David Kulp, late of Bedminster Twp, by widow Mary Kulp.   Bk 7/pg 58   [blank], 1834

Moses T. Fell of Scipio, Seneca Co, NY, son of Jonathan Fell, late of Bucks Co, gives power of attorney to brother Aaron Fell of Buckingham Twp to refuse to accept real estate.   Bk 7/pg 59   Apr 28, 1834

Jacob Stine of Durham Twp. and wife Sarah (late Green), acknowledge payment by her brother John L. Green of share in land of mother bequeathed by her father Dr. Felix Linn.   Bk 7/pg 60   Apr 20, 1834

Elias Koch and wife Sophia, daughter of late Jacob Snyder of Hilltown Twp and heir of Catharine Croll, acknowledge payment of estate by her guardian John Snyder of Hilltown.   Bk 7/pg 61   Mar 4, [1834?]

John Fluck of Richland Twp, guardian of Israel, Elizabeth and Christiana Shaffer, minor children of late Henry Shaffer, and George Walp of Haycock Twp, guardian of William Shaffer, another minor child, acknowledge payment of estate by John Burge/Berger and Abraham Derstine, administrators of John Berger, late of Richland, who was guardian to the Shaffer children. Bk 7/pg 61   Apr 17, 1834

Catharine Gettman of Richland Twp is widow of William Gettman and daughter of Jacob Sease, late of Rockhill Twp. Jacob bequeathed upon his widow's death money to two grandchildren and remainder into three shares, except that Catharine's share to be divided one-fifth to her son George Sheetz and the remainder to her other four children after her decease. Her sons Samuel, Solomon and Michael Gettman have recently purchased Jacob Sease's dwelling house and plantation. Jacob's executors Elizabeth (his widow) and Philip Singmaster are now deceased. Catharine acknowledges payment of estate by Frederick Singmaster. Bk 7/pg 62   Mar 2, 1833

Joseph Shive of Haycock Twp. and wife Hannah, daughter of William Gettman, late of Rockhill Twp and heir of Jacob Sease, late of Rockhill, acknowledge payment of estate by Frederick Singmaster.
Bk 7/pg 64   Apr 12, 1834

Abraham Stout of Rockhill Twp, now 21, acknowledges payment by guardian Frederick Althouse of estate from father Jacob Stout, late of Rockhill.
Bk 7/pg 65   Jan 28, 1832

Isaac Stout of Rockhill Twp, blacksmith, now 21, acknowledges payment by guardian Frederick Althouse of estate from father Jacob Stout, late of Rockhill. Bk 7/pg 65   Jan 19, 1830

Enos Keil of Rockhill Twp. and wife Elizabeth, daughter of Jacob Stout, late of Rockhill, acknowledges payment of estate by guardian Frederick Althouse.
Bk 7/pg 66   Jan 18, 1834

Peter Merkel, guardian of Henry Price, minor child under 14, acknowledges payment by Henry Schleichter, previous guardian, of minor's estate.
Bk 7/pg 66   Aug 9, 1831

John Brunner of Philadelphia assigns his share in estate of late father John Brunner due upon the death of his mother Margaret to Philip Brunner.
Bk 7/pg 67   May 3, 1834

Jacob D. Benner, guardian of Simon Snyder, minor child of Henry Snyder, late of Richland Twp, acknowledges payment of estate by Simon's former guardian Jesse Iden.   Bk 7/pg 67   May 26, 1834

Joseph Heist of Milford Twp, now 21, acknowledges payment by guardian Jacob Boyer of Milford Twp of estate from late father George Heist.
Bk 7/pg 70   Apr 30, 1834

Rachel Harvey, wife of Henry Harvey of Miami Co, OH, gives power of attorney to husband Henry to recover money in hands of Thomas Betts, executor of Henry Harvey, late of Bucks Co.   Bk 7/pg 71   Nov 6, 1833

Abner Harvey, son of Henry Harvey, late of Upper Makefield Twp, and Abner's wife Jane grant to executor Thomas Betts the right to sell Henry's real estate.   Bk 7/pg 72   Sep 27, 1831

John Townsend, Margaret Townsend, William Townsend, Elizabeth (wife of William Dungan), Benjamin W. Townsend and Amos Townsend, children of Mary Townsend, who was sister and heir of Robert Walker, late of Buckingham Twp, acknowledge payment of estate by Robert's brothers Phineas and Benjamin Walker.   Bk 7/pg 76   Jun 16, 1834

Thomas Foster assigns right in estate of Hosemond Crozer to son William Foster.   Bk 7/pg 78   Jun 17, 1834

Peter Hillpot and wife Anne and Samuel Fretz of Plumstead Twp. and wife Elizabeth, legatees of John Fretz, late of Tinicum Twp, acknowledge payment of estate by Henry and John Fretz.   Bk 7/pg 80   Mar 31, 1834

Ann S. McElroy, widow of Jno. McElroy, late of Bensalem Twp, gives power of attorney to son Herbert McElroy of Bristol Borough to recover money due her.   Bk 7/pg 81   Jul 16, 1834

Leonard Kessler of Springfield Twp, now 21, acknowledges payment by Samuel Ruth and Jonas Cressman, administrators of Peter Ruth, late of Springfield Twp, who was Leonard's guardian, of estate due from father Stophel Kessler, late of Northampton Co.   Bk 7/pg 84   Apr 19, 1834

Samuel and Sarah (Kessler) Hafler of Springfield Twp, acknowledge payment by Saml Ruth and Jonas Cressman, administrators of Peter Ruth, late of Springfield Twp, who was Sarah's guardian, of estate due from father Stophel Kessler, late of Williams Twp, Northampton Co.   Bk 7/pg 85   Apr 10, 1834

Hannah Eliza Crouse, daughter of Jacob Crouse, late of Nockamixon Twp, now 21 and married to Benjamin F. Gerhart of Doylestown Twp, acknowledges payment of estate by guardian Isaac Stem.

Bk 7/pg 85   Feb 13, 1834

Thomas Pursel, John Pursel, Brice Pursel, John Fisher Jr. and wife Ann, Eveline Pursel and Thomas Pursel Sr. (guardian of Hugh, Daniel and Hannah Pursel), children of Brice Pursel, late of Nockamixon Twp, agree that the estate will not be sold and the family will continue to live together with their mother Catharine.   Bk 7/pg 89   Aug 15, 1832

Sarah and Balinda Pursel of Laurance Co, IL gives power of attorney to friend Samuel Tomlinson of Knox Co, IN to collect dowry due from estate of father John Pursel, late of Bucks Co. now in the hands of her guardian Brice Pursel, Esq. or in the hands of executors John Williams and George Wiker.

Bk 7/pg 91   Feb 10, 1825

Mercy and Mary Purcil of Butler Co, OH give power of attorney to Samuel Tomlinson of Knox Co, IN to collect from guardian Brice Purcil Esq. of estate from father John Purcil.   Bk 7/pg 93   Aug 29, 1829

Asa Beck of Indiana and wife Ann, daughter of John Pursel, late of Nockamixon Twp, give power of attorney to John Iliff of Hunterdon Co, NJ to recover estate from guardian Brice Pursel of Nockamixon.

Bk 7/pg 95   [not dated]

Jacob Sease, late of Rockhill Twp, yeoman, gave one-third of estate to son Michael of Richland Twp, yeoman, who is also now deceased. George Sease and the widow (who is now deceased) were named Michael's executors. George Sease acknowledges payment by Frederick Singmaster of estate from Jacob Sease.   Bk 7/pg 96   Jun 7, 1834

George H. Pauling of Moreland Twp, Montgomery Co, administrator of Sarah Kimble, late of Plumstead Twp, who was a surviving sister of Christopher Kimble, late of Plumstead, acknowledges payment of estate by Christopher's administrator Richard Kimble.   Bk 7/pg 98   Aug 12, 1834

John H. Watson of Richland Twp, practioner of physic, and wife Hannah, daughter of late Shipley Lester of Richland, assign to brother William Lester of Richland, plowmaker, right in estate due upon death of their mother Margaret.   Bk 7/pg 98   Sep 9, 1834

John and Sarah Roberts of Milford Twp. are now too infirm to support themselves. They assign to son Everard all right in their real estate so that he will support them and also to pay for his support of brother Lewis and sister Sarah.   Bk 7/pg 99   Feb 14, 1834

Samuel Park, surviving executor of William Park, late of Horsham Twp, Montgomery Co, gives power of attorney to friend Lemen Banes of Warminster Twp. to recover any money due the estate.
                    Bk 7/pg 104   Sep 24, 1834

Siblings of Abraham Landes, late of Bedminster Twp: Jacob Landis of Hilltown Twp, Joseph Landis of Bedminster Twp, Christian and Barbara Myers of Springfield Twp, heirs of sister Elizabeth Myers (Isaac Myers of Franconia Twp, Abraham Myers of Towamensing Twp, Jacob and Catharine Hage of Franconia Twp, John and Sarah Hage of Franconia Twp, Peter and Susanna Myer of Towmensing Twp, Michael and Elizabeth Young of Franconia Twp, Mary Young—deceased), heirs of sister Magdalena High (David, Abraham, Sarah High, Anne High of Bedminster, Ralph of Plumstead, Philip of Fayette Co), heirs of sister Mary Myers (Ralph of Franconia, Christian—deceased, Abraham, Isaac and Catharine, all of Bedminster Twp, Joseph and Sarah Leatherman of Plumstead Twp, Jacob and Elizabeth Gehman of Clinton Co, Upper Canada and Daniel and Magdalena Haldeman of New Britain Twp). They acknowledge payment of estate by executors Joseph and Ralph Landis.   Bk 7/pg 106   Jan 26, 1833

Elizabeth Gayman of Clinton Twp, Lincoln Co, Niagara District, Upper Canada, gives power of attorney to friend Joseph Fretz of Louth Twp, Lincoln Co. to recover estate from executor Joseph Landes of Bedminster Twp due from late Abraham Landes of Bedminster Twp. Bk 7/pg 108   Apr 16, 1833

Joseph Fretz and wife Catharine, daughter of Joseph Fretz, late of Bedminster Twp, acknowledge payment of estate by guardian Jacob Stover.
                    Bk 7/pg 110   Sep 30,1834

Catharine Ritter of Haycock Twp. acknowledges payment by administrator Peter Ritter of estate due from her late husband Peter Ritter.
                    Bk 7/pg 111   Feb 18, 1834

Abraham Klinker of Haycock Twp. and wife Susanna, daughter of Peter Ritter, late of Nockamixon Twp, acknowledge payment of estate by administrator Peter Ritter.   Bk 7/pg 111   Feb 18, 1834

Joseph Taylor, late of Lower Makefield Twp, bequeathed estate to son Joseph subject to payment to his surviving sisters and children of deceased sisters Ann Janney and Hannah. Heirs M. Cunningham, Rachel Cunningham, Samuel Bunting, Letitia Bunting, Cyrus Cadwallader, Mary Cadwallader, John Comfort, Sarah T. Comfort, John Palmer, Susanna Palmer, Mahlon Taylor, Benjn. T. Yardly, Harriet K. Yardly, Morris Buckman and Anna M. Buckman acknowledge payment by Joseph Taylor.

Bk 7/pg 112   Apr 12, 1833

Albert Lester of Richland Twp, taylor, is due one-seventh share of estate from father Shipley Lester upon death of mother Margaret. Albert assigns right in share to Abel Lester of Richland Twp, tanner.   Bk 7/pg 114   Oct 22, 1834

John and Henry Kinze of Rockhill Twp, sons of John Kinze, late of Rockhill, acknowledge payment of estate by executors Jacob and Abraham Kinze.

Bk 7/pg 117   May 27, 1833

Joseph Alderfer of Upper Providence Twp, Montgomery Co, yeoman, acknowledges payment by executors Jacob and Abraham Kinze of estate from John Kinze, late of Rockhill Twp.   Bk 7/pg 118   Mar 10, 1832

John Starner of Haycock Twp, executor of Jacob Starner, late of Springfield Twp, acknowledges payment by Adam Starner, one of Jacob's sons, for real estate bequeathed to Adam, due upon the death of widow Catharine.
.   Bk 7/pg 119   Apr 21, 1824

Sarah and Mary Buckman, acting executors of Jonathan Buckman, late of Newtown, give power of attorney to Joshua Mitchell of Middletown Twp. to recover money due the estate.   Bk 7/pg 120   Nov 24, 1834

George Frantz of Bedminster Twp. sold real estate to his son George Jr. subject to a life right. George Jr. recently died leaving a widow and six minor children. George Sr. cancels the life right in the real estate.

Bk 7/pg 121   Dec 6, 1834

Abraham Fretz of Hilltown Twp, John Fretz of Hilltown, Jacob Fretz of Hilltown, Isaac Fretz of Richland Twp and Barbara Fretz, siblings of Hannah Fretz, late of Bedminster Twp, acknowledge payment of estate by administrator William Fretz.   Bk 7/pg 126   Mar 19, 1832

Catharine Gerhart of Doylestown Twp, late Catharine Gebhart, heir of
Hannah Fretz, late of Bedminster Twp, acknowledges payment of estate by
administrator William Fretz.   Bk 7/pg 126   Mar 19, 1832

Jacob Stover, guardian for William and Catharine Fretz, minor children of
Joseph Fretz, late of Bedminster Twp, acknowledges payment by
administrator William Fretz of estate due from Hannah Fretz, late of
Bedminster Twp.   Bk 7/pg 127   Mar 19, 1832

Jacob and John Gebhart of Doylestown Twp, heirs of Hannah Fretz, late of
Bedminster Twp, acknowledges payment of estate by administrator William
Fretz.   Bk 7/pg 128   May 19, 1832

Joseph Yocum of Livingston Co, NY, heir of Hannah Fretz, late of
Bedminster Twp, acknowledges payment of estate by administrator William
Fretz.   Bk 7/pg 128   Nov 19, 1834

David Heastant of New Britain Twp and wife Susanna (late Gebhart),
Abraham Kephart of New Britain and John Shutt of Doylestown Twp and
wife Nancy (late Gebhart), heirs of Hannah Fretz, late of Bedminster,
acknowledge payment of estate by administrator William Fretz.
          Bk 7/pg 129   Mar 19, 1832

Christian Clemens, guardian of Elizabeth Kebhart, daughter of John Kebhart,
late of Doylestown, acknowledges payment by administrator William Fretz of
estate due from Hannah Fretz, late of Bedminster Twp.
          Bk 7/pg 131   Mar 19, 1832

Abraham Fretz, guardian of Abraham Fretz, minor child of Joseph Fretz, late
of Bedminster Twp, acknowledges payment by administrator William Fretz of
estate due from Hannah Fretz, late of Bedminster. Bk 7/pg 131   Mar 19, 1832

George Stoneback of Haycock Twp. died intestate leaving widow Catharine
and nine children. His real estate went to son-in-law George Lightcap.
Widow Catharine is now deceased and the dower is due. The real estate is
now owned by Stephen Weimer. Heirs Joseph and Maria Afflerbach (also
assignees of daughter Catharine Stoneback and daughter Mary—wife of
Henry Steckel and administrator of Peter Niemand who married daughter
Barbara), and John and Susanna Ohl acknowledge payment of dower by
Stephen Weimer.   Bk 7/pg 132   Dec 10, 1834

Jesse Mercer of Belmont Co, OH and wife Jane, daughter of John C. and Elizabeth Closson, both deceased within five years. Jane due one-ninth share of Elizabeth's share of estate of John Praul. They give power of attorney William Rich of Belmont Co, OH to recover estate from Daniel Bilew, administrator of John and Elizabeth Closson.   Bk 7/pg 134   Oct 1, 1834

Jacob and Elizabeth Godshalk sold real estate in Plumstead Twp to Joseph Overhold subject to payment of dower to heirs of Samuel Godshalk upon death of his widow Catharine. One of those heirs, Jacob Godshalk, late of Plumstead Twp but now of OH, assigns his right to Abraham Godshalk of Doylestown Twp.   Bk 7/pg 140   Sep 3, 1834

William C. Hibbs and Thomas M. Hibbs of Middletown Twp, each entitled to one-thirteenth part of estate of Jonathan Hibbs, late of Middletown, assign shares to Joseph C. Leaw of Middletown.   Bk 7/pg 141   Aug 21, 1834

Isaac Shitz of Nockamixon Twp, now 21, acknowledges payment by guardian Conrad Oberbeck of estate due from father and mother.
                                                Bk 7/pg 143   Jan 12, 1835

James Carter, husband of Rebecca Ann, daughter of Jonathan Hibbs, late of Middletown Twp, assign their one-thirteenth share of estate to James G. Hibbs.   Bk 7/pg 144   [blank], 1834

Jacob Fluck, Enos Schlichter and Adam Fluck, guardians of minor children of Jacob Danehower, son of Elizabeth Danehower, late of Rockhill Twp, acknowledge payment of estate by Elizabeth's executors Henry Baringer and Adam Fluck.   Bk 7/pg 145   Oct 5, 1833

Jacob Fluck, Enos Schlichter and Adam Fluck, all of Rockhill Twp, guardians of the minor children of Mary Danehower, late of Rockhill Twp, acknowledge payment of estate by Henry Baringer and Peter Shipe.
                                            Bk 7/pg 146   Aug 27, 1832

Abraham Drissel of Tinicum Twp, only legatee of Susanna Stover, late of Tinicum Twp, acknowledges payment of estate by executor John Drissel.
                                            Bk 7/pg 149   Dec 10, 1834

Peter Scholl, late of Milford Twp, died intestate in May last past. John and Sarah Long of Milford are entitled to one-sixth share of estate and sell that share to John Samsel of Milford Twp, guardian of Catharine Seiler, minor daughter of Peter Seiler, late of Milford Twp.   Bk 7/pg 152   Feb 9, 1835

186

Thomas Smith and wife Elizabeth and James Fisher and wife Sarah, children of George Stoneback, deceased, acknowledge payment of dower by Stephen Wimmer, due now that the widow Catharine is deceased.

Bk 7/pg 156   Jan 13, 1835

Mary Tyson of Bedminster Twp, spinster, and Martin Tyson of Tinicum Twp, both now 21, acknowledge payment by guardian John Fretz of estate due from father Henry Tyson, grandmother Barbary Fretz and sister Barbary Tyson.

Bk 7/pg 157   Feb 21, 1835

Mary Kremer of Milford Twp gives power of attorney to Peter Shelly, Esq. of Springfield Twp. to recover money due from estate of grandfather Philip Dosch and father Abm. Dosch.

Bk 7/pg 161   Feb 14, 1835

Jacob Heston of Upper Makefield Twp. gives power of attorney to son Jesse S. Heston of Wrightstown Twp. to recover money due him.

Bk 7/pg 162   Nov 25,1829

Abraham Wismer established his three sons-in-law, Abraham Overhold, Henry Landis and Christian Gross, as trustees for his daughter Magdalena Wismer, who was also an heir of John High. Christian Gross, the only surviving trustee, acknowledges payment by Jacob, Abraham and Isaac Overholt, administrators of Abraham Overholt.   Bk 7/pg 166   Mar 23, 1835

Margaret Seas of Richland Twp, daughter of Michael Seas, late of Richland, now 21, acknowledges payment by guardian George Custard of estate from father Michael and mother Eva.

Bk 7/pg 167   Apr 1, 1835

John Bare of East Huntington Twp, Westmoreland Co, PA and wife Magdalena (late Kephart), heir of Hannah Fretz, late of Bedminster Twp, acknowledges payment of estate by administrator William Fretz.

Bk 7/pg 173   Aug 25, 1832

Abraham Fretz (eldest son), Joseph Fretz and wife Catharine, children of Joseph Fretz, late of Bedminster Twp, and Jacob Stover, guardian for minor child William C. Fretz, acknowledge payment of estate by administrator William Fretz.

Bk 7/pg 174   Apr 1, 1835

Christian Mann of Haycock Twp. gives power of attorney to Christian Bertels of Haycock Twp. to recover money from estate of George Mann of which John Amey is administrator.

Bk 7/pg 186   Apr 23, 1835

Hillary Senn of Rockhill Twp, son of Jacob Senn, late of Rockhill, now 21, acknowledges payment of estate by guardian George Roudenbush.
Bk 7/pg 186   Mar 21, 1835

John Counselman, William Counselman, Charles Counselman, Sarah Counselman and Rachel Counselman, all of Montgomery Co, MD own real estate in Bucks County that belonged to late John Counselman. They give power of attorney to Samuel Counselman of Montgomery Co, MD to sell the land.
Bk 7/pg 187   Mar 3, 1835

Frederick Fisher, late of Hilltown Twp, bequeathed estate to children Abraham, Jacob and Elizabeth (wife of Henry Overholtzer). Jacob has since died bequeathing his share to his brother and sister. Henry and Elizabeth Overholtzer of Upper Canada have given power of attorney to Daniel Overholtzer of Hatfield Twp, Montgomery Co. who acknowledges payment of estate by Abraham Fisher.
Bk 7/pg 188   Jan 3, 1835

Jacob Mumbouwer of West Kinsingtown, Philadelphia Co. gives power of attorney to Lorentz Stahler, Esq. of Upper Milford Twp, Lehigh Co. to recover father's estate from brothers John and David Mumbower.
Bk 7/pg 189   May 29, 1834

Christian Gross, surviving trustee of Magdalena Wismer, acknowledges payment of estate by Henry Landes, surviving administrator of Henry Landes who was a trustee of Magdalena.
Bk 7/pg 190   Apr 20, 1835

Jacob Landis, Joseph Landis, Daniel Landis (by guardian Jacob Leatherman), Mary Kulp (widow), Jacob and Magdalena Leatherman, Henry and Barbara Landis, Susanna Landis, Abraham and Hannah Leatherman and Elizabeth Landis (by guardian Jacob Overholt), heirs of Henry Landis, late of Plumstead Twp, acknowledge payment of estate by administrator Henry Landis.
Bk 7/pg 191   Apr 20, 1835

Rachel Cary (daughter of Joseph Cary) of Licking Co, OH, legatee of Rachel Ely, late of Buckingham Twp, now 18 (on Nov 28 last), gives power of attorney to grandfather Thomas Cary of Solebury Twp to recover estate from executor Hugh B. Ely.
Bk 7/pg 192   Feb 11, 1835

Jesse Johnson (trustee for Abigail Addis), Sarah Addis and Thomas Purdy (trustee for Nancy Corson), acknowledge payment by assignees of Amos Addis, executor of Ann Summers, deceased. Bk 7/pg 193   Apr 2, 1835

Henry Fabian, John Fabian, Michael Fabian, Samuel Fabian, George and Nancy Strouse and Abraham and Elizabeth Overback acknowledge payment by executor George Fabian of estate from Casper Fabian Sr., late of Durham Twp.   Bk 7/pg 194   Mar 30, 1835

John Harpel, guardian of Mary, Catharine, Aaron and Sarah Sheetz, minor children of Andrew Sheetz and wife Sarah (late Fabian), acknowledges payment by executor George Fabian of estate from Casper Fabian Sr., late of Durham Twp.   Bk 7/pg 195   Mar 30, 1835

Albert Michener of Newgarden Twp, Chester Co, PA, grandson of Jonathan Beans, late of Bucks Co, gives power of attorney to father William S. Michener of Newgarden Twp to recover estate from executors John Beans.
                    Bk 7/pg 196   Aug 11, 1834

Susanna Drissel, Joseph Mease of Springfield Twp (guardian of John and Susanna Drissel) and Abraham Rieff of Hilltown Twp (guardian of Joseph, Isaac and Henry Drissel), widow and minor children of Henry Drissel, late of Tinicum Twp, acknowledge payment by administrator John Drissel.
                    Bk 7/pg 197   Apr 17, 1835

Isaac Wichersham and wife Phebe and Rachel Michener, daughters of Wm S. Michener of Newgarden Twp, Chester Co, PA and legatee of Jonathan Beans, late of Bucks Co, give power of attorney to father William to recover estate from executor John Walton.   Bk 7/pg 201   Aug 11, 1834

William S. Michener acknowledges payment of estate by executor John Walton (husband of Margery, daughter of Jonathan Beans).
                    Bk 7/pg 203   May 8, 1835

Elizabeth Wildonger (widow), John and Mary Swope, Sarah Wildonger, Moses and Hannah Leer and Magdalena Wildonger, all of Tinicum Twp, Joseph and Catharine Fly of Bedminster Twp, and Abraham Worman of Tinicum (guardian of minor children Abraham and Moses Wildonger), heirs of Jacob Wildonger, late of Tinicum, acknowledge payment of estate by executors Jacob Wildonger and Jacob Kilmer.   Bk 7/pg 207   Mar 31, 1835

John Fretz of Bedminster Twp and wife Fronica, daughter of Joseph Shelly, late of Milford Twp, sell their share to Michael Landis of Saucon Twp, Lehigh Co, shoemaker.   Bk 7/pg 209   May 6, 1835

Abraham of Plumstead Twp and wife Sarah, now 21, acknowledge payment by guardian George Fox of estate due from father Leonard Wildonger, late of Plumstead.   Bk 7/pg 211   Mar 2, 1835

Barbara Blank, widow of John Blank, late of Rockhill Twp, and daughter of George Kline, late of Milford Twp, acknowledges payment of estate by brother George Kline of Milford Twp.   Bk 7/pg 211   Apr 6, 1835

Samuel Weir, late of Bucks Co, willed land to son James which after his death was to be sold and proceeds divided among Samuel's grandchildren. James and Mary Griffith (late Simpson) of Clermont Co, OH, Samuel Simpson and Jesse R. and Hannah Grant (late Simpson), both of Georgetown, Brown Co, OH, give power of attorney to Samuel Hart of Doylestown to recover estate from James Finley, executor of James Wier. Bk 7/pg 212   Jun 9, 1835

Margaret Overholt, widow of Abraham Overholt, late of Plumstead Twp, and Peter Laux, guardian of minor son Henry Overholt, acknowledge payment of estate by administrators Isaac, Abraham and Jacob Overholt.
                                           Bk 7/pg 213   Jul 10, 1835

Sarah King, widow of Jeremiah King of Kingwood Twp, Hunterdon Co, NJ, releases dower right in land in Solebury Twp now owned by John E. Kenderdine.   Bk 7/pg 216   Jul 2, 1835

Arther D. Cernea of Buckingham Twp and wife Sarah Ann and Mary Lester, daughters of Thomas Lester, late of Richland Twp, both now 21, acknowledge payment of estate by guardians William Green and Peter Lester.
                                           Bk 7/pg 218   Jul 10, 1835

Edward Roberts of Anderson Twp, Hamilton Co, OH gives power of attorney to friend Edward [Everard?] Foulke to recover money from creditors in Pennsylvania.   Bk 7/pg 219   Jan 29, 1808

Everard Foulke of Richland Twp, attorney for Edward Roberts, acknowledges payment from Evan Roberts of legacy due under will of Nathan Roberts, late of Richland Twp.   Bk 7/pg 220   Apr 26, 1809

Solomon Shull of Fairfield Co, OH gives power of attorney to John Shitz of Milford Twp to recover estate from John Long of Milford, administrator of Peter Shull, late of Milford.   Bk 7/pg 221   Nov 27, 1834

Adam and Susanna Brey of Milford Twp. give power of attorney to John Sheetz of Milford, yeoman, to recover estate from Peter Scholl, late of Milford.   Bk 7/pg 222   Apr 11, 1835

Samuel Rose assigns right in real estate in Doylestown and Charleston, SC to nephew William W. Rose.   Bk 7/pg 227   Aug 17, 1835

Sarah W. Meredith of Highland Co, OH, heir of Mary Meredith of Doylestown, gives power of attorney to Mathias Morris, Esq. of Doylestown to recover estate from acting executor A. Chapman.
                                                    Bk 7/pg 228   Jun 29, 1830

Joseph S. Heany of Tinicum Twp and wife Mary, legatee of John Fretz, late of Tinicum Twp, acknowledge payment of estate by Christian K. Kressman of Nockamixon Twp who now owns a certain mill property.
                                                    Bk 7/pg 230   Apr 1, 1835

Christian and Mary Fretz of Tinicum Twp. sell to Christian K. Kressman of Nockamixon Twp, miller, their right in property jointly owned by Christian and his brother John.   Bk 7/pg 231   Apr 23, 1835

Peter Fulmer, son of Daniel Fulmer, late of Bedminster Twp, now 21, acknowledges payment of estate by guardian Peter Sollowday.
                                                    Bk 7/pg 234   Apr 7, 1833

Enos Roudenbush of Rockhill Twp. and wife Catharine acknowledge payment by guardian Peter Soloday of estate from late father Daniel Fullmer.
                                                    Bk 7/pg 234   Apr 4, 1835

Jesse Iden of Richland Twp and wife Ann soon intend to move to Indiana and give power of attorney to Daniel L. Downing of Richland Twp. to sell their land in Richland.   Bk 7/pg 237   Sep 4, 1835

William Bennet of Tinicum Twp, now 21, acknowledges payment by guardian Abraham Worman of dower from grandmother Long.
                                                    Bk 7/pg 238   Apr 29, 1833

George Swope of Tinicum Twp, legatee of George Keeler, late of Tinicum Twp, acknowledges payment of estate by executors Abraham and Isaac Worman.   Bk 7/pg 239   May 29, 1833

William Shuman Jr. and Jacob Grube of Lower Mt. Bethel Twp, Northampton Co, appointed guardians of William Shuman of Lower Mt. Bethel, an habitual drunkard, after petition by William's brother Harman, acknowledge payment by Abraham and Isaac Worman of estate due from George Keeler, late of Tinicum Twp.   Bk 7/pg 239   Mar 26, 1832

Catharine Wisener, Isaac Wisener and Thomas and Elizabeth Groom, heirs of George Wisener, deceased, acknowledge payment by Joshua Smith, executor of Edmond Smith, of dower due by death of widow Ursula Wisener.
                                        Bk 7/pg 241   Sep 22, 1835

Seth Rodrock of Doylestown, now 21, acknowledges payment by guardian Josiah Y. Shaw, Esq. of estate from late father David Rodrock.
                                        Bk 7/pg 242   Jul 20, 1835

Benjamin Iliff of Greenwich Twp, Warren Co, NJ, now 21, acknowledges payment by guardian John Iliff of estate from grandfather John Iliff, late of Bucks Co.   Bk 7/pg 243   Sep 8, 1835

John Hestant of Halloway Co, Upper Canada and Jacob and Elizabeth Fretz of Hilltown Twp, children of Henry Hestant, late of New Britain Twp, yeoman, acknowledge payment of estate by executors David and Abraham Hestant.
                                        Bk 7/pg 244   Sep 19, 1835

John Beidler of Richland Twp, widower of Barbara, daughter of Henry Hestant, late of New Britain Twp, acknowledges payment of estate by executors David and Abraham Hestant.   Bk 7/pg 245   Mar 28, 1835

Elizabeth Black of Nockamixon Twp, sister of Michael Hartman, late of Montgomery Twp, Montgomery Co, releases executors Philip Hartzel, Andrew Reed and Michael Hartman in consideration that her son Jacob Black has obligated to pay her a yearly stipend.   Bk 7/pg 245   Sep 24, 1835

John Stockham Jr. of Falls Twp, now between 25 and 26 years old, and youngest brother Thomas Stockham, now 21, acknowledge payment by guardian Thomas Stockham of Bristol Twp of estate due from father George Stockham, deceased.   Bk 7/pg 246   Aug 17, 1835

Grace C. Burton of Falls Twp, now 21, acknowledges payment by guardian Joseph Burton of estate due from father John Burton, deceased.
                                        Bk 7/pg 247   Sep 30, 1835

Samuel Iden, Jesse Iden, Margaret Iden, Jane Iden, Sarah Iden and Susanna Iden, children of Randal Iden, late of Richland Twp and widow Eleanor choose friends to value the estate.   Bk 7/pg 247   Mar 11, 1815

Joseph Himmelwright of Milford Twp, guardian of Sarah Ann Lunn, daughter of Dr. Abner T. Lunn, late of Rockhill Twp, acknowledges payment of estate by administrators George Roudenbush and Samuel B. Cressman.
                                                    Bk 7/pg 248   Oct 6, 1835

Samuel Stout, son of Daniel Stout, late of Bedminster Twp, gives power of attorney to John Harpel to refuse to accept the real estate.
                                                    Bk 7/pg 249   Oct 22, 1835

David and Susanna (Mathias) Gehris of Hereford Twp, Berks Co, Henry Mathias (eldest son), Tobias Mathias, Jacob and Eve Kooker and Catharine Bender (widow) give power of attorney to Charles DuBois of Doylestown to refuse to accept real estate of late Henry Mathias. Bk 7/pg 252   Oct 17, 1835

Francis and Jesse Cope and Margaret Landes (widow), children of Abraham Cope, late of Hilltown Twp, and Abraham Reiff, guardian of Catharine Johnson, a minor grandchild, acknowledge payment of estate from administrators Catharine and Henry Cope.   Bk 7/pg 253   Apr 15, 1835

Gilbert Rodman of Washington, DC, executor of Gilbert Rodman, late of Bensalem Twp, gives power of attorney to Hon. John Fox of Doylestown to sell Gilbert's real estate.   Bk 7/pg 253   Sep 29, 1835

David Clayton of Byberry Twp, Philadelphia Co and wife Mary, Norman Clayton of Southampton Twp, Daniel Vanartsdalen of Philadelphia and wife Maria, Garret W. Conover of Freehold Twp, Monmouth Co, NJ and wife Jane and Sarah Clayton of Mooreland Twp, Montgomery Co, children of John Clayton, late of Mooreland Twp, give power of attorney to brothers Jonathan of Southampton and Jacob E. and Joseph of Mooreland to sell the real estate.
                                                    Bk 7/pg 255   Oct 10, 1835

Aaron Christine of Bedminster Twp, heir of Barbara Bryan, late of Bedminster, acknowledges payment of estate by his guardian Abraham Jacoby.   Bk 7/pg 257   Apr 5, 1834

David High of Bedminster Twp, now 21, acknowledges payment by Mary Culp, widow of his guardian David Culp, of estate from father Daniel High.
                                                    Bk 7/pg 259   Nov 14, 1835

Elizabeth Closson and her son Mahlon Closson, late of Bucks County had Daniel Boylue as administrator. Elizabeth left a daughter Grace Adams who died in Preble Co, OH leaving children Mary, Benjamin, Ann and John, last three minors with Jedediah Adams of Warren Co, OH as guardian. Jedediah Adams and Mary Adams (single) give power of attorney to Isaac Lincoln of Warren Co, OH to recover estate from Daniel Boylue.
Bk 7/pg 259   Nov 4, 1835

Mary Kunsman of Springfield Twp, releases Solomon Kunsman of Springfield, bastardy[?], of all debts.   Bk 7/pg 263   Jul 30, 1835

James Winder, late of Lower Makefield Twp, died leaving widow and six children. Heir Thomas Winder of Bucks sells his share of estate to Amos Knight.   Bk 7/pg 263   Dec 14, 1835

Philip Dosh, late of Rockhill Twp, directed that his estate be equally divided among his legatees after the death of his wife and son Abraham. John Kramer (husband of daughter Mary) assigns their right to John Kramer Sr.
Bk 7/pg 264   Dec 14, 1835

Benjamin Jackson of Union Co, IN gives power of attorney to Philip Sipler of Bucks Co. to recover estate due from Rebecca, Jacob and Jesse Jackson, late of Bucks.   Bk 7/pg 265   Feb 19, 1835

Daniel Nicholas and wife Catharine, daughter of John Smith and granddaughter of George Smith, acknowledges payment of estate by guardian Benjamin Jacoby.   Bk 7/pg 268   Oct 10, 1835

Thomas Warner, deceased, devised land in Wrightstown Twp. to Amos Warner, since deceased, subject to privilege of Mary Warner (spinster). Thomas Warner of Warminster Twp, yeoman [heir of Amos?] agrees to let Mary stay in the dwelling.   Bk 7/pg 269   Jan 3, 1835

Elizabeth Hampshire of Livingston Co, NY gives power of attorney to George Overpeck of Springfield Twp. to sell real estate formerly of Anna Maria Overpeck, late of Springfield.   Bk 7/pg 272   Dec 5, 1835

Henry Younken and wife Mary, Jacob Heckman and wife Susanna, Andrew Hickson and wife Nancy, Peter Jacob and wife Sarah, Jacob Overpeck (of Wane Twp, Butler Co, OH) and George and Margaret Houpt (of Augusta Twp, Northumberland Co, PA), children of Anna Mariah Overpeck, late of

Springfield Twp, give power of attorney to George Overpeck of Springfield Twp. to sell real estate. Bk 7/pg 273 Nov 6, 1835

Lewis LeGuen, a citizen of the U.S., now living in Paris, France, gives power of attorney to wife Mary to recover moneys in U.S. Bk 7/pg 276 Dec 6, 1823

Henry Shevler, late of Durham Twp, died intestate. Brother Jacob Shevler of East Huntingdon Twp, Westmoreland Co, PA died leaving children Polly, Catharine, Henry (by first wife) and Jacob, Susannah (wife of Mathew McBrier), Elizabeth (wife of John Brothers), Sarah, John and Lavina (wife of Solomon Sheppard). They give power of attorney to friend Andrew Shaddinger, drover, of Bucks Co. to recover estate due them.
Bk 7/pg 279 Nov 13, 1835

Millicent (wife of David Bradshaw), Rebecca, Letitia, Cornelius and Aaron Bradshaw (on behalf of William Large, minor child of Joseph S. Large, late of Buckingham Twp), release their guardian Thomas Bye of Buckingham Twp.
Bk 7/pg 280 Dec 8, 1835

John Rufe, now 21, son of Jacob Rufe, late of Nockamixon Twp, acknowledges payment of estate by administrator Michael Dech.
Bk 7/pg 281 Feb 23, 1834

Elizabeth, wife of John Shellenberger, and heir of Michael Kulp, deceased, refuses to accept the real estate. Bk 7/pg 284 Mar 9, 1832

William Folwell of Romulus, Seneca Co, NY gives power of attorney to Joseph H. Purdy of Doylestown to recover estate from representatives of William Purdy, late of Doylestown. Bk 7/pg 284 Mar 7, 1836

Susannah Spencer (late Amey), wife of Daniel Spencer Jr. of Kingston Twp, Luzerne Co, PA gives power of attorney to husband to recover estate from late grandfather George Amey of Haycock Twp. Bk 7/pg 288 Jul 11, 1834

Dorothy Ann Spencer (late Amey), wife of Orren Spencer of Kingston Twp, Luzerne Co, PA gives power of attorney to friend Daniel Spencer Jr. to recover estate from grandfather George Amey of Haycock Twp.
Bk 7/pg 288 Jul 15, 1834

Thomas Worthington of Franklin Co, OH gives power of attorney to Adin G. Hibbs of Franklin Co. to recover estate from father Amos Worthington and grandfather David Worthington. Bk 7/pg 289 Feb 6, 1836

Elizabeth Swartz, Jacob and Mary Hendricks and Jacob and Susanna Swartz, children of Joseph Drissel, late of Tinicum Twp, acknowledge payment of estate by acting executor John Drissel.   Bk 7/pg 293   Apr 6, 1836

Samuel Cary, Samuel Shaw and George Custard, guardians of Chapman, Caroline and James Green, children of Dr. James R. Green, late of Richland Twp, acknowledge payment of estate by administrators Ann Green, John Foulke and William Green.   Bk 7/pg 296   Sep 11, 1835

Thomas Folwell, late of Southampton Twp, will land to son William subject to dower of widow Elizabeth and payment to granddaughter Elizabeth W. Hemphill. William and wife Jane and widow Elizabeth sold to William Purdy. Elizabeth is since deceased. Elizabeth W. Hemphill is now of age and married to John Wilkinson, Esq. who is since deceased. William Purdy is also now deceased. Elizabeth Wilkinson acknowledges payment by Thomas Purdy, executor of William Purdy.   Bk 7/pg 297   Apr 12, 1836

William Dalbey of Philadelphia and wife Mary, daughter of Shipley Lester, late of Richland Twp, assign their right in estate to Abel Lester of Richland Twp, tanner.   Bk 7/pg 300   Mar 21, 1836

Andrew Shitz of Plumstead Twp, heir of Adam Shitz, late of Nockamixon Twp, acknowledges payment of estate by executor Michael Shitz.
                                        Bk 7/pg 300   [blank], 1835

William Snyder of Upper Saucon Twp, Lehigh Co, guardian of Mary Ann Zigafoos, acknowledges payment by John O. Campbell, administrator of William Campbell, late of Springfield Twp, who had been Mary Ann's guardian.   Bk 7/pg 307   Apr 29, 1836

Charles and Elizabeth Teterly, Jonas and Susannah Althouse, Henry and Hannah Wismer, John Ott and Henry Ott and Henry Ott as guardian of Daniel, Emanuel and Barbara Ott, children of Elizabeth Ott, daughter of Manuel Solloday, late of Bedminster Twp, acknowledge payment of estate by administrators Daniel and John Solloday.   Bk 7/pg 309   Apr 11, 1834

John Kramer of Bedminster Twp, hatter, and wife Susannah, Henry and Rebecca Kramer, John Kramer, shoemaker, and wife Barbara, Abraham and Catharine Krouthomel, children of Emanuel Solloday, late of Bedminster Twp, acknowledge payment of estate by administrators Daniel and John Solloday.   Bk 7/pg 309   Apr 11, 1834

Catharine Crouse of Nockamixon Twp, now 21, acknowledges payment by guardian John Williams of estate due father Jacob Crouse, late of Nockamixon.   Bk 7/pg 311   Apr 4, 1836

Rev. John Kershaw of Maidstone, Kent County, England and Mark Freeman Kershaw, James Kershaw and Richard Gray and his wife Elizabeth Milner (of Knox Co, OH), being children of John by his wife Elizabeth, deceased, who was the only surviving child of Mark Freeman, late of Philadelphia, merchant, give power of attorney to Samuel Harvey of Germantown, Philadelphia, merchant, to sell the estate.   Bk 7/pg 316   Mar 14, 1835

Anna Matilda Foulke of Richland Twp, now 21, and John and Letitia Roberts of Milford Twp, acknowledges payment by guardians Richard Moore and George Custard of estate due from late father Thomas Foulke.
                                         Bk 7/pg 319   Apr 18, 1836

Jonas Hagey of Bedminster Twp, now 21, acknowledges payment by guardian Abraham Gearhart of estate due from father Jacob Hagey.
                                         Bk 7/pg 320   Apr 5, 1836

Elizabeth, wife of Henry Hasting and daughter of Israel and Martha Monroe, late of Chester Co, gives power of attorney to husband Henry to collect share of mother's estate payable by Jeremiah Dungan. Bk 7/pg 321   Mar 26, 1836

Henry Myers, Abraham Myers, Mary Myers, Ester Myers, Charles Dyer Jr., Edward M. Dyer, Elizabeth Stott, heirs of John Myers, late of Plumstead Twp, acknowledge payment of estate by executor Christian Myers.
                                         Bk 7/pg 326   Jun 8, 1835

Thomas Walton of Chenango Twp, Beaver Co, PA, heir of Rachel Walton, daughter of Garret Vanhorn, late of Springfield Twp, by attorney and brother-in-law Conard Frederick of Moncey Borough, Lycoming Co, PA, acknowledges payment of estate from William Stokes, surviving administrator.   Bk 7/pg 328   Jul 9, 1836

Jacob and Henry Cressman, executors of Jacob Cressman, late of Rockhill Twp, acknowledge payment by heir Abraham Cressman for land willed to him.   Bk 7/pg 329   Jun 10, 1836

Joseph Hartman of Williams Twp, Northampton Co. and wife Elizabeth, daughter of Jacob Trumbauer, late of Richland Twp, acknowledge payment of estate by guardian John Trumbauer.   Bk 7/pg 331   May 26, 1836

John, Jeremiah, William, James, Anne, Citty and Mary Algard, heirs of Lewis Algard, assign their shares in estate to widow Barbara.

Bk 7/pg 332   Feb 16, 1833

Abraham and Magdalena Meyer, children of William Meyer, late of Springfield Twp, acknowledge payment of estate by administrators Samuel Williams and Christian Meyers.   Bk 7/pg 337   Apr 4, 1836

John Myers of Columbiana Co, OH, son of Wm Myers of Springfield Twp, acknowledges payment of estate by administrators Samuel, William and Christian Myers.   Bk 7/pg 338   Mar 14, 1836

David Smith of Lancaster Co. and wife Hannah, daughter of Martha Monrow (formerly Dungan) who was a daughter of Jeremiah Dungan, late of Bucks Co, give power of attorney to Benjamin Penrose of Lancaster Co. to recover estate from executor Jeremiah Dungan Jr.   Bk 7/pg 338   Jul 19, 1836

Salma Bright of Springfield Twp. gives power of attorney to Jacob Bright of Springfield to recover money from estate of her father Daniel Benner.

Bk 7/pg 340   Jul 30, 1836

Jacob Hibbs, late of Bristol Twp, bequeathed his estate in ten shares upon the death of his widow and his daughter Rachel. His daughter Mary has since died intestate and her two shares go to the other children. Joseph Scott of Gates Twp, Monro Co, NY and wife Marian, who was a daughter of Jacob Hibbs, give power of attorney to Amos Scott of Bensalem Twp, yeoman, to recover their share of estate.   Bk 7/pg 342   Jul 25, 1836

Abraham Willdy and wife Charlotte, daughter of John Vanhorn, late of Middletown Twp, assign to Jesse Hellings of Middletown their right in the estate dower due upon the death of widow Elanor.   Bk 7/pg 343   Apr 5, 1836

Ashbel and Susanna Jones of New Britain Twp, due to advanced years and infirmity, give power of attorney to son John J. Jones of New Britain, farmer, and son-in-law Benjamin Fulton of Warrington Twp, wheelwright, to sell their real estate.   Bk 7/pg 343   Aug 30, 1836

Joshua Richardson, Jonathan K. and Mary D. Stackhouse, Thomas and Rachel Livezey, Samuel H. and Sarah Paxson and John D. Richardson, heirs of Joseph Richardson, late of Middletown Twp, acknowledge settlement of several mortgages that served as dower to widow Mary.

Bk 7/pg 353   May 12, 1836

Mary Strawsnider, widow of John, late of Durham, yeoman, who died intestate, Jacob Zigafuse of Nockamixon Twp, guardian of minor son John Strawsnider, Jesse Cawley of Lower Saucon Twp, trustee of Solomon Waggoner and wife Sarah (late Strawsnider), Elizabeth, Mary, Catharine and Hannah Strawsnider, daughter of John, acknowledge payment of estate by administrators Michael Fackenthall Jr. and Joseph Harwick.

Bk 7/pg 354   [not dated]

Samuel B. Keller of Lower Mount Bethel Twp, Northampton Co, school teacher, assigns to John DeYoung of Lower Mount Bethel, merchant, his share in estate of late father John Keller, Esq. of Haycock Twp. due upon death of his mother Margaret.   Bk 7/pg 356   Aug 24, 1836

Joseph and John Schleifer, William and Elizabeth Strunk, Abraham and Mary Stauffer, children of John Schleifer, late of Richland Twp, choose men to value the estate.   Bk 7/pg 359   Apr 15, 1836

Samuel Meyers of Tinicum Twp, son of John Meyers, late of Tinicum, assigns to Abraham Stover of Nockamixon Twp his share of father's estate due upon death of his mother Eve.   Bk 7/pg 372   Nov 12, 1836

John Beidler of Richland Twp, guardian of Peter and Silas Beidler, sons of Henry Beidler and wife Catharine, deceased, who was daughter of Michael Stoneback, deceased and granddaughter of Michael Dieterly, late of Haycock Twp, acknowledges payment of estate by executor Philip Wimmer.

Bk 7/pg 372   May 18, 1836

Margaret Stoneback, John Stoneback of Richland Twp, Elizabeth Stoneback, Jacob and Mary Deily of Richland Twp. and Henry, David and Baltzer Stoneback of Richland Twp, children of Michael Stoneback, deceased, and grandchildren of Michael Dieterly, late of Haycock Twp, acknowledge payment of estate by executor Philip Wimmer.   Bk 7/pg 373   Apr 27, 1836

George M. Kressler of Springfield Twp, son of George Kressler, late of Durham Twp, gives power of attorney to Jacob E. Buck of Springfield to recover estate from executor Henry Kressler.   Bk 7/pg 378   Oct 8, 1836

Samuel E. Buck of Doylestown, merchant, son of Nicholas Buck, late of Nockamixon Twp, entitled to one-sixth share of dower upon the death of his mother Mary, assigns his share to Nicholas Buck of Nockamixon Twp.

Bk 7/pg 379   Jul 28, 1834

Henry Ott, guardian of Joseph Nicholas, minor child of Jacob Nicholas, late of Tinicum, acknowledges payment of estate by administrators Jonathan Leidigh and Isaac Worman.	Bk 7/pg 383	Dec 26, 1836

Jacob and Mariah Slifer, Solomon and Margaret Litzenberger and Barbara Yerger, daughter of Michael Young, late of Philadelphia, release to George Deterley a lot of land in Bedminster Twp. which he purchased of executor Christian Young.	Bk 7/pg 384	Jan 10, 1837

Jesse Carver of Solebury Twp, son of Benjamin Carver, late of Plumstead Twp, and wife Euphema sell their share in Benjamin's estate to Samuel Smith of Plumstead.	Bk 7/pg 385	Jan 19, 1837

John Narragang of Richland Twp, co-executor and only heir of his father Peter Narragang, releases the other executor, John Diehl.	Bk 7/pg 387	Nov 4, 1836

Teana (Christiana) Gerhart of Rockhill Twp, now 21, acknowledges payment of estate from father Adam Gerhart, late of Rockhill, by guardian Henry Schlichter.	Bk 7/pg 389	Jan 28, 1837

Christian Fluck of Haycock Twp, hatter, assigns his share in father's estate, due upon death of his mother and now in hands of executors Philip Fluck and David Housekeeper to David Mumbour of Haycock Twp.	Bk 7/pg 389	Dec 7, 1830

Joseph F., Martin and Elizabeth Tyson and Abraham and Magdalene Holderman, grandchildren of Joseph Tyson Sr., late of Bedminster Twp, acknowledge payment of estate by administrators Joseph Tyson and Abraham High.	Bk 7/pg 390	Nov 11, 1836

Jacob Hockman, guardian of Henry Tyson, minor child of late Henry Tyson of Bedminster Twp and grandson of late Joseph Tyson Sr. of Bedminster Twp, acknowledges payment of estate by administrators Joseph Tyson and Abraham High.	Bk 7/pg 391	Nov 11, 1836

Elias Bissey of Tinicum Twp, now 21, acknowledges payment by guardian Jacob Hoppock of estate due from late father Jacob Bissey.	Bk 7/pg 401	Apr 21, 1836

Lydia Pursell, late of Bristol Borough bequeath estate after the death of her son Isaac Wilson to his children. Executors Joseph Warner and Samuel

200

Swain transfer one-fourth of estate to Garret Lukens and wife Lydia, a
daughter of Isaac.   Bk 7/pg 401   Mar 14, 1832

Abner Torbert of Upper Makefield Twp, yeoman, gives power of attorney to
brothers Jacob/Lamb[?] and Anthony Torbert of Upper Makefield to recover
moneys due him.   Bk 7/pg 406   Apr 27, 1816

Isaac, Israel and George Childs and Jacob and Rachel B. Lukens acknowledge
payment by executor Joshua Michener of estate due to Deborah Childs under
the will of George Michener, late of Plumstead Twp.
                                                Bk 7/pg 406   Apr 9, 1831

John and Hannah Michener acknowledge payment by executor Joshua
Michener of estate due under will of their father George Michener, late of
Plumstead Twp.   Bk 7/pg 407,409   Apr 4, 1831

Joseph Scott of Morrisville, son of Mary Scott, late of Plumstead Twp,
acknowledges payment of estate by guardian Nicholas Swartz.
                                                Bk 7/pg 407   Mar 7, 1837

John Townsend of Plumstead Twp. and Sarah Bradshaw and Aaron
Townsend of Bedminster Twp. give power of attorney to Hiram Burges of
Plumstead to recover moneys due them.   Bk 7/pg 414   Nov 3, 1832

William Swope (assigned of John Strouse), George Strouse, Jacob and
Elizabeth Shuman, Peter and Catharine Shull and Henry and Sophia Shuman,
representatives of George Strouse, late of Tinicum Twp, acknowledge
payment of estate by administrator John Mast. Bk 7/pg 415   May 30, 1829

Margaret Lester of Richland Twp, widow of Shipley Lester, late of Richland,
releases to Abel Lester of Richland her claim in land in Quakertown.
                                                Bk 7/pg 423   Mar 27, 1837

Shipley Lester, late of Richland Twp, left estate to his heirs. Heirs Abel
Lester, William Lester, Shipley Lester, Antrim Lester, Hannah L. Watson and
William and Mary Ann Dalbey all assigned their shares to Abel Lester. Abel
acknowledges payment of estate by executors William Lester and Richard
Moore.   Bk 7/pg 424   Apr 10, 1837

Margaret Lester, widow of Shipley Lester is about to remove to Indiana with
her son Abel and discharges the executors from their trust.
                                                Bk 7/pg 425   Apr 10, 1837

William Lester of Dudly Twp, Henry Co, IN, Shipley Lester of Richmond, Wayne Co, IN, Hannah L. Watson (wife of John H. Watson) of Springborough, Warren Co, OH, and Antrim Lester of Raymond, Hinds Co, MS, assign right in estate to their father Shipley Lester to Abel Lester of Richland Twp.   Bk 7/pg 426   Jan 27, 1837

Mary Lester, widow of John Lester, late of Richland Twp, releases to her son John C. Lester all right in estate of John Lester.   Bk 7/pg 429   Sep 17, 1836

Elizabeth Swartz (widow of Isaac) of Haycock Twp, Jacob and Mary Hendricks of Hilltown Twp, and Jacob and Susanna Swartz of Milford Twp, daughters of Joseph Drissell, late of Tinicum Twp, acknowledge payment of estate by executor John Drissell.   Bk 7/pg 430   May 2, 1837

Jesse Fluck of Hilltown Twp, yeoman and wife Elvira, daughter of David Wambold, late of Rockhill Twp, acknowledge payment of estate by her guardian Andrew Drumbore.   Bk 7/pg 433   Mar 25, 1837

David and Henry Dirstine, Abraham and Catharine Clemmer, Leonard and Sophia Vanfossen, David S. and Anna Heebner and Mary Ruth, children of Isaac Dirstine, late of Rockhill Twp, acknowledge payment of estate by Jacob Dirstine.   Bk 7/pg 434   Apr 1, 1836

Louisa C. Magill, William D. Magill, Robert M. Magill and Benjamin M. Magill, all of Philadelphia, give power of attorney to brother Alfred Magill of Doylestown Twp. to recover money due under several mortgages.
                    Bk 7/pg 435   Apr 1, 1837

Levi N. Leidigh, son of Phillip Leidigh, late of Bucks Co, now 21, acknowledges payment of estate by guardian Isaac Worman.
                    Bk 7/pg 436   Apr 1, 1837

Christian Getman of Rockhill Twp, guardian for Hyginses, Moses and Leanna Barndt, minor children of Frederick Barndt, late of Rockhill Twp, acknowledges payment of estate by administrators Philip Barndt.
                    Bk 7/pg 437   Mar 30, 1835

Philip High, Abraham and Sarah Kinsey and Anna High, children of Philip High, late of Bedminster Twp, acknowledge payment of estate by administrators David, Ralph and Abraham High.   Bk 7/pg 439   Apr 4, 1837

David Ditlow of Center Co, George and Hannah Gunkel of Northampton Co, heirs of Charles Ditlow, late of Bucks Co, yeoman, give power of attorney to their father Abraham Ditlow of Bucks Co. to recover from estate Philip and George Mumbower, executors of Philip Mumbower, late of Bucks Co.
Bk 7/pg 440   Mar 1, 1837

Christian Clymer, late of Milford Twp, yeoman, bequeathed one-fourth share of estate to daughter Susanna Strunk. Jacob and Susanna Strunk of Milford Twp. sell share to John Fretz of Milford Twp.   Bk 7/pg 442   Apr 24, 1837

George Ackerman of Milford Twp gives power of attorney to Jacob Beidler of Milford to recover share of dower from executor Peter Shelly, Esq. due from estate of father John Ackerman, late of Milford Twp. upon the death of his wife Susanna.   Bk 7/pg 444   Mar 31, 1837

Isaac Weaver of Tinicum Twp, assignee of Henry Ulmer, son and heir of Peter Ulmer, late of Nockamixon Twp, acknowledges payment of dower share by the present owners George Shitz, Frederick Stone and others.
Bk 7/pg 449   May 3, 1837

Joseph Fretz of Tinicum Twp, legatee under will of John Fretz, late of Tinicum, acknowledges payment by Christian K. Kressman of Nockamixon Twp. of legacy due from him as present owner of a mill property in Nockamixon Twp.   Bk 7/pg 450   Apr 1, 1837

Peter and Maria Lewis of Rockhill Twp, Magdalena Klinker of Rockhill and Peter Cuffle of Rockhill, yeoman, children of Peter Cuffle, late of Columbian Co, OH, give power of attorney to Jacob Cuffle of Rockhill, yeoman, to recover estate due them.   Bk 7/pg 451   May 17, 1837

Joseph Conard of Whitepain Twp, Montgomery Co, blacksmith, and wife Rebecca, daughter of Joseph Shaw, late of Richland Twp, now 21, acknowledge payment of estate by guardians George Custard and Samuel Shaw.   Bk 7/pg 455   Apr 4, 1836

Thomas Worthington, present guardian of Artis Worthington, acknowledges payment of estate by former guardian Thomas Good.
Bk 7/pg 457   May 13, 1837

Joseph and Mary Rodman and Jacob Street of Muskingam Co, OH, children of James Street, late of Bensalem Twp, give power of attorney to Samuel Hellings of Middletown Twp, to recover estate.   Bk 7/pg 459   Apr 7, 1837

Wilson Hughs, John Hughs, Sylvester Hughs and Howell and Frances
Hoppock, children of Zebedee Hughes who was a brother of George Hughes,
acknowledge payment by George of money due them from the estate of
George's father John Hughes, late of Buckingham Twp.

Bk 7/pg 460   Mar 18, 1834

Franklin P. Sellers assigns to Cornelius Sellers his share in a legacy left to his
mother Sophia Sellers by Peter Bodder and now in hands of Joseph Moore of
Buckingham Twp.   Bk 7/pg 462   Jun 26, 1837

Charles D. Margerum, heir of Martha Hough, late of Lower Makefield Twp,
acknowledges payment of estate by Jolly Longshore of Middletown Twp,
present owner of land originally taken by Israel Margerum and by William
Longshore, guardian of minor children of Benjamin Margerum.

Bk 7/pg 465   Jul 3, 1837

Elias Bright of Hilltown Twp. gives power of attorney to Jacob Bright of
Springfield Twp. to recover estate which will become due after decease of his
mother Salana, widow of Elias Bright.   Bk 7/pg 469   Jul 15, 1837

Eve Myers, widow of John, late of Tinicum Twp, now old and infirm, releases
son Henry of dower obligation as he takes care of her in her old age.

Bk 7/pg 472   Jan 13, 1837

James Gilkyson is incapable of taking care of himself due to great age. His
children Andrew, Aaron and Rachel Larue, Samuel and Elias constitute John
Yardley, Esq. to manage James' affairs.   Bk 7/pg 473   Sep 19, 1837

Henry Myers of Tinicum Twp, guardian for Henry and Catharine Strouse,
minor children of late Henry Strouse Jr. and grandchildren of Henry Strouse,
late of Nockamixon Twp, acknowledges payment of estate by administrators
John and Jacob Strouse.   Bk 7/pg 474   Mar 25, 1837

Michael Kunsman and wife Sarah, daughter of Henry Strouse, late of
Nockamixon Twp, acknowledge payment of estate by administrators John and
Jacob Strouse.   Bk 7/pg 475   Mar 6, 1837

Jacob Strouse of Tinicum Twp, guardian for Samuel Strouse, minor child of
late Nicholas Strouse and grandson of Henry Strouse, late of Nockamixon
Twp, acknowledges payment of estate by administrator John Strouse.

Bk 7/pg 475   Mar 25, 1837

George Hoffman of Philadelphia and wife Julian, daughter of Christian Fritzinger, deceased, give power of attorney to John K. Zeilin of Delaware Co. to recover estate from Catharine Fritzinger and James S. Rich, M.D., executors of John Fritzinger, late of Doylestown Twp.

Bk 7/pg 476   Apr 24, 1837

Mary Zeilin of Philadelphia, heir of John Fritzinger, late of Doylestown Twp. gives power of attorney to John K. Zeilin of Delaware Co. to recover estate from executors Catharine Fritzinger and James S. Rich, M.D.

Bk 7/pg 477   Apr 24, 1837

George Walters and wife Sarah, daughter of John Fritzinger, late of Doylestown Twp, acknowledge payment of estate by executors Catharine Fritzinger and James S. Rich.   Bk 7/pg 477   May 3, 1837

Alfred Magill, guardian of Thomas, Margaret, George W., John and Jacob F. Fritzinger, children of late John Fritzinger and William Smith and wife Maria (late Barclay) and Eliza Springer (late Barclay), grandchildren of John Fritzinger, and Mary Zeiling, Ann Frantz, Henry Fritzinger, Catharine Fritzinger, George and Sarah Walters, Martha (wife of Austin Brittain), children of John Fritzinger, and Moses and Mary Hiple, Juliann (married), Elizabeth (married), John, James S. and Samuel M. Fritzinger, children of Christian Fritzinger and grandchildren of John, late of Doylestown Twp, acknowledge payment of estate by executors Catharine Fritzinger and Dr. James S. Rich.   Bk 7/pg 478   Apr 18, 1837

John Lukens of Vincennes Borough, IN, son of Mary Lukens, legatee of George Michener, gives power of attorney to William Burtch[?] of Knox Co, IN to recover estate from executor Joshua Michener.

Bk 7/pg 482   Jul 6, 1837

Silas Heston of Rockingham Co, NC gives power of attorney to brother Samuel of Bucks Co. to sell his one-third interest in real estate of his late father Isaiah Heston.   Bk 7/pg 484   Sep 21, 1837

Thomas Roberts of Highland Co, OH and wife Hannah (late Burgess) give power of attorney to Thomas C. Rockhill, Esq. of Philadelphia, merchant, to recover estate from William Watson, executor of George Burgess, late of Bucks Co.   Bk 7/pg 485   Sep 8, 1837

Jacob Mitman of Bedminster Twp. and Elizabeth Mitman, children of Conrad Mitman, late of Bedminster Twp, acknowledge payment of estate by executors John and Henry Mitman.   Bk 7/pg 488   Apr 3, 1834

Martin King of Philadelphia, son of Henry King, late of Philadelphia and grandson of Elizabeth King (widow) of Hilltown Twp, acknowledges payment of estate by his father's brother Peter King of Hilltown Twp. that would be due him upon the death of his grandmother.
                                                                Bk 7/pg 491   Oct 3, 1837

Andrew and Mary Creveling of Springfield Twp, Susanna Ruth of Springfield and Jonas Kressman of Springfield, guardian of Elizabeth Ruth, daughters of Henry Ruth of Springfield Twp, acknowledges payment of estate by administrator Francis Ruth.   Bk 7/pg 493   Apr 3, 1837

Jacob Stout of Rockhill Twp, now 21, acknowledges payment by guardian John Gearhart of Franconia Twp, Montgomery Co. of estate from late father Jacob Stout of Rockhill Twp.   Bk 7/pg 495   Nov 9, 1837

Mary White of Montgomery Twp, Montgomery Co. gives power of attorney to son-in-law John Fabian to recover dower money due from son David White out of estate of late husband George White of Nockamixon Twp.
                                                                Bk 7/pg 501   Jun 29, 1837

Samuel Gilbert assigns to his brother Hiel Gilbert his share in dower of estate of late father Samuel Gilbert of Buckingham Twp. due upon the death of their mother Huldah.   Bk 7/pg 502   Feb 7, 1838

Abraham Shelly of Cannceaonces[?] Twp, Butler Co, son of Joseph Shelly, late of Milford Twp, acknowledges payment of estate by executors Jacob and Joseph Shelly.   Bk 7/pg 502   May 1, 1837

Barbarah McDowell of Buckingham Twp. gives power of attorney to grandson John Rous of Buckingham Twp. to recover money due her.
                                                                Bk 7/pg 503   Jan 19, 1838

George Hicks of Haycock Twp. and wife Ann, legatee under will of John Roberts, late of Chester Co. assign her legacy to Penrose Hicks.
                                                                Bk 7/pg 503   Nov 18, 1837

Jacob Grove, John Grove, William and Mary Swink, John and Hannah Selser, Jonathan and Susanna Hough, Henry Grove and Daniel and Catharine Harley, heirs of David Groff, late of Doylestown Twp, acknowledge payment of estate by executor David Grove, excepting the share bequeathed to David's daughter Maria in Virginia.   Bk 7/pg 504   Apr 7, 1836

Tobias Sellers, surviving guardian of William Mayberry, son of William Mayberry, late of Upper Hanover Twp, Montgomery Co, doctor of medicine, gives power of attorney to Abraham Shults of Lower Milford Twp, Bucks Co. to record satisfaction of a mortgage from William Reaser of Lower Milford.
                                                Bk 7/pg 507   Oct 5, 1837

Samuel Nicholas of Tinicum Twp, son of Jacob Nicholas, late of Haycock Twp, gives power of attorney to Samuel A. Smith of Doylestown to acknowledge satisfaction of a bond from Peter Nicholas.
                                                Bk 7/pg 511   Apr 5, 1838

Ann Gaddis of Harrison Co, OH, widow of John Gaddis, late of Plumstead Twp, gives power of attorney to Stow[?] Hutchinson of Harrison Co. to recover money from Joseph Hough.   Bk 7/pg 512   Mar 2, 1838

Joseph Carver, widower of Clarissa Maria, sister of Col. John Hart and daughter of Joseph Hart, late of Warwick Twp, acknowledges payment of estate by Col. John.   Bk 7/pg 513   Apr 5, 1838

James E. and Naomi Hill (late Rodrock), acknowledge payment by Naomi's guardian Josiah Y. Shaw, Esq. of estate from late father David Rodrock.
                                                Bk 7/pg 514   Apr 6, 1838

Mary W. Johnson, wife of Lawrence Johnson of Philadelphia, is due money from estate of late father Aaron Winder of Bucks Co, and asks that the money be paid to her husband.   Bk 7/pg 516   Apr 16, 1838

Deborah Arnold, widow of Frederick Arnold, late of Springfield Twp, releases son Solomon from dower obligation.   Bk 7/pg 517   Oct 16, 1837

Abraham Yoder of Franconia Twp, Montgomery Co, administrator of Mary Yoder, late of Rockhill Twp, gives power of attorney to friend Abraham Allaback of Towamensing Twp, Montgomery Co, yeoman, to receive money due estate.   Bk 7/pg 518   Apr 11, 1838

Andrew Frankenfield, son of Philip and Margaret Frankenfield and grandson of George Snyder, late of Tinicum Twp, now 21, acknowledges payment of estate by guardian Henry Hillpot.   Bk 7/pg 519   Mar 17, 1838

Valentine Hager, Christian Hager, Joseph Hager, Martin and Elizabeth Shive, Michael and Mary Lightcap, and John and Catharine Rufe, children of Valentine Hager Sr., late of Nockamixon Twp, acknowledge payment of estate by administrator John Hager.　　Bk 7/pg 520　Apr 7, 1838

John Uhler of Nazareth, Northampton Co, now 21, acknowledges payment by guardian John Knecht of estate due from father Jacob Uhler, late of Durham Twp.　　Bk 7/pg 521　Apr 16, 1838

Benjamin Dean of Philadelphia gives power of attorney to James G. Hibbs of Middletown Twp. to recover money due from estate of Jacob Hellings, late of Bensalem Twp.　　Bk 7/pg 522　Apr 23, 1838

Elizabeth Dean, mother of late John Worstall, and Owen and Susan Worstall, siblings of John, late of Newtown Twp, acknowledge payment by George Chapman and John Blackfan, executors of Ezra Buckman who was John's administrator.　　Bk 7/pg 523　Apr 6, 1838

Elizabeth Goforth, widow of John, late of Bensalem Twp, releases sons William and Jacob from dower obligation.　Bk 7/pg 524　Nov 1, 1837

Sarah Wood of Saltcreek Twp, Pickaway Co, OH gives power of attorney to Joseph Burton of Bristol Twp. to sell land in Morrisville.　　Bk 7/pg 524　May 2, 1834

Jesse Palmer of Pickaway Co, OH and wife Naomi, daughter of John Wood, late of Bucks Co. give power of attorney to Joseph Burton, Esq. of Bucks Co. to sell land in Bucks Co.　　Bk 7/pg 525　Feb 5, 1834

Joseph Leatherman, John Leatherman, Abraham Leatherman, Peter and Ester Detweiler, Abraham and Elizabeth Wismer and Joseph and Nancy Tyson, heirs of Jacob Overholt, late of Bedminster Twp, acknowledge payment of estate by executor Christian Meyers Sen.　Bk 7/pg 526　Apr 3, 1838

Jacob Fretz, John Fretz, Mark Fretz, Abraham Fretz, Jonas Fretz, David Fretz, Benjamin and Ester Winebury and Joseph and Sarah Wisler, heirs of Jacob Overholt, late of Bedminster Twp, acknowledge payment of estate by executor Christian Meyers Sen.　　Bk 7/pg 527　Apr 3, 1838

Abraham Wismer, guardian for Jacob, John, Joseph, Mary and Anna Gross, children of John and Mary Gross and heirs of Jacob Overholt, late of

Bedminster Twp, acknowledges payment of estate by executors Christian
Meyers Sen.   Bk 7/pg 528   Apr 3, 1838

Joseph Fry, guardian of Ely and Catharine Leatherman, and Abraham
Leatherman, guardian of Mary Leatherman, children of Jacob Leatherman,
late of Plumstead Twp, and heirs of Jacob Overholt, late of Bedminster Twp,
acknowledges payment of estate by executor Christian Meyers Sen.
                                                 Bk 7/pg 528   Apr 3, 1838

Elizabeth Hockman and Magdalene Myers, both of Bedminster Twp, and
Abraham and Mary Shaddinger, heirs of Jacob Overholt, late of Bedminster
Twp, acknowledge payment of estate by executor Christian Meyers Sen.
                                                 Bk 7/pg 529   Apr 3, 1838

Abraham Shaddinger, guardian of Barbara Fretz, daughter of Henry Fretz,
late of Bedminster Twp, and heir of Jacob Overholt, late of Bedminster Twp,
acknowledges payment of estate by executor Christian Meyers Sen.
                                                 Bk 7/pg 530   Apr 3, 1838

Sarah Ann Dean of Middletown Twp. gives power of attorney to her uncle
Jesse Hellings to recover money due her and to attend to the division of estate
between her and her sister.   Bk 7/pg 531   Apr 11, 1838

Joshua Heist of Upper Hanover Twp, Montgomery Co, cordwainer, now 21,
acknowledges payment by guardian Jacob Boyer of estate due from father
George Heist.   Bk 7/pg 532   Apr 7, 1838

James Hartley, now of Columbiana Co, OH, having a legal claim with
siblings to two lots in Bucks Co formerly belonging to father Samuel, gives
power of attorney to Amos Armitage of Solebury Twp. to sell his interest.
                                                 Bk 7/pg 532   Mar 28, 1837

Susanna Trisler, widow, mother of late Isaac Trissel, acknowledges payment
of estate by Isaac's guardian Abraham Reiff. Bk 7/pg 533   Apr 4, 1838

Joseph Nicholas, now 21, acknowledges payment by guardian Henry Ott of
estate due from father Jacob Nicholas, late of Tinicum Twp.
                                                 Bk 7/pg 535   Mar 16, 1838

Mary Booz, widow of John Booz, late of Bristol Twp, releases to Charles
Holmes the dower right in land purchased by Ann Holmes.
                                                 Bk 7/pg 535   Mar 31, 1838

Moses Tomlinson of Highland Co, OH and wife Ruth, and Moorman Butterworth of Warren Co, OH and wife Fanny, daughters of Joseph Smith, late of Upper Makefield Twp, give power of attorney to William H. Anderson of Warren Co, OH to recover estate from executor Ralph Smith.

Bk 7/pg 536   Apr 14, 1838

Benjamin Dean and wife Sarah Ann, daughter of Jacob and Charlotte Hellings, late of Bensalem Twp, transfer estate right to James G. Hibbs.

Bk 7/pg 540   May 23, 1838

Abraham Yoder, John Yoder, Samuel Yoder and Isaac and Barbara Souder, heirs of John Yoder, acknowledge payment of dower by Henry Yoder.

Bk 7/pg 541   May 23, 1838

Samuel Yoder, John Yoder, Henry Yoder and Isaac and Barbara Souder, heirs of Mary Yoder, acknowledge payment of estate by eldest son and administrator Abraham Yoder.   Bk 7/pg 541   May 23, 1838

William Miller, Susan Miller and Nancy Ann Miller of New Haven Twp, Huron Co, OH, give power of attorney to Peter M. Ritter of Bucks Co. to recover legacy left by Bartel and Elizabeth White, late of Bucks Co.

Bk 7/pg 550   Apr 30, 1838

Abraham White, William White, Henry and Mary Fritz, Dr. James Martin and wife Elizabeth, Samuel and Barbary Maust, Lydia White, Sarah White, John and Mary Smith, John and Rebecca Fabian, Peter and Mary Ritter, John and Elizabeth Moyers, John and Catharine Groover, Nicholas H. and Sarah Carty, Elisha and Hannah Miller, grandchildren of Bartle White, late of Bedminster Twp, acknowledge payment of estate by David White Sr. and David White, Esq.   Bk 8/pg 1   Apr 14, 1838

Hugh Ely of Solebury Twp, son of John Ely, late of Solebury, acknowledges payment of estate by executor Asher Ely.   Bk 8/pg 2   Oct 24, 1814

Phineas Ely, grandson of John Ely, late of Solebury Twp, acknowledges payment of estate by executor Asher Ely.   Bk 8/pg 2   Mar 16, 1822

Elizabeth Townsend and Mary, widow of John Paxson (late of Solebury Twp), daughters of John Ely, late of Solebury Twp, acknowledges payment of estate by executor Asher Ely.   Bk 8/pg 3   Sep 27, 1837

James E. Dungan, son of James Dungan, late of Northampton Twp, entitled to one-half of dower upon death of widow, sells his share to Jacob Keyser of Philadelphia.   Bk 8/pg 4   Jul 5, 1838

Samuel Shearer of Upper Milford Twp, Lehigh Co and wife Sarah, Jacob Schlifer of Milford Twp and wife Hannah, Samuel Smith, Mary Smith, both of Milford Twp, Henry Fried of Marlborough Twp, Montgomery Co and wife Elizabeth, Conrad, Solomon and Henry Smith, all of Milford, children of Conrad Smith of Milford Twp and his wife Elizabeth, a daughter of John Stryckers, late of Milford Twp, acknowledge payment of estate by John's executors David Deahl and Henry Trumbower.   Bk 8/pg 5   Apr 6, 1833

Conrad Smith of Milford Twp, blacksmith, and wife Elizabeth, Mary Deahl, widow, of Milford, and Adam Brey of Upper Milford Twp, Lehigh Co, yeoman and wife Barbara (deceased), daughters of John Stryckers, late of Milford Twp, yeoman, acknowledge payment of estate by executors Henry Trumbower and David Deahl.   Bk 8/pg 7   Mar 8, 1834

Saml Sherrer, guardian for Catharine, Hannah, Aaron, Polly, Lewis, Henry, John and Elizabeth Stricker, children of John Stricker Jun., late of Upper Milford Twp, Lehigh Co, acknowledges payment of estate from John Stricker Sr. by executors Henry Trumbower and David S. Diehl.
                                              Bk 8/pg 8   Feb 7, 1835

William Lester of Henry Co, IN and wife Ann (late Wilson) who was a legatee of Jane Lester, late of Bucks Co, give power of attorney to James Wilson of Bucks Co. to recover estate.   Bk 8/pg 11   Apr 9, 1838

William and Mary Fenton of Buckingham Twp. assign to Samuel, Eleazar, James, Randal, Ephraim, Charles P. and Thomas D. Fenton, children of late Ephraim Fenton and to Samuel, Randall and Jesse Fenton and William and Elizabeth Rich, children of late Patrick Fenton, their share in estate of Hannah Fenton.   Bk 8/pg 16   Aug 24, 1838

Hannah Fenton, late of Buckingham Twp, bequeathed estate to Jesse, Samuel and Randall Fenton and Elizabeth Rich, children of late Patrick Fenton, and Henrietta, Ann, Martha, Samuel, Eleazar, James, Randal, Ephraim, Charles P. and Thomas D. Fenton and to William Fenton and his wife Mary. William Fenton contested the will as he was left less than the others. The others agree to give him an equal share if he withdraws his complaint.
                                              Bk 8/pg 17   Aug 24, 1838

Hannah (wife of Elijah Lewis who is absent), Samuel Jarrett, Abel P. Jarrett, Elizabeth Jarrett, of age, and Rebecca, David and Morris Jarrett, children of late Richard Jarrett, acknowledge payment by Isaac Parry, executor of Jonathan Jarrett, late of Warminster Twp. who bequeathed estate to Richard.
Bk 8/pg 24   Apr 30, 1837

Elizabeth Burton of Falls Twp, now 21, and Randall Myers and wife Mary Ann (late Burton), acknowledge payment by guardian Anthony Burton Jun. of estate from father John Burton Jun. and grandfather John Burton Sen.
Bk 8/pg 25   Sep 8, 1838

John Shadinger of Butler Co, OH and wife Elizabeth, daughter of Jacob Wismer, late of Bucks Co, give power of attorney to Abraham Shaddinger of Bucks Co. to recover estate.   Bk 8/pg 26   Jun 2, 1838

Franey Wildonger of Bedminster Twp, now 21, acknowledges payment by guardian George Fox of estate from late father Leonard Wildonger.
Bk 8/pg 27   May 1, 1838

Abigail Johnson of Richland Twp, daughter of Saml Johnson, late of Richland, now 21, acknowledges payment of estate by guardian David Johnson of Richland.   Bk 8/pg 28   Oct 15, 1836

David R. Johnson of Richland Twp, son of Samuel Johnson, late of Richland, now 21, acknowledges payment of estate by guardian David Johnson.
Bk 8/pg 30   Oct 28, 1837

Samuel and Elizabeth Foulke, Andrew and Mary Ambler, daughter of Benjamin Johnson, late of Richland Twp, Ephraim and Abigail Heller and David R. Johnson, children of late Samuel Johnson and grandchildren of Benjamin, Joseph, Gibson[?] and Milton Johnson, sons of late Casper R. Johnson and grandsons of late Benjamin Johnson, acknowledge payment of estate by executors David, Anthony and Benjamin Johnson.
Bk 8/pg 31   Apr 23, 1838

Nathan James of Doylestown Twp. died intestate leaving no widow or issue but mother Rachel and siblings Benjamin W., Margaret Riale, Elizabeth (wife of William Hines), Abiah (deceased, children Caroline—wife of Benjamin Griffith, Barzilla, James, Elizabeth, Levi and Nathan). Mother Rachel assigns her share to the other heirs.   Bk 8/pg 41   Oct 25, 1838

Jacob Dill of Rockhill Twp. gives power of attorney to friend Barbara Blank of Rockhill to receive his share in dower of father Frederick Dill, late of Rockhill Twp, upon death of his mother Catharine.

Bk 8/pg 41   Sep 29, 1838

John Scout, husband of Maria, daughter of Elizabeth Major, acknowledges payment by John Kerr of estate due by will of John Kerr, Esq.

Bk 8/pg 47   Jan 20, 1821

Magdalena Reaser, widow of Abraham Reaser, late of Springfield Twp, acknowledges payment of estate by administrator David Horn.

Bk 8/pg 51   Nov 20, 1833

Imla Drake of Springfield Twp, now 21, acknowledges payment by guardian Dr. James Martin of estate from father Joseph Drake.

Bk 8/pg 51   Dec 8, 1838

Jacob and Elizabeth Leatherman of Guilford Twp, Medina Co, OH give power of attorney to Jacob Leatherman Jr. of Guilford Twp to sell land in Plumstead Twp.   Bk 8/pg 52   Oct 18, 1838

William E. Fretz, now 21, son of Joseph Fretz, late of Bedminster Twp, acknowledges payment of estate by guardian Jacob Stover and of estate from Hannah Fretz, late of Bedminster.   Bk 8/pg 53   Nov 2, 1838

John Park and wife Elizabeth of Warminster Twp. have agreed to separate due to unhappy differences between them.   Bk 8/pg 55   Nov 20, 1838

Abraham Asure and wife Tacy, daughter of Martha Stradling who was a legatee of John Counselman, late of Falls Twp, acknowledge payment of estate by John's executor Joseph Burton.   Bk 8/pg 58   Nov 12, 1838

Robert K. Longstreth of Falls Twp, now 21, acknowledges payment by guardian Joseph Burton of estate from late grandfather Mahlon Milnor.

Bk 8/pg 59   Oct 15, 1838

Charles Armitage of Columbiana Co, OH and Sarah Beans of Bucks Co. are about to be married.   Bk 8/pg 59   May 8, 1838

Sarah Beans of Solebury Twp. gives power of attorney to Jesse Beans, M.D. of Solebury to recover any moneys due her. Bk 8/pg 60   May 8, 1838

213

Elizabeth Stinson of Bucks Co. assigns to her sister Jane Stinson a bond given by John Bothell to Elijah Stinson.   Bk 8/pg 61   Jun 20, 1837

Henry Darrah of Bradford Twp, Steuben Co, NY gives power of attorney to Jacob Cassel of Montgomery Twp, Montgomery Co, yeoman, to sell land in PA.   Bk 8/pg 62   Jan 14, 1839

James Dungan, heir of sister Sarah Dungan, late of Northampton Twp, acknowledges payment of estate by Thomas Purdy, administrator of Daniel Dungan who was executor to Sarah.   Bk 8/pg 65   Apr 4, 1838

Joseph Matchner of Bibery Twp, Philadelphia Co. has separated by mutual consent from his wife Frances of Falls Twp.   Bk 8/pg 67   Jan 7, 1839

Jane Jemison of Richland Twp, widow of John Jemison, late of Milford Twp, released dower right to lands of her husband's son Samuel Jemison, now deceased.   Bk 8/pg 72   Dec 7, 1838

Jacob Edwards and wife Elizabeth, now 21, acknowledge payment by guardian William Gillam of estate of her grandfather Andrew Hunter.
Bk 8/pg 72   Nov 3, 1838

Susanna Weydemeyer, widow, and Sarah Weydemeyer, John Weydemeyer of Greenwich Twp, Warren Co, NJ, Samuel Weydemeyer of Bedminster Twp, Isaac Weydemeyer of Tinicum Twp. and James Kilmer, guardian for Levina and Mary Ann Weydemeyer and Michael Worman, guardian of Jonas Weydemeyer, children of Jacob Weydemeyer, late of Tinicum Twp, acknowledge payment of estate by administrators Jacob Weydemeyer and Samuel Rufe.   Bk 8/pg 73   Jun 23, 1838

Samuel Worstall, Rachel Worstall, Mary Worstall and James Worstall, children of late John Worstall, assign their right in estate to their mother Ruth.
Bk 8/pg 82   Feb 8, 1839

John Swartz of Gwynedd Twp, Montgomery Co. assigns his right in dower due upon death of mother Mary Swartz from estate of father Christian Swartz, late of New Britain Twp, to James White, of Gwynedd Twp.
Bk 8/pg 87   Feb 19, 1839

Isaac Craven, legatee of Thomas Craven of Montgomery Co, acknowledges payment of estate by executors Samuel and Thomas B. Craven.
Bk 8/pg 91   Jan 31, 1839

Charles Brunner of Philadelphia, grandson of Andrew Brunner, late of Springfield Twp, acknowledges payment of dower by Anthony Weirbach.
Bk 8/pg 92   Feb 9, 1839

Frances Detweiler, widow of Christian Detweiler, late of Plumstead Twp. and Daniel Rickert, guardian of only child Isaac, acknowledge payment of estate by administrator John L. Delp.
Bk 8/pg 96   Apr 1, 1834

John Atherholt of Rusk, Monroe Co, NY gives power of attorney to Jonas J. Rotzel of Rusk to recover estate from Levi Markley and Samuel Atherholt, executors of Christian Atherholt, late of New Britain Twp.
Bk 8/pg 97   Apr 9, 1839

Henry Eckel, guardian of Lovina Gerhart, daughter of Abraham Gerhart, late of Bedminster Twp, acknowledges payment of estate by Enos Cassel.
Bk 8/pg 101   Mar 30, 1839

John Romick, husband of Magdalene Trauger, of Williams Twp, Northampton Co, blacksmith, acknowledge payment by her guardian Conrad Kohl of estate from her father Jacob Trauger.   Bk 8/pg 102   Mar 27, 1839

David Carr of West Chester, PA, son of David Carr, late of Plumstead Twp (died 1825), gives power of attorney to John Pugh, Esq. of Doylestown to record satisfaction of a bond from his brother Joseph Carr who inherited their father's land.   Bk 8/pg 102   Mar 30, 1839

Charles M. and Mary R. Griffiths of Northern Liberties Twp, Philadelphia give power of attorney to Abel M. Griffiths, Esq. of Doylestown to sell land in Hilltown Twp.   Bk 8/pg 103   Mar 27, 1839

John Avery and wife Mary W., daughter of Stephen Comfort, late of Falls Twp, give power of attorney to John Vansant of Eugene, Verrmillion Co, IN to recover estate from administrators Hector C. Ivins and Mary Comfort.
Bk 8/pg 107   Mar 11, 1839

John B. Winder, Harman Winder, Abraham and Sarah Knight, Jonathan and Mercy Clayton, and Amos Knight (assignee of Thomas Winder), heirs of James Winder, late of Lower Makefield Twp, acknowledge payment of dower by Elias Gilkyson.   Bk 8/pg 109   Apr 12, 1839

Robert Robinson of Morgan Co, OH and wife Elizabeth, heir of Isabella Simpson, late of Bucks Co, give power of attorney to Ford Sill of Morgan Co. to recover estate.   Bk 8/pg 112   Mar 26, 1839

Margaret Atherholt, widow of Christian, late of New Britain Twp, gives power of attorney to Jonas J. Rotzel of Rusk, Monroe Co, NY to recover debts from Samuel Gehman of Bucks Co.   Bk 8/pg 113   Apr 9, 1839

Thomas Stradling of Lower Makefield Twp. died intestate leaving ten children: James, Thomas, Elizabeth Neeld, Samuel T. Brown [son-in-law?], Abraham, Timothy, Joshua, Samuel, Achilles B. [only nine signed agreement]. The heirs agree that James and Thomas Stradling who be empowered to sell the real estate.   Bk 8/pg 114   Feb 10, 1838

Christianna Cyphert of Springfield Twp, single woman, now 21, releases Levi Weaver, blacksmith, from all responsibility with respect to a bastard child that they had.   Bk 8/pg 115   Dec 24, 1838

Elizabeth Steward of Philadelphia, mantimaker[?], now 21, acknowledges payment by guardian Christian Myers of estate from late grandfather Peter Steward.   Bk 8/pg 116   Nov 18, 1834

Rachel W. Steward of Philadelphia, now 21, acknowledges payment by guardian Christian Myers of estate from late grandfather Peter Stewart.
                                        Bk 8/pg 119   Dec 20, 1836

Thomas S. Stuart of Northern Liberties, Philadelphia, now 21, acknowledges payment by guardian Christian Myers of estate from late grandfather Peter Stuart.   Bk 8/pg 119   Jan 7, 1839

Asa Ridge of Bensalem Twp. gives power of attorney to brother William to recover money due him.   Bk 8/pg 121   Oct 21, 1837

Catharine Frederick, wife of Joseph, due one-sixth of one-fourth part of estate of Jacob Wismer, late of Plumstead Twp. with the other five-sixths to go to her heirs at her death. Her sons Isaac and Jonathan will be due two-fifths of this one-fourth part and sell their shares to their father Joseph Frederick.
                                        Bk 8/pg 122   Apr 15, 1839

Elizabeth Croman, widow of Michael, late of Richland Twp, acknowledges payment of estate by John Diehl, guardian of [her daughter] Elizabeth Croman, deceased.   Bk 8/pg 128   Apr 27, 1839

Garret Vansant, late of Wrightstown Twp, by will dated 1796 and probated 1806 bequeathed estate in trust for daughter Elizabeth Addis and after her death to her three children: Mary, Rebecca McClelland and Elizabeth. Mary is now married to John Phillips, Rebecca is a widow. Elizabeth Addis died intestate on Oct 28, 1832. John and Mary Phillips and Rebecca McClelland, all of Uniontown, Fayette Co. give power of attorney to relative Robert M. Lee of Philadelphia, Esq. to sell land of Garret Vansant in which they have an interest.   Bk 8/pg 130   Apr 13, 1833

Saml Dixson bequeathed estate to his widow Sarah who is now married to William Vansant of Warminster Twp. Robert Ramsey is to be trustee of her estate.   Bk 8/pg 133   Oct 1, 1832

David Spinner and John Eckel Jr., both of Philadelphia and heirs of John Eckel Sen., late of Bedminster Twp, acknowledge satisfaction of a mortgage from Samuel Trumbore of Rockhill Twp.   Bk 8/pg 136   Mar 21, 1839

Aaron and Mercy Eastburn, Thomas and Lydia Hollowell, Thomas Bye, John Bye and Anne Brown, siblings of Elizabeth Scholfield and Sarah Shaw, both of whom died without issue and owning six-tenths of land in Solebury Twp (the other four-tenths owned by Thomas and Lydia Hollowell and Anne Brown), under will of their late father Thomas Bye of Buckingham Twp. Heirs appoint John D. Balderston of Solebury Twp. to divide the estate.
                    Bk 8/pg 138   Dec 18, 1838

Michael Bessey of Wayne Co, OH and wife Mary, daughter of Jacob Wismer, late of Bucks Co, authorize executor Charles Rice to deposit their share in the Doylestown Bank.   Bk 8/pg 139   Apr 19, 1839

Silas Dobins who is due money from estate but supposed to be deceased without any heirs except sister Eliza D. Waggoner and her siblings. She acknowledges payment of her share from John Hough and holds him harmless if Silas should return.   Bk 8/pg 142   Apr 22, 1839

John Hough, Elizabeth Dobins, Dr. and Martha Peckworth, Silas Dobins and David and Eliza D. Waggoner own estate in common. Eliza D. Waggoner has been divorced.   Bk 8/pg 142   Apr 22, 1839

Emily Dobbins, granddaughter of Thomas Dobbins (by guardian Henry McKeen) and Thomas S. and William J. Dobbins, sons of William Dobbins and grandsons of Thomas Dobbins have all received payment of their shares by John Hough as has Martha Peckworth.   Bk 8/pg 143   Jun 3, 1839

Thomas S. Dobbins of Franklin, Portage Co, OH gives power of attorney to William J. Dobbins of Lehigh Co. to recover any moneys due him in PA.
Bk 8/pg 146   Apr 8, 1839

Samuel, Henry and John Stout, and Elizabeth and Magdalene Stout, children of Daniel Stout, late of Bedminster Twp, acknowledges payment of estate from administrator Peter Stout.   Bk 8/pg 148,150   Oct 21, 1837

Joseph Stout and Philip R. and Catharine (late Stout) Crout, grandchildren of Daniel Stout, acknowledge payment of estate by administrator Peter Stout.
Bk 8/pg 149   Dec 28, 1836

John Hager, guardian of Elizabeth Kemmerer, daughter of Jonas and Mary Kemmerer and granddaughter of Daniel Stout, late of Bedminster Twp, acknowledges payment of estate by administrator Peter Stout.
Bk 8/pg 150   Jan 11, 1837

Jacob Fretz, heir of John Fretz, late of Tinicum Twp, acknowledges payment of estate by Christian K. Kressman of Nockamixon Twp. who is owner of a mill property in Nockamixon Twp.   Bk 8/pg 152   Apr 5, 1839

Harvey Shaw, administrator of late wife Sarah W., daughter of Samuel Ely of Bucks Co, acknowledges payment of estate by Sarah's guardian John Blackfan of Solebury Twp.   Bk 8/pg 152   Jun 19, 1839

Isaac Wynkoop of Boone Co, IN is entitled to receive money from Elias Gilkyson of Lower Makefield Twp. by right of wife Ann (late Winder), heir of James Winder. Isaac gives power of attorney to Abraham Knight of Moreland Twp, Montgomery Co. to receive this money.
Bk 8/pg 154   Jun 25, 1839

Henry McCorkle of Washington, DC gives power of attorney to Margaret McCorkel of Newtown to sell property due from late father Archy McCorkle of Newtown.   Bk 8/pg 158   May, 1833

Henry and Rachel Woolbach and Anna Strouse, grandchildren of John Strouse, late of Nockamixon Twp, acknowledge payment of estate by executor Nicholas Strouse.   Bk 8/pg 159   Apr 10, 1839

Jacob Strouse, Frederick Strouse, Isaac Strouse, Martin and Magdalena Hoffman and Samuel and Margaret Yost, children of John Strouse, late of

Nockamixon Twp, acknowledge payment of estate by executor Nicholas
Strouse.   Bk 8/pg 160   Apr 12, 1839

Sarah Kepler, widow of Jacob, late of Haycock Twp, acknowledges payment
of estate by administrators John Kepler and Henry Frankenfield.
                                        Bk 8/pg 161   Apr 1, 1839

John Kepler, heir of Jacob Kepler, late of Haycock Twp, acknowledges
payment of estate by administrator Henry Frankenfield.
                                        Bk 8/pg 161   Apr 1, 1839

Anna Mary Marsh of Northern Liberties, Philadelphia, now 21, acknowledges
payment by guardian Joseph Howell of Falls Twp. of estate from late father
Benjamin Marsh and late grandfather John Parker. Bk 8/pg 162 Jul 24, 1839

George Barron of Philadelphia, son of Jacob Barron, late of Springfield Twp,
yeoman, Andrew Brunner in right of deceased wife Magdalena, Jacob
Brunner in right of wife Mary, Valentine Frankenfield in right of wife
Catharine and Michael Frankenfield in right of wife Rachael acknowledge
payment of estate by administrators Jacob Barron, Philip Barron and Michael
Fackenthall Jr.   Bk 8/pg 163   Aug 14, 1839

Michael Guth, John Guth, Henry Guth, George Guth, John and Elizabeth
Reasly, Samuel and Margaret McHose and John O. and Sarah Campbell,
children of Henry Guth, late of Durham twp, yeoman, acknowledge payment
of dower from George Mill of Durham Twp. due upon death of widow
Catharine.   Bk 8/pg 170   May 22, 1839

William Ramsey the elder, late of Warwick Twp, bequeathed real estate to
nephew William R. Blair and to nephew Robert Ramsey and niece Elizabeth
Ramsey subject to life estate of William Ramsey the youngest who is lately
deceased. Elizabeth Ramsey of Warwick gives power of attorney to her
brother Robert to refuse to accept the real estate. Bk 8/pg 175   Oct 21, 1839

James M. Roberts and wife Susanna S. (late Furman) acknowledge payment
by guardian John Comfort of estate from her late father William Furman.
                                        Bk 8/pg 178   Apr 8, 1834

James M. Roberts, present guardian of Deborah, Sarah and William Furman,
children of late Wm, acknowledges payment of estate by previous guardian
John Comfort.   Bk 8/pg 179   Apr 10, 1838

Sophia Foster of Wrightstown Twp, spinster, gives power of attorney to Jonathan K. Breece of Wrightstown to recover moneys due her.
Bk 8/pg 180   Mar 2, 1839

John Harpel, guardian of John Swartz, minor child of Isaac Swartz, late of Haycock Twp, acknowledges payment of estate by administrator Joseph Swartz.
Bk 8/pg 182   Feb 23, 1839

Henry G. Stover, guardian of Catharine Swartz, minor child of Isaac Swartz, late of Haycock Twp, acknowledges payment of estate by administrator Joseph Swartz.
Bk 8/pg 183   Feb 23, 1839

Jacob and Mary Fretz, Henry G. and Susan Stover and Elizabeth Swartz, children of Isaac Swartz, late of Haycock Twp, acknowledge payment of estate by administrator Joseph Swartz.
Bk 8/pg 183   Feb 23, 1839

Jacob Hendricks, guardian of Lydia Swartz, minor child of Isaac Swartz, late of Haycock Twp, acknowledges payment of estate by administrator Joseph Swartz.
Bk 8/pg 184   Feb 23, 1839

Charlotte Clark of Philadelphia, widow of Joseph Clark, late of Doylestown Twp, released part of her estate to James Clark of Doylestown Twp. in return for his dropping his dispute of Joseph's will.   Bk 8/pg 185   Dec 7, 1839

Joseph Richardson of Bensalem Twp, grandson of Samuel Richardson, late of Falls Twp, acknowledges payment of estate by executor Joseph Burton.
Bk 8/pg 187   Oct 7, 1839

Albert G. Beeks of Plumstead Twp, now 21, acknowledges payment by Ephraim and John Walter, administrators of his former guardian Michael Walter, Esq. of estate from late father Samuel Beeks/Becks.
Bk 8/pg 188   Mar 29, 1839

Samuel and Mercy White of Champaign Co, OH give power of attorney to Stacy Watson of Bucks Co. to recover money from Edward Watson of Middletown Twp. due to Mercy from estate of her brother Ezra Watson, late of Middletown.
Bk 8/pg 189   Jun 11, 1839

Thomas and Hannah (late Burgess) Roberts of Highland Co, OH give power of attorney to William Watson, executor of George Burgess, to pay her estate to Daniel Deals Co. of Philadelphia.   Bk 8/pg 190   Oct 14, 1839

Martha Opdyke of Philadelphia, daughter of Robert Merrick, late of Bucks Co, gives power of attorney to brother James Merrick of New Hope to receive money from executors of Isaac Chapman who was administrator of Robert Merrick.   Bk 8/pg 191   Jul 15, 1839

Starr and Mary H. Baldwin of Newark, Licking Co, OH release dower right in land in Buckingham Twp. to Cornelia, Henry Irwin and Theodore Vanhorn, all of Newark, OH, children of William B. Vanhorn, late of Newark, OH. Mary H. Baldwin was the widow of William B. Vanhorn.
                                    Bk 8/pg 191   Nov 19, 1839

Henry Huber, Charles Huber, Henry and Hannah Bodder, Abraham and Maria Leister, Charles and Catharine Leister and LeaAnne Huber, children of Catharine Huber, late of Springfield Twp. who was widow of Henry Huber, acknowledge payment of estate by Catharine's administrator Joseph Huber.
                                    Bk 8/pg 193   Dec 16, 1839

Margaret (late Heft) Messemer of Springfield Twp. gives power of attorney to Peter Shive of Haycock Twp. to recover estate from Peter and Nicholas Heft, administrators of William Heft.   Bk 8/pg 196   Jan 4, 1840

Jesse Fenton of Pleasant Twp, Franklin Co, OH, yeoman, gives power of attorney to Isaiah Michener of Buckingham Twp, farmer, to recover money from Samuel and James Fenton, executors of Hannah Fenton, late of Buckingham Twp. as well as estate from late aunt Martha Fenton and late father Patrick Fenton and late brother Ephraim Fenton, all of Buckingham Twp.   Bk 8/pg 200   Jan 10, 1840

Joseph Singmaster of Walke Twp, Juniata Co. gives power of attorney to John Samsel, Esq. of Bucks Co. to petition Orphans Court to value real estate of father Jacob Singmaster, late of Milford Twp.   Bk 8/pg 201   Dec 30, 1839

Oliver Childs of Philadelphia, Jefferson Co, NY and wife Edith S. give power of attorney to John Ball of Richland Twp. to sell real estate bequeathed to Edith by her late grandfather Nathan Ball of Richland Twp. along with her brothers Nixon and Lewis B. Shaw (being the surviving children of John and Elizabeth Shaw).   Bk 8/pg 203   Oct 28, 1839

John Overpeck of Durham Twp, guardian for Edward Overpeck, minor son of Jacob Overpeck, late of Springfield Twp. acknowledges payment by former guardian Benjamin Jacoby of Springfield Twp.   Bk 8/pg 205   Jan 20, 1838

Samuel Fluck and wife Catharine, daughter of Conrad Yost, late of Bedminster Twp, acknowledge payment of estate by administrators Peter Yost and George Hillpot.   Bk 8/pg 206   Jan 13, 1840

Elizabeth Walton, widow of Joshua Walton, late of Warminster Twp, yeoman, releases son Jonathan Walton from dower right.
                                   Bk 8/pg 207   Feb 8, 1840

Catharine Stover, widow of Ralph Stover, is now deceased and the dower is due. Children Christian and Mary Fretz, Philip and Elizabeth Fretz, John and Ann Arndt and William Stover acknowledge payment by current owner Andrew Heller, Esq.   Bk 8/pg 209   May 29, 1838

William F. Swift of Bristol Borough is due estate from grandfather John Swift, late of Bensalem Twp, upon death of his uncle John Swift and his mother Ann Swift. He sells his share to Martha W. Tombs of Bristol Borough.   Bk 8/pg 210   Nov 22, 1823

Peter Hoffman of Northampton Borough, Lehigh Co, John and Catharine Matts of Richland Twp, Moses and Barbara Heft of Springfield Twp, Margaret Hoffman of Richland Twp, and Lewis and Mary Micke, Esq. of Plainfield Twp, Northampton Co, children of John Hoffman, late of Richland Twp, acknowledge payment of estate by executor John Hoffman.
                                   Bk 8/pg 213   Oct 12, 1839

John McEwen and wife Eleanor, daughter of Elijah Stinson, late of Bucks Co, sell their share to Elizabeth Stinson.   Bk 8/pg 216   Mar 11, 1840

Elizabeth Joyce, widow, (late Elizabeth Moyer), Abraham Moyers, Samuel and Mary Freis, Magdalena Kneedler, Amos Wilson (assignee of Levi and Rachel Cooper) and Joseph Myers, heirs of Joseph Myers, acknowledge payment by Charles Hinkle of dower due upon death of widow.
                                   Bk 8/pg 222   Dec 31, 1839

Ralph Stover bequeathed real estate to son William Stover subject to dower right by widow Catharine. William sold this land to Henry Stover who subsequently died intestate and the land was adjudged to his son-in-law Abraham Stover who sold it to Enos Fretz. Ralph's heirs Abraham F. Stover, Christian and Mary Fretz, Philip and Elizabeth Fretz, John and Ann Arndt and William Stover acknowledge payment of dower by Enos Fretz.
                                   Bk 8/pg 224   May 17, 1838

Martha Hartley, now of Philadelphia, has joint interest with siblings in land formerly belonging to late father Samuel Hartley. She gives power of attorney to Joseph D. Armitage of Solebury Twp. to sell her interest.
Bk 8/pg 227   Nov 28, 1839

Catharine Johnson of Hilltown Twp, intermarried with Jeremiah Rhoad, now 21, acknowledges payment by guardian Abm Reiff of estate from grandfather Abraham Cope.   Bk 8/pg 229   Apr 1, 1840

William Beck of Plumstead Twp, shoemaker, now 21, acknowledges payment by guardian Michael Walter of estate from late father Samuel Beck.
Bk 8/pg 233   Feb 16, 1835

John Walter and wife Mary, now 21, acknowledge payment by guardian Michael Walter of estate from late father Samuel Beck.
Bk 8/pg 233   Apr 1, 1837

Catharine Walter, widow, and William Hinkle, Jordon D. Cope, Isaiah Bissey, Tobias Walter, William Hinkle (guardian of Rachel Walter) and Isaac Fretz (guardian of minor children of Rebecca Fretz), all heirs of Michael Walter, late of Plumstead Twp, acknowledge payment of estate by administrators Ephraim and John Walter.   Bk 8/pg 234   Apr 7, 1840

Abi Gilbert and William and Elizabeth Blakey (late Gilbert) acknowledge payment by guardian Jesse James of estate from late father David Gilbert and late grandfather Joshua Gilbert, both of Byberry Twp, Philadelphia Co.
Bk 8/pg 234   [not dated]

J. Adrian Cornell of Northampton Twp. gives power of attorney to son David Cornell of Northampton to manage his affairs. Bk 8/pg 237   May 29, 1840

Harriet Hellings of Bensalem Twp. gives power of attorney to uncle Jesse Hellings of Middletown Twp. to recover moneys due her.
Bk 8/pg 239   Apr 15, 1840

Abraham and Mary Fisher and John L. and Anne Delp, heirs of Ann Detweiler who was the daughter of Christian Atherholt, late of New Britain Twp, John Lightcap and wife Sarah, daughter of Christian, John A. and Christian Loux, two of the three heirs of Rebecca Loux who was a daughter of Christian, Samuel Moffly and Peter Loux (guardians of Margaret, Elizabeth, Catherine and Mary Ann Atherholt, minor children of Jacob

Atherholt, son of Christian) and John Atherholt, son of Christian, acknowledge payment of estate by Levi Markley and Samuel Atherholt.

Bk 8/pg 240   Apr 4, 1840

Joseph Slocum and Hezekiah Parsons, appointed by Luzerne Co. court as guardians for John D. Shaffer, son of Solomon Shaffer, late of Springfield Twp, acknowledge payment of dower due upon death of widow Eve.

Bk 8/pg 242   Apr 17, 1840

Samuel and Nancy Watson, Sarah Percy of Wrightstown Twp, Jane Percy of Northampton Twp. and Eliza Percey of Bucks Co. acknowledge payment of legacy under will of Thomas Percy, late of Wrightstown by executors Gilbert, Garret and William Percy.

Bk 8/pg 243   Apr 10, 1840

Catharine Lund was appointed by court of Franklin Co, OH as guardian to Lewis B. Long, aged 8 years. She gives power of attorney to David Evans of Philadelphia to recover moneys due from Lewis' great-grandfather Ephraim Thomas.

Bk 8/pg 245   Apr 15, 1840

Elizabeth Mann of Haycock Twp, widow of Christian Mann of Haycock and former wife of Michael Smell of Haycock, acknowledges payment of dower by son Michael Smell of Haycock Twp.

Bk 8/pg 247   Apr 18, 1840

Henry G. Stover, John Harpel and Jacob Hendricks, guardians of Catherine, John and Lydia Swartz, minor children of Isaac Swartz, late of Haycock Twp, acknowledge payment of estate by administrators Joseph Swartz and Jacob Fretz.

Bk 8/pg 248   Apr 1, 1839

Henry G. and Susan Stover and Elizabeth Swartz, children of Isaac Swartz, late of Haycock Twp, acknowledge payment of estate by administrators Joseph Swartz and Jacob Fretz.

Bk 8/pg 249   Apr 1, 1839

Stephen W. Jones and wife Rebecca (late Hunter), now 21, acknowledge payment by guardian William Gillam of estate due from her grandfather Andrew Hunter.

Bk 8/pg 250   Mar 30, 1840

Abraham Derstine of Hilltown Twp, John Derstine, Michael Derstine, Samuel Derstine, Samuel and Mary Gayman, John W. and Catharine Delp, heirs of George Derstine, late of Rockhill Twp, acknowledge payment of estate by administrators Jacob and Henry Derstine.

Bk 8/pg 251   Apr 1, 1840

Mary Canby, widow of Joshua C. Canby, Esq., late of Middletown Twp, acknowledges payment of estate by son and administrator Joseph Canby.
Bk 8/pg 252   Feb 24, 1840

Henry W. Miller of Springwells Twp, Wayne Co, MI gives power of attorney to wife Sarah E. Miller to recover estate from late father Henry Miller, formerly of Bucks Co. as well as legacies due under wills of Bartle and Elizabeth White.   Bk 8/pg 253   Apr 20, 1840

Elias, Jonathan and Jesse Hinkel, children of John Hinkel, late of Richland Twp, acknowledge payment of estate by executor John Snyder.
Bk 8/pg 255 Mar 14,1840

John Harpel, Abraham Zeganfuse and Samuel Fluck, guardians of Levi, Martin, Matthias and Silas Althouse, minor children of Martin Althouse, late of Bedminster Twp, acknowledge payment of estate by administrators Jonas and Tobias Althouse.   Bk 8/pg 255   May 11, 1840

John and Elizabeth Lutz, daughter of Martin Althouse, late of Bedminster Twp, and widow Catharine acknowledge payment of estate by administrators Jonas and Tobias Althouse.   Bk 8/pg 256   May 1, 1840

Andrew Brunner acknowledges payment by Jacob Barron of estate due to Magdalena Brunner from her late father Jacob Barron.
Bk 8/pg 259   Jun 11, 1840

James and Dinah Hartley of Columbiana Co, OH give power of attorney to Amos Armitage of Solebury Twp. to sell land in Lumberville in which they have right along with his siblings, heirs of Samuel Hartley.
Bk 8/pg 260   May 11, 1840

Rebecca Kinsey, now wife of John C. Swain of Chengo, NY, Joseph Kinsey of Philadelphia, Joseph Hayes of Burlington Co, NJ (guardian of Ann Eliza, Mary and Joseph Vansant, minor children of Joseph Vansant), heirs of Garret H. Vansant, acknowledge payment of estate by Samuel Scott of Bensalem Twp.   Bk 8/pg 261   Aug 15, 1836

Garret J. Vansandt of Rebles Co, OH, heir of Garret H. Vansandt, late of Bensalem Twp. who died without will or heirs of his body, gives power of attorney to Joseph Shaw of Philadelphia to recover estate from administrator John Paxson.   Bk 8/pg 262   Jul 23, 1836

J. Robert Allen of Smith Co, TN gives power of attorney to son Joseph W. Allen to recover estate from Garret Vansandt due to his wife Alethea, daughter of Archibald Vanhorn. Clarissa Vanhorn of Smith Co, TN but now in Summer Co, another daughter of Archibald, also gives power of attorney to Joseph W. Allen.   Bk 8/pg 263   Sep 6, 1836

Adaliza Bruce of Washington, DC, daughter of Gabriel Vanhorn who was son of Mary Vanhorn (late Vansant) and heir of Garret H. Vansant and James W. Breckenridge of Montgomery Co, MD in right of wife Eliza, another heir of Garret H. Vansant, acknowledge through attorney John Paxson payment of estate by Samuel Scott.   Bk 8/pg 266   Feb 11, 1837

Sarah Stackhouse, Garret H. Vansant (son of Joseph Vansant, late of Bristol), Ellen Siddle (late Vansant, daughter of late Joseph Vansant), heirs of Garret H. Vansant, acknowledge payment of estate by Samuel Scott.
                                        Bk 8/pg 267   Apr 12, 1836

Mary (late Kinsey), wife of James Vansant, now of Bensalem Twp, and Elizabeth (late Kinsey), wife of Aaron Ridge, now of Northampton Twp, heirs of Garret H. Vansant, acknowledges payment of estate by Samuel Scott.
                                        Bk 8/pg 268   Apr 18, 1836

Tacy Vansant, daughter of Joseph Vansant, late of Bristol Borough and heir of Garret H. Vansant, acknowledges payment of estate by Samuel Scott.
                                        Bk 8/pg 269   Oct 30, 1838

Uriah and Evelina Agton Bonser (late Vanhorn) of Scioto Co, OH and Jonathan and Marietta Jane Mead (late Vanhorn) of Kanhawa Co, VA give power of attorney to John Paxson to recover from Samuel Scott estate due as heirs of Garret Vanzandt.   Bk 8/pg 270   Aug 23, 1837

Benjamin and Martha Yates of Montgomery Co, daughter of Joseph Vansant, late of Bristol Borough and heir of Garret H. Vansant, acknowledges payment of estate by Samuel Scott.   Bk 8/pg 275   Oct 1, 1836

Ellen Wood, Sarah Cox, Ann Polhemus, John Paxson (trustee to estate of Jacob Rampson), Amos Wood (trustee to estate of Catharine Johnson), heirs of Garret H. Vansant, late of Bensalem Twp, acknowledge payment of estate by Samuel Scott.   Bk 8/pg 275   Apr 11, 1836

James and Ann Howard (late Vanzandt, daughter of Joseph) of Bristol
Borough and heir of Garret H. Vanzandt, acknowledge payment of estate by
Samuel Scott.   Bk 8/pg 276   Apr 9, 1836

Joseph R. Willett of Prince George Co, MD in right of his wife acknowledge
payment by Samuel Scott of a bond due upon the death of Tacy Vansant,
widow of Garret H. Vansant, late of Bensalem Twp.
                                       Bk 8/pg 277   May 6, 1836

Elizabeth Stinson, single woman, heir of Elijah Stinson and assignee of John
and Eleanor McEwen, now assigns the share receive from the McEwens to
Jane Stinson, single woman.   Bk 8/pg 277   May 6, 1840

Mahlon and Sarah Moon of Miami Co, OH give power of attorney to Isaac
Duckeminor[?] of Bucks Co. to recover money due from estate of Mahlon
Wharton.   Bk 8/pg 279   Jul 7, 1840

Isaac and Mary Walton and Sarah Hallowell, heirs of Thomas Spencer, late of
Northampton Twp. acknowledge payment by William Spencer of estate due
upon the death of their mother.   Bk 8/pg 282   Jun 9, 1820

Mary Meredith, late of Doylestown, bequeathed estate to children of sons
Charles and Thomas and daughter Elizabeth Chapman. Grandson Hamilton
Meredith, late of Hannibal, Marion Co, MO died a minor. Susan C. Meredith,
Campbell D. Meredith and Hugh Meredith of Jefferson Twp, Monroe Co, MO
give power of attorney to Dr. Charles H. Meredith of Doylestown to recover
their portion of Hamilton's share from executor Abraham Chapman, Esq.
                                       Bk 8/pg 283   Dec 24, 1839

Cornilea B. Meredith of New Petersburg, Highland Co, OH gives power of
attorney to Walker M. Yeatman of Cincinnati to recover estate from Abraham
Chapman, Esq. of Doylestown, executor of grandmother Mary Meredith,
widow of Dr. Hugh Meredith.   Bk 8/pg 288   Dec 28, 1839

John and Mary Matilda Spencer, Courtland T. Meredith, Thomas H. and Ann
E. McCarty and John and Sarah W. Freshoun, children of Dr. Tho. N.
Meredith of Highland Co, OH, give power of attorney to Foote & Bowler of
Cincinnati, merchants, to recover estate from A. Chapman, Esq. of
Doylestown, due by death of Hambilton Meredith, son of Dr. Charles
Meredith, by will of Mary Meredith, widow of Dr. Hugh Meredith, late of
Doylestown.   Bk 8/pg 289   May 25, 1840

Henry Stover (minor child of Henry Stover, late of Bedminster Twp), now 21, acknowledges payment of estate by guardian Mathias Stover.

Bk 8/pg 291   Feb 29, 1840

Isaac Frankenfield, minor child of Philip and Margret Frankenfield and grandson of George Snyder, late of Tinicum Twp, now age 21, acknowledges payment of estate by guardian Henry Hillpot.   Bk 8/pg 292   Apr 4, 1840

Catharine Stinson, widow of Elijah Stinson, late of Warwick Twp, yeoman, agrees on settlement of estate with children Elizabeth Stinson, John Stinson, Robert Stinson, Isaac and Margaret Kirk, Henry and Martha Darrah, Jane Stinson and John and Eleanor McEwen.   Bk 8/pg 293   Mar 12, 1840

Joseph and Elizabeth Jones and Pamela James, heirs of Nathaniel Jones, late of Hilltown Twp, acknowledge payment of estate by executor Jonathan Jones.

Bk 8/pg 295   Apr 7, 1840

Sarah Hager, widow of Philip Hager, late of Durham Twp, yeoman, and children Abraham, John, Ralph, George and Susana Trauger, William and Mary Fausbenner, Catharine Hager and John K. Adams (guardian for children Peter, Elizabeth, Hannah and Sarah Hager), acknowledge payment of estate by administrator Michael Fackenthall Jr.   Bk 8/pg 296   Mar 30, 1840

Samuel B. Stout of Milford Twp, tobacconist, acknowledges payment by guardian John Gearhart of estate due from late father Jacob Stout.

Bk 8/pg 297   Oct 9, 1840

Thomas Cooper, late of Solebury Twp, died intestate leaving children Joseph, Thomas, Samuel, William, Rachel, Martha (wife of Benjamin Walton) and Phebe (wife of William L. Knox), all still living. Heirs agree that administrator Thomas Cooper should sell the real estate.

Bk 8/pg 299   Sep 1, 1840

Isaac Meyer of Plumstead Twp, singleman, now 21, acknowledges payment by guardian Jacob Stover Sen. of estate due to him.

Bk 8/pg 302   Feb 11, 1831

Thomas Spencer, late of Northampton Twp, bequeathed land to Thomas Spencer the younger, subject to payment to Sarah Hallowell and children of Margaret Worthington. Sarah Hallowell and William Worthington, Jesse Worthington, Spencer Worthington, Zenas and Mary Buckman and Esther

228

Worthington (children of Margaret Worthington, deceased) acknowledge payment of estate by Thomas Spencer the younger.

Bk 8/pg 303   Oct 25, 1824

Abraham and Hannah Overholt and Jacob and Anna Overholt and John Shutt, heirs of Jacob Shutt, late of Doylestown Twp, acknowledge payment of estate by executor Samuel Shutt.   Bk 8/pg 304   Apr 4, 1840

Jonathan Shaw, guardian appointed by the court of Columbiana Co, OH of Rebecca Bradshaw, daughter of late James Bradshaw who was a brother to Susanna Bradshaw, late of Plumstead Twp, gives power of attorney to Joseph Moore of Buckingham Twp. to recover estate.   Bk 8/pg 308   Dec 24. 1840

Edmund Badger of Philadelphia is indebted to brother Samuel Badger and due estate under will of Bela Badger, late of Bristol Twp. who left money to his niece Lucretia Badger (daughter of brother Edmund) or to Edmund upon Lucretia's death. Edmund signs over his share of estate to brother Samuel.

Bk 8/pg 309   Dec 31, 1840

Jacob Eckert, Hannah Deis, widow, Carlina Fulmer of Hilltown Twp, widow, and Enos Eckert of Hilltown Twp, give power of attorney to Jacob Kremer of Bedminster Twp. and Eve Eckert of Hilltown Twp, administrators of Michael Eckert, late of Hilltown Twp, to sell Michael's land.

Bk 8/pg 311   Nov 30, 1839

John Bleim of Richland Twp, son of John Bliem, late of Richland, acknowledges payment of estate by administrator Jacob Bleim.

Bk 8/pg 314   Dec 14, 1839

Henry Bartholomew of Lower Milford Twp. and wife Anna, daughter of John Bleim, late of Richland Twp, acknowledge payment of estate by administrator Jacob Bleim.   Bk 8/pg 314   Dec 14, 1839

Mary Ann Boyd of Bristol Borough, spinster is about to be married to Horatio Nelson Bostwick of Bristol Borough, storekeeper. Robert Cabeen of Bristol, storekeeper, Samuel Vanderson of Philadelphia, merchant and her brother John Boyd of Bristol, storekeeper are to be her trustees.

Bk 8/pg 315   Apr 5, 1826

Ephraim Brunner of Plum Twp, Allegheny Co. gives power of attorney to Thomas Brunner of Warrington Twp. to recover money due him.

Bk 8/pg 317   Oct 5, 1840

Rachel Vansant, widow of Wilhelmus Vansant, late of Warminster Twp, releases administrator William Vansant of the dower obligation.

Bk 8/pg 318   Nov 20, 1840

Joseph K. Craven of Horsham Twp, Montgomery Co. and wife Alice, daughter of Wilhelmus Vansant, late of Warminster Twp, acknowledge payment of estate by administrator William Vansant.

Bk 8/pg 319   Jan 2, 1841

Christopher Strouse of Tinicum Twp. gives power of attorney to Jonathan Strouse of Tinicum, cordwainer, to recover all moneys due him.

Bk 8/pg 320   Jan 18, 1841

James Foulke, Samuel and Sidney Shaw, Thomas and Abigail Wright, Ann Green, Hannah Foulke, Keziah Foulke, Mary Foulke, children and Nathaniel Kinsey, grandchild of John Foulke, late of Richland Twp, choose men to value John's real estate.   Bk 8/pg 323   May 19, 1840

John Brunner died leaving widow Margaret with a dower right in real estate. Margaret is now deceased and heir Abraham Brunner sells his share of dower to Philip Brunner.   Bk 8/pg 327   Mar 11, 1841

Margaret Yerkes, widow of Harman Yerkes, late of Warminster Twp, releases dower right to Joseph Moorehead of Spring Garden District, Penn Twp, Philadelphia Co, merchant.   Bk 8/pg 327   Feb 10, 1841

Jesse Black of Southwark District, Philadelphia Co. and wife Elizabeth, now 21, daughter of Ann Carver (wife of David Carver) and legatee of Asenath Walker, late of Buckingham Twp, acknowledges payment of estate by trustees Amos and Stacy Walker.   Bk 8/pg 328   Oct 8, 1838

Asenath Walker, late of Buckingham Twp, give money in trust to sons Amos and Stacy Walker to pay to children of daughter Ann (wife of David Carver) when they became 21. Ann is now deceased and her daughter Asenath (wife of Alfred H. Barber of Plumstead Twp.) is now 21. She acknowledges payment of estate by Amos and Stacy Walker. Bk 8/pg 329   Dec 19, 1840

Ann Niblick, spinster and widow of James Niblick of Buckingham Twp. gives power of attorney to Benjamin Hyde of Buckingham to recover moneys due her.   Bk 8/pg 337   Mar 22, 1841

Susanna Swartz of Milford Twp. gives power of attorney to Samuel Slutter of Milford Twp. to recover estate of her daughter Lydia Swartz, late of Hilltown Twp.   Bk 8/pg 338   Feb 13, 1841

Peterson Tomlinson, now 21, acknowledges payment by guardian John Davis of estate from father John E. Tomlinson and grandfather Anthony Tomlinson.
                                                     Bk 8/pg 342   Mar 25, 1841

Joshua M. Lukens of Louisville, KY, son of Mary Lukens who is a legatee of George Michener, gives power of attorney to Thos. F. Evans of Philadelphia to recover estate from executor Joshua Michener.   Bk 8/pg 343   Nov 3, 1840

Daniel Strawn of Bucks Co. and Jason and Eleanor Livezey of Montgomery Co, children of Daniel Strawn, late of Haycock Twp, acknowledge payment of estate by executor William L. Strawn.   Bk 8/pg 344   Jun 28, 1831

Catharine Heft of Springfield Twp, now 21, acknowledges payment by guardian Joseph Amey of estate from grandfather Philip Heft, late of Springfield.   Bk 8/pg 345   Mar 14, 1840

Sarah Ely (widow) and Robert, Jervas, Mercy, George and Smith Ely give power of attorney to William Carr, Esq. of Doylestown to record satisfaction of dower mortgage by Amasa and Robert Ely.   Bk 8/pg 347   Apr 3, 1841

Samuel and Paulina Myers of Columbiana Co, OH give power of attorney to Thomas E. Longshore of Columbiana Co. to recover money from estate of George Iden, late of PA.   Bk 8/pg 349   Mar 27, 1841

Anne Child of Philadelphia, widow, gives power of attorney to Robert S. Child of Philadelphia, carpenter, to recover from William Edwards, farmer, of Bucks Co. money due her from estate of George Iden.
                                                     Bk 8/pg 350   Apr 14, 1841

George Hillpot, John G. Hillpot and Jacob Hillpot, all of Tinicum Twp, and John and Sarah Mood, George and Elizabeth Leer, Rebecca Heaney (widow) and Samuel and Catharine Rufe, children of Elizabeth Hillpot, late of Tinicum, acknowledge payment of estate by administrator Frederick G. Hillpot.   Bk 8/pg 351   Apr 3, 1841

John Hager and wife Elizabeth, daughter of William Heaney, late of Tinicum Twp, acknowledge payment of estate by her guardian Samuel Rufe.
                                                     Bk 8/pg 352   Jan 2, 1841

John G. Hillpot, Jacob Hillpot, John and Sarah Mood, George and Elizabeth Leer, Rebecca Heaney (widow), all of Tinicum Twp. and Samuel and Catharine Rufe of Durham Twp, heirs of George Hillpot, late of Tinicum Twp, acknowledge payment of estate by administrators George and Frederick G. Hillpot.   Bk 8/pg 353   Apr 3, 1841

Rebecca Heaney of Tinicum Twp, widow of William Heaney, late of Tinicum, acknowledges payment of estate by administrators John H. Heaney and Frederick G. Hillpot.   Bk 8/pg 354   Jan 2, 1841

Isaac Heaney of Tinicum Twp, son of William Heaney, late of Tinicum, and Samuel Rufe of Durham Twp. and Nicholas Buck of Nockamixon Twp. (guardians for William's children Elizabeth, Nicholas, Sarah, Helanah, Catharine, Frederick, Rebecca, Salome, Mary Ellen and Matilda), acknowledge payment of estate by administrators John H. Heaney and Frederick G. Hillpot.   Bk 8/pg 355   Jan 2, 1841

George Blank and wife Mary Ann, daughter of Henry Trumbower, late of Milford Twp, acknowledge payment of estate by her guardian John Trumbower.   Bk 8/pg 358   Mar 15, 1841

James E. Cooper of Punxsutawney, Jefferson Co. and wife Mary give power of attorney to Thomas Cooper of Falls Twp. to recover estate from Thomas Cooper Sr. and wife Jane, both late of Falls Twp. Bk 8/pg 363   Apr 26, 1839

Jacob Bleam and Henry and Nancy Bartholomew, heirs of John Bleam, late of Richland Twp, acknowledge payment of estate by John Bleam.
                                                Bk 8/pg 364   Mar 27, 1841

Sarah Hallowell acknowledges payment by Amos Spencer of estate due under will of Thomas Spencer.   Bk 8/pg 369   Jun 9, 1827

Thomas Pricket of Philadelphia, merchant and his wife Lydia, granddaughter of late William Delaney and Mary McClure, daughter of William Delaney, give power of attorney to James Young of Philadelphia, merchant, to record satisfaction of mortgage.   Bk 8/pg 372   May 11, 1841

John Beatty Margerum, heir of Martha Hough, late of Lower Makefield Twp, acknowledges payment of estate by Jolly Longshore of Lower Makefield.
                                                Bk 8/pg 373   Mar 1, 1841

Leonard Wildonger of Philadelphia, now 21, acknowledges payment by guardian George Fox of estate from father Leonard Wildonger.

Bk 8/pg 376   Apr 2, 1841

Charlotte Bissey, now 21, acknowledges payment by guardian Jacob Nash of estate from father Jacob Bissey.   Bk 8/pg 377   May 8, 1841

Phebe Knox, wife of William L. Knox of Lambertville, NJ is due estate from Thomas Cooper and asks that it be paid to her husband.

Bk 8/pg 378   Apr 26, 1841

Martha Walton, wife of Benjamin Walton of Solebury Twp. is due estate from Thomas Cooper and asks that it be paid to her husband.

Bk 8/pg 378   Apr 26, 1841

Jacob and Elizabeth Detisman, John and Eve Wart, John and Susanna Drumbauer, and George and Anna Mumbower, daughters of Conrad Shellenberger, late of Hilltown Twp, and Samuel H. and Eve Hillpot and Mary Droger, grandchildren, acknowledge payment of estate by administrators John L. and Jacob L. Shellenberger.

Bk 8/pg 381   May 18, 1841

Joseph Burrows of Philadelphia, dealer, gives power of attorney to William H. Slack of Bucks Co, farmer, to recover estate from Jesse Heston of Bucks, executor of his father Nathaniel Burrows, late of Bucks.

Bk 8/pg 386   Jun 18, 1841

Hellen Taggart, sister and only heir of Mary Taggart, late of Bucks Co, acknowledges payment of estate by Ann Lefferts, executrix of Jonathan Lefferts, Esq. who was administrator to Mary Taggart.

Bk 8/pg 387   Mar 4, 1841

Glancy Jones of Gadsden Co, Florida Territory is entitled by right of wife Anna to estate of her father William Rodman, late of Bensalem Twp. They sell their share to John Ruan, M.D. of Philadelphia.

Bk 8/pg 388   Jun 14, 1841

Jacob Kramer, guardian of Jeremiah and Mary Fetter, minor children of Jacob Fetter, acknowledges payment of estate by administrator John Kramer.

Bk 8/pg 394   Apr, 1841

Robert P. Lovett, father and guardian of Joseph B., Anna Mary, Daniel and Robert P. Lovett, acknowledges payment by Samuel Brown of estate due the children by will of their grandfather Joseph Brown, late of Bristol Twp, their mother Rebecca being deceased.   Bk 8/pg 394   May 21, 1840

John Custard of Rockhill Twp. sells to Joel Evans of Philadelphia his share in estate of his father Morgan Custard situate in Rockhill and Richland Twps.
                                                  Bk 8/pg 397   Aug 20, 1841

Thomas Twining Hutchinson of Northampton Twp. assigns to Dr. David Hutchinson of Newtown Twp. his share in estate of his grandfather David Twining, late of Newtown Twp.   Bk 8/pg 399   Nov 24, 1824

John Patterson of Philadelphia was heir by his mother Rebecca Patterson to one-sixth share of a farm in Bristol Twp. John died intestate leaving six children: John R., Charles E., Joseph H., James E., Martha M. and Rebecca Ann. The children give power of attorney to John R. Patterson to recover rents from the current tenant.   Bk 8/pg 400   Feb 14, 1838

Jacob Heft and wife Anna, daughter of Christian Mann, deceased, acknowledge payment by Joseph Mann of Haycock Twp. of dower due upon the death of widow Elizabeth.   Bk 8/pg 406   May 31, 1841

Peter Shive and George Walp, guardians of Sarah, Elizabeth, Margaret and Mariah Mann, minor children of George Mann, deceased, and heirs of Christian Mann, late of Haycock Twp, acknowledge payment by Joseph Mann of Haycock of dower due upon the death of widow Elizabeth.
                                                  Bk 8/pg 406   May 31, 1841

Jonathan Leidy of Philadelphia and wife Clarisa, daughter of Isaac Weaver, late of Tinicum Twp, and Sheridan Weaver, son of Isaac (by guardian Jonathan Leidy), acknowledge payment of estate by administrators Reed C. Weaver and William Stokes.   Bk 8/pg 408   [blank], 1841

Margaret N. Shirley of Alexandra, District of Columbia gives power of attorney to son Charles P. Shirley of Philadelphia to recover money due from father's estate in Bristol.   Bk 8/pg 409   Jun 1, 1841

Levina Weydemeyer, now 21, acknowledges payment by guardian Jacob Kilmer of estate from father Jacob Weydemeyer, late of Tinicum Twp.
                                                  Bk 8/pg 410   Apr 4, 1840

Jonathan Burton Jr., now 21, acknowledges payment by guardian Joseph Burton, Esq. of estate from mother Rosanna.　Bk 8/pg 413　Sep 21, 1841

Evan Green of Columbia, Lancaster Co, son of Benjamin Green, late of Richland Twp, sells his share of estate to sister Lydia Green of Richland.
　Bk 8/pg 414　Feb 16, 1830

Joseph Scarborough of Hancock Co, OH gives power of attorney to Jacob Twining of Bucks Co. to recover dower from his mother, the widow Joseph Scarborough, late of Solebury Twp.　Bk 8/pg 414　Aug 3, 1841

John Weaver of Richland Twp, blacksmith, gives power of attorney to John Weaver Jr. of Richland to recover dower due from Samuel Weaver after decease of Catharine Weaver.　Bk 8/pg 418　Oct 18, 1841

Joseph Hough, late of Warwick Twp, bequeathed income from estate to widow Eleanor and after her death to children of his brothers Thomas and John and sisters Mary Walker and Charlotte Meredith. Robert H. Walker, a son of Mary Walker, sells his share (one-third of one-fourth) to Benjamin McVaugh of Doylestown Twp.　Bk 8/pg 419　Oct 28, 1841

Anna Margaret Kruger, late of Bucks Co, bequeathed estate to estate Elizabeth, wife of Lawrence Shick of Muskinjum Co, OH. Lawrence and Elizabeth acknowledge payment of legacy by executor Michael Dech.
　Bk 8/pg 422　Jul 15, 1840

Charles and Mary Logan of Trumbull Co, OH, Elizabeth Vanhorn and John Logan, both of Northampton Twp, children of George Logan, late of Northampton, give power of attorney to Samuel Beans of Northampton to sell George's real estate.　Bk 8/pg 423　Nov 1, 1841

Latitia Watson of Lower Makefield Twp. gives power of attorney to Malachi White to recover money from estate of brother Nathan Brelsford, late of Middletown Twp.　Bk 8/pg 424　Oct 22, 1840

Henry Landes of Richland Twp. died intestate leaving no issue or father but widow Phryne and widowed mother Hannah of Plumstead Twp. Hannah transfers her share of estate to Phryne.　Bk 8/pg 425　Nov 15, 1841

Elizabeth Buck, widow of John Buck, late of Tinicum Twp, releases her dower right to eldest son Aaron Buck and other heirs of John.
　Bk 8/pg 427　Oct 30, 1841

Samuel Crouse, saddler and harnessmaker of Frenchtown, NJ, now 21, acknowledges payment by guardian John Williams of estate from father Jacob Crouse, late of Nockamixon Twp.   Bk 8/pg 428   Jul 31, 1841

Michael Fackenthall Sen. of Durham Twp. and wife Mary mutually agree to separate and Mary agrees to relinquish all right to Michael's estate.
                                            Bk 8/pg 429   Sep 22, 1841

Frederick and Abigail Christine, David and Jane Young, Jacob Andres, Abraham Andres, John Andres and Samuel Andres, heirs of John Andrews, late of Tinicum Twp, release to widow Sarah, now of Williams Twp, Northampton Co, their right to dower after her death.
                                            Bk 8/pg 430   Mar 25, 1839

Sarah Andres of Williams Twp, Northampton Co, widow of John Andres, late of Tinicum Twp, acknowledges payment of estate by administrator John Laubenstine of Tinicum Twp.   Bk 8/pg 431   Dec 25, 1840

Samuel Andres of Williams Twp, Northampton Co, son of John Andres, late of Tinicum Twp, acknowledges payment of estate by administrator John Laubenstine.   Bk 8/pg 432   Dec 26, 1840

Michael Snyder and wife Anna, William and Magdalena Snyder, Jacob High, Catharine High, single woman, Samuel High, Michael High, Aaron and Hannah Kern, Zachariah Leidy (guardian of Elizabeth and Margaret High), children of Jacob High, late of Hilltown Twp, acknowledge payment of estate by executrix Catharine High.   Bk 8/pg 434   Apr 26, 1840

Harriet Hellings of Bensalem Twp, single woman, previously gave power of attorney to Jesse Hellings of Middletown Twp. to petition Orphans Court for partition of estate of her late father Jacob Hellings. Harriet now revokes that power of attorney and gives power of attorney to Moses LaRue of Bristol Twp. to settle estate of father and aunt Mary Wilson, late of Bensalem Twp.
                                            Bk 8/pg 440   Dec 3, 1841

Francis Howe (guardian of Caroline M. Howe), Francis Howe, Charles and Amanda M. Adams and William W. and Harriet Knight, heirs of Jedidiah Howe, late of Philadelphia, give power of attorney to Joseph S. Paxson of Philadelphia to record payment of estate by administrator Jesse L. Stillwaggon.   Bk 8/pg 447   Dec 29, 1841

Jonathan Leidy of Buckingham Twp. and wife Clarisa, daughter of Isaac Weaver, late of Tinicum Twp, acknowledge payment of estate by Isaac's son Reed C. Weaver. Jonathan also acknowledges as guardian of Sheridan Weaver, son of Isaac.	Bk 8/pg 453	Dec 21, 1837

William Stover of Buckingham Twp, yeoman, and wife July Ann, daughter of Isaac Weaver, late of Tinicum Twp, acknowledge payment of estate by Isaac's son Reed C. Weaver.	Bk 8/pg 454	Apr 13, 1838

Jacob Overpeck and Andrew Overpeck (by guardian Jacob Barron) request men to divide the land of their father Andrew Overpeck, late of Springfield Twp.	Bk 8/pg 457	Feb 10, 1816

William Roberts deeded land to Samuel Roberts in trust for Margaret Edwards and after her death to her children. Margaret requests Samuel to sell this land.	Bk 8/pg 459	Mar 23, 1842

Hannah Kinsey of Cincinnati, OH, daughter of John Griffith, late of Richland Twp, and wife of Nathaniel Kinsey, and Abraham and Rachael Griffith of Morgan Co, OH, son of John, give power of attorney to friend Caleb Foulke of Quakertown to recover money due from father's estate.
	Bk 8/pg 460	Dec 18, 1841

Michael and Elizabeth (formerly Nace) Hedrick of Bedminster Twp. assign a legacy from Elizabeth's grandfather Jacob Stout, late of Bedminster Twp. to John Kramer of Rockhill Twp. and John Garis of Bedminster Twp.
	Bk 8/pg 463	Dec 11, 1839

Richard D. Sutphin and Andrew Knepper, guardians of Joshua and Clayton K. Riale, children of John W. Riale, late of Fairfield Co, OH, give power of attorney to Henry Louard of Fairfield Co. to recover estate from grandfather Joshua Riale, late of Bucks Co.	Bk 8/pg 469	Feb 19, 1842

Abraham Overholt of Columbianna Co, OH gives power of attorney to Joseph Fry of Plumstead Twp. to recover his one-seventh share of dower from John Gross, due upon death of Elizabeth Overholt, widow of Joseph Overholt.
	Bk 8/pg 470	[not dated]

Joseph Overholtz, Martin Overholtz, Jacob and Margaret Leatherman and Abraham and Mary Beam, all of Medina Co, OH, give power of attorney to Jacob Leatherman Jr. to recover dower from John Gross, due upon death of Elizabeth Overholt, widow of Joseph Overholt.	Bk 8/pg 471	Nov 27, 1839

Sarah Leatherman, widow and Elizabeth Overholt, single woman, daughters of late Joseph Overholt, acknowledge payment by John Gross of dower due upon death of widow Elizabeth.   Bk 8/pg 472   Apr 15, 1839

Elizabeth Overholt, widow of Joseph Overholt, acknowledges payment of dower by John Gross.   Bk 8/pg 475   Apr 15, 1839

Eliza Apple, daughter of Jacob Apple, late of Springfield Twp, acknowledges payment of estate by guardian Anthony Wireback.
     Bk 8/pg 475   Feb 22, 1842

Jacob Janney assigns his right in father's estate, due upon death of his mother, to Jesse Hough.   Bk 8/pg 477   Mar 30, 1842

John Vanhorne, late of Middletown Twp, died leaving widow Phebe and children James, Garret, Joshua and Elizabeth (wife of Jonathan Watson). Widow is now deceased and children acknowledge payment of dower by John LaRue.   Bk 8/pg 479   Mar 29, 1842

Elias Horn of Richland Twp, cordwainer, now 21, acknowledges payment by guardian Jacob Horn of estate from father Sebastian Horn.
     Bk 8/pg 480   Dec 28, 1841

John Stouffer, Benjamin Fredrick, Hannah Fredrick, John Titlow, John Freed, George H. Gearhart, William Gotshalk, Susannah Gearhart, John Wisler, Michael Wireman, Catherine Wireman, Isaac Overholser, Rachel Overholser, Samuel Gehman, Henry Walt, Elizabeth Walt, Henry Hinsecker, Hannah Hunseker, John Markley, Ann J. Markley, Eli Stouffer, Hannah Stouffer, Hannah Swartley, Jacob Wisler, Isaac Wisler and Robert F. Potts, heirs of Henry Stouffer, give power of attorney to friend Isaac Howland of Montgomery Twp, Montgomery Co. to sell land in Hilltown Twp.
     Bk 8 pg 480   Apr 20, 1841

Henry Bittz and wife Mary Ann, now 21, acknowledge payment by her guardian Jacob Kilmer of estate from her father Jacob Weydemeyer, late of Tinicum Twp.   Bk 8/pg 483   Mar 28, 1842

Townsend Bradshaw and Aaron and Rebecca T. Hinchman, of Columbiana Co, OH, children of late James Bradshaw who was brother and heir to Susanna Bradshaw, late of Plumstead Twp, give power of attorney to James Bradshaw of Columbiana Co. to recover estate from Susanna's administrators William Bradshaw and George Fell Jr.   Bk 8/pg 483   Mar 23, 1842

Crispin Wood died intestate leaving no issue so estate went to siblings. Mary Woolverton of Buckingham Twp, daughter of Martha Woolverton who was a sister to Crispin, gives power of attorney to Samuel Bradshaw of Plumstead Twp. to recover estate administrators Henry Wood and Green Sergent.

Bk 8/pg 486   Apr 6, 1842

Sheridan Weaver, now 21, acknowledges payment by guardian Jonathan Leidy of estate due from father Isaac Weaver, late of Tinicum Twp.

Bk 8/pg 487   Apr 7,1842

Philip Seiple of Delaware Co, OH gives power of attorney to John Johnson of Bucks Co. to recover money from estate of his father Henry Seiple, late of Bucks Co, from administrators Samuel and David Seiple.

Bk 8/pg 489   Dec 24, 1841

Thomas Jackson of Millcreek Hundred, New Castle Co, DE and wife Jane, daughter of late John Griffith, formerly of Richland Twp, give power of attorney to William Griffith of Richland Twp. to recover her share of estate due now that the widow Rachel Griffith is deceased.

Bk 9/pg 1   Apr 16, 1842

Nathaniel Kinsey of New Castle Co, DE sells to Thomas Stapler and Jonas Pusey, both of Wilmington, DE, the one-fifth share of dower of late Rachel Griffith (widow of John Griffith) due to his wife Hannah who was Rachel's daughter.

Bk 9/pg 2   Jul 23, 1839

Ajax Osmond, late of Solebury Twp, bequeathed estate to wife Rachel and daughter Margaret Knowles and then to his grandchildren upon their deaths. Margaret's son Osmond Engles sells his share to James Ruckman.

Bk 9/pg 3   Apr 7, 1842

Jeremiah Roudenbush left widow Margaret with dower. Executors George Roudenbush and Henry Leidy obtain release for payment of estate to heirs of daughter Charlotte (wife of John Harr): Margaret Bernt, David Harr, George Harr's heirs (John, Margaret, Jonas), Elizabeth (wife of Henry Wenhold), Mary (wife of John Getman).

Bk 9/pg 5   Apr 4, 1842

Morris Neeld acknowledges payment of money due from guardian William Palmer.

Bk 9/pg 8   May 14, 1834

Oliver Neeld, now 21, acknowledges payment by guardian William Palmer of estate from late father John B. Neeld.

Bk 9/pg 8   Sep 18, 1841

Anna Eliza Neeld of Lower Makefield Twp, now 21, acknowledges payment by guardian William Palmer of estate from late father John B. Neeld.
Bk 9/pg 9   Apr 2, 1839

Rhoda Neeld of Newtown Twp, spinster, now 21, acknowledges payment by guardian William Palmer of estate from late father John B. Neeld.
Bk 9/pg 9   Apr 1, 1840

Daniel Trumbower of Milford Twp, cordwainer, and wife Catharine, daughter of Henry Trumbower, late of Milford Twp, acknowledge payment of estate by administrator Frederick A. Trumbower.   Bk 9/pg 12   Oct 27, 1838

Enos Artman of Milford Twp, yeoman, guardian of Henry and Eliza Trumbower, minor children of Henry Trumbower, late of Milford Twp, yeoman, acknowledges payment of estate by administrators Frederick A. and Daniel Trumbower.   Bk 9/pg 13   Oct 27, 1838

Mary Trumbower of Milford Twp, widow of Henry Trumbower, late of Milford Twp, yeoman, acknowledges payment of estate by administrators Frederick A. and Daniel Trumbower.   Bk 9/pg 13   Oct 27, 1838

John Trumbower of Richland Twp, yeoman, guardian of Mary Ann Trumbower, minor daughter of Henry Trumbower, late of Milford Twp, yeoman, acknowledges payment of estate by administrators Frederick A. and Daniel Trumbower.   Bk 9/pg 14   Oct 27, 1838

George Brown of Solebury Twp. sells his share of estate of Benjamin Brown, late of Falls Twp, to Elizabeth Brown of Falls Twp.
Bk 9/pg 15   Apr 25, 1842

Elisha W. Smith of Buckingham Twp. sells to Simpson Thompson and Jacob Twining of Bucks Co. his share of estate of his late father Gen. Samuel Smith.
Bk 9/pg 16   Apr 30, 1842

Alfred S. Carver and Harriet Carver, minor children of Mary Carver (late Paxson), deceased, acknowledge payment by guardian William Stradling of estate from late grandfather Samuel Paxson.   Bk 9/pg 18   May 7, 1842

John Loux, late of Plumstead Twp, died intestate leaving widow and four children. The dower is now due by the recent death of widow Ann. John's land was adjudged to Peter and Abraham Loux who sold part of it. Heirs Peter Loux (administrator of estate of late Catharine Delp), Moses Loux and

Abraham Loux acknowledge payment of dower by present owners Charles Selner, Jonas Fry and Mathias Kepler.   Bk 9/pg 19   May 23, 1842

Susanna Derstine, wife of Henry Derstine of Genesee Co, NY, daughter of John Landes, late of Rockhill Twp, gives power of attorney to friend George Springer of Rockhill Twp. to recover estate due her at the death of stepmother Elizabeth Landes.   Bk 9/pg 20   May 11, 1842

Abraham Landes, Henry and Susanna Derstine, George and Catharine Drumbore, children of John Landes, late of Rockhill Twp, acknowledge payment by John's son Samuel of estate due them by the death of widow Elizabeth.   Bk 9/pg 21   May 19, 1842

Catharine Trauger, widow of Christian Trauger, late of Nockamixon Twp, yeoman, acknowledges payment of estate by executor Michael Fackenthall Jr.
        Bk 9/pg 23   Mar 19, 1842

Jacob and Mary Blim and Barbara Letherman, daughter of Jacob Hockman, late of Bedminster Twp, give power of attorney to Jacob's heir Ulrich Hockman to record satisfaction of a mortgage given to Jacob by Isaac Schlichter.   Bk 9/pg 25   Apr 4, 1842

William P. Jenks of Baltimore, MD gives power of attorney to brother Michael H. Jenks of Newtown Twp. to record satisfaction of mortgage from Elizabeth Story.   Bk 9/pg 32   Jul 11, 1842

Erwin Kennedy acknowledges payment of estate by testamentary guardians John Kirkbride and Rachel Kennedy.   Bk 9/pg 33   Jul 23, 1842

Thomas Jackson of Millcreek Hundred, New Castle Co, DE gives power of attorney to son James C. Jackson of Millcreek Hundred to receive one-fifth share of dower of his mother-in-law Rachel Griffith (recently deceased), late of Richland Twp.   Bk 9/pg 36   Sep 18, 1841

William Griffith, son and administrator of John Griffith, late of Richland Twp, acknowledges payment by William Green of money due estate now that the widow Rachel is deceased.   Bk 9/pg 37   Sep 20, 1841

Thomas Jackson of Millcreek Hundred, New Castle Co, DE and wife Jane, daughter of John and Rachel Griffith, late of Richland Twp, acknowledge payment of estate by William Green.   Bk 9/pg 38   Sep 23, 1841

Thomas Stapler and Jonas Pusey of Wilmington, DE, assignees of Nathaniel Kinsey who married Hannah Griffith, daughter of John Griffith, late of Richland Twp, and John's son Abraham Griffith by attorney Caleb Foulke, acknowledge payment of estate by William Green who purchased land from John G. and Abigail Griffith subject to dower for John Griffith's widow Rachel.   Bk 9/pg 39   Apr 13, 1842

Jacob Dillinger of Northampton Borough, Lehigh Co, trustee under the insolvency laws of John G. Griffith, son of John Griffith, late of Richland Twp, acknowledges payment of dower by William Green.
                                           Bk 9/pg 41   May 17, 1842

Jacob Regle, Elizabeth Overpeck, Sarah Overpeck, Jacob Stehle and Frederick Rufe acknowledge payment of dower by Jacob Overpeck.
                                           Bk 9/pg 42   Nov 15, 1841

Samuel Landes of Rockhill Twp (guardian of Mary Clymer, daughter of Jacob Clymer, late of Rockhill Twp), Jacob Gerhart of Rockhill (guardian of Jacob's son Abraham) and Abraham Shelley of Colebrook Twp, Berks Co. (guardian of Jacob's daughter Elizabeth) acknowledge payment of estate by Jacob's administrator Enos Schlichter.   Bk 9/pg 45   Apr 23, 1842

William and Elizabeth Arthurs, Rebecca Arthurs (widow of John Arthurs) and Mary Ann Wheeler (widow of Ignatius Wheeler), all of Cincinnati, OH, legatees of Jacob Vansant, late of Bensalem Twp, give power of attorney to John Paxson of Bensalem Twp. to recover mortgage from Samuel Scott.
                                           Bk 9/pg 46   Dec 7, 1841

John Paxson, attorney of Alexn. McCormick of Princes Georges Co, MD and wife Eliza (late Vanhorn), daughter of Archibald Vanhorn, deceased, who was an heir of Gerret H. Vansant, acknowledges payment of mortgage by Samuel Scott.   Bk 9/pg 49   Oct 15, 1836

Sarah Burton of Falls Twp, now 21, acknowledges payment by guardian Anthony Burton of estate due from late father John Burton Jr. and from late grandfather John Burton Sr.   Bk 9/pg 50   Apr 1, 1842

Samuel Cressman, Philip Cressman, Peter and Catharine Roudenbush, Abel and Mary Kerr and Hannah Cressman, children of Jacob Cressman, late of Rockhill Twp, yeoman, and Andrew and Lydia Barnet, Reinhard and Phebe Keeler, Peter and Magdalena Fritz and Philip and Elizabeth Hartzel, daughters of Magdalena Kerr, late wife of Henry Kerr and daughter of late Jacob

Cressman, acknowledge payment of estate by executors Jacob, Abraham and Henry Cressman.   Bk 9/pg 51   Apr 2,1842

Thomas Wolverton of Crawford Co, OH gives power of attorney to Jacob B. Smith of Hunterdon Co, NJ to recover money due from estate of Crispin Wood, late of Bucks Co, who was brother to Thomas's mother Martha Wolverton, deceased.   Bk 9/pg 52   Jun 29,1842

Elizabeth Ely and Sarah Ely, daughters of Jonathan Ely, late of Solebury Twp, and John Kitchin, guardian of Harriet, Richard C., Crispin P. and Gershom M. Ely, children of late Seneca Ely, a son of Jonathan, acknowledge payment of estate by administrators Jonathan and Isaiah Ely.
                        Bk 9/pg 53   Jul 27, 1841

Edward Wolf of Springtown, Bucks Co. and wife Elizabeth (late Amey) acknowledge payment by Elizabeth's guardian Jacob Kooker of estate due from her late grandfathers Conrad Hess and George Amey.
                        Bk 9/pg 54   Nov 27, 1841

John Cyphert of Springfield Twp, now 21, acknowledges payment by guardian Jacob Kooker of estate from late father William Cyphert.
                        Bk 9/pg 55   Apr 4, 1841

George Budd of Lambertville, NJ and wife Elizabeth (late Wolverton) give power of attorney to Jacob B. Smith of Hunterdon Co, NJ to recover money from estate of Crispin Wood, late of Bucks Co. Bk 9/pg 55   Apr 30, 1842

Harriet A. Hellings of Bensalem Twp, single woman, gives power of attorney to uncle Jesse Hellings of Middletown Twp. to recover money due her.
                        Bk 9/pg 56   Mar 8, 1842

William P. Morgan of Edgmont Twp, Delaware Co, executor of Isaac Morgan, late of Richland Twp, acknowledges payment by Isaac's assignees George Custard, William H. Ball, William Green and Richard Moore.
                        Bk 9/pg 57   Sep 12, 1842

Sarah Shatinger, Andrew S. and Catharine Michener, Hiram and Barbara Michener and Esther Shatinger, all of Plumstead Twp, daughters of Andrew Shatinger, late of Plumstead Twp, acknowledge payment of estate by administrators Abraham, Henry and Jacob Shatinger.
                        Bk 9/pg 58   Aug 12, 1842

Elizabeth P. Wilson, guardian of minor child of Samuel Wilson, late of Philadelphia, gives power of attorney to Samuel Hart of Bucks Co, magistrate, to record satisfaction of mortgage. Bk 9/pg 59   Oct 14, 1842

John Harpel, guardian of Julyann Fabian, minor child of George Fabian, late of Nockamixon Twp, acknowledges payment of estate by George's administrator John Fabian.   Bk 9/pg 60   Apr 11, 1842

Mary Fabian, widow of George Fabian, late of Nockamixon Twp, acknowledges payment of estate by administrator John Fabian.
                                                Bk 9/pg 60   Apr 14, 1842

Jacob Fabian, George Fabian, Catharine Fabian, Eliza Fabian, John and Maryann Burgstresser, heirs of George Fabian, late of Nockamixon Twp, acknowledge payment of estate by administrator John Fabian.
                                                Bk 9/pg 61   Apr 9, 1842

Daniel Boileau, guardian of Jacob Wilson Fabian, Elizabeth Fabian and Mary Jane Fabian, minor children of late Casper Fabian and grandchildren of George Fabian, late of Nockamixon Twp, acknowledges payment of estate by administrator John Fabian.   Bk 9/pg 62   Apr 9, 1842

Enos Barndt, Samuel Barndt, Nery Barndt, John K. and Rachel Heany, Michael and Lidya Nase, Benjamin and Elizabeth Coppe, children of Samuel Barndt the elder, late of Rockhill Twp, acknowledge payment of estate by administrator Margaret Barndt.   Bk 9/pg 64   Sep 16, 1842

Ephraim and Margaret Brunner of Plumb Twp, Alleghany Co. give power of attorney to brother Thomas Brunner of Doylestown Twp. to sell land in Houghville inherited from mother Ann Margaret Cooper.
                                                Bk 9/pg 67   Apr 4, 1842

Elizabeth Amey, widow of Joseph Amey, late of Springfield Twp, and Joseph's only child William, agree to selection of men to value Joseph's real estate.   Bk 9/pg 70   Nov 15, 1842

John Johnson of Bristol Borough, due to inherit house in Bristol by will of Francis Mechlar upon death of present wife of Thomas Sargeant, sells his interest to William Davis, present owner of the house.
                                                Bk 9/pg 70   Nov 14, 1842

Witnesses acknowledge marriage of William J. Jewell of Solebury Twp, son of Warford and Achsah Jewell of Solebury, and Catharine Armitage, daughter of Amos and Rebecca Armitage of Solebury Twp. on Oct 20, 1842 before Mathias Shaw, justice of the peace.   Bk 9/pg 74   Oct 20, 1842

Griffith Williams of Newtown Borough, now 21, acknowledge payment by guardian Dr. David Hutchinson of estate from late father Griffith Williams.
Bk 9/pg 76   Apr 26, 1842

Hannah Weaver of Springfield Twp, widow of Martin Weaver, and Elias Bechtel of Springfield Twp, mason, intend to be married. They agree to settlement of Hannah's property.   Bk 9/pg 84   Dec 12, 1842

Joseph B. Margerum, heir of Martha Hough, late of Lower Makefield Twp, acknowledges payment of his share of Martha's lien on property which Jolly Longshore of Lower Makefield purchased from William Longshore (guardian of minor children of Benjamin Margerum) and Israel Margerum.
Bk 9/pg 86   Dec 6, 1842

Christian G. Strein of Warwick Twp. owns land in trust for self and wife Fronia and at their death for the use of their four youngest children: Margareta Elizabeth Schwartz, Rosina Catharina Strein, John Jacob Strein and Maria Elizabeth Strein.   Bk 9/pg 90   Oct 15, 1842

Frederick Christine of Doylestown Twp. and wife Abigal, daughter of John Andrews, late of Tinicum Twp, acknowledge payment of estate by Jonas Laubenstein, administrator of John Laubenstein, late of Tinicum Twp, who was administrator of John Andrews.   Bk 9/pg 92   Nov 24, 1842

Elisha W. Smith (by attorneys Jacob Twining and Simpson Thompson), Samuel A. Smith, Isaac Vanhorn (husband of late Mary Ann), Andrew J. Smith (by attorney Phineas J. Smith) and Phineas J. Smith, heirs of Gen. Samuel A. Smith, late of Buckingham Twp, agree to men to value the real estate.   Bk 9/pg 94   Dec 29, 1842

Benjamin Williams, Susan Williams, Abel Lester, Margaret Lester and Jeremiah Williams, all of Monroe Twp, Coshocton Co, OH, give power of attorney to John E. Kenderdine of Solebury Twp. to recover money due from estate of Jeremiah Williams, late of Tinicum Twp. Bk 9/pg 99   Aug 2, 1839

Isaac B. Williams of Solebury Twp. gives power of attorney to Newberry D. Williams of Tinicum Twp. to recover money due from estate of Jeremiah Williams, late of Tinicum Twp.   Bk 9/pg 100 · Apr 14, 1840

John Loux, guardian of Susanna Loux, minor child of Peter and Elizabeth Loux, acknowledges payment of estate by Samuel Harwick, administrator of Samuel Harwick, late of Springfield Twp, who was previously Susanna's guardian.   Bk 9/pg 108 Feb 23, 1843

Henry Harwick, Jacob and Catharine Strouse and Peter and Elizabeth Loux, heirs of Samuel Harwick, late of Springfield Twp, acknowledge payment of estate by administrator Samuel Harwick.   Bk 9/pg 109 Feb 23, 1843

Francis and Merry Davidson of New London Twp, Chester Co. give power of attorney to son William of Warrington Twp. to recover money due from estate of William Carnahan of Warrington Twp.   Bk 9/pg 110 Feb 2, 1842

Ann Gregg, widow of Dr. Amos Gregg, late of Bristol Borough, and Amos's children John and Deborah Philips and John P. and Ann Eliza Kirkbride, sell part of their land to Delaware Division of the Pennsylvania Canal.
    Bk 9/pg 113 May 2, 1828

Benjamin and Caroline Griffith, Bazilla James, Elizabeth James, Levi James and Benjamin Griffith (guardian of Nathan James), all children of late Abiah James, and Joseph and Rachel Evans, Elizabeth Lunn, David and Sarah Ann Stephens and Abiah J. and Miranda Riale, all children of late Margaret Riale, and William and Elizabeth Hines, sell to Benjamin W. James land that was willed by Abiah James to Nathan and Benjamin W. James.
    Bk 9/pg 116 Mar 3, 1843

Samuel Nonnemaker sells to Thomas Craig his right in estate due to Catharine (wife of James Nonnemacher), daughter of Valentine Kramer, late of Hilltown Twp.   Bk 9/pg 118 Feb 22, 1843

Jonathan Levy of Buchanan Co, MO, son of John Adam Levy, late of Milford Twp, gives power of attorney to David Spinner, Esq. of Milford Twp. to petition Orphans Court to value the real estate. Bk 9/pg 120 Oct 19, 1842

Barbary Fretz of Plumstead Twp, spinster, now 21, acknowledges payment by guardian Abraham Shadinger, drover, of money due from estate of her late father Henry Fretz, uncle of Jacob Overholt, late of Bedminster Twp.
    Bk 9/pg 123 Mar 14, 1843

Jacob Strouse of Tinicum Twp, guardian of Samuel Strouse, minor child of Nicholas Strouse, late of Nockamixon Twp, acknowledges payment of estate by administrator Henry Strouse.　　　　Bk 9/pg 124　Mar 1, 1828

David W. McNair of Northampton Twp, now 21, acknowledges payment by guardian Isaac Vanartsdalen of money due him.　Bk 9/pg 138　Apr 8, 1843

David Carr Price and wife Margaret (late Wildonger) of Plumstead Twp, Margaret now being 21, acknowledge payment by her guardian George Fox of money due from estate of her father Leonard Wildonger, late of Plumstead Twp.　　　　Bk 9/pg 138　Mar 30, 1843

Michael Baum, Charles Baum, Conrad and Margaret Metzger, Leonard and Barbara Metzger, Peter and Elizabeth Emery (Elizabeth deceased leaving children Samuel, Mary, Margaret, Peter, Charles), Benjamin and Catharine Sells (Catharine deceased leaving children Michael, Mary, Samuel, John, Barbara, Sarah, Susanna, Catharine, Joseph and Benjamin) and Peter and Mary Dewit (Mary deceased leaving children Sarah, John, Henry, William, Thomas, Reuben, Joseph, Susanna and Mary) and Thomas and Susanna Jones (Susanna deceased leaving children Sarah, Barbara, Susanna, Isaac, Mary and Cynthia), all children of Charles Baum, late of Clermont Co, OH who was a brother of Philip Baum, late of New Britain Twp, give power of attorney to John S. Bryan, Esq. of Doylestown to recover estate due them.
　　　　Bk 9/pg 141-3　May 10, 1842

Witnesses acknowledge marriage of Joseph D. Armitage of Solebury Twp, son of Samuel and Elizabeth L. Armitage of Solebury, and Emeline Small of Solebury Twp, daughter of Jonah Small of Philadelphia on Mar 13, 1839.
　　　　Bk 9/pg 145　Mar 13, 1839

Crispin Wood, late of Bucks Co, died in 1841 intestate leaving no widow or children but siblings Martha, Mary, Joseph, Jesse H. and Uriah (deceased, children Thomas, Henry and Robert). Robert Wood of Philadelphia, entitled to one-third part of one-fifth part of the estate sells his share to Samuel Green of Doylestown Borough.　　　　Bk 9/pg 148　May 18, 1843

Sheridan Weaver of Tinicum Twp. acknowledges payment by Reed C. Weaver of dower due to his mother Elizabeth, widow of Isaac Weaver, late of Tinicum Twp.　　　　Bk 9/pg 150　Apr 7, 1842

247

Elizabeth Weaver, widow of Isaac Weaver, late of Tinicum Twp, acknowledges payment by Isaac C. Weaver of interest due her on Sheridan Weaver's share of her dower.   Bk 9/pg 151   Apr 7, 1842

Andrew Reed sells land in Hilltown Twp. to Isaac Hinley that he purchased of David Cope who inherited the land from his father Jacob Cope. Andrew agrees to indemnify Isaac against any claim by Jacob's daughters Hannah Rule or Rebecca Myers against this real estate.   Bk 9/pg 152   Apr 8, 1843

Caroline Mathews (wife of John Mathews Jr. of Doylestown Twp.), daughter of late Jacob Smith, released Conrad Oberbeck of Nockamixon Twp. of any claim she or her husband might have against him.   Bk 9/pg 156   Apr 18, 1843

Robert Flack, late of New Britain Twp, bequeathed land to sons James and Henry subject to payment of interest to daughter Sarah (wife of Jacob Picker) and to her children after her death. James and Henry sold this land to their brother Robert. Sarah is since deceased leaving only child Ann (wife of Abraham Ruth). Abraham and Ann Ruth of Moreland Twp, Montgomery Co. acknowledge payment of estate by William Flack of New Britain Twp, executor of Robert Flack Jr.   Bk 9/pg 158   Apr 8, 1843

Nicholas Heany, now 21, acknowledges payment by guardian Samuel Rufe of money due from estate of his father William Heany.
                    Bk 9/pg 160   Jan 21, 1843

Ephraim Sidney Thomas of Warren Co, IN, son of Erasmus Thomas who was a son of Ephraim Thomas, late of Bucks Co, gives power of attorney to Charles M. Thomas of Warren Co. to recover estate due him.
                    Bk 9/pg 162   May 19, 1843

Charles M. Thomas of Iroquois Co, IL and formerly of Philadelphia, grandson of Ephraim Thomas, late of New Britain Twp, and son of Erasmus Thomas, acknowledges payment of estate.   Bk 9/pg 163   Apr 2, 1839

Horatio J. Thomas, E. Darwin Thomas and Frederick A. Thomas, all of Warren Co, IN (the two former lately of Philadelphia and the latter lately of Bucks Co), grandson of Ephraim Thomas, late of New Britain Twp, and sons of Erasmus Thomas, acknowledge payment of estate.
                    Bk 9/pg 164   Apr 10, 1839

Jonathan and Jacob Frederick, grandchildren of Jacob Wismer, late of Plumstead Twp, will be due part of their mother Catharine Frederick's one-

fourth share of her father's estate but sell their interest to their father Joseph
Frederick.   Bk 9/pg 166   Feb 12, 1842

Benjamin M. Thomas of Vincennes, Knox Co, IN, formerly of Philadelphia,
grandson of Ephraim Thomas, late of New Britain Twp, and son of Erasmus
Thomas, acknowledges payment of estate.   Bk 9/pg 167   Mar 25, 1839

Rebecca and Hiram A. Williams, administrators of Thomas Williams, late of
Tinicum Twp, who was a son of Jeremiah Williams, late of Tinicum Twp,
acknowledge payment of estate by Jeremiah's executors.
                                               Bk 9/pg 168   Apr 24, 1843

Mary Ann Chambers, daughter of Robert Wood, late of Buckingham Twp,
who is now 18 years old and entitled to receive her legacy, acknowledges
through her attorney William Kitchen that she has received payment by Henry
Wood and Greene Sergeant, administrators of Crispin Wood who was
executor of Robert Wood.   Bk 9/pg 181   Apr 25, 1843

Maryann Chambers of Clinton Co, IL, daughter of Robert Wood, late of
Bucks Co, gives power of attorney to William Kitchin of Solebury Twp. to
recover estate.   Bk 9/pg 182   Sep 6, 1842

Mary Knowles, widow of Joseph Knowles, late of Lower Makefield Twp,
gives power of attorney to son Mahlon K. Knowles to recover money due her.
                                  Bk 9/pg 183   Mar 15, 1843

Mary Magdalena Adams, widow of John K. Adams, late of Durham Twp,
yeoman, John Knecht (guardian of minor son Henry Adams), John Slida (in
right of wife Elizabeth), John Boyer (guardian of minor daughter Catharine),
John Fackenthall (guardian of minor daughters Hannah and Christeana), John
Overpeck (guardian of minor daughters Mary Ann and Sarah), acknowledge
payment of estate by administrator Michael Fackenthall Jr.
                                  Bk 9/pg 184   Apr 8, 1843

Jacob Swenk and wife Mary, widow of Jacob Landes who was son of John
Landes, late of Rockhill Twp, and Jacob's only daughter Elizabeth Landes
acknowledge payment by John's son Samuel Landes of dower due upon the
death of John's widow Elizabeth (who is now deceased).
                                  Bk 9/pg 190   Apr 5, 1843

Rachel Deily (formerly Sames) of Haycock Twp, spinster, now 21, acknowledges payment by guardian Peter R. Mann of money due from estate of her grandparents Michael and Elizabeth Smell.

Bk 9/pg 192   Apr 10, 1843

John L. Bailey of Milford, Hunterdon Co, NJ, now 21, acknowledges payment by guardian Daniel Boileau of money due from estate of his late father John Bailey.   Bk 9/pg 193   Apr 26, 1843

Charles Paxson, Jonathan Pickering, G. Pickering, Joseph S. Pickering, Elihu Pickering (administrator of Samuel Pickering), Holcomb Ely (administrator of Isaac Pickering), heirs of Jonathan Pickering, acknowledge payment by Moses Eastburn and Knowles Lancaster, present owners of the estate of dower due upon death of Jonathan's widow.   Bk 9/pg 194   Apr 5, 1843

Philip Miller, late of New Britain Twp, willed that his real estate to be sold subject to dower for the widow which after her death would be payable to his seven children: John D., William G., Henry L., P. Washington, Tirzah, Margaret and Catharine. The widow is now deceased and the heirs (including Tirzah's husband Stephen Snare, Margaret's husband Daniel Harrar and Catharine's husband Joseph Harrar) acknowledge payment of dower by present owner Levi James.   Bk 9/pg 195   Jan 16, 1840

Henrietta Disborough of Philadelphia, widow, formerly Henrietta Nottnagle, gives power of attorney to John L. Newbold of Philadelphia to record satisfaction of a mortgage.   Bk 9/pg 196   May 25, 1843

Anna Parry of New London Twp, Chester Co, granddaughter of Jonathan Pickering, late of Bucks Co, gives power of attorney to uncle Charles Paxson of New London Twp. to recover dower due now that the widow Mary is deceased.   Bk 9/pg 197   Mar 27, 1843

Henry Herpst and wife Margaret, daughter of Isaac Weirback, late of Springfield Twp, acknowledge payment of estate by executor Henry Weirback, due upon the death of widow Anna.   Bk 9/pg 200   Jun 8, 1843

Heil Wood of Plumstead Twp, son of Jonathan Wood, late of Plumstead Twp, give power of attorney to William Heacock of Plumstead Twp. to recover estate from administrator Moses Ridge of Tinicum Twp.

Bk 9/pg 201   Jun 10, 1843

Mary and Joseph Canby, administrators of Joshua C. Canby, late of Middletown Twp, sell land to Thomas Lownes, Joseph Lownes, Beulah Lownes, Rebecca Lownes and Susannah Lownes, children of William Lownes of Upper Makefield Twp.   Bk 9/pg 203   Apr 1, 1840

Susanna Laubenstine of Tinicum Twp, acknowledges payment by Jonas Laubenstine, administrator of John Laubenstine, late of Tinicum, who was executor to her father Peter Laubenstine, late of Tinicum Twp.
                                                              Bk 9/pg 206   Apr 3, 1843

Henry Scholl of Bensalem Twp, son of George Scholl, late of Gwyned Twp, Montgomery Co, acknowledges payment of estate by executors Tobias and George Scholl.   Bk 9/pg 207   Mar 28, 1826

Peter C. Bailey, son of Samuel Bailey, late of Lower Makefield Twp, sells his share of estate (due upon death of his mother Rachel) to Joshua Vansant in order to pay debts.   Bk 9/pg 210   May 26, 1843

Samuel Wilson, executor of Samuel Baum, late of New Berlin, Union Co, who was an heir of Philip Baum, late of Bucks Co, gives power of attorney to John E. Baum of Philadelphia to recover estate from administrator Samuel Overholt.   Bk 9/pg 211   Jun 20, 1843

Margaret Heft of Haycock Twp, spinster, gives power of attorney to Danl. Applebach, Esq. of Haycock to recover money due from estate of Henry Kramer of Bedminster Twp. and from estate of Henry's widow Sarah.
                                                              Bk 9/pg 212   Aug 1, 1843

George Wyker of Tinicum Twp. gives power of attorney to son Samuel Wyker to recover money due him.   Bk 9/pg 212   Apr 2, 1843

Hester L. Aaronson, Abraham Perkins, Hannah (wife of Albert S. Mendenhall), David Perkins, Elizabeth (wife of Joseph Hall), Samuel Perkins, George Perkins, William Perkins and Amos Hutchin Deacon (guardian of Rebecca Deacon, minor daughter of Rebecca Deacon—late Perkins), heirs of Martha Perkins (late Sipler), give power of attorney to Joseph Hall to refuse to accept Martha's release estate.   Bk 9/pg 216   [blank], 1843

Joseph Radcliff, late of Warrington Twp, died about March 1843 intestate leaving children John, Robert, Seth, Rudolph, William, Sarah (wife of Isaac Milnor), Rebecca (wife of William Lilly who is dead) and Susan (wife of

Jacob Marple). Seth Radcliff of Hamilton Co, OH sells his share to Rudolph
Radcliff. Bk 9/pg 223   Oct 14, 1843

Abraham Leatherman of Sewickley[?] Twp, Westmoreland Co. gives power
of attorney to Abraham Shaddinger of Bucks Co. to receive estate from Henry
Leatherman of Bucks Co, executor of Ann Delp (formerly Leatherman).
Bk 9/pg 225   Jul 19, 1843

Conrad Kohl of Nockamixon Twp. died intestate leaving widow and eight
children, including Samuel S. Kohl of Wallpack Twp, Sussex Co, NJ. Samuel
gives power of attorney to Michael Dech of Nockamixon Twp. to refuse to
accept his father's real estate. Bk 9/pg 226   Sep 5, 1843

William Vanartsdalen, Joseph Vanartsdalen, Joseph Eastburn, Rebecca
Vanartsdalen, Mary Vanartsdalen and Rachel Vanartsdalen, give power of
attorney to Christopher Vanartsdalen of Bucks Co. to record satisfaction of a
mortgage. Bk 9/pg 230   Mar 25, 1843

Isaac Wynkoop and wife Ann, heir of James Winder, late of Lower Makefield
Twp, acknowledges payment by Aaron Larue (present owner of the real
estate) of dower due now that the widow is deceased.
Bk 9/pg 230   Jun 25, 1839

John B. Winder, Harman Winder, Abraham and Sarah Knight, Jonathan and
Mercy Clayton and Amos Knight (assignee of Thomas Winder), heirs of
James Winder, late of Lower Makefield Twp, acknowledge payment by
Aaron Larue (present owner of the real estate) of dower due now that the
widow is deceased. Bk 9/pg 231   Apr 13, 1839

John and Mary Trauger of Nockamixon Twp, Benjamin and Elizabeth
Dotterer of Durham Twp, Abraham and Susanna Trauger of Haycock Twp,
Joseph and Rachel Stover of Nockamixon Twp. and Leah Mill of
Nockamixon, daughters of Elizabeth Mill (formerly Summers), daughter of
George Fulmer, late of Nockamixon Twp, acknowledge payment of estate by
executor John Fulmer. Bk 9/pg 235   Aug 29, 1837

Mary Yost of Williams Twp, Northampton Co, daughter of John Yost who
married Magdalena Fulmer, daughter of George Fulmer, late of Nockamixon
Twp, acknowledges payment of estate by executor John Fulmer.
Bk 9/pg 236   Nov 15, 1841

John King of Bethlehem Twp, Northampton Co. and wife Rosena, daughter of Abraham and Elizabeth Mills and granddaughter of George Fulmer, late of Nockamixon Twp, acknowledge payment of estate by executor John Fulmer.

Bk 9/pg 237   May 4, 1839

Jacob Yost of Springfield Twp, son of John Yost who married Magdalena Fulmer, daughter of George Fulmer, late of Nockamixon Twp, acknowledges payment of estate by executor John Fulmer.

Bk 9/pg 237   Aug 26, 1836

George Fulmer of Haycock Twp, Frederick Fulmer of Nockamixon Twp, Jacob Fulmer of Tinicum Twp, Catharine Yost, Philip and Sarah Hoffman, children of George Fulmer, late of Nockamixon Twp, acknowledge payment of estate by executor John Fulmer.   Bk 9/pg 238   Nov 6, 1841

James Transue of Lower Saucon Twp, Northampton Co, carpenter, and wife Mary, daughter of John Yost who married Magdalena Fulmer, daughter of George Fulmer, late of Nockamixon Twp, acknowledge payment of estate by executor John Fulmer.   Bk 9/pg 240   Oct 17, 1836

Joseph Aderhold of Willington Twp, Bucks Co[?] and wife Susanna, daughter of George Fulmer, late of Nockamixon Twp, acknowledge payment of estate by executor John Fulmer.   Bk 9/pg 241   Jun 12, 1841

William Yost of Tinicum Twp, son of John Yost and his late wife Magdalena, daughter of George Fulmer, late of Nockamixon Twp, acknowledges payment of estate by executor John Fulmer.   Bk 9/pg 241   Mar 26, 1836

Abraham Mill of Nockamixon Twp, grandson of George Fulmer, late of Nockamixon Twp, acknowledges payment of estate by executor John Fulmer.

Bk 9/pg 242   Oct 23, 1841

Frany Mill of Nockamixon Twp, daughter of Elizabeth Mill who was daughter of George Fulmer, late of Nockamixon Twp, acknowledges payment of estate by executor John Fulmer.   Bk 9/pg 243   Mar 7, 1840

Abraham Frankenfield of Williams Twp, Northampton Co, carpenter, and wife Catharine, daughter of John Yost, deceased, who was married to Magdalena Fulmer, deceased, daughter of George Fulmer, late of Nockamixon Twp, acknowledge payment of estate by executor John Fulmer.

Bk 9/pg 243   Oct 3, 1836

Silas and Elizabeth (late Ridge) Mudge of Lycoming Co. and Catharine Niece, Ann Niece, Eliza Niece, William Niece, Henry Niece, John Niece, John and Mary (late Niece) Meace, Henry and Levina (late Niece) Southard, Abraham and Rebecca (late Niece) Tallman, heirs of John and Mary (late Ridge) Niece of Lycoming Co (along with Latitia Rathmell), give power of attorney to Amariah Rathmell of Lycoming Co. to recover money due from estates of Elizabeth and Mary's brothers Thomas, William and Edward Ridge.
Bk 9/pg 245   Oct 28, 1843

Henry Landes of Chester Co, son of Mary Landes (late Kulp), David and John Yoder, sons of Dorety Yoder (late Kulp), Jacob and Ann Moyer (daughter of Henry Kulp), David, Henry and Abraham Kulp and Elizabeth High (children of Henry Kulp), acknowledge payment by their uncle Abraham Kulp of Bedminster Twp. of estate due from his brother Jacob Kulp, late of Bedminster Twp.
Bk 9/pg 249   May 28, 1825

John B. Taylor inherited land from father Charles Taylor, late of Upper Makefield Twp, subject to payment of share to brother George Taylor. George is now deceased leaving no widow or issue but mother Mary Taylor. Mary Taylor acknowledges payment of estate by current owner Joseph Janney.
Bk 9/pg 256   Sep 16, 1843

Michael Dech, guardian of Henry Dech (minor son of late Jacob Dech), acknowledges payment by Michael and Jacob Kohl, administrators of late Conrad Kohl who was Henry's previous guardian.
Bk 9/pg 265   Dec 16, 1843

Marriage is intended between Phebe Skelton of Solebury Twp, single woman, and Thomas Stradling of Solebury Twp. and they agree to settlement of Phebe's estate.
Bk 9/pg 267   Apr 13, 1843

George Richards bequeathed land to Margaret (nee Richards) Mackey, wife of Philip Mackey and to her children Charles and Robert Matty (who assumed the name of their stepfather Philip Matty). Robert Mackey of Warminster Twp. acknowledges payment by his stepfather Philip Matty for his share of this land.
Bk 9/pg 269   Jun 21, 1843

Isaac J. Beans and wife Mary, daughter of John Harman, late of Upper Makefield Twp, sell their interest in estate of her father and estate of Enoch Harman, late of Upper Makefield Twp. to John C. Beans and Stacy W. Brown to pay debts.
Bk 9/pg 271   Jan 6. 1844

254

Peter George and wife Elizabeth, daughter of late Philip Harpel, assign enough of their share to executor Philip R. Harpel to pay debts which Philip owed to Joseph Stover and Joseph Gruver on their behalf.

Bk 9/pg 275   Jan 30, 1844

Peter and Elizabeth George assign their interest in estate of Philip Harpel to Aaron George in order to pay debts.   Bk 9/pg 276   Jan 30, 1844

Henry Fluck and Peter and Eve (nee Fluck) Yost, grandchildren of John Fluck, late of Bedminster Twp, acknowledge payment of estate by executor Samuel Fluck.   Bk 9/pg 276   Apr 4, 1843

David Fluck and George and Catharine (nee Fluck) Weisel, heirs of John Fluck, late of Bedminster Twp, acknowledge payment of estate by executor Samuel Fluck.   Bk 9/pg 277   Apr 4, 1843

Henry Eckel, Esq., guardian of Aaron Fluck, minor child of Philip Fluck, late of Bedminster Twp, and grandchild of John Fluck, late of Bedminster Twp, acknowledges payment of estate by John's executor Samuel Fluck.

Bk 9/pg 278   Apr 4, 1843

Peter Yost, testamentary guardian of Samuel Fluck and Soloma Fluck, minor children of late Frederick Fluck and grandchildren of John Fluck, late of Bedminster Twp, acknowledges payment of estate by executor Samuel Fluck.

Bk 9/pg 279   Apr 4, 1843

Philip Hoffman, testamentary guardian of Levi Fluck, minor child of late Frederick Fluck and grandchild of John Fluck, late of Bedminster Twp, acknowledges payment of estate by executor Samuel Fluck.

Bk 9/pg 280   Apr 4, 1843

Elias Fluck, Ephraim and Elizabeth (nee Fluck) Ott and Jacob and Mary Ann (nee Fluck) Egolf, grandchildren of John Fluck, late of Bedminster Twp, acknowledge payment of estate by executor Samuel Fluck.

Bk 9/pg 280   Apr 4, 1843

Samuel Ott, George and Lydia (Ott) Maugle, Peter and Catharine (Ott) Shive, George and Susanna (Ott) Yost, William and Anna (Ott) Allum and Samuel and Rebecca (Ott) Trumbore, grandchildren of John Fluck, late of Bedminster Twp, acknowledge payment of estate by executor Samuel Fluck.

Bk 9/pg 281   Apr 4, 1843

Barbara Shipe, wife of Jacob Shipe of Augusta Twp, Northumberland Co, daughter of late John Flook of Bucks Co, gives power of attorney to son Abraham Shipe to recover estate from executor Samuel Fluck.
Bk 9/pg 282   Mar 23, 1843

Henry Trumbower of Williams Twp, Northampton Co, now 21, acknowledges payment by guardian George Custard of estate from late father Jacob Trumbower.
Bk 9/pg 287   Jul 6, 1843

Jacob Stone, Henry Stone (for himself and as assignee of brother John), Adam and Elizabeth (Stone) Clemens and Philip and Mary Magdalena (Stone) Christman acknowledge payment by Adam Barntz and Jacob Delp, executors of late Peter T. Barntz who was executor of late Jacob Barntz of legacy due to their mother Elizabeth Stone under Jacob's will. Bk 9/pg 293   May 20, 1843

Else Crouse, widow of Henry Crouse, late of Tinicum Twp, and Stephen and Elizabeth Gano, James and Lucy Snyder, Harbet S. and Sarah Engle, Charles B. and Rachel Snyder and Mary Crouse, Ann Crouse, John Crouse and Thomas Crouse, children of Henry, acknowledge payment of estate by administrators Amos Hunt.
Bk 9/pg 295   Oct 26, 1843

David Atherholt, administrator of Gabriel Atherholt, late of Bucks Co, acknowledges payment by Joseph Fretz and Jacob S. Kratz, administrators of late William Fretz, of Gabriel's share in estate of his father Frederick Atherholt which was due at the death of Frederick's widow.
Bk 9/pg 297   Mar 4, 1844

Jonah Heacock, William Heacock, Joel Heacock, Joseph Heacock, Enos Heacock, John and Margaret Good, children of Jesse Heacock, late of Rockhill Twp, agree to selection of men to value their father's real estate.
Bk 9/pg 299   Oct 13, 1841

John Lutz (in right of wife Susanna), George W. Jones (in right of wife Sarah) and John L. Radcliff (guardian of Charlotte Frederick, Sarah Frederick and Matilda Frederick), legatees of Jacob Grove, late of Warrington Twp, acknowledge payment of estate by executors David Grove and Daniel Harley, excluding their share of legacy given to Jacob's sister Maria in Virginia.
Bk 9/pg 303   Apr 22, 1843

Abraham Grove, Mary (wife of James Madison Lacy) and Barbarah Grove, children of John Grove, acknowledge payment of estate by David Grove and Daniel Harley, executors of late Jacob Grove. Bk 9/pg 304   May 11, 1842

David Connard, Jacob Connard, Samuel Connard (who is now absent), Mary (wife of Absalom Wilson), Ann Connard, Hannah Connard and Susan Connard, children of Elizabeth Connard, agree that David Grove, surviving executor of late David Grove, should pay the legacy given to their mother Elizabeth by her father David, rather than having it held in trust.

Bk 9/pg 305   Apr 8, 1842

William Long, Esq. of Durham Twp. and Nancy Hughs of Greenwich Twp, Warren Co, NJ at intending soon to be marriage and agree to the settlement of Nancy's property.   Bk 9/pg 308   Jan 17, 1832

Eve Heft of Richland Twp, widow and mother of Samuel and Julyann Heft, late of Richland, lunatics, acknowledges payment of estate by Tobias Landes, trustee of the estates of Samuel and Julyann.   Bk 9/pg 314   Dec 1, 1843

Samuel Sliffer of Springfield Twp, farmer, and wife Eva agree to separate due to unhappy contests and differences between them. Jacob Gehman of Springfield Twp. agrees to serve as Eva's trustee. Bk 9/pg 315   Mar 29, 1836

Charles Baum of Vermilion Co, IL, heirs of Philip Baum, late of Bucks Co, gives power of attorney to Michael Baum of Clermont Co, OH to recover estate due him.   Bk 9/pg 322   Feb 21, 1844

Jacob Leidigh and Jacob and Mary M. Stearly of Montgomery Co. acknowledge payment of estate by Jonathan Leidigh and Isaac Worman, administrators of Henry Leidigh, late of Bucks Co.

Bk 9/pg 324   Nov 3, 1842

Elizabeth Seaber and John Leidich of Philadelphia acknowledge payment of estate by Jonathan Leidigh and Isaac Worman, administrators of Henry Leidigh, late of Bucks Co.   Bk 9/pg 325   Oct 21, 1842

Jacob Bertolet of Montgomery Co. and Jacob L. Bertolet, Francis and Mary Kline, Hester Bertolet, John L. Bartolet and Samuel L. Bartolet of Philadelphia acknowledge payment of estate by Jonathan Leidigh and Isaac Worman, administrators of Henry Leidigh, late of Bucks Co.

Bk 9/pg 325   Nov 5, 1842

A.N. Leidigh and L.N. Leidigh of Philadelphia, children of late Philip Leidigh, acknowledge payment of estate by Jonathan Leidigh and Isaac Worman, administrators of Henry Leidigh, late of Bucks Co.

Bk 9/pg 327   Nov 24, 1842

Ann Landis of Livonia Twp, Livingston Co, NY, heir of Philip Baum, late of Bucks Co, gives power of attorney to John Landis of Warren Co, NJ to recover estate from Abraham Baum or administrators of Philip.

Bk 9/pg 328   Aug 21, 1843

Stephen Acor of Buckingham Twp, husband of Hannah Atherholt, (late McCarthy), daughter of John G. McCarty, late of Haycock Twp, acknowledges payment of estate by administrators Allen McCarty and David White   Bk 9/pg 329   Apr 3, 1844

Jacob Thomas, late of Northampton Twp, bequeathed estate to widow Rachel and after her death to his children, leaving Jonathan Thomas (since deceased) and William Carr as executors. Eldest son Richard L. Thomas, who was in debt due to fire and other casualties, assigns his share to William Carr in exchange for an advancement of money.   Bk 9/pg 330   Apr 4, 1844

Abraham Moyer Sen. of Hilltown Twp. agrees to sell land to his son Samuel Moyer.   Bk 9/pg 331   Sep 2, 1841

Daniel Atherholt of Nockamixon Twp, husband of Caroline McCarty, daughter of John G. McCarty, late of Haycock Twp, acknowledges payment of estate by administrators Allen McCarty and David White.

Bk 9/pg 333   Apr 4, 1844

Henry Nase, Andrew and Margaret Auchey, Enos and Elizabeth Cope, Conrad and Anna Renninger, Thomas and Hanna Heller, John and Sarah Kremer and Abraham Cressman (guardian of Sophia Nase), children of John Nase, late of Rockhill Twp, acknowledge payment of estate by administrators Anna and Michael Nase.   Bk 9/pg 334   Apr 2, 1844

Joseph Ott, William Ott, Michael Ott, Henry and Mary Fisher, legatees of Mary Ott, late of Bedminster Twp, acknowledge payment of estate by executors Samuel Fluck.   Bk 9/pg 336   Apr 11, 1844

Jacob and Lydia (Swartz) Johnson, acknowledge payment by Lydia's guardian Jacob Hendricks of estate due from Lydia's father Isaac Swartz, deceased.   Bk 9/pg 336   Apr 2, 1844

Jacob Gayman and Benjamin Gehman, sons of Jacob Gahman, late of Springfield Twp, acknowledge payment of estate by Abraham Gahman who held money during the life of Ann Gahman as directed by Jacob's will. Abraham Angeny, Samuel Angeny, William Angeny, David Angeny,

Elizabeth Angeny and guardians of children of late Jacob Angeny, children of late Barbary Angeny, daughter of Jacob Gehman, also acknowledge payment.
Bk 9/pg 339   Apr 5, 1844

Jacob Gross, guardian of Hannah, Isaac and Ephraim Meyers, and Simeon Kratz, guardian of Eliza and John Meyers, minor children of John O. Meyers, late of Bedminster Twp, acknowledge payment of estate by administrators Abraham Holderman and Samuel Meyers.   Bk 9/pg 340   Apr 6, 1844

John Autherholt of Haycock Twp, husband of Elizabeth McCarty, daughter of John G. McCarty, late of Haycock, acknowledges payment of estate by administrators Allen McCarty and David White.   Bk 9/pg 342   Apr 8, 1844

Henry Clymer of Milford Twp. gives power of attorney to friend Thomas Cope of Richland Twp. to obtain a bond as security for his son-in-law Thomas Hartzel.   Bk 9/pg 344   Jan 19, 1844

Jacob Shipe of Augusta Twp, Northumberland Co, farmer, gives power of attorney to son Abraham Shipe to recover money from father's estate now in hands of brother Peter Shipe of Bucks Co.   Bk 9/pg 345   Mar 20, 1844

Jacob and Joseph Shelly, executors of Joseph Shelly, late of Milford Twp, acknowledge payment of Joseph's son Joseph Shelly in payment for late bequeathed to him.   Bk 9/pg 345   Apr 4, 1844

Elizabeth, Andrew, David, Rachel, Robert, Albert and Rebecca, children of late William Flowers (the latter two being minors), acknowledge payment of mortgage by Andrew Flowers.   Bk 9/pg 346   Mar 28, 1844

Josiah S. Doan, heir of late Eleazer Doan, gives power of attorney to Thomas Stradling of Plumstead Twp. to recover from Ephraim Jones of Plumstead Twp. the share due to Josiah by right of his father Joshua Doan.
Bk 9/pg 348   Aug 29, 1842

David and Sarah Doan of Athens Co, OH give power of attorney to friend Lutheran L. Backer of Morgan Co, OH to recover legacy due to Sarah from John and Joseph Meredith, administrators of James Meredith.
Bk 9/pg 349   Mar 18,1844

Mary Green and her children Elizabeth Stuart/Stucat, Martha Green, Mary Green and Samuel Green acknowledge payment of estate by Thomas Brown, present owner of land previously owned by Robert Wood who bequeathed money to Mary Green.   Bk 9/pg 351   Apr 11, 1844

Simon M. Snyder and wife Barbara, daughter of Henry Barndt, late of Hilltown Twp, now 21, acknowledge payment of estate by her guardian Joseph Weisel.   Bk 9/pg 353   Mar 22, 1841

Henry Barndt of Hilltown Twp, now 21, acknowledges payment by guardian Joseph Weisel of estate from late father (excluding the widow's dower).
                Bk 9/pg 354   Dec 17, 1839

James Gold and wife Anna, heirs of Henry Barndt, late of Hilltown Twp, acknowledge payment of estate by her guardian Joseph Weisel.
                Bk 9/pg 354   Apr 6, 1844

Samuel and Eliza Carver of Clinton Co, OH give power of attorney to William Rhenemans of Clinton Co. to collect moneys due from James Townsend and Ezra Croasdale, administrators of Benjamin Croasdale, late of Bucks Co.   Bk 9/pg 357   Jul 19, 1843

Henry, Abraham, and Joseph Fretz, Jacob and Mary Hockman, Isaac and Susanna Detwiler, Philip and Catharine Leatherman and John and Vonacre[?] High, heirs of Joseph Fretz, late of Bedminster Twp, agree to sell Joseph's land to Abraham Meyers of Bedminster Twp.   Bk 9/pg 358   Nov 27, 1843

Mariah Ahlum of Haycock Twp, widow of Aaron Ahlum, late of Haycock, acknowledges payment of estate by administrator Samuel Roudenbush.
                Bk 9/pg 359   Oct 21, 1843

John Fluck, of Richland Twp, guardian of Samuel and Lewis Ahlum, sons of Aaron Ahlum, late of Haycock Twp, acknowledges payment of estate by administrator Samuel Roudenbush.   Bk 9/pg 360   Oct 21, 1843

Cornelius Mahan of Middletown Twp. gives power of attorney to nephew Cornelius Mahan Jr. of Middletown to recover money due him.
                Bk 9/pg 360   May 2, 1842

Abraham Fluck, David and Hanna Mumbouer, Elizabeth Housekeeper (widow), Samuel and Susanna Scholl, Jesse Housekeeper (attorney for Catharine Housekeeper), children of Hanna Fluck, widow, late of Hilltown Twp, acknowledge payment of estate by executor Abraham Heany.
                Bk 9/pg 363   Apr 10, 1844

260

James B. Smith, guardian of Thomas and Mary Fluck, acknowledges payment of estate by Abraham Heany, executor of Hannah Fluck, late of Hilltown Twp.   Bk 9/pg 365   Apr 26, 1844

Ann H. Williams of Newtown Borough, now 21, acknowledges payment by guardian Dr. David Hutchinson of estate from late father Griffith Williams.
                                    Bk 9/pg 366   Apr 24, 1844

Charles Kletzing of Franconia Twp, Montgomery Co, now 21, acknowledges payment by guardian Samuel Horning of estate from uncle Henry Lawrence.
                                    Bk 9/pg 367   Apr 5, 1844

John and Christian Cressman, both of Lower Mount Bethel Twp, Northampton Co, and Abraham Cressman of Nockamixon Twp, Jonas Cressman of Springfield Twp, Peter and Catharine Steely of Durham Twp, children of Christian Cressman, late of Springfield Twp. and Jacob Dietterich of Upper Mount Bethel Twp, Northampton Co, guardian of Elizabeth Heft, minor child of Elizabeth Heft, late of Upper Mt. Bethel and grandchild of Christian Cressman, acknowledge payment of estate by George Cressman of Springfield Twp. (guardian of Samuel Cressman, minor son of Jacob Cressman, late of Springfield) and Joseph Fry Sen. of Springfield Twp. (guardian of William and Jacob Cressman, minor sons of late Jacob) due by will of Christian from his son Jacob who inherited the real estate.
                                    Bk 9/pg 368   Jan 1, 1840

Elizabeth James and Levi James, children of late Abiah James Jr., release their guardian Benjamin Griffith of Richland Twp. of any responsibility.
                                    Bk 9/pg 370   Mar 14, 1844

Jacob and Daniel Landes, sons of Daniel Landes, late of Bedminster Twp, acknowledge payment by Abraham Landes, Benjamin Landes, Samuel Landes, Mary Landes, Magdalena Landes and Sarah Landes of estate due from dower of their late mother Mary Landes.   Bk 9/pg 372   Apr 22, 1844

Jonah Heacock, Jesse Heacock, Joseph Heacock, Jonah Heacock (attorney for Nathan Heacock and Aaron Heacock of Indiana) acknowledge payment of estate by William Heacock, Joel Heacock, Enos Heacock and Richard Moore, executors for their father Jesse Heacock, late of Rockhill Twp.
                                    Bk 9/pg 373   Apr 8, 1844

Nathan Heacock and Aaron Heacock, both of Ripley Twp, Rush County, Indiana, sons of Jesse Heacock, late of Rockhill Twp, give power of attorney to Jonah Heacock of Upper Dublin Twp, Montgomery Co. to recover estate.
Bk 9/pg 374   Apr 14, 1842

Robert N. Taylor and wife Eveline, late Doan, heir of Eleazor Doan, deceased, give power of attorney to Thomas Stradling of Plumstead Twp. to recover estate from Ephraim Jones of Plumstead Twp. due to Emeline by right of her father Joshua Doan.   Bk 9/pg 375   Sep 24 1842

John Michener, Mary Worthington, Mary Michener, Jacob Shaddinger and Thomas Stradling (executors of Jonah Doan), Susanna Michener, Samuel Tomlinson, Jonathan Doan, Sarah Doan, Thomas Stradling (attorney for Josiah T. Doan and Robert N. and Eveline Taylor), heirs of late Eleazor Doan, acknowledge payment of dower of Eleazor's widow Mary by Ephriam Jones, current owner of the real estate.   Bk 9/pg 377   Apr 2, 1838

David Snyder of Blockley Twp, Philadelphia Co. and wife Mary Ann Josephine (late Jardella) give power of attorney to Samuel Hart, Esq. of Doylestown Twp. to enter satisfaction of a mortgage.
Bk 9/pg 380   May 23, 1844

Henry Funk, husband of Catharine Stover, of Turbit Twp, Northumberland Co. gives power of attorney to John Clemmens of Doylestown Borough to petition Orphans Court for partition of real estate of Jacob Stover, late of Bedminster Twp.   Bk 9/pg 381   Jul 2, 1844

John Beaumont, late of Upper Makefield Twp, bequeathed by codicil land to his executors Elizabeth Beaumont and Merrick Reeder, Esq. in trust for his daughter Sarah Ann. Elizabeth is since deceased. Sarah Ann married after 1835 to John C. Schenck. Sarah Ann asks that land she purchased in 1835 from Horatio N. Beaumont be sold to Merrick Reeder for her benefit.
Bk 9/pg 381   Aug 8, 1844

Abel Penrose of Richland Twp. died intestate Dec, 1824 leaving widow and siblings but no issue. Widow is now married to Jesse Heacock. After her death, the dower is due to heirs William Penrose, Benjamin Penrose, Morris Penrose, Margaret (wife of Jesse Vickert), Garner Faul and Sarah Bower (only child of late Eberhard Penrose, wife of Reuben Bower). Reuben and Sarah Bower of Ruscomb Manor Twp, Berks Co, blacksmith, sell their share of dower to Charles Levan of Ruscomb Manor Twp, yeoman.
Bk 9/pg 383   May 28, 1844

Henry Cope of Hilltown Twp, Margaret Landes of Bucks Co, Francis Cope of Montgomery Co, Jesse Cope of Hilltown Twp, Jeremiah and Catharine (late Johnson) Rhoad, heirs of late Abraham Cope, acknowledge payment of dower by Samuel Detwiler. Bk 9/pg 384 Apr 4, 1844

Levi Kramer of Bedminster Twp, administrator of Sarah Kramer, widow of Henry Kramer, acknowledges payment of dower by John Kramer, administrator of Henry. Bk 9/pg 385 Aug 1, 1844

Samuel Yost of Haycock Twp, guardian of Jacob and Levi Kramer, minor children of Henry Kramer, late of Bedminster Twp, acknowledge payment of estate by administrator John Kramer. Bk 9/pg 386 Jul 20, 1844

Daniel Bartholomew of Bedminster Twp, guardian of [blank] Kramer, minor child of Henry Kramer, late of Bedminster Twp, acknowledges payment of estate by administrator John Kramer. Bk 9/pg 386 Aug 2, 1844

John Heist of Milford Twp, now 21, acknowledges payment by guardian Jacob Boyer to estate from late father George Heist.
Bk 9/pg 387 Apr 18, 1843

Benjamin Foulke of Gwynedd Twp, Montgomery Co, blacksmith, due one-sixth share of farm of late grandfather Casper Johnson of Richland Twp, now about to be occupied by his parents, upon the death of his mother Catharine Foulke. Benjamin assigns his share to Martha Foulke of Richland Twp. in order to pay debts. Bk 9/pg 388 Apr 15, 1844

Levina Fluck, now 21, acknowledges payment by guardian Philip Hoffman of estate from late grandfather John Fluck of Bedminster Twp.
Bk 9/pg 389 Jul 24, 1844

John W. Stewart of Philadelphia, cordwainer, now 21, acknowledges payment by guardian Christian Myers of estate from late grandfather Peter Stewart.
Bk 9/pg 390 Aug 10, 1844

Nicholas Mensch of Kent Co, MD gives power of attorney to friend John Smith of Springfield Twp. to sell land in Haycock Twp.
Bk 9/pg 391 Apr 19, 1843

Jacob Fulmer, John Fulmer, Peter Fulmer, Daniel Fulmer, Tobias and Barbara Gerhard, Joseph and Mary Weisel, John and Dinah Steiner Sr., John and Nancy Steiner, Esq., Enos and Catharine Roudenbush, Aaron and Sarah Ann

Moll and Joseph Weisel (guardian of children of late Samuel Fulmer), heirs of Catharine Fulmer, late of Rockhill Twp, widow of Daniel Fulmer, acknowledge payment of dower by George Hager. Bk 9/pg 391 Apr 6, 1844

William Wade Bleecher, Lieutenant of U.S. Navy married to Lucretia Ann, daughter of Edmund Badger of Philadelphia, Innkeeper, sometime prior to Sep 15, 1840. Lucretia Ann was due a legacy by will of Bela Badger, late of Bristol. William and Lucretia Ann assign her legacy to her father Edmund to reimburse him for the expenses he incurred to educate and maintain Lucretia.
Bk 9/pg 394   Sep 15, 1840

Jacob Fulmer, John Fulmer, Peter Fulmer, Daniel Fulmer, Tobias and Barbara Gerhard, Joseph and Mary Weisel, John and Denah Steiner Sen., John and Nancy Steiner, Enos and Catharine Roudenbush, Aaron and Sarah Ann Moll and Joseph Weisel (guardian of children of late Samuel Fulmer), heirs of Catharine Fulmer, late of Rockhill Twp, widow of Daniel Fulmer, acknowledge payment of dower by John Yost. Bk 9/pg 396   Apr 6, 1844

Same heirs acknowledge payment of dower by Daniel Bartholomew.
Bk 9/pg 398   Apr 6, 1844

Henry Cope of Hilltown, Margaret Landes of Bucks Co, James Cope of Montgomery Co, Jesse Cope of Bucks Co, Jeremiah and Catharine (late Johnson) Rhoad, heirs of Abraham Cope, acknowledge payment of dower by Michael Zeigler.   Bk 9/pg 397   Apr 4, 1844

Jacob Slifer of Richland Twp. and wife Mary have agreed to separate due to unhappy differences between them. Jacob agrees to give property to Balladin Diehl and George Ziegler in trust for Mary. Bk 9/pg 403   Sep 25, 1844

William Neece, Catharine Neece, Eliza Neece and Abraham and Rebecca Tallman, children of John Neece of Lycoming Co. and wife Mary who was sister to Thomas, William and Edward Ridge, late of Bucks Co, who died without issue, give power of attorney to John Neece of Lycoming Co. to recover estate from administrators Daniel Boileau and William Ridge.
Bk 9/pg 405   Oct 22, 1844

Samuel Jacoby of Northumberland Co, indebted to estate of Catharine Jacoby, transfers to Catharine's executor Benjamin Jacoby his share in estate of his late father Peter Jacoby.   Bk 9/pg 407   Oct 9, 1844

Thomas Wood of Holmes Co, OH gives power of attorney to William C. Hutchinson of Holmes Co. to recover estate from Henry Wood and Green Sargeant, administrators of Crispin Wood, late of Bucks Co.

Bk 9/pg 409   Oct 5, 1844

Alexander Fenner, Charles Fenner, Julian (wife of Peter Trauger) and Mary Fenner, grandchildren of Nicholas Kruger, late of Nockamixon Twp, and heirs by right of their late mother Margaret Fenner, all over 21, acknowledge payment of estate by administrators Henry Kruger.

Bk 9/pg 410   Apr 5, 1844

Nicholas Kruger Jr. of White Deer Twp, Union Co, yeoman, son of Nicholas Kruger, late of Nockamixon Twp. who died intestate, acknowledges payment of estate by administrator Henry Kruger.   Bk 9/pg 411   Apr 12, 1844

John Kruger of Durham Twp, yeoman, son of Nicholas Kruger, late of Nockamixon Twp, acknowledges payment of estate by administrator Henry Kruger.   Bk 9/pg 412   Apr 8, 1844

Real estate of late Thomas K. Biles in Lower Makefield Twp. sold to Thomas Jenks subject to payment of interest to Thomas Bailey during his life and to his children after this death, by direction of will of Edward Bailey. Thomas Bailey is now deceased and land is now in possession of Howard Jenks, son of Thomas. John Barton (administrator of Hester Barton), Enoch Bailey, Ann Bailey, Henry Worthington (attorney for David and Sarah Worthington) and Benjamin Atkinson (administrator of Letitia Atkinson), children of Thomas Bailey, acknowledge payment by Howard Jenks.

Bk 9/pg 413-17   Apr 8, 1841

John and Caroline (Kohl) Taylor of Nockamixon Twp. due a debt from estate of Abraham Stover, late of Nockamixon Twp, but assign their share of estate to administrators Barbara and Isaac Stover.   Bk 9/pg 418   Oct 28, 1844

Abraham Fluck, Christian Fluck, Elizabeth Housekeeper (widow), Catharine Housekeeper (widow), John Shive (widower of Magdalena), David and Hannah Mumbower, Abraham and Barbara Gearhart and Samuel and Susanna Scholl, heirs of Christian Fluck, late of Hilltown Twp, acknowledge payment of estate by Philip Fluke who inherited the real estate.

Bk 9/pg 419   Apr 4, 1839

Henry Trumbower of Milford Twp, son of Henry Trumbower Sen., late of Milford Twp, now 21, acknowledges payment of estate by guardian Enos Eartman.　　　　　　　　　　　　　　Bk 9/p 421　Apr 26, 1843

Joseph Halderman, by a paper of writing purporting to be his will, left money to his widow Elizabeth and his son Michael and daughter Rachel (wife of Samuel Griffith). The other children (Samuel, John, Mary, Silas, Jacob, Elizabeth and Benjamin) agree to honor these bequests.
　　　　　　　　　　　　　　Bk 9/pg 422　Nov 6, 1844

John Maugle of Waterloo, Seneca Co, NY gives power of attorney to Joseph Weisel of Bedminster Twp. to appoint men to appraise the estate of his later father Daniel Maugle.　　　　　　Bk 9/pg 424　Jul 1, 1844

E.T. McDowell (attorney for Ely Paxson of Hancock Co, OH) acknowledges payment by Joseph Dilworth of dower due by death of Mary Paxson.
　　　　　　　　　　　　　　Bk 9/pg 426　Mar 22, 1843

Aaron George (assignee of Peter George and wife Elizabeth, daughter of Philip Harpel, late of Tinicum Twp) acknowledges payment of estate by executor Philip R Harpel.　　　　Bk 9/pg 427　Dec 2, 1844

Magdalena Harpel, widow of Philip Harpel, late of Tinicum Twp, acknowledges payment of estate by executors Philip R. Harpel and Peter George.　　　　　　　　　　　Bk 9/pg 428　Dec 6, 1844

Mary Ann Harpel, daughter of Philip Harpel, late of Tinicum Twp, acknowledges payment of estate by executors Philip R. Harpel and Peter George.　　　　　　　　　　　Bk 9/pg 429　Dec 6, 1844

Peter Stout, John Stout, Henry Stout, Samuel Stout, Magdalene Stout, Joseph Stout, Philip R. and Catharine Krout, John Hager (guardian of Elizabeth Kemmerer), heirs of Daniel Stout, late of Bedminster Twp, acknowledge payment of estate by Elizabeth Stout of dower due by death of widow Sevilla.
　　　　　　　　　　　　　　Bk 9/pg 433　Nov 16, 1844

Adam Frankenfield of Scioto, Delaware Co, OH, son of Michael Frankenfield, late of Springfield Twp, gives power of attorney to George Cyphert, Esq. of Springfield Twp. to recover estate from administrators Michael and William Frankenfield.　　　　Bk 9/pg 435　Nov 25, 1844

George W. Brown of New York City gives power of attorney to John S. Brown of Doylestown Borough to recover estate from father and mother, both late of Bucks Co.   Bk 9/pg 439   Dec 14, 1843

Josiah Brown of Trumbull Co, OH gives power of attorney to John S. Brown of Doylestown Borough to recover estate from father and mother, both late of Bucks Co.   Bk 9/pg 439   Jul 8, 1843

John S. Brown (attorney for George W. Brown, Josiah Brown and Thomas Brown) acknowledges payment by Charles Smith of estate from Josiah Brown Sr.   Bk 9/pg 440   Jun 3, 1844

Jacob Stearly and Jonathan Leidigh, attorneys for Elizabeth Seaver, Levi N. Leidigh, Aaron N. Leidigh, Francis and Mary Kline, heirs of Henry Leidigh, late of Nockamixon Twp, acknowledge payment of dower by Franklin Nice due by the death of widow Elizabeth Leidigh.   Bk 9/pg 442   May 24, 1844

Jacob S. Bartolet, attorney for Samuel Bartolet, Ater[?] Bartolet and John L. Bartolet, heirs of Henry Leidigh, late of Nockamixon Twp, acknowledge payment of dower by Franklin Nice due by death of widow Elizabeth.
     Bk 9/pg 443   Nov 2, 1844

Solomon Hess and wife Catharine, daughter of Philip Leidigh, late of Durham Twp, acknowledge payment of dower by Franklin Nice, due by death of Elizabeth Leidigh, widow of Henry Leidigh. Bk 9/pg 444   Jun 3, 1844

Daniel Zeigler of Tinicum Twp. and wife Mary, heirs of Henry Leidigh, late of Nockamixon Twp, acknowledge payment of dower by Franklin Nice due by death of widow Elizabeth.   Bk 9/pg 444   Apr15, 1844

John O. Campbell, trustee of Sarah Ernst, daughter of Philip Leidigh, late of Durham Twp, acknowledges payment of dower by Franklin Nice due by death of Elizabeth Leidigh, widow of Henry Leidigh.
     Bk 9/pg 445   Apr 15, 1844

Ebenezer M. Cord, attorney for John Leidigh of Easton, brother of Henry Leidigh, late of Nockamixon Twp, acknowledges payment of dower by Franklin Nice due by death of widow Elizabeth.   Bk 9/pg 445   Apr 26, 1844

Catharine Horn of Upper Saucon Twp, Lehigh Co, now 21, acknowledges payment by guardian Jacob Horn of estate due from late father Sebastian Horn.   Bk 9/pg 446   Jun 11, 1844

Peter Ott of Bedminster Twp, mason, acknowledges payment by Elizabeth Fetter of estate from Jacob Kramer, late of Bedminster Twp, mason.
Bk 9/pg 448   Feb 11, 1845

George Chapman and Jonathan K. Bonham of Bucks Co, having purchased from Joseph A. Donovan of Baltimore a slave named Samuel called in Bucks Co. "Big Ben" of Black or very dark complexion and of uncommonly large height and size, being about six feet eight inches in height, who was formerly owned by William Anderson, residing near Newtown, MD, now set this slave free.
Bk 9/pg 450   Oct 16, 1844

Elias Bright of Springfield Twp. died intestate leaving widow Salome and four children: John, Elias, Jacob and issue of Samuel. Son Jacob of Milford Twp. gives power of attorney to brother John of Springfield Twp. to recover dower from Jacob Ertman, John Bright and Joseph Minchinger, current owners of the real estate.
Bk 9/pg 452   Jan 9, 1845

Charles and John Wildman, executors of John Wildman, late of Bensalem Twp, and John's son Joshua K. Wildman acknowledge payment by John's son Ellwood Wildman for land Ellwood inherited.   Bk 9/pg 455   Feb 12, 1845

John Fretz, son of Joseph Fretz, late of Bedminster Twp, gives power of attorney to Jacob Fretz of Bedminster Twp. to petition Orphans Court for partition of Joseph's estate.
Bk 9/pg 461   Apr 12, 1844

Lewis Malone of Buckingham Twp, now 21, acknowledges payment by guardian Abner Walton of estate from late father James Malone and from late sister Alice Malone.
Bk 9/pg 461   Apr 2, 1844

Agnes Davis, tenant in common with Salome Davis, late of New Britain Twp, gives power of attorney to Amos Griffith, Salome's administrator, to sell the land they owned in common.
Bk 9/pg 463   Dec 2, 1844

Caleb Edwards of Richland Twp, yeoman, and wife Sarah, daughter of William Penrose, late of Richland Twp, acknowledge payment of estate by executor Evan Roberts.
Bk 9/pg 466   Apr 2, 1845

William Neace, Henry Neace and Ann Neace, heirs of John and Mary (late Ridge) Neace, all of Lycoming Co, give power of attorney to Amariah Rathwell of Lycoming Co. to recover money due them from the estates of

Thomas Ridge, William Ridge, Edward Ridge and Henry Ridge, late of Bucks
Co.   Bk 9/pg 467   Mar 21, 1845

Levi Bearinger, now 21, acknowledges payment by guardian John Kramer of
estate from late father Henry Baringer.   Bk 9/pg 476   Apr 12, 1845

Ann Carrell, widow of Samuel Carrell, late of Tinicum Twp. and heir of
Samuel Carrel the younger, late of Allen Twp, Northampton Co,
acknowledges payment of estate by Hugh Horner, administrator of Robert
Horner who was Samuel's guardian.   Bk 9/pg 481   Oct 9, 1844

James Kennedy of Allen Twp, Northampton Co, guardian of Uriah Carrell
and Jane Ann Carrell, minor children of Samuel Carrel, late of Tinicum Twp,
acknowledge payment by Hugh Horner, administrator of their previous
guardian Robert Horner.   Bk 9/pg 481   Apr 18, 1845

James Carrell of Easton, now 21, acknowledges payment by Hugh Horner,
administrator of his former guardian Robert Horner, late of Allen Twp,
Northampton Co, of estate due from late father Samuel Carrel.
                                     Bk 9/pg 482   Oct 14, 1844

Hugh Horner Abernathy of Allen Twp, Northampton Co, son of Samuel
Abernathy, Esq., late of Tinicum Twp, acknowledges payment of estate by
guardian Hugh Horner.   Bk 9/pg 483   Jul 2, 1830

Ann Kitchen, late of Solebury Twp, bequeathed money to daughter Sarah
Duer to be put out at interest. Her husband Joseph acknowledges that he has
done so.   Bk 9/pg 484   Apr 2, 1845

Christian Fluck (by attorney Samuel Shive), David Mumbauer (in right of
wife Hannah), Francis Gerhart, Samuel Gerhart (by guardian Joseph Hedrick)
and Abraham Gerhart (father of Francis, Samuel and Thomas—deceased),
Samuel Fluck, Enos and Jacob Fluck (by guardian Abraham Kramer),
Thomas and Mary Fluck (by guardian James B. Smith), heirs of Philip Fluck
who was an heir of Christian Fluck, acknowledge payment of dower by
Samuel A. Smith and John Fluck, administrators of Philip Fluck who was
Christian's executor.   Bk 9/pg 484   Apr 9, 1844

Abraham Fluck, Elizabeth Housekeeper, Catharine Housekeeper (by attorney
Jesse Housekeeper), Elias and Levi Shive (heirs of late Magdalene Shive),
Samuel and Susanna Scholl, heirs of Christian Fluck, late of Hilltown Twp,

acknowledge payment of dower by Samuel A. Smith and John Fluck, administrators of Philip Fluck who was Christian's executor.

Bk 9/pg 485   Apr 4, 1844

Joseph Reeder of Wrightstown Twp. gives power of attorney to brother Isaac Reeder of Newtown Twp. to recover any moneys due him.

Bk 9/pg 487   May 4, 1844

Isaac Fretz, Martin Fretz, Abraham Fretz, Henry and Anna Meyers, Joseph F. and Barbary Myers, Benjamin and Elizabeth Hendricks, heirs of Abraham Fretz, late of Bedminster Twp, acknowledge payment of estate by executors Christian and John Fretz.   Bk 10/pg 1   Apr 4, 1845

Benjamin Hendricks of Bedminster Twp. releases his right to a legacy given to his wife Elizabeth by her late father Abraham Fretz if executors Christian and John Fretz will purchase a house for the benefit of his wife.

Bk 10/pg 1   Apr 4, 1845

William P. and Elizabeth (Story) Jenks and Mary Story, all of Baltimore Co, MD, give power of attorney to Dr. Ralph Lee of Newtown Borough to recover proceeds of a mortgage from executors of John Story, late of Newtown Twp.   Bk 10/pg 2   Feb 24, 1845

David Stover of Bethlehem Twp, Northampton Co, son of David Stover, late of Nockamixon Twp, acknowledges payment by Jacob Reigle of dower due by the death of David's widow Barbara Kunsman (widow of Philip Kunsman, late of Lower Saucon Twp, Northampton Co).   Bk 10/pg 3   Mar 31, 1845

Abraham Fulmer, guardian of Julyann Tatesman, minor child of Samuel Tatesman, late of Tinicum Twp, acknowledges payment of estate by administrator Henry Frankenfield.   Bk 10/pg 4   Apr 4, 1845

Moses Knight of Moreland Twp, Philadelphia Co, now 21, acknowledges payment by guardian Benjamin Knight of estate from late father Aaron Knight.   Bk 10/pg 4   Apr 10, 1845

Joseph Fretz, Jacob and Mary Hockman, Isaac and Susanna Detwiler, Abraham and Sarah Meyers, Philip and Catharine Leatherman, John and Franey High and Jacob Fretz (attorney for John Fretz), heirs of Joseph Fretz, late of Bedminster Twp, acknowledge payment of estate by administrator Henry Fretz.   Bk 10/pg 5   Mar 24, 1845

Joseph Fretz, guardian of John and Abraham Fretz, minor children of Abraham Fretz, late of Plumstead Twp, acknowledges payment of estate by Henry Fretz, administrator of Joseph Fretz, late of Bedminster Twp.
Bk 10/pg 6   Mar 24, 1845

Abraham Meyers, guardian of Joseph, Mary and Sarah Fretz, minor children of Abraham Fretz, late of Plumstead Twp, heirs of Joseph Fretz, late of Bedminster Twp, acknowledges payment of estate by administrator Henry Fretz.   Bk 10/pg 7   Mar 24, 1845

Peter and Mary Ann Gwinner of Newtown acknowledge payment of trust by Dr. John H. Gordon and David Hutchinson to their son Henry W. Gwinner.
Bk 10/pg 8   Mar 7, 1845

Elizabeth P. Waddell of Philadelphia, widow of Henry L. Waddell of Morrisville, releases to executors George W. Richards and Pemberton Waddell her estate right for benefit of her children. Bk 10/pg 9 Apr 21, 1836

Benjamin Johnson, son of Benjamin Johnson, late of Richland Twp, elects certain portions of his father's real estate after the selection of his brother Anthony.   Bk 10/pg 10 Sep 4, 1837

Maria Gearhard of Rockhill Twp, now 21, acknowledges payment by guardian Henry Schlichter of estate due from father Adam Gearhart, late of Rockhill Twp.   Bk 10/pg 12   Apr 13, 1839

Hillary Senn of Rockhill Twp. and wife Eliza, acknowledge payment by her guardian Henry Schlichter of estate due from her father Adam Gearhart, late of Rockhill Twp.   Bk 10/pg 13   Mar 9, 1840

Jacob Moyer of Franconia Twp, Montgomery Co, guardian of Lana Landes, and Jacob Heckler of Franconia, guardian of Sarah Landes, and Henry Moyer, guardian of Benjamin and Mary Landes, and Abraham Moyer, guardian of Jacob and Elizabeth Landes, both of Upper Salford Twp, Montgomery Co, acknowledge payment of estate by Abraham Fretz, administrator of Eve Georgian/Georgen, late of Bedminster Twp. Bk 10/pg 14   Apr 12, 1845

John G. and Isaac Landes, Elizabeth (Landes) Fretz, Abraham and Mary (Landes) Stout, Tobias and Lydia (Landes) Hanicka/Hanga, John and Sarah Beck Jr., grandchildren of Eve Georgen, late of Bedminster Twp, receive payment of estate by administrator Abraham Fretz.
Bk 10/pg 14   Apr 10, 1845

271

Christian and Barbary Meyers, Thomas and Magdalena Trower and Joel and Catharine Strawn, heirs of William Fretz, late of Bedminster Twp, acknowledge payment of estate by administrators Joseph S. Fretz and Jacob S. Kratz.   Bk 10/pg 15   Apr 11, 1845

Henrietta Desborough, widow of Leopold Nottnagle, and as administrator for William Godfried Nottnagle and Bernard Wykoff Nottnagle, Samuel Badger (trustee for Jacob and Lisette Julia Walton—nee Nottnagle) and William Kinsey (assignee of Bernard W. Nottnagle) give power of attorney to Frederick Augustus Raybold to record satisfaction of a mortgage.
                                              Bk 10/pg 16   Apr 30, 1845

Jacob Rensheimer of Medina Co, OH gives power of attorney to George Cyphert, Esq. of Springfield Twp. to recover estate due from late father [not named] of Springfield Twp.   Bk 10/pg 17   Dec 2, 1843

Abraham Frederick, son of Joseph Frederick and grandson of Jacob Wismer, late of Plumstead Twp, assigns his share of Jacob's estate to Abraham Shaddinger, drover.   Bk 10/pg 19   Mar 25, 1845

William Rungan and wife Mary Ann, now of Wilmington, DE, daughter of late William Green, acknowledge payment by John Phillips, M.D. who was surety of Mary Ann's guardian James F. Hood.   Bk 10/pg 20   May 23, 1844

John and Elias Fretz of Plumstead Twp, Henry and Mary Shaddinger, Daniel and Sarah Gotwals (by her guardian Henry Shaddinger) and Susanna Fretz (by her guardian Abraham Shaddinger, drover), all of Plumstead Twp. and children of John Fretz Sen., late of Plumstead Twp, acknowledge payment of estate by administrators Tobias, Henry and Jonas Fretz.
                                              Bk 10/pg 20   May 9, 1845

Mary Zeilin of Philadelphia, widow, daughter of John Fritzinger, late of Bucks Co, gives power of attorney to John K. Zeilin of Delaware Co. to recover estate from administrator David Riale and also to recover the share of Mary S. (wife of Moses K. Kiple) who was a daughter of late Christian Fritzinger, a son of John, which share they assigned to Mary Zeilin.
                                              Bk 10/pg 22   Apr 19, 1845

Hannah J. Thomas of Hatboro Twp, Montgomery Co. and Samuel Thompson, M.D. of Northampton Twp. are about to be married and agree to settlement of Hannah's property.   Bk 10/pg 23   May 15, 1845

Charles Armitage and Sarah Beans entered into a marriage agreement on May 8, 1837 in which they agreed to maintain Sarah's property separately. Sarah Armitage of Smith Twp, Columbianna Co, OH gives power of attorney to Samuel Beans of Solebury Twp. to recover all moneys due her.

Bk 10/pg 26   May 24, 1845

Henry Leidigh, late of Nockamixon Twp, farmer and storekeeper, died intestate leaving widow Elizabeth and no children but siblings and deceased siblings' children. The widow died on Nov 10, 1843 and the dower is now payable. Jacob Leidigh of Frederick Twp, Montgomery Co, farmer, gives power of attorney to Francis Leidigh of Frederick Twp. to recover estate due him as a brother of Henry.   Bk 10/pg 28   Mar 30, 1844

Francis Leidigh of Montgomery Co. (attorney for Jacob Leidigh of the same place) acknowledges payment by Franklin Nice of dower of late Elizabeth Leidigh, widow of Henry Leidigh, late of Nockamixon Twp.

Bk 10/pg 29   Apr 7, 1845

John Swift of Bensalem Twp. bequeathed estate to brother Joseph Swift and nephew Samuel Swift in trust for son Joseph and Joseph's widow Ann after his decease and Joseph's children after Ann's deceased. Joseph survived his father and Ann survived Joseph. Joseph left several children including William F. Swift of Bristol Borough who in 1823 assigned his share to Martha W. Tombs of Bristol Borough. Martha W. Tombs of Bristol now assigns this share to William Bache of Philadelphia.

Bk 10/pg 29   Nov 22, 1844

John Keller of Northampton Co, son and administrator of John Keller, late of Haycock Twp, assigns his share of estate to Joseph Hunsberger and John Algard, executors of Henry Algard, in order to pay debts.

Bk 10/pg 31   May 26, 1845

David Worthington bequeathed land to his son Amos who died before his father. Amos' heirs asked that the land be sold. Seth Worthington (David's executor) acknowledges payment by Joseph F. Tyson who bought the land.

Bk 10/pg 33   Jun 3, 1845

Louisa C. Feaster, late of Bucks Co, widow, purchased land in Newtown Borough in 1835 and subsequently married Dr. William B. Watson. Louisa died intestate on Feb 15, 1836 leaving minor son John Feaster and her husband. Dr. William B. Watson of Michigan releases his right of tenancy to David Feaster, guardian of John Feaster.   Bk 10/pg 34   May 9, 1845

Henry Reigle and wife Catharine, daughter of Joseph Fulmer, late of Haycock Twp, now 21, acknowledges payment of estate by her guardian Jacob Stover.
Bk 10/pg 35   Mar 31, 1845

Hannah Walker, widow of Benjamin Walker and Benjamin's children Robert, Charles W. and Sarah Allen, Henry E. and Mary Ann Eisenbrey, Cyrus and Rachel Hartley, Beulah Walker, Charles, Samuel and Jane Walker, acknowledge payment of dower by William Stokes and others, current owners of Benjamin's real estate.   Bk 10/pg 35   Apr 5, 1845

Jacob Ott, son of Mary Ott, late of Bedminster Twp, acknowledges payment of estate by executor Samuel Fluck.   Bk 10/pg 37   Feb 17, 1845

Leonard Wildonger, David C. and Margaret Price and Charles and Franey Leedom acknowledge payment of legacies by Abraham King, executor of Henry Krout, late of Plumstead Twp.   Bk 10/pg 38   Apr 5, 1845

Amos Smith of Washington Twp, Munroe Co, OH gives power of attorney to Charles Smith of Plumstead Twp. to sell land of father Aaron Smith, late of Plumstead Twp.   Bk 10/pg 39   Mar 28, 1845

Samuel M. Pearson of New Jersey and wife Juliann (late Peters) assign her share of estate of her late father Warner Peters to estate of Dr. Jesse Beans, late of Buckingham Twp, to pay debt.   Bk 10/pg 40   Apr 25, 1843

William and Anne Wharton, William and Ann Richards and Jane Richards (administrator of Henry Richards), children of Joachim Richards, acknowledge payment of dower by Charles Moon due by death of Joachim's widow Elizabeth in April, 1845.   Bk 10/pg 41   May 9, 1845

George Ullery of Darke Co, OH and wife Rebecca (late Moon) give power of attorney to Jacob Shull of Preble Co, OH to recover money from Rebecca's guardian Mahlon Kirkbride of Bucks Co.   Bk 10/pg 42   Apr 17, 1845

Susanna Gruver of Springfield Twp, administrator of Tobias Gruver, late of Springfield, gives power of attorney to Joseph Weaver of Lower Saucon Twp. to settle her affairs.   Bk 10/pg 43   Aug 2, 1845

Samuel Brunner of Springfield Twp, guardian of Tobias Huber, minor son of Adam Huber, acknowledges payment by Joseph Weaver (agent of Susanna Gruver, administrators of Tobias Gruver) of money due from Tobias's prior guardian Tobias Gruver.   Bk 10/pg 43   Mar 30, 1845

David S. Siner, Thomas S. Hinkle, Charles Hinkle, William Breish, Leonard W. Hinkle, James G. Hinkle and Jonas Ruth, children [and sons-in-law?] of late George Hinkle are entitled to estate upon death of their mother Mary Hinkle. They assign their rights to John Breish in return for his care of their mother and give him power of attorney to collect estate from George's executors Andrew Heller.   Bk 10/pg 44   Jul 14, 1845

John Fretz, son of Isaac Fretz, late of Tinicum Twp, acknowledges payment of estate by administrators Abraham, Enos and Isaac Fretz.
                                         Bk 10/pg 46   May 17, 1845

John, Jacob and Anna Leatherman, heirs of Abraham Leatherman, late of Bedminster Twp, acknowledge payment of estate by executors Philip and Abraham Leatherman.   Bk 10/pg 46   May 15, 1845

Philip Person of Upper Saucon Twp, Lehigh Co, assigns to his son Henry Pearson of Upper Saucon Twp, the share of estate coming from Philip's father Henry Person, late of Springfield Twp, yeoman, in order to pay debts.
                                         Bk 10/pg 47   Aug 19, 1845

Elizabeth Tatesman, widow of Samuel Tatesman, late of Tinicum Twp, acknowledges payment of estate by administrator Henry Frankenfield.
                                         Bk 10/pg 48   Jun 7, 1845

Elizabeth Kohl, widow of John Kohl, late of Nockamixon Twp, Isaiah and Lavina (Kohl) Kramer, Elizabeth Kohl and Isaac Kohl, heirs of John, give power of attorney to Nicholas G. Kohl to sell the real estate.
                                         Bk 10/pg 48   Aug 7, 1845

William H. Ellis and wife Ann M. of Upper Makefield Twp. have agreed to separate due to unhappy differences between them and agree to settlement of property.   Bk 10/pg 49   Sep 6, 1845

Thomas Rice and wife Mary (late Sein) of Springfield Twp, daughter of July Ann Litzenberger, late of Haycock Twp, acknowledge payment of estate by administrator Solomon Litzenberger.   Bk 10/pg 51   Oct 10, 1845

Michael Deemer, guardian of Levi and Christian Hager, minor sons of John Heager, late of Nockamixon Twp, acknowledge payment of estate by executors Samuel Heager and Michael Dech (excluding dower of John's widow Magdalena).   Bk 10/pg 52   Apr 5, 1842

John Hutchinson of Harrison Co, OH gives power of attorney to Joshua P. Watson of Harrison Co. to recover estate from sister Sarah Hutchinson, late of Bucks Co. Bk 10/pg 54 Aug 18, 1845

John Hutchinson of Harrison Co, OH (attorney for Joshua P. Watson) acknowledges payment by Samuel G. Watson who purchased part of the estate of Sarah Hutchinson. Bk 10/pg 55 Sep 5, 1845

Solomon Trauger of Springfield Twp, laborer, grandson of Christopher Trauger, late of Nockamixon Twp, acknowledges payment of estate by executors Jacob and Joseph Trauger. Bk 10/pg 56 Jun 23, 1845

Henry Mitchell of Millcreek Hundred, New Castle Co, DE gives power of attorney to nephew Henry Mitchell Jun. of Wilmington, DE to recover money due him in Bucks Co. Bk 10/pg 57 Jul 23, 1845

Henry Leidigh, late of Nockamixon Twp, farmer and storekeeper, died intestate leaving widow Elizabeth and no children but siblings and deceased sibling's children. Widow died on Nov 10, 1843. Samuel, John and Esther Bartolet, children of Catharine Bartolet (late Leidigh), late of Montgomery Co, give power of attorney to Jacob L. Bartolet of Limerick Twp, Montgomery Co. to recover dower. Bk 10/pg 60 Mar 18, 1844

Abisha Jenkins, formerly of Philadelphia but lately of Bucks Co, bequeathed money to sister Lydia and rest of estate to siblings Miriam, Jonathan, Lydia, Benjamin, George, Mathew and Joseph. Miriam (wife of Elihu S. Bunker) died before Abisha leaving children William J., Bethuel, Frederick E. and Robert S. Joseph died before Abisha leaving children Mary (wife of Edwin Townsend in NY), Caroline (wife of William Jordan in Hudson, NY), Francis (minor and unmarried). The other heirs acknowledge the right of Miriam and Joseph's children to collect their parent's shares. Bk 10/pg 61 Dec 26, 1845

John A. and Hannah Gross, heirs of Henry Leidich, late of Nockamixon Twp, acknowledge payment of dower by Franklin Nice, due by death of widow Elizabeth. Bk 10/pg 62 Aug 30, 1845

William Johnson, M.D. and wife Elizabeth (late Decker) of Philadelphia acknowledge payment by Elizabeth's trustee Henry Mitman of estate from her grandfather Jacob Nicholas, late of Haycock Twp. Bk 10/pg 63 Oct 15, 1845

John S. Klotz of Nockamixon Twp. and wife Juliann (late Yost) release their right in estate of Abraham Stover, late of Nockamixon Twp. to his administrators Barbara and Isaac Stover.   Bk 10/pg 66   Oct 7, 1845

Jacob Fulmer of Tinicum Twp. and wife Elizabeth, heir of Henry Leidich, late of Nockamixon Twp, acknowledge payment of dower by Franklin Nice, due by death of widow Elizabeth.   Bk 10/pg 72   Nov 7, 1845

Jacob Dubler/Tobler and wife Hannah Jane (late Raisner) acknowledge payment by her guardian Samuel Lutz of estate from her late grandfather Adam Shitz.   Bk 10/pg 73   Oct 2, 1842

Isaac and Mary (Nixon) Parry and Tacy (Nixon) Shoemaker of Warminster Twp, sisters of Abel Nixon, late of Richland Twp, give power of attorney to George Custard of Richland Twp. to sell his real estate.
     Bk 10/pg 77   May 5, 1845

Evan and Sarah Foulk of Morgan Co, OH [heirs of Abel Nixon?] give power of attorney to George Custard of Richland Twp. to sell the estate of Abel Nixon, late of Richland Twp.   Bk 10/pg 78   Feb 13, 1845

William M. Vickers, son of Ablegate (Nixon) Vickers, gives power of attorney to George Custard of Richland Twp. to sell the estate of Abel Nixon, late of Richland Twp.   Bk 10/pg 80   Apr 22, 1845

Margaret Lester, Hannah Lancaster, William Nixon, Martha Nixon, Samuel Nixon, Barbara Nixon, Beulah Patterson, Edwin Vickerts, Maryann Vickers and Thomas Vickers give power of attorney to George Custard of Richland Twp. to sell land of Abel Nixon, late of Richland Twp.
     Bk 10/pg 81   Jan 13, 1845

John Atkinson of Indiana, Benjamin S. Atkinson of NJ and Mary of PA, heirs of Sarah Atkinson who was a legatee of John Severns, late of Bensalem Twp, acknowledge payment of estate by executors Abraham Severns and Charles Walton.   Bk 10/pg 85   Jun 18, 1842

Henry Sassaman, George and Catharine Stone, John and Elizabeth Riegle, heirs of Jacob Sassaman Sr., late of Nockamixon Twp, acknowledge payment of estate by Samuel Sassaman, another of the heirs.
     Bk 10/pg 85   Apr 12, 1845

Peter Fluck, son of John Fluck, late of Bedminster Twp, acknowledges payment of estate by executor Samuel Fluck.   Bk 10/pg 88   Nov 12, 1845

Silas Mudge of Hephun[?] Twp, Lycoming Co. and wife Elizabeth, daughter of William Ridge, give power of attorney to Adolphus D. Wilson of Williamsport, Lycoming Co. to recover estate from William's executors and from administrators of Elizabeth's brothers Thomas, William and Edward Ridge.   Bk 10/pg 89   Jan 29, 1846

Thomas and Ann J. Paxson, daughter of Samuel Johnson, late of Buckingham Twp, acknowledge payment of estate by Samuel's son William H. Johnson.
                                                      Bk 10/pg 92   Sep 4, 1845

Thomas Paxson acknowledges payment by William H. Johnson, executor of Samuel Johnson, late of Buckingham Twp, of money to be held in trust for Samuel's daughter Elizabeth Pickering.   Bk 10/pg 93   Jan 22, 1846

Jonas Stover of East Rockhill Twp. and wife Ann and Enos Stout of Hilltown Twp. and wife Catharine, daughters of John Kratz, late of Plumstead Twp, acknowledge payment of estate by executors Phillip Kratz Jr. and Isaac Kratz.
                                                      Bk 10/pg 93   Jan 31, 1846

Jacob Moyer of Hilltown Twp, yeoman, gives power of attorney to Abraham Moyer of Bedminster Twp. to recover estate from late father Samuel Moyer Sen.   Bk 10/pg 95   Apr 1, 1845

Casper J. Foulke of Richland Twp. is due to inherit one-sixth share of estate of his grandfather Casper Johnson, late of Richland Twp, upon the death of his parents Hugh and Catharine Foulke. He assigns his share to Jacob Benner of Richland Twp. in order to pay debts.   Bk 10/pg 95   Apr 10, 1844

John D. and Mary McCarty, Thomas D. and Mary D. McCarty, Abner and Louisa McCarty, Allen and Lidia McCarty and David and Caroline Autherhold, Stephen and Hannah Acre and John and Elizabeth Autherhold (last three daughters of John G. McCarty) give power of attorney to Nicholas H. McCarty to sell land of Nicholas McCarty, late of Haycock Twp.
                                                      Bk 10/pg 96   May 1, 1845

Moses and Prudence Thomas and William and Lucy Cooper, children of David Thomas, late of Solebury Twp, give power of attorney to brother Joseph Thomas to sell the real estate.   Bk 10/pg 97   Dec 24, 1845

Elmina and Mary Ann Munday of Solebury Twp, now 21, acknowledge payment by guardian Amos Armitage of estate from aunt Sarah Hambleton, late of Canada.　　　　Bk 10/pg 100　Mar 3, 1840

William Roberts, Hannah Roberts, Maria Roberts, John and Paulina (Roberts) Penrose, Amos Edwards, Joseph and Margaret (Edwards) Foulke, grandchildren of Mary Penrose, late of Richland Twp, acknowledge payment of estate by executor Richard Moore.　　Bk 10/pg 101　Apr 3, 1845

Hugh Foulke Jun. of Richland Twp, blacksmith, owes money of Martha Foulke of Rockhill Twp. and is due money under will of his grandfather Casper Johnson of Richland Twp. at the decease of his father Hugh and mother Catharine. He transfers his right to this money, now in hands of trustee Samuel D. Foulke.　　　　Bk 10/pg 101　Jan 1, 1834

William and Margaret Cornell of Northampton Twp. sell to William Cornell Jun. of Northampton land which William inherited from his father Adrian Cornell.　　　　Bk 10/pg 102　Aug 27, 1845

Mahlon and Amelia Lloyd of Henry Co, IL give power of attorney to Benjamin Lloyd of Bucks Co. to sell their one-fourth interest in land in Newtown Borough belonging to late Ann Lloyd who left four children: Mahlon, Benjamin, William and Elizabeth.　Bk 10/pg 104　Dec 30, 1845

Abraham Meyers, guardian of Joseph, Mary Ann and Sarah Fretz, and Joseph Fretz, guardian of John and Abraham Fretz, minor children of Abraham Fretz, late of Plumstead Twp, acknowledge payment of estate by administrator Ephraim Walter.　　　　Bk 10/pg 106　Apr 8, 1845

Anna Fretz, widow of Abraham, late of Plumstead Twp, receivess payment of estate from administrator Ephraim Walter.　Bk 10/pg 106　Apr 8, 1845

Jacob Hockman, John Hockman, Isaac and Catharine Wisler and Jacob Hockman as guardian for Mary Hockman, heirs of Jacob Hockman, late of Bedminster Twp, acknowledge payment of dower by Christian Fretz, due by death of their mother Elizabeth Young, late of Bedminster Twp.
　　　　　　　　　Bk 10/pg 108　Mar 5, 1846

Henry Swartley, administrator of estate of his late wife Elizabeth, heir of Jacob Hockman, late of Bedminster Twp, acknowledges payment of dower by Christian Fretz, due by death of her late mother Elizabeth Young.
　　　　　　　　　Bk 10/pg 109　Mar 5, 1846

Letitia G. Munday of Solebury Twp, now 21, acknowledges payment by guardian Amos Armitage of legacy from aunt Sarah Hambleton, late of Upper Canada. Bk 10/pg 111   Jul 22, 1844

Elizabeth Eiler, Rebecca Gerhard and Mary Steiner/Sterner of Schuylkill Co, heirs of late Peter Gruger, give power of attorney to Adam P. Gruger of Bucks Co. to recover legacy due by will of Peter's father Phillip Gruger. Bk 10/pg 112   Apr 1, 1843

Jesse Groover, Phillip Groover, John and Sarah Kaiser, Henry and Catharine Meyers, children of Elias Groover, late of Haycock Twp. and grandchildren of Phillip Groover, late of Tinicum Twp, acknowledge payment of estate by executors Andrew Groover, Joseph Groover and Arnold Lear. Bk 10/pg 113   Apr 4, 1845

Adam Groover, son of Peter Groover and grandson of Phillip Groover, late of Tinicum Twp, acknowledges receipt of estate on behalf of Elizabeth Eiler, Rebecca Gearhard and Mary Sterner/Steiner from Andrew Groover, Joseph Groover and Arnold Lear, executors of Phillip Groover. Bk 10/pg 113   Apr 5, 1844

John Groover, son of Phillip Groover, late of Tinicum Twp, acknowledges payment of estate by executors Andrew Groover, Joseph Groover and Arnold Lear. Bk 10/pg 114   Apr 6, 1844

Adam Groover of Nockamixon Twp, son of Phillip Groover, late of Tinicum Twp, acknowledges payment of estate by executors Andrew Groover, Joseph Groover and Arnold Lear. Bk 10/pg 115   Apr 4, 1844

Joseph and Susanna McDonald of Franklin Co, OH give power of attorney to Adin G. Hibbs of Franklin Co. to recover money due them from estate of Susanna's father, John Kratz, late of Bucks Co. Bk 10/pg 117   Nov 28, 1845

Charles Taylor Jr. took part of the real estate of Charles Taylor, late of Upper Makefield Twp. and sold a portion of this to David B. Taylor which portion was sold by sheriff's sale to Joseph Janney who then sold it to Mahlon R. Taylor. Heirs J.B. Taylor, Mary Taylor (widow), Sarah H. Taylor and Elizabeth Taylor release their dower right to Mahlon R. Taylor. Bk 10/pg 121   Nov 17, 1845

Samuel H. Dungan and James Dungan, entitled to portion of real estate of late James Dungan, release their right to the grantees of the real estate and acknowledge payment of their shares by the administrator.

Bk 10/pg 123   Apr 6, 1846

George and Agnes Montgomery, Henry Blaker, William Blaker, Thomas Blaker and Levi, Peter, Belinda, George and Samuel S. Blaker by their guardian John Davis Esq., heirs of Peter Blaker, late of Northampton Twp, acknowledge payment of estate by Joshua C. Blaker, Paul Blaker, Benjamin Blaker and Hogeland Barcalow, representatives of Peter's late brother Paul Blaker who inherited property from his father Paul Blaker Sr. subject to payment of dower on death of mother Sarah Griffiths.

Bk 10/pg 130   Oct 22, 1841

Margaret Jones, legatee of Nathaniel Jones, late of Hilltown Twp, acknowledges payment of estate by John Shutt, attorney for executor Jonathan Jones.   Bk 10/pg 132   Nov 16, 1840

Robert B. Forten, formerly of Philadelphia but now of Bucks Co, and Mary Hanscome, formerly of SC but now of Bucks Co, intend to be married soon and agree to settlement of Mary's estate.   Bk 10/pg 133   Nov 4, 1845

Benjamin and Temperance Harwick, Reuben Drake, Dr. James Martin (guardian of Sarah C. Drake) and Benjamin Harwick (guardian of Evine L. Drake), heirs of late Joseph Drake (excluding Imla Drake), acknowledge payment of dower by Rev. C.P. Miller.   Bk 10/pg 134   Apr 2, 1846

Mary Waldman of Richland Twp, widow of John Waldman, late of Richland Twp, infirm and of advanced age, gives power of attorney to Richard Moore of Richland Twp. to manage her affairs.   Bk 10/pg 138   Apr 7, 1845

Francs A. Wilson of Vernon Twp, Crawford Co. and wife Mary, daughter of James Gibson, late of Plumstead Twp, give power of attorney to Haislet Gibson of Bucks Co. to recover estate due them.   Bk 10/pg 138   Jan 26, 1846

Ameriah Rathwell of Lycoming Co, attorney for Silas and Elizabeth (Ridge) Mudge, acknowledges payment of estate by William Ridge and Daniel Boileau, administrators of Thomas, William and Edward Ridge.

Bk 10/pg 139   Apr 11, 1845

Isaac Summers, Samuel and Elizabeth Ott, John and Sarah Stahr, Isaac and Catharine Wolfinger, Leidy and Mary Worman, Tobias and Magdalena

Worman and Samuel Ott (guardian for Summers Smith, minor son of Aaron and Susanna Smith), heirs of Lewis Summers, late of Tinicum Twp, acknowledge payment of estate by executor Lewis Summers.

Bk 10/pg 140   Apr 4, 1846

Aaron Green, son of William Green, late of Falls Twp, now 21, acknowledges payment of estate by guardian Samuel McCracken.

Bk 10/pg 142   Apr 6, 1846

Christian Young, Mary Sleiffer, John and Barbara Fetter, John and Mary Stone, Michael Shaffer, Hannah Shaffer, Thomas and Catharine Leister, Gabriel and Susan Rohn and Abraham Kramer (administrator of William Young, late of Bedminster Twp), heirs of Michael Young, late of Northern Liberties Twp, Philadelphia Co, acknowledge payment of dower of late Elizabeth Young by Christian Fretz, guardian of Rachel E. Mitman, minor child of George Mitman, late of Bedminster Twp. who held the dower.

Bk 10/pg 142   Apr 10, 1846

Christian Fretz, John Fretz, Isaac Fretz, Martin Fretz, Henry and Anna Meyers, Benjamin and Elizabeth Hendricks, Joseph F. and Barbary Meyers, heirs of Abraham Fretz, late of Bedminster Twp, acknowledge payment of estate by Abraham Fretz.   Bk 10/pg 144   Apr 9, 1846

John A. and Hannah Gross, Daniel and Mary Zeigler of Tinicum Twp, Jonathan Leidigh, Jacob Stearly of Philadelphia (attorney for Elizabeth Seaber, Levi N. Leidigh, Aaron N. Leidigh and Mary Kline), Francis Leidigh of Montgomery Co. (attorney for Jacob Leidigh of Montgomery), John O. Campbell (trustee for Sarah Ernst), Jacob S. Bartolet of Montgomery Co. (attorney for Samuel Bartolet, Esther Bartolet and John S. Bartolet of Berks Co.), Jacob and Elizabeth Fulmer of Tinicum Twp, Solomon and Catharine Hess of Springfield Twp, Jonathan Leidigh of Philadelphia (attorney for Jacob and Mary M. Steerly), Charles Kitchen (attorney for Thomas Leidigh, executor of John Leidigh, late of Easton), heirs of Henry Leidigh, late of Nockamixon Twp, acknowledge payment by John Emery of dower due by death of widow Elizabeth.   Bk 10/pg 145-50 Aug 30,1845

Isaac Kressman of Springfield Twp. and wife Tillana (formerly Sames), granddaughter of Elizabeth Mann (formerly Smell), late of Haycock Twp, acknowledge payment of estate by guardian Peter R. Mann.

Bk 10/pg 152   Apr 5, 1846

Mary Maugle (widow) and David Maugel, Joseph Maugel, Mary Kramer (widow), Christina Zeigler (daughter of Hannah Zeigler), Daniel and Susana Hoffert, George and Anna Keiper and George Maugle (guardian of William and Amanda Maugle, minor children of late William Maugle), children of Daniel Maugel, late of Rockhill Twp, acknowledge payment of estate by administrator Abraham Heaney.   Bk 10/pg 152   Apr 6, 1846

Eber Thomas, late of Hilltown Twp, died intestate leaving farm taken by eldest son Eli Thomas who sold it to Mr. Rhodes, subject to dower for widow who is since deceased. Heir Enos Thomas of Mill Creek Twp, Erie Co. gives power of attorney to James Thomas of Court[?], Seneca Co, NY to recover dower from Mr. Rhodes.   Bk 10/pg 157   Feb 11, 1846

Samuel Halderman, Mary Halderman, Silas Halderman, Jacob Halderman, Samuel Griffiths (guardian of Elizabeth and Benjamin Halderman) and John Halderman, legatees of Joseph Halderman, late of Warrington Twp, acknowledge payment of estate by executors John Garner and Benjamin Fulton.   Bk 10/pg 159   Apr 25, 1846

C.W. Everhard and wife Elizabeth of Rockhill Twp, now 21, acknowledge payment by guardian Frederick Althouse of estate from her late father Thomas Van Buskirk.   Bk 10/pg 161   Apr 13, 1839

Jacob L. Staufer of Rockhill Twp, son of late John Staufer, now 21, acknowledges payment by guardian Frederick Althouse of estate from late father and from late grandfather Jacob Staufer. Bk 10/pg 162   Apr 10, 1846

Abraham Leatherman and Anna Leatherman, heirs of Abraham Leatherman, late of Bedminster Twp, acknowledge payment of estate by Phillip Leatherman, John Leatherman and Jacob Leatherman.
Bk 10/pg 163   May 3, 1844

Esther McIlvain, widow and William R. McIlvain, sole heir of late Edward S. McIlvain, give power of attorney to Alexander M. McIlvain to record satisfaction of a mortgage.   Bk 10/pg 166   May 12, 1846

Elizabeth Fetter, sister [should be niece] of Jacob Kramer, late of Bedminster Twp, entitled to one-seventh part of Jacob's estate, acknowledges payment of estate by administrators Aaron and Levi Kramer. Heirs George Baringer, John Baringer (on his own behalf and on behalf of wife Magdalena) and Joseph Kramer also acknowledge payment. Bk 10/pg 166   May 15, 1846

John Baringer Jr. of Lower Saucon Twp, Lehigh Co, heir of late John Baringer, and John Jr.'s children Enos Baringer, Elizabeth Baringer and Hannah (wife of John Ritter), acknowledge payment of estate by executor George Baringer.   Bk 10/pg 167   Jun 21, 1845

Aaron Baringer, Reuben Baringer, Levi Baringer and John Kramer (guardian of Mahlon Baringer), grandchildren of John Baringer Sen., late of Hilltown Twp, acknowledge payment of estate by executor George Baringer.
                                                    Bk 10/pg 168   Jun 21, 1845

Michael Rinehard, nephew of Jacob Kramer, late of Bedminster Twp, acknowledges payment of estate by administrators Aaron and Levi Kramer.
                                                    Bk 10/pg 168   May 18, 1846

Robert and Margaret Arthur, heirs of Jacob Kramer, late of Bedminster Twp, acknowledge payment of estate by administrators Aaron and Levi Kramer.
                                                    Bk 10/pg 169   May 19, 1846

John Kramer, brother of Jacob Kramer, late of Bedminster Twp, and Christian Stout (on behalf of wife Susanna), acknowledge payment of estate by administrators Aaron and Levi Kramer.   Bk 10/pg 169   May 19, 1846

Jacob Grove bequeathed estate to sister Mary (who is now deceased) and after her death to Susan (wife of John Lutz of Montgomery Co.), Sarah (wife of George W. Jones of Warrington Twp.) and Elizabeth Frederick (of Philadelphia) and Elizabeth's children. Heirs (Elizabeth by her attorney James Gilkyson and Elizabeth's children Charlotte, Sarah and Matilda by their guardian John Ratcliff) acknowledge payment of estate by executors David Grove and Daniel Harley.   Bk 10/pg 170   May 20, 1846

Samuel Lay, present trustee of John and Elizabeth Lay, acknowledge payment by their prior trustee Abraham Heaney, Esq. Bk 10/pg 171   May 25, 1846

David Geisinger of Hilltown Twp. and wife Margaret and Jacob Detwiler Jun. and wife Catharine, daughters of Christian Clemmer, late of Rockhill Twp, acknowledge payment of estate by executors George, Abraham and Christian Clemmer.   Bk 10/pg 171   Mar 23, 1844

Mary Seesemyer/Geesemyer, niece of Jacob Kramer, late of Bedminster Twp, acknowledges payment of estate by administrators Aaron and Levi Kramer.
                                                    Bk 10/pg 173   May 26, 1846

John S. Kratz of Fairfield Co, OH, son of John Kratz, late of Plumstead Twp, acknowledges payment of estate by executors Isaac Kratz and Phillip Kratz Jr.
Bk 10/pg 174   May 21, 1846

Evan and Sarah Foulke of Penn Twp, Morgan Co, OH give power of attorney to Caleb Foulke of Richland Twp, yeoman, to recover money from son Charles of Monroe Co, PA and from Zachariah Flagler of Monroe Co. and estate of Sarah's late brother Abel Nixon (now in hands of George Custard of Richland Twp).
Bk 10/pg 175   May 18, 1846

Polly Bahl, widow of Joseph Bahl, late of Milford Twp, acknowledges payment of dower by Jacob Bach.
Bk 10/pg 176   Jun 1, 1846

Joel and Amy Wright of Morrisville are heirs of Benjamin Wright, late of Falls Twp, through a mortgage given by Mark Wright to the eleven children of Benjamin, due upon death of widow Esther. Joel and Amy acknowledge payment of their share by Mark Wright.
Bk 10/pg 177   Apr 8, 1846

Ann Nicholas, late of Upper Makefield Twp, wife of Joseph Nicholas, died intestate leaving two children: Joshua C. and Elizabeth Ann (wife of Aaron Bradshaw). Joshua C. Nicholas of Upper Makefield and wife Catharine sell their share to Aaron Bradshaw.
Bk 10/pg 178   Jun 1, 1846

Henry Kemmerer of Richland Twp, trustee of Daniel William Ale, minor son of Daniel Ale, acknowledges payment by his previous guardian Jacob Kachline of Lower Saucon Twp, Northampton Co.
Bk 10/pg 179   Apr 13, 1846

Martha Brady of Kensington District, Philadelphia gives power of attorney to William Bready of Warwick Twp. to recover her one-sixth share of land of Robert Jamison taken by his nephew William C. Jamison, from William's executors Josiah and George Hart.
Bk 10/pg 180   May 2, 1846

Sarah Mann of Rockhill Twp, spinster, now 21, acknowledges payment by guardian Peter Shive of estate from late father George Mann and late grandfather Christian Mann.
Bk 10/pg 181   May 2, 1846

David Davis (administrator of his late wife Eliza), Susan (wife of John Ratzel) and Martha (single woman), heirs of Abraham Cope Sen., late of Hilltown Twp, acknowledge payment of estate by administrators Benjamin and Tobias Cope.
Bk 10/pg 181   May 2, 1846

Samuel W. Twining of Hampton, Rock Island Co, IL gives power of attorney to Watson Twining of Warminster Twp. to recover dower from William W. Warner of Warwick Twp. due now that Samuel's mother Elizabeth is deceased.   Bk 10/pg 182   May 28, 1846

Samuel B. Brown of Trumbull Co, OH is due yearly interest from estate of Susanna Bradshaw, late of Plumstead Twp, in right of wife Mary Ann Bradshaw (now deceased) and sells this right to Albert Phillips of Plumstead Twp.   Bk 10/pg 183   May 3, 1843

Jacob Hartman, Frederick Hartman, George Hartman and Anthony and Catharine Effrich, children of late Phillip Hartman, acknowledge payment of estate by administrators John and Samuel Hartman.
                                                          Bk 10/pg 187   May 23, 1846

Eber Thomas, late of Hilltown Twp, left land adjudged to eldest son Ely Thomas subject to payment of dower upon death of widow Zillah who is now deceased. Christian Snyder of Philadelphia, assignee of son Eli gives power of attorney to Charles E. DuBois to recover dower.
                                                          Bk 10/pg 190   Apr 3, 1846

Malichi Twining of Wrightstown Twp. and wife Ann have agreed to separate due to unhappy differences between them and agree to settlement of their estate.   Bk 10/pg 190   Sep 18, 1834

Henry B. Myers of Wayne Co, OH and Henry and Elizabeth Kindigh of Columbia Co, OH, heirs of Magdalena Myers, late of Plumstead Twp, give power of attorney to Jacob O. Myers of New Britain Twp. to ask Orphans Court for an inquest to partition Magdalena's estate.
                                                          Bk 10/pg 196   Jun 13, 1846

Sarah P. Chapman, widow of John Chapman, late of Upper Makefield Twp, releases William R. Chapman from dower obligation.
                                                          Bk 10/pg 197   Aug 26, 1846

Jacob B. Kreamer of New York City, nephew of Jacob Kramer, late of Bedminster Twp, acknowledges payment of estate by administrators Aaron and Levi Kramer.   Bk 10/pg 199   Jun 13, 1846

Charles Wright of Moore Twp, Northampton Co, Lidy Wright and Rudolph Wright of Lower Nazareth Twp, Northampton Co, children of Susan

(Kramer) Wright, heir of Jacob Kramer, late of Bedminster Twp, acknowledge payment of estate by administrators Aaron and Levi Kramer.
Bk 10/pg 199   Jun 15, 1846

Jonas Wolf of Allentown, husband of Sarah Wolf, heir of Jacob Kramer, late of Bedminster Twp, acknowledges payment of estate by administrators Aaron and Levi Kramer.
Bk 10/pg 201   Jun 2, 1846

Henry Kramer, Israel Kramer, John Kramer (blacksmith), Mary Funk, John Wright, Tobias Wright, Charles and Mary Ziegenfoos, William and Nancy Roth, heirs of Jacob Kramer, late of Bedminster Twp, acknowledge payment of estate by administrators Aaron and Levi Kramer.
Bk 10/pg 202   Jun 1, 1846

Josiah Winder, Thomas Winder, Amos B. Winder, Robert W. Winder and Jonathan and Elizabeth Beans, children of Joseph Winder, late of Lower Makefield Twp, acknowledge payment of dower of widow Ruth Winder by current owner Daniel Lovett.
Bk 10/pg 202   May 7, 1846

William Shoemaker of Springfield Twp, now 21, acknowledges payment by guardian Jacob Barron of estate from late grandfather Conrad Shoemaker.
Bk 10/pg 207   Aug 13, 1846

Catharine Shoemaker, now 21, acknowledges payment by guardian Jacob Barron of estate from late grandfather Conrad Shoemaker.
Bk 10/pg 207   Feb 24, 1845

Miles and Hannah Strickland and William and Margaret Hawk, daughters of late Sarah Gilkyson, give power of attorney to Britton L. Gilkison of Upper Makefield Twp. to record satisfaction of a mortgage.
Bk 10/pg 208   May 6, 1846

Peter H. and Jane (Gilkyson) Anderson of Miami Co, OH give power of attorney to Britton L. Gilkyson to record satisfaction of mortgage given to George Harrison as trustee of Sarah Gilkyson, wife of Andrew Gilkyson.
Bk 10/pg 208   Oct 30, 1843

Wilson Malone of Buckingham Twp, now 21, acknowledges payment by guardian Abner Walton of estate from late father James Malone and late sister Alice Malone.
Bk 10/pg 212   Apr 4, 1846

Christian and Elizabeth Kressman of Nockamixon Twp, yeoman, Elizabeth (Kressman) Fisher of Nockamixon and Margaret Kressman of Durham Twp. give power of attorney to Michael Fackenthal of Durham Twp. to sell land in Durham Twp. of which their brother John Kressman died seized intestate and without issue.   Bk 10/pg 212   Oct 9, 1846

Rachel Hillpot of Tinicum Twp, Joseph and Juliann Stout, Aaron and Mary Ott and Jacob D. and Eve Ott, daughters of Henry Hillpot, late of Tinicum Twp, acknowledge payment of estate by administrators Adam Hillpot and George Zeigler.   Bk 10/pg 214   Apr 2, 1846

Jacob Fluck of Spring Garden District, Philadelphia, son of Ludwick Fluck, late of Richland Twp, assigns his legacy to Jesse H. Snyder of Northern Liberties Twp, Philadelphia Co. Jesse then assigns this legacy to Samuel Fluck.   Bk 10/pg 217   Jul 31, 1846

William T. Vandegrift, late of Bensalem Twp, bequeathed land to sons Allen and William subject to payment to widow Charlotte. Charlotte acknowledges receipt of the required payments.   Bk 10/pg 223   Nov 17, 1846

Charles and Elmira Cone, Daniel and Frances Keen and LaFayette Jones, all of Cincinnati, OH, give power of attorney to Chauncey Pratt of Covert, Seneca Co, NY to recover estate of Sarah Jones, late of Cincinnati from administrator James Thomas of Covert.   Bk 10/pg 223   Jul 29, 1846

David Grove bequeathed estate to daughter Maria and after her death to his other children. Maria is now deceased and her siblings, John Grove of Warrington Twp, Susanna Hough of Buckingham Twp, Elizabeth Connard of Philadelphia, William and Mary Swenk of Hilltown Twp, Daniel and Catharine Harley of Warwick Twp, Henry Grove of Philadelphia and John and Hannah Selsor of Montgomery Co, acknowledge payment of estate by David's surviving executor, David Grove.   Bk 10/pg 225   Oct 7, 1846

Joseph Eyre of Newtown gives power of attorney to wife Elizabeth C.B. Eyre to recover estate from executors of Isaac Eyre, late of Middletown Twp.
                         Bk 10/pg 226   Dec 12, 1846

Jacob Weidner and Anne (widow of John Seider, late of Upper Saucon Twp, Lehigh Co), children of Daniel Weidner, late of Milford Twp, acknowledge payment of dower due to widow Edith Weidner by their brother Daniel Weidner who purchased the real estate.   Bk 10/pg 231   Apr 10, 1840

Joseph Weidner, heir of Daniel Weidner, late of Milford Twp, acknowledges payment of dower by Daniel and Jacob Weidner.

Bk 10/pg 232   Mar 27, 1843

George S. Knipe of Honesdale Borough, Wayne Co. and wife Mary (late Halderman) give power of attorney to Joseph Knipe to agree to appoint of men to value estate of Jacob Halderman, late of New Britain Twp.

Bk 10/pg 233   Jan 7, 1847

Phineas B. Morris of Hamilton Co, OH gives power of attorney to Henry S. Morris of Lower Makefield Twp. to sell land he inherited from late father Jesse Morris of Bristol Borough.   Bk 10/pg 234   Jan 8, 1842

Susanna, wife of Christopher Sell of Upper Saucon Twp, Lehigh Co, daughter of Christian Bleam, late of Milford Twp, now 21, acknowledges payment of estate by guardian John Heistand.   Bk 10/pg 235   Oct 5, 1846

Joseph Fretz of Haycock Twp. and wife Catharine have agreed to separate and agree to settlement of their property.   Bk 10/pg 236   Nov 3, 1846

John Calf, late of Nockamixon Twp, left a widow Elizabeth and three daughters: Margaret (wife of Peter Cosner), Anna and Elizabeth, all over 21. They agree to settlement of the estate.   Bk 10/pg 237   May 24, 1824

Henry Baringer of Richland Twp and William Kramer of Forks Twp, Northampton Co, heirs of Jacob Kramer, late of Bedminster Twp, acknowledge payment of estate by administrators Aaron Thomas and Levi Kramer.   Bk 10/pg 239   Jan 20, 1847

Susan Fretz of Tinicum Twp, legatee of John Fretz, late of Tinicum Twp, acknowledges payment of estate by Christian K. Kressman of Nockamixon, present owner of a certain mill there.   Bk 10/pg 240   Apr 1, 1842

Levi Fulmer of Haycock Twp. and wife Mary, daughter of late Jacob Hartman, acknowledge payment of estate by her guardian John Shive.

Bk 10/pg 240   Apr 4, 1846

Henry Means acknowledges payment of estate by Abraham Wismer, administrator of his late wife Barbara Means.   Bk 10/pg 243   Jun 1, 1846

Sarah Ann, wife of John V. Schenck of St. Louis, MO and daughter of John Beaumont, late of Upper Makefield Twp, gives power of attorney to her

brother John A. Beaumont of Upper Makefield Twp. to recover estate due
her.   Bk 10/pg 243   Oct 2, 1844

John Owen of Wheatfield Twp, Perry Co, Esq. gives power of attorney to son
Grifith Owen to recover estate of late Agnes Davis due to his wife Amelia
from administrator David Todd of Bucks Co.   Bk 10/pg 243   Jun 6, 1846

Henry Frederick, son of Joseph Frederick and grandson of Jacob Wismer, late
of Plumstead Twp, assigns his share of Jacob's estate to Abraham Shaddinger.
drover.   Bk 10/pg 243   Jan 30, 1847

Isaac and Catharine (Hockman) Wisler, she an heir of Elizabeth Young, late
of Bedminster Twp, acknowledge payment of estate from executors Jacob and
John Hockman.   Bk 10/pg 244   Mar 2, 1847

William C. Jamison of Warwick Twp. is entitled to dower as sole heir of late
Matthew C. Jamison as his widow Ann is now deceased. William received
payment from William Bready.   Bk 10/pg 246   May 20, 1844

George Adam Kober, late of Rockhill Twp, bequeathed estate to daughter
Christina, wife of Daniel Nicholas of Bedminster Twp. who assigns this share
to his son Daniel K. Nicholas of Bedminster. Bk 10/pg 246   Mar 13, 1847

John Detweiler of Hilltown Twp, yeoman and wife Anna and Samuel Clemer
of Rockhill Twp. and wife Elizabeth, daughters of Jacob Detweiler the elder,
late of Rockhill Twp, acknowledge payment of estate by executors Samuel
and Jacob Detweiler.   Bk 10/pg 250   Mar 8, 1847

William Cressman of Springfield Twp, now 21, acknowledges payment by
guardian Joseph Frey of estate from late father Jacob Cressman.
                                            Bk 10/pg 251   Mar 13, 1847

John and Catharine Berndt of New Britain Twp, George and Sarah Berndt and
Adam Cressman of Rockhill Twp (guardian of Mary and John Server),
children of David Server, late of Rockhill Twp, acknowledge payment of
estate by administrator Abraham Server.   Bk 10/pg 251   Apr 1, 1847

William S. and Robert M. Magill, two of the heirs of William Magill,
innkeeper, late of Doylestown, in 1836 assigned their shares to the other three
heirs, Alfred M. Magill, Louisa C. Magill and Benjamin M. Magill. Those
three sell their rights to certain bonds and mortgages to William and Robert.
                                            Bk 10/pg 253   Feb17, 1847

William Long, Esq. of Durham Twp, deceased, and wife Nancy (late Hughes) in 1834 sold land to James M. Long of Greenwich Twp, Warren Co, NJ. William's administrators, William Stokes, Thomas Long and Abraham Houpt, agree to hold the estate harmless for any claims arising from this sale.

Bk 10/pg 255   Jul 23, 1845

Jacob Allum of Bedminster Twp. lately died instate leaving no widow but five sons: Henry, John O., Jesse, Jacob O. and William. They agree to an equal division of the estate.

Bk 10/pg 255   Sep 13, 1845

Hannah Johnson, now of Philadelphia, widow of Henry Johnson, late of Richland Twp, yeoman, and Henry Johnson, only son and heir of Grey Johnson (one of the sons of Henry), Benjamin Johnson, Henry Johnson, Sarah Johnson, Hannah Logan and Jane Johnson, children of Henry, and heirs of Henry's daughter Lydia, now deceased, assign their shares of Lydia's estate to Jane in payment of debts that Lydia owed her.   Bk 10/pg 256   Mar 22, 1847

Jacob and Samuel Sumstone, sons of Jacob Sumstone, late of Nockamixon Twp, now 21, acknowledge payment of estate by Thomas Long, Abraham Houpt and William Stokes, administrators of their late guardian William Long.

Bk 10/pg 258   [blank], 1845

Isaac Craven, late of Warminster Twp, bequeathed part of his farm to son Abraham and another part to son-in-law John Finney who is since deceased and his son Isaac C. Finney now owns John's portion. Abraham and Isaac agree to close a road that has been made a part of the bequest.

Bk 10/pg 259   Mar 31, 1847

Sophia Nase of Rockhill Twp, now 21, acknowledges payment by guardian Abraham Cressman of estate from late father John Nase.

Bk 10/pg 260   Apr 2, 1847

John S. Klotz of Easton, tanner, married to July Ann, daughter of Adam Yost, late of Nockamixon Twp, sells their share of estate to Christian Henning of Easton.

Bk 10/pg 261   Mar 19, 1847

Jacob Hendricks, married to Mary Drissel, and Jacob Swartz, married to Susanna Drissel, daughters of late Joseph Drissel, acknowledge payment by Nicholas H. McCarty, guardian of Leah Drissel, daughter of Abraham Drissel (who inherited Joseph's land) of their shares of estate.

Bk 10/pg 263   Apr 6, 1847

Carey Smith of Buckingham Twp. and wife Sarah P., daughter of Aaron Paxson, late of Solebury Twp, acknowledge payment of estate by executors Aaron T. Paxson and Ezra Paxson.   Bk 10/pg 263   Apr 5, 1847

Jonas Weydemeyer, minor child of Jacob Weydemeyer, late of Tinicum Twp, now 21, acknowledges payment of estate by guardian Michael Worman.
          Bk 10/pg 264   Apr 5, 1847

Thomas Brown, Martha Brown, John Brown and Anne Brown, children of Abraham Brown, late of Falls Twp, release their guardian Thomas Bye Sen. of Buckingham Twp. of any obligations.   Bk 10/pg 265   Dec 4, 1846

Jacob Kindig of Springfield Twp. and Maria Frankenfield, widow of Abraham Frankenfield, late of Springfield Twp, are about to be married and agree to settlement of their property.   Bk 10/pg 268   Jan 30, 1846

Christian Nicholas, late of Haycock Twp, owned land which went to his eldest son Daniel, subject to dower of widow Susanna. Daniel sold his share of dower to Jacob Ott and Michael Keller. Widow Susanna is now deceased and Jacob Ott and Michael Keller acknowledge payment of dower by current owner John Strouse.   Bk 10/pg 274   Apr 6, 1847

John Kline of Hatfield Twp, Montgomery Co, John and Elizabeth Fretz of Hilltown Twp. and Charles and Mary Ann Ruth of Perkiomen Twp, Montgomery Co, children of late Henry Kline of Hatfield Twp. who was a legatee of late Abraham Herman, and legatees Jacob Fretz of Moreland Twp, Montgomery Co, John Fretz of Hilltown Twp, Andrew and Catharine (Fretz) Swartz of Towamensin Twp, Montgomery Co, and Jacob and Elizabeth (Heistand) Fretz of Hilltown Twp, acknowledge payment of estate by executors David Heistand and Abraham Heistand. Bk 10/pg 276 Apr 8, 1847

Robert Hall, Isaac W. Hall, Edward C. Hall, Samuel S. Hall, Benjamin Hall, Edward and Sarah C. Spain and Edward and Mary S. Wallace, children of late Rebecca Hall, acknowledge payment of estate due by will of Sarah Church to Rebecca and then to her children from George Spangler, present owner of Sarah's land.   Bk 10/pg 279   Nov 13, 1838

Sarah C. Drake of Plumstead Twp, daughter of Joseph Drake, late of Nockamixon Twp, now 21, acknowledges payment of estate by guardian James Martin.   Bk 10/pg 283   Apr 10, 1847

Chas. Ziegenfoos, in right of wife Mary, heir of Jacob Kramer, acknowledges payment of estate by administrators Aaron Thomas and Levi Kramer.

Bk 10/pg 283   May 1, 1847

Juliann Summers of Philadelphia, now 21, acknowledges payment by guardian John Geil of estate from late father Isaac Summers.

Bk 10/pg 285   Apr 27, 1847

Mary Jane Doan, daughter of late Joel Doan who was a son of Eleazer Doan, late of Plumstead Twp, acknowledges payment of dower by Dr. William M. James, administrator of Ephraim Jones who owned the property.

Bk 10/pg 286   May 11, 1847

Jeremiah Fetter of Bedminster Twp, son of late Jacob Fetter, acknowledges payment by guardian Henry Shive of Bedminster of legacy from will of John Wert, late of Bedminster Twp.   Bk 10/pg 286   Apr 6, 1847

John Strouse, Jacob Strouse, Michael and Sarah Kunsman, Henry Meyers (guardian of Henry and Catharine Strouse, minor children of late Henry Strouse Jr.), Jacob Strouse (guardian for Samuel Strouse, minor child of late Nicholas Strouse), heirs of Henry Strouse, late of Nockamixon Twp, acknowledge payment by Ephraim Yost of dower of widow Magdalena.

Bk 10/pg 287   May 10, 1847

Samuel Shive of Richland Twp. and wife Sarah, daughter of Ludwick Fluck, late of Richland Twp, give power of attorney to Reuben Benner of Richland Twp. to recover estate from executors John Fluck, Abraham Fluck and Charles Wolf.   Bk 10/pg 288   Oct 12, 1846

Philip S. Gerhard of Whitpain Twp, Montgomery Co, grandson of Susanna Singmaster, late of Milford Twp, acknowledges payment of estate by executor Frederick Singmaster.   Bk 10/pg 289   Nov 30, 1846

Sarah Vickers, late of Solebury Twp. bequeathed estate to Benjamin Youells of Solebury Twp. He sells his share to Amos Youells of Solebury and Cyrus Youells of New Hope.   Bk 10/pg 289   Jun 15, 1847

Jacob Wright of Medina Co, OH, nephew of Jacob Kramer, late of Bedminster Twp, acknowledges payment of estate by administrators Aaron Thomas and Levi Kramer.   Bk 10/pg 290   Apr 15, 1847

Oliver Wilson, late of Buckingham Twp, died intestate leaving widow Ann W. and two children: Oliver H. and Mary T. Wilson. Ann, Oliver and Mary acknowledge payment of estate by their guardian Samuel Wilson.
Bk 10/pg 290   Jun 21, 1847

Elizabeth Swartley of New Britain Twp, now 21, acknowledges payment by guardian Henry Swartley of estate from late father John Swartley.
Bk 10/pg 292   Apr 5, 1847

Thomas Snyder of Richland Twp, now 21, acknowledges payment by guardian John Shive of estate from late father John Snyder and brother Tobias Snyder.
Bk 10/pg 292   Feb 23, 1847

John Heft, trustee of Philip Heft of Richland Twp, acknowledges payment by previous trustee Joseph Mann of estate from Henry Heft, late of Richland Twp.
Bk 10/pg 293   May 21, 1847

Samuel Wolfinger and wife Sarah, daughter of Frederick Wolfinger, late of Tinicum Twp, acknowledge payment of estate by Isaac Wolfinger.
Bk 10/pg 293   Feb 10, 1847

Sarah and Mary Rankin of Warminster Twp, John and Elizabeth Bothwell of Warminster Twp. and John Bothwell (guardian of Joseph and Charles Croasdale, children of late Rebecca Croasdale—nee Rankin) and Joseph and Hannah Knowles of Warminster Twp, daughters of John Rankin, late of Warminster Twp, acknowledges payment of estate by executor James Rankin as well as estate due from late brother John Rankin who died without issue.
Bk 10/pg 294   May 22, 1847

Catharine Starh, widow of Rev. Samuel Starh and daughter of Frederick Wolfinger, late of Tinicum Twp, acknowledges payment of estate by Isaac Wolfinger.
Bk 10/pg 297   Feb 10, 1847

Joseph Merrick, Fanny Merrick, Sarah Merrick and Elizabeth Merrick, children of Enos Merrick, late of Upper Makefield Twp, acknowledge payment of estate by their brother Isaac Merrick who inherited Enos' land.
Bk 10/pg 298   Aug 22, 1846

John Swartz, Henry G. and Susan Stover, Benjamin and Elizabeth Hendricks, Jacob and Mary Fretz, John and Catharine Keisinger and Jacob and Lydia Johnson, heirs of Elizabeth Swartz, late of Haycock Twp, receive payment of estate from administrator Joseph Swartz.   Bk 10/pg 300   Jun 5, 1847

Elizabeth Ray, now of Breckenridge Co, KY, gives power of attorney to Thomas Ray of same place to recover money due her from Ezra Croasdale Sen., James Townsend and Ezra Croasdale Jun., administrators of Benjamin Croasdale, late of Southampton Twp.   Bk 10/pg 302   Apr 21, 1847

John Sorver of Rockhill Twp, John and Catharine Barnett, George and Sarah Barnett, Abraham Barnett (in right of late wife Mary), children of David Sorver, late of Rockhill, acknowledge payment by Abraham Sorver of dower due to widow Elizabeth.   Bk 10/pg 302   Apr 8, 1847

John and Mary C. Hutchinson of Sangaman Co, IL give power of attorney to his brother Elias Hutchinson of Bucks Co. to sell their interest in land belonging to late Isaac Hutchinson.   Bk 10/pg 304   Jun 9, 1847

John W. and Mary Lattimore of Groveland, Livingston Co, NY give power of attorney to Amos Armitage of Salisbury [Solebury?], Bucks Co. to sell their interest in land belonging to late Isaac Hutchinson of Salisbury.
                              Bk 10/pg 305   Oct 12, 1846

Joseph and Martha Hutchinson of Rostraren/Rostraver[?] Twp, Westmoreland Co, son of Isaac Hutchinson, late of Solebury Twp, gives power of attorney to his brother Elias Hutchinson of Solebury to sell their interest in Isaac's land.
                              Bk 10/pg 306   Oct 10, 1846

John H. Johnson, Jacob Knight and Christina Frey (late Fackenthall), wife of Joseph Frey, legatees of Michael Fackenthall, late of Durham Twp, acknowledge payment of estate by executor John Fackenthall.
                              Bk 10/pg 308   Apr 5, 1847

Hannah Adams, daughter of John K. Adams, late of Durham Twp, now 21, acknowledges payment of estate by guardian John Fackenthall.
                              Bk 10/pg 308   Jun 11, 1847

Christian Trauger, John Trauger, Emanuel and Elizabeth Worman, children of Christopher Trauger, late of Nockamixon Twp, acknowledge payment of estate by executors Jacob and Joseph Trauger.   Bk 10/pg 309   Jun 11, 1847

James Jamison of Buckingham Twp. died intestate about 1837 leaving widow and children Andrew, William, James, Robert (since deceased), Sarah Ann and Mary (wife of George B. Smith). George B. and Mary Smith sell their interest in estate to Andrew and William Jamison.
                              Bk 10/pg 311   Apr 19, 1847

Rebecca Yost, widow of William Heaney, late of Tinicum Twp, and now wife of Samuel Yost, agrees to take a dower bond from the heirs in place of dower in William's land.　　　　　　　　　　　Bk 10/pg 312　Apr 6, 1847

Henry Allem, John Allem, Jesse Allem, Jacob Allem and William Allem, all of age and only heirs of Jacob Allem, late of Bedminster Twp, give power of attorney to David White of Bedminster to record satisfaction of a mortgage from John Lutz.　　　　　　　　　　　Bk 10/pg 312　Jun 7, 1847

Samuel M. Wiggins in right of wife Matilda acknowledges payment of estate by Aaron and Levi Kramer, administrators of Jacob Kramer, late of Bedminster Twp.　　　　　　　　　　　Bk 10/pg 313　Feb 26, 1847

Ann P. Swift, widow of Thomas R. Swift of Norfolk, VA, gives power of attorney to Lewis Swift, Esq. of Bucks Co. to manage her affairs. Signed before Greenbury Ridgely Stringer, notary public in New Orleans, LA.
　　　　　　　　　　　Bk 10/pg 315　Apr 22, 1847

John P. Croasdale gives up the right to administer the estate of his late brother Wm Croasdale to Benjamin Croasdale of Northampton Twp. and Joseph Comly of Southampton Twp.　　　　　　　Bk 10/pg 316　May 27, 1847

Mary Frantz of Philadelphia, daughter of Peter Frantz, late of Hilltown Twp, now 21, acknowledges payment by guardian Ephraim Sellers of estate from father and from late grandfather John Frantz.　Bk 10/pg 317　Apr 15, 1847

Samuel Wright of Harris Twp, Centre Co, son of Susanna Kramer who was a sister of Jacob Kramer, late of Bedminster Twp, acknowledges payment of estate by administrator Aaron Kramer.　　　　Bk 10/pg 318　Sep 20, 1847

Joakim Richards, late of Falls Twp, died leaving farm in Falls Twp. Heirs William and Ann Wharton, Henry and Jane Richards, William and Ann Richards and John Richards sold the land to Charles Moon, subject to dower for widow Elizabeth. John Richards of Hamilton Co, OH, gives power of attorney to Anthony Burton of Bucks Co. to recover his share of dower.
　　　　　　　　　　　Bk 10/pg 319　Jun 1, 1847

Mary R. Livingston of Philadelphia, Charles A. and Julia (Livingston) Peabody and Louisa Livingston, all of New York City, acknowledge payment by John Green of Falls Twp. of a mortgage he took from them.
　　　　　　　　　　　Bk 10/pg 320　Jun 3, 1847

Mathias Althouse, son of Martin Althouse, late of Bedminster Twp, now 21, acknowledges payment of estate by guardian Samuel Fluck.
Bk 10/pg 321   Oct 2, 1847

Isaac Heaney, Nicholas H. Heaney, John and Elizabeth Hager, Samuel and Sarah Calvin, James R. and Halenah Wiggins, children of William Heaney, late of Tinicum Twp, acknowledge payment of estate by administrators John H. Heany and Frederick G. Hillpot.   Bk 10/pg 322   Oct 23, 1847

Joseph Nicholas of Forks Twp, Northampton Co, son of Christian Nicholas, late of Haycock Twp, acknowledges payment of dower by John Strauss who purchased the real estate, now that the widow Susanna is deceased.
Bk 10/pg 323   Nov 5, 1847

Nicholas Buck of Nockamixon Twp, guardian of Frederick, Rebecca and Mary Ellen Heaney, minor children of William Heaney, late of Tinicum Twp, acknowledges payment of estate by administrators John H. Heaney and Frederick G. Hillpot.   Bk 10/pg 323   Oct 23, 1847

Henry Marian acknowledges payment by guardian John Miller Jr. of one-third share of estate from late father (including estate received from Germany), and asks that one-third share be paid to his mother.   Bk 10/pg 324   Jul 8, 1847

William Marian of Morrisville, now 21, acknowledges payment by Thomas Miller (one of the administrators of William's guardian John Miller Jr.) of estate from late father Christopher Marian.   Bk 10/pg 324   May 24, 1847

Maria Louisa, wife of John B. Davies of Dinwiddie Co, VA, is entitled to share of estate of Joseph Lantz in Bucks Co. and consents that her share be paid to her husband.   Bk 10/pg 325   Nov 1, 1847

William Durell of Philadelphia and wife Eliza (late Shelly), granddaughter of Joseph Shelly, late of Milford Twp, acknowledge payment of estate by executors Jacob and Joseph Shelly.   Bk 10/pg 326   Oct 1, 1844

Jacob Moyer of Richland Twp. and wife Anna, daughter of Joseph Shelly, late of Milford Twp, acknowledges payment of estate by executors Jacob and Joseph Shelly.   Bk 10/pg 326   Mar 30, 1844

Peter Meyer of Washington Twp, Berks Co. and wife Eve, daughter of Joseph Shelly, late of Milford Twp, acknowledge payment of estate by executors Jacob and Joseph Shelly.   Bk 10/pg 327   Mar 27, 1844

Mary Landis of Saucon Twp, Lehigh Co, daughter of Joseph Shelly, late of Milford Twp, acknowledges payment of estate by executors Jacob and Joseph Shelly.   Bk 10/pg 327   Apr 3, 1844

Jacob Shelly of Milford Twp, son of Joseph Shelly, late of Milford, acknowledges payment of estate by executors Jacob and Joseph Shelly.
Bk 10/pg 328   Mar 30, 1844

Peter Snyder of Heidelberg Twp, Lehigh Co, and wife Barbara, daughter of Joseph Shelly, late of Milford Twp, acknowledge payment of estate by executors Jacob and Joseph Shelly.   Bk 10/pg 328   Mar 23, 1844

Margaret Sabohm, formerly of Burlington Co, NJ but now of Louisville, KY, gives power of attorney to brother James S. Woodward of Philadelphia to sell land in Bristol Twp.   Bk 10/pg 329   Sep 8, 1847

Barbara Geisinger of Milford Twp, widow, due to old age and infirmities assigns all her property to Susanna Geisinger of Milford in exchange for Susanna pledging to take care of Barbara.   Bk 10/pg 331   Oct 28, 1847

Andrew Fetter, late of Bedminster Twp, bequeathed estate to granddaughter Catharine Davis (daughter of Mary) when she married or reached the age of 18. Catharine Davis acknowledges payment of estate by executor John Fetter.
Bk 10/pg 332   Apr 17, 1847

Benjn. Thompson (for himself and as assignee of Wm Burton), J.W. Thompson, Wm Thompson, Hector C. Robins, John Robbins, Thos. McLaughlin (for self and as attorney for Allen and Sarah Glasgow), Robt. McBride, George Thompson, Jonathan P. Burton (attorney for Sargeant J. Severance), William A. White, Latitia M. Burton, Margaret Thompson, Robt. R. Lovett, Jane Robins (for Ann Robins, deceased), Hector Thompson Jr. and Rosina Thompson, legatees of Hector Calbraith, late of Falls Twp, acknowledge payment by executor Hector Thompson.
Bk 10/pg 332   Apr 3, 1846

Howard and Sarah Ivins of Falls Twp. assign to John Robins their share in estate of Howard's father Isaac Ivins.   Bk 10/pg 333   Jul 10, 1847

Joseph and Catharine Fretz had assigned property to Henry Frankenfield, Esq. of Haycock Twp. to pay debts and now acknowledge receipt of the remaining money from Henry.   Bk 10/pg 334   Nov 22, 1847

Alexander Brubaker of Somerset Co. and wife Drusilla and Juliann Hoffly, daughters of John and Barbara Hoffly, said Barbara being a daughter of Abraham and Elizabeth Swartz, said Elizabeth being a daughter of Christian Rohr, late of New Britain Twp, acknowledge payment of estate by Ephraim Sellers, current owner of the real estate.   Bk 10/pg 336   Nov 5, 1847

Alexander and Drusilla Brubaker, Julian Hoffly and John Hoffly, all of Somerset Co. give power of attorney to Jacob H. Baer of Hatfield Twp, Montgomery Co. to recover from Ephraim Sellers of New Britain Twp. a legacy due them from estate of Christian Rohr, late of New Britain.
Bk 10/pg 337   Nov 30, 1847

Frederick S. Hillpot, George Samuel Hillpot, Samuel and Leah Rachel Leer and Solomon and Sipra Ann Mill, children, and Barbara Hillpot, widow of Barnet Hillpot, late of Tinicum Twp, farmer, who died January 2, 1848, agree to settlement of estate.   Bk 10/pg 337   Jan 27, 1848

Thomas Craig of Lower Towamensing Twp, Carbon Co. gives power of attorney to Samuel Nonemacher of Upper Towamensing Twp, Carbon Co. to recover estate from heirs of Catharine Nonemacher of Hilltown Twp.
Bk 10/pg 341   Feb 7, 1848

Catharine Ann Galloway Burton of Middlesex Co, England, spinster, Adelaide Sophia Burton of Middlesex, spinster, Sir Charles William Cuff Burton of Vollerton, Carlow Co, Ireland, baronet, and Adolphus William Desart Burton of Middlesex, Esq., only children of Ann Grace Burton, late of Gloucester Place, Portman Square, Middlesex Co, widow, give power of attorney to William Rawle of Philadelphia to sell land they inherited located in Philadelphia, Bucks and Northampton Co.   Bk 10/pg 344   Jan 8, 1848

Henry Fretz, Joseph Fretz, Jacob Fretz, Samuel and Elizabeth Fretz, Joseph S. and Mary Heaney and Susannah Fretz, children of Christian Fretz, late of Tinicum Twp, acknowledge payment of estate from Peter Hillpot, attorney for administrator Henry Fretz.   Bk 10/pg 348   Nov 6, 1847

Mary Smith of Buckingham Twp, widow of Benjamin Smith, late of Buckingham, acknowledges payment of annuity by Henry Woodman, on covenant of his wife Mary.   Bk 10/pg 349   Jul 26, 1845

Abraham Fluck of Nockamixon Twp, Isaac Fluck of Upper Saucon Twp, Lehigh Co, Michael and Elizabeth Weiss of Lower Saucon Twp, Northampton Co, James and Catharine Walp of Upper Saucon Twp, Samuel and Christina Farrell of Manyunk, Philadelphia Co, heirs of John Fluck, late of Springfield Twp, acknowledge payment of dower by John Fluck due for widow Christina Fluck.   Bk 10/pg 349   Oct 25, 1847

Martin Althouse, minor child of Martin Althouse, late of Bedminster Twp, now 21, acknowledges payment of estate by guardian Abraham Ziegenfuss.
                                        Bk 10/pg 350   Mar 16, 1846

Nicholas Buck was appointed guardian of Catharine, Salome and Matilda Haney, minor daughters of William Haney, late of Tinicum Twp, all of whom since died in their minority. William's widow Rebecca acknowledges payment of their estate by Nicholas Buck.   Bk 10/pg 351   May 13, 1843

John Leer and wife Magdalena, daughter of Frederick Wolfinger, late of Tinicum Twp, acknowledge payment of estate by Isaac Wolfinger.
                                        Bk 10/pg 351   Nov 9, 1847

Jacob Sames of Haycock Twp, now 21, acknowledges payment by guardian Peter R. Mann of estate from late grandmother Elizabeth Mann.
                                        Bk 10/pg 352   Apr 2, 1847

Adam Hillpot, Rachel Hillpot, Joseph and Juliann Stout, Aaron and Mary Ott and Eve Hillpot (late Ott), heirs of Henry Hillpot, late of Tinicum Twp, who died intestate leaving widow and six children, and whose widow Elizabeth died Aug 11, 1847, acknowledge payment of dower by George Ziegler.
                                        Bk 10/pg 352   Feb 19, 1848

William and Rebecca Wilson, David and Martha White, Mary Smith, Susan Smith, William D. Smith and Samuel Bissey (guardian of James and Mary Smith, minor children of Robert Smith), acknowledge payment of estate by Samuel A. Smith, acting administrator [of James Smith].
                                        Bk 10/pg 354   Jan 17, 1848

John Riale Sr., late of Doylestown Twp, bequeathed land to son John Jr. subject to payment to daughter Martha (wife of Artemus T. Rowland). Artemus and Martha acknowledge payment by John Jr.
                                        Bk 10/pg 354   Mar 7, 1848

Samuel Detweiler of Bedminster Twp, son of late Anna Detweiler who was a daughter of Christian Atherholt, late of New Britain Twp, acknowledges payment of estate by executor Samuel Atherholt.
                                        Bk 10/pg 356   Feb 26, 1847

Henry D. Overholt, administrator of Henry Yothers, late of Westmoreland Co, gives power of attorney to David N. Yothers of Montgomery Co. to recover money due estate from David and Abraham Yothers.

Bk 10/pg 356   Dec 27, 1847

Franklin M. Diehl of Richland Twp, now 21, acknowledges payment by guardian John Matts of estate from late father Daniel Diehl.

Bk 10/pg 358   Feb 14, 1848

Sydney Van Buskirk of Richland Twp, singlewoman, now 21, acknowledges payment by guardian Frederick Althouse of estate from late father Thomas Van Buskirk.   Bk 10/pg 360   Feb 15, 1847

John S. Klotz of Forks Twp, Northampton Co. and wife Juliann, heirs of Adam Yost, late of Nockamixon Twp, sell to Abraham Knecht of Forks their share of dower.   Bk 10/pg 360   Mar 25, 1848

Adam Hillpot, Rachel Hillpot, Joseph and Juliann Stout, George and Elizabeth Ziegler, Aaron and Mary Ott and Eve Hillpot (late Ott), heirs of Henry Hillpot, late of Tinicum Twp, acknowledge payment of dower by Isaac Heaney, due by death of their mother Elizabeth. Bk 10/pg 361   Feb 19, 1848

Richard T. Williams of Newtown Borough, now 21, acknowledges payment by guardian David Hutchinson of estate from late father Griffith Williams.

Bk 10/pg 362   Jun 7, 1847

Casper and Susan Foulk and Enos and Sarah Heacock of Henry Co, IN, children of Catharine Foulke who was a daughter of Casper Johnson, give power of attorney to Joel Heacock of Rockhill Twp. to sell (along with Catharine's other children) land she inherited from her father.

Bk 10/pg 362   Mar 9, 1848

Hezekiah B. Malone of Cincinatti, OH, now 21, acknowledges payment by guardian Abner Walton of estate from late father James Malone and late sister Alice Malone.   Bk 10/pg 364   Apr 4, 1848

Monroe Housekeeper of Springfield Twp, now 21, acknowledges payment by guardian Peter Shive of estate from later father Mathias Housekeeper.

Bk 10/pg 365   Mar 3, 1848

Aaron Housekeeper of Lower Saucon Twp, Northampton Co, now 21, acknowledges payment by guardian Peter Shive of estate from late father Mathias Housekeeper. Bk 10/pg 366 Apr 5, 1844

Henry Mumbower of Upper Dublin Twp, Montgomery Co, now 21, acknowledges payment by guardian Abraham Fluck of estate from father David Mumbower, late of Haycock Twp. Bk 10/pg 368 Mar 10, 1848

Henry Kratz, son of William Kratz, late of Hilltown Twp, now 21, acknowledges payment by guardian Abraham Reiff of estate from late father and late grandfather. Bk 10/pg 368 Apr 6, 1848

Mary Matilda Funk of Springfield Twp, daughter of Henry Funk, late of Springfield, acknowledges payment of estate by executors Joseph Schleiffer. Bk 10/pg 371 Feb 1, 1848

Kaufman Funk of Springfield Twp, guardian of Henry and Elizabeth Funk, minor children of Henry Funk, late of Springfield Twp, acknowledges payment of estate by executor Joseph Schleiffer. Bk 10/pg 371 Feb 1, 1848

John Frick Sr. of Hatfield Twp, Montgomery Co, gentleman, gives power of attorney to son Peter Frick of Hatfield, taylor, to recover money due him. Bk 10/pg 374 Mar 2, 1847

James Bleiler and wife Susan, daughter of Thomas Geary, late of Plumstead Twp, sell their share in Thomas' estate to Elias Benner of Plumstead. Bk 10/pg 375 Apr 17, 1845

Mary Snyder of Hilltown Twp, daughter of Henry Savecool and now wife of Francis Snyder, now 21, acknowledges payment of estate by guardian Jacob Savacool. Bk 10/pg 375 Apr 1, 1848

Jacob Race, son of late Henry Race, acknowledges payment of estate by guardian Jacob Savacool. Bk 10/pg 376 Nov 12, 1847

Henry Herpst, husband of Margaret Herpst who died leaving seven children who are entitled to a share of estate of Anna Weirbach, late of Springfield Twp, acknowledges payment by administrators Jacob and John J. Weirbach. Bk 10/pg 378 Jun 8, 1843

David Jarrett bequeathed estate to brother Jesse and to his children. Jesse had five children including Tacy (wife of James Kirk). James Kirk sells his share of estate to Jacob Kirk of Montgomery Co. Bk 10/pg 379 Dec 3, 1847

Elizabeth Ray of Breckenridge Co, KY gave power of attorney to son Thomas Ray to recover money from Ezra Croasdale Sr., James Townsend and Ezra Croasdale Jr., administrators of Benjamin Croasdale, late of Southampton Twp. Elizabeth now revokes this power of attorney and gives power instead to Samuel Croasdale of Bucks Co. Bk 10/pg 381 Apr 10, 1848

Eliza Trumbower of Milford Twp, now 21, acknowledges payment by guardian Enos Artman of estate from late father Henry Trumbower, including bond from brother Frederick A. Trumbower. Bk 10/pg 385 Apr 1, 1848

Mary Funk of Springfield Twp, singlewoman, heir of late Henry Funk, acknowledges payment of estate by guardian Caufman Funk.
Bk 10/pg 385 Dec 31, 1847

Nathan James of New Britain Twp, now 21, acknowledges payment by guardian Benjamin Griffith of estate from late father Abiah James Jr.
Bk 10/pg 386 Apr 17, 1848

John G. Penrose, Clayton & Eleanor Foulke, Benjamin F. & Maria Roberts, all of Richland Twp, children of Joseph & Margaret Penrose, late of Richland and grandchildren of John Jemison, late of Milford Twp, acknowledge payment of estate by trustee Samuel Roberts. Bk 10/pg 386 Apr 2, 1840

Charles Jemison, John Jemison and David Jemison, grandsons of John Jemison, late of Milford Twp, acknowledge payment of estate by trustee Samuel Roberts. Bk 10/pg 387 Dec 13, 1847

Margaret Jemison, daughter of Samuel Jemison, late of Milford Twp. and granddaughter of John Jemison, late of Milford, acknowledges payment of estate by trustee Samuel Roberts. Bk 10/pg 388 May 30, 1840

Elias Durn and wife Angelina (late Barndt), of Richland Twp, acknowledge payment by her guardian Peter Solliday of estate from late father Henry Barndt. Bk 10/pg 389 Apr 8, 1848

Samuel Strouse, son of Nicholas Strouse, late of Nockamixon Twp, now 21, acknowledges payment of estate by guardian Jacob Strouse.
Bk 10/pg 389 Apr 10, 1848

Able Satterthwaite of Abington Twp, Montgomery Co, William Satterthwaite Jr. of Falls Twp, executors of Giles Satterthwaite, acknowledge payment by Joseph Canby of Bensalem Twp. of a mortgage given to their father.

Bk 10/pg 390   Jun 7, 1848

Franklin Nyce, trustee of Sarah, wife of Philip Nyce and daughter of late Christopher Trauger of Nockamixon Twp, acknowledges payment of estate by executor Joseph Trauger.   Bk 10/pg 391   Apr 18, 1848

Christian Kressman and Elizabeth Fisher of Nockamixon Twp, Margaret Kressman of Durham Twp, siblings of John Kressman, late of Durham Twp, acknowledge payment of estate by administrator Michael Fackenthall.

Bk 10/pg 392   Mar 10, 1848

Mary Ann Downing, wife of Joseph M. Downing and daughter of Mary Warner, late of Bristol Borough, requests executor Joseph Warner (the other executors, William Milnor, now deceased) to sell her mother's land.

Bk 10/pg 393   Jan 1, 1848

Joseph Strawn, trustee of Phebe Mumbower, widow of Conrad Mumbower, acknowledges payment of estate by Conrad's executor Michael Dech.

Bk 10/pg 396   May 2, 1848

Adin G. and Pamila Hibbs and John and Eliza Walton, all of Columbus, OH give power of attorney to Charles Shade of Doylestown to collect on a bond given them by Charles J. Shade due upon the death of Christiana Shade, widow of Jacob Shade.   Bk 10/pg 396   Apr 22, 1848

Joel Strawn of Haycock Twp. and wife Catharine, Christian Myers of Bedminster Twp. and wife Barbara, Thomas Trowers of Buckingham Twp. and wife Magdalena, and Jacob S. Kratz of Plumstead Twp. and wife Elizabeth, daughters of William Fretz, late of Bedminster, acknowledge payment of dower by Joseph S. Fretz of Bedminster.

Bk 10/pg 397   Jan 5, 1848

John Hafler and wife Solemy, daughter of Frederick Fluck, late of Bedminster Twp and legatee of grandfather John Fluck, late of Bedminster, acknowledge payment of estate by guardian Peter Yost.   Bk 10/pg 402   Apr 4, 1846

Jacob Fluck of Northern Liberties Twp, Philadelphia Co, shoedealer, sells to Christopher and George Bockius of Northern Liberties his share in estate of late brother Joseph Fluck of Richland Twp who died intestate without widow or issue.   Bk 10/pg 403   Apr 19, 1848

John Miller Jr. of Lower Milford Twp, son of late Maria Miller, acknowledges payment of estate by executor Charles Dickenshied.
                                    Bk 10/pg 404   Apr 5, 1848

Aaron and Ann Zelner of Plumstead Twp, weaver, about to emigrate to Canada, have agreed to sell land to Saml Sine of Bedminster Twp. and give power of attorney to Samuel Nash of Plumstead Twp. to execute the sale.
                                    Bk 10/pg 407   Oct 12, 1847

Samuel Hibbs, late of Bensalem Twp, bequeathed land to wife Maria and after her death to his two children. Son Stephen G. Hibbs of Bristol Borough and his wife Mary sell their share to James Vanzant of Bensalem Twp.
                                    Bk 10/pg 411   Aug 11, 1848

Catharine Baum of Milford Twp, widow of Peter Baum of Milford, acknowledges payment of estate by John Shelly Sr., guardian of Hannah Baum, a minor daughter of Peter who is since deceased.
                                    Bk 10/pg 414   Sep 2, 1843

Silas Fretz, now 21, acknowledges payment by guardian Jacob Nash of estate from late grandfather Jacob Bissey.   Bk 10/pg 417   Apr 12, 1848

Ashbel Jones, John J. Jones, Oliver Jones, Benjamin and Elizabeth Fulton and Albert G. and Lucinda Beck, children of late Asbhel Jones, and Ashbel's grandchildren John J. Jones (son of late Thomas), Oliver Jones (by guardian George Brunner), Mary Jones (by guardian John D. James), Rachel Mathias (by guardian Mark Darrah), Thomas, Susan and Mary Mathias (by guardian Jesse Armstrong, children of Rowland Mathias), acknowledge payment of dower by Jacob Detweiler, current owner of estate.
                                    Bk 10/pg 418   Apr 6, 1848

Hester Hill, widow, and Abraham Hill, David Hill, Michael and Elizabeth Hoffard, Peter and Margaret Ott, Sarah Hill, James and Rebecca Clymer and Permelia Hill, children of Richard Hill, late of New Britain Twp, agree to sale of Richard's land.   Bk 10/g 420   Aug 16, 1848

Lydia Miller of Nockamixon Twp, now 21, acknowledges payment by guardian Frederick Stone of estate from late father George Miller of Nockamixon.   Bk 10/pg 421   Mar 31, 1846

Sarah Sheets of Nockamixon Twp, daughter of George Sheetz, late of Nockamixon, acknowledges payment of estate by Jacob Stone, executor of Frederick Stone who was George's administrator.

Bk 10/pg 422   Oct 1, 1847

Aaron and Isaac Ulmer of Nockamixon Twp, sons of Samuel Ulmer, late of Nockamixon, acknowledges payment of estate by Jacob Stone, executor of Frederick Stone who was Samuel's administrator.

Bk 10/pg 422   Mar 9, 1848

Samuel Roberts, late of Upper Makefield Twp. died intestate about 15 years ago leaving widow Hannah and two children: William and Cyrus. Hannah agrees to her dower interest.   Bk 10/pg 424   Sep 25, 1848

John P. Hood releases son James F. Hood and daughter Isabella Bunting from all debts to him.   Bk 10/pg 424   May 18, 1848

John McElroy, late of Bucks Co, bequeathed estate to widow and after her death to children Herbert, Samuel, John, Sarah, James, Archibald, Richard and Thomas. Widow and Herbert, Samuel, Archibald and Thomas are since deceased. Sarah has since married Levi Vandegrift who has since died without issue. Heirs Charles C. McElroy, James McElroy, John McElroy and Richard D. McElroy, assign to Sarah Vandegrift their interest in her share should she die without issue.   Bk 10/pg 425   Mar 28, 1848

Catharine Weimer, late of Upper Makefield Twp, died intestate leaving one sister, Elizabeth Groom, widow of Thomas Groom, late of Columbia, Lancaster Co. Elizabeth sells her interest to Charlotte Wiggins, wife of Thomas Wiggins.   Bk 10/pg 429   Sep 11, 1848

Barbara Shelly, widow of Jacob Shelly, late of Milford Twp. who died in September, 1847, agrees to accept dower in Jacob's land.

Bk 10/pg 430   Nov 6, 1848

John Fulmer, Daniel Fulmer, George Fulmer, Abraham Fulmer and Mariah Fulmer, children of Abraham Fulmer (by guardian John Sleffer), George and Elizabeth Cressman, Susana Autherholt, Levina (wife of Joseph Ritter) and Mariah Ritter, Daniel Ritter, Enos Ritter and Lucy Ritter, children of Mary Ritter (by guardian George Heft), John and Sarah Dieterly, heirs of George and Catharine Fulmer, late of Haycock Twp, blacksmith, acknowledge payment of dower by George's executor William Stokes.

Bk 10/pg 432   May 15, 1847

306

Michael Yost of Whitedeer Twp, Union Co, yeoman, and wife Catharine, daughter of George Fulmer, late of Haycock Twp, acknowledge payment of dower by executor William Stokes.   Bk 10/pg 433   Nov 7, 1848

David W. Hess of Springfield Twp, son of Joseph Hess, late of Springfield, acknowledges payment of estate by executors Isaac and Jacob Hess.
                                                     Bk 10/pg 435   Jan 3, 1848

Charles Apple of Springfield Twp. and wife Anna, Joseph Frey of Lower Saucon Twp, Northampton Co. and wife Susanna and Nathan Kressman of Springfield and wife Ablona, daughters of Joseph Hess, late of Springfield Twp, acknowledge payment of estate by executors Isaac and Jacob Hess.
                                                     Bk 10/pg 436   Dec 13, 1847

Rachael E. Moyer, of full age, wife of Dr. Joseph Moyer and daughter of Susan Mitman, late of Bedminster Twp, acknowledge payment of estate by executor Jacob Fretz. Also releases guardian Christian Fretz for payment of estate from late father George Mitman.   Bk 10/pg 440   Dec 28, 1848

Thomas and Robert Service, sons of Robert Service, late of Warrington Twp, release each other from any estate claim.   Bk 10/pg 443   Jan 6, 1848

John H. Harlan, Pamelia (widow of William Pusey), William and Sarah Roberts, all of Linonia Twp, Wayne Co, MI, and Mary H. Harlan, Joseph Harlan and Benjamin and Hannah H. Moore, all of Farmington Twp, Oakland Co, MI, children of Hannah Harlan, along with their mother Hannah, who is an heir of David Jarret upon death of David's widow Rebecca, agree to settlement with David's trustee Benjamin Cadwallader.
                                                     Bk 10/pg 446   Sep 4, 1848

Thomas Kramer (guardian of Amanda Althouse) and Jacob Gearhart (guardian of Peter Althouse), minor children of John Althouse, late of Hilltown Twp, acknowledge payment of estate by Peter Gerhart, current husband of the widow Ann.   Bk 10/pg 452   Mar 28, 1848

Emanuel Trauger of Nockamixon Twp, William H. Trauger of Nockamixon, and Michael and Hannah Dech, children of Frederick Trauger, late of Nockamixon, acknowledge payment of estate by administrator Henry Kruger.
                                                     Bk 10/pg 453   Apr 1, 1848

Samuel H. Trauger and Felix and Elizabeth Fenner, all of Plymouth Twp, Richland Co, OH, heirs of Magdalena Trauger, late of Nockamixon Twp, acknowledge payment of estate by administrator Emanuel Trauger.

Bk 10/pg 454   Dec 29, 1848

Clayton Newbold and William F. Newbold, executors of Rebecca Richardson, release her son Clayton N. Richardson of any claims by the estate.

Bk 10/pg 454   Apr 10, 1840

Lewis Garner assigns to John Morris his right in estate of father George Garner including proceeds from Fountain Inn and payment due at death of his mother.

Bk 10/pg 455   Mar 2, 1849

Felix Fenner of Plymouth Twp, Richland Co, OH and wife Elizabeth, daughter of Frederick Trauger, late of Nockamixon Twp, receive payment of estate from administrator Henry Kruger.   Bk 10/pg 456   Dec 29, 1848

Sarah Ann Wilson, widow of Isaac Wilson, gives power of attorney to Anthony Swain to acknowledge satisfaction of a mortgage.

Bk 10/pg 456   Feb 3, 1849

Joel Evans, late of Philadelphia, grocer, took a mortgage in 1820 from John Miller who assigned this in 1836 to Elizabeth Troxell who subsequently married John O. James. John O. and Elizabeth James of Philadelphia, merchant, give power of attorney to Isaiah James of Hilltown Twp. to record satisfaction of the mortgage.   Bk 10/pg 457   Feb 8, 1849

Peter Loux, Christian S. Loux, Martin Loux, John Loux, Abraham Shadinger (administrator of Henry Loux), Catharine Loux and Jesse Allem, heirs of Jacob Loux, late of Bedminster Twp, acknowledge payment of dower by Samuel Rufe due by death of widow Mary. Bk 10/pg 459   Dec 11, 1843

William H. Trauger, Henry and Mary Kruger, Michael and Hannah Dech Jr., all of Nockamixon Twp, children of Magdalena Trauger, late of Nockamixon, acknowledge payment of estate by administrator Emanuel Trauger.

Bk 10/pg 469   Dec 20, 1848

Samuel and Adah P. Lewis of Harrison Co, OH give power of attorney to Hiram H. Pearson of Bucks Co. to recover money due Adah from Samuel Watson as heir to Sarah Hutchinson.   Bk 10/pg 472   Mar 24, 1849

Elizabeth Hutchinson sold land to Samuel G. Watson subject to payment to heirs of Sarah Hutchinson, including Hannah Pearson and Samuel and Ada Lewis. Hannah has since died leaving Hiram H. Pearson as executor who is also attorney for Samuel and Ada Lewis. Hiram acknowledges payment by Samuel G. Watson. Bk 10/pg 473   Apr 7, 1849

Jacob Deetz, Frederick and Catharine Hildebrand, Abraham and Elizabeth Leister, Samuel and Sarah Nase, John and Hannah Nase and Henry Deetz, heirs of Henry Deetz, late of Upper Salford Twp, Montgomery Co, agree to sell land that was bequeathed to Henry. Bk 10/pg 475   Apr 11, 1848

Elias Kramer, Zeno Kramer, Henry Kramer, Elias and Nancy Hinkle, Daniel and Mary Ott and Lydia Kramer, children of John Kramer, late of Bedminster Twp, and grandchildren of Jacob Kramer, late of Bedminster, acknowledge payment of estate by Jacob's executors Ephraim Meyers and Joseph Crouthamel. Bk 10/pg 478   Apr 7, 1849

John Kramer of Bedminster Twp, guardian of Samuel, Reuben and Catharine Althouse, minor children of Elizabeth Althouse, late of Bedminster, and of Mary Fetter, minor daughter of Jacob Fetter, late of Bedminster, and Daniel Bartholomew, guardian of Daniel Kramer and Samuel Yost of Haycock Twp, guardian of Jacob and Levi Kramer, minor sons of Henry Kramer, late of Bedminster, acknowledge payment of estate by Ephraim Meyers and Joseph Crouthamel, executors of Jacob Kramer, late of Bedminster.
Bk 10/pg 478   Apr 7, 1849

Samuel and Mary Yost, daughter of Jacob Kramer, late of Bedminster Twp, acknowledge payment of estate by executors Ephraim Meyers and Joseph Crouthamel. Bk 10/pg 479   Apr 7, 1849

Reuben Stover of Bedminster Twp, now 21, acknowledges payment by guardian Joseph Stover of estate from late father Henry Stover.
Bk 10/pg 485   Apr 19, 1849

John Staufer of Upper Salford Twp, Montgomery Co. gives power of attorney to son Jacob Staufer of Franconia Twp, Montgomery Co. to acknowledge satisfaction of a mortgage. Bk 10/pg 486   Apr 17, 1849

Jacob Kressman of Nockamixon Twp, now 21, acknowledges payment by guardian Joseph Fry of estate from late father Jacob Kressman.
Bk 10/pg 486   Mar 22, 1849

Jacob R. Cressman of Rockhill Twp. and wife Elizabeth, daughter of George Mann, late of Haycock Twp, now 21, acknowledges payment of estate by guardian George Walp.   Bk 10/pg 489   Apr 2, 1849

Jane Eliza Vandegrift, now 21, acknowledges payment by guardian Amos V. Scott of estate due her.   Bk 10/pg 490   Apr 4, 1849

Mary Moyer, widow of William Moyer, and John Yoder of Upper Saucon Twp, Lehigh Co. and wife Catharine, Abraham Moyer of Bedminster Twp. and wife Anna and Jacob Moyer of Hilltown Twp. and wife Hannah, daughters of William Moyer, late of Springfield Twp, and Joseph Baum of Bedminster, Samuel and Mary (Baum) Detweiler of Plumstead Twp, Henry and Elizabeth (Baum) Meyer of Springfield, Enos and Lydia (Schans) Reichenbach of Upper Milford Twp, Lehigh Co. and Sarah and Abraham Schantz (by guardian Joshua Stahler of Upper Milford) and William Baum of Richland Twp. and Henry Baum of West Buffalo Borough, Union Co, grandchildren of William, acknowledge payment of estate by administrators Abraham D. Moyer and John Yoder.   Bk 10/pg 494-499   Apr 2, 1849

Lewis Eckel, grandson of John Leidy, late of Hilltown Twp, acknowledges payment of estate by executors Zachariah Leidy and George Sheip.
                                        Bk 10/pg 506   Apr 27, 1849

William J. Smith of Nockamixon Twp. and wife Catharine Ann, now 21, daughter of late John Hager, acknowledge payment of estate by her guardian Joseph Trauger.   Bk 10/pg 506   Mar 31, 1849

John Detweiler, Jacob Detweiler, Christian Detweiler, Barbara Shellenberger, Susanna Detweiler and Anna Keil, heirs of Samuel Detweiler who was due one-sixth share of estate of Anna Detweiler, late of Rockhill Twp, acknowledge payment of estate by executor Samuel Detweiler.
                                        Bk 10/pg 507   Apr 27, 1849

William Bean, Michael Bean and Mary Appenzeller, heirs of late John Bean, Abraham Bean and Mary Bean, heirs of Jacob Bean, who were heirs of Anna Detweiler, late of Rockhill Twp, acknowledge payment of estate by her executor Samuel Detweiler.   Bk 10/pg 508   Apr 27, 1849

Samuel Harr, Tobias Harr, Jacob Harr, David Harr, Elizabeth Shellenberger and Hannah Bean, heirs of Anna Harr who was an heir of Anna Detweiler, late of Rockhill Twp, acknowledge payment of estate by executor Samuel Detweiler.   Bk 10/pg 508   Apr 27, 1849

Abraham Bean, Elizabeth Fry, Susanna Appenzeller, Phrany Bean, heirs of Mary Bean who was due one-sixth part of the estate of Anna Detweiler, late of Rockhill Twp, acknowledge payment of estate by executor Samuel Detweiler.   Bk 10/pg 509   Apr 27, 1849

Samuel Detweiler, Henry Detweiler, John Detweiler, Anna Kinsey, Catharine Landis, Barbara Detweiler, Magdalena Detweiler, Hannah Detweiler, Leah Ruth and Rachel Detweiler, heirs of John Detweiler who was due one-sixth share of estate of Anna Detweiler, late of Rockhill Twp, acknowledge payment by executor Samuel Detweiler.   Bk 10/pg 510   Apr 27, 1849

Jacob Detweiler, Anna Detweiler and Elizabeth Clemmer of Hilltown and Rockhill Twp, heirs of Jacob Detweiler Sr., who was due one-sixth share of estate of Anna Detweiler, late of Rockhill Twp, acknowledge payment by executor Samuel Detweiler.   Bk 10/pg 511   Apr 27, 1849

Leonard Detweiler of Hilltown Twp. and Samuel Rosenberger of Hatfield Twp, Montgomery Co, heirs of Anna Detweiler, late of Rockhill Twp, acknowledge payment by executor Samuel Detweiler.
                                        Bk 10/pg 511   Apr 27, 1849

John L. Boyer of Williams Twp, Northampton Co, yeoman, grandson of John Boyer, late of Durham Twp, acknowledges payment of estate by executors Jacob Boyer, John Boyer and John Knecht.   Bk 10/pg 512   Feb 1, 1849

Catharine Shuyler, widow, George R. Kressler, Mary Shugan/Shuger/Shuyler, widow, of Spring Garden and Kensington, Philadelphia Co, heirs of late George Kressler, acknowledge payment of estate by Henry L. Kressler, administrator of Henry Kressler, late of Springfield Twp.
                                        Bk 10/pg 514   Apr 10, 1849

Elizabeth (wife of William W. Kucher of Philadelphia), daughter of late George Kressler, and heir of her grandfather George Kressler, late of Durham Twp, acknowledges payment of estate by Henry K. Kressler, executor of George's estate.   Bk 10/pg 514   Apr 4, 1849

Samuel Hoffman of New Jersey and wife Elena, daughter of George Kressler, acknowledge payment of estate by executor Henry Kressler.
                                        Bk 10/pg 515   Mar 30, 1848

Leah (wife of Henry Wolfinger of Philadelphia), daughter of George Kressler and heir of her grandfather George Kressler, late of Durham Twp, acknowledges payment of estate by executor Henry K. Kressler.

Bk 10/pg 515   Apr 4, 1849

John R. Kressler of Alexandria Twp, Hunterdon Co, NJ, son of late George Kressler and heir of his grandfather George Kressler, late of Durham Twp, acknowledges payment of estate by executor Henry K. Kressler.

Bk 10/pg 516   Apr 2, 1849

Henry R. Kressler of Easton, son of George Kressler and grandson of George Kressler, the elder, acknowledges payment of estate by executor Henry Kressler.   Bk 10/pg 517   Apr 10, 1848

Ely Kressler of Greenwich Twp, Warren Co, NJ, son of George Kressler and heir of his grandfather George Kressler, late of Durham Twp, acknowledges payment of estate by executor Henry Kressler.   Bk 10/pg 517   Apr 24, 1848

Mary Shuger of Fremont, Schuylkill Co. gives power of attorney to George R. Kressler of Spring Garden, Philadelphia Co. to recover her share of a mortgage due to George M. Kressler, late of Haycock Twp, upon the farm of Henry Kressler, late of Springfield Twp.   Bk 10/pg 518   Jul 10, 1848

John Kratz, Abraham Kratz, Mary (widow of Isaac Huntsberger), Barbara (wife of Abraham Huntsberger), Elizabeth (wife of John Huntsberger), Magdalena (wife of Jacob Kolb), Catharine Kratz, Margaret (wife of Daniel High), children of late Valentine Kratz, and Susan (wife of Moses Overholt) and Margaret (wife of Jacob High), children of late Anna Huntsberger who was also a daughter of Valentine Kratz, John Albright, Abraham Albright, Margaret (wife of Jacob Moyer), Anna (wife of David Moyer), Mary (wife of Jacob Swartz), Susanna (wife of Daniel Clendennan), Magdalena (wife of Abraham High), children of late Amos Albright, all of Niagara District, Canada, heirs of late Amos King, and Maria Albright who are legatees of Jacob Letherach, late of Hilltown Twp, by attorney Abraham Huntsberger, acknowledge payment of estate by Jacob Overholt and Jacob Landes, executors of Jacob Letherach.   Bk 10/pg 519   May 4, 1849

John B. and Sarah Williamson of New Albany, IN, son of Mahlon Williamson, late of Falls Twp, give power of attorney to Peter Williamson of Falls Twp. (another son) to sell their interest in land in Falls Twp.

Bk 10/pg 520   Apr 19, 1849

William Mitchel Kirk of Buckingham Twp, husband of Elmira (late Johnson), who is now 21, acknowledges payment by her guardian Charles Thompson of estate from her late father Charles Johnson.   Bk 10/pg 523   May 22, 1849

Susanna Funk of Springfield Twp, widow of Henry Funk, acknowledges payment by executor Joseph Schleiffer of estate due to eldest son Enos Funk who died in his minority without issue.   Bk 10/pg 524   Mar 31, 1849

Susanna Funk of Springfield Twp, widow of Henry Funk and daughter of Henry Schleiffer, late of Springfield Twp, acknowledges payment of estate by executor Joseph Schleiffer.   Bk 10/pg 524   Mar 31, 1849

Barbara Gerhart, daughter of Joseph Moyer and now married to Francis Gerhart, acknowledges payment of estate by her guardian John S. Moyer.
Bk 10/pg 526   Feb 17, 1849

Leonard Knight, surviving executor of Inglish Knight, acknowledges payment by Aaron Knight of money to be paid out of the farm willed by late Inglish Knight to his son Samuel.   Bk 10/pg 527   Apr, 1849

Joseph B. Lovett, Anna Mary Lovett, Daniel Lovett and Robert P. Lovett (by guardian Daniel L. Brown), grandchildren of late Joseph Brown, acknowledge payment by current owner Benjamin Woolston (who bought from the minors' father Robert P. Lovett who bought from Samuel Brown) of their share of estate of Joseph due upon the death of the widow Mary.
Bk 10/pg 529   Jun 1, 1849

Abraham Warner, Charles Y. Warner (by guardian Robert Yardley) and Hannah Warner, heirs of William F. Warner, Charles Yardley (in right of wife, late Warner), William C. and Hannah (Warner) Thomas, George Warner and Yardley Warner, acknowledge payment by Lydia Yardley of a mortgage due them.   Bk 10/pg 530   Jul 22, 1848

Asa and Susannah Ridge of Muskingum Co, OH and Jonathan R. and Euphimia Johnson of Dayton, Montgomery Co, OH give power of attorney to William Ridge Jun. of Bucks Co. to recover money due them from estate of late William Ridge.   Bk 10/pg 532   Apr 24, 1849

William D. Rosenberger of Hatfield Twp, Montgomery Co, storekeeper, and wife Malinda, daughter of John Medary, late of Warrington Twp, acknowledge payment of estate by administrators Burgess Medary and Josiah Markley.   Bk 10/pg 532   Jun 21, 1849

Jonathan and Sarah Read of OH, Duncan and Rebecca E. Eldridge of IA, John and Ann Hines and Joseph and Mary Cain of NJ and William and Sarah Lippincott of PA, heirs of Kajah Lippincott, lately of Evesham Twp, NJ, give power of attorney to William Roberts of Bensalem Twp. to sell land in Bensalem Twp.   Bk 10/pg 534   Mar 2, 1848

Jesse Rice and wife Catharine, heir of Jacob Mann, sell their share of dower to Henry Frankenfield, Esq.   Bk 10/pg 538   Feb 22, 1849

William S. Hilles of Wilmington, DE and Sarah L. Allen of Attleborough, Middletown Twp. intend to be married. Sarah owns a lot of woodland bequeathed to her by her aunt Ann Richardson. They agree to settlement of her estate.   Bk 10/pg 538   May 5, 1849

Isaac Drumbore of Rockhill Twp, Enos Drumbore of Milford Twp, Enos Schlichter (attorney for Tobias Drumbore), Catharine Drumbore of Rockhill, Sarah (wife of John Sechrist) and Mary (wife of Michael Leister of Milford Twp), heirs of Andrew Drumbore Sen., late of Rockhill Twp, acknowledge payment of estate by executors Abraham and Andrew Drumbore Jr.
                               Bk 10/pg 542   Jun 18, 1849

Austin W. and Achsah Knight of Muskingum Co, OH give power of attorney to John Lukens of Bucks Co. to recover their share of estate of Benjamin Croasdale, late of Southampton Twp.   Bk 10/pg 543   Jan 28, 1843

Jonathan Leidigh, Levi Leidigh, Aaron Leidigh, Jacob and Elizabeth Fulmer, Daniel and Mary Zeigler, John and Hannah Gross, Jacob and Sarah Arnst, Solomon and Catharine Hess, children of Philip Leidigh, late of Durham Twp, acknowledge payment of dower by Abraham Fulmer, administrator of Philip Fulmer, late of Nockamixon Twp.   Bk 10/pg 544   Apr 30, 1849

Dr. Albert Pearson of Solebury Twp. sells to Hiram H. Pearson of Solebury his interest in dower of mother Jane Pearson. Bk 10/pg 545   Apr 22, 1848

John Sisom bequeathed land in Bristol Borough to daughter Martha (now Martha W. Tomb) and if she should die without issue then to his granddaughter Jane Sisom (daughter of his son Joseph). Jane married Samuel Vanschuyver and she and her husband are both deceased leaving children Wesley Vanschuyver of Logansport, Cass Co, IN and Jane Anna Mack (widow of William Mack of Springfield, MA) who give power of attorney to Daniel Wood, Esq., counselor at law in Rochester, Monroe Co, NY to sell their interest in this land.   Bk 10/pg 546   Feb 1, 1849

John High of Hilltown Twp, Anna (widow of Samuel Moyer Sen.), Jacob and Mary Fretz of Doylestown Twp, and Barbara (widow of Samuel Moyer Jun.), heirs of David High, late of Hilltown, acknowledge payment of estate by administrators Philip and Jacob High.   Bk 10/pg 547   Apr 5, 1849

John L. and James M. Barclay, both of KY, children and only heirs of John Barclay, late of Northern Liberties Twp, Philadelphia Co, give power of attorney to A.W. Gilkison of Bristol Borough to enter satisfaction of a mortgage.   Bk 10/pg 548   May 16, 1849

Joseph Kline, guardian of Lawrence Kern, minor children of Lawrence Kern, late of Milford Twp, gives power of attorney to Charles Dubbs to refuse to accept real estate of Lawrence Sr.   Bk 10/pg 550   Sep 10, 1849

Barzillai Hare, alias John Robbarts, late of New Britain Twp, died intestate leaving widow Christiana and no issue but collateral heirs Elizabeth (wife of Thomas Keeble of Ipswich, Suffolk Co, England, gardner) and Sarah (wife of William Moss of Derby, Derby Co, England). Thomas and Elizabeth Keeble and William and Sarah Moss give power of attorney to Caleb E. Wright of Doylestown to recover estate from administrator Samuel Darrah.
       Bk 11/pg 1   May 25, 1849

Henry S. Sellers of South Bethlehem, Lehigh Co, son of John Sellers, late of Haycock Twp, acknowledges payment of estate by administrators Abraham Sellers and Michael Smith.   Bk 11/pg 7   Sep 1, 1848

Jacob Worman, guardian of Dianna and Mary Ann Sellers, minor children of John Sellers, late of Haycock Twp, acknowledges payment of estate by administrators Abraham Sellers and Michael Smith.
       Bk 11/pg 8   Jul 24, 1848

Frederick Kiser, Samuel Kiser, John and Mary Huffman, William and Catharine Campbell, Jacob and Elizabeth Trough, John and Sarah Selner, Mary Kiser and David Ott (attorney for George S. and Susanna Ott), children of Frederick Kiser, late of Nockamixon Twp, acknowledge payment of estate by administrators Jacob and John Kiser.   Bk 11/pg 10   Sep 29, 1849

Thomas H. Moon of Preble Co, OH, son of James Moon, late of Lower Makefield Twp, gives power of attorney to Frederick Kramer of Preble Co. to recover estate from his guardian Mahlon Kirkbride of Bucks Co.
       Bk 11/pg 10   Jan 26, 1849

David Wilson Small, now 21, had Marden Wilson as guardian and Jonathan Wilson as Marden's surety. Marden is now insolvent and acknowledges payment of estate by Jonathan Wilson.   Bk 11/pg 11   Nov 16, 1849

Patrick Mulvany, late of Tinicum Twp, bequeathed estate to sister Ann (wife of Dennis Sheridan) and after her death to her children James, Patrick, John, Bryan, Mathew, Thomas, Dennis, Bridge Glanin, Catharine Sheridan and Elizabeth Sheridan. Ann's son John Sheridan of Fort Wayne, IN gives power of attorney to Mathew Sheridan of Tinicum Twp. to recover estate from executors Joseph Hough and Daniel Barr.   Bk 11/pg 12   Feb 11, 1847

Anne Sheridan and her children James, Patrick, Bryan, Thomas, Dennis, Bridged Glonin, Catharine Sheridan and Elizabeth Sheridan of Drumhanon, Kills Parish, Upper Kills Barony, Meath Co, Ireland give power of attorney to Mathew Sheridan of Tinicum Twp. to recover estate from Joseph Hough and Daniel Barr, executors of Patrick Mulvany, late of Tinicum Twp.
Bk 11/pg 12   Aug 3, 1848

Moses Kramer of Haycock Twp, son of Lawrence Kramer, acknowledges payment of estate by Benjamin Kramer.   Bk 11/pg 14   Mar 25, 1837

Nancy, wife of Samuel Koon of Montgomery Co, OH, daughter of Jonathan Loride, late of Bucks Co, gives power of attorney to husband Samuel to recover estate from administrators John Loride and Daniel Daily.
Bk 11/pg 14   Sep 19, 1849

Jonathan Leidich, Levi Leidich, Aaron Leidich of Philadelphia, Jacob and Elizabeth Fulmer, Daniel and Mary Zeigler of Tinicum Twp, John A. and Hannah Gross of Northampton Co, Jacob and Sarah Ernst, Solomon and Catharine Hess of Springfield Twp, heirs of Philip Leidich, acknowledge payment of dower by Abraham Dilgard.   Bk 11/pg 17   Apr 3, 1849

Amos King of Hilltown Twp. sells to John King of Hilltown Twp. his right to estate of grandparents Martin and Elizabeth King.
Bk 11/pg 17   Jan 9, 1850

John Mill of Durham Twp. died intestate leaving widow Elizabeth and no issue but siblings George Mill of Durham, Solomon Mill of Tinicum Twp, Magdalena Teel of Wilkes Barre, and heirs of Catharine Trauger (husband George of Durham and children Levi, John M., George and Eliza Shick, Abraham and Frederick M.). Widow and siblings agree to settlement of estate.   Bk 11/pg 18   Dec 14, 1849

Josephine Collam of Doylestown Borough, heir of Jacob Servor, acknowledges payment of estate by her guardian George W. Brown of Fallsington. Bk 11/pg 19 Feb 5, 1850

Mary Anganey, widow and mother of Samuel Anganey, deceased, acknowledges payment by Samuel's guardian Henry Letherman of Samuel's share in estates of Jacob Anganey, Anna Gayman and Barbarah Anganey. Bk 11/pg 24 Aug 24, 1844

Achsah Walton of Spring Garden district, Philadelphia Co. gives power of attorney to Israel Walton of Byberry, Philadelphia Co. to sell land in Southampton Twp. lately belonging to her brother Ezra Croasdale, deceased. Bk 11/pg 25 Nov 30, 1849

Jacob W. George of Tinicum Twp, now 21, acknowledges payment by guardian Samuel S. Hillpot of estate from late father Jacob George. Bk 11/pg 25 Jan 26, 1850

Charles Kile of Richland Twp. sells to Samuel Lay of Richland his share in estate due upon decease of his mother Elizabeth Lay. Bk 11/pg 26 Apr 8, 1850

John S. Klotz of Moore Twp, Northampton Co. and wife Julian, daughter of Adam Yost, late of Nockamixon Twp, assign her right to share of widow's dower to Daniel Kleckner of Moore Twp. to pay back rent due on a tavern which John has rented from Daniel. Bk 11/pg 27 Jan 19, 1849

Catharine Sheetz, widow of Michael Sheetz, late of Nockamixon Twp, in return for all the goods she brought to her husband and an additional sum, releases her claim in her husband's estate to his heirs David C. Sheetz, Samuel Raisner, Mary Lutz and Jacob Nicholas. Bk 11/pg 28 Feb 27, 1850

Joseph D. Rosenberger, son of John Rosenberger, late of Hatfield Twp, Montgomery Co, now 21, acknowledges payment of dower due upon death of his mother Sarah by Zachariah Leidy of Hilltown Twp. who received the fund from Francis Frantz. Bk 11/pg 34 Apr 1, 1850

John Park of Pickaway Co, OH gives power of attorney to David Lloyd of Horsham Twp, Montgomery Co. to sell property received by will of late William Park. Bk 11/pg 34 Mar 8, 1850

John and Christianna Crouthamel, Moses and Mary Texter, Elias and Barbara Hartzel, daughters of Leonard Eckert, late of Rockhill Twp, acknowledge payment of estate by executors Leonard Eckert Jr. and George Beltz.
Bk 11/pg 37   Apr 4, 1850

Levi Yost, Lafayette Yost, Silas and Ann Schlichter, Franey Yost and Henry Frankenfield (guardian of Edward Yost), heirs of Adam Yost, late of Nockamixon Twp, acknowledge payment of dower by Ephraim Yost.
Bk 11/pg 37   Mar 30, 1850

John Wolfinger, guardian of Samuel Wolfinger, minor child of Samuel Wolfinger, late of Nockamixon Twp, acknowledges payment of estate by administrator Emanuel Trauger.   Bk 11/pg 38   Mar 30, 1850

George N. Nutz of Southwark District, Philadelphia Co, currier, and wife Maria, daughter and only heir of late Magdaline Wilson who was a daughter of Jacob Reed, late of New Britain Twp, acknowledge payment of estate by Henry Bruner.   Bk 11/pg 41   Apr 8, 1850

William W. Bleecker, now of Erie Co. sells to Albert G. Allen of Philadelphia, accountant, the estate belonging to late Bela Badger which was bequeathed to his wife Lucretia Badger.   Bk 11/pg 42   Jan 23, 1850

Milton Johnson and Evan Penrose Jun. of Richland Twp, guardians appointed by will of John J. Penrose, late of Richland, to his son Evan R. Penrose, acknowledge payment of estate by executors Clayton Foulke and David Johnson.   Bk 11/pg 43   [blank], 1849

William McNair of Howard Co, MO, heir of John McNair, late of Southampton Twp, who was a brother of Rebecca McNair, late of Bucks or Montgomery Co, gives power of attorney to James Finney of Bucks Co. to recover estate from Rebecca's executor Samuel McNair Sen.
Bk 11/pg 44   Mar 31, 1849

John Harwick of Richland Twp, legatee of Ludwick Fluck, late of Richland, acknowledges payment of estate by executors John Fluck, Abraham Fluck and Charles Wolf.   Bk 11/pg 45   Mar 30, 1850

Margaret Fretz, now 21, acknowledges payment by guardian Jacob Nash of estate from late grandfather Jacob Bissey.   Bk 11/pg 45   Sep 29, 1849

Frederick Rufe of Bedminster Twp, guardian of William Rufe, minor son of Levi Rufe and grandson of David White, late of Bedminster Twp, acknowledges payment of estate by administrator Elizabeth White.

Bk 11/pg 46   Apr 5, 1850

Ephraim Yost, Levi Yost, Lafayette Yost, Silas and Ann Schlichter, Frany Yost and Henry Frankenfield, Esq. (guardian of Edward Yost), heirs of Adam Yost, late of Nockamixon Twp. (John S. Klotz and wife Julian previously paid), acknowledge payment of dower by John Harpel, Esq.

Bk 11/pg 47   Mar 18, 1850

John S. Klotz and wife Julyann, heirs of Adam Yost, late of Nockamixon Twp, acknowledge payment of dower by John Harpel.

Bk 11/pg 47   Dec 5, 1849

Levi Rufe, administrator of Lydia Rufe, late of Bedminster Twp, daughter of David White, late of Bedminster Twp, acknowledges payment of estate by administrator Elizabeth White.   Bk 11/pg 47   Apr 5, 1850

Abraham White, William White, Henry and Mary Fretz, Dr. James and Elizabeth Martin, Samuel and Barbary Maust and Sarah White, heirs of David White, late of Bedminster Twp, acknowledge payment of estate by administrator Elizabeth White.   Bk 11/pg 48   Apr 5, 1850

Christian and Barbara Gross and Christian Gross as guardian for Magdalena Wismer, Hannah Landes (nee Wismer) and John Letherman (attorney for Elizabeth Overholt—late Wismer), legatees of Jacob Letherach, late of Hilltown Twp, and Abraham Overholt and Peter Loux (attorney for Isaac and Henry Overholt), children of Margaret Overholt (nee Wismer), legatee of Jacob Letherach, acknowledge payment of estate by executors Jacob Overholt and Jacob Landes.   Bk 11/pg 48   Jun 18, 1849

Sarah S. Allen (late Taylor) of Middletown Twp. gives power of attorney to Caleb N. Taylor to record satisfaction of a mortgage.

Bk 11/pg 50   Apr 11, 1850

Abraham Fluck, Lewis Fluck, Jesse Fluck, Jacob Fluck, Samuel Fluck, Maria Snyder, Elizabeth Hinkle, Catharine Durn, Hannah Ahlum, Nancy Wolf and Sarah Shive, give power of attorney to Charles Wolf to acknowledge satisfaction of a mortgage from Herman Ahlum. Bk 11/pg 50   Apr 1, 1850

Peter Gares of Bedminster Twp. and wife Elizabeth, daughter of Frederick Trauger, late of Haycock Twp, sell to William Trauger of Haycock Twp. their right in widow's dower. Bk 11/pg 52 Apr 26, 1850

Ezra Croasdale of Southampton Twp. died last August 20 intestate, unmarried and without issue but leaving two sisters: Grace Knight (widow of Asa Knight) and Achsah Walton (widow of James Walton) and deceased sister Sarah (wife of John Larue, also deceased, children Marmaduke, Mary Knight, Ezra, Carey, Asa and Moses). Grace Knight of Bristol Borough, Marmaduke and Sarah Larue of Southampton Twp, Joseph P. and Mary Knight of Bensalem Twp, Ezra and Mary Ann Larue of Lower Makefield Twp, Carey and Mary Larue of Mansfield Twp, Burlington Co, NJ and Moses Larue of Clearfield Co. give power of attorney to Caleb N. Taylor of Bristol Twp. to sell their shares of the real estate. Bk 11/pg 53 Oct 27, 1849

Jacob S. Shelly of Milford Twp. and William B. Shelly (guardian of John W. Shelly, minor son of Michael Shelly), Samuel and Elizabeth Moyer of Springfield Twp, Samuel K. and Susanna Harley of Salford Twp, Montgomery Co, Levi and Barbara Shelly of Milford Twp, children of Jacob Shelly, late of Milford Twp, acknowledge payment of estate by administrators Joseph S. Shelly, David S. Shelly and William H. Oberholtzer.
Bk 11/pg 55 Apr 1, 1850

William Rymond, Paul Rymond and David and Anna Rapp, children of Michael Rymond, late of Nockamixon Twp, acknowledge payment of estate by executors Samuel and George Rymond. Bk 11/pg 60 Nov 30, 1849

Samuel Fulmer, Enos Fulmer, Joseph Fulmer, Peter and Elizabeth Nicholas, Levi and Mary Strouse, Abraham S. and Sarah Stover, Henry and Catharine Reigle, heir of Joseph Fulmer, late of Haycock Twp, acknowledge payment of dower by Anna Fulmer. Bk 11/pg 61 Apr 3, 1850

Enos Fulmer, Joseph Fulmer, Peter and Elizabeth Nicholas, Levi and Mary Strouse, Abraham S. and Sarah Stover, Henry and Catharine Reigle and Anna Fulmer, heirs of Joseph Fulmer, late of Haycock Twp, acknowledge payment of dower by Samuel Fulmer. Bk 11/pg 61 Apr 3, 1850

Enos Fulmer, Joseph Fulmer, Peter and Elizabeth Nicholas, Levi and Mary Strouse, Abraham S. and Sarah Stover, Henry and Catharine Reigle and Anna Fulmer, heirs of Catharine Fulmer, late of Haycock Twp, acknowledge payment of estate by executor Samuel Fulmer. Bk 11/pg 62 Apr 3, 1850

Jacob and Joseph Fretz, brothers of John Fretz, late of Nockamixon Twp, acknowledge payment by Christian R. Kressman for lien on property he purchased from John Fretz and Henry and Elizabeth Fretz.

Bk 11/pg 62   May 22, 1850

Henry M. Puff of Doylestown Twp. and Elizabeth Bowers of Doylestown Twp. are intended to be married soon. They agree to settlement of Elizabeth's property.

Bk 11/pg 63   Feb 24, 1848

James Chapman bequeathed estate after decease of his widow to daughters Elizabeth Iden, Abigail Chapman and granddaughter Juliann Maria Chapman and appointed son-in-law Samuel Iden as executor. Samuel and Elizabeth Iden are both deceased leaving children James C. and Ellen Iden. John P. Thornton of Solebury Twp. and wife Juliann Maria acknowledge payment of estate by Samuel Iden (during his lifetime) and his two children since his death.

Bk 11/pg 66   Jun 24, 1850

E. Morris Lloyd and Henry C. Lloyd of Doylestown Borough, grandsons of late Enos Morris, Esq., acknowledge payment of estate by guardian James Gilkyson of Doylestown Borough.

Bk 11/pg 67   Jul 3, 1850

John Frantz, son of Peter Frantz, late of Hilltown Twp, now 21, acknowledges payment of estate by guardian Ephraim Sellers.   Bk 11/pg 68   Apr 2, 1849

Samuel and Elizabeth Fretz of Montville Twp, Medina Co, OH give power of attorney to Lewis Fretz of Somerville, Somerset Co, NJ to recover from executors of John Fretz a legacy due to Elizabeth.   Bk 11/pg 68   Jun 7, 1850

Lewis Fretz (attorney for Samuel and Elizabeth Fretz, said Elizabeth being heir to her uncle John Fretz, late of Nockamixon Twp) acknowledges payment by Christian K. Kressman, current owner of the estate, a lien due now that the widow Ann is remarried.   Bk 11/pg 69   Jul 5, 1850

Jacob and Joseph Fretz, brothers of John Fretz, late of Nockamixon Twp, acknowledge payment of dower by Charles Trauger and Nathan Wolfinger, current owners of John's land.   Bk 11/pg 69   May 22, 1850

Ann Eliza Ulrich, granddaughter of Andrew Fetter, late of Bedminster Twp, acknowledges payment of estate by executor John Fetter.

Bk 11/pg 71   Aug 1, 1850

Lydia Howell of Bristol Twp, daughter of William Howell, late of Bristol Twp, acknowledges payment of estate by executors Joseph M. Howell, Amos B. Howell and Harvey Howell.   Bk 11/pg 72   Apr 27, 1850

William Vansant of Bristol Twp. and wife Elizabeth, daughter of William Howell acknowledges payment of estate by executors Joseph M. Howell, Amos B. Howell and Harvey Howell.   Bk 11/pg 73   Apr 27, 1850

Phebe Howell, widow of William Howell, late of Bristol Twp, acknowledges payment of estate by executors Joseph M. Howell, Amos B. Howell and Harvey Howell.   Bk 11/pg 73   Apr 26, 1850

Ulrich Hockman Sen. and Ulrich Hockman Jr., guardians of Ulrich and Anna Hockman, children of Jacob Hockman, deceased, acknowledge payment of estate by Philip Letherman, executor of Catharine Letherman.
           Bk 11/pg 74   May 16, 1850

Abigail Chapman of Solebury Twp, daughter of James Chapman, acknowledges payment of estate by executor Samuel Iden and by his children James C. and Ellen Iden.   Bk 11/pg 75   Jun, 1850

William Heffley, son of late Barbara Heffley, acknowledges payment by Ephraim Sellers, current owner of land previously owned by Christian Rohr, of estate due by Christian's will.   Bk 11/pg 75   Sep 6, 1850

Samuel Landes of Rockhill Twp, guardian of Mary Stouffer, minor daughter of John Stouffer, late of Rockhill Twp, acknowledges payment of estate by Mary's former guardian Samuel Wampole.   Bk 11/pg 76   Aug 16, 1850

Jacob Dirstine (guardian of Mary Horning), Henry Dirstine (guardian of Samuel Horning) and Manassah Bean (guardian of Sarah and Enos Horning), all of Rockhill Twp, minor children of late Samuel Horning, acknowledge payment of estate by administrators Joseph and Abel Horning.
           Bk 11/pg 76   Apr 21, 1849

William R. Strawn of Greene Co, son of Abel Strawn, late of Bucks Co, gives power of attorney to Josiah Hart of Doylestown to recover money due from Abel's estate.   Bk 11/pg 77   Jan 31, 1850

Josiah Hart (attorney for William R. Strawn) acknowledges payment of estate by executors Daniel Strawn and Joel Strawn.   Bk 11/pg 77   Feb 25, 1850

Joseph Strawn of Doylestown, James and Ann Johnson of Milford Twp, Lehigh Co, Mary Strawn of Haycock Twp, David and Elizabeth Hill of Doylestown Twp. and Charles and Esther Johnson of Richland Twp, children of Abel Strawn, late of Haycock Twp, acknowledge payment of estate by executors Daniel and Joel Strawn.   Bk 11/pg 78   Nov 26, 1849

David C. Sheetz, Jacob Nicholas and Mary Lutz, legatees of Michael Sheetz of Nockamixon Twp, acknowledge payment of estate by Samuel S. Raisner.
                                              Bk 11/pg 78   Jun 15, 1850

Abel Swartzlander and Catharine Swartzlander of Doylestown Twp. and Henry Leicey of Hilltown Twp. (guardian of Elizabeth and Mary Swartzlander), legatees of Abel Strawn, late of Haycock Twp, acknowledge payment of estate by executors Daniel Strawn and Joel Strawn.
                                              Bk 11/pg 79   Apr 3, 1850

George and Elizabeth Sheib, Jacob and Fronica Swink, Jacob and Sarah Reed and David and Hannah Backman, daughters of John Leidy, late of Hilltown Twp, acknowledge payment of estate by executor Zachariah Leidy.
                                              Bk 11/pg 80   Apr 5, 1850

David Comfort of Philadelphia previously transferred to Stephen W. Comfort his right in estate of mother Sarah Comfort. Stephen further assigns this right to Jeremiah Comfort of Philadelphia Co.   Bk 11/pg 81   Oct 2, 1850

William Addis, administrator of Henry Raisner, late of Warwick Twp, who was a legatee of John Morris of Bucks Co, acknowledges payment of estate by executor Morris Morris.   Bk 11/pg 81   Oct 12, 1850

Mary Rose, wife of Samuel Rose of Solebury Twp, entitled to estate from late father Joseph Scarborough, transfers her right to husband Samuel.
                                              Bk 11/pg 82   Oct 12, 1850

Deborah Balderston, daughter of John W. Balderston, late of Solebury Twp, acknowledges payment of estate by brother Oliver Balderston.
                                              Bk 11/pg 82   Sep 16, 1850

Assenath Walker, late of Buckingham Twp, bequeathed one-fifth of her estate in trust to sons Amos and Stacy Walker to pay to the children of her daughter Ann (wife of David Carver) when they became 21. Ann Carver is deceased and her daughter Sarah Ann Carver of Solebury Twp, now 21, acknowledges payment of estate by Amos and Stacy Walker. Bk 11/pg 84   Sep 28, 1850

John Beaumont, late of Upper Makefield Twp, requested his executors Elizabeth Beaumont and Merrick Reeder to hold estate in trust for his daughter Sarah Ann Beaumont or sell it on her behalf. Elizabeth is since deceased and Merrick Reeder sold the land to benefit Sarah Ann (now wife of John B. Schenck) and purchased other land with the proceeds. Should Sarah Ann die without issue, this land will pass to H. Nelson Beaumont, A. Jackson Beaumont, George H. Beaumont and John A. Beaumont. These four release their right to the land to Sarah Ann Schenck. Bk 11/pg 85   Apr 12, 1850

John A. Beaumont of Upper Makefield Twp, son of John Beaumont, late of Upper Makefield, releases executor Merrick Reeder from responsibility as his brother Horatio N. Beaumont has promised to pay his share.
Bk 11/pg 86   Jan 26, 1843

William H. Long of Warrington Twp, son of John Long, late of Warwick Twp, transfers his share of estate to Moses Lukens of Montgomery Co.
Bk 11/pg 86   Nov 1, 1850

Sarah Kohl, widow of Conrad Kohl, late of Nockamixon Twp, and John Kohl, Thomas Kohl, Samuel Kohl, Michael Kohl Sen. (guardian of Aaron Kohl), Levi and Catharine Trauger and Frederick and Alvina Trauger, children of Conrad, acknowledge payment of estate by administrators Michael and Jacob Kohl.   Bk 11/pg 86   Apr 13, 1844

Lydia Savacool of Hilltown Twp, now 21, acknowledges payment by Elias and Jacob Harr, administrators of her former guardian David Harr Sen., deceased.   Bk 11/pg 87 Nov 26, 1850

Thomas Dunlap, guardian of John C. Craig (a minor), gives power of attorney to Edward J. Fox of Doylestown Borough to acknowledge satisfaction of a mortgage from John Dunlap.   Bk 11/pg 91   Dec 17, 1850

Elizabeth K. Ott, now 21, acknowledges payment by guardian Abraham Ott of estate due from late grandparents Michael and Mary Kulp and from late uncle Andrew Kulp.   Bk 11/pg 92   Apr 8, 1845

John Fell, late of Plumstead Twp, bequeathed land to daughters Hannah, Martha and Jane, subject to payment to son Samuel and daughter Ann. Samuel Fell and Ann (Fell) Townsend acknowledge payment of their shares and release Charles Smith (who purchased the land) from any obligation.
Bk 11/pg 93   Nov 14, 1850

Joseph Letherman of Hilltown Twp. is about to move to the western states and gives power of attorney to John Letherman of Bedminster Twp. to settle affairs for him. Bk 11/pg 99 Apr 4, 1840

James Jamison, late of Buckingham Twp, died leaving widow Ann and children Andrew S., Sarah Ann, William, Mary S. (wife of George B. Smith) and James. George B. Smith of Cecil Co, MD and wife Mary S. give power of attorney to Richard Watson of Doylestown Borough to sell their right to estate. Bk 11/pg 99 Jan 25, 1851

Andrew S. Jamison of Cheraw, Chesterfield District, South Carolina gives power of attorney to Richard Watson of Doylestown Borough to sell his share of estate of his father James Jamison, late of Buckingham Twp. Bk 11/pg 100 Jan 28, 1851

John Lay Jr. of Haycock Twp. sells to Samuel Lay of Richland Twp. his share of estate due upon the death of his mother Elizabeth Lay. Bk 11/pg 100 Feb 4, 1851

Samuel Stout of South Whitehall Twp, Lehigh Co, brother of Elizabeth Stout, late of Bedminster Twp, acknowledges payment of estate by administrator Henry Stout. Bk 11/pg 101 Aug 14, 1846

Peter and John Stout and Magdalena Stout, siblings of Elizabeth Stout, late of Bedminster Twp, and Joseph Stout and Philip K. and Catharine Krout, children of late Daniel Stout, another brother, and John Hager, guardian of Elizabeth Kemerer, daughter of late Mary Kemerer [sister of Elizabeth?], acknowledge payment of estate by administrator Henry Stout. Bk 11/pg 101 Sep 25, 1846

Christian Myers, guardian of Elias Hager, son of Mary Stout, late of Bedminster Twp, acknowledges payment of estate by executor Henry Stout. Bk 11/pg 102 Feb 25, 1851

Jonathan Beans (in right of wife Elizabeth), Charles E. DuBois (assignee of Benjn. Moore, in right of wife Rachel), Joseph Winder, Thomas Winder, Amos B. Winder and P. Robert Winder, heirs of Joseph Winder, late of Lower Makefield Twp, acknowledge payment by Jonathan T. Schofield of estate due upon death of widow Ruth. Bk 11/pg 103 Oct 7, 1846

325

Charles Yeakle of Upper Hanover Twp, Montgomery Co. and wife Susanna, daughter of David Yeakle, late of Milford Twp, acknowledge payment of dower by Jacob Clymer, Esq. (assignee of Henry M. Shelly).
Bk 11/pg 105   Mar 13, 1851

Harman Yerkes of Warminster Twp, farmer, acknowledges payment of estate by Stephen Yerkes of Warminster Twp, due by will of his father Harman Yerkes,   Bk 11/pg 109   Mar 31, 1851

Tamar Betts and Hannah H. Betts acknowledge payment of legacy by brother Cyrus Betts, as instructed by will of their father Thomas Betts, late of Buckingham Twp.   Bk 11/pg 109   Apr 2, 1851

Lewis Willard of Southampton Twp. executes a bond to Hannah Willard, widow of his father Jacob Willard, late of Wrightstown Twp. to pay a legacy given to Hannah by Jacob's will.   Bk 11/pg 110   Apr 1, 1851

Hannah Long of Warrington Twp, spinster, now 21, acknowledges payment by guardian Amos Scarborough of estate from late father Andrew Long.
Bk 11/pg 112   Apr 5, 1851

Charles Kemerer of Richland Twp. and wife Elizabeth, now 21, daughter of late Samuel Leidy and legatee of John Leidy, late of Durham Twp, acknowledge payment of estate by testamentary guardian Benjamin Riegle.
Bk 11/pg 112   Mar 24, 1851

Catharine Eckhart, widow of George Eckhart of New Britain Twp, Jacob and Elizabeth Wisler of Hatfield Twp, Montgomery Co, Samuel and Mary Donehower of Montgomery Twp, Montgomery Co, Sarah King of Hilltown Twp, daughters of Martin King Sen., late of Hilltown Twp, and Samuel King and Elizabeth Wagner, children of Henry King, late of Philadelphia Co, who was a son of Martin, and John F. King of New Britain Twp. and John and Catharine Kimble of Buckingham Twp, children of late Martin King, who was another son of Martin Sen., acknowledge payment of estate by administrators Peter and John King.   Bk 11/pg 113   Apr 8, 1851

Nathan Mack and wife Rachel (nee Kortz) and Susanna Kortz, granddaughters of John Keller, late of Haycock Twp, acknowledge payment of dower by Abraham Stover of Haycock Twp, due by death of widow Margaret.   Bk 11/pg 114   Apr 5, 1851

John Keller, Thomas Keller, William Keller, Hannah Amey (widow), Mary Kerch (widow), Henry and Margaret Gearhard and Jacob and Sarah Dreisbach, children of John Keller, late of Haycock Twp, acknowledge payment of dower by Abraham Stover of Haycock Twp, due by death of widow Margaret.   Bk 11/pg 115   Apr 5, 1851

John D. Young, Esq., attorney for Samuel B. Keller, son of John Keller, late of Haycock Twp, acknowledges payment of dower by Abraham Stover of Haycock Twp, due by death of widow Margaret.   Bk 11/pg 116   Apr 5, 1851

Mariah Muss of Haycock Twp, spinster, now 21, acknowledges payment by guardian Nicholas Heft of estate from late mother Catharine Muss.
                               Bk 11/pg 116   Apr 13, 1849

Thomas Jones, late of Hilltown Twp, bequeathed that his land be sold subject to dower for wife Susanna and at her death to be paid to his four daughters: Philadelphia, Mary, Clarissa and Lavina. Susanna died Jul 12, 1850. Daughter Mary Jones died leaving a will dated Sep 3, 1825 with Griffith Jones as executor. John and Philadelphia Jones of Buckingham Twp, Griffith Jones (trustee for Clarissa Jones), Griffith Jones (executor of Mary Jones) and Manuel and Lavina Gibbs of New York City acknowledge payment of dower by John Sheip, executor of Christian Frederick Fisher who owned part of the land.   Bk 11/pg 117   Apr 14, 1851

Elizabeth Musselman, Fanny Clymer, Mary Fretz and Barbara Landes, daughters of Henry Landis, late of Haycock Twp, acknowledge payment of estate by executors Tobias and Daniel Landis.   Bk 11/pg 118   Apr 4, 1851

Magdelane Hager of Nockamixon Twp, now 21, acknowledges payment by guardian John Trauger of estate from late father John Hager.
                               Bk 11/pg 119   Apr 5, 1851

Isaiah B. Terry and wife Rebecca of Wrightstown Twp. have agreed to separate due to unhappy differences between them and agree to settlement of property.   Bk 11/pg 120   Apr 19, 1851

John and Ellen Service, John and Rachel McNair, Elizabeth Service and Mary Service (single women), all of Warrington Twp, all daughters of Robert Service, late of Warrington Twp, acknowledge payment of estate by Robert's sons and executors Robert and Thomas Service.   Bk 11/pg 125   Apr 6, 1850

Eveline Twining and Samuel and Mary (Scarborough) Rose, heirs of Joseph Scarborough, late of Solebury Twp, acknowledge payment of estate by administrators Sarah Scarborough and _____ Scarborough.

Bk 11/pg 126   Apr 3, 1851

Samuel Scheetz, Lewis Scheetz, Hannah (Scheetz) Walp and Olivia (Scheetz) Link of Richland Twp. give power of attorney to William Benner of Richland Twp. to record satisfaction of a mortgage from George Stanner.

Bk 11/pg 130   Apr 2, 1851

William Green of Quakertown gives power of attorney to son Richard Green of Quakertown to recover moneys due him.   Bk 11/pg 131   Jan 24, 1851

Isaiah and Esther Michener, Benjamin Good, Sarah Ann Good, Charles Good (in Indianapolis), Joel Heacock and Jonathan and Margaret Carr acknowledge payment of dower by John Good on property formerly of late John Good, for the benefit of John's wife Margaret.   Bk 11/pg 132   Apr 23, 1847

Joseph and Lena Larzalere of Springfield Twp, Muskingkum Co, OH and Ann Larzalere of Bristol Twp, the two eldest children of Benjamin and Sarah (Brown) Larzalere, both late of Bristol Twp, acknowledge payment of estate by administrators William Larzalere and James Harrison.

Bk 11/pg 134   Apr 18, 1851

Charles Lovett transfers to William Neal his right in the dower of his mother Margaret Lovett, now in hands of George Ettinger.

Bk 11/pg 136   Apr 2, 1851

Allen and Beulah South, Isaac and Sarah South, William Neal (attorney for Charles Lovett) and Charles White (guardian of Aaron Lovett), all of Lower Makefield Twp. and children of late Samuel Lovett who died intestate leaving a widow and four children, give power of attorney to Anthony Burton of Bristol Twp. to recover money due from George Ettinger who purchased the real estate.   Bk 11/pg 136   Apr 2, 1851

Peter Leer, George Leer, Samuel Leer, Catharine Snyder (widow of Barnet Snyder), Frederick and Elizabeth George, Susannah Gary (widow of George Gary), Mary Maust (widow of George Maust), children of Joseph Leer, late of Tinicum Twp. and Franklin B. Leer, son of late John Leer and grandson of Joseph, acknowledge payment of estate by administrator Joseph Leer Jr.

Bk 11/pg 137   Dec 25, 1850

Susanna Funk, widow of Henry Funk Jr., late of Springfield Twp, heir of Enos Funk, late of Springfield Twp (minor son of Henry) acknowledges payment of estate by Enos' guardian Kaufman Funk.

Bk 11/pg 138   Dec 13, 1849

Aaron Meyers and wife Barbara, daughter of Isaac Rickert, late of Hilltown Twp, acknowledges payment of estate by her guardian John Hackman.

Bk 11/pg 139   Apr 4, 1851

John Shive of Doylestown Twp, brother and legatee of Elizabeth Shive, late of Bedminster Twp, acknowledges payment of estate by executors George and Henry Shive.   Bk 11/pg 140   Apr 5, 1851

Charles R. Hess, Tobias Hess, George R. Hess, Elizabeth (widow of Henry Brunner), Catharine (widow of David Ruckle), Hannah (wife of Levi O. Kolb, Esq.), heirs of George Hess, late of Springtown, acknowledge payment of estate by administrators Joseph, David and Solomon Hess.

Bk 11/pg 141   Apr 1, 1850

Christian Kressman and Elizabeth Fisher, siblings of Margaret Kressman, late of Durham Twp. who died intestate and without issue, acknowledge payment of estate by administrator Michael Fackenthall. Bk 11/pg 143   May 15, 1851

Charles Banes, Esther Banes, Hannah Brown (late Banes, wife of Joel Brown), of White and Pulaski Counties, IN and Joseph Banes of Clinton Co, OH by their attorney William T. Banes of Pulaski Co, IH acknowledge payment of estate by Joseph Carver, surviving administrator of the estate of William McDowell, late of Buckingham Twp, due by the death of William's widow Esther Blaker (late McDowell).   Bk 11/pg 144   Jun 24, 1851

Charles Banes, Esther Banes and Joel and Hannah (Banes) Brown of White and Pulaski Counties, IN and Joseph Banes of Clinton Co, OH give power of attorney to William T. Banes of Pulaski Co. to recover estate from Esther Blaker, late of Bucks Co, mother of Eliza Ann (McDowell) Banes who is married to their father William T. Banes.   Bk 11/pg 145   May 12, 1851

David Seip, late of Nockamixon Twp, died intestate leaving widow Mary and eight children: William, John, David, Maria (wife of William Maxwell), Margaret Seip, Rosanna Wright (widow), Elizabeth (wife of William Oldham) and Catharine (wife of Frederick Steely), release Michael Dech and John Seip (who purchased the real estate) of any dower obligation.

Bk 11/pg 147   Apr 21, 1851

Tobias Drumbore of Madison Twp, Franklin Co, OH acknowledges payment by his attorney Enos Schlichter of Rockhill Twp, of estate due from his late father Andrew Drumbore Sen.   Bk 11/pg 148   Jan 24 1851

Thomas Stockham, late of Bristol Twp, willed that his real estate be sold one year after the decease of his widow with one-third of the proceeds to go to Eliza Booze, one-third to John and George Stockham and one-third to various other persons.   John Stockham sells his one-sixth share to John Phillips, M.D. of Bristol Borough.   Bk 11/pg 148   Jul 3, 1851

Henry Wentzel of Germantown Twp, Philadelphia Co. and wife Keziah (late Young), legatee of John Crawford, late of Warrington Twp, acknowledge payment of estate by executor William Carr.   Bk 11/pg 149   Jul 28, 1851

Leidy Eckel of Chester Co, legatee of John Leidy, acknowledges payment of estate by executors Zachariah Leidy and George Sheip.
                                                        Bk 11/pg 150   May 8, 1851

Leidy Eckel of Chester Co, now 21, acknowledges payment by guardian Zachariah Leidy of estate from late father Samuel Eckel.
                                                        Bk 11/pg 150   May 8, 1851

Washington Boucher of Bensalem Twp, now 21, acknowledges payment by guardian William B. Vandegrift of estate from late father Benjamin Boucher.
                                                        Bk 11/pg 151   Apr 4, 1846

John K. Paxson of Solebury Twp. and wife Achsah L. agree to separate due to unhappy differences between them and agree to settlement of their property.
                                                        Bk 11/pg 151   Aug 25, 1851

Samuel Detweiler of Plumstead Twp, yeoman, revokes previous power of attorney given to John L. Delp of Plumstead Twp. and gives power of attorney to his son Abraham F. Detweiler of Plumstead Twp. to recover moneys due him, especially those held by John L. Delp.
                                                        Bk 11/pg 152   Aug 27, 1851

Uzziel U. Jamison of Northampton Twp, now 21, acknowledges payment by guardian James Jamison of estate from late father William Jamison.
                                                        Bk 11/pg 153   Aug 12, 1851

William T. Vandegrift, late of Bensalem Twp, willed farm to son William subject to payment to daughters Sarah, Martha and Ann.   William and Sarah

Bresley, Jonathan and Martha Vandegrift and Ann Lake acknowledge payment of estate by their brother William Vandegrift of Bristol Twp.
Bk 11/pg 155   Mar 28, 1851

Elizabeth Major of Tinicum Twp, daughter of Samuel Major, late of Tinicum, acknowledges payment of estate by mother Sarah and Hugh R. Major who are Samuel's executors.   Bk 11/pg 156   Jun 18, 1851

Jacob D. Sigafoose/Ziegenfuss of Nockamixon Twp. and Susanna Frankenfield of Tinicum Twp. are soon intended to be married and agree to keep Susanna's property separate for her use.   Bk 11/pg 157   Jun 21, 1851

Reuben Kurtz of Easton, grandson of John Keller, late of Haycock Twp, acknowledges payment of payment of dower by Abraham Stover on his behalf and as attorney for John and Eliza Shug, John's granddaughter.
Bk 11/pg 161   May 13, 1851

Mahlon Hendricks and wife Mary, daughter of late Mark Fretz, now 21, acknowledge payment by guardian Jacob Nash of estate from late grandfather Jacob Bissey.   Bk 11/pg 161   Oct 16, 1851

George and Margaret Comly of Bustletown, Philadelphia Co, farmer, Jonathan and Jane Stevens of Smithfield, Philadelphia Co, farmer, and Ann Lake of Smithfield, widow, daughters of William T. Vandegrift, late of Bensalem Twp, acknowledge payment of estate by William's son Allen.
Bk 11/pg 162   Aug 10, 1851

Enoch Strawn, late of Richland Twp, bequeathed estate to seven children: John, William, Miles, Myra (wife of Nathan Dolbey), Elizabeth (wife of Enos Roberts), Joseph and Mary (wife of Samman[?] Penrose). Myra's son Barton Dolbey gives power of attorney to Daniel Dolbey of Philadelphia Co, innkeeper, to recover his share of his grandfather's estate.
Bk 11/pg 164   Aug 26, 1851

Elias L. Helwig of Roaring Creek Twp, Montour Co. gives power of attorney to Jacob Fretz of Solebury Twp. to collect money due from Elias Ott, Abraham Ent and John Kirk, that is now due and which becomes due upon the death of Mary Helwig, widow of John Helwig, late of Roaring Creek Twp.   Bk 11/pg 165   Apr 14, 1851

David K. Kressler, Charles K. Kressler, John and Maria Youngken, Sarah Kressler and Catharine Ann Kressler, children of Henry Kressler, late of

Springfield Twp, acknowledge payment of estate by administrator Henry K. Kressler. Bk 11/pg 167 Apr 1, 1851

Thomas Amey, George Amey, Margaret Felman, Matilda Johnson and Mariah Sollada, children of Anthony Amey, late of Richland Twp, acknowledge payment of estate by executors William Amey and Abel S. Johnson. Bk 11/pg 168 Nov 17, 1849

Euphemia Willet of Bensalem Twp, single woman, gives power of attorney to Charles Willet of Bensalem Twp, yeoman, to appear at the Orphans Court and accept the real estate of her late sister Margaret Longstreth.
Bk 11/pg 174 Sep 6, 1851

William Cyphert, late of Springfield Twp, owned property in common with George Cyphert and John Cyphert. William died intestate leaving children Sarah (wife of Joseph Funk of Springfield Twp, yeoman), Susanna (wife of George Kunsman of Lower Saucon Twp, Northampton Co, yeoman), Christianna (wife of Samuel Zeiner of Lower Saucon Twp.) and John. William's four children agree with Bartel and George W. Seifert, administrators of George Cyphert Esq., late of Springfield Twp, agree to division of this land. Bk 11/pg 178 Dec 6, 1851

John Shelly, son of Samuel Shelly, late of Hilltown Twp, now 21, acknowledges payment of estate by guardian John Heckler.
Bk 11/pg 180 Dec 15, 1851

Mary Strawsnider (widow), John Strawsnider the younger (a lunatic), Solomon and Sarah Wagner, Samuel and Elizabeth Campbell, Elias and Mary Ruch, Henry and Catharine Super and Aaron and Hannah Kramer, widow of children of late John Strawsnider who was executor of John Strawsnider who held a mortgage against Henry and Catharine Ziegenfuss, give power of attorney to John Dixon of Durham Twp. to file settlement of the mortgage.
Bk 11/pg 181 Jan 2, 1852

Sarah S. Reeder, widow of Merrick Reeder, late of Solebury Twp, releases Merrick's sons Joseph E. Reeder, David K. Reeder and William P. Reeder of any dower obligation. Bk 11/pg 181 Dec 19, 1851

David Herr, Elizabeth (wife of Michael Derstine), Mary Ann (wife of Aaron Appenzeller), Catharine (wife of Joel Thomas), Tobias Fluck (guardian of John and Maria Herr) and Henry Troxell (guardian of Daniel and Christiana

Herr), heirs of David Herr, late of Rockhill Twp, acknowledge payment of estate by administrators Elias and Jacob Herr.   Bk 11/pg 182   [blank] 1851

Smith Carver, Joseph Carver and wife Eliza, all of Hancock Co, OH, give power of attorney to William Carver of Bucks Co. to sell their interests in the estate of Robert Carver, lately deceased, father to Smith and Joseph.
Bk 11/pg 185   Jan 10, 1851

Solomon McNair, late of Upper Makefield Twp, bequeathed estate to children. Daughter Eliza has since died intestate leaving mother and siblings. Widow Sarah and children Solomon McNair of Lancaster Co, William McNair of Michigan, John McNair of Lancaster, Charles V. and Mary Craven of Livingston Co, NY, James and Martha Love of Chester Co. and Daniel and Sarah Ann Kirkwood of Pottsville acknowledge payment of estate by Solomon's son and executor James M. McNair.   Bk 11/pg 185   Jan 27, 1851

William Heft died intestate leaving real estate in hands of administrators Nicholas and Peter Heft and a sum in the hands of Nicholas Heft, the interest to be paid to Margaret Massamer during her life and to Jacob Heft after her decease. Jacob Heft assigns his right to Nicholas Heft.
Bk 11/pg 187   Jan 20, 1852

Jane (Eugenie) Mourier, at present residing at Beziers Department de Therault in France, widow of John P. Mourier, recently deceased in Illinois and formerly of Philadelphia, gives power of attorney to John Sanderson, Esq. of Philadelphia to settle John's estate.   Bk 11/pg 188   Jul 29, 1851

Michael Sigafoose and wife [not named], George and Mary Sigafoose, John Sigafoose and wife [not named], Jacob Sigafoose and wife, Samuel Sigafoose and wife, Frederick and Catharine Strouse and Elizabeth Strouse (widow of Leonard Strouse), heirs of Henry Sigafoose Sen., late of Nockamixon Twp, acknowledge payment of estate by administrator William Sigafoose.
Bk 11/pg 189   Oct 26, 1844

Robinson Stackhouse of San Francisco, CA, late of Philadelphia, gives power of attorney to William Kinsey of Bristol Borough to sells his share in estate of late father Ebenezer Stackhouse.   Bk 11/pg 190   Oct 1, 1851

Silas Althouse, now 21, acknowledges payment by guardian Samuel Fluck of estate from father Martin Althouse, late of Bedminster Twp.
Bk 11/pg 192   Oct 27, 1851

Joseph Drissel of Tinicum Twp. acknowledges payment by guardian
Abraham Reiff.   Bk 11/pg 193   Apr 9, 1848

Henry Drissel of Tinicum Twp. acknowledges payment by guardian Abraham
Reiff.   Bk 11/pg 194   Jan 16, 1852

Jesse and Thomas Schlichter of Rockhill Twp, Isaac Schlichter and Catharine
Van Buskirk, children of Andrew Schlichter, late of Northern Liberties Twp,
Philadelphia Co, acknowledge payment of estate by executors Henry and
Enos Schlichter and Frederick Althouse.   Bk 11/pg 196   Apr 4, 1850

Charles Frederick Fisher of New Orleans, LA gives power of attorney to
brother Christian Frederick Fisher of Rockhill Twp. to recover money due
him.   Bk 11/pg 196   Sep 30, 1846

George Landes, Jacob and Barbara Baringer, George and Catharine Baringer,
Henry and Sarah Rosenberger, Jacob and Elizabeth Benner, Samuel and Mary
Frick, Charles Frick, John Frick, Tobias and Catharine Shive, and Anna Frick
(by guardian Peter Frick), children and grandchildren of George Landes, late
of Haycock Twp, whose widow Anna is now deceased, acknowledge payment
of estate by George's son John who inherited his father's land.
                                                  Bk 11/pg 197   Mar 20, 1850

John Neice of Moncey Twp, Lycoming Co. acknowledges payment of estate
by William Ridge and Daniel Boileau, administrators of Thomas, William and
Edward Ridge.   Bk 11/pg 200   Nov 4, 1844

John Neice of Moncy Twp, Lycoming Co, attorney for William Neice,
Catharine Neice, Eliza Neice and Abraham and Rebecca (Neice) Tollman, all
of Lycoming Co, acknowledges payment of estate by William Ridge and
Daniel Boileau, administrators of Thomas, William and Edward Ridge.
                                                  Bk 11/pg 200   Nov 4, 1844

Ameriah Rothwell of Lycoming Co, attorney of Henry Niece and Ann Niece
of Lycoming Co. and in right of wife Latitia, all heirs of John Neice and wife
Mary (late Ridge), acknowledge payment of estate by William Ridge and
Daniel Boileau, administrators of Thomas, William and Edward Ridge.
                                                  Bk 11/pg 201   Apr 11, 1845

Charles C. Jennings of Easton, guardian of Anna Margaret Carrell and Sarah
Carrell, minor children of James Carrell Jr. and great-grandchildren of James
Carrell the elder, late of Tinicum Twp, gives power of attorney to Uriah W.

Carrell of Easton to appear at Orphans Court and refuse to accept the real estate.   Bk 11/pg 201   Sep 6, 1851

James Kennedy of East Allen Twp, Northampton Co, guardian of Jane Anne Carrell, minor daughter of Samuel Carrell Jr. and granddaughter of James Carrell, late of Tinicum Twp, gives power of attorney to Uriah Carrall of Easton to appear at Orphans Court and refuse to accept the real estate.
                                                Bk 11/pg 201   Aug 17, 1851

James W. Carrall of Freeport, Stevenson Co, IL but now in Easton gives power of attorney Rev. Benjamin Carrell of Somerset Co, NJ to appear at Orphans Court and refuse to accept the real estate of James Carrell, late of Tinicum Twp.   Bk 11/pg 202   Jun 27, 1851

Lydia Hill of Doylestown Twp, spinster, now 21, acknowledges payment by guardian Josiah Rich of estate from late father Isaac Hill.
                                                Bk 11/pg 202   Mar 3, 1852

Samuel Landis, guardian for Barbara Stover, minor child of John Stover, late of Rockhill Twp, acknowledges payment of estate by her former guardian Enos Schlichter.   Bk 11/pg 203   Feb 4, 1852

Martin Myers, heir of John Myers, late of Bedminster Twp, acknowledges payment of estate by administrator Joseph Myers.
                                                Bk 11/pg 203   Mar 8, 1852

Mary Stouffer (late Clymer), now 21, acknowledges along with her husband Samuel L. Stauffer payment by her guardian Samuel Landis of estate from late father Jacob Clymer.   Bk 11/pg 210   Nov 3, 1851

Eli Fell of Buckingham Twp, guardian of Daniel and James P. Hough, minor children of Richard P. Hough, late of Solebury Twp, acknowledges payment of estate by administrator William Hough.   Bk 11/ pg 212   Apr 3, 1852

Francis Swartz, John K. and Eliza (Swartz) Shellenberger, Caroline Swartz, Lydia Swartz, Levi Kreamer (guardian of Sarah Swartz), children of Jacob Swartz, late of Bedminster Twp, acknowledge payment of estate by administrators Jefferson Swartz and Aaron Ott.   Bk 11/pg 212   Apr 3, 1852

Rebecca C. Betts, daughter of Thomas Betts, late of Buckingham Twp, acknowledges payment of estate by Thomas' son Cyrus.
                                                Bk 11/pg 213   Apr 5, 1852

Henry Johnson of Travis Co, TX and wife Jane G. (late Denyer) and John Pratt of Gonzales Co, TX and wife Elizabeth (late Denyer), heirs of Mark Fretz, late of New Britain Twp, give power of attorney to friend Ebenezer W. Denyer/Denzer of Gonzales Co. to recover estate due from executors John Geil and Henry Fretz.   Bk 11/pg 217   Jul 31, 1851

Ebenezer W. Denyer of Gonzales Co, TX, heir of Mark K. Fretz, late of New Britain Twp, and as attorney for sisters Elizabeth (wife of John Pratt) and Jane (wife of Henry Johnson), acknowledges payment of estate by executors Henry Fretz and John Geil. Also acknowledges payment by Henry Fretz as administrator for Mark's widow Elizabeth Fretz.   Bk 11/pg 218   Apr 12, 1852

Thomas Dungan, late of Northampton Twp, bequeathed estate to widow and daughter Jane Gill and to Jane's children after her death. Jane's son James Gill of Philadelphia sells his share to his brothers John Jr. and Samuel Gill of Northampton Twp. John then sells his share to Samuel in 1852.
                                   Bk 11/pg 220   Feb 16, 1849

Edwin K. Wambold of Rockhill Twp, son of Abraham Wambold, late of Rockhill, acknowledges payment of estate by his guardian George Schwenk.
                                   Bk 11/pg 222   Nov 14, 1851

Elizabeth Kober, Philip and Christiana Steer of Gwynedd Twp, Montgomery Co, Samuel and Lydia Hartman of Richland Twp, Peter and Mary Frank of Rockhill Twp, Andrew and Esther Haines of Franconia Twp, Montgomery Co, and Michael and Sarah Benner of Rockhill Twp, children of Abraham Kober, late of Rockhill Twp, acknowledge payment of estate by executors George A. Kober, Abraham Cressman and George Beltz.
                                   Bk 11/pg 223   Mar 29, 1852

John and Elizabeth Kilmer, Henry and Rebecca Wolfinger and Elisha and Anna Miller (of Plumstead Twp), daughters of George Wagner, late of Tinicum Twp, acknowledge payment of estate by administrators Henry, John and George F. Wagner.   Bk 11/pg 223   Apr 13, 1852

William White of Bedminster Twp, guardian of Aaron Maust, minor son of Samuel Maust, late of Tinicum Twp, acknowledges payment of estate by Samuel's administrator Michael Worman of Tinicum Twp.
                                   Bk 11/pg 225   Apr 3, 1852

James Martin, medicine doctor, of Nockamixon Twp, guardian of Lydia Maust, minor daughter of Samuel Maust, late of Tinicum Twp, acknowledges payment of estate by administrator Michael Worman.
Bk 11/pg 225   Apr 3, 1852

John Fellman of Richland Twp, Mary Metz[?] of Lower Saucon Twp, Northampton Co, Catharine Clymer of New Britain Twp. and Nancy Derstine of Hilltown Twp, children of Henry Fellman, late of Richland Twp, acknowledge payment of estate by executor Samuel Fellman.
Bk 11/pg 226   Apr 9, 1852

Samuel Maust, now 21, son of Jacob Maust, late of Nockamixon Twp, acknowledges payment of estate by administrator Frederick Rufe.
Bk 11/pg 226   Apr, 1838

Joseph Fulmer of Nockamixon Twp, yeoman, and wife Sarah, daughter of George Ruff, late of Nockamixon, acknowledges payment of estate by executors Frederick and John Ruff.   Bk 11/pg 227   Dec 14, 1833

Frederick Gantzert certifies that he and his wife have decided to separate and that he will not intrude on her.   Bk 11/pg 227   Aug 21, [1843?]

Edward Yost of Plumstead Twp, now 21, acknowledges payment by guardian Henry Frankenfield of estate from late father Adam Yost.
Bk 11/pg 228   Apr, 1852

David W. Kelly, William Kelly and Anna Kelly, children of Jesse Kelly, late of Morrisville, release to the widow Sarah their rights to Jesse's estate.
Bk 11/pg 232   Apr 2, 1852

Henry H. Kulp of Philadelphia Co, son of Isaac Kulp, late of Hilltown Twp, now 21, acknowledges payment of estate by guardian Henry Hackman, also of estate from late grandparents Isaac and Mary Kulp Sen.
Bk 11/pg 232   Apr 23, 1852

Sarah Benner, daughter of Gerret Benner, late of Hilltown Twp, now 21, acknowledges payment of estate by guardian Jesse Fluck.
Bk 11/pg 233   Mar 20, 1852

Jacob Smith of Falls Twp, yeoman, and wife Eliza, daughter of Jacob Vanhart, late of Falls, acknowledge payment of estate by executors Thomas Vanhart, Aaron Ivins and William Smith.   Bk 11/pg 234   Apr 7, 1852

Samuel Horning of Doylestown Borough, now 21, acknowledges payment by guardian Henry Dirstine of estate from late father Samuel Horning.

Bk 11/pg 235   Apr 9, 1852

Ephriam Thomas, late of New Britain Twp, bequeathed money to son Elias to be held in trust by Levi James and James Polk. James Polk subsequently died and was replaced by John M. Potts. John M. Potts and Walter F. Maines[?] and wife Mary Ann, only child of Elias Thomas, late of New Britain Twp, acknowledge payment of estate by Isaiah James of New Britain Twp, present owner of the land.   Bk 11/pg 235   Mar 9, 1852

Abraham Housekeeper of Warren Co, OH, coach trimmer, now 21, acknowledges payment by guardian Abraham Fluck of estate from late father Mathias Housekeeper.   Bk 11/pg 239   May 14, 1852

Samuel Carey, M.D., of Richland Twp, guardian of Mary McCray, granddaughter of William Green, late of Richland Twp, acknowledges payment of estate by executors Richard R. Green, Edward Foulke and Joshua Foulke.   Bk 11/pg 240   Apr 6, 1852

John Hutchinson, Rebecca Hutchinson of Rostravin[?] Twp, Westmoreland Co, Joseph Hutchinson of Elizabeth Twp, Allegheny Co, Ira Hutchinson of Fayette Co, heirs of Joseph Hutchinson, late of Elizabeth Twp, Allegheny Co, who was a brother of Sarah Hutchinson, late of Bucks Co, give power of attorney to Joseph Hutchinson of Rostraven[?] Twp. to recover estate in hands of Samuel Watson.   Bk 11/pg 241   May 8, 1852

James and Mary Wallace, William and Priscilla Hart, Charles and Jane Shewell, children of Robert and Mary Wallace, late of Warwick Twp, and Joseph Ford, husband of late Isabella (daughter of Robert and Mary) who left children Mary Ford, William Ford, Eliza (wife of Isaac Davis), Amanda (wife of Riley Patterson) and Priscilla Ford, and Robert and James Ford (by their guardian John Borthwell), and Samuel Polk and Thomas and Isabella (Polk) Hough, children of Eliza (Wallace) Polk and minors John, Jane and Mary Alice Ward, children of Rebecca (Wallace) Ward, give power of attorney to William Carr of Doylestown to sell the real estate.

Bk 11/pg 244   Sep 27, 1851

George L. Hood acknowledges payment of estate by Samuel B. Wood, executor of his late father John P. Wood.   Bk 11/pg 247   Jun 30, 1852

Emanuel O. Soliday of Bedminster Twp. and wife Mary, daughter of Jacob Fetter, late of Bedminster, and legatee of John Wert of Bedminster, acknowledge payment of estate by her guardian Henry Shive of Bedminster.
Bk 11/pg 247   Apr 27, 1852

Louis P. Rousseau, Theodore Rousseau, Elwin Rousseau, Alfred Rousseau, Mary (wife of William Percy), Alice (wife of Jacob Whildy), Margaret (wife of Samuel Arrison) and Elizabeth and Constance G. Rousseau, children of Dr. Clet Rousseau, late of Morrisville, assign their right to the estate to the widow Elizabeth.
Bk 11/pg 249   Nov 6, 1851

Susan Jane Wood of Solebury Twp, only heir of Grace Ridge, late of Solebury Twp, acknowledge payment of estate by executor John N. Solliday.
Bk 11/pg 249   Jun 1, 1852

Sarah W. Bachman of Durham Twp, heir of late John Bachman, now 21, acknowledges payment by guardian Jacob A. Bachman of estate from late father.
Bk 11/pg 250   Jun 19, 1852

Mercy M. Taylor, widow of Bernard Taylor, yeoman, late of Upper Makefield Twp, releases dower right to Bernard's children Jonathan and Maria B. (Taylor) Brock, Watson and Hannah H. (Taylor) Malone, Jacob H., Robert F. and William S.
Bk 11/pg 251   Aug 21, 1852

Philip Barron bequeathed estate to daughter Julianna, wife of Philip Lambach, and to her children after her decease. Julianna died July 6, 1837 leaving children including Elizabeth (wife of John Crader) who resides in Kalamazoo Co, MI who is entitled to one-fourth of Julianna's share. John and Elizabeth Crader acknowledge payment of their share by Jacob Barron of Springfield Twp.
Bk 11/pg 252   Jan 8, 1850

Maria Stone of Tinicum Twp, daughter of Henry Stone, late of Tinicum Twp, now 21, acknowledges payment of estate by guardian Michael Worman.
Bk 11/pg 253   Aug 10, 1852

William Wireman of Franconia Twp, Montgomery Co, Abraham and Mary Krupp of Franconia Twp. and Catherine Wireman of Franconia Twp, legatees of John Berge, late of Rockhill Twp, acknowledge payment of estate by executors Abraham Fretz and Abraham Hunsicker.
Bk 11/pg 257   Apr 6, 1852

John Delp of Philadelphia Co, Michael Delp of Hatfield Twp, Montgomery Co. and Thomas and Anna Wilson of Montgomery Twp, Montgomery Co, legatees of John Berge, late of Rockhill Twp, acknowledge payment of estate by executors Abraham Fretz and Abraham Hunsicker.

Bk 11/pg 257   Apr 17, 1852

Aaron and Magdalena Berge of Lower Salford Twp, Montgomery Co. and Susanna Anthony, legatees of John Berge, Rockhill Twp, acknowledge payment of estate by executors Abraham Fretz and Abraham Hunsicker.

Bk 11/pg 258   Apr 12, 1852

Daniel W. Ehl of Milford Twp, now 21, acknowledge payment by guardian Henry Kemerer.   Bk 11/pg 259   Sep 20 1852

John Good of Plumstead Twp. executed a mortgage to Robert Shaw of Montgomery Twp, Montgomery Co, his brother Elias Shaw and their sisters Sarah Gibson (wife of Moses Gibson of Gloucester Co, NJ) and Rachel (wife of James Sands of Buckingham Twp), due upon the death of Martha B. Shaw, widow of John Shaw, late of Buckingham Twp. Martha died Apr 15, 1851. Moses and Sarah Gibson and James and Rachel Sands acknowledge payment of their shares by Robert Shaw.   Bk 11/pg 259   Apr 3, 1852

Jesse and Adrianna Dungan, J. Craven and Martha Cornell, Catharine Terry and Jane Twining, heirs of Gilliam Cornell, late of Southampton Twp, give power of attorney to friend Isaac Vanhorn of Northampton Twp. to sell land which John Cornell bequeathed to his son Gilliam Cornell.

Bk 11/pg 261   Sep 9, 1852

Henry Weiss of Milford Twp, yeoman, guardian of Milton, Henry, Amelia and Hannah Heist, minor children of Aaron Heist, late of Milford Twp, blacksmith, acknowledges payment of estate by administrators Henry Clymer and Susanna Heist.   Bk 11/pg 262   Apr 4, 1846

Franklin B. Sacket of Warwick Twp, heir of late John Sacket, acknowledges payment of estate by his guardian Strickland Bennett of Buckingham Twp.

Bk 11/pg 264   Oct 19, 1852

Samuel Moyer the elder and wife Elizabeth of Rockhill Twp, sawmiller, sell land to Samuel Moyer the younger subject to payment to the heirs upon the death of Samuel and Elizabeth.   Bk 11/pg 264   Apr 24, 1837

Stephen Kirk of Buckingham Twp. and wife Anna, daughter of Ebenezer Large, late of Solebury Twp, release their right to John Carver of Buckingham Twp. any claim to land he purchased from Joseph and Cynthia Large, eldest son of Ebenezer. Bk 11/pg 265 Oct 21, 1852

Jacob Warner of Lower Saucon Twp, Northampton Co, yeoman, Frederick Warner of Springfield Twp, weaver, Christian Cyphert, widow of William of Springfield Twp. and Sarah Cyphert, widow of George of Springfield Twp, heirs of Henry Warner, late of Springfield Twp, acknowledge payment of estate by administrator George W. Seifert. Bk 11/pg 266 Feb 16, 1852

Benjamin Williams, son of William Williams, late of Bucks Co, now 21, acknowledges payment of estate by John Adams, Esq, trustee of Benjamin's father, who replaced James Burson, the trustee appointed by will of Jeremiah Williams. Bk 11/pg 267 Apr 16, 1847

Mary Horning of West Rockhill Twp, now 21, acknowledges payment by guardian Jacob Dirstine of estate from late father Samuel Horning.
Bk 11/pg 268 Dec 26, 1848

Elizabeth Caufman of Springfield Twp. gives power of attorney to Abraham Benner of Springfield Twp. to settle estate of Christian Cauffman of whom she is administrator and to attend a court trial that she has with Abraham Cauffman. Bk 11/pg 268 Feb 24, 1852

Alfred M. Magill, Louisa C. Magill and Benjamin W. Magill, children of William Magill, late of Doylestown, assigned to William D. Magill and Robert M. Magill their rights to various bonds held to secure dower of William's widow Mary. William D. Magill now assigns his right to John Fell of Buckingham Twp. Bk 11/pg 268 Apr 5, 1847

Isaac Mathews, administrator of John Fell, late of Buckingham Twp, assigns the right gained in the prior entry to Eli Fell of Buckingham Twp.
Bk 11/pg 269 Nov 14, 1852

John Swartley of New Britain Twp, cigar maker, now 21, acknowledges payment by guardian Abraham Gearhart of estate from late father John Swartley. Bk 11/pg 270 Nov 26, 1852

Jane Gill, widow of John Gill, late of Solebury Twp, acknowledges payment of estate by administrators Lemen Banes and Samuel Gill.
Bk 11/pg 270 Dec 1, 1852

Peter and Anna (Detweiler) Stouffer of Upper Milford Twp, Lehigh Co, farmer, and Barbara (Detweiler) Stouffer, heirs of Leonard Detweiler Sen., late of Hilltown Twp, acknowledge payment of estate by executors Samuel and John Detweiler.   Bk 11/pg 271   Nov 27, 1852

Sarah Stepel/Staples, granddaughter of Christian Mann, late of Haycock Twp, now 21, acknowledges (along with her husband Reuben B.) payment by her guardian Nicholas Heft of estate from late mother Catharine Mus [Miess].
                                                  Bk 11/pg 271   Oct 5, 1852

John Hough of Solebury Twp, William and Mary Pursell, George and Amey Morris and Samuel and Jane Frock of Luzerne Co, children of Richard P. Hough, late of Solebury Twp, acknowledge payment of estate by administrator William Hough.   Bk 11/pg 272   Sep 30, 1852

Daniel Kramer, son of Henry Kramer, late of Bedminster Twp, now 21, acknowledges payment of estate by guardian Daniel Bartholomew.
                                                  Bk 11/pg 273   Dec 4, 1852

Henry A. Hartley of Knox Twp, Columbiana Co, OH gives power of attorney to Amos Armitage of Solebury Twp. to recover estate from late father from his guardian John Armitage.   Bk 11/pg 274   Nov 2, 1852

Henry A. Hartley of Stack Co, OH, now 21, acknowledges payment by guardian John Armitage of estate from late father Samuel Hartley.
                                                  Bk 11/pg 274   Dec 7, 1852

Mahlon Hartley of Columbiana Co, OH, now 21, acknowledges payment by guardian John Armitage of estate from late father Samuel Hartley.
                                                  Bk 11/pg 275   Dec 7, 1852

Michael H. Jenks, administrator of Jesse Leedom, late of Newtown Twp, gives power of attorney to brother-in-law George Yardley, Esq. to record satisfaction of a mortgage.   Bk 11/pg 275   Dec 8, 1852

Elizabeth (wife of Joseph Vankirk), Isaac Hutchinson and Charity Forsyth, children of Joseph Hutchinson, late of Elizabeth Twp, Allegheny Co, give power of attorney to Joel K. Vankirk of Rostrun Twp, Westmoreland Co. (now of Philadelphia) to recover from Samuel Watson of Bucks Co. the money due them from estate of Sarah Hutchinson, late of Bucks Co, who was Joseph's sister.   Bk 11/pg 277   Oct 28, 1852

Eleazer B. Shaw, John Shaw, sons of James Shaw, late of Plumstead Twp, and the children of James' late son Jonathan: John Shaw, Elizabeth Shaw, James Shaw, Jacob and Rachel Danenhower, John and Mary Danenhower, and Charlotte Shaw (deceased, children Moses and Charlotte by guardian Moses Rich), acknowledge payment by Rachael, Mary and Elizabeth Shaw, daughters of James, of dower due by death of James' widow Elizabeth.

Bk 11/pg 279   Apr 5, 1850

Isaac Comly, Zebedee Comly, Thomas and Ann (Comly) Buckman, Charles and Keziah (Comly) Roberts, Alfred Comly, Clement Comly and Joseph B. Comly acknowledge payment of estate by Amos Jones Comly, administrator of Clement Comly, late of Warminster Twp.   Bk 11/pg 281   Jan 17, 1853

Mary Dixon (now wife of Moses W. Dillon) assigns to her husband her right to real estate bequeathed to her by Barnet Peringer, late of Tinicum Twp.

Bk 11/pg 283   Feb 3, 1853

John Wirt Sen. of Hilltown Twp. sells land to Peter Wirt of Hilltown subject to payment upon John's death to John's heirs, Peter to take his share.

Bk 11/pg 283   Feb 3, 1853

Margaret (Vandegrift) Vansant, Nicholas L. Vansant, Hester Ann (Vandegrift) Plumly, Jane Eliza (Vandegrift) Scott and Francis A. Scott, heirs of Jacob J. Vandegrift, late of Bensalem Twp, acknowledge payment of dower by Mahlon B. Vandegrift, due upon the death of their mother Rachel.

Bk 11/pg 284   Jan 27, 1853

Phillip Barron of Springfield Twp. bequeathed land to son Jacob subject to payment of heirs of daughter Julianna Landbach upon her death. Julianna died in 1838 leaving children including Samuel who died Mar 22, 1851. Samuel's share was unpaid at his death and the land now owned by Jacob's son Jacob the younger. Aaron Landbach acknowledges payment by Jacob Barron of Samuel's one-fourth share of this legacy.

Bk 11/pg 284   Feb 8, 1853

Rebecca Miller of Lower Makefield Twp, now 21, acknowledges payment by guardian John Wildman of estate from her late father John Miller Jr.

Bk 11/pg 285   Feb 9, 1853

Stephen C. Vansant of Philadelphia, now 21, acknowledges payment by guardian Anthony Burton of estate from deceased parents.

Bk 11/pg 286   Jun 18, 1852

Jacob Bigonet (attorney for Dr. Richard Wilson), Henry H. Wilson (attorney for Dr. Elias Wilson), Henry H. Wilson, Ruth Anna Ely, Margaret W. Ely and Richard Randolph and Oliver Parry (guardians of Richard Elias Ely), heirs of Dr. John Wilson, late of Buckingham Twp, acknowledge payment of estate by Joseph O. Ely, C. Bennington Ely and Moses Eastburn, administrators of Hugh B. Ely who was Dr. Wilson's administrator.

Bk 11/pg 288   Apr 10, 1852

John Moyer of Hilltown Twp, now 21, acknowledges payment by guardian Simson Kratz of estate from late father Joseph Moyer.

Bk 11/pg 289   Oct 5, 1850

Silas A. Todd of Peoria Co, IL gives power of attorney to Samuel Darrah of Doylestown Twp. to recover estate from his late father David Todd and to take the real estate which he intends to convey to David's widow Mary.

Bk 11/pg 289   Feb 24, 1853

Isaac Kern of Philadelphia, son of Henry Kern, late of Rockhill Twp, acknowledges payment of estate by guardian Henry Schlichter, including estate from late grandfather John Kern.   Bk 11/pg 290   Jan 20, 1853

William Lohr of Alexandria Twp, Hunterdon Co, NJ and wife Catharine, daughter of John K. Adams, late of Durham Twp, acknowledges payment of estate by John Boyer.   Bk 11/pg 291   Jan 31, 1853

Bennett Hutchinson of Dallas Co, IA gives power of attorney to Amos Walton of Bucks Co. to recover from Samuel Watson of Solebury Twp. the money due him from estate of Sarah Hutchinson, late of Bucks Co.

Bk 11/pg 291   Feb 14, 1853

Elizabeth R. Richardson authorizes Samuel Hulme, Esq. to sell to Israel Allen of Bristol Borough the property she inherited from her mother Mary Hulme.

Bk 11/pg 293   Oct 10, 1848

Henry H. Althouse of Milford Twp, tavernkeeper and his mother Ann Althouse of Milford agree that Henry will provide her a piece of ground on which to build a house which will revert to Henry on Ann's death.

Bk 11/pg 294   Feb 2, 1849

Mary Overholtzer, widow of Abraham, and otherwise called Mary Funk of Springfield Twp, becoming aged and feeble, gives power of attorney to John Shimmel and Joseph Urmy to handle her affairs. Bk 11/pg 295   Feb 10, 1853

Hannah C. Bennett, wife of James T. Bennett, is entitled to proceeds from sale of real estate of John Whitcomb of Bucks Co. and agrees to have this paid to her husband.   Bk 11/pg 296   Aug 4, 1852

Joel Medary, son of John Medary, late of Warrington Twp, acknowledges payment of estate by administrators Burgess Medary and Josiah Markley.
                                                        Bk 11/pg 302   Mar 31, 1853

Franklin P. Sellers of Norristown, guardian of Samuel G. Mathews, minor son of Edmund Mathews, deceased, and legatee of Mary Polk, late of Doylestown Twp, acknowledges payment of estate by executor William Godshalk.
                                                        Bk 11/pg 303   Apr 1, 1853

Benjamin Godshalk of Northampton Co, legatee of Mary Polk of Doylestown Twp, acknowledges payment of estate by executor William Godshalk.
                                                        Bk 11/pg 303   Apr 1, 1853

Charles C. Cox, now 21, acknowledges payment by guardian James S. Rich of estate from late father William Cox.   Bk 11/pg 304   Apr 2, 1853

Caroline Teuhlon of Macungie Twp, Lehigh Co, Sarah Jacoby of Berwick, Columbia Co. and Enoch Kurtz of New York City, entitled to share of dower of Margaret Keller, widow of John Keller, late of Haycock Twp, having given power of attorney to Reuben Kurtz of Easton, Reuben acknowledges payment of dower by current owner Abraham Stover. Bk 11/pg 304   May 6, 1852

Samuel Bolinger, husband of Elizabeth Fryling, deceased, daughter of Martin Fryling, late of Plumstead Twp, assigns his right to estate to Elias and Leonard Fryling.   Bk 11/pg 304   Jun 18, 1852

Sarah Kratz of Hilltown Twp. acknowledges payment by guardian Abraham Reiff of estate from late father and grandfather. Bk 11/pg 305   Apr 4, 1853

James V. and Sarah Foster of Bristol Borough, William and Grace Sickle of Northampton Twp, Silas and Euphemia Vanartsdalen and Hannah Cox of Philadelphia give power of attorney to Samuel Willet Cox of Green Co, OH to sell land in Cincinnati, OH formerly belonging to Horatio G. Cox, late of Hamilton Co, OH.   Bk 11/pg 309   Apr 2, 1853

Augustus H.S. Beck of Haycock Twp, now 21, acknowledges payment by guardian Martin Bewighouse of estate from late father Henry Beck.
                                                        Bk 11/pg 309   Apr 4, 1853

Martin Bewighouse, guardian of Sarah Fabian, minor child of Henry Fabian, late of Tinicum Twp, acknowledges payment of estate by Sarah's prior guardian Phillip Strouse.   Bk 11/pg 309   Apr 2, 1853

Peter Shelly of Richland Twp. gives power of attorney to Peter Shelly, Esq. to recover money due from late grandfather Abraham Gahman who bequeathed money to his daughter Amy who was Peter's mother.
                                        Bk 11/pg 310   Feb 7, 1853

Samuel Firman of Solebury Twp. and wife Hannah, Eli Fell of Buckingham Twp. and wife Mary and Wilson Doan of Solebury Twp, children of Jonathan Doan, late of Buckingham Twp, acknowledge payment of estate by executors Henry Carver and Thomas Stradling.   Bk 11/pg 312   Apr 7, 1853

Abraham Benner and wife Mary, daughter of John Stauffer, late of Rockhill Twp, acknowledge payment of estate by her guardian Samuel Landes.
                                        Bk 11/pg 314   Jan 28, 1853

Isaac Deaterly, guardian of Mary Kilmer, minor daughter of Samuel Kilmer, late of Bedminster Twp, acknowledges payment of estate by administrators Jacob Kilmer and Jacob Deaterly, including share of estate of John Kilmer.
                                        Bk 11/pg 315   Apr 2, 1853

John A. Bissey, Samuel Bissey, Jesse Bissey, Henry Bissey, Samuel and Catharine Yost, children of Henry Bissey, late of Tinicum Twp, acknowledge payment of dower by John Harpel, Esq. of Bedminster Twp.
                                        Bk 11/pg 315   Apr 6, 1853

Jacob and Mary Bachman, heirs of Elizabeth (Cope) Bachman, late of Hilltown Twp, Margaret (Cope) Leidy, Mary (Cope) Cope, Catharine (Cope) Cope and Polly (Cope) Leidy, all of Hilltown Twp, daughters of Jacob Cope, late of Hilltown, acknowledge payment of estate by executor Henry Leidy.
                                        Bk 11/pg 316   Apr 4, 1853

Jacob and Mary Bachman, heirs of Elizabeth (Cope) Bachman, late of Hilltown Twp, Margaret (Cope) Leidy, Mary (Cope) Cope, Catharine (Cope) Cope and Polly (Cope) Leidy, all of Hilltown, daughters of Catharine Cope, late of Hilltown, acknowledge payment of estate by administrator Henry Leidy.   Bk 11/pg 316   Apr 4, 1853

Jonathan Leedom, Rebecca Leedom, Anna Leedom and Sarah Leedom, all of Moreland Twp, Philadelphia Co, give power of attorney to Richard Leedom of Moreland to record payment of a mortgage.   Bk 11/pg 317   Apr 18, 1853

John Mathews, legatee of Mary C. Polk, late of Doylestown Twp, acknowledges payment of estate by executor William Godshalk.
Bk 11/pg 317   Apr 21, 1853

Joel R. Vankirk of Westmoreland Co. (attorney for Charity Forsyth, Joseph and Elizabeth VanKirk and Isaac Hutchinson, heirs of Sarah Hutchinson, late of Solebury Twp), acknowledges payment of estate by Samuel Watson of Solebury Twp.   Bk 11/pg 318   Dec 29, 1850

John D. Balderston, administrator of Isaac Hutchinson, late of Bucks Co, and Stor Hutchinson of Harrison Co, OH acknowledge payment by Samuel G. Watson, current owner of land now adjudged to Elizabeth Hutchinson, of their share in estate of Sarah Hutchinson.   Bk 11/pg 319   Apr 8, 1852

Samuel G. Watson of Solebury Twp. purchased land of Samuel Beans subject to payment to Hannah Pearson and Samuel and Ada Lewis after the death of Elizabeth Hutchinson who is now deceased. Hannah Pearson is now deceased and Hiram H. Pearson is her executor. Hiram H. Pearson (also as attorney for Samuel and Ada P. Lewis) acknowledges payment by Samuel G. Watson.
Bk 11/pg 319   Mar 17, 1853

John Hutchinson, Rebecca Hutchinson, Joseph Hutchinson and Ira Hutchinson, heirs of Joseph Hutchinson, late of Allegheny Co, are due money from Samuel G. Watson of Solebury Twp. Their attorney Joseph Hutchinson acknowledges payment on their behalf.   Bk 11/pg 320   May 25, 1852

Amos Walton of Solebury Twp. (attorney for Bennett Hutchinson) acknowledges payment by Samuel G. Watson of money due by death of Elizabeth Hutchinson on property Samuel owns. Bk 11/pg 321   Mar 10, 1853

Catharine Laubach, widow of Frederick Laubach, late of Durham Twp, and David Laubach, William Laubach, Aaron Laubach of Durham Twp, David B. and Sarah Eschbach of Kensington District, Philadelphia, Abraham and Catharine Cressman of Springfield Twp, William and Christianna Cressman of Nockamixon Twp, Susannah Laubach of Durham and Matilda Laubach (by her guardian John Fackenthall of Durham Twp), children of Frederick, acknowledge payment of estate by administrators Charles and Samuel Laubach.   Bk 11/pg 321   Mar 23, 1853

Joel Wright, Grace (wife of Robert Crozer), Ann Wright, Catherine B. (wife of Thomas Butcher), Ruth Wright, Sarah B. Wright and Rachel Wright (wife of Joseph Howell), mortgages of Mark Wright, give power of attorney to Charles E. Dubois, Esq. of Doylestown to record satisfaction of the mortgage.
Bk 11/pg 324 Apr 5, 1853

John A. Bissey, Jesse Bissey, Samuel Bissey, Henry Bissey, Samuel and Catharine Yost, children of Henry Bissey, late of Tinicum Twp, acknowledge payment of dower by Jacob Kilmer of Tinicum Twp.
Bk 11/pg 324   Apr 6, 1853

John Wildonger, Rachel Root and Leah Stone, heirs of Elizabeth Wildonger, late of Tinicum Twp, acknowledge payment of estate by administrator Moses Wildonger.
Bk 11/pg 325   Apr 17, 1852

John Swope, Jacob Swope, David Swope, George Swope and Elizabeth (Swope) Swartz, heirs of Elizabeth Wildonger, late of Tinicum Twp, acknowledge payment of estate by administrator Moses Wildonger.
Bk 11/pg 325   Apr 17, 1852

John Swope, Jacob Swope, David Swope, George Swope and Elizabeth (Swope) Swartz, heirs of Jacob Wildonger, late of Tinicum Twp, acknowledge payment of estate by executor Jacob Kilmer.
Bk 11/pg 326   Apr 17, 1852

John Wildonger, Rachel Root and Leah Stone, heirs of Jacob Wildonger, late of Tinicum Twp, acknowledge payment of dower by executor Jacob Kilmer.
Bk 11/pg 326   Apr 17, 1852

Mary Ann Fosbender, now 21, acknowledges payment by guardian Jacob Kiser of estate from late father Jonas Fosbenner. Bk 11/pg 327 Mar 18, 1853

Francis Dennison, Rachel Sellers, Christianna Price and Sidney Pearson, all of PA, sisters of Mary Polk, late of Doylestown Twp, acknowledge payment of estate by executor William Godshalk.   Bk 11/pg 327 Apr 1, 1853

Jesse Tomlinson, Charles Tomlinson and Joseph and Rhoda (Tomlinson) Walton agree to sell land and split the proceeds. Bk 11/pg 328 May 4, 1853

Hannah Bennett, widow of Miles Bennett, late of Upper Makefield Twp, releases her right to dower to John Bennett of Upper Makefield.
Bk 11/pg 329 Jul 29, 1847

Christian Cressman, late of Springfield Twp, bequeathed money in trust for daughter Mary (wife of Adam Wimmer) to be held by executors John, Abraham, Jonas and George Kressman. Mary is deceased leaving children Samuel Berger of Springfield, Andrew Wimmer of Haycock Twp, George Wimmer of Rockhill Twp, Joseph Wimmer of Hilltown Twp, Abraham Wimmer of Upper Saucon Twp, Lehigh Co, Daniel Wimmer of Rockhill, Mary Rothrock (wife of Samuel) of Haycock, Elizabeth Quatenfield (wife of Jesse) of Haycock and Samuel Rothrock (guardian of Dianna, Matilda, Edwin, Levi, John, Frederick and Amanda Hemmerly, children of Catharine Hemmerly, late of Springfield Twp). Mary's heirs acknowledge payment by Michael Kressman and Joseph Kressman, late of Lower Mount Bethel Twp, Northampton Co [administrators of John Kressman, late of Lower Mount Bethel?], Abraham Cressman of Durham Twp, Jonas Kressman of Springfield, George Kressman of Springfield. Bk 11/pg 332   Apr 4, 1853

Henry Moyer, late of Plumstead Twp, blacksmith, died intestate leaving widow and seven children. Son John G. Moyer of Plumstead Twp. transfers his share of dower to Henry Benner of Plumstead Twp. to pay debts.
                                        Bk 11/pg 333   Jan 13, 1853

Joseph Hutchinson of Rostravin[?] Twp, Westmoreland Co, son of Isaac Hutchinson, late of Bucks Co, gives power of attorney to Amos Walton of Bucks Co. to recover father's estate in hands of Jacob Wilson.
                                        Bk 11/pg 334   [blank] 16, 1853

John Hutchinson of Sangaman Co, IL gives power of attorney to Amos Walton of Solebury Twp. to recover money from Jacob Wilson due him as an heir of late Isaac Hutchinson.   Bk 11/pg 334   Apr 8, 1853

Jacob Wilson purchased land from estate of Isaac Hutchinson, subject to dower for widow Sarah who died Aug 14, 1853. Letitia Hamilton, Dorothy (Hutchinson) Rozel, Joseph Hutchinson (by attorney Amos Walton), John W. and Mary (Hutchinson) Lattimore (by attorney Amos Armitage), Phebe (Hutchinson) Walton, William and Mercy H. (Hutchinson) Kirk, John Hutchinson (by attorney Amos Walton), Oliver and Hannah (Hutchinson) Hough and John E. Kenderdine (administrator of Elias Hutchinson), heirs of Isaac Hutchinson, acknowledge payment of dower by Jacob Wilson.
                                        Bk 11/pg 335   Apr 6, 1853

Mary E. Hough, daughter of late Robert Hough, acknowledges payment of estate by her guardian Thomas Hough of Doylestown Twp.
                                        Bk 11/pg 336   May 18, 1853

William B. Cooper of Falls Twp. died Jan 6, 1843 leaving widow Rachel P. and sons Mahlon C. and Erwin. Rachel P. Cooper and Mahlon C. Cooper of Morrisville give power of attorney to Erwin Cooper to record satisfaction of a mortgage. Bk 11/pg 337 May 17, 1853

Samuel Hinkle of Springfield Twp, administrator of Jacob [Horn?], late of Richland Twp, acknowledges payment by former administrator John Matts of money which he was to hold during the life of Mary Miller, Jacob's widow. Bk 11/pg 338 May 5, 1853

Michael Headman of Rockhill Twp, yeoman, guardian of Rebecca Wenholt, and Michael Althouse of Rockhill, guardian of Caroline Wenholt, minor daughters of Jacob Wenholt, late of Rockhill, acknowledge payment of estate by administrators Moses Texter and Samuel Roudenbush. Bk 11/pg 338 Apr 5, 1853

Sophia Wenholt, widow of Jacob Wenholt, late of Rockhill Twp, acknowledges payment of estate by administrators Moses Texter and Samuel Roudenbush. Bk 11/pg 339 Apr 5, 1853

Jacob Vanhart, late of Biles Island, Falls Twp, bequeathed money to his son Jacob who died before his father leaving five children: Sarah Elizabeth (wife of John S. Hutchinson of Trenton), Ann M. (wife of Christiannus Lupotis of Trenton), Rebecca (wife of Joseph/Josiah Comly of Jersey City), Jacob Vanhart of Morrisville and Anna Pennelia (wife of Benj. K. Knowles of Trenton). Jacob Jr.'s heirs acknowledge payment of estate by executors Aaron Ivins, Thomas Vanhart and William Smith. Bk 11/pg 341 Jan 10, 1853

Isaac O. Person, Sarah (Person) Leith and Catharine (Person) Kopline, children of late Henry Person Jr., and Allen Leith (by guardian Jacob F. Leith), son of Mary Person who was a granddaughter of Henry Person Sen., acknowledge payment of dower by Jacob Person, third son of Henry Person Sen. who inherited the estate, due now that the widow is deceased. [Abraham Person also signed but was not listed.] Bk 11/pg 343 Mar 7, 1853

Abraham E. Fretz, John and Anna (Fretz) Fretz, Christian and Elizabeth (Fretz) Fretz, Dr. Joseph and Rachel (Mitman) Moyers (granddaughter), heirs of Abraham Fretz, late of Bedminster Twp, acknowledge payment of dower by Jacob and Phillip K. Fretz. Bk 11/pg 346 Apr 4, 1853

Susannah Funk of Springfield Twp, heir of late Elizabeth Funk who was a minor daughter of late Henry Funk, acknowledges payment of estate by Elizabeth's guardian John Kaufman Funk.   Bk 11/pg 347   Apr 1, 1853

James B. Jardine petitions court to recognize contract he had with Michael Guth of Durham Twp. to purchase land, which contract was made before Michael Guth was declared by the court to be incompetent due to be an habitual drunkard. The Court acknowledges the contract.
Bk 11/pg 348   Feb 14, 1853

David and John Magill, brothers of William Magill, late of Solebury Twp, and Jonathan Magill, Jonathan J. and Mary Watson, Mary Magill, Susan Magill, Charles Magill and Sarah Magill, heirs of Jacob Magill, late of Solebury Twp, another brother of William, acknowledge payment of estate by Joseph E. Magill of Solebury Twp, another legatee of William.
Bk 11/pg 353   Mar 29, 1853

John A. Hanks of Pittsboro, Chatam[?] Co, NC, administrator of his wife Euphemia, gives power of attorney to C. Moris Lloyd of Doylestown to recover money due him.   Bk 11/pg 354   Apr 13, 1853

John Mortimer, late of Newtown, intended to bequeath money to George Barton and his wife Matilda but this was left out of the will inadvertently. John's children John, George, Thomas and William and Betsey Good agree to give them part of the estate.   Bk 11/pg 355   [blank] 8, 1853

Thomas and Susan (Tomlinson) Warwick of Hempstead, AR, heir of her uncle Joseph Tomlinson and her sister Elizabeth Tomlinson, give power of attorney to Anthony Swain to sell their interest in the land in Bristol.
Bk 11/pg 361   Aug 29, 1852

Hannah Balderson, daughter of John W. Balderson, late of Solebury Twp, acknowledges payment of legacy by brother Oliver.
Bk 11/pg 362   Apr 7, 1853

Elizabeth Ely of Solebury Twp, daughter of Joshua Ely, late of Solebury, due money from brother Nathan who inherited the real estate but he sold part to Oliver Balderson. Elizabeth acknowledges payment by Oliver of her share.
Bk 11/pg 363   Apr 7, 1853

Sarah Gerhart of Rockhill Twp, now 21, and her husband Zeno Gerhart acknowledge payment by her guardian Manasoch Bean of estate from her late father Samuel Horning.   Bk 11/pg 365   Mar 19, 1853

Joseph Overholt, administrator of Samuel Landis, late of Medina Co, OH, gives power of attorney to friend Abraham Leatherman of Medina Co. to recover money from Jacob Leatherman, administrator of Samuel's mother Hannah Landis, late of Bucks Co.   Bk 11/pg 366   May 17, 1853

Henry and Barbara Landis, Mary (Landis) Kulp, Susan Landis, Elizabeth Landis and Abraham Leatherman (guardian of children of Hannah Leatherman, late Landis), daughters of Henry and Hannah Landis, late of Bucks Co, and Abraham Leatherman as attorney for administrator of Samuel Landis, late of Medina Co, son of Henry and Hannah, acknowledge payment of estate by administrator Jacob Leatherman.   Bk 11/pg 366   Jun 3, 1853

Philip Jacoby, late of Hilltown Twp, died intestate leaving land which was sold to John Snyder, Jacob Weiser, John Slutter and Jacob Slutter, subject to dower for widow Catharine who died Jul 6, 1852. Philip's heirs Samuel A. Smith and Mary Jacoby (executors of Abraham Jacoby), Susan Jacoby (administrator of Samuel Jacoby), Joseph Hendershot (administrator of John Jacoby), John Server (administrator of Enos Jacoby), George and Mary Shull, Jacob Friedly (administrator of Susan Friedly), John and Hannah Snyder, acknowledge payment of dower.   Bk 11/pg 368   [blank], 1853

Joseph W. Hendershot, administrator of John Jacoby, late of Bloomsburg, Columbia Co, who was son of Philip Jacoby, late of Bucks Co, gives power of attorney to Oliver Jacoby of Bloomsburg to recover dower.
                                        Bk 11/pg 369   Jun 6, 1853

Jacob Kratz of Milton Twp, Warne[?] Co, OH, legatee of Abraham Kratz of Richland Twp, gives power of attorney to Jacob Clymer of Milford Twp, to recover estate from executor William B. Myers. Bk 11/pg 371   Mar 26, 1853

Henry and Elizabeth Feaster, Jacob and Maria Cornell, Jesse and Adriana Dungan, Catharine Terry, Jane K. Twining, James C. and Martha Cornell, Mahlon B. and Mary Ann Cornell, Isaac and Christiana Craven, Anthony and Ellen Flack, Cornelia Cornell, James D. and Sarah Cornell and Jesse and Hester Cornell, heirs of Cornelia Cornell, late of Southampton Twp, give power of attorney to friend John C. Cornell of Northampton Twp. to sell real estate.   Bk 11/pg 372   Nov 28, 1853

Michael Dech Sen. of Nockamixon Twp. and wife Catharine have agreed to separate due to unhappy differences between them and agree that Catharine is to keep the property she brought at the time of their marriage.
Bk 11/pg 377   Sep 15, 1853

Catharine Weckerly (widow of Abraham), niece of Christian Auchinbach, late of Springfield Twp, acknowledges payment of legacy by Christian's executor Joseph Baum.
Bk 11/pg 378   May 4, 1853

Samuel Atherholt and Levi Markley, executors of Christian Atherholt, late of New Britain Twp, have paid the heirs: Samuel A. Detweiler and Ann (wife of John L. Delp), children of Christian's daughter Ann, Samuel D. Fisher, Mary Ann (wife of Samuel H. Myers/Moyer) and Christian Myers/Moyer (guardian of Elizabeth Fisher), grandchildren of Ann by her late daughter Mary, son Jacob's children (Catharine—wife of Jesse Fluck, Mary Ann—wife of Henry Hulshiser, Samuel Muffly—guardian of Margaret—wife of William Myers, Elizabeth—wife of Levi Fosbenner), daughter Rebecca Loux's children (John A. Loux, Christian Loux, Samuel—to his son Oliver), daughter Elizabeth Ruth, daughter Sarah Lightcap.
Bk 11/pg 379   Apr 5, 1852

Lafayette Yost, Silas and Anna Schlichter, Samuel Bissey (guardian of Franey Yost), Henry Frankenfield (guardian of Edward Yost), heirs of Adam Yost, late of Nockamixon Twp, acknowledge payment of estate by administrators Ephraim and Levi Yost.
Bk 11/pg 380   Apr 7, 1847

Henry Nase of Richland Twp. and wife Mary Ann, daughter of Andrew Headman, late of Rockhill Twp, acknowledge payment of estate by administrators Samuel and Thomas Headman.   Bk 11/pg 382   Apr 9, 1853

Anna Kulp (widow) and Jacob Kulp, Joseph Kulp, Isaac Kulp and David and Elizabeth Angeny, children of Henry Kulp, late of Hilltown Twp, acknowledge payment of estate.
Bk 11/pg 382   Aug 1, 1853

John Jones of Buckingham Twp. and Philadelphia Jones, formerly of Philadelphia but now of Buckingham, intend to be married and agree to settlement of their property.
Bk 11/pg 383   May 18, 1832

Sarah Ann Kline, spinster, of Milford Twp, now 21, heir of William Kline, late of Milford, acknowledges payment of estate by her guardian John Graber.
Bk 11/pg 385   Jan 15, 1853

Daniel Rosenberger, Mary Gehman and Christiana Kulp, children of Jacob Rosenberger, late of Hatfield Twp, Montgomery Co, and Jacob Landes, Ephraim Landes, George Landes and John Landes, sons of Jacob's late daughter Barbara, acknowledge payment of dower by George Roudenbush of Rockhill Twp.   Bk 11/pg 385   Mar 28, 1853

Aaron W. Leister and wife Sarah (late Zeigenfuse) of Granville, Milwaukee Co, WI give power of attorney to Mathias Zeigenfuse of Haycock Twp. to sell their interests.   Bk 11/pg 386   Oct 8, 1853

Elizabeth Barron of Springfield Twp, heir of Henry Schleiffer, late of Springfield, acknowledges payment of estate by executor Joseph Schleiffer.
Bk 11/pg 387   Dec 14, 1853

Frederick Wolfinger, Abraham Wolfinger, Michael Wolfinger, Nicholas Wolfinger, Peter and Elizabeth Deemer, Jeremiah and Catharine Mill, Daniel and Mary Lee, children of Solomon Wolfinger, late of Nockamixon Twp, acknowledge payment of dower by Emanuel Trauger.
Bk 11/pg 388   Nov 5, 1853

Sarah Mathews, legatee of Jonas Fell of Buckingham Twp, acknowledges payment of estate by Jesse Fell.   Bk 11/pg 388   Jan 2, 1854

Sophia Haring of Milford Twp (widow) and Catharine (wife of Joseph Kline), Rachel Trumbower and Mary (wife of William P. Smith) of Milford Twp, daughters of Henry Haring, late of Milford Twp, acknowledge payment of estate by administrators Amos and Aaron W. Haring.
Bk 11/pg 388   May 16, 1853

Ann Catherine Craig, only daughter and heir of Henry Sigafoose, late of Ohio Co, VA, and her husband William Craig give power of attorney to William Sigafoose of Nockamixon Twp to recover estate due them.
Bk 11/pg 392   Mar 15, 1852

William Sigafoose acknowledges payment by administrator Samuel Poulton.
Bk 11/pg 393   Feb 22, 1854

Mercy M. Taylor, widow of Bernard Taylor, late of Upper Makefield Twp, acknowledges security for dower received by Bernard's children Jacob H., Robert F., William S., Jonathan and Maria B. Brock and Watson and Hannah H. Malone.   Bk 11/pg 397   Jun 2, 1853

Henry Overholtzer, Rachel Overholtzer and Ellen Overholtzer (married to Jacob March), children of late Isaac Overholtzer and grandchildren of Owen Overholtzer, all of Chester Co, give power of attorney to their brother Owen Overholtzer of East Pikeland Twp, Chester Co. to recover estate due them.
Bk 11/pg 397   Feb 20, 1854

Mary A. Sayler, Susan Lessig/Zessey and Elizabeth Overholtzer, children of late Henry D. Overholtzer, give power of attorney to Owen Overholtzer of Chester Co. to recover estate due them now in hands of John Shimel.
Bk 11/pg 398   Feb 18, 1854

Maria (Mann) Roudenbush, wife of Henry Roudenbush of Hilltown Twp, now 21, acknowledges payment by guardian Peter Shive of estate from late father George Mann.
Bk 11/pg 398   Mar 18, 1854

William Comfort of Philadelphia, but now at Pittsburg, gives power of attorney to brother Edmund Comfort of Philadelphia to sell land in Bucks County on Delaware River which he received from Charles Comfort in 1837.
Bk 11/pg 399   May 12, 1852

Samuel Fosbenner, now 21, acknowledges payment by guardian Jacob Kiser of estate from late father Jonas Fosbenner.   Bk 11/pg 399   Mar 17, 1854

James Paxson Hough, having attained his majority, acknowledges payment by guardian Eli Fell Jr. of estate from late father Richard Hough.
Bk 11/pg 400   Mar 30, 1854

Mary Anna I. Vansant, now 21, acknowledges payment by guardian Anthony Burton of estate from late parents.   Bk 11/pg 400   Oct 29, 1853

Ann Ivins, widow of Aaron Ivins, late of Falls Twp, is recently deceased and the dower now due from Charles Ellis and George F. Ivins, present owners of the estate. Aaron's children Aaron Ivins, Barclay Ivins Jr., Aaron Ivins (as trustee for estate of Eliza Ivins and as assignee of Caleb Ivins), Sarah B. Ivins and Aaron B. Ivins and Robert Ivins (administrators of George M. Ivins), Minor and Lydia J. Harvey and Ann C. (Ivins) Wharton acknowledge payment of dower.   Bk 11/pg 400   Nov 26, 1852

John J. Hall of Plumstead Twp, mason, now 21, acknowledges payment by guardian Josiah Rich of estate from late father Isaac Hall.
Bk 11/pg 401   Mar 27, 1854

Joseph Black of Plumstead Twp, about to go to California, gives power of attorney to Joseph Swartz of Plumstead Twp. to recover money due him.
Bk 11/pg 402   Sep 15, 1852

Henry and Abraham Yonker of Nockamixon Twp, now 21, acknowledge payment by guardian Enos Snyder of estate from late father Nicholas Yonken.
Bk 11/pg 403   Mar 30, 1854

Jonas Bailey of Nockamixon Twp, now 21, acknowledges payment by guardian Jacob Adams of estate from late father John Bailey.
Bk 11/pg 404   Aug 31, 1852

Joseph and Elizabeth Satterthwaite, daughter of Samuel Crozer, late of Falls Twp, release claim to land in Falls Twp. which Thomas and Catharine C. Crozer sold to Phineas Jenkins, being part of a tract which Samuel's brother Robert Crozer and his wife Grace sold to Samuel, excluding the dower due to Samuel's widow Martha.
Bk 11/pg 406   Apr 1, 1854

Charles B. Schlichter, Jacob A. Schlichter, Augustus B. Schlichter and Michael Nees (guardian of Mary Margaret Schlichter), children of Enos Schlichter, late of Rockhill Twp, acknowledge payment of estate by executors Henry Troxel and Sophia Schlichter.
Bk 11/pg 407   Mar 30, 1854

Sophia Schlichter, widow of Enos Schlichter, late of Rockhill Twp, and Enos' children Charles B., Jacob A., Augustus B. and Mary Margaretta (by guardian Michael Nase) acknowledge payment by Andrew Schlichter and Henry Hendricks, executors of Isaac Schlichter of money due Enos as an heir of Andrew Schlichter, Esq.
Bk 11/pg 407   [not dated]

John S. Cornell, late of Bucks Co. but now of San Francisco, CA, gives power of attorney to M.B. Cornell of Montgomery Co. to sell his share of estate of his late aunt Cornelia Cornell situate in Southampton Twp, bequeathed to her by her late husband Gilliam M. Cornell.
Bk 11/pg 407   Feb 11, 1854

Samuel Johnson, late of Buckingham Twp, bequeathed estate to son William H. Johnson subject to payment to daughters Ann J. (wife of Thomas Paxson) and Elizabeth Pickering. They acknowledge payment by William.
Bk 11/pg 408   Apr 3, 1854

Catharine Althouse, daughter of Tobias Althouse, now 21, acknowledges payment by guardian John Kramer of estate from late mother out of estate of Jacob Kramer.
Bk 11/pg 409   Mar 25, 1854

Phillip Person of Lehighton, Carbon Co, sells his right in dower of widow of Henry Person to Jacob Person in payment of a debt.

Bk 11/pg 410   Apr 1, 1854

Henry Person of Coopersburgh, Lehigh Co, drover, assigns to Jacob Person all his right in dower of widow of Henry Person, late of Springfield Twp.

Bk 11/pg 410   Apr 1, 1854

Thomas Stradling, recently appointed guardian of Mary R. Good, minor child of John Good, late of Plumstead Twp, acknowledges payment of estate by John J. Moore and Gilbert Ball, administrators of Joel Heacock, late of Rockhill Twp, who was the previous guardian.   Bk 11/pg 411   Apr 3, 1854

Edwin Fretz of Doylestown Borough acknowledges payment by guardian George McIntosh of estate from late grandfather John Swartzley.

Bk 11/pg 411   Apr 5, 1854

Zenes Buckman, late of Newtown Twp, left issue including Spencer and William. Spencer Buckman and wife Sarah Ann sell their share to William Buckman.   Bk 11/pg 412   Apr 1, 1842

Abraham Berge, Elizabeth Berge of Hilltown Twp, Christian Souder and Isaac Berge of Franconia Twp, Montgomery Co. (guardians of Anna Berge) and Susanna Berge, children of Susanna Berge, late of Hilltown Twp, acknowledge payment of estate by administrator Henry B. Moyer.

Bk 11/pg 412   Apr 3, 1854

John O. Myers, late of Bedminster Twp. left widow Elizabeth (now married to Abraham Dirstine) and several children named Eliza and John and others, with Simeon Kratz serving as Eliza and John's guardian. Eliza died in the summer of 1853, shortly before arriving at the age of 21. Elizabeth Dirstine acknowledges payment of estate by Simeon Kratz.

Bk 11/pg 413   Apr 1, 1854

Jesse Tomlinson, Charles Tomlinson and Joseph and Rhoda Walton, heirs of Jesse Tomlinson, late of Bensalem Twp, acknowledge payment by Caleb N. Taylor of proceeds from the sale of the real estate. Bk 11/pg 415 Apr 6, 1854

Mary, daughter of Adam Nunemaker, late of Rockhill Twp, now over 21, wife of Jefferson Mood, acknowledges payment of estate by her guardian Henry Frederick.   Bk 11/pg 415   Apr 5, 1854

357

Peter D. Barthe of Spring Garden Twp, York Co, gentleman, and Mary T. Clement, niece of Michael W. Ash of York Town, attorney, are about to be married and agree to financial matters. Bk 11/pg 416   Jun 28, 1825

John Foust of Nockamixon Twp. sells to Francis Rapp of Nockamixon his share in estate of his mother Ann Margaret Foust as well as land in Nockamixon bequeathed to Ann Margaret by John Trittenbauch.
Bk 11/pg 417   May 3, 1851

Martha Collins, widow of Enoch Collins, late of Buckingham Twp, releases her right to dower to her children Sarah (wife of John Short), Mary Ann (wife of Dr. John McManus), Letitia (wife of Abraham Thompson), Jane Collins, Ellen Collins and John Collins. Bk 11/pg 417   Apr 15, 1854

Charles Levy, attorney for Joseph Singmaster, Mary Singmaster and Mariah Miller (alias Hinkel), heirs of Jacob Singmaster, late of Milford Twp, acknowledges payment by George A. Singmaster of dower due to late widow Susanna. Bk 11/pg 418   Apr 22, 1854

John Kepler of Haycock Twp. acknowledges payment by Christian Hager of Haycock of dower on his plantation during life of Sarah Kepler.
Bk 11/pg 418   Apr 6, 1854

Samuel Funk of Springfield Twp. agrees with Elizabeth Funk, Barbara Funk and Anna Funk of Springfield to share property which they paid for together.
Bk 11/pg 419   Apr 1, 1854

Sarah Rauch of Springfield Twp, daughter of John Hoffman, late of Springfield Twp, acknowledge payment of estate by executors Elizabeth Hoffman and Daniel Landis. Bk 11/pg 419   Apr 15, 1854

Fietta Kline, Maria Gerhart, Catharine Gerhart, Barbara Gerhart and Jacob Barndt (guardian of Sarah and John Gerhart), children of Phillip Gerhart acknowledge payment of estate by administrators Sefernus and Abner Gerhart. Bk 11/pg 420   [not dated]

Daniel and Margaret (Delp) Bartholomew and Charles Bowers, heirs to estate of George Delp, late of Bedminster Twp, acknowledge payment of estate by executors Jacob Delp. Bk 11/pg 421   Oct 22, 1853

Daniel and Margaret (Delp) Bartholomew, heirs of Margaret Delp, late of Bedminster Twp, acknowledge payment of estate by administrator Jacob Delp.   Bk 11/pg 421   Oct 22, 1853

George Hockman, James and Margaret (Hockman) Harris, Samuel and Isabella (Hockman) Hockman and Maria Hockman, grandchildren of George Delp, late of Bedminster Twp, acknowledge payment of estate by executor Jacob Delp.   Bk 11/pg 421   Oct 22, 1853

Lydia Zeigenfuse, daughter of Abraham Zeigenfuse, late of Bedminster Twp, now 21, acknowledge payment of estate by guardian Emanuel C. Salliday.
                    Bk 11/pg 422   Apr 7, 1854

George Miller of Nockamixon Twp, son of George Miller, late of Nockamixon, acknowledges payment of estate by Jacob Stone, executor of Frederick Stone, late of Nockamixon, who was George's guardian.
                    Bk 11/pg 422   Dec 28, 1850

Ann Barbary Shitz, daughter of George Shitz, late of Nockamixon Twp, acknowledges payment of estate by Jacob Stone, executor of Frederick Stone, late of Nockamixon, who was George's administrator.
                    Bk 11/pg 423   Mar 19, 1850

Franey Ulmer of Tinicum Twp, daughter of Samuel Ulmer, late of Tinicum Twp, acknowledges payment of estate by Jacob Stone, executor of Frederick Stone, late of Nockamixon Twp, who was Samuel's administrator.
                    Bk 11/pg 423   Dec 20, 1851

Samuel Major and wife Catharine, daughter of George Shitz, late of Nockamixon Twp, acknowledges payment of estate by Jacob Stone, executor of Frederick Stone, late of Nockamixon, who was George's administrator.
                    Bk 11/pg 423   Feb 14, 1854

Isaac Amey of Allentown, laborer, John Amey of Allentown, laborer, Susannah (wife of Tobias Deaterly) of Springfield Twp, Elizabeth (wife of Nicholas Heft) of Haycock Twp, Rebecca Amey of Springfield and Hannah (wife of Joshua Frey) of Springfield, heirs of John Amey, late of Springfield Twp, acknowledge payment of estate by executors Levi Amey of Springfield, yeoman, George Amey of Springfield, yeoman, and Joseph Amey of Springfield, yeoman.   Bk 11/pg 424   Apr 1, 1854

George and Joseph Amey of Springfield Twp, executors of John Amey, late of Springfield Twp, acknowledge payment of estate by executor Levi Amey.
Bk 11/pg 425   Apr 1, 1854

Robert McMasters, son of John McMasters, late of Bucks Co, sells to Daniel Poor, Esq. of Upper Makefield Twp. his share of dower.
Bk 11/pg 426   Apr 1, 1854

Peter Joseph Marx of Lower Makefield Twp. and wife Aleshia have agreed to separate due to unhappy differences between them and agree to settlement of estate.
Bk 11/pg 427   Apr 7, 1854

James R. Vansant of Cincinnatti, OH, George and Mary W. Scott of Steubenville, Jefferson Co, OH and Mercy Jane Vansant of Philadelphia give power of attorney to Edward D. Woodruff of Philadelphia to sell their interest in land in Newtown Borough.
Bk 11/pg 428   Apr 15, 1850

William Green, late of Richland Twp, bequeathed money to daughter Jane (wife of Jervis Thomas) to be held in trust by brother-in-law Samuel Cary and nephews Benjamin G. Foulke and Aaron Penrose. Jane divorced from Jervis in 1849. Jane R. Thomas acknowledges payment of estate by executors Richard R. Green, Edward Foulke and Joshua Foulke.
Bk 11/pg 431   Apr 7, 1854

Caroline G. Foulke, wife of Joshua Foulke of Richland Twp, and daughter of William Green, late of Richland, acknowledges payment of estate by executors Richard R. Green, Joshua Foulke and Edward Foulke.
Bk 11/pg 432   Apr 29, 1854

Elizabeth McCray of Richland Twp, Grace R. Shaw of Plumstead Twp. and Mary Green and Alice Walton of Stroudsburg and Matilda Foulke of Richland Twp, daughters of William Green, late of Richland Twp, acknowledge payment of estate by executors Richard R. Green, Joshua Foulke and Edward Foulke.
Bk 11/pg 433   Apr 10, 1854

Tobias Fishler of Tinicum Twp. and wife Sarah, daughter of Samuel Major, late of Tinicum Twp, now 21, acknowledge payment of estate by her guardian Joseph Leer.
Bk 11/pg 435   Apr 24, 1854

Elias Major, son of Samuel Major, late of Tinicum Twp, now 21, acknowledges payment of estate by guardian Joseph Leer.
Bk 11/pg 435   Mar 25, 1852

Jacob H. Atkinson, Mary Atkinson, Eliza Trego, John L. Atkinson, Amy Ellis, Thomas C. Atkinson, Abraham Atkinson and Ann Daniels, children of John Atkinson, late of Upper Makefield Twp, acknowledge payment of estate by administrator Samuel Atkinson.   Bk 11/pg 436   Apr 18, 1854

Naieta Marsteller of Hamilton Twp, Monroe Co, now 21, acknowledges payment by guardian Jacob Pearson of estate from late father Paul Marsteller.
Bk 11/pg 436   Apr 24, 1854

Samuel Lambert, Christian Lambert, Mary Transue, Sarah Transue, Elizabeth Rhoad, Catherine Dickson, Susanna Brotzman, Margaret Hartzel and Elenora Ruth, children of Christian Lambert, late of Durham Twp, acknowledge payment of estate by Michael Fackenthall, administrator of Anthony Transue who was Christian's administrator.   Bk 11/pg 438   May 1, 1854

Enos Renner, Henry Renner, Samuel Renner, William and Elizabeth Ott, John and Sally Nase, Nathan and Hannah Thomas, Adam and Lydia Nyce, Jacob and Catharine Drollinger and John Renner, heirs of Adam Renner, late of Hilltown Twp, acknowledge payment of dower by John Hingbey[?] of Hilltown Twp, due by death of their mother.   Bk 11/pg 440   Apr 1, 1851

Charles Selner of Durham Twp, son of John Selner, late of Nockamixon Twp. and heir of Charles Selner, late of Plumstead Twp, being weak in body and unable to go to Doylestown, gives power of attorney to Peter Selner of Springfield Twp. to recover estate from executor Jacob Herring.
Bk 11/pg 443   May 30, 1854

John Atherholt of Lapeer Co, MI, son of Christian Atherholt, late of New Britain Twp, acknowledges payment of dower by executors Levi Markley and Samuel Atherholt, due by death of his mother Margaret.
Bk 11/pg 444   Sep 30, 1851

Mary (wife of Francis Wagoner), Sarah Atherholt, Jacob Atherholt, Isaac Atherholt, Christian Atherholt, Margaret (wife of Joseph Paisley) and Joseph Paisley (guardian of Samuel Atherholt), children of Christian Atherholt who was a son of Christian Atherholt, late of New Britain Twp, acknowledge payment of dower by executors Levi Markley and Samuel Atherholt.
Bk 11/pg 445   Apr 7, 1852

Siblings of Charles Selner, late of Plumstead Twp: Catherine Deaterly, Mary Deaterly, Susanna (deceased, children Charles Haring, Hannah Wasser), Magdalena Berger (deceased, son Joseph), Elizabeth Shuman (deceased, children Joseph and Jacob), John (deceased, children John, Peter, Hannah Fabian, Sarah Reiser), Daniel (deceased, children John, Joseph, Elisha, Mary Conard) acknowledge payment of estate by trustee Jacob Haring.

Bk 11/pg 445   Jun 3, 1854

Silas Althouse of Bedminster Twp. sells to Mathias Althouse his share in dower of his father Martin Althouse's estate.   Bk 11/pg 446   Jun 9, 1854

Nathan T. Knight, late of Philadelphia, who died May 18, 1853 intestate, owned land in Bristol Borough. Widow Elizabeth and children John and Sidney Wood, Sarah Knight, Ellen Knight, Mary Elizabeth Knight and Anna Knight (last three minors) acknowledge payment of proceeds from real estate by Walter Laing, Mordecai Thomas and Susan Wilson.

Bk 11/pg 447   Apr 1, 1854

Mary James of New Britain Twp, widow of Levi James, renounces right to Levi's estate.   Bk 11/pg 448   Feb 3, 1854

Henry M. Laing, executor of Henry Moore and testamentary trustee of Catharine R. Laing, gives power of attorney to Anthony Swain to record satisfaction of a mortgage.   Bk 11/pg 448   May 9, 1854

Abraham Roudenbush, Jesse Roudenbush, Enos Roudenbush, Samuel Roudenbush, Sarah Cressman, Anna Althouse, Matilda Clymer and Elizabeth Leidy, heirs of George Roudenbush, late of Rockhill Twp, acknowledge payment of estate by executors Jacob and George Roudenbush.

Bk 11/pg 449   Apr 7, 1854

Levi and George Amey of Springfield Twp, executors and sons of John Amey, late of Springfield Twp, acknowledge payment of estate by executor Joseph Amey.   Bk 11/pg 450   Apr 1, 1854

Magdalena Gearhart of Franconia Twp, Montgomery Co, widow of George Mann, late of Haycock Twp, and children Sarah (wife of Henry Bradford of Providence Twp, Montgomery Co), Elizabeth (wife of Jacob Cressman of Rockhill Twp), Margaret (wife of John Cressman of Rockhill Twp), Maria (wife of Henry Roudenbush of Hilltown Twp), acknowledge payment of dower by Levi, George and Joseph Amey.   Bk 11/pg 451   Mar 18, 1854

Alfred Shaw of New Orleans, LA, son of late Sarah Ann Shaw, who was a sister of Thomas Carver, late of Solebury Twp, gives power of attorney to

Matthias Shaw of Solebury Twp. to recover estate from administrator Richard Watson.   Bk 11/pg 451   Apr 14, 1854

Matilda Laubach of Durham Twp, now 21, acknowledges payment by guardian John Fackenthall of estate from late father Frederick Laubach.
                                                                       Bk 11/pg 453   Mar 27, 1854

William Hagaman of Plain Twp, Wayne Co, OH, heir of John J. Vanhorn, late of Northampton Twp, gives power of attorney to Barnet Barnes of Warminster Twp. to recover estate from administrator Levi Temple.
                                                                       Bk 11/pg 454   Oct 23, 1852

John McMasters, late of Upper Makefield Twp, died intestate leaving widow Ann and six children: William, Hannah, James, Robert, John and Rachel. Son John recently died leaving children William and Mary. William McMasters sells his share of dower to David Conrad of Northern Liberties Twp, Philadelphia Co, flour merchant.   Bk 11/pg 455   Apr 15, 1845

Emma Comfort of Philadelphia, now 18 and entitled to estate from grandfather Harvey Gillingham, acknowledges payment by guardian Redman Hance.   Bk 11/pg 456   Aug 13, 1854

Christiana Waltman, daughter of Jacob Waltman, late of Richland Twp, now 21, acknowledges payment of estate by guardian Peter Harris.
                                                                       Bk 11/pg 456   Aug 19, 1854

Harvey Summers of Philadelphia, now 21, acknowledges payment by guardian John Geil of estate from late father Isaac Summers.
                                                                       Bk 11/pg 457   Aug 31, 1854

Charles Alexander of Lower Makefield Twp, son of Robert and Rachael, and Sarah Fish, daughter of Elijah and Elizabeth Fish of Lower Makefield Twp, were married at Elijah's house on Nov 4, 1841.   Bk 11/pg 458   Nov 4, 1841

Jacob and Carolina Myers, Lydia Zeigenfuss, Emmanuel C. Salliday (guardian of James and Catherine Zeigenfuss), children of Abraham Zeigenfuss, late of Bedminster Twp, acknowledge payment of estate by administrators Aaron Zeigenfuss and Emanuel Ott.
                                                                       Bk 11/pg 459   Apr 7, 1854

Columbia E. Dobynes of Jefferson Co, MS, sole surviving child of Josiah Simpson, is entitled to estate from grandfather William Simpson, formerly of

Bucks Co, gives power of attorney to David S. Seavis[?] of Bucks Co. to recover estate due her. Bk 11/pg 460   Aug 24, 1854

Joseph S. Shelly of Milford Twp, David S. Shelly of Saucon Twp, Lehigh Co, Jacob S. Shelly of Upper Milford Twp, Lehigh Co, Samuel H. and Susanna Harly of Salford Twp, Montgomery Co, Levy S. and Barbara Shelly of Milford Twp, William H. and Fanny Oberholtzer of Milford Twp, Samuel and Elizabeth Moyer of Springfield Twp, William B. Shelly (guardian of John Shelly, son of late Michael S. Shelly), children of Jacob Shelly, late of Milford Twp, farmer, acknowledge payment of dower by George Klein due by the recent death of the widow Barbara.   Bk 11/pg 463   Apr 2, 1853

John Vanartsdalen, late of Northampton Twp, bequeathed estate to wife Jane and sons Francis and John. Jane releases son John from claim to real estate. Bk 11/pg 464   Aug 28, 1854

Thomas E. Baines of Cooper Co, MO, son of Eliza Ann Banes, late of White Co, IN, gives power of attorney to William M. McDowell of Bucks Co. to recover estate due him. Bk 11/pg 465   Feb 27, 1854

Sarah Thomas, widow of Jonathan Thomas, late of Bristol Borough, releases dower right to Walter Laing of Bristol Twp. Bk 11/pg 466   Mar 29, 1852

Jacob Wenholt of Lower Salford Twp, Montgomery Co, acknowledges payment by Moses Texter and Samuel Roudenbush, administrators of Jacob Wenholt, late of Rockhill Twp. who was his guardian, of estate from late father Isaac Wenholt. Bk 11/pg 467   [not dated]

Joshua P. Lovett of Halls Cross Roads, Harford Co, MD, gives power of attorney to David Brown of Falls Twp. to recover dower due from Samuel Sutton due by recent death of Bulah Lovett, widow of Owen Lovett. Bk 11/pg 467   Apr 5, 1854

Thomas Chapman Harvey of Philadelphia, Esq. and Elizabeth Gibbes of Cheltenham, Gloucester Co. [NJ or England?], spinster, are about to be married and agree to settlement of estate as Elizabeth possesses money lent out to her uncles Edward and John Sealy of Bridgewater, Somerset Co, bankers. Bk 11/pg 468   Mar 29, 1842

Adam Walp of Shreveport, LA gives power of attorney to Charles Walp of Richland Twp. to acknowledge payment by Felix Walp of estate due from his late father David Walp. Bk 11/pg 472   Sep 25, 1854

Clarissa Clymer of Hilltown Twp, daughter of Jonathan Wood, late of Plumstead Twp, acknowledges payment of estate by her mother Catherine Wood. Bk 11/pg 473 Oct 14, 1854

Edmond Roberts of Rockhill Twp. assigns to Hugh Foulke of Richland Twp. his share in estate of his aunt Susanna Roberts, late of Richland Twp. Bk 11/pg 475 Nov 4, 1854

John Buck, son of John Buck, late of Tinicum Twp, now 21, acknowledges payment of estate by guardian Nicholas Buck. Bk 12/pg 1 Nov 17, 1848

Rebecca Heaney, daughter of William Heaney, late of Tinicum Twp, now 21, acknowledges payment of estate by guardian Nicholas Buck. Bk 12/pg 1 Apr 8, 1854

Alfred Buck and wife Lenah (late Buck), now 21, acknowledge payment by her guardian Nicholas Buck of estate from her late grandfather Jacob Buck and late father John Buck. Bk 12/pg 2 Apr 7, 1848

Jacob Buck, son of John Buck, late of Tinicum Twp, now 21, acknowledges payment by guardian Nicholas Buck of estate from late father and late grandfather Jacob Buck. Bk 12/pg 3 Nov 17, 1848

Samuel Yost of Tinicum Twp. and wife Rebecca (late Haney), mother of Frederick Haney, minor son of William Haney, late of Tinicum Twp, who died unmarried and without issue, acknowledge payment of estate by Frederick's guardian Nicholas Buck. Bk 12/pg 3 Dec 16, 1848

David Smith, late of Spring Garden District but now of Philadelphia, druggist, assigns to Joshua W. Ash of Philadelphia, physician, his share of estate of father Jonathan Smith, late of Solebury Twp, in the hands of administrators Elizabeth and John Smith. Bk 12/pg 4 Nov 23, 1854

John Weydemeyer, Samuel Weydemeyer, Isaac Weydemeyer, Thomas and Sarah Dungan, John and Susan Garron and Levina Weydemeyer, heirs of Jacob Weydemeyer, late of Tinicum Twp, acknowledge payment of estate by Jacob Weydemeyer. Bk 12/pg 5 Apr 5, 1841

Jacob Kilmer (guardian of Mary Ann Weydemeyer) and Michael Worman (guardian of Jonas Weydemeyer) , minor children of Jacob Weydemeyer, acknowledge payment of estate by Jacob Weydemeyer. Bk 12/pg 6 Apr 5, 1841

Samuel and Elizabeth Rufe, heir of Jacob Weydemeyer, late of Tinicum Twp, acknowledge payment of estate by Jacob Weydemeyer.

Bk 12/pg 7   Apr 5, 1841

George and Julia Ann Ashbauch of Hartsville, Stuben Co, NY give power of attorney to Thomas P. Ball of Quakertown to recover estate from Gilbert Ball, administrator of Joseph Foltz.   Bk 12/pg 11   Nov 28, 1854

Jacob Foltz of Norristown, Elias Foltz, Samuel Foltz, Jonas Foltz, Sarah Foltz and Catharine Charles of Springfield Twp, heirs of Joseph Foltz, late of Richland Twp, acknowledge payment of estate by administrator Gilbert Ball.

Bk 12/pg 12   Sep 27, 1854

Sarah Cyphert (widow), Joseph Seifert of Springfield Twp, Leonard Cyphert of Lower Saucon Twp, Northampton Co (guardian of David W. Cyphert) and Kroft Fisher of Springfield Twp (administrator of his wife Elizabeth), children of George Cyphert, late of Springfield Twp, acknowledge payment by administrators Bartel and George W. Seifert.   Bk 12/pg 13   Apr 1, 1853

John Kohl of Durham Twp, yeoman, gives power of attorney to son Henry Kohl of Durham Twp. to record satisfaction of a mortgage.

Bk 12/pg 16   Jan 9, 1855

William C. Souder of Waterloo Twp, Waterloo Co, Canada, yeoman, Joseph S. Souder of Waterloo Twp, yeoman, and John S. Souder of Waterloo Twp, gentleman, sons of John Souder, formerly of Rockhill Twp, yeoman and late wife Catharine Sarah Souder, give power of attorney to brother Jacob S. Souder of Upper Salford Twp, Montgomery Co. to sell the real estate.

Bk 12/pg 19   Oct 24, 1854

Richard Roberts of Philadelphia, son of Jesse Roberts, late of Richland Twp, acknowledges payment of estate by executors Hersillia J. Roberts and Benjamin G. Foulke.   Bk 12/pg 20   Oct 12, 1854

Rebecca Heston, Esther Michener, Mercy Walton and Hannah Stackhouse, heirs of John Heston, late of Wrightstown Twp, acknowledge payment of estate by administrators Absalom Michener, Thomas Walton and Charles Stackhouse.   Bk 12/pg 21   Jan 18, 1855

Jacob Vanhart of Biles Island, Falls Twp, bequeathed estate to son James Vanhart upon the arrival of son William S. at age of 21. James, late of Ohio, died before his father leaving five children: Samuel, Eliza (wife of Hamilton

Hitchins), Jacob (and wife Jane), Thomas (and wife Susanna) and Emanuel (and wife Jane), all of Cincinatti, OH. They acknowledge payment of estate by executors Aaron Ivins, Thomas Vanhart and William Smith.

Bk 12/pg 23   Jun 1, 1854

Levi and Joseph Amey of Springfield Twp, sons and executors of John Amey, late of Springfield, acknowledge payment of estate by executor George Amey.   Bk 12/pg 26   Apr 1, 1854

Joel Wright of Falls Twp, executor of Benjamin Wright, late of Falls Twp, renounced right of administration to the other named executor, Mark Wright.

Bk 12/pg 27   Jan 25, 1855

Sarah Price and Martha B. Smith of Philadelphia, daughters of Samuel Brown, late of Solebury Twp, acknowledge payment of estate by administrator John S. Brown.   Bk 12/pg 34   Nov 16, 1854

Thomas P. Ball of Richland Twp (attorney for Julia Ann and George Eschbach of Steuben Co, N) acknowledge payment of estate by Gilbert Ball, administrator of Joseph Foltz, late of Richland Twp.

Bk 12/pg 34   Jan 6, 1855

Thomas P. Ball (attorney for Mary Amos—late Foltz—of North Dansville, Livingston Co, NY) acknowledges payment of estate by Gilbert Ball, administrator of Joseph Foltz, late of Richland Twp.

Bk 12/pg 36   Feb 8, 1855

Mary Amos of North Dansville, Livingston Co, NY, heir of Joseph Foltz, late of Bucks Co, gives power of attorney to Thomas P. Ball of Bucks Co. to recover estate from administrator Gilbert Ball, Esq.

Bk 12/pg 37   Jan 13, 1855

David Howell, late of Upper Makefield Twp, bequeathed estate to sons Samuel and Charles. Charles died in Jan, 1829 leaving widow Mary C. and son David. Samuel, Mary C. and David (by guardian Mahlon K. Tahlor) agree to men to partition the real estate.   Bk 12/pg 38   Jan 23, 1830

Mary Hough, widow of William M. Hough, late of Lower Makefield Twp, Charles and Susan Hough, Jesse and Maria Hough, James and Rachel Vernartesdale, heirs of William, give power of attorney to Thomas S. Cadwallader of Lower Makefield to sell the real estate.

Bk 12/pg 40   Aug 15, 1854

Mahlon Long of Harrisburg, administrator of Hugh Long, late of Warminster Twp, gives power of attorney to his brother Charles Long of Bucks Co. to enter satisfaction of a mortgage.   Bk 12/pg 41   May 9, 1850

Samuel W. Downing of Bristol Twp. gives power of attorney to wife Eliza Clark Downing and nephew William Milner Downing of Bristol Borough to sell all his property.   Bk 12/pg 43   Mar 13, 1855

John Kratz, Barbara Kratz, Catharine Yeakel, Samuel W. Moyer (guardian of Barbara and John Moyer, minor children of Mary Moyer late of Hilltown Twp), all of Hilltown Twp, and Jacob Kratz of Milton Twp, Wayne Co, OH, heirs of Jacob Kratz, late of Hilltown Twp, acknowledge payment of estate by administrator Henry Leicy.   Bk 12/pg 47   Mar 17, 1855

Stephen K. Price of Philadelphia sells to Daniel T. Moore of Philadelphia his share in estate of Rachel Kirk, late of Bucks Co.   Bk 12/pg 48   Mar 21, 1855

Sarah B. Simpson of Solebury Twp, daughter of late Stephen Twining, gets payment of estate from Charles Twining.   Bk 12/pg 52   Mar 24, 1855

Sophia Wireman, Christianna David, Catharine Hines, John and Elizabeth McKinney and John Apple (administrator of Ann Apple), children of Henry Wierman, late of New Britain Twp, acknowledge payment of estate by executors Isaac and Michael Wireman.   Bk 12/pg 55   Apr 8, 1851

Richard C. and Charlotte Bye of Buckingham Twp, Isaiah and Marcy W. Ely of Philadelphia and James M. and Susan M. Wilkinson of Solebury Twp, children of John Bye, late of Buckingham Twp, agree to settlement of estate.
          Bk 12/pg 57   Mar 31, 1855

Isaac W. Staily of New Britain Twp, son of late Jacob Staily, acknowledges payment of estate by guardian Daniel Hill of New Britain Twp.
          Bk 12/pg 59   Apr 3, 1855

Hesther Landes of New Britain Twp, heir of Magdalena Overholt, late of Plumstead Twp, acknowledges payment of estate by administrator Charles Bryan.   Bk 12/pg 60   Mar 23, 1855

Abraham Overholt, Elizabeth Overholt of Plumstead Twp, Hester Landes of New Britain Twp, John Overholt and Isaac Overholt of Buckingham Twp, heirs of Magdalena Overholt, late of Plumstead Twp, acknowledge payment of estate by administrator Charles Bryan.   Bk 12/pg 60   Jan 13, 1855

Frederick G. Hillpot, Esq. and Charles Furnece, guardians of Silas and Levina Ulmer, minor children of Felix Ulmer, late of Tinicum Twp, acknowledge payment of estate by administrator Abraham Ulmer.

Bk 12/pg 61   Jan 7, 1854

William Miller, Susanna Miller and Nancy Ann Miller of Newhaven Twp, Huron Co, OH gave a power of attorney to Peter M. Ritter of Nockamixon Twp. to collect money from estates of Bartel and Elizabeth White. They acknowledge payment by Peter.   Bk 12/pg 66   Mar 12, 1855

Luissa A. (wife of Silas Kroner) and James C. Hill (guardian of Sarah and Sophia Evans), children of James Evans, late of Doylestown Twp, acknowledge payment of estate by Yates Y. Evans who inherited the real estate and was to pay James' daughters (including Rebecca) after the death of his widow.   Bk 12/pg 67   Apr 5, 1855

Sarah Ann Swartz of Doylestown Borough, now 21, acknowledges payment by guardian Levi Kramer of estate from father Jacob Swartz, late of Bedminster Twp.   Bk 12/pg 68   Apr 7, 1855

Rebecca A. Dean (late Flowers), wife of George Dean of Middletown Twp. and co-holder of a mortgage from Daniel Trump to Elizabeth, Andrew, David, Rachel, Robert B., Albert and Rebecca A. Flowers, children of William Flowers, late of Middletown Twp, gives power of attorney to husband George to record satisfaction of the mortgage.   Bk 12/pg 70   Apr 3, 1855

Henry N. Groff, Noah Groff (attorney for Christiana Fulmer), Jacob N. Groff, Thomas N. Groff, Noah Groff, Aaron Groff (by guardian Abraham Groff), heirs of Jacob Groff, late of Rockhill Twp, acknowledge payment of estate by administrators John and George N. Groff.   Bk 12/pg 70   Mar 17, 1855

Rebecca G. Taylor of White Haven Borough, Luzerne Co. gives power of attorney to husband John Taylor to recover money due her.

Bk 12/pg 71   Apr 2, 1855

John M. Potts of New Britain Twp, about to move to Illinois, gives power of attorney to David Ridle of Doylestown Twp. to recover money due him.

Bk 12/pg 72   Apr 14, 1854

Mahlon Hartly of Columbia Co, OH gives power of attorney to Samuel Armitage of Bucks Co. to recover share of father's estate in hands of guardian John Armitage.   Bk 12/pg 72   Jan 29, 1851

369

Aaron Wambold of Rockhill Twp, guardian of Milton, Rachel and Catharine Schlichter, minor children of Jesse Schlichter, acknowledges payment of estate by administrators Henry Troxel and Henry Schlichter.

Bk 12/pg 73   Apr 10, 1855

Mary L. Stauffer, widow of Samuel L. Stauffer of Rockhill Twp, acknowledges payment of estate by administrators Henry Troxel and George Trumbore.   Bk 12/pg 74   Apr 9, 1855

Catharine Schlichter, widow of Jesse Schlichter, late of Rockhill Twp, acknowledges payment of estate by administrators Henry Troxel and Henry Schlichter.   Bk 12/pg 74   Apr 10, 1854

Samuel Landes of Rockhill Twp. and Abraham Clymer of Milford Twp. acknowledge payment of estate by Henry Troxel and Henry Schlichter, administrators of Samuel L. Stover, late of Rockhill Twp.

Bk 12/pg 75   Apr 9, 1855

William B. Kemerer of Richland Twp, Paul H. Hartzel and Neri Barndt of Rockhill Twp, guardians of Maria, Sophia and Amanda Heller, minor children of Tobias Heller, acknowledge payment of estate by administrator Henry Troxel.   Bk 12/pg 76   Apr 11, 1855

Hannah Heller, widow of Tobias Heller, late of Rockhill Twp, acknowledges payment of estate by administrator Henry Troxel.   Bk 12/pg 76   Apr 11, 1855

James Darrah, late of Warminster Twp, bequeathed real estate to son Henry subject to payment to wife Rebecca. Henry is since deceased and land sold to Joseph Carrell of Warminster Twp, subject to dower. Widow Rebecca is also now deceased. Henry's heirs James E. Darrah and Mary H. Whitaker acknowledge payment of dower by Joseph Carrell.

Bk 12/pg 79   Feb 13, 1855

Jacob Groff of Richland Twp, yeoman, and Hannah Moore of Richland Twp, widow of William Moore, late of Richland, are about to be married and agree to settlement of estate.   Bk 12/pg 81   Feb 13, 1851

Franklin Wimmer of Richland Twp, now 21, acknowledges payment by guardian John Diehl of estate from late father Philip Wimmer.

Bk 12/pg 82   Apr 4, 1855

Jacob M. Kaufman of Springfield Twp, now 21, acknowledges payment by guardian Joseph M. Myers of estate from late father Michael Kaufman.
Bk 12/pg 83   Feb 12, 1855

Hersillia J. Roberts, Hannah L. Roberts, Benjamin G. Roberts, Jesse Roberts and Isabella G. Roberts, all of Richland Twp, children of Jesse Roberts, late of Richland Twp, acknowledge payment of estate by executor Benjamin G. Foulke.
Bk 12/pg 87   Jan 8, 1855

Samuel Neice and John N. and Mary Solliday, siblings of Tobias Neice/Nace, late of Tinicum Twp, acknowledge payment of estate by administrator Frederick G. Hillpot.
Bk 12/ pg 90   Feb 24, 1854

Elizabeth Sacks of Milford Twp, spinster, daughter of Michael Sacks, recently gave birth to a male bastard and has charged Edward Reiter of Milford Twp. as the father of the child. Edward agrees to pay for upbringing of child.
Bk 12/pg 91   Apr 16, 1855

Abigail Althouse of Philadelphia, now 21, acknowledges payment by guardian Henry Troxel of estate from father Frederick Althouse, late of Rockhill Twp.
Bk 12/pg 93   Apr 17, 1855

Jonathan Paxson of Bensalem Twp, guardian of Edward and Charles Laing, gives power of attorney to Anthony Swain of Bristol to record satisfaction of a mortgage.
Bk 12/pg 96   Jul 12, 1854

Daniel K. Nicholas, guardian of Emma Elizabeth Fox, minor child of Joseph Fox, late of Haycock Twp, acknowledges payment of estate by administrator Henry Frankenfield.
Bk 12/pg 97   Mar 13, 1855

Nelson Cooper of Tinicum Twp. acknowledges payment by Charles Fellman, Esq., trustee appointed to sell land of Bethell Cooper for benefit of his heirs.
Bk 12/pg 98   Apr 27, 1855

Anna Leatherman, entitled by bequest to one-fourth of estate of Philip Leatherman of Bedminster Twp, acknowledges payment by executors Abraham and Jacob Leatherman.
Bk 12/pg 99   Dec 8, 1854

Elizabeth Price and Sybilla Tyson (by guardian John Proctor), legatees of Isaac Godshalk, late of New Britain Twp, acknowledge payment of estate by executors Jacob Gross and Samuel Anglemoyer.   Bk 12/pg 99   Apr 2, 1855

Lea Miller of Lower Milford Twp, daughter of late Maria Miller, acknowledges payment of estate by executor Chas. F. Dickenshied.
Bk 12/pg 102   Apr 3, 1850

Ann McDowell, late of Buckingham Twp, left children James (and wife Elizabeth), Henry (and wife Angeline), Sarah (widow of Joseph Mathews), Martha Bewley (widow), Mary (widow of Watson Mathews), all of Philadelphia, Margery (wife of William Mathews), Phebe (wife of Jonathan Mathews), both in Buckingham, Elizabeth (wife of Jacob Wright of Camden, NJ) and one grandchild, Letitia (only child of Thomas McDowell, deceased, wife of Aaron Carver of Solebury Twp). Heirs give power of attorney to Jonathan Mathews to sell the real estate.   Bk 12/pg 105   Nov 30, 1854

Francis Fretz, guardian of Lydia Maust, minor child of late Samuel Maust, acknowledges payment of estate by Elizabeth Martin and Henry Frankenfield, executors of her former guardian James Martin.   Bk 12/pg 107   Apr 5, 1855

John Swarts, Dinah Swarts of Bedminster Twp, Isaac Swarts of Philadelphia, Michael and Elizabeth Beck of New Britain Twp, legatees of Ann Swarts, late of Bedminster Twp, acknowledge payment of estate by executors Abraham Swarts and Isaac Rosenberger.   Bk 12/pg 108   Apr 26, 1853

Henry Frankenfield of Richland Twp, tobacconist, now 21, acknowledges payment by guardian Henry Baringer of estate from late grandfather Daniel Horn and of Michael Diehl.   Bk 12/pg 111   Jun 4, 1855

Mary Flack of Newtown Twp, mother and sole heir of Martha Flack, recently deceased, acknowledges payment of estate by Martha's guardian Seruch Titus.   Bk 12/pg 114   Apr 4, 1855

James Cooper of Kingwood Twp, Hunterdon Co, NJ acknowledges payment by Charles Fellman, Esq. of his share of proceeds from sale of the real estate of Bethell Cooper.   Bk 12/pg 114   Jun 9, 1855

Rachael Cooper, Hannah M. Lamb, Harrison E. Cooper and David H. Cooper of Richmond Twp, Tioga Co, PA, heirs of Mary Myers, acknowledge payment of money owed by Abraham Myers.   Bk 12/pg 115   Mar 2, 1855

Mary Cressman of Rockhill Twp, Magdalena Stout, Elizabeth Raudenbush and Anna Fluck of Hilltown Twp, daughters of Henry H. Stout, late of Hilltown Twp, acknowledge payment of estate by administrators Enos Stout and Tobias Fluck, Esq.   Bk 12/pg 118   Jun 15, 1855

Hannah (Stout) Stouffer, Lydia (Stout) Kramer, Ruben Y. Strausberger, Henry Strausberger (by attorney Elias Harzell), Andrew S. Strausberger, Lucy Ann Hartzell, Elizabeth Shelly and Mary Hartzell, heirs of Henry H. Stout, late of Hilltown Twp, acknowledge payment of estate by administrators Enos Stout and Tobias Fluck. Bk 12/pg 119 Jun 15, 1855

Mary Knight of Southampton Twp (widow) gives power of attorney to son Jonathan Knight of Southampton to recover money due her. Bk 12/pg 119 Apr 25, 1855

July Ann Strong (late Cooper), granddaughter of William Cooper, late of Tinicum Twp, acknowledges payment of estate by Charles Fellman, High Sherriff of Bucks Co. who is trustee for the heirs. Bk 12/pg 120 Jun 27, 1855

William S. Hutchinson of Northampton Twp, son of Thomas T. Hutchinson, late of Northampton, was bequeathed estate after the death of Thomas's wife Ester who died before Thomas. William gives up his bequest to his sisters Sarah, Ann, Elizabeth Martin (and her children Joseph and Sarah), Rebecca and Matilda. Bk 12/pg 122 Jun 17, 1854

Josiah D. and Sarah E. Brooks and Margaret L. Dixey, only children of Capt. Charles Dixey, acknowledge payment of estate by their uncle Thomas Dixey who was Charles' executor. Bk 12/pg 130 Aug 13, 1855

George Linton sells to Charles F. Linton of Philadelphia, painter, his share of estate of James Linton of Bucks Co. Bk 12/pg 135 Nov 7, 1854

Mary Elizabeth Russell (formerly Banes) of White Co, IN gives power of attorney to William McDowell of Bucks Co. to recover money from Joseph Carver Sen., executor of Esther Blaker, late of Bucks Co. Bk 12/pg 136 Jul 17, 1855

Jacob and Sarah Crater of Seneca Co, OH give power of attorney to Lewis Haycock of Montgomery Co. to recover legacy from estate of Mary Overhulzer, late of Bucks Co. Bk 12/pg 138 Jul 10, 1855

Lewis Haycock of Lower Salford Twp, Montgomery Co, acknowledges payment by John Shimel and Joseph Ormey, administrators of Mary Overholzer of estate due to Jacob and Sarah Crator of Seneca Co, OH. Bk 12/pg 139 Jul 24, 1855

Abia Logan (wife of Samuel Logan) and Jane (wife of Benajah Raylman of Upper Makefield), daughters of Henry Raylman, late of Upper Makefield Twp, acknowledges payment of mortgage by George W. Trego, farmer, of Upper Makefield Twp.   Bk 12/pg 142   Oct 4, 1855

Mahlon Diehl of Richland Twp, now 21, acknowledges payment by guardian John Matts of estate from late father David Diehl.
                                                Bk 12/pg 146   Oct 27, 1855

Samuel Cooper of Tinicum Twp. acknowledges payment by Charles Fellman, Esq., trustee of real estate on behalf of Bethel Cooper's heirs.
                                                Bk 12/pg 148   Oct 22, 1855

William Cooper of Sussex Co, NJ, grandson of William Cooper, late of Tinicum Twp, acknowledges payment of his share by Charles Fellman, High Sheriff of Bucks Co. who was trustee for the heirs.
                                                Bk 12/pg 149   Apr 9, 1855

Jacob Landis and wife Mary, daughter of Michael Hotel, late of Richland Twp, acknowledge payment of estate by administrators Joseph B. and Henry Hottel.   Bk 12/pg 154   Apr 6, 1855

Margaret Myers (late Atherholt) of Richland Twp, now 21, acknowledges payment by guardian Samuel Moffley of estate due her.
                                                Bk 12/pg 155   Apr 27, 1853

Lafayette Solliday and wife Catharine, daughter of Michael Huddle, late of Richland Twp, acknowledges payment of estate by administrators Joseph and Henry Huddle.   Bk 12/pg 156   Dec 5, 1854

Henry Moyer of Hilltown Twp, guardian of Elizabeth Atherholt, acknowledges payment of estate by her previous guardian Samuel Muffley.
                                                Bk 12/pg 156   Apr 2, 1855

Elizabeth (Huddle) Stoneback of Richland Twp. and Henry Stoneback, guardian of Susannah Huddle, daughter of Michael Huddle, late of Richland Twp, acknowledge payment of estate by administrators Joseph and Henry Huddle.   Bk 12/pg 157   Nov 18, 1854

Frederick G. Hillpot, guardian of Reed Fox, acknowledges payment by Charles Fellman, Esq., trustee appointed to sell real estate of Bethell Cooper's heirs.   Bk 12/pg 157   Nov 23, 1855

Peter Hartman of Huron Co, OH gives power of attorney to Samuel Hartman of Bedminster Twp. to recover estate from father Jacob Hartman, late of Rockhill Twp, and dower of widow Mary who is now deceased.

Bk 12/pg 159   Sep 12, 1855

Garret V. and Elizabeth Carver of Northampton Twp, Joel and Hannah Carver, Aaron and Rebecca V. Walton, Thomas W. and Rachel Bye and Joseph Bye of Buckingham Twp, Allen R. and Margaret Bye of Solebury Twp, John and Martha Fretz of Doylestown Twp and Benjamin and Sarah Ann Buckman of Newtown Twp, heirs of Joseph E. Carver, late of Solebury Twp, give power of attorney to Benjamin S. Rich of Buckingham Twp. to sell the real estate.   Bk 12/pg 160   Sep 22, 1855

Nathan L. Hill of Doylestown, now 21, acknowledges payment by guardian Josiah Rich of estate from late father Isaac Hill.   Bk 12/pg 161   Dec 10, 1855

Jonathan Pearson bequeathed land in Solebury Twp. to wife until youngest child was of age. The heirs sold this land in 1844 to Hiram H. Pearson, one of the heirs, subject to payment to the widow of Cyras Pearson. Cyrus's widow, now Eliza Ramsey of Clermont Co, OH acknowledges payment by Hiram H. Pearson.   Bk 12/pg 170   Sep 28, 1855

Mary A. Gilham of Wayne Co, OH, formerly of Bucks Co, widow of William Gilham, late of Bucks Co, gives power of attorney to Tilghman Schluder of Wayne Co, OH to recover estate from executor William Wierbeck of Lehigh Co.   Bk 12/pg 172   Oct 26, 1854

Tilghman Sleider of Wayne Co, OH, attorney for Mary A. Gilliam of Wayne Co, widow of William Gilliam, late of Durham Twp, acknowledges payment of estate by executor William H. Weireback.   Bk 12/pg 173   Nov 13, 1854

Barbara Stover (now Fulmer) of Richland Twp, daughter of John Stover, now 21, acknowledges payment of estate by guardian Samuel Landes.

Bk 12/pg 173   Jan 3, 1856

Charlotte Duer of Miami Co, OH gives power of attorney to George S. Duer of Miami Co. to rent land in Lower Makefield Twp. that she inherited from William Duer.   Bk 12/pg 179   Jan 8, 1856

Lewis B. Taylor of Springfield Twp, now 21, acknowledges payment by guardian Abraham T. Myers of estate from late father Joseph Taylor.

Bk 12/pg 186   Dec 14, 1855

Allen Tomlinson, Silas Tomlinson of Northampton Twp. and Mary
Tomlinson of Moreland Twp, Montgomery Co, now 21, acknowledge
payment by guardian Silas Tomlinson Sen. of estate from late father A.
Tomlinson.   Bk 12/pg 188   Jan 19, 1856

Margaret Welding of Bensalem Twp. and John Bethell of Philadelphia,
children of John Bethell, late of Wrightstown Twp, acknowledge payment of
estate by Thomas E. Bethell and Sarah Bethell.   Bk 12/pg 190   Mar 28, 1846

Henry Hunsberger, late of Hilltown Twp, died leaving widow Catharine (who
is since deceased) and ten children: Abraham, Anna (deceased, wife of
Christian Landes, son Benjamin), John, Elizabeth (wife of Moses Landes),
Henry, Isaac, Catharine, Frances (wife of Jacob H. Meyer), Jacob and Mary
(wife of Joshua Histand). The heirs acknowledge payment of estate by son
Jacob.   Bk 12/pg 191   Sep 1, 1855

George W. Hogeland of Lower Makefield Twp. assigns his share in estate of
late father Henry Hogeland to Samuel G. Slack of Yardleyville to pay a debt.
                                            Bk 12/pg 193   Mar 1, 1856

Andrew Margerum of Lower Makefield Twp, now 21, acknowledges
payment by guardian John Wildman of estate from late grandmother Grace
Margerum.   Bk 12/pg 194   Mar 14, 1856

Simon James, late of New Britain Twp, died intestate in 1815 leaving a
widow and five children: Cynthia (wife of John Althouse), John H., Eliza
(wife of Samuel McCorkle), Lydia (wife of Henry L. Miller) and Ebenezer.
The widow died Apr 8, 1842. The children acknowledge payment of dower
by current owner Benjamin James Sen.   Bk 12/pg 199   May 2, 1843

Abiah James of Hilltown Twp, tavern keeper, son of Benjamin M. James,
acknowledges payment of estate by Oliver P. James, M.D. who inherited the
real estate.   Bk 12/pg 200   Apr 2, 1855

Samuel Eckel died intestate leaving widow and children. Son Lewis Eckel of
Philadelphia assigns his share of dower to Zachariah Leidy of Hilltown Twp.
to pay a debt.   Bk 12/pg 206   Mar 24, 1856

Charles Baum of Hilltown Twp. and wife Elizabeth (late Aaron), now 21,
acknowledge payment by her guardian Derostus Aaron of estate due her.
                                            Bk 12/pg 215   Apr 3, 1856

William Craven of Philadelphia, heir of Lydia McNeal, late of Southampton Twp, sells to Wilhelmus Corson of Southampton his share in land in Southampton. Bk 12/pg 217   Apr 20, 1855

Daniel Haldeman, guardian of Anna and Catharine Grove, grandchildren of Phillip Brunner, late of Warrington Twp, children of late Margaret Grove, acknowledges payment of estate by administrators George, John and Joel Brunner. Bk 12/pg 218   Apr 8, 1856

Joel Swartz, heir of Phillip Brunner, late of Warrington Twp, son of late Lydia Swartz who was a daughter of Phillip, acknowledges payment of estate by administrators George, John and Joel Brunner.
Bk 12/pg 219   Apr 8, 1856

Monroe Hockman, guardian of Anna Margaret, Adaline G. and Harry S. Swartz, minor children of late Lydia Swartz who was a daughter of Phillip Brunner, late of Warrington Twp, acknowledges payment of estate by administrators George, John and Joel Brunner.   Bk 12/pg 219   Apr 8, 1856

Deborah Kephart, Ann E. Magill, Mary Ann Reigel and Julia Ann Rodrock, children of Phillip Brunner, late of Warrington Twp, acknowledge payment of estate by administrators George, John and Joel Brunner.
Bk 12/pg 220   Apr 8, 1856

Elizabeth Sellers, widow of Enos Sellers, late of Rockhill Twp, acknowledges payment of estate by administrators Henry Troxel and Francis Sellers.
Bk 12/pg 230   Apr 7, 1856

Tobias Walter, William and Elizabeth (Walter) Hinkle, Jourdan D. and Mary (Walter) Cope and Caroline Slichter and Catharine Fluck, daughters of Mary (Walter) Fretz, and Catharine Bissey (minor child of Lydia Bissey—late Walter, by guardian Tobias Nash), and Catharine, Isaac, Theodore, Hannah and Mary Holcombe, minor children of Rachel (Walter) Holcombe (by guardian Jourdan D. Cope), children of Michael Walter, Esq., late of Plumstead Twp, acknowledge payment of estate by administrators Ephraim and John Walter. Bk 12/pg 231   Apr 4, 1856

Elizabeth Miller and Mary Long of Rockhill Twp, daughters of late Phillip Raezer, acknowledge payment of estate by executor George Berringer.
Bk 12/pg 232   Apr 3, 1856

Charles R. Grove, David Grove and Phillip Grove, grandchildren of Phillip Brunner, late of Warrington Twp. and children of late Margaret Grove, acknowledge payment of estate by administrators George, John and Joel Brunner.　　　　　　　　　　　　　　　Bk 12/pg 233　Apr 12, 1856

Elizabeth Rheader/Reeder of Philadelphia, daughter of late Catharine Muse, acknowledges payment of estate by guardian Jacob R. Cressman.
　　　　　　　　　　　　　　　Bk 12/pg 235　Apr 12, 1856

Mary Elizabeth Atherholt of Buckingham Twp, now 21, acknowledges payment by guardian David Atherholt of estate from John G. McCarty.
　　　　　　　　　　　　　　　Bk 12/pg 237　Apr 17, 1856

Joseph Seifert, David W. Seifert and William Fisher (by guardian John Fluck), all of Springfield Twp, heirs of Bartel Seifert, late of Springfield, acknowledge payment of estate by administrator George W. Seifert.
　　　　　　　　　　　　　　　Bk 12/pg 238　Apr 19, 1855

Ludwig Barndt, late of Bucks Co, died by 1813 intestate leaving widow Elizabeth and six children. Son Elias sells his share of dower to Jonathan Cressman.　　　　　　　　　　　　Bk 12/pg 240　Feb 27, 1845

Dr. Charles Waage and wife Mary Ann, now 21, daughter of late Peter Heisler, acknowledge payment of estate by her guardian Jacob L. Sholl.
　　　　　　　　　　　　　　　Bk 12/pg 241　Apr 15, 1856

Allamanda Hearing of Milford Twp, daughter of Jonathan Cressman, late of Rockhill Twp, acknowledges payment of estate by administrators Levi and Josiah Cressman.　　　　　　　　　Bk 12/pg 242　Mar 25, 1856

Lewis Sellers, George and Eliza Smith, Michael Headman (guardian of James Sellers), Nathaniel Heany (guardian of Susanna and Israel Sellers), Aaron K. Wambold (guardian of Harvey and Enos Sellers), heirs of Enos Sellers, late of Rockhill Twp, acknowledge payment of estate by administrators Henry Troxel and Francis Sellers.　　　　Bk 12/pg 243　Apr 7, 1856

Mary Ann Heisler, wife of Dr. Charles Waage of Upper Hanover Twp, Montgomery Co, and granddaughter of Peter Blyler, late of Milford Twp, acknowledges payment of estate by executors Henry Troxel and Jacob L. Sholl.　　　　　　　　　　　　　Bk 12/pg 245　Apr 15, 1856

378

Jeremiah Esbach of Richland Twp, son of Jesse Esbach, late of Berks Co, and grandson of Christian Eshbach, acknowledges payment of estate by guardian Abraham Deihl. Bk 12/pg 248   May 4, 1855

Charles Brown, Joseph Brown, Catharine Brown, Anna Mann, Elizabeth Ahlum and Sarah Diehl acknowledge payment of dower by Daniel Diehl due by the death of Magdalena Brown, widow of Joseph Brown, late of Haycock Twp. Bk 12/pg 249   Apr 5, 1856

Hannah Heller, widow of Tobias Heller, late of Rockhill Twp, wheelwright, gives power of attorney to Hugh Kintner of Doylestown to record satisfaction of a mortgage from Samuel Gerhart. Bk 12/pg 250   Apr 17, 1856

Catharine Fluck of Bedminster Twp. and Elizabeth Hillpot of Tinicum Twp, daughters of late Catharine Yost, widow of Conrad Yost, late of Bedminster Twp, acknowledge payment of dower by Peter Yost of Bedminster Twp.
Bk 12/pg 254   Apr 13, 1856

Hannah Heller, widow of Tobias Heller, late of Rockhill Twp, acknowledges payment of estate by Paul H. Hartzel, guardian of late Sophia Heller, a minor child of Tobias. Bk 12/pg 256   Apr 10, 1856

George Miller and Henry A. Moyer of Hilltown Twp, guardians of James M. and Sarah Kline, children of Jesse Kline, late of Hilltown Twp, acknowledge payment of estate by administrators John F. Kline and Henry Allbright.
Bk 12/pg 257   Apr 4, 1856

Charles R. Hess of Lower Saucon Twp, Northampton Co, guardian of Amanda Rockel, daughter of Catharine Fluck, late of Springfield Twp, acknowledges payment of estate by administrator de bonis non John Fluck.
Bk 12/pg 258   Mar 27, 1856

Elias Worman, Aaron Worman, John N. and Catharine Solliday, all of Tinicum Twp, heirs of Henry Worman, late of Tinicum Twp, and John Harpel, guardian of Henry, Mary Ellen, Samuel and William Summers, minor children of Henry's late daughter Hannah Summers, and Daniel Boileau, assigned of Henry's son Jonas Worman, acknowledge payment of estate by administrators Michael, Tobias and Lewis Worman.
Bk 12/pg 263   Mar 28, 1856

Enos Shive, Jesse Shive, Hannah Soladay and Elizabeth Benner, children of Mary Shive, late of Bedminster Twp, acknowledge payment of estate by administrators Joseph and Thomas Shive.   Bk 12/pg 265   Mar 28, 1856

Jonathan Paxson, Joseph Paxson, Samuel Paxson and Joseph Canby, administrators of John Paxson, late of Bensalem Twp, give power of attorney to Caleb N. Taylor to record satisfaction of a mortgage.
Bk 12/pg 265   Apr 21, 1856

John Bethel, late of Wrightstown Twp, bequeathed estate to son James Bethel when John's youngest daughter reached the age of 21, to be paid by John's two youngest children Thomas E. and Sarah Bethel. James released this legacy to John's widow Rebecca. Rebecca acknowledges payment of Thomas's share by his assigned Robert Ramsey.
Bk 12/pg 269   Feb 18, 1856

John Kramer of Bedminster Twp, guardian of Samuel and Reuben Althouse, minor children of Tobias Althouse and heirs of Catharine Althouse, late of Bedminster Twp, acknowledge payment of estate by administrator Mathias Althouse.   Bk 12/pg 271   Jan 26, 1856

Catharine Clymer of New Britain Twp, heir of Catharine Althouse, late of Bedminster Twp, acknowledges payment of estate by administrator Mathias Althouse.   Bk 12/pg 272   Feb 6, 1856

Jonas and Silas Althouse, sons of Catharine Althouse, late of Bedminster Twp, acknowledge payment of estate by administrator Mathias Althouse.
Bk 12/pg 272   Jan 26, 1856

John B. Missimer of Richland Twp, guardian of Catharine, Enos, Frederick, Elizabeth and John Lutz, minor children of Elizabeth Lutz, late of Bucks Co, acknowledge payment of estate by Mathias Althouse of Richland Twp, administrator of Catharine Althouse, late of Bucks Co.
Bk 12/pg 273   Jan 26, 1856

Ephraim Walter, John Walter, William and Elizabeth (Walter) Hinkle, Jourdan D. and Mary (Walter) Cope, and Caroline Slichter and Catharine Fluck, daughters of late Rebecca (Walter) Fretz, and Hannah, Rachel and Catharine Bissey, daughters of late Lydia (Walter) Bissey (by guardian Tobias Nash), and Catharine, Isaac, Theodore, Hannah and Mary Holcomb, minor children of Rachel (Walter) Holcomb (by their guardian Jourdan D. Cope), children of Catharine Walter, late of Plumstead Twp, acknowledge payment of estate by administrator Tobias Walter.   Bk 12/pg 274   Apr 10, 1856

Nero S. Strassburger of Pottstown Borough, Montgomery Co, grandson of Henry Stout, late of Hilltown Twp, acknowledges payment of estate by administrators Enos Stout and Tobias Fluck.   Bk 12/pg 276   Jul 11, 1855

Jonas Maust, now 21, acknowledges payment by guardian Mahlon C. Lear of estate from grandfather.   Bk 12/pg 276   Apr 29, 1856

Mahlon Long, Rachel Long and Ann Eliza Long of Warwick Twp, John and Mary Polk of Warrington Twp, children of Mary Long, late of Warminster Twp, acknowledge payment of estate by executor Charles Long.
Bk 12/pg 277   May 9, 1856

Mary Bigoney, granddaughter of Phillip Brunner, late of Warrington Twp, daughter of late Margaret Grove, acknowledges payment of estate by administrators George, John and Joel Brunner.   Bk 12/pg 279   May 12, 1856

In 1835 Samuel Harbison assigned property to James Kelly and Henry Moore in trust for benefit of himself, his wife Jane and their children and to be distributed to his wife and children after his death. James Kelly has since died and Henry Moore was discharged as trustee and replaced by Dr. James S. Rich. Samuel Harbison acknowledges payment of trust by Dr. Rich.
Bk 12/pg 280   May 6, 1856

Mary Bennet of the Eleventh Ward of Philadelphia gives power of attorney to son Richard C. Bennet of Warminster Twp. to sell her land in Southampton Twp.   Bk 12/pg 286   Feb 1, 1856

Jacob Wildonger, Abraham Wildonger, Jacob and Elizabeth Kilmer, Moses and Hannah Lear, Joseph and Catharine Fly, Henry and Sarah Wagner, Jacob and Mary Hufferd, heirs of Elizabeth Wildonger, late of Tinicum Twp, acknowledge payment of estate by administrator Moses Wildonger.
Bk 12/pg 289   [not dated]

Jacob Wildonger, Abraham Wildonger, Moses Wildonger, Moses and Hannah Lear, Joseph and Catharine Fly, Henry and Sarah Wagner, Jacob and Mary Hufferd, heirs of Jacob Wildonger, late of Tinicum Twp, acknowledge payment of estate by administrator Jacob Kilmer.   Bk 12/pg 289   Apr, 1852

John H. Snyder, Amos H. Snyder, Andrew Snyder, Thomas Snyder, Caroline Brong and Catharine Cressman, heirs of John Snyder, late of Richland Twp, acknowledge payment of dower by the heirs of Samuel Hartman, late of Richland Twp, due upon the death of the widow Sarah Snyder.

Bk 12/pg 294   Mar 27, 1855

Mary King of Hilltown Twp, now 21, acknowledges payment by guardian John F. King of estate from father John King, late of Hilltown Twp.

Bk 12/pg 295   Apr 5, 1856

Aaron Fretz, William Fretz, Francis and Catharine Scheetz, George and Elizabeth McIndosh, Jacob Kratz (guardian of Mary Fretz), John Fretz (guardian of Isaak Fretz), Christian Meyers (guardian of Henry H. Fretz), heirs of Joseph S. Fretz, late of Bedminster Twp, acknowledge payment of estate by executors Margaret Fretz and Joseph F. Myers.

Bk 12/pg 299   Apr 5, 1856

Mahlon Williamson of Philadelphia, attorney for Edward Roberts of Warren Co, OH, acknowledges payment by Benjamin C. Foulke, executor of Susanna Roberts, of legacy given to Edward.   Bk 12/pg 300   Jun 5, 1856

Edward Roberts of Warren Co, OH, legatee of his sister Susanna Roberts, late of Richland Twp, gives power of attorney to Mahlon Williamson of Philadelphia to recover estate from executor Benjamin C. Foulke.

Bk 12/pg 301   May 31, 1856

Elvina Swink of Hilltown Twp, now 21, acknowledges payment by guardian Jacob Race of estate from late father Jacob Swink.

Bk 12/pg 304   May 19, 1856

Jacob Booz, Daniel Booz, Joseph Booz, Samuel Booz, Lavina Doble, Sarah Stockham, Peter Booz and James Booz, children of John Booz, late of Bristol Twp, Ann Subers, Samuel L. Booz, Isaac L. Booz, Hannah Stackhouse and William Booz, children of late John Booz (son of the previous John Booz), John Booz, Isaac Booz, Ellen Booz and Edward Booz, children of late Isaac Booz (son of John Booz Jr. and grandson of John Booz Sr., by guardians Thomas Montany and James M. Boileau), John S. Booz, Albert Booz, Jesse Booz, Henry Booz and Anna Mary Booz, children of Joseph L. Booz (son of John Booz Jr. and grandson of John Booz Sr., the last two by their guardian Joseph Stackhouse), Wallace and Mahlon Dungan, children of Rebecca Dungan (daughter of John Booz Jr. and granddaughter of John Booz Sr., by their guardian Thomas Dungan), Rebecca and Edward Booz, children of late

Ann Booz (daughter of late Rebecca Girton and granddaughter of John Booz Sr.), Mary Stackhouse (daughter of late Rebecca Girton), John Anderson, Mary Ann Anderson, Sarah Anderson, Elizabeth Anderson and William Anderson (by his assignee Joseph Booz), children of late Elizabeth Anderson (daughter of John Booz Sr.), George H. Vanzant, Joseph Vanzant, John W. Vanzant and Susan M. Vanzant, children of Susan Vanzant (daughter of late Mary Wright and granddaughter of John Booz Sr.), Susan Wright, daughter of late Wilson Wright (son of late Mary Wright), Ann Carver, Seth Wright, Elizabeth Bennet, Mary E. Wright, Samuel C. Wright and Harriet Thile, children of late Mary Wright, David C. Booz, Edward G. Booz, Elizabeth Dungan, Thomas Booz, John Booz, Martin Booz and Frank Booz (the last three by their guardian Caleb N. Taylor), children of late William Booz (son of John Booz Sr.), John McCluskey (husband of late Mary Booz, daughter of late William Booz), Mary Elizabeth Roberts and William Booz, children of late Amos Booz (son of John Booz Sr.), all heirs of John Booz Sr. who died about 1821 leaving dower to widow Mary Booz who is now deceased. The heirs give power of attorney to Andrew W. Gilkeson of Bristol Borough to recover dower from the persons now owning the real estate.
Bk 12/pg 305   Mar 28, 1855

Samuel Detweiler, John Detweiler, Ann Kinsey, Leah Ruth, Catharine Landis, Hannah Detweiler, Rachael Detweiler and Magdaline Detweiler, all heirs of Barbara Detweiler, late of Rockhill Twp, acknowledge payment of estate by administrator Henry Detweiler.   Bk 12/pg 314   Jun 21, 1856

William T. Vandegrift, late of Bensalem Twp, bequeathed legacy to daughter Ann Lake to be paid by his son William who inherited the farm in Bristol Twp. Ann Lake acknowledges payment of legacy by William Vandegrift.
Bk 12/pg 320   Mar 28, 1854

Mary Harding (wife of Charles Harding), Henry Hicks, William Hicks, Anne Jackson (wife of George W. Jackson), Aaron Hicks and Rebecca Hicks, heirs of Rebecca Hicks, late of Bensalem Twp, acknowledge payment of estate by administrator George Hicks.   Bk 12/pg 320   Apr 15, 1856

Anna Shelly (now Overholtzer) of Hilltown Twp, acknowledges payment by guardian John Allebach of money due her.   Bk 12/pg 322   Apr 7, 1856

Samuel Rufe, late of Durham Twp, bequeathed real estate to sons Frederick H. and Samuel H. Rufe. Widow Eve Catharine refuses to accept the terms of the will but instead prefers to take her dower. She releases Frederick and Samuel of dower obligation.   Bk 12/pg 322   Aug 27, 1856

Joel Thomas of Hilltown Twp. assigns to Catharine Thomas of Hilltown Twp. his share in estate of father Josiah Thomas, late of Bucks Co, to pay a debt.
Bk 12/pg 330   Oct 9, 1856

Anna Kinsey (widow) and John D. Kinsey, Jacob D. Kinsey, Catharine (wife of Leonard Detweiler), Michael Nace (guardian of Mary and Nancy Kinsey, minor children of late Henry D. Kinsey), children of John Kinsey, late of Rockhill Twp, acknowledge payment of estate by administrators Henry Troxel and Samuel D. Kinsey.
Bk 12/pg 333   Sep 26, 1856

John Foster, Alfred C. Foster, Mele Ann (wife of Bryan Woorell), Latitia (wife of Samuel Clark) and Tacy Ann (wife of Charles Hart), all of Bucks Co, acknowledge payment of legacies by Joseph Morrison, executor of Mele Kruson, late of Bristol Borough.
Bk 12/pg 334   May 29, 1856

Sarah Worstall, late of Newtown Twp, bequeathed estate to brother Amos Smith with the desire that after his death the interest thereof to be paid to Sarah Smith, widow of her late brother Jacob B. Smith and after Sarah's death to Jacob's children. Amos Smith agrees to abide by this intent.
Bk 12/pg 341   May 8, 1852

Annie Margaret Grove of Doylestown Twp, now 21, acknowledges payment by guardian Daniel Haldeman of estate from late grandfather Phillip Brunner.
Bk 12/pg 343   Nov 17, 1856

John Good of Lower Saucon Twp, Northampton Co, guardian of Matilda Good, daughter of Manassa H. Good, late of Springfield Twp, acknowledges payment of estate by administrator David R. Hess.
Bk 12/pg 343   Apr 2, 1855

Susanna Foulke of Sixth Ward of Philadelphia, daughter of late Evan Foulke who was a nephew of Susanna Roberts, late of Richland Twp, acknowledges payment of estate by executor Benjamin C. Foulke. Susanna Foulke's mother Sarah Brown and her siblings Lewis and Sarah Foulke pledge to repay the legacy to Benjamin C. Foulke if he needs to pay debts of the estate.
Bk 12/pg 345   Oct 7, 1856

William H. Ball of Whitemarsh Twp, Montgomery Co, guardian of Ann Amanda Edwards, daughter of late John Edwards and granddaughter of Nathan Edwards, late of Milford Twp, acknowledges payment of estate by executor Benjamin G. Foulke.
Bk 12/pg 346   Nov 12, 1856

John E. Knowles, now 21, acknowledges payment by guardian Stephen K. Betts of estate due him. Bk 12/pg 350   Dec 2, 1856

John Bartholomew, Daniel Bartholomew, Samuel Bartholomew, William Bartholomew, Mary Ann Krouthamel, Mary Bartholomew, Lydia Bartholomew and Nancy Bartholomew, all of Bucks Co, siblings of Henry Bartholomew, late of Bedminster Twp, acknowledge payment of estate by administrators Thomas Bartholomew and George Walp.
Bk 12/pg 351   Dec 1, 1856

Esther McDowell left heir Eliza Ann McDowell (wife of William T. Banes) who died leaving six children including George Banes of Warren Co, IN. George gives power of attorney to William McDowell to recover estate.
Bk 12/pg 352   Sep 1, 1856

Christian Clymer, late of Milford Twp, bequeathed estate to Henry Hearing of Milford Twp in trust for daughter Catharine. Surviving executor Jacob Clymer (the other executor, Jacob Strunk, being deceased) appoints Dr. Aaron Shelly of Milford Twp. as trustee as Henry Hearing is deceased.
Bk 12/pg 352   Sep 24, 1856

Henry J. Bissey, William Bissey and Mary E. Bissey, heirs of Jonas Bissey, late of Clay Co, IL, and grandchildren of Henry Bissey, late of Tinicum Twp, acknowledge payment by John Harpel, Esq. of Bedminster Twp, Jacob Kilmer of Tinicum Twp. and John Welder of Tinicum Twp. of their share of the purchase of Henry's real estate. Bk 12/pg 354   Dec 8, 1856

Lydia Croman of Richland Twp, Elizabeth Cope of Milford Twp, Catharine Croman of Upper Hanover Twp, Montgomery Co, daughters of Jacob Benner, late of Richland Twp, and John J. Moore (guardian of William, Joseph and Jacob Smith, children of late Mary Smith, another daughter of Jacob Benner) and Solomon Scheetz of Milford Twp (guardian of Diannah Scheetz, daughter of late Christian Scheetz, another daughter of Jacob Benner), acknowledge payment of estate by administrators Aaron, Jonas and David Benner.
Bk 12/pg 359   Jun 21, 1856

Patrick Mulvany, late of Tinicum Twp, bequeathed estate to sister Ann (wife of Dennis Sheridan) and after her death to her children James, Patrick, Bryan, Mathew, Thomas, Dennis, Bridget Glanin, Catharine Sheridan and Elizabeth Sheridan. The heirs, living in Drumborrow in the Parish of Kills, Barony of Upper Kills, County of Meath, Ireland, give power of attorney to Mathew

Sheridan of Tinicum Twp. to recover estate from executors Joseph Hough and
Daniel Barr. Bk 12/pg 360 Feb 20, 1847

Mathew and Hannah Hughes of Philadelphia, Elizabeth (Hughes) Hellyer,
Lucy Ann (Hughs) Scott of Solebury Twp, and Mary (Huges) Paff of
Indianapolis, IN (by her attorney William R. Evans), children of Mathew
Hughes, late of Plumstead Twp, confirm Mathew's bequest of real estate to
his grandson Hugh Hughes. Bk 12/pg 366 Dec 23, 1856

Missouri (wife of Milton Roberts), Cornelia (wife of David R. Jamison),
Matilda Foulke and Jane Foulke, children of Joshua and Caroline G. Foulke,
ratify their parents' sale to Henry Trumbower Jr. of land that Caroline
inherited from William Green. Bk 12/pg 373 Dec 3, 1855

John Gaddes, late of Plumstead Twp, bequeathed estate to son William
together with his brothers and after William's death to William's children.
William is since deceased leaving seven children including Horatio Gaddes of
Putnam Co, VA and Samuel Gaddes (who gave power of attorney to Horatio).
Horatio acknowledges payment of their shares by present owner William
Banger. Bk 12/pg 374 Mar 18, 1852

John Geddes, late of Plumstead Twp, bequeathed estate to daughter Levina
Scott, she to receive the interest and the principal to be paid out of his real
estate to her children after her death. Levina Scott died in Oct, 1830 leaving
children who gave powers of attorney to Aaron P. Tomlinson of Jefferson Co,
OH. Aaron acknowledges payment of principal by present owners William
Banger and Elias Morris. Bk 12/pg 376 Mar 22, 1851

William Geddes, son of late John Geddes of Plumstead Twp, died in June,
1843 leaving seven children including William and John Geddes who gave
power of attorney to their brother Hamilton Geddes of Morgan Co, OH.
Hamilton acknowledges payment of estate by present owners William Banger
and Elias Morris. Bk 12/pg 378 Apr 7, 1851

Moses Geddes, executor of John Geddes, acknowledges payment by current
owner William Banger (who bought from Joseph Cowell who bought from
Joseph Hough who bought from the estate) of dower due upon the death of
John's widow Ann. Bk 12/pg 380 May 16, 1843

John Geddes of Ohio gives power of attorney to Hamilton Geddes to recover
money due under will of John Geddes of Plumstead Twp to his father William
Geddes. Bk 12/pg 381 Nov 4, 1850

Samuel Geddes of DeWitt Co, IL gives power of attorney to Horatio Geddes to recover estate from grandfather John Geddes, late of Bucks County.
Bk 12/pg 382   Mar 25, 1848

George and Mary Ann (Scott) Green of Fulton Co, IL, daughter of Levina Scott who was a daughter of John Geddes, late of Bucks Co, and who died in Oct, 1830 leaving Mary Ann and six other children, give power of attorney to Aaron P. Tomlinson of Jefferson Co, OH to recover their share.
Bk 12/pg 382   May 21, 1850

John G. Scott, Henry Scott and Charles and Rebecca Burke, all of Belmont Co, OH, children of Lavina Scott who was a daughter of John Gaddes, late of Bucks Co, who died in Oct, 1830, give power of attorney to Aaron P. Tomlinson of Jefferson Co, OH to recover their share.
Bk 12/pg 384   Apr 8, 1850

Harrison R. Scott, Elizabeth Scott and Peter and Sarah Jane Balderston, all of Belmont Co, OH, children of Leviney Scott who was a daughter of John Gaddes, late of Bucks Co, give power of attorney to Aaron P. Tomlinson of Jefferson Co, OH to recover their share of John's estate.
Bk 12/pg 386   Feb 15, 1847

William Geddes of Washington Co, OH gives power of attorney to Hamilton Geddes to recover his share of estate of John Geddes of Plumstead Twp. left to his father William Geddes.
Bk 12/pg 388   Mar 6, 1851

Moses Geddes and Steward McNott, residents of Windsor Twp, Morgan Co, OH testified before William Bestwick, a Justice of the Peace in Windsor Twp, that Samuel Geddes, William Geddes, John Geddes, Horatio Geddes, Hambleton Geddes, Sarah Hany and James Geddes are legal heirs of the estate of William Geddes, late of Windsor Twp, who died June 16, 1843.
Bk 12/pg 389   Nov 9, 1850

Joseph Roberts and Jonathan Balderston of Belmont Co, OH testify before Elijah Combs, a Justice of the Peace in Belmont Co, that Harrison R. Scott, Elizabeth Scott and Sarah Jane (wife of Peter Balderston) are grandchildren of John Geddes, late of Bucks County, and children of Leviney Scott, late wife of John Scott.
Bk 12/pg 390   Feb 15, 1847

Moses Hughes and Joseph Roberts testify before Elijah Combs that John G. Scott, Henry Scott and Rebecca (wife of Charles Burke) are also children of Levina Scott, late wife of Job Scott.
Bk 12/pg 391   Mar 27, 1850

Alfred Strickler of Bucks Co, farmer, assigns to his mother Susan, widow of Bernard Strickler, his share in his father's real estate.

Bk 12/pg 391   Feb 18, 1857

Mahlon B. Janney of Falls Twp. and his wife Charllotte B. have agreed to separate due to divers unhappy differences between them and agree to settlement of their property.   Bk 12/pg 393   Mar 18, 1857

Mary Warwick, Catharine Ann Tomlinson and Thomas N. Tomlinson of Bristol Twp. and Gilbert Tomlinson and Joseph H. Tomlinson of Bristol Borough agree to the settlement of the estates of their two uncles Thomas and Pierson Tomlinson, both late of Bristol Twp, as well as their aunts and uncles Sarah Tomlinson, John Tomlinson, Elizabeth Tomlinson, Joseph Tomlinson, Hannah Tomlinson and Israel Tomlinson and their cousin Joseph Henry Tomlinson (infant son of the last named Joseph Tomlinson), all of whom (except Thomas and Pierson) died intestate. They and their sister Susan Warwick jointly owned (through their late father Gilbert Tomlinson) one-sixth part of land in Bristol Twp. They also own one-fourth part of land belonging to their late uncle Joseph Tomlinson, subject to dower for Joseph's widow Olinda (now Nelson).   Bk 12/pg 395   Feb 9, 1857

Alevia Bertles of Wilkesbarre, Luzerne Co. gives power of attorney to William B. Bertels of the same place to recover dower due from estate of her late father Jacob Trumbower in Richland Twp.   Bk 12/pg 400   Feb 4, 1857

Sarah Longshore (late Solliday) of Plumstead Twp, now 21, acknowledges payment by guardian Samuel Bradshaw of estate from late father [blank] Salliday and grandfather Daniel Solliday.   Bk 12/pg 409   Jul 12, 1854

Isaac Bradshaw and Phebe Ann Hand, children of late William Bradshaw and grandchildren of late David Bradshaw, acknowledge payment of estate by David's executor William Watson, one-third of the proceeds of the farm which David willed to Sarah Bradshaw, William Bradshaw and Ruth Meredith.   Bk 12/pg 411   Apr 3, 1857

Anna L. McMasters of Upper Makefield Twp, Esther B. Yardley and Elizabeth B. Briggs of Lower Makefield Twp. and Susan B. Dawes of Newtown Borough give power of attorney to Joseph H. Yardley of Lower Makefield Twp. to record satisfaction of a mortgage given by Wilson Large to the heirs of Jacob Knowles, the interest payable to Rachel Knowles during her life.   Bk 12/pg 414   Apr 2, 1857

Mary Bickell (late Trimby) of Philadelphia gives power of attorney to William H. Karz/Katz[?] of New Britain Twp. to record satisfaction of a mortgage given to her by Joseph Trimby of New Britain Twp.

Bk 12/pg 415   Mar 27, 1857

Nancy Meyers, widow of Abraham T. Meyers, late of Springfield Twp, and Abraham's children John K. Meyers of Plumstead Twp, Jacob K. Meyers of Plumstead, Mary Fryling of Springfield, Sarah Moyer of Upper Salford Twp, Montgomery Co. and William K. Meyers and Henry K. Meyers of Springfield Twp. agree to settlement of estate.   Bk 12/pg 417   Mar 23, 1857

Wilson Carver of Buckingham Twp, son of late John Carver, acknowledges payment of estate by his guardian Strickland Bennet of Buckingham Twp.

Bk 12/pg 419   Apr 4, 1857

Mary Haldeman, Michael Haldeman, Samuel Haldeman, Silas Haldeman, Benjamin G. Haldeman (for himself and as guardian of Samuel G. and Benjamin H. Pole, minor children of Elizabeth Pole), heirs of Joseph Haldeman, late of Warrington Twp, acknowledge payment of estate by executors John Garner and Benjamin Fulton.   Bk 12/pg 421   Apr 6, 1857

Sarah Doan, Charity Conard, Samuel and Phebe Carter, Joseph and Mary Bennett, Michael and Eliza Leister and Amy Worthington, all of Bucks Co, and Charles and Rebecca Mathews of Cecil Co, MD, heirs of Israel Worthington, who bequeathed estate after death of his wife to his sons-in-law Jesse Worthington and Oliver (or Robert) Doan, for the benefit of his seven daughters, acknowledge payment of estate by Oliver Doan (the widow and Jesse Worthington being deceased).   Bk 12/pg 426   Apr 7, 1857

Edward S. Fitch of Harford Co, MD, guardian of Benjamin Morris Magill and Edward F. Magill, minor children of Benjamin Magill, late of Philadelphia, gives power of attorney to E. Morris Lloyd of Doylestown to recover money due him as guardian, especially from Louisa C. Magill, John G. Mann and Jane S. Magill, executors of Alfred M. Magill, and Mabelda[?] Ann Magill, administrator of Benjamin Morris Magill, the estate being payable on the death of William Magill's widow Mary.   Bk 12/pg 432   Mar 23, 1857

Abraham Roudenbush, Jesse Roudenbush, Enos Roudenbush, Samuel Roudenbush, Elizabeth Leidy, Sarah Cressman, Anna Althouse and Matilda Clemmer, heirs of George Roudenbush and his widow Elizabeth, acknowledge payment of estate by executors Jacob and George Roudenbush.

Bk 12/pg 435   Mar 31, 1857

Amy Large of Buckingham Twp, wife of Aaron Large and legatee of Elizabeth Stirk, late of Buckingham Twp, acknowledges payment of estate by executor James Kirk.   Bk 12/pg 437   Jun 5, 1856

Sarah Reiter of Quakertown, now 21, receives payment from guardian Jacob L. Sholl of estate from late father Samuel Reiter.   Bk 12/pg 438   Apr 8, 1857

James Wambold, Jacob Wambold and Abraham Wambold (by guardian Michael Nase), Maria Nase, Lydia Weber and Rebecca Hoff, heirs of Tobias Wambold, late of Rockhill Twp, acknowledge payment of estate by administrator Henry Troxel.   Bk 12/pg 439   Apr 6, 1857

Catharine Trauger (widow) and John K. Trauger, Eve (wife of Samuel S.T. Hillpot), Christian and Mary Magdalene Stealy and William and Catharine Cressman, children of Jacob Trauger Sen., late of Nockamixon Twp, acknowledge payment of estate by executors Jacob K. Trauger and Samuel S.T. Hillpot.   Bk 12/pg 441   Mar 23, 1857

The real estate of Abraham Wambold, late of Rockhill Twp, was awarded by the Orphans Court to his son Noah. His daughter Mary (wife of Charles A. Schwink) died intestate without issue. Charles A. Schwink repays the principal (subject to their paying him interest during his life) to Mary's heirs Noah Wambold, Aaron Wambold, Edwin Wambold and Catharine and Oliver Weikel.   Bk 12/pg 444   Apr 14, 1857

Thomas Taylor, guardian of William Taylor, gives power of attorney to Anthony Swain to record satisfaction of a mortgage.
                    Bk 12/pg 447   Apr 7, 1857

Jane James (widow) and Elizabeth Gilbert, Augustena B. James, Mary Townsend and Phebe Croasdale, children of Samuel James, late of Bensalem Twp, acknowledge payment of estate by administrators Heil Gilbert, Paul Townsend and Edward Croasdale.   Bk 12/pg 452   Mar 19, 1857

William R. Beans, administrator of Francis Vansartsdalen, late of Northampton Twp, and Isaac Vanhorn, guardian of Francis' minor children, agree to hold harmless Joseph K. Young who purchased the real estate of any claim for dower by the widow Mary Jane.   Bk 12/pg 454   Apr 6, 1857

Mary Jane Vanartsdalen of Northampton Twp, widow of Francis Vanartsdalen, releases Joseph K. Young (who purchased the real estate) of any dower right.   Bk 12/pg 455   Apr 6, 1857

Peter L. Jacoby, guardian of Silas, son of Samuel S. Stover, late of Springfield Twp, farmer, and Samuel's widow Sarah acknowledge payment of estate by administrators Jacob Gehman and Eli Stover.   Bk 12/pg 456   Apr 1, 1857

Sarah A. Mease of Bethlehem, daughter of Daniel Mease, late of Richland Twp, and John Schleiffer of Richland Twp. (guardian of Alevia Mease, daughter of the said David [sic]) acknowledge payment of estate by administrator Joseph Mease.   Bk 12/pg 461   Feb 6, 1857

Samuel Brunner assigns all his property to Mrs. Maria before leaving to go to Europe and likely not returning.   Bk 12/pg 462   Oct 13, 1856

Jacob Kiser, guardian of Juliann and Abraham, children of Michael Fabian, late of Durham Twp, mason, and John Deemer, guardian of Michael's son Eli, get payment of estate from William Kressman.   Bk 12/pg 466   Apr 1, 1857

Thomas P. Ball, attorney for Margaret Lloyd of King Twp, York Co, Province of Canada, acknowledges payment of estate by Gilbert Ball, administrator of her deceased brother Joseph Foltz.   Bk 12/pg 467   Nov 10, 1856

Sarah Vanartsdalen acknowledges payment by her guardian Simon Vanartsdalen of money due her.   Bk 12/pg 470   Apr 4, 1856

Hugh Folke of Richland Twp, administrator of Elizabeth Roberts (alias Zelnor or Zellers), late of Northumberland Co, who was a niece of Susanna Roberts, late of Richland Twp, acknowledges payment of estate by Susanna's executor Benjamin G. Foulke.   Bk 12/pg 470   Apr 4, 1857

Daniel Roberts of Zorie Twp, West Canada and Lewelly Roberts of Buckingham Twp, legatees of Susanna Roberts, late of Quakertown, give power of attorney to Susan Green of Quakertown to recover estate from executor Benjamin G. Foulke.   Bk 12/pg 472   Nov 3, 1855

Mary Schlichter (widow) and Elizabeth (wife of Silas Bilger), daughter of Henry Schlichter, late of Rockhill Twp, acknowledge payment of estate by administrator William Schlichter.   Bk 12/pg 477   Apr 6, 1857

Benjamin L. Richardson of Clay Twp, Muskingum Co, OH, grandson of Benjamin Larzelere of Bristol Twp, entitled to one-half of his mother's share in the hands of his guardian Joseph Burton, Esq., gives power of attorney to James Harrison of Bristol Borough to recover the estate from Joseph Burton.   Bk 12/pg 479   Aug 8, 1856

Tobias H., Phillip, Jonas and John Cressman, Jacob Cressman (by trustee Jacob Cressman Sen.), Hannah Sholl, Lydia Gerhart, Mary Gerhart, Elizabeth Shellenberger and Sarah Cressman, heirs of Mary Cressman, Mark K. Hartzel, Jacob Hartzel, Philip Hartzel (by guardian Abraham Groff), Henry Hartzel, Franklin Hartzell, William Harvey Hartzell (by guardian Nero Barndt), Alfred Hartzell, Richard Hartzell and Lydia Hartzell (by their guardian Henry Cressman), Mariah Schlichter and Eliza Barndt, heirs of Philip Hartzel Jr., acknowledge payment of estate by Abraham G. Hartzel, administrator of Philip Hartzel Sen., including the estate due them at the death of Philip Jr.'s widow Elizabeth. Bk 12/pg 481 Nov 15, 1856

Elizabeth Hartzel, Barbara Hartzel, Hannah Hartzel, Lydia Leidy, Catharine Veil, Abbey Hartzel (by trustee Samuel Veil) and Mary Cressman (by her children Tobias H., Philip, Jonas and John Cressman, Jacob Cressman—by trustee Jacob Cressman Sen., Hannah Sholl, Lydia Gerhart, Mary Gerhart, Elizabeth Shellenberger, Sarah Cressman) and the children of late Philip Hartzel (Mark K., Jacob, Philip—by guardian Abraham Groff, Henry, Franklin, William Harvey—by guardian Nero Barndt, Alfred, Richard and Lydia Ann—by guardian Henry Cressman, Maria Schlichter and Eliza Barndt), heirs of Philip Hartzel Sen., late of Rockhill Twp, get payment of estate from administrator Abraham G. Hartzel. Bk 12/pg 482 Nov 15, 1856

Isaac Summers, guardian of Mary Ann Lear, Sarah Ann Lear and William Lear, children of late William Lear, entitled to a legacy from their grandfather Arnold Lear, acknowledges receipt of estate from executors Mary Lear, John Lear, Joseph Lear and F.G. Hillpot. Bk 12/pg 485 Apr 3, 1857

Barnet Lear, grandson of Barndt Hillpot, late of Tinicum Twp, now 21, acknowledges payment of estate by guardian Mahlon C. Lear.
Bk 12/pg 486 Apr 6, 1857

Ann Cadwallader, daughter of Jacob Cadwallader, late of Upper Makefield Twp, acknowledges payment of estate by brother and executor Samuel C. Cadwallader. Bk 12/pg 487 Apr 4, 1843

Isaiah P. Large of Hunterdon Co, NJ, son of Ebenezer Large, late of Bucks Co, gives power of attorney to Stephen Kirk of Bucks Co. to recover estate due him. Bk 12/pg 488 Apr 1, 1857

A portion of the real estate of late Enos Morris was adjudged to heir Theodore Morris, subject to payment to John Feaster in right of his wife Louisa C. who was a daughter of Enos. Aaron Feaster, administrator of John Feaster, gives

392

power of attorney to David Feaster of Northampton Twp. to acknowledges
payment by Theodore.   Bk 12/pg 497   May 8, 1857

John Geil of Rockingham Co, VA gives power of attorney to Henry Geil of
Bucks Co. to recover estate from deceased mother Mary Geil and from
deceased father Abraham Geil.   Bk 12/pg 499   May 11, 1857

John Booze, late of Bristol Twp, died intestate about 1821 leaving widow
Mary and fourteen children: John, Jacob, Daniel, Joseph, William, Samuel,
Rebecca (wife of Peter Girton), Mary (wife of Seth Wright), Elizabeth (wife
of Levi Anderson), Amos, Peter, James, Lavina and Sarah Booze. Widow
Mary died about May 1, 1854. Heirs Jacob, Daniel, Joseph and Samuel
Booze, Lavina Doble, Peter Booze, Sarah Stockham and James Booze,
children of John Booze Sr., Ann Subers, Samuel L. Booze, Isaac L. Booze,
Hannah Stackhouse and William Booze, children of John Booze Jr., John
Booze, Isaac Booze, Ellen Booze and Edward Booze, children of Jesse L.
Booze (another son of John Jr.), John S. Booz, Albert Booze, Jesse Booz,
Henry Booz and Anna Mary Booz, children of Joseph L. Booz (another son of
John Jr.), Wallace and Mahlon Dungan, children of Rebecca Dungan (a
daughter of John Jr.), Rebecca and Edward Booz, children of Ann Booz
(daughter of Rebecca Girton), Mary Stackhouse (daughter of Rebecca
Girton), John Anderson, Mary Ann Anderson, Sarah Anderson and William
Anderson (children of Elizabeth Anderson), John W. Vanzant, George H.
Vanzant, Joseph L. Vanzant and Susan U. Vanzant, children of Susan
Vanzant (daughter of Mary Wright), Susan Wright, daughter of Wilson
Wright (a son of Mary Wright), Ann Carver, Seth Wright, Elizabeth Bennett,
Mary E. Wright, Samuel C. Wright and Harriet Thearle, children of Mary
Wright, David C. Booz, Edmund G. Booze, Elizabeth Dungan, Thomas Booz,
John Booz, Martha Booz and Frank Booz (last three by guardian Caleb N.
Taylor), children of William Booz (son of John Sr.), John McCloskey
(husband of Mary Booz, daughter of William), Mary Elizabeth Roberts and
William Booz, children of Amos Booz (son of John Sr.) all gave power of
attorney to Andrew W. Gilkeson, Esq. to recover dower. Andrew
acknowledges payment of dower from the current owners of the real estate.
                              Bk 12/pg 500   Apr 4, 1855

John Eakin, only surviving parent of Jacob K. Eakin and Martha Eakin who
died under the age of eleven, acknowledges payment of estate by their
guardian Jacob Clemens.   Bk 12/pg 514   May 21, 1857

Hannah Heller, daughter of Elizabeth Fish, late of Haycock Twp, receives
payment of estate from administrator Jacob Kohl. Bk 12/pg 515   Apr 3, 1857

Peter Wert of Hilltown Twp, yeoman, and wife Susannah, sister of Phillip Mumbauer, late of Upper Hanover Twp, Montgomery Co, acknowledge payment of estate by administrator Reuben Mumbauer.

Bk 12/pg 516   Nov 8, 1856

Peter Wert of Hilltown Twp, yeoman, and wife Susannah, sister of Maria Trumbauer [Mumbauer?], late of Milford Twp, acknowledge payment of estate by administrator Reuben Mumbauer.   Bk 12/pg 517   Apr 11, 1857

Peter Wert of Hilltown Twp, yeoman, and wife Susannah, daughter of Philip Mumbauer, late of Milford Twp, acknowledge payment of estate by executor Reuben Mumbauer.   Bk 12/pg 518   Apr 3, 1856

Henry Troxel of Rockhill Twp, guardian of Henry Housekeeper, minor son of Lydia Housekeeper, legatee of Maria Mumbauer, late of Milford Twp, and of sister of Philip Mumbauer, late of Upper Hanover Twp, Montgomery Co, acknowledges payment of estate by administrator Reuben Mumbauer.

Bk 12/pg 519   Nov 1, 1856

Mary Swartley (widow) and William Swartley, John Swartley, Sarah (wife of Abraham Kratz), Magdalena (wife of Henry Ruth), Levi Swartley and Mary Swartley, children of John Swartley, late of New Britain Twp, acknowledge payment of estate by administrators Joseph and Jacob M. Swartley.

Bk 12/pg 522   Apr 4, 1857

Peter Barnet (husband) and Henry Barnet, William Barnet and Hannah Barnet, children of Elizabeth Barnet, late of Nockamixon Twp, authorize administrator Henry Frankenfield to settle a mortgage with Henry Kruger.

Bk 12/pg 522   Apr 6, 1857

Anthony T. Morris, son of Enos Morris, late of Bucks Co, now of Columbia, TX, appointed E. Morris Lloyd, Esq. of Doylestown Borough to record payment of estate by Theodore Morris who inherited the real estate.

Bk 12/pg 523   May 19, 1857

Henry Shoemaker of Floid Co, VA assigns to Joseph Pritchard of Roanoke Co, VA his share of estate of father Conrad Shoemaker, formerly of Bucks County.   Bk 12/pg 525   Nov 14, 1854

Philip Fluck of Haycock Twp, now 21, acknowledges payment by guardian Samuel Stahr of estate from grandmother Hannah Fluck, late of Hilltown Twp.   Bk 12/pg 526   Mar 30, 1857

Joseph Brown, late of Philadelphia County, died on August 27, 1852 intestate with administration granted to Sarah Ann Brown, George W. Kuhn and Thomas Hudson and Charles H. Mason was appointed guardian of the minor children.　　　　　　　　　　　　　　　　Bk 12/pg 527　Dec 3, 1852

Catharine Ann Fox (late Bessonett), widow of James Fox of Natchez, MS, Edwin and Sophia Bessonett of Copiah Co, MS, George and Margaret E. Bessonett of Natchez, Joseph P. Armstrong of Mobile, AL and Charles H. and Elizabeth Bessonett of Richmond, MS give power of attorney to John Bessonett Jr. of Philadelphia to sell land in Bristol Borough which John Bessonett sold in 1825 to Robert Cabeen in trust for wife Mary and after her death to her children. Mary died in 1830 leaving seven children: Charles, John, Clotilda Armstrong (now deceased, leaving one child who died in its minority leaving Joseph Armstrong as representative), Catharine Ann Fox, Edwin, Theodore (now deceased) and George.　Bk 12/pg 530　Apr 28, 1857

David C. Strunk of Richland Twp, son of Henry Strunk, late of Richland, assigns his one-fifth share of estate to John B. Missimer, Esq. of Richland.
　　　　　　　　　　　　　　　　Bk 12/pg 538　May 18, 1857

Nelson Beans, son of Jesse Beans, M.D., late of Buckingham Twp, assigns his estate to Henry L. Corson of Buckingham.　Bk 12/pg 539　Feb 26, 1857

William and Susanna H. Burton of Falls Twp. and their children Elizabeth H. Burton, Jane Burton, Edwin J. Burton, Samuel B. Burton and Mary B. (wife of Abel B. Sattherthwaite Jr.), acknowledge payment to Susanna of money to her from her trustee David Brown of Falls Twp.　Bk 12/pg 540　May 1, 1857

James Wright died intestate in 1832 leaving widow Rebecca and five children: Robert, Rebecca (since married to William B. Rodgers), Joshua (since deceased), James (since deceased) and John and deceased daughter Elizabeth Bunting (children James, Joseph, Joshua and John Bunting). Son Richard inherited the real estate subject to dower for widow Rebecca who is now deceased. Heirs William B. and Rebecca Rodgers and Phebe Ann Wright, James H. Wright and Elizabeth Wright, children of late Joshua Wright, and James H. Wright, Robert Wright and William Wright (by guardian William Hawk), children of late James Wright, and James Bunting, Joseph Bunting, Joshua Bunting and John Bunting, children of late Elizabeth Bunting, receive payment of dower from current owners Lewis Rue, Richard Rue, George W. Rue and Johannes Watson.　Bk 12/pg 542　May 30, 1856

Mary Hampton of Solebury Twp, now 21, acknowledges payment by guardian Samuel Bradshaw of estate from late father James Hampton.
Bk 12/pg 545   Apr 25, 1857

William Watson, administrator of late wife Louisa who was a daughter of Enos Morris, late of Bucks Co. and who was also the widow of late John Feaster, gives power of attorney to Louisa's son John J. Feaster of New York City to acknowledge payment by Theodore Morris, son of Enos, of Louisa's share of estate, signed in Clinton Co, MI.   Bk 12/pg 547   Jul 10, 1857

Christian Funk (guardian of Abraham Funk), George A. Hess (guardian of Anna Malinda and Elizabeth Funk), children of Jacob Funk, late of Springfield Twp, miller, acknowledge payment of estate by administrator Absalom Cawley.   Bk 12/pg 548   Apr 1, 1857

Andrew J. and Adaline Hellings and Thomas J. Hellings, all of Mercer Co, IL, give power of attorney to Isaac P. Hellings of Bucks Co. to sell their share of real estate of their late father Thomas Hellings.   Bk 12/pg 550   Mar 10, 1857

Eve Hager, widow of John Hager, late of Tinicum Twp, and John's children Samuel, Elizabeth (wife of Isaac Fox) and Sarah Kohl release executors F.G. Hillpot from collecting $100 of a $500 mortgage due from Samuel Cooper.
Bk 12/pg 552   Jan 27, 1857

Joshua and Caroline G. Foulk have sold to Lewis B. Thompson land in Quakertown which Caroline received from executors of William Green. Missouri Roberts (wife of Milton), Cornelia Jamison (wife of David R.), Matilda Foulk and Jane Foulk, children of Joshua and Caroline, ratify this sale.   Bk 12/pg 554   Apr 2, 1856

Patrick Mulvany, late of Tinicum Twp, bequeathed estate to sister Ann (wife of Dennis Sheridan) and to her children after her deceased. Patrick Sheridan, Bryan Sheridan, Thomas Sheridan and Catharine (wife of Robert Martin), children of Ann Sheridan of Drumbarrow, Kills Parish, Upper Kills Barony, Meath CO, Ireland give power of attorney to James Fleming of Nockamixon Twp. to recover their shares from executors Joseph Hough and Daniel Ban or from current owner Mathew Sheridan.   Bk 12/pg 555   Jul 13, 1857

Lewis Sellers of Philadelphia, Daniel Sellers of 22nd Ward, Philadelphia, Rachel Walters of Nazareth, Northampton Co, Charles Sellers of Nazareth, Philip Sellers of Hatfield Twp, Montgomery Co, Elizabeth Albright of Luzerne Co. (by attorney Charles Sellers), Hannah Amanda Masser of

Luzerne Co. (by attorney Charles Sellers) and Francis R. Sellers of Kent Co, MD (by attorney Daniel Sellers), the eight children of Hannah Sellers, late of Whitemarsh Twp, Montgomery Co, who was the daughter of Enoch Roberts, late of Richland Twp, acknowledge payment of estate by surviving executor Joel B. Roberts.   Bk 12/pg 556   Apr 3, 1855

Elizabeth S. Albright and Hannah Amanda Masser of Luzerne Co, daughters of Philip and Hannah Sellers, late of Whitemarsh Twp, Montgomery Co. and granddaughter of late Enoch Roberts, gives power of attorney to brother Dr. Charles Sellers of Nazareth, Northampton Co. to recover estate due her from uncle Joel Roberts, executor of Enoch, late of Quakertown.
                                              Bk 12/pg 558   Mar 27, 1855

Francis R. Sellers of Kent Co, MD, mason, gives power of attorney to Daniel H. Sellers of 22nd Ward Philadelphia, teacher, to recover estate from late grandfather Enoch Roberts.   Bk 12/pg 559   Feb 21, 1855

Hannah Fulmer of Haycock Twp, Michael Soliday of Bedminster Twp, Henry Shisler, Jacob Shisler of Plumstead Twp, Catharine Rickert of Plumstead, Henry K. Myers of Plumstead (guardian of Michael and Samuel Shisler), heirs of Henry Benner, late of Rockhill Twp, acknowledge payment of estate by administrators Michael and Elias Benner. Bk 12/pg 560   Aug 16, 1856

Ann Miller of Warsaw Co, AL gives power of attorney to Samuel Bilger of Philadelphia to recover money due her from estates of John and Henry Cramer of Philadelphia.   Bk 12/pg 560   Nov 26, 1856

Elizabeth Hart of Durham Twp, daughter of late Ann Sheridan, gives power of attorney to James Fleming of Nockamixon Twp. to recover estate due her from Joseph Hough and Daniel Barr, executors of Patrick Mulveney, late of Tinicum Twp, who bequeathed estate to her mother, or from Mathew Sheridan, current owner of the estate.   Bk 12/pg 568   Sep 12, 1857

Joseph Thomas, son of Erasmus Thomas and grandson of Ephraim Thomas, late of New Britain Twp, now 21, acknowledges payment of his bequest by his father Erasmus, signed in Warren Co, IN.   Bk 12/pg 569   Jul 21, 1857

Jonas Lear of Herrick Twp, Bradford Co. gives power of attorney to Abraham Lear, Esq. of Tinicum Twp. to recover his share of estate of late father Arnold Lear of Tinicum Twp.   Bk 12/pg 570   Sep 12, 1857

SURNAME INDEX

Surnames are indexed once per page but may appear multiple times on each page. Entries involving negro slaves are indexed under "Slave".